Roberto Petrosino, Pietro Cerrone, Harry van der Hulst (Eds.)
From Sounds to Structures

Studies in Generative Grammar

Editors
Norbert Corver
Harry van der Hulst

Founding editors
Jan Koster
Henk van Riemsdijk

Volume 135

From Sounds to Structures

Beyond the Veil of Maya

Edited by
Roberto Petrosino
Pietro Cerrone
Harry van der Hulst

ISBN 978-1-5015-2131-7
e-ISBN (PDF) 978-1-5015-0673-4
e-ISBN (EPUB) 978-1-5015-0663-5
ISSN 0167-4331

Library of Congress Control Number: 2018016485

Bibliographic information published by the Deutsche Nationalbibliothek
The Deutsche Nationalbibliothek lists this publication in the Deutsche Nationalbibliografie;
detailed bibliographic data are available on the Internet at http://dnb.dnb.de.

© 2020 Walter de Gruyter, Inc., Berlin/Boston
This volume is text- and page-identical with the hardback published in 2018.
Typesetting: Integra Software Services Pvt. Ltd.
Printing and binding: CPI books GmbH, Leck

www.degruyter.com

Roberto Petrosino, Pietro C. Cerrone and Harry van der Hulst
Preface

This volume is dedicated to Andrea Calabrese, Professor of Linguistics at the University of Connecticut, on the occasion of his sixtieth birthday, in recognition of his inspirational and foundational contributions to the understanding of languages, *from sounds to structures*.

The subtitle of the volume, *Beyond the Veil of Maya*, is inspired by Andrea's approach to investigating languages, and, more generally, discovering the world. The term '*Maya*', in Indian traditions, refers to our sensory perception of the world and, as such, to a superficial reality that we must look beyond to find the inner essence of things. Similarly, when studying languages we perceive *sounds* – *Maya* – and then we strive to discover, or to *un-veil* the *structures* – what lies *beyond the veil* – in what we call phonology, morphology and syntax and their interfaces. This domain-general approach to investigation permeates Andrea's entire work, which deals with a highly broad range of linguistic *issues*, as he likes to say – a term that we have adopted for the title of the four parts of this volume.

The first part, Issues in Phonology, focuses on phonological theory and its connections to phonetics. Since his MIT dissertation in 1988, Andrea has pursued a consistent path in developing a general theory of phonology in which phonological activity (i.e., processes, rules) may be causally triggered by universal constraints. The resulting model, called the *constraint-and-repair* (CR) model, in which phonological processes are brought about either by positive instructions (*rules*), or as *repair* operations acting on language-specific, illicit configurations (*constraints*, or *filters*; for a review, Calabrese 2009). Andrea was one of the first, and remains the current major architects of this approach. Today, after more than 30 years since its beginnings (among others, Calabrese 1988, 1992, 1995), his framework is the foundational model for complex phonological processing, including Andrea's own important contributions to the understanding of phenomena like metaphony and palatalization across languages (in Romance in particular; see Calabrese 2005).

The contributions by Stefano Canalis, Harry van der Hulst and Elizabeth Pyatt follow this path. In his chapter "The status of Italian glides in the syllable", Canalis describes the distribution of Italian glides and their interaction with various phonological processes and phonologically conditioned allomorphy, and argues that the available evidence points to an analysis of them as phonologically vocalic elements. In "Metaphony with unary elements", Harry van der Hulst analyzes several cases of metaphony, using unary elements. His main goal is not to show that unary features deliver superior accounts (as compared to binary feature systems), but to ask if we use unary elements, which set of such features is required and how metaphony is best formally represented given that choice of features. Elizabeth Pyatt, "Many sons of Aodh: Tracing multiple phonological outcomes of the Scottish and Irish clan name MacAoidh/O'hAodha", describes the multiple phonological outcomes for a Middle Irish clan name *Mac A'ed*, which can be accounted for as possible repair outcomes as predicted in Calabreses framework.

Phonetics, and its relation with phonology in sound perception and recognition are also among Andrea's interests. Hemanga Dutta & Michael Kenstowicz, "The phonology and phonetics of laryngeal stop contrasts in Assamese", investigate the expression of the voicing and aspiration contrasts in the stop systems of Hindi, Bengali, and Assamese, with a special focus on the latter. Mirko Grimaldi's "The phonetics-phonology relationship in the neurobiology of language" hints at Andrea's interests in the neurophysiological correlates of phonology and phonetics. The chapter tries to lay the groundwork for explaining sound discretization and phonological abstraction in the light of recent neurophysiological data, and proposes that it results from a continuous process that converts spectro-temporal (acoustic) states into neurophysiological states.

The remaining parts of the volume reflect the importance that Andrea's work has also enjoyed outside phonology. The second part, *Issues in Morpho-Phonology*, examines the hotly debated topic of morpho-phonological alternations, to which Andrea has contributed at length in the last few decades.

Jonathan Bobaljik, "Disharmony and decay: Itelmen vowel harmony in the 20th century", traces the development, over the course of the 20th century, of the dominant-recessive vowel harmony pattern of Chukotko-Kamchatkan languages. By way of a quantitative comparison of two historical stages of Itelmen, he reveals that the harmony process, though never exceptionless, qualified in 1910 as a learnable, productive rule, but failed to qualify as such in 1994. A massive influx of disharmonic Russian loans over the same period is offered by the author as a plausible factor that rendered the harmony rule unlearnable.

David Embick and Kobey Shwayder, "Deriving morphophonological (mis)applications", deal with exceptionality in morpho-phonology. Morpho-phonological alternations may be defined either phonologically or morphologically, depending on the locality conditions under which the alternations occur. The article examines the problem of German Umlaut, which cannot be defined in these terms because of its "hybrid" nature from the perspective of trigger/target interactions.

Irina Monich, "Distribution of falling tones in Mabaan", accounts for the distribution of falling tones in Mabaan as being realized in specific morphophonological environments, and discusses the role of affix attrition in the development of this pattern.

J. Joseph Perry & Bert Vaux, "Vedic Sanskrit accentuation and readjustment rules", and Roberto Petrosino "Allomorphy of Italian determiners at the morphology-phonology interface", argue for the necessity of readjustment, i.e. morphologically-conditioned processes which alter phonological properties of some exponent. While recent work has questioned whether readjustment or analogous mechanisms are necessary or desirable, Perry & Vaux and Petrosino show that allomorphic alternations from Vedic Sanskrit and Italian, cannot be dealt with using alternative mechanisms. Specifically, the authors show that interactions between accentuation, syllabification and ablaut for Vedic, and between morphological (i.e., *phi*-features) and phonological information (i.e., syllabic structure) in Italian cannot be accounted for by using a combination of suppletive allomorphy and "regular" phonology; rather, at least some purely phonological processes must be interleaved together with morphophonological processes implemented by readjustment.

The significance of Andrea's treatment of constraints, and his enduring interest for Romance linguistics, have also percolated into morpho-syntax, as the third part of this volume, *Issues in the Morpho-Syntax*, shows. In his chapter, "Subject and impersonal clitics in northern Italian dialects", Diego Pescarini focuses on the interaction between the impersonal *si/se* and subject clitics in northern Italian dialects. In western dialects, *si* co-occurs with a non-agreeing clitic form (while it cannot co-occur with object clitics in the so-called passive-*si* construction); in Venetian dialects, the co-occurrence of *se* and subject clitics is degraded/ungrammatical, while in Friulian the combination is acceptable, but the subject clitic is dropped. The author argues that the peculiar behavior of northern Italian dialects results from the multiple agree relation holding between T, si_{arb}, and the argument of passive-like constructions, coupled with language-specific constraints on the realization of T's features.

Similarly, Andrew Nevins and Susi Wurmbrand adopt Andrea's constraints in their contributions. In "Copying and resolution in South Slavic and South Bantu conjunct agreement", Nevins deals with a case of Cross-modular Structural Parallelism, a hypothesis about the reuse of operations such as featural agreement, featural deletion, and feature co-occurrence constraints across domains of morphosyntactic and phonological features (Calabrese 1998). Wurmbrand's "Markedness as a condition on feature sharing" analyzes the availability of fake indexicals (bound first and second person pronouns) in English, Dutch, German and Icelandic and their correlation with the richness of agreement displayed by the head DPs and relative pronouns, arguing for a markedness account (using ideas from Calabrese 2011).

In "Diachronic and synchronic aspects in the expression of temporal distance in the past: A process of grammaticalization in Italian compared with other

Romance languages and English", Paola Benincà, Mariachiara Berizzi and Laura Vanelli compare expressions used to localize an event in the past in Modern Italian (namely, *fa* and *prima*) with Old Italian, Spanish, other Romance varieties and English, and propose a cartographic account.

M. Rita Manzini & Leonardo M. Savoia, "N-inflections and their interpretation: Neuter *-o* and plural *-a* in Italian varieties", propose a syntactic analysis of the so-called neuter inflection *-o* and *-a* in Central and South varieties of Italian.

Finally, the fourth part of the volume, *Issues in Syntax*, reflects how noteworthy Andrea's work has been in syntactic research too. As a young researcher, Andrea contributed to the analysis of sentential complementation, and of the interaction between the information structure and phonological structure in standard and non-standard Italian (especially in Salentino) – an '*issue*' that has paved the way to the current framework of cartography, represented by the first four chapters of this volume. Adriana Belletti, "On *a*-marking of object topics in the Italian left periphery", analyzes the main distributional and interpretive properties of Italian *a*-marked topics, which overall behave like non-*a*-marked topics as far as their distribution and their interpretive possibilities are concerned but involve some supplementary feature, such as e.g. affectedness or involvement.

Giuliano Bocci & Silvio Crushina, "Postverbal subjects and nuclear pitch accent in Italian wh-questions", discuss two properties that characterize *wh*-question in Italian and that were first described and analyzed in Calabrese (1982): subject inversion and the assignment of the nuclear pitch accent (NPA). Both properties are the reflexes of the derivational history of the *wh*-movement, and, as experimental data show, the result of a direct interaction between the syntactic and the phonological component.

Guglielmo Cinque, "On the Merge position of additive and associative plurals", addresses a particular aspect of the syntax of additive and associative plurals, namely their Merge position within the extended projection of the NP. Crosslinguistic analysis suggests that while the additive plural is merged below DP, the associative plural is merged above DP (and below Case).

Finally, Luigi Rizzi, "Subjects, topics and the interpretation of *pro*", addresses the interpretive properties of null pronominal subjects, and the related issue of the similarities and differences between subjects and topics. The paper argues for a "subject criterion" associated with a particular structural position in the clausal spine, and involving both formal and interpretive properties. The criterial approach leads to discussing similarities and differences between subjects and topics with respect to anaphora resolution, conditions for appropriate use, and other formal and interpretive properties.

The broad variety of contributions in this volume strongly testifies to the diversity of Andrea's influence. We are thankful to all the contributors to this volume for joining us in acknowledging the significance of Andrea's work across many areas of linguistics, for (mostly) sticking to the tight deadlines, for reviewing each other's papers, and for being extremely supportive of the whole project since the beginning. We are equally grateful to the scholars who devoted their expertise and valuable time in reviewing all contributions anonymously, thus making this volume stronger in its argumentations and contents. Finally, we thank Morris Halle for his encouragement in the preparation of this volume. As Andrea's mentor and friend, he wished to express his deep affection for him, noting: "Andrea has always been interested in problems which are a little bit different from the problems that other people are interested in. That's part of the reason why I always found him good company to talk to. He's always been more like a friend than a student of mine". We are all looking forward, as his students, colleagues and friends, to learning more from Andrea's experience and guidance in the years to come.

We express our gratitude to the editors of the SGG series and, in particular to Lara Wysong at De Gruyter Mouton, for their assistance, without whom this volume would not have been possible.

References

Calabrese, Andrea. 1982. Alcune ipotesi sulla struttura informazionale della frase in Italiano e sul suo rapporto con la struttura fonologica. *Rivista di Grammatica Generativa* 13. 489526.

Calabrese, Andrea. 1988. Towards a theory of phonological alphabets. Cambridge, MA: MIT, PhD thesis.

Calabrese, Andrea. 1992. A constraint-based theory of phonological inventories. In J. Rennison (ed.), *Phonologica,* 35–54. Torino: Rosenberg & Sellier.

Calabrese, Andrea. 1995. A constraint-based theory of phonological markedness and simplification procedures. *Linguistic Inquiry* 26(3). 373–463.

Calabrese, Andrea. 1998. Some remarks on the Latin case system and its development in Romance. In J. Lema and E. Trevino (eds.), *Theoretical advances on Romance languages,* 71–126. Amsterdam: John Benjamins.

Calabrese, Andrea. 2005. *Markedness and economy in a derivation model of phonology.* Berlin/New York: Mouton de Gruyter.

Calabrese, Andrea. 2009. Markedness theory versus phonological idiosyncrasies in a realistic model of language. In E. Raimy and C. E. Cairns (eds.), *Contemporary views on architecture and representations in phonology,* 261–304. Cambridge, MA/London, England: The MIT Press.

Calabrese, Andrea (2011). "Investigations on markedeness, syncretism and zero exponence in morphology". In: *Morphology* 21.2, pp. 283–325.

Calabrese, Andrea and Diego Pescarini (2014). "Clitic metathesis in the Friulian dialect of Forni di Sotto". In: *Probus* 26.2.

Contents

Part I: *Issues* in Phonology

Stefano Canalis
The status of Italian glides in the syllable —— 3

Hemanga Dutta and Michael Kenstowicz
The phonology and phonetics of laryngeal stop contrasts in Assamese —— 30

Mirko Grimaldi
The phonetics-phonology relationship in the neurobiology of language —— 65

Harry van der Hulst
Metaphony with unary elements —— 104

Elizabeth J. Pyatt
Many sons of *Aodh*: Tracing multiple outcomes of the Scottish and Irish clan name *MacAoidh/Ó hAodha* —— 129

Part II: *Issues* in Morpho-Phonology

Jonathan David Bobaljik
Disharmony and decay: Itelmen vowel harmony in the 20th century —— 161

David Embick and Kobey Shwayder
Deriving morphophonological (mis) applications —— 193

Irina Monich
Distribution of falling tones in Mabaan —— 249

J. Joseph Perry and Bert Vaux
Vedic Sanskrit accentuation and readjustment rules —— 266

Roberto Petrosino
Allomorphy of Italian determiners at the morphology-phonology interface —— 295

Part III: *Issues* in the Morpho-Syntax

Paola Benincà, Mariachiara Berizzi, Laura Vanelli
Diachronic and synchronic aspects in the expression of temporal distance in the past: A process of grammaticalization in Italian compared with other Romance languages and English —— 329

M. Rita Manzini and Leonardo M. Savoia
N inflections and their interpretation: Neuter -*o* and plural -*a* in Italian varieties —— 357

Andrew Nevins
Copying and resolution in South Slavic and South Bantu Conjunct Agreement —— 391

Diego Pescarini
Subject and impersonal clitics in northern Italian dialects —— 409

Susi Wurmbrand
Markedness as a condition on feature sharing —— 432

Part IV: *Issues* in Syntax

Adriana Belletti
On *a*-marking of object topics in the Italian left periphery —— 445

Giuliano Bocci and Silvio Cruschina
Postverbal subjects and nuclear pitch accent in Italian wh-questions —— 467

Guglielmo Cinque
On the Merge position of additive and associative plurals —— 495

Luigi Rizzi
Subjects, topics and the interpretation of *pro* —— 510

Index —— 531

Part I: *Issues* in Phonology

Stefano Canalis
The status of Italian glides in the syllable

1 Introduction

Italian glides pose several phonological problems, which are mainly due to the fact that they seem to exhibit properties of both vowels and consonants. While their phonetic nature is fairly well understood and consistent with findings from other languages, their phonological status is a matter of controversy, enough to remind of Larry Hyman's statement that "[p]erhaps the most problematic segment type for all theories of phonology is the class of glides" (Hyman 1985: 77).

This paper aims to address the nature of their role within the syllable. In section 2 I will briefly discuss their relationship with diphthongs and hiatuses. In section 3 I will succinctly describe the phonetics and distribution of Italian glides. In section 4 some general information about their phonology will be provided, and in section 5 I will discuss falling diphthongs. In section 6 I will present some of the previous proposals about the syllabic role of Italian on-glides, as well as my own hypothesis. While previous analyses have argued that Italian glides are basically consonantal (on-glides belonging to the onset, and off-glides belonging to the coda), I will try to show that they are essentially vocalic in nature. On-glides are always syllabified within the nucleus, and form a single complex vocalic segment with the following root node (with the exception of the glide [w] after velar stops, which forms a complex consonantal segment with the latter). I will also argue that off-glides too are part of the nucleus, but as an independent segment of the diphthong they belong to. In order to prove these claims, I will present evidence from assimilatory processes, article allomorph selection, phonotactic distribution, and vowel duration.

2 Diphthongs and hiatuses

Before discussing glides in detail it may be useful to briefly examine their complex relationship with hiatuses. Glides typically occur next to a vowel, the two forming a diphthong – traditionally, diphthongs are defined as combinations of a vowel and a preceding or following glide (called 'on-glide' and 'off-glide' respectively) within

https://doi.org/10.1515/9781501506734-001

the same syllable.[1] When dealing with vocoid sequences, the question often arises whether they are diphthongs or hiatuses, the latter being defined as sequences of two syllabic nuclei. In fact, as simple and straightforward as they may be in theory, these definitions sometimes run into practical difficulties. Practically distinguishing Italian hiatuses from diphthongs may prove to be a tall order (see Marotta 1987 for a detailed discussion), mainly because the phonetic difference between the two categories is basically a continuum (Salza, Marotta, and Ricca 1987). Furthermore, underlying hiatuses may be realized as diphthongs (this possibility also occasionally extends to hiatuses with initial mid vowels, as (1b) shows).

(1) a. *b*[i]*ologia* 'biology' in slow speech → *b*[j]*ologia* in fast speech
    b. *parto cesar*[e]*o* 'Cesarean section' → *parto cesar*[j]*o* (non-standard)

It has to be added, however, that in Italian the change is unidirectional; hiatuses may optionally become diphthongs, but underlying diphthongs never become hiatuses. A realization as in (2) would only be possible at an unnatural, artificially slow speech rate.

(2) a. *p*[j]*ede* 'foot' → ?* *p*[i]*ede*

Vowel/glide alternations seem to be affected by various factors (Marotta 1987: 871–877). One of them is lexical stress, as hiatuses tend to be preserved if one their vowels is stressed (a typologically common pattern – see e.g. Casali 1997); for instance, *b*[j]*ologìa* is more likely than *b*[j]*òlogo* 'biologist', *ubr*[i]*àco* 'drunkard' is more likely than *ubr*[i]*acàrsi* 'to get drunk'. Another factor is sociolinguistic variation; in fast, *allegro* speech and informal contexts the diphthongization of hiatuses is more common. Finally, morphological boundaries also play a role, as the diphthongization of a hiatus is blocked (or at least is much less likely, even in fast speech) if a morphological boundary occurs between the two vowels: *appendiabiti* / ap'pɛndi#'abiti/ [ap'pɛndi'aːbiti] 'coat hanger', *riarmare* /ri+ar'mare/ [riar'maːre] 'rearm', *antiacari* /'anti+'akari/ ['anti'aːkari] 'antiacarian'. There is also some geographical variation; for example, the standard Italian pronunciation of *viaggio* 'journey' is *v*[i]*aggio*, but in northern Italy *v*[j]*aggio* is very common.

In Italian, the difference between falling diphthongs and hiatuses is even more elusive than between hiatuses and rising diphthongs, as phonetically

---

[1] This 'combination' can also be seen as a complex vowel with two distinct articulatory targets over its duration. Triphthongs – clusters made of a vowel and two glides – are less common but also attested in many languages (see section 3 about triphthongs in Italian).

there is little difference between an unstressed vowel and the gliding part of a falling diphthong (see the phonetic data discussed in the next section). Especially word-finally, it is difficult to establish conclusively which phonological category high vocoids belong to.

3 Phonetics and distribution of Italian glides

Diphthongs (together with the closely related category of hiatuses) form a significant portion of the phonological material of Italian lexicon. According to Marotta (1987: 848), about 30% of Italian words have at least a diphthong or a hiatus. She also observes that her count probably underestimates diphthongs and hiatuses, since it is based on the entries of a dictionary; this implies that only citation forms were counted, but inflection – especially verbal – fairly often creates diphthongs and hiatuses in Italian.

Five phonetic glides are differentiated in the literature:
1. the palatal on-glide [j]
2. the labio-velar glide [w]
3. the labio-palatal on-glide [ɥ][2]
4. the palatal off-glide [i̯]
5. the labio-velar off-glide [u̯]

In general, Italian glides have a shorter duration when compared to high vowels.[3] Salza, Marotta, and Ricca (1987) found that /i, u/, even when unstressed, all else equal are longer than both on- and off-glides. Glides (especially on-glides) also seem to be more centralized than vowels; F2 was found to be lower in front glides than in /i/, and to be higher in labiovelar glides than in /u/ – which implies a more centralized realization that nuclear /i/ and /u/. Glides are also more constricted than high vowels, and their formant patterns are much less stable.

---

2 This glide has a much more restricted distribution than the others, usually only being an optional variant of [w] in Glide-Glide-Vowel clusters (e.g. in *quieto* [ˈkɥjɛːto] 'calm', *reliquia* [reˈliːkɥja] 'relics', Marotta 1987: 880–881). Calamai and Bertinetto (2006) report that in the same clusters [ɥ] may also be a variant of [j] instead of [w], and sporadically the two glides may even coalesce (e.g. *continuiamo* [kontiˈnwjaːmo] / [kontiˈnɥaːmo] 'we continue').

3 This is sometimes seen as an inherent property of glides; however, it may be useful to add that glides do not necessarily have to be short segments. Geminate glides do exist (see Maddieson [2008] for a review), and they can also be found in some varieties of Italian, such as Rome Italian; for example [ˈmɛjːo] 'better', [ˈpajːa] 'straw'.

Within glides, off-glides display a more vocoid-like nature than on-glides. Salza, Marotta, and Ricca (1987), and Salza (1988) found that Italian off-glides are longer than on-glides; in fact, phonetically they basically are non-nuclear vocalic articulations (Mioni 2001: 176). Marotta (2010) reports a mean duration of 50 ms for on-glides and 80 ms for off-glides, compared with 120 ms for stressed vowels. Therefore, although some authors ignore the phonetic difference between Italian on-glides and off-glides in their phonetic transcriptions and use the IPA symbols [j] and [w] for both, in this paper these symbols are restricted to on-glides.

As for the distribution of Italian glides, most glide-vowel and vowel-glide combinations are phonologically licit, but there are some co-occurrence constraints (see Marotta 1987, 1988, 2010; Mioni 1993; Bertinetto and Loporcaro 2005; Krämer 2009). Among rising diphthongs, high clusters *[ji], *[wu] are impossible. Every other combination is attested: [ja], [jɛ], [je], [jɔ], [jo], [ju], [wa], [wɛ], [we], [wi], [wɔ], [wo]. The illicitness of *[ji] is not only inferable from the static distribution of on-glides, but is also confirmed by a cluster simplification process occurring when a root-final front glide is followed by an inflectional /i/; the resulting cluster *[ji] is reduced to [i], while inflectional [o], [a] and [e] do not cause the deletion of the preceding glide.

(3) a. *ampio* 'wide-M.SG'   /'ampj + o/ → ['ampjo]
    b. *ampia* 'wide-F.SG'   /'ampj + a/ → ['ampja]
    c. *ampie* 'wide-F.PL'   /'ampj + e/ → ['ampje]
    d. *ampii* 'wide-M.PL'   /'ampj + i/ → ['ampi], *['ampji]
    e. *cambio* 'I change'   /'kambj + o/ → ['kambjo]
    f. *cambia* 's/he changes' /'kambj + a/ → ['kambja]
    g. *cambi* 'you change'   /'kambj + i/ → ['kambi], *['kambji]

Falling diphthongs have more restrictions on their internal structure. They share with rising diphthongs the constraint against same-height clusters (*[ii̯], *[uu̯]), but also have two other constraints of their own. A back vowel cannot be followed by [u̯] (that is, *[ɔu̯] and *[ou̯] are impossible – a third option, *[uu̯], is ruled out both by this and the preceding constraint), and /i/ cannot be the first element of a falling diphthong (that is, *[iu̯] and *[ii̯] are impossible (*[ii̯] being also ruled out by the constraint against homorganic diphthongs). The allowed combinations therefore are [ai̯], [ɛi̯], [ei̯], [ɔi̯], [oi̯], [ui̯], [au̯], [ɛu̯], [eu̯]. However, it is not obvious whether the last two constraints are synchronically active or rather are mere lexical gaps resulting from accidental diachronic patterns. In fact, in a small number of words (acronyms, loanwords, foreign proper names) such diphthongs are attested; for example the surname (*Fernando*) *Couto* – a Portuguese former footballer who played in Italy for years – was usually pronounced as [ˈkɔṷto] by Italian journalists and supporters. Additionally, falling diphthong cannot be followed by a tautosyllabic consonant:

(4a) i.   daino   [ˈdai̯no] 'fallow deer'   ii.   trauma   [ˈtrau̯ma]   'injury'
      iii. feudo   [ˈfɛṷdo] 'fief'   iv.   faida   [ˈfai̯da]   'feud'

(4b) i.   *dairno   ii.   *traurma
      iii. *guailna   iv.   *faidda

This restriction seems to follow from a more general constraint; in Italian, codas can only consist of a single consonant, be it a sonorant or the first half of a geminate.[4]

(5)   a. can.to 'song'   b. cam.po 'field'   c. por.to 'harbour'
      d. col.tre 'blanket' e. lat.te 'milk'   f. map.pa 'map'
      g. pac.co 'pack'

It has to be added that if the diphthong is in the word-final syllable a following consonant, usually /s/, is possible (e.g. mouse [ˈmau̯s] 'mouse (pointing device)', mais [ˈmai̯s] 'corn'). However, probably this is not a real counterexample to the generalization stated above that falling diphthong cannot be followed by a tautosyllabic consonant. First, as mentioned in section 2 above it is difficult to ascertain whether word-final vocalic sequences are diphthongs or hiatuses – and if mouse, mais and so on have a hiatus they do not constitute a counterexample. Second, Italian allows more consonants word-finally than word-internally; whereas word-internally only one coda consonant at most is permitted, word-finally up to two are possible (sport, volt, (go) kart, and so on – all these examples entered the Italian lexicon as loanwords, but nowadays they belong to the everyday vocabulary). Therefore, falling diphthongs are also in this case parallel to rhymes made of a simple vowel plus a coda consonant; in both cases no further coda consonants are possible word-internally, and one further consonant is possible word-finally (this may indicate that word-final consonants are extra-syllabic in Italian, but we will not explore this issue any further here). The only seeming exception to this generalization thus are the clusters /sC(C)/, which may follow a falling diphthong (6).

---

4 Leaving aside the problem of how word-internal /CsC/ clusters such as in insperato 'unhoped for' are syllabified.

(6) a. *fausto* 'auspicious'
    b. *auspicare* 'to wish for'
    c. *caustico* 'caustic'
    d. *Australia* 'Australia'

These clusters are usually considered heterosyllabic, with /s/ being in coda position (e.g. *pas.ta* 'pasta', *mos.tro* 'monster'). However, the syllabification of Italian /sC(C)/ clusters is a controversial issue (see e.g. Bertinetto 1999); therefore, a syllabification *Fau.sto*, *Au.stra.lia* and so on cannot be excluded *a priori* (actually, /sC(C)/ clusters are licit word-initially). Furthermore, apparently /sC(C)/ clusters are possible after a diphthong only if the latter is [au̯], which makes this exception, if it exists at all, very circumscribed.⁵

Finally, triphthongs, although infrequent in the lexicon, are also attested (Marotta 1987: 880–881; Marotta 2011). They mostly fall into two groups: [ɥjV] clusters after a velar stop (e.g. *reliquia* [reˈliːkɥja], *quieto* [ˈkɥjɛːto]), and clusters on-glide+vowel+off-glide (e.g. *miei* [ˈmjɛi̯] 'my-M-PL', *suoi* [ˈswɔi̯] 'his/her-M-PL').

4 Some preliminary remarks about the phonological status of Italian glides

A recurring question about Italian glides is whether they are two independent phonemes /j, w/ or rather non-syllabic allophones of /i/ and /u/. This has been a controversial issue in the phonology of Italian (among others, see Castellani 1956; Lepschy 1964; Romeo 1968; Tekavčić 1972; Mioni 1993; Krämer 2009), and Romance languages more generally (see for example Hualde 2004 for Spanish). The debate usually revolves about alleged 'minimal pairs' (or lack thereof) between high vowels and glides. Sometimes examples as in (7) are presented as minimal pairs which would justify the assumption of a lexical contrast between glides and high vowels.

(7) a. *spianti* [ˈspjanti] 'you uproot'   *spianti* [spiˈanti] 'spying-PL'
    b. *piano*   [ˈpjaːno] 'slowly/piano' *piano*   [piˈaːno] 'of Pius'

---

5 However, they are true diphthongs and not hiatuses; if [au̯] in *caustico* were a hiatus, stress would be ante-antepenultimate (*[ˈka.us.ti.ko]), a configuration not allowed in Italian (save for cliticized words and few and well-defined verbal forms).

c. *la quale* [laˈkwaːle] 'the one who-F.SG' *lacuale* [lakuˈaːle] 'lacustrine'
d. *Arcuata* [arˈkwaːta] 'town name' *arcuata* [arkuˈaːta] 'bent-F.SG'
e. *riuscire*⁶ [rjuʃˈʃiːre] 'to succeed' *riuscire* [riuʃˈʃiːre] 'to exit again'

However, there are several observations to be made about these data. First, several of the items having a hiatus (e.g. *piano* 'of Pius', *lacuale*) are low frequency words, in some cases altogether missing from the lexicon of many speakers – at least the less educated. Second, as discussed in section 2 above many supposed hiatuses are actually often pronounced with a glide, especially in fast, informal speech – which again makes the supposed minimal pair highly dubious.

Most importantly, the morphological blocking effect described in section 2 is also relevant here. In all the words in the right column of (7) (where a vowel instead of a glide is present) /i, u/ are followed by a morphological boundary, which as seen above blocks diphthongization. The data in (7) are reproduced as (8) with morphological boundaries added.

(8) a. [ˈs+pjant+i] vs. [spi+ˈant+i]
opposite.of-plant-2SG.PRS.IND spy-PRS.PTCP-PL
b. [ˈpjaːno] vs. [pi+ˈaːn+o]
slowly Pius-ADJECTIVIZER-M.SG
c. [laˈkw+aːl+e] vs. [la#ku+ˈaːl+e]
lake-ADJECTIVIZER-SG the.F.SG who-SG
d. [arˈkwaːta] vs. [arku+ˈaːt+a]
town name bend-PST.PTCP-F.SG
e. [rjuʃʃ+iːre] vs. [ri+uʃʃ+iːre]
succeed-INF again-exit-INF

Clearly, morphological boundaries block gliding. Therefore, it is difficult to consider the word pairs in (7) as real minimal pairs; all the hiatuses there cross a morphological boundary, whereas the diphthongs in the left columns never do (as noted among others by Marotta 1988 and Mioni 1993).

Nevertheless, this does not imply that the appearance of a glide or of a vowel is always predictable from morphological boundaries; hiatuses can be present even within the same morpheme, which means that some (if few, and mostly restricted to stressed syllables) near-minimal pairs exist:

---

6 The standard pronunciation of *riuscire* 'to succeed' is [riuʃʃire] according to many dictionaries (e.g. the prescriptive *Dizionario di Ortografia e Pronunzia*, which adopts a rather conservative notion of standard Italian), but this word is pronounced as [rjuʃʃire] by many speakers.

(9) a. *miasma* [mi'azma] 'miasma'   vs.   *chiasmo* ['kjazmo] 'chiasm'
    b. *duello* [du'ɛllo] 'duel'   vs.   *quello* ['kwɛllo] 'that'

However, hiatuses with a [+high] vowel are present in a low number of lexical items, and as seen above in fast speech they may become diphthongs – all facts that, to a smaller or larger degree, make it problematic to interpret them as independent phonemes.[7]

Ultimately, their analysis depends on the definitions of contrast, minimal pair and syllable adopted. Against the claim that a phonological contrast between glides and high vowels exists in Italian, it might be countered that even word pairs like *miasma/chiasmo*, *duello/quello* are not true (near-)minimal pairs, as we are comparing three-syllable words with two-syllable words. A possible solution may be to assume that syllable structure is already present – partially or completely – in underlying representations (see e.g. Golston and van der Hulst 1999; Vaux 2003; Calabrese 2005: 71, 150). A possible implementation of this idea consists in specifying syllable nuclei underlyingly, the difference between e.g. *miasma* and *chiasmo* therefore depending on the presence of three syllable nuclei in /mi$_N$a$_N$sma$_N$/ vs. only two in /kia$_N$smo$_N$/ (underlying nuclei are indicated by the subscript $_N$ after the nuclear vowel).

In what follows I will adopt this position, and I will therefore assume that Italian glides are allophones of /i, u/; /i/ and /u/ may be the only element in the nucleus (being phonetically realized as [i, u]) or share it with another vowel (being phonetically realized as [j, w] before it, and as [i̯, u̯] after it). However, this assumption about the allophonic nature of glides is not crucial for the following discussion.

5 The role of off-glides within the syllable

As mentioned in section 3 above, Italian off-glides are phonetically closer to vowels that on-glides. However, they seem to function phonologically as consonants; codas can only consist of a single consonant (either a sonorant or the first half of a geminate), and likewise off-glides can never be followed by a tautosyllabic consonant.

---

[7] This is a recurrent problem in the phonology of many languages, including many Romance languages – cf. for example Hualde's (2004) definition of Spanish glides as 'quasi-phonemes'.

In fact, at least three different syllabic representations of off-glides (and hence of falling diphthongs) are conceivable: off-glides as coda consonants (10a), as members of a complex vocalic segment (10b), and as independent vowels within the nucleus (10c). In this section I will argue for the latter representation.

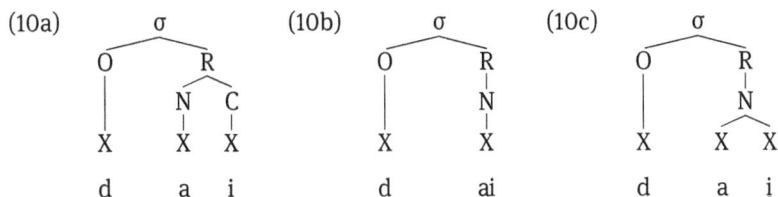

The representation (10a) is adopted by Marotta (1988: 405–407) and van der Veer (2006: 81–82). One argument for this solution is the distributional generalization described in section 3 above: falling diphthongs are never followed by geminates or tautosyllabic consonants, making it reasonable to assume that off-glides occupy the coda position. As observed by van der Veer (2006: 81–82), this phonotactic restriction also implies that stressed word-final falling diphthongs differ from stressed final simple vowels with respect to *Raddoppiamento Fonosintattico* – a word-initial consonant gemination process triggered by a preceding word. While all final-stress words (as well as a closed class of other words – see e.g. Loporcaro 1997 for a description of the contexts of application of *Raddoppiamento*) trigger *Raddoppiamento* if the stressed vowel is a monophthong or a rising diphthong (11a), word-final stressed falling diphthongs do not (11b).

(11a) i. *sa capire* /ˈsa kaˈpire/ [ˈsakkaˈpiːre] 's/he knows how to understand'
 ii. *può capire* /ˈpwɔ kaˈpire/ [ˈpwɔkkaˈpiːre] 's/he can understand'

(11b) i. *sai capire* /ˈsai̯ kaˈpire / [ˈsai̯ kapiːre] 'you know how to understand'
 ii. *vuoi capire* /ˈvwɔi̯ kaˈpire/ [ˈvwɔi̯ kaˈpiːre] 'you want to understand'

Another argument for (10a) is phonetic. Off-glides have a longer duration than on-glides (Salza, Marotta, and Ricca 1987; Salza 1988), and their duration following stressed vowels is not significantly different from that of off-glides following unstressed vowels. They therefore seem to behave as autonomous segments rather than as parts of a complex vocalic element with the preceding vowel. Marotta's (1988) and van der Veer's (2006) arguments convincingly rule out (10b); if falling diphthongs were complex segments, both their durational properties and the impossibility of a following tautosyllabic consonant (including the failure to trigger *Raddoppiamento*) would be unexpected.

However, their arguments are consistent not only with (10a), but also with (10c). The duration of off-glides seems to show that they are autonomous segments rather than parts of a complex vowel (as both (10a) and (10c) assume), but says nothing about the syllabic role of off-glides as either vowels or consonants. As for the fact that off-glides can never be followed by a tautosyllabic consonant, it can alternatively be seen as a restriction on rhyme – rather than coda – complexity; it could be restated as 'in Italian a rhyme cannot have more than two phonemes' (that is, it can be V, VC or VV, but not VCC or VVC). It is thus necessary to resort to other evidence in order to decide between the two competing analyses.

A testing ground is provided by intervocalic /s/ voicing in northern Italian (L. Vanelli, p.c.). Standard Italian contrasts intervocalic /s/ and /z/ (although the contrast is neutralized in any other position). However, most Italian speakers do not have this contrast; for example, in northern Italian only [z] occurs intervocalically (12),[8] whereas (as in Standard Italian) after a consonant only [s] occurs (13).

(12) a. *casa*   ['kaːza]   'home/house'   (cf. standard ['kaːsa])
     b. *mese*   ['meːze]   'month'   (cf. standard ['meːse])
     c. *peso*   ['peːzo]   'weight'   (cf. standard ['peːso])
     d. *chiese* ['kjɛːze]   's/he asked'   (cf. standard ['kjɛːse])

(13) a. *penso*   ['pɛnso]   'I think'
     b. *orso*   ['orso]   'bear'
     c. *polso*   ['polso]   'wrist'

Interestingly, in northern Italian the realization of /s/ between a falling diphthong and a vowel is the same as between two vowels (and rising diphthongs – see

---

8 Actually, this is an oversimplification of the facts. First, 'northern Italian' is a rather vague label; second, even if intervocalic, /s/ usually remains voiceless next to a morphological boundary between a prefix and a root (for example in *risalire* [risaˈliːre] 'to climb again' – cf. *salire* 'to climb' [saˈliːre]), but not always (for example in *disonesto* [dizoˈnɛsto] 'dishonest' – cf. *onesto* [oˈnɛsto] 'honest'), and speakers may have lexical exceptions (for example *presidente* [presiˈdɛnte] 'president', in which a synchronic morphological boundary before [s] is no longer obvious). However, for our goals it is sufficient to know that a morpheme-internal intervocalic /s/ is usually realized as [z] by most speakers in northern Italy.

(12d)); [z] is always found (14), whereas [s] would be expected if it were a post-consonantal environment.⁹ This is strongly suggests that Italian falling diphthongs are phonologically VV rather than VC, which is evidence in favour of the representation (10c). At the same time it is at odds with the assumption in (10a) that off-glides occupy the coda, and hence are consonantal.

(14) a. *eleusino* [eleu̯'ziːno] 'Eleusinian'
 b. *pausa* ['pau̯za] 'pause'
 c. *causa* ['kau̯za] 'cause'
 d. *ausilio* [au̯'ziːljo] 'aid'

6 The role of on-glides within the syllable

The representation of on-glides is debated too. At least three analyses (plus various combinations of them) exist, depending on which syllabic constituent (onset or nucleus) the on-glide is assumed to belong to, and whether it is seen as an independent segment or as a part of a complex segment.

One possibility (15) is that on-glides are not independent segments, but secondary articulations of consonants (and thus are part of the onset). An alternative (16) is that they are part of the onset as independent segments (Marotta 1987: 867). Other proposals claim that on-glides are part of the nucleus, either (17) as one of two separate segments (the other of course being the following vowel), or (18) as the first element of a single complex vocalic segment (which is the hypothesis advocated in this paper). Finally, combinations of these proposals exist. For example, Marotta (1988) holds that the glide [j] belongs to the onset, but [w] either belongs to the nucleus or is the secondary articulation of labio-velar stops; van der Veer (2006: 80) adopts a representation akin to (18) for unstressed vowels, but akin to (17) for stressed ones.

---

9 Most available examples have the diphthong [au̯], but this seems to be more a fortuitous gap than a real phonological restriction. Indeed, the sparse examples with other falling diphthongs also regularly show [z] – for example *Eusebio* [eu̯'zɛːbjo] 'Eusebius', *Freisa* ['frei̯za] 'a wine grape variety', and the southern Italian word *paisà* [pai̯'sa] 'fellow countryman', which is usually pronounced as [pai̯'za] in northern Italy.

(15)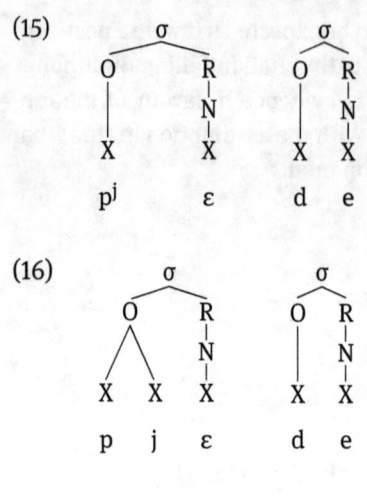

(16)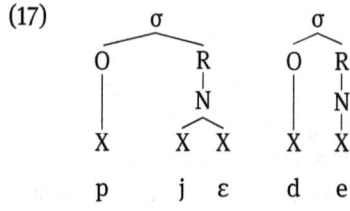

(17)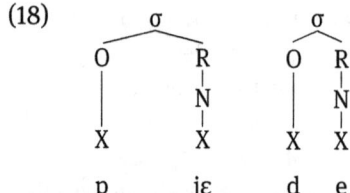

(18)

```
          σ                    σ
        ⌒                    ⌒
       O   R                O   R
       |   |                |   |
       |   N                |   N
       |   |                |   |
       X   X                X   X
       p   jɛ               d   e
```

6.1 On-glides in the onset?

I will argue that (18) is the most convincing solution, but before discussing it in sections 6.2.1 to 6.2.7 I will first critically examine the hypotheses that on-glides belong to the onset - i.e, (15) and (16) in sections 6.1.1 to 6.1.5.

6.1.1 On-glides as secondary articulations?

The hypothesis that on-glides are secondary articulations of onset consonants is probably the easiest to disprove. While it is a reasonable assumption for much older synchronic stages of Italian, or even Proto-Romance (the early gemination of consonants before front glides – e.g. SEPIA > *seppia* 'cuttlefish' – suggests that [j] lost its segmental status and the previous consonant was thus compensatorily lengthened, Calabrese 2005: 319–339), its validity for modern Italian is debatable; the most compelling argument against it is the possibility of word-initial glides (*ieri, uomo*, and so on), which cannot be secondary articulations of a non-existent consonant (Marotta 1987: 868–869).

6.1.2 Differences between [j] and [w]

The main motivation for Marotta's (1988) idea that [j] and [w] have differing syllabic affiliations lies in their asymmetric distribution. The front glide may be preceded by any consonant ([pj], [tj], [kj], [mj], and so on) and followed by any vowel save /i/ ([ja], [jɛ], [je], [jɔ], [jo], [ju]). On the other hand, if a consonant other than [k] or [g] precedes [w], only [ɔ] may follow. However, when [k] or [g] precede [w] any vowel (save /u/, see section 3 above) may follow. The fact that [w] is intimately related to [ɔ] but has no co-occurrence restrictions with the preceding consonant (unless the consonant is a velar stop) indicates that [wɔ] is a unit, while [Cw] is not; therefore, [w] has to belong to the syllable nucleus. Furthermore, word-initial [wɔ] (19a) selects the same definite article allomorph as word-initial vowels (19b), namely *l'* [l], whereas word-initial consonants select *il* (19c).

(19) a. i. *l'uomo* 'the man' ii. *l'uovo* 'the egg'
 b. i. *l'ora* 'the hour' ii. *l'occhio* 'the eye'
 c. i. *il gatto* 'the cat' ii. *il suono* 'the sound'

The opposite holds for [w] after velar stops; since [w] combines freely with any vowel if and only if it is preceded by [k] or [g], this suggests the stops and the glide form complex segments – i.e., labio-velar stops /kʷ/ and /gʷ/. Indeed, distribution is not the only argument to support this analysis of [kw] and [gw]. Another is provided by the so-called *gorgia toscana* of Tuscan Italian,[10] a lenition process that targets intervocalic /k/ (as well as the other intervocalic voiceless stops /p/ and /t/). When *gorgia* applies, the most common realization of intervocalic /k/ is [h]; intervocalic /kʷ/ may become [hw], but interestingly also [h] – the same output of intervocalic /k/ – is a possible realization (for example /di kwɛsto/

---

10 What follows is a highly stylized description of *gorgia toscana*. For a detailed picture, see e.g. Giannelli and Savoia (1978), Marotta (2008).

'of this' → [diˈhɛsto], Giannelli [1976] 2000: 32). This (near) parallelism between the velar and labiovelar voiceless stop again suggests that the [w] of the latter is actually part of the consonant, and [kw] is best analyzed as single complex consonant /kʷ/ rather than as a cluster /kw/.[11] Therefore, following Marotta (1988), from now on I will assume that Italian has the labio-velar stops /kʷ/ and /gʷ/ in its phonological inventory, and therefore [w] is part of a complex consonantal segment if the preceding segment is a velar stop. I will also assume that [w] is syllabified with the nucleus if it precedes [ɔ] (but see below about other nuclei starting with [w]). As duly noted by Marotta (1988: 401), adopting her analysis a handful of ambiguous cases remain, namely words with both a preceding velar stop and a following [ɔ] (for instance *cuore* 'heart', *cuoco* 'cook', *scuola* 'school'); the representation she argues for is not able to tell us if their [w] belongs to the onset or the nucleus.[12]

With regard to the glide [j], according to Marotta (1988) its phonological nature is significantly different from [w]; the palatal on-glide is claimed to always belong to the onset. She bases her claim mainly on three types of evidence. One is phonetic; according to Marotta (1987, 1988), the relatively contoid-like phonetic nature of on-glides suggests that phonologically they are consonants rather than vowels. The second is distributional; unlike [w], [j] has no combinatorial restrictions with the following vowel – just as Italian prevocalic consonants. The third is again based on the article allomorph selected by [j]; whereas, as seen above, word-initial [w] is followed by the same allomorph required by word-initial vowels (*l'uomo*, as *l'occhio*), word-initial [j] selects the same allomorph required by /s+C(C)/, clusters, i.e. *lo* /lo/ (*lo iato* [loˈjaːto] 'the hiatus', as *lo spillo* 'the pin').

---

11 Since [gw] has the same distribution as [kw], the same analysis is supposed to be valid for the voiced stop as well. A reviewer asks what is the proposed relationship between dialect data and the standard, and how argumentation with data from non-standard dialects can inform the discussion about Standard Italian. The inclusion of data from non-standard varieties is motivated by the fact that, whatever the other phonological differences, the phonological nature of glides seems to be broadly the same in all the varieties of Italian discussed here. There may be minor lexical discrepancies, as mentioned in section 3, but the distribution and phonetics of glides, as well as their role in other processes (such as word-initial /s/ voicing – see section 6.2.4) largely coincide. However, some non-standard varieties have more phonological processes sensitive to glide properties than Standard Italian has. Therefore these processes can reveal properties of glides that would otherwise remain invisible if only the standard language were observed, but which reasonably are basically the same across dialects.

12 However, this may be a minor problem; having two equally valid phonological representations available for a sound sequence is much less a source of difficulty than not being able to offer a single representation – indeed, this ambiguity may simply reflect the fact that even speakers themselves are actually uncertain.

However, in what follows I will try to argue that [j], as well as [w] when it is not part of a labiovelar stop, are nuclear, and more precisely that they form a complex vocalic segment with the following vocalic element. Therefore, I will try to show that the arguments for assigning on-glides to the onset are either not relevant or empirically questionable.

6.1.3 Limits of the phonetic argument

It is hardly deniable that Italian on-glides are more contoid-like than off-glides (as eloquently shown by the data in Salza, Marotta, and Ricca 1987, and Salza 1988). But we may legitimately ask to what extent this is relevant to their phonological analysis. Multiple examples across the world's languages suggest that phonetics alone cannot explain the phonological behaviour of glides. For instance, two phonetically identical glides may function differently in two different languages: Italian [w] word-initially selects the article used with word-initial vowels (*l'uomo*), but English word-initial [w] selects the article used with word-initial consonants (*th*[ə] *war*).

Another mismatch between the phonetics and phonology of glides is exemplified by a diachronic example from other Romance languages. In many Romance languages the Latin intervocalic stops underwent voicing (e.g. Spanish *lobo* 'wolf' < LUPUS, *lado* 'side' < LATUS, *juego* 'game' < JOCUS 'joke'); interestingly for our discussion, stops between a vowel and a dorsal on-glide were voiced (e.g. *agua* 'water' < AQUA), but stops followed by an off-glide were not (e.g. Spanish *poco* 'a little' < PAUCUS rather than *pogo – the monophthongization of AU to [o] occurred after the voicing process). This suggests that off-glides, since they blocked intervocalic voicing just as non-intervocalic environments did, were phonologically consonants in Spanish (as well as in the other Romance languages having intervocalic voicing), in spite of them being phonetically more vocoid-like than the on-glide in *agua* (and in spite of off-glides arguably being phonologically vowels in other languages, closely related Italian included – see section 5 above).

Equally significantly, the same phonetic glide may realize two different phonological elements within the same language. Marotta's (1988) own analysis argues that [w] is the first half of a diphthongs if followed by [ɔ], but is the secondary articulation of a consonant if preceded by [k] or [g]; only distribution and other phonological arguments allow us to assign it to either category. In Sundanese (Levi 2008: 1967–1968) vowels are nasalized if a nasal consonant precedes them, but the spreading of nasalization is blocked by non-laryngeal consonants; glides that are inserted to break hiatuses are nasalized, while phonetically identical underlying glides are not. In fact, Levi's (2008) general claim is that both underlying glides (i.e., sonorant consonants) and derived glides (i.e., non-syllabic allophones of vowels) exist, in some cases even within the same language, which implies that the same phonetic glide may be the realization of two different phoneme categories.

Furthermore, the phonological nature of a glide can change without necessarily causing a change in its phonetic realization; as argued by Calabrese (2005: 324–326) the appearance of a constraint */Cj/ in Proto-Romance caused clusters of labial consonants and palatal glides to be re-interpreted as palatalized consonants (so triggering the compensatory gemination of the consonant), but presumably the phonetic realization of the glide remained the same. In general, we can conclude that the phonological status of glides seems not to be dictated by its phonetic properties alone, making the shorter and more constricted realization of Italian [j] and [w] hardly decisive to understand their phonological status.[13]

6.1.4 Why [j] and [w] are not so different

The presence of combinatorial restrictions is a strong argument to group segments together – if the occurrence of a certain element is inextricably linked to another, they presumably form a constituent – but their absence does not necessarily imply the opposite. Furthermore, it is not completely correct that [j] has no co-occurrence restrictions with the following vowel; as shown in section 2, the rising diphthong *[ji] is illicit, although Italian consonants can be followed by any vowel. At the same time, the apparent restriction of [w] to the diphthong [wɔ] or to labio-velar stops might be more a gap due to historical reasons than a real synchronic constraint. Whereas [j] in Italian rising diphthongs has two main diachronic sources – [ɛ] diphthongization to [jɛ] in open stressed syllables and gliding of /l/ in /Cl/ onsets – [w] only has the former, i.e. [ɔ] diphthongization in stressed open syllables. As a consequence, [w] almost exclusively occurs in [wɔ] diphthongs (as for labiovelar stops, voiceless [kw]

---

[13] A reviewer asks what is the proposed relationship between phonetics and phonology, since elsewhere in the paper phonetic properties are often referred to as inherent clues to the phonological status of glides. The crucial difference is that the other phonetic properties referred to are the output of phonological processes or depend on syllabic constituency, while the shorter and more constricted realization of on-glides with respect to off-glides seems to be a universal phonetic tendency, without a deterministic relationship with the phonology of glides.

preserves the glide which was already present in Latin – e.g. *quanto* 'how much' < QUANTUS – and the voiced labiovelar stop [gw] is usually the outcome of the fortition of [w] in Germanic loanwords – e.g. *guancia* 'cheek' < *wankja). However, over time [w] has appeared in other environments too. As observed by van der Veer (2006: 78), words such as *affettuoso* 'tender', *continuo* 'continuous', *perpetuare* 'to perpetuate', *puntualità* 'punctuality' (but the list could also include *attuale* 'current', *suadente* 'persuasive', *assuefare* 'to accustom to', *insinuare* 'to insinuate', and so on) are realized with a diphthong [wo], [wa] [we] by many speakers (although they have a hiatus [uV] in standard Italian). Further counterexamples include acronyms (for instance *UIL* [wil] *Unione Italiana Lavoratori* 'Italian Workers Union') and loanwords such as *(Kinder) Bueno* 'a snack', *twist*, *Twitter* (which also yields the fully integrated verb *twittare* 'to send a message on Twitter').

6.1.5 The (non-)significance of article allomorph selection

Article allomorph selection in Italian probably is, at least in this case, a poor diagnostic criterion, as its conditioning no longer appears to be purely phonological (see Krämer 2009: 85–87; van der Veer 2006: 79–80). Spelling probably plays a role; it is true that word-initial [wɔ] selects the allomorph also used for word-initial vowels, but [w]-initial words such as *whisky* and *weekend* select the allomorph [il]. This is unlikely to be due to the fact that the word-initial diphthong is not [wɔ], as *Word* (the name of the Microsoft word processor, which in Italian is often pronounced with the spelling pronunciation [wɔrd]) too selects *il*; Google reports several examples of this use, for instance the sentence *Se però il word che usano per leggere è più datato* "but if the Word (version) they use to read [it] is less recent". Furthermore, while words starting with [j] usually do not select *l'* (that is, the allomorph required by word-initial vowels), the allomorph they select is *lo*, which is otherwise used before /SC(C)/ clusters and geminate consonants; although [j] is never geminate in standard Italian, the allomorph *il* that would be required by word-initial simple consonants is very rarely used before [j].

There is also a certain amount of variation (for example also *lo whisky* is attested along with *il whisky*), which seems to be larger among children; Marotta (1993) reports an experiment with a group of 61 Pisan children aged of 13–14, in which 77.6% of the subjects produced *lo iato*, 20.7% produced *l'iato*, and 1.7% produced *il iato*. More generally, Marotta (1993) argues that the selection of the definite article allomorph is governed not only by phonological conditions, but also by morphological factors.

6.2 Arguments for on-glides in the nucleus

In the previous section I have presented counter-arguments against the hypothesis that on-glides belong to the onset. This leaves representations (17) and (18); I will now offer positive evidence for the idea that on-glides are in the nucleus. This evidence for the essentially vocalic nature of Italian glides includes the distribution of the so-called 'intrinsic' geminates, glide duration, article allomorph selection and the role of on-glides in two different processes involving word-initial and intervocalic /s/ voicing.

However, before presenting this evidence it may be useful to clarify in advance that what may appear at first glance a strong argument for the nuclear status of on-glides, namely the existence of the so-called 'mobile' diphthongs, is probably not pertinent to our discussion. The diphthongs [jɛ] and [wɔ] usually alternate with simple vowels, the former two occurring in stressed open syllables while the latter occur in all the other environments (since the contrast between mid-low and mid-high vowels is neutralized in unstressed syllables, they actually alternate with unstressed [e] and [o] rather than with [ɛ] and [ɔ]). While this is a significant piece of evidence for assigning Old Italian rising diphthongs (or [jɛ] and [wɔ], at least) to the nucleus, it not necessarily valid for modern Italian. In fact, there are numerous cases of simple vowels in stressed open syllables (e.g. *trovo* 'I find'), and even more numerous cases of diphthongs in unstressed syllables (*suonavo* 'I played', *chiederò* 'I will ask', *lievissimo* 'very light' and many others). It can be safely concluded that this alternation ceased to be phonologically productive long ago, and therefore cannot be used as a proof of the syllabic nature of on-glides in modern Italian (see also Bertinetto 1999, van der Veer 2006, Booij and van der Veer 2015 for a similar point; the (un)productive nature of stressed syllable diphthongization is also a debated issue in the analysis of other Romance languages – see e.g. Albright et al. 2001 on Spanish).

6.2.1 Distribution of intrinsic geminates

If [j] and [w] occur in contexts that arguably are intervocalic, and at the same time they are absent from clearly consonantal positions, we can suppose they are vocalic. This is shown for example by the so-called 'intrinsic geminates'. In Standard Italian the consonants /ts, dz, ʃ, ɲ, ʎ/ never contrast for length, but intervocalically they are always realized as geminates. When the distribution of on-glides is also considered, it can be seen that in the environment V__j the consonants /ts, dz/ are long, just as when intervocalic (e.g. *azione* [atˈtsjoːne] 'action', *razziamo* [ratˈtsjaːmo] 'we plunder'). The sequences */ʃj/, */ʎj/ and

*/ɲj/ are not possible (neither with a long nor a short consonant), but this is probably unrelated to the role of [j] within the syllable; /ʃ/, /ʎ/, ɲ/ being palatal consonants, these clusters are plausibly ruled out by a constraint against two successive palatal segments.

6.2.2 Glide duration

Studies specifically addressing the duration of Italian diphthongs include Salza (1988) and van der Veer (2006). Both find that durations of simple vowels and rising glides are similar, especially if relative duration is considered; "[a]lthough rising diphthongs are longer than monophthongs, their durations relative to the total word duration are strikingly parallel" (van de Veer 2006: 50 – also see Figure 1).

This parallelism suggests that rising diphthongs are a subclass of vowels, and hence wholly belong to the nucleus. Moreover, the duration of [wɔ] was not found to be significantly different from the duration of other diphthongs with a [w] glide (van de Veer 2006: 47), suggesting that the representation of [wɔ] does not differ from the other diphthongs.

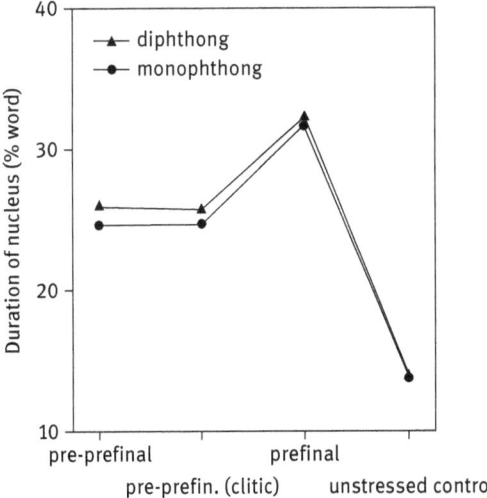

Figure 1: Mean relative durations of monophthongs and diphthongs accumulated over nine speakers, broken down by stress and syllable position in the word (all words are quadrisyllabic except those with prefinal stress, which are trisyllabic). Reproduced from van der Veer (2006: 48).

6.2.3 Intervocalic /s/ voicing

In section 5 /s/ voicing in northern Italian was a diagnostics of the vocalic status of off-glides. A similar argument holds for on-glides; /s/ between a vowel and a rising diphthong (20a) is voiced, exactly as between two vowels (or a vowel and a falling diphthong, for that matter); it is useful to add that the mere presence of a rising diphthong does not cause voicing if /s/ is not intervocalic (20b). Therefore, the glide seems to pattern phonologically as a vowel also with respect to intervocalic /s/ voicing.

(20a) i.   casuale   [kaˈzwaːle]   'casual'
       ii. risiera   [riˈzjɛːra]   non-standard by-form of *riseria* 'rice paddy'
       iii. osiamo   [oˈzjaːmo]   'we dare'
       iv. visione   [viˈzjoːne]   'vision'

(20b) i.   pensione   [penˈsjoːne] 'pension'
       ii. ansia   [ˈansja]   'anxiety'
       iii. intarsio   [inˈtarsjo]   'marquetry'
       iv. insieme   [inˈsjɛːme]   'together'

6.2.4 Glides and word-initial /s/ voicing

As mentioned in section 5 above, in Italian /s/ and /z/ only contrast in intervocalic position (and even this contrast is absent from virtually all non-standard varieties); in all the other phonological environments it is predictable whether [s] or [z] occurs. For example, word-initial /s/ is always voiceless if followed by a simple vowel:

(21) sano [ˈsaːno] 'healthy'   *[ˈzaːno]

If /s/ is followed by another consonant, the [voice] value of the former is automatically determined by that of the latter; /s/ surfaces as voiceless if the following consonant is voiceless (22a), but as voiced if the following consonant is voiced (22b).

(22a) i.   [sp]*eranza* 'hope'   ii. [st]*rano* 'strange'
       iii. [sk]*udo* 'shield'   iv. [sf]*era* 'sphere'

(22b) i.   [zb]*arcare* 'to land'   ii. [zd]*entato* 'toothless'
       iii. [zg]*raziato* 'clumsy'   iv. [zv]*asso* 'grebe'

v. [zn]*ello* 'slender' vi. [zm]*ettere* 'to stop/to give up'
vii. [zr]*otolare* 'to unroll'

This phonological restriction can be represented as a right-to-left voicing assimilation process having as its domain the onset (23); the [voice] feature value of the following segment spreads to a preceding /s/, provided that they both belong to the onset. Reference to the onset as the domain of the process is necessary, as an immediately following vowel – which is voiced but is not part of the onset – does not trigger /s/ voicing. The fact that voicing is not contrastive in vowels cannot be the reason, since sonorant consonants too (22b v–vii) cause /s/ to be voiced – a case of 'visibility' of non-contrastive features (Calabrese 2005: 353–444).

(23)

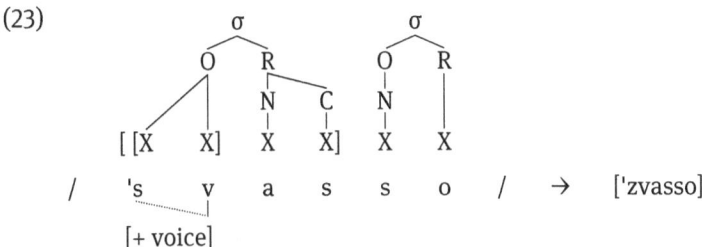

In fact, this restriction seems to follow from a universal property of voicing (and laryngeal features, more generally). As argued by Kehrein and Goldston (2004: 325), "laryngeal features are properties not of segments, but of the onsets, nuclei and codas that dominate them"; within a syllabic constituent made of two or more segments, voicing (as well as the other laryngeal features) occurs contrastively only once. This does not entail that phonetically voiced and voiceless segments can never co-exist within one and the same syllabic constituent, but that the phasing of voicing is never used contrastively.

Adopting the representation of on-glides assumed in (16), the /s/ voicing rule should apply to /#sG/ clusters; such clusters would be predicted to surface as [zG], since /s/ would be followed by a glide (i.e., a voiced segment) within the same onset. On the other hand, (17) and (18) predict that voicing should not occur – just as it does not in [saːno] – because /s/ would not be followed by other (voiced) segments within the same onset, but by (the first half of) a vowel. Crucially for our discussion, word-initial /s/ followed by a glide can never be voiced in Italian:

(23) a. *siero* 'whey'   [ˈsjɛːro]   *[ˈzjɛːro]
     b. *siedo* 'I sit'   [ˈsjɛːdo]   *[ˈzjɛːdo]

c. *suono* 'sound' [ˈswɔːno] *[ˈzwɔːno]
d. *suocero* 'father-in-law' [ˈswɔːtʃero] *[ˈzwɔːtʃero]

It has to be added that failure to voice /s/ before on-glides does not follow from an overall prohibition against any [zj] and [zw] clusters; such clusters do occur word-internally in Italian, for example in *occasione* [okkaˈzjoːne] 'occasion' and *casuale* [kaˈzwaːle] 'casual'.

6.2.5 /s/+glide clusters and article allomorph selection

A further argument to demonstrate the nuclear nature of on-glides is provided by another aspect of article allomorph selection. As seen in sections 6.1.2 and 6.1.5, the singular definite masculine article is /lo/ if the following word starts with an /sC(C)/ cluster (*lo scudo* 'the shield', *lo svasso* 'the grebe', *lo spreco* 'the waste'); before any other /C(C)/ cluster it is /il/ (*il cane*, 'the dog', *il prato* 'the meadow', *il braccio* 'the arm'). Likewise, the singular indefinite masculine article is /uno/ if the following word starts with an /sC(C)/ cluster (*uno scudo*, *uno svasso*, *uno spreco*), otherwise it is /un/ before any other /C(C)/ cluster (*un cane*, *un prato*, *un braccio*). Once more, on-glides behave as vowels rather than onset consonants; before a /sG/ cluster the article selected is /il/ (or /un/), as expected if the glide is vocalic and /s/ alone forms the onset (*il siero*, *il suono*, *il suocero*); it is virtually never[14] /lo/ (or /uno/), which would be expected if /sj/ and /sw/ were /sC/ onset clusters just as [sk]*udo* or [zm]*emorato* are.

The use of this data to support my hypothesis may appear contradictory; while I have discarded article allomorph selection before word-initial glides as a reliable diagnostic criterion in section 6, I am now using article allomorph selection before /sC(C)/ clusters. But arguably the two cases are not identical; whereas the selection of *il/lo*, *un/uno* before glides probably no longer depends on a productive phonological rule (as witnessed by lexical variation and by the numerous exceptions to the supposed rule), the complementary distribution of *il/lo*, *un/uno* before /sC(C)/ and /C(C)/ clusters is still very regular. Whereas *l'uovo* and *il Word* peacefully co-exist in Italian, the latter allomorph selection seems to be regular and much less affected by the problems described above. For example, even loanwords behave as predicted: *lo Swarosky*, *lo Sputnik*, *lo spread*, while sequences such as **il spread* or **il Sputnik* are virtually unattested.

---

[14] It is fair to add that a minority of Italian speakers seem to be comfortable with *lo suocero* – but **lo siero*, **lo suono* and so on are unattested among modern Italian speakers.

6.2.6 Are rising diphthongs complex vowels or bisegmental?

The arguments in sections 6.2.1 to 6.2.7 aim to show that Italian on-glides belong in the syllable nucleus. However, they do not say anything about the difference between (17) and (18); are Italian rising diphthongs complex vowels or bisegmental units? According to van der Veer (2006: 80), they are both; he argues that unstressed diphthongs are monosegmental, while stressed vowels are bisegmental. His conclusion decisively depends on the assumption that Italian is a moraic language. The issue of quantity-sensitivity in Italian is too vast to be treated here, but it is not uncontroversial; see Canalis and Garrapa (2012) for some arguments to the contrary. However, assuming mono- or bisegmental rising diphthongs also makes some more specific empirical predictions about diphthong duration and triphthongs, which may help choose between the two solutions. First, according to my hypothesis rising diphthongs are monosegmental (18), while falling diphthongs are bisegmental (10c). It follows that, all other things equal, the former should be shorter than the latter. Indeed, the data in Salza (1988) show precisely this for almost all rising/falling diphthong pairs (although it must be added that Salza's data come from a single speaker). Second, if both rising and falling diphthongs were bisegmental, triphthongs would be problematic; they would be trisegmental, exceeding the maximal size of Italian rhymes (van der Veer (2008) avoids this paradox because he argues that off-glides are in coda position – but see section 5). On the other hand, if rising diphthongs only occupy one segmental positions they should be able to be followed by another vocalic segment, given (10c) and (18). As discussed in section 3, triphthongs are rare but attested. Although clusters of two on-glides and a vowel after a velar stop do not count as 'true' triphthongs (since the first glide belongs to the labiovelar stop), and word-final triphthongs (e.g. *miei* ['mjɛi̯]) might alternatively be seen as hiatuses whose first element is a diphthong, a few 'true' triphthongs remain – for example *mariuolo* [ma'rjwɔːlo] 'scoundrel', *maieutica* [ma'jɛu̯tika] 'maieutics'. Their paucity seems to depend on their relative complexity and especially on the absence of diachronic paths for their development, more than on an outright synchronic prohibition. This view is also corroborated by evidence from loanwords; word such as *K-way*, *wow* and *wi-fi* are adapted in Italian as [ki'wɛi̯], [wau̯] and [wai̯'fai̯] respectively, preserving their triphthong.

6.2.7 A residual argument for (16)? No glide after obstruent + liquid clusters

If on-glides are essentially vocalic – part of a complex vowel segment – there should be no co-occurrence restrictions between on-glides and consonants.

Conversely, if on-glides where phonologically consonants they should occupy the rightmost position within onsets, and be subject to the general phonotactic restrictions on Italian onsets. Italian onsets can have no more than two segments, and the order can only be obstruent+liquid[15] (a preceding /s/ is additionally possible if the onset is word-initial). However, if there is an on-glide the number of preceding consonants seems to be limited to one (two if the first consonant is a word-initial /s/). Obstruent+liquid onsets seemingly can only be followed by a vowel, suggesting that on-glides are not nuclear and rather fill the rightmost position of the onset. In fact, traditional grammars state that words as in (24) are always realized with a hiatus rather than a diphthong.

(24) a. *Adriano* [adriˈaːno] 'Adrian' b. *striato* [striˈaːto] 'striped'
 c. *trionfo* [triˈoɱfo] 'triumph' d. *cliente* [kliˈɛnte] 'client'

However, at closer inspection this phonotactic constraint appears to be fairly weak, being describable as a tendency at most (Marotta 1987: 875). As she points out, when the [+high] segment preceded by a complex onset belongs to a suffix it is usually realized as as glide (25a), and in some lexical items glides freely alternate with vowels (25b).

(25a) i. *s+copr+iamo* [skoˈprjaːmo] 'we discover'
 ii. *destr+ier+o* [desˈtrjɛːro] 'steed'

(25b) i. *truogolo* [ˈtrwɔːgolo] / [truˈɔːgolo] 'trough'
 ii. *fluoro* [ˈflwɔːro] / [fluˈɔːro] 'fluorine'
 iii. *proprio* [ˈprɔːprjo] / [ˈprɔːprio] 'precisely/own'

It can also be added that, even in lexemes that usually have a hiatus when its [–high] vowel is stressed, a glide seem to be possible when the vowel is unstressed (although these impressionistic judgments would benefit from an experimental confirmation).

(26) a. *congr*[u]*ènza* 'congruency' b. *còngr*[u/w]*o* 'congruent'
 c. *ubr*[i]*àco* 'drunkard' d. *ubr*[i/j]*acàrsi* 'to get drunk'
 e. *cl*[i]*ènte* 'client' f. *cl*[i/j]*entèla* 'clientele'

---

[15] Onsets such as [ps], [pt] are present in a very limited number of words.

7 Conclusions

In the previous sections I have attempted to show that, despite their phonetically ambiguous nature, both Italian on-glides and off-glides are phonologically vocalic. On-glides are the first element of complex vowels; off-glides also belong to the nucleus, but as independent vocalic segments preceded by a non-high vowel. The only case in which a (back) glide belongs to the onset is after a velar stop, because phonologically they together form a labiovelar stop. These claims are based on the distribution of glides, their duration, their role in various phonological processes and in phonologically conditioned allomorphy, which all suggest Italian glides have a phonologically vocalic nature.

These results also suggest some directions for further research. One aspect is the investigation of phonetic duration; detailed studies about the duration of Italian glides already exist (among others Salza, Marotta, and Ricca 1987; Salza 1988; van der Veer 2006), but my proposal predicts that rising and falling diphthongs should differ in their length, and more data are needed to confirm this.

Second, many underlying vowels in hiatus may be optionally realized as glides, but the precise extent of this variability is still partly unknown.

Finally, an hypothesis about the make-up of the phonological rhyme is also a potential hypothesis about the poetic rhyme; if in a rising diphthong G_1V_1 the on-glide G_1 is part of the nucleus (and hence of the rhyme), the diphthong should rhyme only with G_1V_1 but not with the simple vowel V_1 or the diphthong G_2V_1 (that is, [wɔ] should rhyme with [wɔ], but not with simple [ɔ] or [jɔ]). At least for literary periods when rhyming conventions were strictly adhered to, poetic texts would offer a further kind of data to test my predictions.

Acknowledgments: I would like to thank Martina Da Tos, Jacopo Garzonio, Laura Vanelli and two anonymous reviewers for their comments and suggestions. Of course, the usual disclaimers apply.

References

Albright, Adam, Argelia Andrade & Bruce Hayes. 2001. Segmental environments of Spanish diphthongization. *UCLA Working Papers in Linguistics 7 (Papers in Phonology 5)*. 117–151.

Bertinetto, Pier Marco. 1999. La sillabazione dei nessi /sC/ in italiano: un'eccezione alla tendenza 'universale?'. In Paola Benincà, Alberto Mioni & Laura Vanelli (eds), *Fonologia e morfologia dei dialetti d'Italia. Atti del XXXI congresso della Società di Linguistica Italiana, Padova 25–27 settembre 1997*, 71–96. Roma: Bulzoni.

Bertinetto, Pier Marco & Michele Loporcaro. 2005. The sound pattern of standard Italian, as compared with the varieties spoken in Florence, Milan and Rome. *Journal of the International Phonetic Association* 35(2). 131–151.

Booij, Gert & Bart van der Veer. 2015. Allomorphy in OT: the Italian mobile diphthongs. In Eulalia Bonet, Maria-Rosa Lloret & Joan Mascaró (eds.), *Understanding Allomorphy: Perspectives from Optimality Theory*, 45–69. London: Equinox.

Calabrese, Andrea. 2005. *Markedness and economy in a derivational model of economy*. Berlin: Mouton de Gruyter.

Calamai, Silvia and Pier Marco Bertinetto. 2006. Per uno studio articolatorio dei glides palatale, labio-velare e labio-palatale dell'italiano. In Veronica Giordani, Valentina Bruseghini & Piero Cosi (eds.), *Scienze vocali e del linguaggio. Metodologie di valutazione e risorse linguistiche. Atti del III convegno nazionale dell'Associazione italiana di scienze della voce*, 43–56. Torriana: EDK.

Canalis, Stefano & Luigia Garrapa. 2012. Stressed vowel duration in Italian: What paroxytones and proparoxytones have in common. In Irene Franco, Sara Lusini & Andrés Saab (eds.), *Romance Languages and Linguistic Theory 2010*, 87–113. Amsterdam/Philadelphia: John Benjamins.

Casali, Roderic F. 1997. Vowel elision in hiatus contexts: Which vowel goes? *Language* 73(3). 493–533.

Castellani, Arrigo. 1956. Fonotipi e fonemi in italiano. *Studi di Filologia Italiana* 14. 435–453.

Giannelli, Luciano. 2000 [1976]. *Toscana*, 2nd edn. Pisa: Pacini.

Giannelli, Luciano & Leonardo M. Savoia. 1978. L'indebolimento consonantico in Toscana, I. *Rivista Italiana di Dialettologia* 2. 23–58.

Golston, Chris & Harry Van der Hulst. 1999. Stricture is structure. In Ben Hermans & Marc van Oostendorp (eds.), *The derivational residue in phonological Optimality Theory*, 153–174. Amsterdam: John Benjamins.

Hualde, José Ignacio. 2004. Quasi-phonemic contrasts in Spanish. In Vineeta Chand, Ann Kelleher, Angelo J. Rodríguez & Benjamin Schmeiser (eds.), *WCCFL 23: Proceedings of the 23rd West Coast conference on formal linguistics*, 374–398. Somerville, MA: Cascadilla Press.

Hyman, Larry. 1985. *A theory of phonological weight*. Dordrecht: Foris.

Kehrein, Wolfgang & Chris Golston. 2004. A prosodic theory of laryngeal contrasts. *Phonology* 21(3). 325–357.

Krämer, Martin. 2009. *The phonology of Italian*. Oxford: Oxford University Press.

Lepschy, Giulio. 1964. Note sulla fonematica italiana. *L'Italia Dialettale* 27. 53–67.

Levi, Susannah. 2008. Phonemic vs. derived glides. *Lingua* 118. 1956–1978.

Loporcaro, Michele. 1997. Lengthening and Raddoppiamento Fonosintattico. In Martin Maiden & Mair Parry (eds.), *The dialects of Italy*, 41–51. London/New York: Routledge.

Maddieson, Ian. 2008. Glides and gemination. *Lingua* 118. 1926–1936.

Marotta, Giovanna. 1987. Dittongo e iato in italiano: una difficile discriminazione. *Annali della Scuola Superiore* 3rd series, 17. 847–887.

Marotta, Giovanna. 1988. The Italian diphthongs and the autosegmental framework. In Pier Marco Bertinetto & Michele Loporcaro (eds.), *Certamen phonologicum. Papers from the 1987 Cortona phonology meeting*, 389–420. Torino: Rosenberg & Sellier.

Marotta, Giovanna. 1993. Selezione dell'articolo e sillaba in italiano: un'interazione totale? *Studi di Grammatica Italiana* 15. 255–296.

Marotta, Giovanna. 2008. Lenition in Tuscan Italian (*gorgia toscana*). In Joaquim Brandão de Carvalho, Philippe Ségéral & Tobias Scheer (eds.), *Lenition and fortition*, 235–272. Berlin: Mouton de Gruyter.

Marotta, Giovanna. 2010. Dittongo. In Raffaele Simone (ed.), *Enciclopedia dell'Italiano*, vol. 1. Roma, Istituto dell'Enciclopedia Italiana G. Treccani.
Marotta, Giovanna. 2011. Trittongo. In Raffaele Simone (ed.), *Enciclopedia dell'Italiano*, vol. 2. Roma: Istituto dell'Enciclopedia Italiana G. Treccani.
Mioni, Alberto. 1993. Fonetica e fonologia. In Alberto Sobrero (ed.), *Introduzione all'italiano contemporaneo: le strutture*, 101–139. Roma: Laterza.
Mioni, Alberto. 2001. *Elementi di fonetica*. Padova: Unipress.
Muljačić, Žarko. 1972. *Fonologia della lingua italiana*. Bologna: Il Mulino.
Romeo, L. 1968. A phonemic inventory of the Italian bivocalic sequences. *Forum Italicum* 2. 117–143.
Salza, Pier Luigi. 1988. Durations of Italian diphthongs and vowel clusters. *Language and Speech* 31. 97–113.
Salza, Pier Luigi, Giovanna Marotta & Davide Ricca. 1987. *Duration and formant frequencies of Italian bivocalic sequences*. In *Proceedings of the eleventh international congress of phonetic sciences (ICPhS) (August 1–7, 1987, Tallinn, Estonia)*, 113–116. Tallinn: Academy of Sciences of the Estonian SSR, 6 vols., vol. 3.
Tekavčić, Pavao. 1972. *Grammatica storica dell'italiano. Fonematica*. Bologna: Mulino.
Vaux, Bert. 2003. Syllabification in Armenian, Universal Grammar, and the lexicon. *Linguistic Inquiry* 34(1). 91–125.
van der Veer, Bart. 2006. *The Italian 'mobile diphthongs'. A test case for experimental phonetics and phonological theory*. Utrecht: LOT.

Hemanga Dutta and Michael Kenstowicz
The phonology and phonetics of laryngeal stop contrasts in Assamese

1 Introduction

Contrasts in voicing and aspiration are among the most common phonological distinctions in stop inventories (Ladefoged and Maddieson 1996: 47). They are typically distributed over the entire system (Feature Economy of Clements 2003), though there are occasional gaps at particular points of articulation such as Arabic /t/ vs. /d/ but /b/ vs. */p/ and /k/ vs. */g/. Voicing and aspiration contrasts share similar phonetic resources, in particular VOT (voice onset time, Lisker and Abramson 1964). These features may function as alternative expressions of the same historical contrast, as in Dutch [±voice] vs. German [±spread gl] reflexes of Proto-Germanic (Jessen and Ringen 2002). Also, the same underlying phonemic category may distribute its allophones at different points along the VOT dimension, as in Korean where the underlying lax stops are realized with voicing intervocalically as [b, d, g] but as voiceless unaspirated [p, t, k] word or phrase initially, and as aspirated [pʰ, tʰ, kʰ] in the current Seoul dialect of younger speakers, where they are distinguished from underlying aspirated stops by lower F0 in the following vowel (Silva 2006). Finally, voicing and aspiration contrasts have cross-linguistically similar distribution profiles with optimal realization before a modally voiced sonorant but a tendency towards neutralization at the end of the word or before an obstruent. Various researchers, most notably Lombardi (1995), unified such distributional restrictions in terms of feature licensing in the syllable onset, with a default to the unmarked voiceless, unaspirated categories in the complementary set of prosodic positions where consonants may be subject to additional assimilation to neighboring segments. This syllable-licensing model of laryngeal contrasts was challenged by Steriade (1997, 2009) who called attention to languages like Lithuanian, where an obstruent voicing contrast is preserved before sonorants (R) but is neutralized before other obstruents (O). Syllable licensing implies that OO and OR clusters differ in syllabification as hetero vs. tautosyllabic. But such a parsing is inconsistent with evidence from the prosody of the language. For example, standard grammars such as the *Lietuviu kalbos gramatika* and Senn (1966: 61) state that prefix and compound junctures coincide with a syllable boundary. Nevertheless, O#R clusters preserve a voicing contrast while O#O clusters show neutralization and voicing assimilation in these contexts: *stab-meldyste* 'idolatry' vs. *silk-medis* 'silk-tree' but *smulk-žemis* [gž] 'landowner'. In the face of this finding, Steriade (1997) proposes an alternative string-based model for the licensing of laryngeal contrasts as a function of the segmental contexts in which the auditory cues to the contrasts are most robust. The optimal context is between sonorants (R___R), especially vowels, followed by less optimal word-final (___#) position, and finally least optimal pre-obstruent (___O) position. The string-based model predicts more fine-grained distinctions in the distribution of laryngeal contrasts compared to the essentially binary onset vs. coda division of the prosodic model. Steriade (1997) finds that the segmental contexts that license contrasts for voicing largely align with the contexts that license contrasts for aspiration, since VOT is a major cue for both features.

The Indic languages spoken in the North of the Indian subcontinent are particularly relevant to this line of inquiry since their stop systems are well known for freely combining phonological contrasts in both voicing and aspiration across three to five places of articulation. Phonologically, voiced and voiceless aspirates behave in tandem for a couple of significant alternations in Assamese (see section 2 below), showing that the aspirates form a natural class. Further evidence for this point is furnished by a dialect split in which an aspirated stop has been deaspirated when the preceding syllable contains another aspirate (Goswami 1966: 6): cf. deaspirating Eastern Assamese *pʰopola* 'hollow' and *bʰok* 'hunger' vs. Western *pʰapʰla* and *bʰakʰ*. Also, /Cʰ/ acts as a single consonant rather than as a cluster in the schwa syncope of Hindi-Urdu that applies in the context VC___CV (Narang and Becker 1971, Bhatia and Kenstowicz 1972) and for the raising of open mid vowels in the context ___CV in Assamese (Goswami 1966: 75, Mahanta 2007). These processes suggest that the aspirates cannot be reduced to a sequence of C plus /h/. Finally a couple of phonotactic constraints in Assamese make the same point. First, the voiceless and voiced aspirates parallel plain stops in combining with a following liquid /r/ in the formation of word-initial #CR clusters. Second, as observed by an anonymous reviewer, in word-initial Ch structures, the C must be a stop, a restriction that follows automatically if Ch is a single segment. In sum, in terms of phonological structure the Indic aspirates behave as single segments and [±voice] and [±spread gl] are independent distinctions that crosscut the stop systems.

Phonetically, the Indic /b/ vs. /p/ vs. /pʰ/ contrasts align with the cross-linguistically common prevoiced vs. short lag vs. long lag VOT spectrum seen in languages like Thai (Lisker and Abramson 1964). But the voiced aspirates are anomalous from this VOT perspective. Phonetically, the abduction of the vocal folds implementing aspiration is prima facie antagonistic to the adduction required to generate phonation. This fact led Ladefoged (1975) to propose that voiced aspirates are murmured sounds: produced with one portion of the glottis open during stop closure and another portion adducted, comparable to the voiced /ɦ/ in English "ahead". An alternative approach to this articulatory conundrum appeals to phasing: voiced aspirates are like plain voiced stops in showing voicing during closure but are like voiceless aspirates in having an open glottis after release of the oral closure (Ingemann and Yadav 1978). Another phonetic issue concerns whether the extent of VOT is derivative from the magnitude of glottal opening, as proposed originally by Kim (1965) for Korean, or rather must be stipulated as a separate timing target. The fiber optic studies of Kagaya and Hirose (1974) for Hindi and Ingemann and Yadav (1978) for Maithili find a much larger glottal opening for the voiceless aspirates compared to the voiced ones; both reach their maxima in the vicinity of the release of the oral closure and, for the most part, terminate at comparable points in the following vowel. This finding suggests that for the Indic languages the point of resumption of glottal closure cannot be predicted from the degree of glottal opening, as proposed for Korean by Kim (1965).

In sum, the stop inventories of the Indic languages give rise to the following questions that are particularly relevant for the Licensing by Cue model of Steriade (1997, 2009). How are the phonetic cues apportioned for the two separate phonological distinctions of [±voice] and [±spread gl]? Will we find the same hierarchy of licensing contexts for both features? If not, is one contrast more susceptible to neutralization? If so, why?

In this paper we address these questions with respect to four members of the Indic family. Our principal focus is Assamese and Bengali with comparisons to what is known from the literature on Hindi-Urdu and Sanskrit. We argue that each language represents a distinct niche in the overall typology of the licensing of the voicing and aspiration contrasts in prepausal, word-final position. In all three of the modern languages voicing contrasts are stable in this position while aspiration contrasts are more varied in their realization. In particular, we show that in Assamese the underlying contrast between aspirated and plain stops is maintained by various enhancement strategies while in Bengali the contrast is largely neutralized. In Hindi-Urdu the aspiration contrast is maintained along with the voicing contrast; but even here there is evidence that the aspiration contrast is less secure in word-final position. Finally, in Sanskrit both the voicing and the aspiration contrasts are neutralized word-finally. What is noticeably missing from the typology is a language that retains the aspiration contrast but neutralizes voicing in final position. We propose that this gap is not accidental but reflects a UG (universal grammar) bias that is grounded in the phonetic correlates to the two contrasts.

The rest of this paper is organized as follows. In section 2, we overview the phonological distribution of the laryngeal stop contrasts in Assamese.

Section 3 reports the phonetic correlates of these contrasts in both word-medial and word-final positions. The motivation for a spirantization process is argued to be acoustic-auditory in nature in section 4. Section 5 examines the laryngeal stop contrasts in presonorant vs. preobstruent positions and shows that the predictions of the cue-licensing model are largely consistent with our data. Sections 6 and 7 compare the Assamese treatment of the laryngeal stop contrasts in word-final position with those of Bengali and Hindi-Urdu, respectively. Section 8 summarizes our findings and analyses and concludes.

2 Assamese phonemic inventory

Assamese phonology has the phonemic inventory shown in (1) below (Mahanta 2012). While there are a variety of dialects, the table represents the contrasts for the standard eastern variety. The data discussed in this paper are based on the speech of the first author, who is a native speaker of this variety from the Sonitpur region of Upper Assam.

(1) Phonemic inventory of Assamese

	Vowels		Consonants				
	Front	Back		Bilabial	Alveolar	Palatal	Velar	Glottal
High	i	u, ʊ	Plosive	p	t		k	
Mid	e	o		b	d		g	
	ɛ	ɔ		pʰ	tʰ		kʰ	
Low		a		bʰ	dʰ		gʰ	
			Nasal	m	n		ŋ	
			Fricative		s, z		x	h
			Approximant		ɹ	j	w	
			Lateral		l			

Ignoring loanwords, the close mid vowels /e/ and /o/ are allophones of the corresponding open vowels /ɛ/ and /ɔ/ when the following syllable contains a high vowel or another /e/ and /o/. See Mahanta (2007) for documentation and analysis. Stop and nasal place contrasts are restricted to the labial, alveolar, and velar regions. As in Hindi-Urdu, voicing and aspiration are fully crossed in Assamese resulting in 12 contrasting stops. (However, the voiced velar /gʰ/ seems to be relatively infrequent compared to the other stops.) The aspirates are found in both the native *tadbhava* vocabulary ([bʰori] 'foot', [pʰoriŋ] 'cricket') as well as in Sanskrit (*tatsama*) loans ([bʰɔsmɔ] 'ashes', [pʰagun] 'February-March'). Fricatives appear at the alveolar and velar positions but are absent from the labial region (a fact that will be come important later). For the fricatives the laryngeal contrasts are governed by common markedness preferences. There are no aspiration contrasts in the fricative series, showing the cross-linguistic bias against aspirated fricatives. A voicing contrast is found for the alveolars while the velar fricatives are restricted to the unmarked voiceless. Finally, voiced /z/ is optionally realized as a palatal affricate.

Figure 1 from Mahanta (2012) shows minimal quadruples at the three places of articulation for the laryngeal contrasts in stops.

CONSONANT	TRANSCRIPTION	ORTHOGRAPHY	GLOSS
p	pal	পাল	'to rear'
pʰ	pʰal	ফাল	'to split'
b	bal	বাল	'male child'
bʰ	bʰal	ভাল	'good'
t	tal	তাল	'palmyra tree'
tʰ	tʰal	থাল	'plate'
d	dal	দাল	'branch'
dʰ	dʰal	ধাল	'shield'
k	kal	কাল	'time'
kʰ	kʰal	খাল	'ditch'
g	gal	গাল	'cheek'
gʰ	gʰat	ঘাত	'stroke'

Figure 1. Minimal pairs illustrating laryngeal stop contrasts of Assamese in word-initial position (Mahanta 2012: 218).

The table in (2) gives more examples from our data of these contrasts in word-medial, intervocalic position.

(2) Assamese laryngeal contrasts: (near) minimal pairs in intervocalic position

[kɔpal]	'forehead'	[bɔta]	'prize'	[pɔka]	'concrete'
[baba]	'father'	[badam]	'almonds'	[bɔga]	'white'
[sɔpʰa]	'clean'	[bɔtʰa]	'oars'	[pɔkʰa]	'weed'
[xɔbʰa]	'meeting'	[badʰa]	'setback'	[pɔgʰa]	'rope'

In word-final position there is a striking modification of the aspirated stops along the dimensions of place and manner of articulation (Goswami 1966, Dutta Baruah 1992, Rhee 1998). We summarize the phenomenon in (3) based on our data. Examples appear in (4). See 3.2 for discussion of dialectal variation.

(3) a. bilabial aspirate stops are realized as labio-dental fricatives [f] and [v]
   b. alveolar aspirate stops are realized as dental stops [t̪] and [d̪]
   c. the voiceless aspirated stop /kʰ/ is optionally realized as the fricative [x]

(4) realization of laryngeal contrasts in word-final position

/p/	[sap̚]	'pressure'	/t/	[bɔt̚]	'tree'	/k/	[mak̚]	'mother'
/pʰ/	[saf]	'clean'	/tʰ/	[kat̪]	'wood'	/kʰ/	[sɔx≈sɔkʰ]	'interest'
/b/	[dab]	'coconut'	/d/	[rod]	'sun'	/g/	[dag]	'spot'
/bʰ/	[lav]	'profit'	/dʰ/	[bɔd̪]	'kill'	/gʰ/	[bagʰ]	'tiger'

The Assamese aspirate shift occasions alternations in the inflectional and derivational phonology of both nouns and verbs. Examples appear in (5).

(5) alternations in the realization of underlying aspirates in Assamese

noun inflection
citation	[lav]	[bɔrɔf]	[krʊd̪]	[kat̪]	[dukʰ]≈[dux]
ergative	[labʰ-ɛ]	[bɔrɔpʰ-ɛ]	[krʊdʰ-ɛ]	[katʰ-ɛ]	[dukʰ-ɛ]
accusative	[labʰ-ɔk]	[bɔrɔpʰ-ɔk]	[krʊdʰ-ɔk]	[katʰ-ɔk]	[dukʰ-ɔk]
	'profit'	'ice'	'anger'	'wood'	'sadness'

verb inflection
imper. familiar	[lʊv]	[saf]	[rand̪]	[gat̪]	[lɛkʰ]≈[lɛx]
imper. formal	[lʊbʰ-ɔk]	[sapʰ-ɔk]	[randʰ-ɔk]	[gatʰ-ɔk]	[lɛkʰ-ɔk]
infinitive	[lʊbʰ-i]	[sapʰ-i]	[randʰ-i]	[gatʰ-i]	[lɛkʰ-i]
	'be greedy'	'to clean'	'to cook'	'to tie'	'to write'

derivation
[maf]	'forgive, imper.'	[mapʰ-i]	'forgiving'
[lʊv]	'be greedy, imper.'	[lʊbʰ-i]	'greedy person'
[kat̪]	'wood'	[katʰ-oni]	'wooded place'
[band̪]	'bind, imper.'	[bandʰ-oni]	'bond'
[lɛkʰ]≈[lɛx]	'write, imper.'	[lɛkʰ-ɔk]	'writer'

In sum, both the voicing and aspiration contrasts are stable in prevocalic word-initial and word-medial (syllable-onset) positions but differ in their realizations word-finally. The [±voice] distinction is expressed in essentially the same way across all three of these positions while the aspirates exhibit a striking modification in their manner and minor places of articulation in word-final position.

3 Phonetic correlates

In this section we report the phonetic correlates of the Assamese voicing and aspiration contrasts based on an analysis of the speech of the first author.

3.1 Word-medial position

A corpus of 130 words (see Appendix A) was constructed that varied the voicing and aspiration stop contrasts across the labial, alveolar, and velar places of articulation for intervocalic and word-final positions. Where possible the adjacent vowels were restricted to nonhigh and back to provide a consistent context for segmentation. Each word was recorded in a randomized list with five repetitions to give a total of 650 data points. The words were recorded in a sound insulated booth with a Shure Unidirectional Head-Worn Dynamic Microphone and USB 2 Preamp at a sampling rate of 44.1 kHz, 16 bits. Statistical analyses (t-tests and linear regressions) were done in R (Bates and Maechler 2013). The following measurements were taken in Praat version 5.3.39 (Boersma and Weenink 1992–2013): the duration of stop closure as well as the interval from stop release to the onset of voicing in the following vowel (VOT) as determined by visual inspection of the waveforms and spectrograms. For this measure of VOT the cessation of random energy in the waveform was taken to coincide with the onset of the vowel even though there may have been some voicing during the aspiration period. Deciding where to draw the line within the aspiration period itself was deemed to be too tricky. The duration of voicing during stop closure until the cessation of oscillation above and below the baseline was estimated and then the ratio of closure voicing to total closure duration was calculated. Measures of the duration of the vowel preceding the stop as well as the F0 in the first observable pitch period of the vowel following release of the stop were also collected. These factors are known to be phonetic correlates of a voicing contrast in many languages (Lisker 1986, Kingston and Diehl 1994). Our results are summarized in the following tables in (6). The first shows the correlates for the voicing and aspiration contrasts across all consonants while the second breaks them down for the four individual sets. The first table also reports independent T-tests over the phonetic correlates as a function of the voicing and aspiration categories.

(6) Averages (and standard deviations) for phonetic correlates of laryngeal stop contrasts in medial position; T-tests of laryngeal categories

closure dur (ms)	[+voice]	[–voice]	[+spread gl]	[–spread gl]
mean (sd)	75 (16)	109 (18)	88 (23)	97 (24)
F-statistic: 316.2 on 1 and 337 df, $p < 0.001$			F-statistic: 12.04 on 1 and 337 df,	
Adjusted R-squared: 0.48			$p = 0.005$; Adjusted R-squared: 0.03	

voice ratio	[+voice]	[−voice]	[+spread gl]	[−spread gl]
mean (sd)	.80 (.20)	.09 (.07)	.39 (.35)	.50 (.40)
F-statistic: 1782 on 1 and 337 df, $p < 0.001$ Adjusted R-squared: 0.84			F-statistic: 6.9 on 1 and 337 df, $p = 0.008$; Adjusted R-squared: 0.01	

V1 duration (ms)	[+voice]	[−voice]	[+spread gl]	[−spread gl]
mean (sd)	84 (22)	67 (15)	76 (20)	75 (21)
F-statistic: 72.15 on 1 and 337 df, $p < 0.001$ Adjusted R-squared: 0.17			F-statistic: .23 on 1 and 337 df, $p = 0.63$; Adjusted R-squared: 0.002	

V2 F0 (Hz)	[+voice]	[−voice]	[+spread gl]	[−spread gl]
mean (sd)	135 (8)	144 (10)	140 (10)	138 (10)
F-statistic: 73.87 on 1 and 337 df, $p < 0.001$ Adjusted R-squared: 0.17			F-statistic: 4.52 on 1 and 337 df, $p = 0.03$; Adjusted R-squared: 0.01	

VOT (ms)	[+voice]	[−voice]	[+spread gl]	[−spread gl]
mean (sd)	47 (45)	63 (41)	89 (25)	12 (11)
F-statistic: 11.5 on 1 and 337 df, $p < 0.001$ Adjusted R-squared: 0.03			F-statistic: 1847 on 1 and 337 df, $p < 0.001$; Adjusted R-squared: 0.84	

medial	p, t, k	p^h, t^h, k^h	b, d, g	b^h, d^h, g^h
closure dur	115 (15)	103 (19)	80 (18)	70 (11)
voice ratio	.10 (.06)	.08 (.07)	.85 (.21)	.74 (.18)
V1 duration	63 (15)	70 (15)	86 (21)	83 (23)
V2 F0 (Hz)	142 (11)	145 (10)	134 (8)	135 (8)
VOT	19 (11)	97 (15)	6 (6)	88 (25)

Voiced stops have significantly shorter closure duration than voiceless ones, presumably reflecting the difficulty of sustaining voicing during the oral closure. There is a substantial difference in closure voicing, with the voiced stops showing phonation over roughly 80% of their duration compared to the voiceless stops' c. 9%. The duration of the preceding vowel and the F0 just after the release of oral closure also distinguish voiced from voiceless stops in the expected directions, with shorter vowels preceding the voiceless stops and higher F0 following them. Thus, the [±voice] contrast is associated with a variety of cues (acoustic correlates), with closure voicing being most robust in magnitude and significance and supported by smaller differences in the duration of the preceding vowel and F0 in the following vowel.

As far as the contrast in aspiration is concerned, the most reliable correlate is, not surprisingly, VOT. There is a large and statistically reliable difference between the aspirated C^h 89 (25) ms. vs. plain C 12 (11) ms. stops. There is also a small effect of voicing, with voiceless stops having longer VOT values than voiced ones in both the aspirated and the unaspirated categories. Unpaired t-tests found these differences to be significant: [b^h, d^h, g^h] vs. [p^h, t^h, k^h] (t = 2.8; F-statistic: 8.4 on 1 and 177 df 135, p = .004; Adjusted R-squared = 0.04) and [b, d, g] vs. [p, t, k] (t = 9.1; F-statistic: 82.23 on 1 and 158 df, p = < 0.001; Adjusted R-squared = 0.33). Maddieson and Gandour (1976) found a small difference in the length of the vowel before the voiced aspirates (longer) compared to their plain voiced counterparts in Hindi-Urdu, but no such difference holds in our Assamese data. The voiced aspirates [b^h, d^h, g^h] have shorter closure durations and smaller voicing ratios compared to their plain counterparts. Unpaired t-tests found these differences to be significant: closure duration (t = 4.2; F-statistic: 17.71 on 1 and 167 df, p < 0.001; Adjusted R-squared = 0.09) and voicing ratio (t = 5.37; F-statistic: 28.85 on 1 and 166 df, p = < 0.001; Adjusted R-squared = 0.14). These results would be consistent with the assumption that during the articulation of the voiced aspirates the glottis starts opening during the stop closure phase, as suggested by the fiber optic studies of Hindi by Kagaya and Hirose (1974) and of Maithili by Ingemann and Yadav (1977). Finally, voice quality (breathiness) in the following vowel was shown by Dutta (2007) to be another significant correlate of the aspirated stops in Hindi. We made a smaller number of measurements of this factor (H1 – H2) in the low back vowels in our corpus that follow a word-initial stop and found a similar result (not reported here).

In sum, both the [±voice] and the [±spread gl] contrasts are reliably distinguished in intervocalic position. They differ however in that there are more cues for the voicing contrast and the most robust one (closure voicing) is internal to the stop itself while the [±spread gl] distinction is signaled primarily by cues found in the following vowel, requiring a sequencing of the glottal closing and opening gestures.

3.2 Word-final prepausal position

In comparison to what is reported for other Indic languages (in particular Hindi-Urdu), the Assamese word-final aspirated stops undergo a shift in their manner and place of articulation, as indicated in section 2. Based on the preceding literature, there appears to be a significant amount of dialectal variation in the details of the process. But what is striking is that the shift only affects underlying aspirates and is confined to final position. Word-initial and word-medial aspirates are stable. We first summarize what is reported by Goswami (1966) and then by Dutta Baruah (1992).

Goswami (1966) states that while the present-day standard variety of Assamese is based on the eastern dialect of Sibsagar, in earlier stages of the language the western dialect prevailed over the entire country. The author is from the west. He reports that all aspirates word-finally are lenis. "There is a tendency to spirantize in some of the dialects, all except /dɦ/ and /gɦ/ into their homorganic spirants, i.e. /pʰ, tʰ, kʰ, bɦ/ have the allophones [ɸ, θ, x, β] respectively" (p. 14). The author adds in a footnote that the realizations of /tʰ/ as [θ] and /kʰ/ as [x] are "dialectal", commenting further that the former is not very frequent or rather is a free variant and the latter is always distinctive of some caste dialects. In (7) below are examples of the spirantization excerpted from Goswami's discussion, using his notation.

(7) mapʰ   [maɸ]   ≈ [mapᵒ]   'remission, weight'
    sapʰ   [saɸ]   ≈ [sapᵒ]   'clean'
    alɛ́p   [alɛ́ɸ]   ≈ [alɛ́pᵒ]   'inverted comma'
    labʰ   [laβ]   ≈ [lab ᵝ]   'income, gain'
    lobʰ   [loβ]   ≈ [lob ᵝ]   'greed'
    kʰjobʰ   [kʰjoβ]   ≈ [kʰjob ᵝ] 'anger'
    zetʰ   [zeθ]   'second month of the Assamese year'
    pitʰ   [pit ᶿ]   ≈ [pitʰ]   'place, region'
    dɛkʰ   [dɛkʰ]   'to see'

Dutta Baruah's (1992) description of the eastern Sibsagar dialect reports spirantization of the word-final labials (pp. 41, 44), citing examples such as those in (8).

(8) nipʰ   [niɸ]   'nib'
    mapʰ   [maɸ]   'excuse'
    sapʰ   [saɸ]   'clean'
    labʰ   [laβ]   'profit'
    xulɐbʰ   [xulɐβ]   'cheap'
    pabʰ   [paβ]   'a kind of fish'

From these two prior descriptions we infer that spirantization of the word-final labial aspirates is more widespread, while for the alveolars and velars the process is more "dialectal". Also, for younger, more educated speakers, the bilabials seen in (7) and (8) are being replaced by labio-dentals. Below, we summarize the state of affairs for the first author's speech, who is representative of this younger generation. Clearly, more research is needed to document the range of dialectal variation. For our purposes, the important point is that spirantization only affects underlying aspirates and is restricted to word-final position.

First, the voiceless velar stop /kʰ/ is optionally realized as the fricative [x] (9). As indicated earlier, /x/ is an independent phoneme in the language and so the free variation between [kʰ] and [x] leads to a neutralization. It should be noted that for the words in (9), underlying /x/ never alternates with [kʰ]. Aside from /x/ itself, only /kʰ/ may be realized as [x]; /k/ may not. Minimal pairs include /dukʰ/ > [dukʰ] ≈ [dux] 'sadness' vs. /dux/ > [dux], *[dukʰ] 'fault' and /rakʰ/ > [rakʰ] ≈ [rax] 'to keep' vs. /rax/ > [rax], *[rakʰ] 'a Hindu festival'. Moreover, the spirantization of /kʰ/ is not found word-medially or in initial position.[1]

(9) realizations of /kʰ/ and /x/ in different positions of the word

	/kʰ/		/x/	
initial	/kʰaru/	[kʰaru,] *[xaru] 'bangles'	/xɔkʰa/	[xɔkʰa], *[kʰɔkʰa] 'friend'
medial	/akʰɔr/	[akʰɔr], *[axɔr] 'letter'	/ɔxɔmia/	[ɔxɔmia], *[ɔkʰɔmia] 'Assamese'
final	/makʰ/	[makʰ] ≈ [max] 'unit of measure'	/bax/	[bax], *[bakʰ] 'to dwell'
	cf./mak/	[mak], *[max] 'mother'		

Second, the aspirated bilabial stops are obligatorily realized as labio-dental fricatives (10). The fricatives [f] and [v] are only found in this position in Assamese and may not appear word-initially or word-medially. Indeed, loanwords with /f/ and /v/ in these positions are adapted as aspirated stops (see below). Furthermore, it is only the underlying aspirates that are fricativized. Plain stops /p/ and /b/ do not alter their manner of articulation.

(10) realizations of /pʰ/ and /bʰ/ vs. /p/ and /b/ in different positions of the word

/sapʰ/	[saf]	'to clean'	/pap/	[pap̚]	'sin'
/mapʰ/	[maf]	'to forgive'	/sap/	[sap̚]	'pressure'
/bɔrɔpʰ/	[bɔrɔf]	'ice'	/dʰap/	[dʰap̚]	'slope'
/labʰ/	[lav]	'profit'	/bab/	[bab]	'designation'
/lʊbʰ/	[lʊv]	'greed'	/dub/	[dub]	'to drown, sink'
/xourɔbʰ/	[xourɔv]	'fame'	/kabab/	[kabab]	'kabab'

Third, the underlying coronal stops change their place of articulation from alveolar to dental (11). This change in point of articulation only affects the aspirates.

---

[1] Mahanta's (2012:219) description of the speech of an eastern Assamese speaker from Jorhat indicates that spirantization for the velar /kʰ/ occurs in word-medial position. The process is said to be dependent on the individual speaker and speech rate and formality.

Plain /t/ and /d/ remain alveolar. The dentalization of /tʰ/ and /dʰ/ does not apply to word-initial or word-medial stops. Only in word-final position does this process apply. We assume that the dentalized [t̪] corresponds to what Goswami (1966) transcribes as [tᶿ].

(11) realizations of /tʰ/ and /dʰ/ vs. /t/ and /d/ in different positions of the word

/katʰ/	[kat̪]	'wood'	/bɔt/	[bɔt̚]	'Indian banyan'
/mɔtʰ/	[mɔt̪]	'temples'	/dʰɔpat/	[dʰɔpat̚]	'tobacco'
/zɛtʰ/	[zɛt̪]	'May-June'	/dupat/	[dupat̚]	'pair'
/bɔdʰ/	[bɔd̪]	'to kill'	/rod/	[rod]	'sunshine'
/krʊdʰ/	[krʊd̪]	'anger'	/mɔd/	[mɔd]	'alcohol'
/bʊdʰ/	[bʊd̪]	'Wednesday'	/dɔrɔd/	[dɔrɔd]	'pain'

/tʰɔga/	[tʰɔga]	'artefact'
/matʰa/	[matʰa]	'head'
/dʰɔni/	[dʰɔni]	'wealthy'
/radʰa/	[radʰa]	'Radha'

A final relevant point is that words ending in /h/ are not modified. Only aspiration as a secondary feature in the stop system leads to a change.

(12) realization of word-final /h/

/kɔpah/	[kɔpah]	'cotton'
/bɔtah/	[bɔtah]	'wind'
/sah/	[sah]	'tea'
/dɔh/	[dɔh]	'ten'

In sum, word-final position is the site of three disparate modifications of the place and manner of articulation of underlying aspirate stops in Assamese. The voiceless velar /kʰ/ is optionally spirantized to [x], merging with underlying /x/. The bilabials /pʰ/ and /bʰ/ are fricativized to [f] and [v], and lastly the alveolars /tʰ/ and /dʰ/ are realized as dentals [t̪] and [d̪]. Plain stops do not participate in these modifications nor does /h/.

3.3 [±voice] in word-final position

The plain stops retain the voicing contrast in word-final position. Mahanta (2012: 218) states that syllable-final voiceless stops are unreleased while Goswami (1966) reports variation in release for word-final position. For a sample of the first three repetitions of our data, the nonrelease of plain voiceless stops varied as a function of place of articulation: [p̚] 23/24, [t̚] 10/19, [k̚] 10/24. The table in (13) shows that closure voicing and preceding vowel duration continue to distinguish the [±voice] contrast. We also provide the results for the plain consonants, which have been separated out from the spirantized aspirated stops. They have essentially the same differences as the overall set and so the various spirantization effects noted above do not alter the voicing contrast. The magnitude of the closure voicing is reduced compared to word-medial position but is still significantly different from the corresponding voiceless stops. The duration of the preceding vowel is almost twice as long as in medial position, presumably reflecting a lengthening before pause. We also checked the F0 in the vowel offset and found that it has a small effect in the expected direction (higher before voiceless).

(13) Averages (and standard deviations) for phonetic correlates of underlying laryngeal stop contrasts in word-final prepausal position

voice ratio	[+voice]	[−voice]	[b,d,g]	[p,t,k]
mean (sd)	.58 (.26)	.07 (.08)	.66 (.22)	.09 (.09)
t	−24.83			
F-statistic: 616.5 on 1 and 308 df, $p < 0.001$				
Adjusted R-squared: 0.66				

V1 duration (ms)	[+voice]	[−voice]	[b,d,g]	[p,t,k]
mean (sd)	151 (28)	126 (24)	151 (27)	124 (24)
t	−8.1			
F-statistic: 67.05 on 1 and 308 df, $p < 0.001$				
Adjusted R-squared: 0.66				

V1 F0 (Hz)	[+voice]	[−voice]	[b,d,g]	[p,t,k]
mean (sd)	140 (12)	144 (12)	138 (11)	140 (13)
t	3.03			
F-statistic: 9.17 on 1 and 308 df, $p = 0.002$				
Adjusted R-squared: 0.02				

final	p	pʰ	b	bʰ
voice ratio	.09 (.09)	.04 (.05)	.66 (.22)	.45 (.28)
V1dur	124 (24)	129 (24)	151 (27)	152 (29)
F0	140 (13)	148 (10)	138 (11)	142 (14)

In sum, the word-final [±voice] contrast in Assamese is robust and is expressed with the same phonetic correlates as in word-medial position. On the other hand, the aspirates are noticeably modified in their phonetic realization as either spirants or dentals. In the next section we discuss the motivation for this shift.

4 Motivation for aspirate shift

What is the motivation for the shift in the realization of the underlying aspirates in word-final position compared to their stable realization word-medially and initially? Our suggestion is that it is a maneuver of the phonology/phonetics designed to maintain/enhance the plain vs. aspirate contrast in a context where the cues to the contrast are either unavailable or significantly minimized in quantity and/or magnitude. Recall that in medial position the major correlates of [±spread gl] are the stop-external cues of VOT and the voice quality effects on the following vowel. In word-final, prepausal position there is no following vowel and so the acoustic/auditory reflexes of the open glottis will be significantly reduced. We can see this effect with the velar stop /k^h/, which has two variants in final position: the spirantized [x] and unspirantized [k^h]. The average intensities of the aspiration for a period of 30 ms after stop release in the medial prevocalic and word-final contexts for [k^h] were as follows: word-medial 55.21 dB (2.78) vs. word-final 49.54 dB (2.71). Remembering that the decibel scale is not linear, this is a significant difference in magnitude: Welch two sample t-test: t = 5.81, 24 df, p = < 0.001.

Given that there is motivation to enhance the aspiration contrast beyond simple release vs. unreleased, why is spirantization chosen rather than other possible changes such as preaspiration? First, there is cross-linguistic evidence for a close relationship between aspirated stops and the corresponding fricatives. In the loanword adaptation of fricatives into languages that lack the fricative but have a plain vs. aspirated contrast, the aspirate adaptation is chosen. This is seen in the examples in (14). Recall from the table of Assamese phonemes in (1) that the language lacks fricatives in the labial and interdental regions. English loans with these sounds are adapted as the corresponding aspirated stops in word-initial and medial positions. But due to the aspirate shift in final position, they can be accommodated directly in the case of the labials and as a dental stop in the case of /θ/. Korean lacks the labio-dental [f] entirely but has a three-way contrast of plain (lax), tense (fortis), and aspirated voiceless stops. The systematic choice of [p^h] rather than [p] reflects preservation of the frication in the aspirated release of the stop.

(14) Assamese
f > pʰ   [pʰrai] 'fry', [pʰɛn] 'fan', [telipʰun] 'telephone', [kɔf] 'cough'
v > bʰ   [bʰɛn] 'van', [bʰut] 'vote', [bʰɛlu] 'value', [lav] 'love'
θ > tʰ   [tʰri] 'three', [tʰiŋkar] 'thinker', [eit̪] 'eighth'

Korean
f > pʰ   film > [pʰilɨm] (not [pilɨm]), coffee > [kʰapʰi], chef > [sjɛpʰu]

The Nilotic language Dinka lacks fricatives but has a dental vs. alveolar contrast in its stops and affricates (Remijsen and Manyang 2009). Arabic loans with /t, d/ are adapted as alveolar stops, while /s/ is nativized to a dental stop. This choice of dental over alveolar for the adaptation of /s/ parallels the Assamese realization of the aspirated /tʰ/ as a dental. In both cases the alveolar (apical) place of articulation is replaced by a dental (laminal) one.

(15) (examples from Idris 2004)
cá̯a̯at̪ < šaahid 'witness'
rêeet̪ < raʔiis 'president'
t̪úuk < suuk 'market'

Also, well known sound changes in the history of the Indo-European languages shift aspirates to the corresponding fricatives such as PIE *bʰ, *dʰ, *gʰ > Greek Φ, θ, x and the Old-High German consonant shift of Proto-Germanic *pʰ, *tʰ, *kʰ > f, tˢ/s, x. See Vaux (1998) and Vaux and Samuels (2005) for more discussion of the connection between aspiration and fricatives.

Another question concerns the basis of the spirantization. Both the /pʰ/ -> [f], and /kʰ/ -> [x] alternations involve change to a continuant manner of articulation. Such changes are often associated with lenitions. But, as observed by Rhee (1998), the Assamese consonant shift does not have the profile of a typical lenition since it does not apply intervocalically – the canonical lenition site – nor does it affect the plain stops. We might view the spirantization as a reassociation of the opening gesture implemented by the glottis in the release and post-release phase of the aspirated stop to coincide with the oral constriction gesture implemented by the lips and tongue dorsum, changing the degree of constriction from closure to narrow stricture. But this would not explain the change of alveolar to dental where the consonant remains a stop. Moreover, it would be inconsistent with Padgett's (1991) generalization that the assimilation or spread of a stricture gesture only occurs when accompanied by an assimilation of place as well. See however Scheer (2003) for an analysis along these lines.

Our suggestion is that the similarity between the aspirated stops and the corresponding segments involved in the Assamese shift is rather to be found in the acoustic (auditory) domain. Both involve a significant degree of turbulent airflow distributed through the spectrum. This can be seen in the screenshots of the waveforms and spectrograms in (16) below. The first pair shows a word-medial aspirated [pʰ] from the word [epʰal] 'one piece' and its spirantized allophone [f] in final position from the word [saf] 'clean'. The second pair illustrates the two alternative realizations of a word-final velar aspirate from the word /makʰ/ 'unit of measurement'. In each case the fricative is associated with significant turbulence that is comparable to the random energy found in the aspirate.

(16)

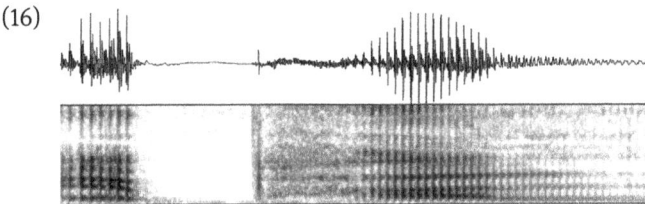

Figure 2: [epʰal] 'one piece'.

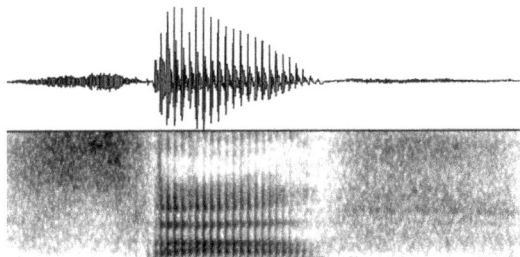

Figure 3: [saf] 'clean'.

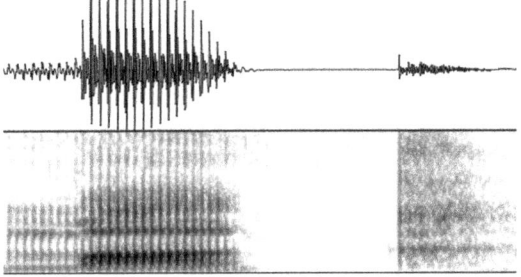

Figure 4: [makʰ] 'unit of measure'.

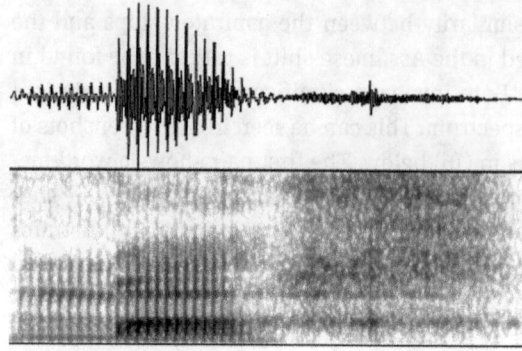

Figure 5: [max] 'unit of measure'.

Turning now to the coronal stops, we propose that the change from an alveolar to dental point of articulation is also motivated by acoustic similarity. The alveolar fricative [s] corresponding to the stop [tʰ] has its turbulence concentrated in the upper region of the frequency spectrum while the dental [θ] mentioned by Goswami (1966) and the release phase of our [t̪] have a more diffuse spectrum that provides a better acoustic match to the aspiration. This is apparent from comparison of the /s/ in [saf] 'clean' in (16) with the release phases of [tʰ] of [matʰa] 'head' and the [t̪] in /mɔtʰ/ > [mɔt̪] 'temple' in (17) and their corresponding FFT's. The [s] has energy concentrated in the central region of the spectrum around 10,000 Hz while the release phases of [tʰ] and [t̪] concentrate their energy in the lower regions. In other words, [t̪] is a closer acoustic match for [tʰ] than [s] is. In addition, as noted by an anonymous reviewer, the shift to dental point of articulation enhances the contrast with the plain stops, which retain their alveolar place.

(17)

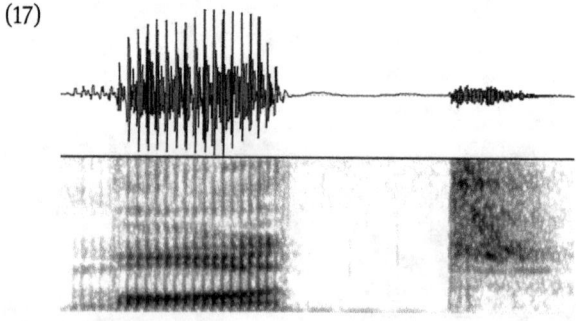

Figure 6: [matʰa] 'head'.

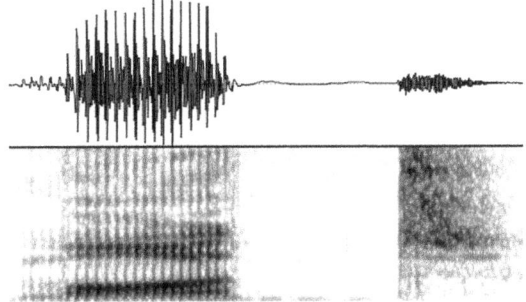

Figure 7: /mɔtʰ/ > [mɔt̪] 'temple'.

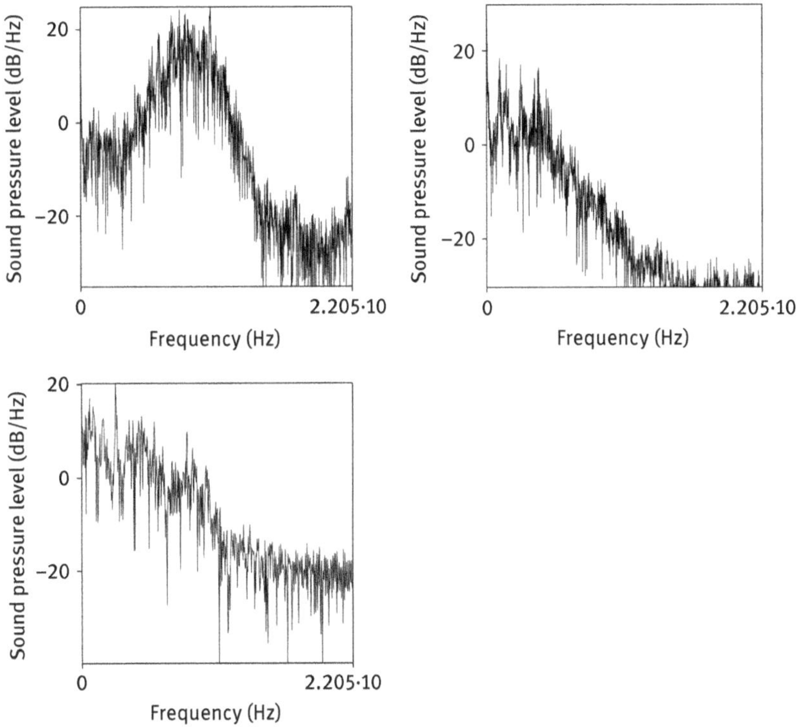

[s] of [saf] 'clean' [tʰ] of [matʰa] 'head'
[t̪] of [mɔt̪] 'temple'

Figure 8: FFT's of three turbulent coronal consonants.

The table in (18) shows center of gravity and skew measurements taken over 20 ms. intervals of the word-final segments involved in the Assamese spirantization using a Praat script due to Hoole (ND). For the stops the measurements were made over the release phases.

(18) center of gravity and skew measures of various word-final segments

segment	N	center of gravity	skew
f	15	4412 (1212)	0.41 (0.56)
v	11	2569 (950)	1.99 (1.16)
k^h	14	1780 (282)	3.41 (1.55)
x	16	2453 (1212)	2.86 (3.16)
s	10	8453 (502)	−.94 (.32)
t̪	12	4182 (1141)	.45 (0.59)
d	8	2722 (783)	1.0 (1.39)
d̪	9	1950 (301)	1.7 (.45)

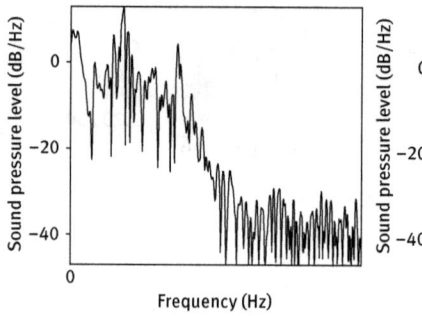

Figure 9: Spectrum of [d].

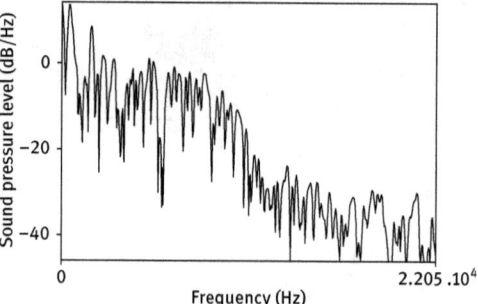

Figure 10: Spectrum of [d̪].

The alveolar [s] has a high center of gravity and a negative skew indicating that most of the turbulence is concentrated in the upper region of the spectrum, reinforcing the point that it is a poor acoustic match for the aspiration of [tʰ] compared to the release phase of [t̪]. Comparison of [f] vs. [v] and the release phases of [t̪] vs. [d̪] indicate that voicing appears to concentrate more energy in the lower part of the spectrum, suggesting an overall decrease in intensity. Also, comparison between the releases of word-final (plain) alveolar [d] vs. underlying aspirate [d̪] found a significant difference in the center of gravity (t = 2.8, 15 df, p = 0.02) but not the skew (t = 1.42, 15 df, p = 0.17). Paired t-tests found small but significant differences in F2 trajectories from vowel mid point to vowel offset over a set of 25 /CaX/ minimal pairs (Appendix B): F2 alveolar [t] 148 Hz (54 Hz) vs. dental [t̪] 98 Hz (46 Hz), (t = 4.25, 24 df, p < 0.001). The shallower F2 slopes for the dental [t̪] is consistent with a more anterior point of articulation. Ijaz and Anwar (ND) report a similar result for the dental vs. alveolar distinction in Urdu, where the low vowel [a] has an F2 offset of 1500 Hz before dental [t̪] vs. 1700 Hz for alveolar [t]. Finally, we have the impression that the dental [t̪] and [d̪] differ from the alveolar [t] and [d] as laminal vs. apical. This difference in tongue posture would be consistent with the flatter spectra of the release phases of [d̪] vs. the more peaked spectra of [d] seen in the samples in Figures 9 and 10 above and observed by Dart (1990: 139) for a similar contrast in 'O'odham.

Our phonological analysis of the Assamese shift is couched in the Optimality model (Prince and Smolensky 2004) and has the following ingredients. First, we assume that there is an auditory-acoustic based feature of [±turbulence] whose acoustic signature is randomly distributed energy in the spectrum. Aspirated stops and [h] share this feature with fricatives and the release phases of affricates and the Assamese dental stops [t̪] and [d̪]. In the face of the markedness constraint banning word-final aspirates, Assamese preserves the turbulence of the aspirate in the fricative at the cost of infidelity for [continuant] and [distributed], which are demoted below Ident-[turbulence].

(19) *Cʰ#, Ident-[turbulence] ≫ Ident-[contin], Ident-[distr]

/labʰ/	*Cʰ#	Ident-[turbulence]	Ident-[contin]
> lav			*
labʰ	*!		
lab		*!	

/katʰ/	*Cʰ#	Ident-[turbulence]	Ident-[distr]
> kat̪			*
katʰ	*!		
kat̚		*!	
kas		*!	

As seen in (20) below, for the velar /kʰ/ the rankings between *Cʰ# and the faithfulness constraints are variable, producing two outputs: the faithful [kʰ] and the spirantized [x]. In addition to the fact that the fricative [x] is already present in the phonemic inventory, the velar stop typically has a longer VOT than coronal and labial stops cross-linguistically, which could help to explain why its aspiration is (optionally) retained vis a vis the labial and coronal stops, which obligatorily shift their manner and/or place. For our Assamese data, the VOT measures in medial position align with this place hierarchy: [pʰ] 88 (14) ms, [tʰ] 96 (14) ms, [kʰ] 105 (19) ms.

(20) *kʰ#, Ident-[turbulence] ≫ Ident-[contin]

/makʰ/	*kʰ#	Ident-[turbulence]	Ident-[contin]
makʰ	*!		
☞ max			*
mak̚		*!	

Ident-[contin], Ident-[turbulence] ≫ *kʰ#

/makʰ/	Ident-[contin]	Ident-[turbulence]	*kʰ#
☞makʰ			*!
max	*!		
mak̚		*!	

5 Preconsonantal position

If Assamese follows Lithuanian, Russian, and Klamath, we expect that the laryngeal stop contrasts will be preserved before (modally voiced) sonorant consonants but will be neutralized before obstruents. To pursue this point we collected and analyzed two data sets. First, we looked at word-initial stop sonorant clusters. Such structures are limited in number in Assamese. The liquid is restricted to the rhotic and quite a few of the aspirates arise from loanwords. Examples appear in (21). See the Appendix C for the full data set, which were recorded in five repetitions. In these data the aspiration overlapped the [r]. In order to estimate the effect of the aspiration compared to clusters with a plain stop, the duration from stop release to the onset of the vowel was measured. On average, the rhotic is 30 ms longer in the aspirated condition: aspirate 99 ms (37), plain 70 ms (31), Welch two-sample t-test: $t = 3.17$, F-statistic: 10.1, 55 df, $p = 0.002$; Adjusted R-squared: 0.14. This suggests that the C vs. Cʰ contrast is maintained in the presonorant context.

(21) [prɔtʰɔm]   'first'   [pʰrai]   'fry'
      [bristi]   'rain'   [bʰrɔmɔn]   'journey'
      [tritijɔ]   'third'   [tʰristar] 'three-star'
      [dristi]   'vision' [dʰrubɔ]   'universal'

To further investigate the laryngeal contrast in preconsonantal position, a set of 24 words whose final stops were balanced for place, voicing, and aspiration was constructed (see Appendix D). They were followed by the particles –nai 'no, none', -tʊ definite marker, and –dur hol 'away went' and repeated five times to give a data set of 360 items.

The table below shows the results before the sonorant –nai. The voicing contrast is maintained for the same factors that operate word-medially before a vowel, especially the closure-voicing ratio. And the plain vs. aspirated contrast is most reliably expressed by VOT.

(22) phonetic correlates of [±voice] and [±spread gl] before –nai: mean (st dev) and t-test

C1 / -nai	closure dur	voice ratio	V1 duration	F0	VOT
[+voice]	97 (27)	.53 (.36)	133 (23)	142 (12)	13 (20)
[–voice]	125 (37)	.08 (.02)	115 (22)	137 (21)	44 (41)
[–spread gl]	106 (29)	.39 (.39)	128 (23)	142 (14)	18 (26)
[+spread gl]	120 (41)	.17 (.28)	117 (24)	136 (20)	42 (42)
t-test p: (63 df)					
[±voice]	0.001	<0.001	0.002	0.296	<0.001
[±spread gl]	0.115	0.012	0.058	0.125	0.007

Before the voiceless consonant of –tʊ there is neutralization of the voicing contrast for C1 with apparent assimilation of the voicelessness of the following consonant. This can be seen in the .08 closure voicing ratio for underlying voiced stops.

(23) phonetic correlates of underlying [±voice] before -tʊ: mean (st dev) and t-test

C1 / -tʊ	closure dur	voice ratio	V1 duration	F0
[+voice]	113 (18)	.08 (.18)	135 (22)	133 (23)
[–voice]	119 (15)	.03 (.07)	127 (30)	133 (28)
t-test p: (58 df)	0.204	0.115	0.276	0.968

But before the voiced stop of –dur, the underlying voicing contrast for C1 seems to be retained for the key correlates of closure duration and voicing ratio, suggesting that there is incomplete assimilation of voicing in the context of the voiced stop.

(24) phonetic correlates of underlying [±voice] before –*dur*: mean (st dev) and t-test

C1 / -dur	closure dur	voice ratio	V1 duration	F0
[+voice]	80 (13)	.89 (.29)	138 (24)	139 (19)
[–voice]	96 (25)	.49 (.45)	134 (28)	136 (25)
t-test p: (58 df)	0.003	< 0.001	0.530	0.630

But when the data are broken down in terms of the plain vs. aspirated categories for C1 then there is a significant difference for the voicing ratio, with underlying plain stops showing an average closure-voicing ratio of .84 while underlying aspirates lag behind at .52, a significant difference (t = –3.17, 58 df, p = 0.002). This suggests that the underlying [+spread gl] gesture for the aspirated consonants may inhibit C1's assimilation of voicing from C2. More data are needed to test this hypothesis; see Kenstowicz, Abu-Mansour, and Törkenczy (2000) and Wetzels and Mascaró (2001) for examples of voicing assimilation restricted to just [+voice] or to just [-voice].[2]

In sum, our data are largely consistent with the predictions made by the Licensing by Cue model. Before the nasal of –*nai* the closure voicing ratio, closure duration, and V1 duration distinguish the voiced from voiceless stops on an order of magnitude and reliability comparable to word-final position. And for the aspiration contrast, while the 42 ms VOT of aspirated stops is quite a bit less than the c. 90 ms found word-medially before a vowel, it is still reliably distinct from the plain stops' 18 ms. In position before the voiceless stop –*tu* there is neutralization of the underlying voicing contrast in C1. Before the voiced stop of –*dur*, underlying plain stops assimilate the voicing of the following voiced stop while underlying aspirates do so to a significantly smaller degree.

6 Bengali

Bengali is cited (Kenstowicz 1994: 193–4) as a language with a dialect split with one variant following Hindi in maintaining the voicing and aspiration contrasts in word final position while the other neutralizes the aspiration contrast but pre-

---

[2] It should be noted that the –*tʊ*, -*nai*, and –*dur* morphemes do not derive from the same underlying syntactic structures. In particular, while – *tʊ* is a suffix, the items with -*nai* and with -*dur* are subject-predicate structures. Differences in junctural cohesion could thus conceivably have influenced the results. But in no case was there a pause between the target word and the following particle.

serves the voicing contrast.[3] As observed by Steriade (1997), this asymmetry is expected in the licensing by cue model if the major cues to the aspiration contrast are the stop-external ones of VOT and burst intensity while the voicing contrast relies on the internal correlates of closure voicing and duration as well as V1 duration. We attempted to document this dialect asymmetry by collecting data from three female speakers of Colloquial Bengali from Bangladesh. The speakers are students at MIT and range in age from 20 to 25 years. In terms of language background, the speech of the first two subjects is based on the capital Dhaka while the third is from Dinajpur in the northwest. A word list of 66 items (Appendix E) was constructed that distributed the voicing and aspiration contrasts across three stop places of articulation in medial and final positions. The speakers pronounced each target word in isolation and before the negative particle –*nai*.

In word-medial intervocalic position the four-way contrast was reliably supported by voicing ratio (with only a trend for closure duration) and by VOT for aspiration. In our statistical modeling the predictor variables were the aspiration and voicing categories of the stops and their interactions while word and speaker were random intercepts. P values were estimated with R's pvals.fnc.

(25) phonetic correlates of [±voice] and [±spread gl] in word-medial position: mean (st dev) and linear regression

closure dur (ms)	[+voice]	[−voice]
mean (sd)	71 (28)	91 (19)
asp	t = 0.08,	p = 0.934
voice	t = 1.45,	p = 0.152
asp*voice	t = 0.30,	p = 0.765
voice ratio	[+voice]	[−voice]
mean (sd)	.99 (.02)	.11 (.13)
asp	t = 0.35,	p = 0.729

---

3 In their structural phonemic analysis of Standard Colloquial Bengali based on data collected from a speaker from Calcutta, Ferguson and Chowdhury (1960:45) state that "In (prejunctural) position there is a greatly reduced contrast between unaspirated and aspirated stops, and between h and zero. It is almost possible to say that there is no contrast here, since it is only in very careful speaking styles or in dialectally colored pronunciations that any contrast at all is made". They also note that /ph/ and /bh/ are optionally realized as spirants [ɸ] and [β] and that /th/ is sometimes pronounced with affrication as [tθ] (p. 45). As noted by one of our reviewers, the neutralization of word-final aspiration but maintenance of voicing contrasts in Bengali was also observed by Chatterji (1926: 441–442) and Pattanyak (1966).

voice	t = 25.09,	p < 0.001
asp*voice	t = 0.44,	p = 0.661

V1 dur (ms)	[+voice]	[−voice]
mean (sd)	121 (23)	111 (23)
asp	t = 0.51,	p = 0.611
voice	t = 0.08,	p = 0.936
asp*voice	t = 1.04,	p = 0.301

VOT (ms)	[+spread gl]	[−spread gl]
mean (sd)	85 (22)	8 (13)
asp	t = 10.41,	p < 0.001
voice	t = 1.06,	p = 0.445
asp*voice	t = 2.58,	p = 0.015

In word-final, prepausal position the voicing contrast was significantly correlated with the stop closure duration, closure voicing, and V1 duration (26).

(26) phonetic correlates of [±voice] in word-final position: mean (st dev) and linear regression

closure dur (ms)	[+voice]	[−voice]
mean (sd)	107 (29)	144 (35)
asp	t = −0.46,	p = 0.624
voice	t = 2.60,	p = 0.011
asp*voice	t = 1.80,	p = 0.074

voice ratio	[+voice]	[−voice]
mean (sd)	.91 (.18)	.08 (.15)
asp	t = 0.86,	p = 0.386
voice	t = 17.81,	p < 0.001
asp*voice	t = 0.23,	p = 0.818

V1 dur (ms)	[+voice]	[−voice]
mean (sd)	121 (23)	111 (23)
asp	t = 1.61,	p = 0.108
voice	t = 2.65,	p = 0.009
asp*voice	t = 0.68,	p = 0.492

As for the aspiration contrast, there was a significant effect of VOT (as measured by the duration of turbulence visible in the narrow band spectrograms) and burst intensity (27).

(27) phonetic correlates of [±spread gl] in word-final position: mean (st dev) and linear regression

VOT (ms)	[+spread gl]	[−spread gl]
mean (sd)	80 (36)	55 (36)
asp	t = 2.60,	p = 0.011
voice	t = 0.31,	p = 0.761
asp*voice	t = 0.47,	p = 0.637
burst (dB)	[+spread gl]	[−spread gl]
[+spread gl]	52.8 (5.9)	51.1 (6.3)
asp	t = 0.58,	p = 0.563
voice	t = 2.26,	p = 0.026
asp*voice	t = 2.47,	p = 0.015

However, when the data were broken down by subject with multiple comparisons (Tukey), only the third speaker from Dinajpur evidenced a reliable difference in VOT, as seen in (28) below. We may therefore conclude that compared to the voicing contrast, the aspiration contrast is less reliable in word-final position.

(28) VOT by speaker in word-final position: mean (st dev) and linear regression with multiple comparisons (Tukey)

	Speaker 1	Speaker 2	Speaker 3
[+spread gl]	98 (36)	65 (37)	66 (25)
[−spread gl]	84 (30)	40 (23)	31 (24)
Pr (>|t|)	0.12	0.14	<0.001
Tukey	Sp 1 − Sp 2	Sp 1 − Sp 3	Sp 2 − Sp 3
Pr (|z|)	0.642	<0.001	<0.001

In order to test the contrast before the sonorant −*nai*, the data had to be restricted to words terminating in a voiceless stop since voiced stops often lacked a measurable release in this context. We took two measures to estimate the aspiration. The first was simply the interval between stop release and the onset of voicing in the following nasal. With this measure there was no significant difference between underlying aspirated vs. plain voiceless stops. We also estimated the aspiration by the duration of the visible frication after the release of the stop in narrow band spectrograms, a period that was typically shorter than the classic VOT definition. In this case, a reliable difference emerged, as seen below in (29).

(29) phonetic correlates of aspiration before –*nai*

	VOT	Turbulence period
[+spread gl]	96 (33)	67 (29)
[–spread gl]	82 (42)	44 (26)
Pr (>|t|)	–0.44	0.003

We tentatively conclude that, at least for two of our Bengali speakers, the [±spread gl] contrast is not reliably maintained in word-final position compared to the stability of the [±voice] contrast. It should be noted that the apparent neutralization of C^h vs. C does not clearly result in the unmarked unaspirated variant but rather in more uncertainty and gradience. For these speakers the ranking in (30) may be proposed.

(30) *C^h#, Ident-[continuant] ≫ Ident-[turbulence]

7 Hindi-Urdu

Hindi-Urdu is described as a language that preserves both the voicing and aspiration contrasts of stops in word-final as well as word-initial and word-medial positions (Ohala 1983). Concrete evidence affirming the presence of the voicing and aspiration contrasts word-finally is presented by Ahmed and Agrawal (1968). In their study a set of 870 CVC nonsense syllables varying the 29 consonantal phonemes of Hindi-Urdu in onset and coda were constructed. The syllables were recorded by three speakers (two males and one female) and presented to six native speaker listeners. The authors provide confusion matrixes summarizing the 15,660 responses. We extracted from their tables the responses for the bilabial, alveolar, and velar stops and categorized them for [±spread gl] and [±voice] for both positions. The data are summarized in (31). What is remarkable is the high hit rate, affirming the presence and stability of the laryngeal contrasts. Nevertheless, even here there are more errors with the aspiration contrast than with the voicing contrast in word-final position.

(31) confusion matrices for [±spread gl] and [±voice] based on data from Ahmed and Agrawal (1968); P = voiceless stop (plain and aspirated) and B = voiced stop (plain and aspirated)

Word-initial

	C	Cʰ		P	B
C	3234	6	P	3217	22
Cʰ	11	3230	B	32	3203
d'	5.60			4.79	

Word-final

	C	Cʰ		P	B
C	2903	72	P	2947	42
Cʰ	191	2810	B	10	2973
d'	3.49			4.90	

Linear regression with the probit link finds the difference in position within the word to be at the edge of significance for the aspiration contrast in comparison to no reliable difference for the voicing contrast (32). This suggests that the distinction between internal and external cues still shows up in what otherwise is a very high (near ceiling) response pattern.[4]

(32) regression statistics on [±spread gl] and [±voice] contrasts by position in word

[±spread gl]	Estimate	Std. Error	z value	Pr (>|z|)
intercept	0.02311	0.01124	2.056	0.039
position	0.04274	0.02248	1.901	0.057

[±voice]	Estimate	Std. Error	z value	Pr (>|z|)
intercept	0.002953	0.011243	0.263	0.793
position	−0.00387	0.022487	−0.151	0.880

---

4 Analysis of the confusion matrices in Bhatia's (1976) study of Hindi stops found a similar asymmetry for word-final position: [±voice] d' = 2.85 vs. [±spread gl] d' = 2.02.

Hindi-Urdu thus occupies the third niche in the possible rankings of the markedness constraints banning an aspiration contrast in final position (33). Marathi (Pandharipande 1997) also maintains a fully crossed voicing and aspiration contrast: [saap] 'snake' vs. [saapʰ] 'clean'; [ved] 'the Veda (sacred text)' vs. [vedʰ] 'attraction'. Punjabi (Bhatia 1993) has lost the doubly marked voiced aspirates but maintains a ternary voiced, plain voiceless, and voiceless aspirated contrast in initial, medial, and final position. Examples of the latter include [jad] 'when', [rat] 'blood', [ratʰ] 'chariot'.

(33) Ident-[continuant], Ident-[turbulence] » *Cʰ#

8 Summary and conclusion

In this paper we have documented a three-way distinction in the typology of laryngeal stop contrasts in the modern Indic languages instantiated by the constraint rankings in (34).

(34) Hindi-Urdu: Ident-[continuant], Ident-[turbulence] » *Cʰ#
　　　 Assamese: *Cʰ#, Ident-[turbulence] » Ident-[continuant]
　　　 Bengali: *Cʰ#, Ident-[continuant] » Ident-[turbulence]

Second, we have proposed that the basis of the Assamese spirantization of the aspirates is acoustic-auditory in nature. Aspirated stops share with fricatives the random distribution of acoustic energy in the frequency spectrum during their release and post-release phases. We also suggested that this helps to explain loan-word adaptations and sound changes linking these two sound classes. Third, the typology makes sense given the Licensing by Cue model of Steriade (1997, 2009). The aspirated stops are enhanced or neutralized in a context where the cues to the contrast are diminished. A striking additional fact is that in all three languages reviewed here the voicing contrasts are maintained in word-final, prepausal position. We can understand the stability of the [±voice] contrasts vis a vis the relative instability of the [±spread gl] contrasts by the phonetic correlates associated with these laryngeal oppositions. The voicing contrast is associated with an ensemble of cues (closure duration, closure voicing ratio, V1 duration) that are distributed across a broad region within which the stop is realized while the [±spread gl] opposition is signaled primarily by the turbulence after stop release and secondarily by voice quality in the beginning of the following vowel. These cues are diminished or absent before pause. This suggests in turn a default UG ranking of Ident-[voice] » Ident-[spread gl] that predicts the absence of a language that neutralizes a distinction in [±voice] while preserving a contrast in [±spread gl] in final position. To the best of our knowledge, such a language is not attested in Indic or elsewhere.

For the languages in (34) Ident-[voice] dominates the markedness constraint banning final voiced obstruents *[+voice]# and this ranking holds for other Indic languages such as Maithili, Punjabi, and Marathi. In this regard Sanskrit becomes interesting since this language neutralized not only [±spread gl] but also [±voice] in word-final position (Allen 1953: 70). Thus, in comparison to Sanskrit the modern languages have promoted faithfulness for voicing. Possibly related to this difference is the fact that Sanskrit – at least at its earliest stages – was a pitch accent language with lexical contrasts signaled by F0. In the modern Indic languages stress is predictable from syllable weight or distance from the edge of the word and F0 is associated with a rising contour across the accentual phrase. If the phonetic correlates of the Sanskrit laryngeal stop contrasts were similar to what is found in the modern languages (except possibly for F0) then closure voicing should have been available to distinguish /b/ from /p/. According to the "default model" of voicing proposed by Westbury and Keating (1986), in prepausal position closure voicing in a stop consonant will naturally cease at some point before oral release unless additional articulatory actions are taken to sustain phonation. From this perspective, the modern languages such as Hindi-Urdu must draw on more articulatory resources to maintain the laryngeal contrasts. A key objective of future research should be to determine if this is true and if so, how it is done. More generally, while the laryngeal stop contrasts in the Indic languages have been studied for over forty years with a variety of instrumentations, research has (quite properly) focused on the contexts in which the contrasts are most clearly expressed. This has provided a firm foundation for investigations like this one into how the contrasts are realized in different contexts, particularly those that are relevant to cue-based vs. prosody-based models of laryngeal licensing.

References

Ahmed, Rais & S. S. Agrawal. 1969. Significant features in the perception of (Hindi) consonants. *Journal of the Acoustical Society of America* 45(3). 758–63.
Allen, William Sidney. 1953. *Phonetics in ancient India*. London: Oxford University Press.
Bates, Douglas & Martin Maechler. 2013. Lme4: Linear Mixed Effects Models using S4 classes. R Package Version 0.999999–2. http://cran.rproject.org/web/packages/lme4/index.html
Bhatia, Tej. 1976. On the predictive role of the recent theories of aspiration. *Phonetica* 33. 62–74.

Bhatia, Tej. 1993. *Punjabi: a cognitive-descriptive grammar*. New York: Routledge.
Bhatia, Tej & Michael Kenstowicz. 1972. Nasalization in Hindi: a reconsideration. *Papers in Linguistics* 5. 202–12.
Boersma, Paul, Weenink, David, 1992–2011 Praat: Doing phonetics by Computer. Version 5.2.21, http://www.praat.org
Chatterji, S. K. 1926. *The origin and development of the Bengali language*. London: George Allen.
Clements, George N. 2003. Feature economy. *Phonology* 20. 287–333.
Dart, Sarah. 1991. *Articulatory and acoustic properties of apical and laminal articulation*. Los Angeles: UCLA Working Papers in Phonetics 79.
Dutta Baruah, P.N. 1992. *Assamese phonetic reader*. Central Institute of Indian Languages, CIL Phonetic Reader Series 27.
Dutta, Indranil. 2007. *Four-way stop contrasts in Hindi: an acoustic study of voicing, fundamental frequency, and spectral tilt*. Urbana: University of Illinois Ph.D. dissertation.
Ferguson, Charles & Munier Chowdhury. 1960. The phonemes of Bengali. *Language* 36. 22–59.
Goswami, Golok Chandra. 1966. *An introduction to Assamese phonology*. Poona: Deccan College.
Hoole, Phil. ND. http://www.phonetik.uni-muenchen.de.
Idris, Hélène Fatima. 2004. *Modern developments in the Dinka language*. Göteborg University: Göteborg Africana Informal Series 3, Department of Oriental and African Languages.
Ijaz, Adnan & Muhammad Awais Anwar. ND. Acoustic differences between dental and alveolar stops of Urdu. http://www.cle.org.pk/Publication/Crulp_report/CR03_02E.pdf.
Ingemann, Francis & Ramawatar Yadav. Voiced aspirated consonants. *Papers from the 1977 Mid-America Linguistics Conference*, 337–44.
Jessen, Michael & Catherine Ringen. 2002. Laryngeal features in German. *Phonology* 19. 189–212.
Kagaya, Ryohei & Hajime Hirose. 1975. Fiberoptic electromyographic and acoustic analyses of Hindi stop consonants. *Annual Bulletin, Research Institute of Logopedics and Phoniatrics, University of Tokyo* 9. 27–46.
Kenstowicz, Michael. 1994. *Phonology in generative grammar*. Oxford: Blackwell Publishers.
Michael Kenstowicz, Mahasen Abu-Mansour & Miklós Törkenczy. 2000. Two notes on laryngeal licensing. In Stefan Ploch (ed.), *Living on the edge: phonological essays commemorating the radical career of Jonathan Kaye*, 259–282. Berlin: De Gruyter Mouton.
Kim, Chin-Wu. 1965. On the autonomy of the tensity feature in stop classification. *Word* 21. 339–359.
Kingston, John & Randy Diehl. 1994. Phonetic knowledge. *Language* 70. 419–54.
Ladefoged, Peter. 1975. *A course in phonetics*. New York: Harcourt Brace Jovanovich.
Ladefoged, Peter & Ian Maddieson. 1996. *The sounds of the world's languages*. Oxford: Blackwell Publishers.
Lietviu kalbos gramatika. 1965. Vilnius: Mintis.
Lisker, Leigh. 1986. "Voicing" in English: a catalogue of acoustic features signaling /b/ versus /p/ in trochees. *Language and Speech* 29. 3–11.
Lisker, Leigh & Arthur Abramson. 1964. A cross language study of voicing in initial stops: acoustical measurements. *Word* 20. 384–422.
Lombardi, Linda. 1995. Laryngeal neutralization and syllable well-formedness. *Natural Language and Linguistic Theory* 13. 39–74.

Mahanta, Shakuntala. 2007. *Directionality and locality in vowel harmony*. Utrecht: LOT Publications.
Mahanta, Shakuntala. 2012. Assamese. *Journal of the International Phonetics Association* 42. 217–224.
Maddieson, Ian & Jack Gandour. 1977. Vowel length before aspirated consonants. *Indian Linguistics* 38. 6–11.
Narang, G. & D. Becker. 1971. Aspiration and nasalization in the generative phonology of Hindi-Urdu. *Language* 47. 647–67.
Ohala, Manjari. 1983. *Aspects of Hindi phon*ology. Delhi: Motilal Banarsidass.
Padgett, Jaye. 1991. *Stricture in feature geometry*. Amherst: University of Massachusetts Ph.D. dissertation.
Pattanayak, Debi Prasanna. 1966. *A controlled historical reconstruction of Oriya, Assamese, Bengali and Hindi*. The Hague: Mouton.
Pandharipande, Rajeshwari. 1997. *Mararthi*. New York: Routledge.
Prince, Alan & Paul Smolensky. 2004. *Optimality theory*. Cambridge, MA: MIT Press.
Remijsen, Bert & Caguor Adong Manyang. 2009. Illustrations of the IPA: Luanyjang Dinka. *Journal of the International Phonetics Association* 39. 113–24.
Rhee, Soek-Chae. 1998. *Aspects of release and nonrelease in phonology*. Urbana: University of Illinois Ph.D. dissertation.
Scheer, Tobias. 2003. On spirantization and affricates. In Stefan Ploch (ed.), *Living on the edge: phonological essays commemorating the radical career of Jonathan Kaye*, 283–301. Berlin: Mouton de Gruyter.
Senn, Alfred. 1966. *Handbuch der Litauischen Sprache*. Heidelberg: Carl Winter.
Silva, David. 2006. Acoustic evidence for the emergence of tonal contrast in contemporary Korean. *Phonology* 23. 287–308.
Steriade, Donca. 1997. Phonetics in phonology: the case of laryngeal neutralization. UCLA: Unpublished ms.
Steriade, Donca. 2009. The P-map and its consequences for constraint organization. In Kristin Hansen & Sharon Inkelas (eds.), *The nature of the word*, 151–179. Cambridge, MA: MIT Press.
Vaux, Bert. 1998. The laryngeal specifications of fricatives. *Linguistic Inquiry* 29. 497–511.
Vaux, Bert & Samuels, Bridget. 2005. Laryngeal markedness and aspiration. *Phonology* 22. 395– 436.
Westbury, John & Patricia Keeting. 1986. On the naturalness of stop consonant voicing. *Journal of Linguistics* 22. 145–166.
Wetzels, W. Leo, & Mascaró, Joan. 2001. The typology of voicing and devoicing. *Language* 77. 207–244.

Appendix A

ɔpɔra	personal name	zux	'to measure'
kɔpah	'cotton'	max	'unit of measurement'
kɔpal	'forehead'	nɔx	'nails'
sɔpɔnia	'dependent son-in-law'	sɔx	'interest'

pʰɔpɔra	'dappled'	mux	'face'
pap	'sin'	jukʰ	'to measure'
sap	'pressure'	makʰ	'unit of measurement'
bap	'father'	nɔkʰ	'nails'
dʰap	'slope'	sɔkʰ	'interest'
rap	'interest'	mukʰ	'fact'
map	'measurement'	pɔka	'ripe'
bʰap	'vapors'	ɔkɔra	'stupid'
sɔp	food item	dɔbɔka	placename
dɔba	'chess'	suka	'brilliant'
ɛbar	'one time'	kɔka	'grandfather'
baba	'small child'	bɔk	'crane'
buba	'dumb'	kak	'whom'
duba	'to drown'	zak	'group'
suburi	'neighborhood'	zʊk	'leech'
subua	'to chew'	mak	'mother'
bab	'designation'	kɔkak	'grandfather'
kabab	meat item	pɔta	'flattened grinder'
kub	'to whip'	bɔta	folk culture item
dub	'to drown'	bɔtɔl	'bottle'
dab	'coconut sp.'	bɔtah	'wind'
bʰab	'thoughts'	bɔtɔr	'weather'
dɔrɔb	'medicine'	tɔpɔt	'hot'
ɛpʰal	'one piece'	kɔpɔt	'shrewd'
xopʰura	folk culture item	dʰɔpat	'tobacco'
kupʰa	'omen'	dupat	'two piece item'
sɔpʰa	'clean'	bɔt	'tree sp.'
dɔpʰa	'chapter'	katʰi	'toothpick'
dʰɔpɔla	'dappled'	kɔtʰa	'talks'
sapʰ	'clean'	matʰa	'head'
mapʰ	'to forgive'	bɛtʰa	'grief'
bɔrɔpʰ	'ice'	bɔtʰa	'oars'
kɔpʰ	'phlegm'	katʰ	'wood'
dupʰ	'to get hurt'	mɔtʰ	'temple'
ɛbʰar	'unit of measure'	rɔtʰ	'chariot'
ɛbʰori	'unit of measure'	zɛtʰ	name of month
ɔbʰab	'scarcity'	badam	'almonds'
xɔbʰa	'meeting'	bɔdɔn	'body'
gabʰoru	'young girl'	bodoru	personal name
labʰ	'profit'	bidai	'farewell'
kʰjobʰ	'anger'	rod	'sun'
lʊbʰ	'greed'	mɔd	'alcohol'
xourɔbʰ	'fragrance'	dɔrɔd	'pain'
badʰa	'obstacle'	bad	'to avoid'
radʰa	mythological character	bɔga	'white'
adʰa	'half'	bɔgɔra	'to wrestle'

lɛdʰa	'lazy'	tʰɔga	folk culture item
sidʰa	'straight'	sɔga	'bird'
ɔdʰɔm	'man of bad character'	dɔga	'unit of measurement'
bɔdʰ	'to kill'	sagoli	'goat'
krʊdʰ	'anger'	ag	'front part'
budʰ	'Wednesday'	dag	'mark'
akʰɔr	'alphabets'	bʰag	'share'
akʰɔra	'practice'	bʰʊg	'to enjoy'
pɔkʰɔra	'shabby'	ɛgʰɔr	'one household'
pokʰila	'butterfly'	ogʰori	'gypsy'
pɔkʰa	'plant'	pɔgʰa	'rope'
xɔkʰa	'friend'	ɔgʰɔtɔn	'untoward incident'
nɔikʰɔtrɔ	'star'	logʰun	'to fast'
zɔkʰɔla	'ladder'	bagʰ	'tiger'
		sagʰ	'reduplicated word'

Appendix B

kat	'to cut'	patʰ	'path'
katʰ	'wood'	mat	'voice'
bat	'way'	matʰ	'nonsense'
batʰ	'bath'	tat	'there'
pat	'leaves'	tatʰ	'nonsense'

Appendix C

prɔtʰɔm	'first'	bʰrismɔ	name of a character
pristʰa	'page'	dristi	'vision'
pʰrai	'to fry'	drɔibbɔ	'substance'
pʰrend	'friend'	dʰrubɔ	'universal'
tritijɔ	'third'	dʰritiman	'patient'
tʰri:star	'three-star'	grɔhɔn	'acceptance'
brihɔt	'large'	gram	'village'
bristi	'rain'	gʰrina	'hatred'
brikkʰɔ	'tree'	gʰran	'scent'

Appendix D

bap	'father'	dɔrɔd	'pains'
pap	'sin'	kɔtʰ	'mat'
kub	'whip'	katʰ	'woods'
bab	'post'	rɔtʰ	'charriot'

kɔpʰ	'phlegm'	krʊdʰ	'anger'
bɔrɔpʰ	'ice'	mak	'mother'
labʰ	'profit'	zuk	'leech'
lʊbʰ	'greed'	dag	'mark'
dʰɔpat	'tobacco'	sɔkʰ	'interest'
kut	'coat'	nɔkʰ	'nail'
rod	'sun'	bagʰ	'tiger'

Appendix E

tʃʰagɔl	'goat'	tʃap	'pressure'
kɔpʰ	'plegm'	tʰakur	'community'
pakʰa	'fan'	atʰ	'eight'
apel	'apple'	lobʰ	'greed'
kādʰ	'shoulder'	agʰat	'wound'
bɔropʰ	'ice'	labʰ	'profit'
mapʰ	'to forgive'	ʃak	'leafy greens'
paʈʰa	'goat'	kʰam	'envelope'
aʈa	'wheat'	kɔtʰa	'talk'
sapʰ	'clean'	ʃat	'seven'
maʈʰ	'ground'	budʰ	'Wednesday'
pʰasi	'to hang'	bidʰan	'ways'
dag	'stain'	nɔkʰ	'nails'
pat	'plate'	dɛkʰ	'to see'
hoʈʰat	'suddenly'	rakʰ	'to keep'
sɔpʰor	'journey'	ɔbak	'surprised'
nɔkʰ	'nails'	kak	'crow'
badʰa	'obstacles'	nak	'nose'
dʰan	'paddy'	ʃak	'nonsense'
ʃadʰ	'wedding'	ʈak	'bald'
ada	'ginger'	bad	'to avoid'
pap	'sin'	tʃad	'roof'
ɔbʰab	'to think'	mɔrod	'male'
kaʈʰ	'wood'	ʃud	'nonsense'
pʰul	'flower'	bɔdʰ	'to kill'
radʰa	personal name	budʰ	'Wednesday'
tarikʰ	'date'	bɔb	personal name
bagʰ	'tiger'	ʃob	'all'
bad	'avoid'	ʈɔb	'flower vase'
ʃaban	'soap'	kʰobʰ	'anger'
adab	'greetings'	lobʰ	'greed'
adekʰ	'inexperienced'	labʰ	'profit'
paʈʰ	'lesson'	durlɔbʰ	'rare'
pʰāki	'excuse'		

Mirko Grimaldi
The phonetics-phonology relationship in the neurobiology of language

1 Introduction

1.1 The linguistic perspective

In the beginning, phonetics and phonology did not constitute independent disciplines and their underlying notions were mutually interchangeable. With the emergence of the synchronic approach, phonetics and phonology were progressively separated: so, the assumption – immanent in all alphabetic writing systems – that the sounds of speech (*phones*) might be analyzable into separate units (*phonemes*) has taken root within contemporary linguistics (see Durand & Laks 2002; van der Hulst 2013 for a discussion). Both phonetics and phonology have the aim of describing and explaining sound patterns of human languages, but the way in which the two disciplines addressed this issue has been generally counterposed. So, the relationship between phonetics and phonology has been consistently puzzled.

Jakobson, Fant & Halle's (1952) work prompted, in same way, the connection of phonetics substance with phonological mental representations. The crucial idea was that distinctive features (i.e., the abstract link between articulatory plans and acoustic outputs) are universal, binary, and must have correlates in terms of both articulation and audition: "The distinctive features would be more than a universal schema for classifying phonemes in all their diversity across languages; the features would be 'real' in the sense of being universal neural mechanisms for producing and for perceiving sounds of speech" (Teuber 1967 cited in Jakobson & Waugh 1979: 123). From this perspective, the relevant representational linguistic primitives are not single segments, but rather smaller segments are composed of: i.e., distinctive features. Accordingly, the work of the phonologist had to be interdisciplinary, as s/he needed to treating and interpreting data from language acquisition or loss, experimental phonetics, and psycholinguistics. However, the Jakobson's approach remained programmatic and phonetics and phonology followed their own ways.

The *analysis by synthesis* framework offered another chance to reconcile the two levels of analysis according to Jacobson's ideas (Stevens & Halle 1967; Stevens 2002). The analysis by synthesis theory assumes top-down processes in which potential signal patterns are internally generated (synthesized) and compared to the incoming signal which is continuous and does not present markers for phonemes boundaries. Thus, perceptual analysis crucially contains a step of synthetically generated candidate representations (a form of hypothesis-and-test model). The model proceeds from the assumption that cues from the input signal trigger guesses about "landmarks" that serve to identify phoneme boundaries: consequently, the internal synthesis of potential phonemes is compared to the input sequence. Thus, landmarks are intrinsic to the signal and provide evidence for different kinds of segments (vowels, glides, and consonants): e.g., a peak in low-frequency amplitude for a vowel, a minimum in low-frequency amplitude, without acoustic discontinuities, for a glide, and two acoustic discontinuities for a consonant, one of which occurs at the consonant closure and one at the consonant release (Stevens 2002: 1873; see also Poeppel et al. 2008).

For example, vowels may be classified on the basis of the first two formant peaks (F1, F2) on the spectral envelopes (Peterson & Barney 1952). The F1 is inversely correlated with articulatory tongue height, while the F2 (but also F3) reflects the place of articulation (PoA) along the horizontal (front-back and unrounded-rounded) dimension. The major features for vowels are the features specifying the position of the tongue body and lip rounding: the features [±high], [±low], [±back] and [±round] (as showed in Fig. 1). In consonants, beyond formants, additional physical parameters are essential for discriminative performance: e.g., formant transitions, energy bursts, and the vibrations of the vocal chords occurring before and during the consonant burst.

The publication of Chomsky & Halle's (1968) volume sanctioned the separation of the two disciplines. This work emphasized the phonological component, that is, the system of rules, based on distinctive features, that applies to a surface structure and assigns to it a certain phonetic representation drawn from the universal class provided by linguistic universals. The phonological component is abstract (collocated at the level of the mental representation) as compared with phonetic representations, although both are given in terms of phonetic features. Therefore, the phonological principles that speakers acquire and control determine the phonetic shape of phonemes, words, and sentences. Words are represented as a series of phonemes each of which is a bundle of distinctive features that indicate the acoustic-articulatory configuration underlying phonological segments. In principle, the framework initially developed did not consider that the subject matter of phonology should be empirically verified since distinctive features (and their implications) were taken for granted (but see Halle 2002). This mainstream approach survived notwithstanding, for example, Halle (1983: 94–95) clearly suggested that distinctive feature representation comes both from articulatory and from acoustic/auditory aspects of speech sounds and that they are instantiated in the brain: « [...] we spoke not of 'articulatory features' or of 'acoustic features,' but of 'articulatory' and/or 'acoustic correlates' of particular

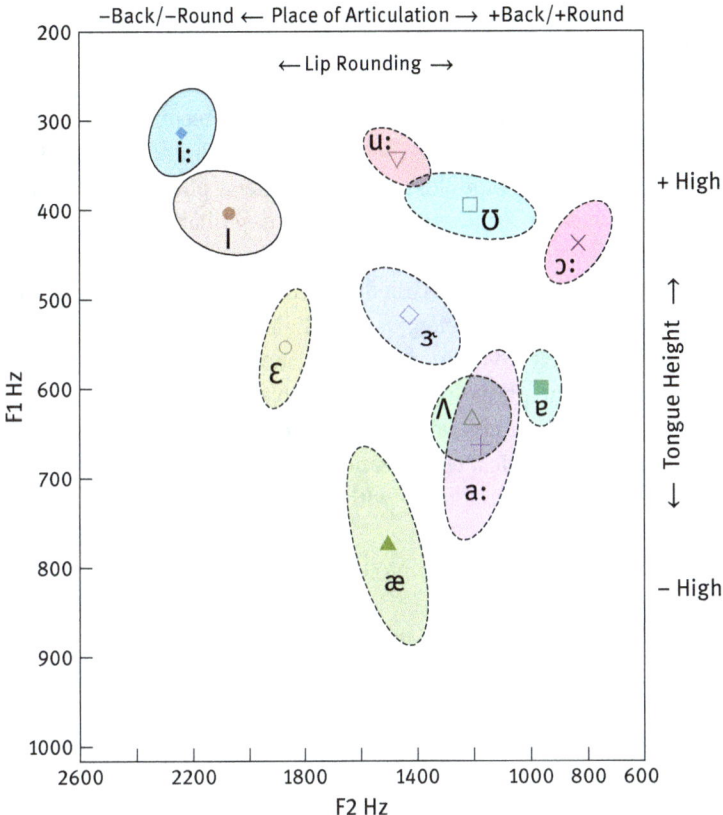

Fig. 1: F1-F2 Hz scatterplot of the stressed British English vowels produced by a native 50-year-old male speaker (recorded at CRIL). 68.27% confidence ellipse corresponding to ±1 standard deviation from the bivariate mean (the symbol within the ellipse indicates the mean formant value). F1 is inversely correlated with articulatory tongue height (+high/−high), while F2 reflects place of articulation in the horizontal (−back/+back and −round/+round) dimension.

distinctive features. [...] On this view, the distinctive features correspond to controls in the central nervous system which are connected in specific ways to the human motor and auditory systems ».

Hence, phonetics continued to be interested in describing speech sounds as a physical phenomenon (from acoustic, articulatory and auditory perspectives), whereas phonology developed increasingly formal apparatuses to describe the distinctive sounds used by language systems to build their words and the speaker's mental representation of these sounds and words together with the rules controlling phonological processes (for a deep discussion of these issues cf. Durand & Laks 2002). Successive attempts advocated a sort of alliance of the traditional approaches represented by phonetics and phonology (Lindblom 1986). However, Lindblom's model did not represent an alliance that strive for a theory showing how phonological units receive different phonetic realizations (articulatory and acoustic) under different contexts, or how acoustical information can serve to reconstruct the phonological representations responsible for their production (Bromberger & Halle 1986). The alliance proposed by Lindblom was essentially a physicalist alliance, which treats units of phonology as illusory by-products describable in articulatory and acoustic terms, so that phonological unit may be identifiable as phonetic ones.

Notwithstanding different scholars called for an *interface* (Blumstein 1991), an *interaction* (Keating 1991) or an *integration* (Ohala 1990) of the two disciplines (see also Pierrehumbert 1990), many phoneticians yet felt that the mental (abstract) entities posited in phonology are not subject to rigorous scientific investigation while phonologists argued that phonetics is a relatively uninteresting subfield of biology and physics, which is not useful to describe and explain certain linguistics aspects of human mind (with some notable exceptions as, for example, Archangeli & Pulleyblank 1994).

This mismatch has been crystallized into typical approaches which counterpose phonetics to phonology:
- Phonetics ended up being committed to describing/investigating pure acoustic, articulatory and perceptive properties of speech.
- Phonology is conversely involved in computational operations integrating the properties of speech into abstract (mental) representations subjected to categorical (discreet) processes.

1.2 The neurobiological perspective

While phoneticians and phonologists continued to separately investigate their subject matter, neuroscientists started exploring the phonetic and the phonological point of views from the neurobiological perspective. Indeed, the general issue of the neural representation of complex patterns is common to all neuroscience and has been investigated in many sensory modalities. In fact, if the spectro-temporal properties of speech are really converted into discrete (phonological) representations and these representations into appropriate motor commands to generate sequences of sounds, the brain is the unique responsible for the computational processes involved.

We have to note that the ability to categorize speech seems an ancient trait shared with many mammalian species. Studies on animals (chinchillas, gerbils, marmosets, ferrets, etc.) show clear evidence of categorical perception of speech sounds and conspecific vocalizations suggesting that the categorical processing is a general feature of auditory perception in vertebrates (Kuhl & Miller 1978; Ohl & Scheich 2005; Lu, Liang & Wang 2001; Mesgarani et al. 2008; Zoloth et al. 1979; Nelson & Marler 1989; see also Fitch 2010 for a discussion of these data). Also, animals vocalize modulating formant frequencies by changing the shape of their vocal tract: for instance, a cat may mew modulating formant frequencies to generate consonant-vowel-like 'miaow' sounds (Carterette et al. 1984).

Despite this shared property with animals, only humans have the ability to associate a finite sequence of sounds with potentially infinite concepts *signing* the external and internal world, and only humans can recursively combine sequences of signs (words) producing potentially infinite sentences. Moreover, the animal findings required massive training regimes in order to obtain categorical behavior patterns; conversely, human infants complete this task in the first stages of post-natal life (cf. Section 2.1). Crucially, animals do not need to convert these categories into representation structures that can make contact with higher-level levels of representations, e.g., morphemes, words, etc. Therefore, while the superficial behavior between the species may appear similar, the underlying computations required are likely to be quite different.

As suggested by Darwin (1871), the primary evolutionary changes required for human language were neural, not changes in vocal or auditory anatomy. What emerged as unique properties of the *Homo Sapiens* brain is the synchronization of neuronal activity along a functional cortico-thalamic network through a reentrant neural activity where neural information can be continuously interchanged between clusters of neurons: that is, for what concerns language computations, the synchronization of fronto-temporo-parietal clusters of neurons among themselves and with the thalamic nuclei (Edelman & Tononi 2000). Reentrant activity is present in all vertebrate brains but it is not synchronized with long-term and working memory. Reentrant activity per se is sufficient to generate primary conceptualization and categorization of the world (i.e., primary consciousness) but it cannot lead to effective learning processes. However, high-order conceptualization and categorizations are possible only when long-term memory may be synchronously integrated with working memory to result in continuous computational and representational processes (i.e., secondary consciousness) and then in learning (Edelman & Tononi 2000).

Accordingly, at one extremity of the speech perception process, in the inner ear, is the acoustic representation of speech, which, as we have seen, represents a general property of animal and humans. At the other extremity of the process are discrete (abstract) phonological representations, which can be manipulated by symbolic processes. Between these extremities there are multiple phonetic representations, which organize speech sounds into linguistically-relevant categories (Phillips 2001: 713–714). Thus, the analog representation of the acoustic of speech is converted in the digital representation of discrete (phonological) categories through the processing of phonetics categories, which are also analog, but which organize speech sounds into linguistically-relevant categories: the processing of the invariant properties of phonetic categories (i.e., distinctive features) leads to abstract representations.

In line with this perspective, the neural understanding of the high-resolution system for acoustic decoding and phonological encoding, tied to the ability for abstraction and an efficient memory mechanism, raises fundamental questions such as (i) whether spatially and temporally distributed activation patterns within the auditory cortex are directly implicated in speech sound processing; (ii) whether speech decoding is generated by pure bottom-up reflection of acoustic differences or whether they are additionally affected by top-down processes related to phonological categories and distinctive features. From this perspective, it seems that the phonetics-phonology relationship may be investigated according to Jacobson's program unifying the two level of analysis within the neural patterns activations (cf. Manca & Grimaldi 2016).

1.3 Aims of the present work

After briefly introducing the different neurophysiological techniques used to investigate the auditory brain, I critically review the studies on speech perception (but also production data are taken into consideration). The findings of these studies are re-examined to understand how direct measurements of temporal and spatial brain activation can clarify the phonetics-phonology relationship. On the base of a recent work on speech processing computations and operations (Giraud & Poeppel 2012), I sketch a preliminary proposal aiming at explaining bottom-up and top-down processing. The idea is that discretization and phonological abstraction are the result of a continuous process that convert spectro-temporal states into neurophysiological states represented by nested cortical oscillatory rhythms spatially distributed in the auditory cortex.

2 Investigating the auditory brain

2.1 Techniques and methods

In auditory neuroscience, two techniques are widely used: electroencephalography (EEG) and magnetoencephalography (MEG), as they are the most powerful non-invasive tools with high temporal reliability (Roberts et al. 2000). Recently, also electrocorticography (ECoG) – an invasive approach used in clinical contexts where pre-surgical evaluation of cognitive processes is needed – is increasingly used to directly record auditory activity (Poeppel & Hickok 2015; Leonard & Chang 2016). MEG and EEG research into language processing is based on event-related potentials (ERPs) and event-related magnetic fields (ERMFs) recorded while the subjects are performing a cognitive task. Thereby stimuli are administered to subjects and markers are set into the EEG trace whenever a stimulus is presented. Then a short epoch of EEG/MEG around each marker is used to average all these segments. This is based on the logic that in each trial there is a systematic brain response to a stimulus. Practically, this means that one typically repeats a given experimental paradigm a number of times (say, >30 times), and then one averages the EEG/MEG recordings that are recorded time-locked to the experimental event.

However, this systematic response cannot be seen in the raw EEG, as there it is overlaid by unsystematic background activity (which is simply considered as noise). By averaging all the single epochs that are time-locked to the experimental event, only the systematic brain response should remain (i.e., those generate neural action potentials related to the stimuli), but the background EEG/MEG should approach zero (Sauseng & Klimesch 2008). The noise (which is assumed to be randomly distributed across trials) diminishes each time a trial is added to the average, while the signal (which is assumed to be stationary across trials), gradually emerges out of the noise as more trials are added to the average. These brain responses are named event-related potentials (ERPs) and event-related magnetic fields (ERMFs) reflecting the summated activity of network ensembles active during the task. ERPs/ERMFs are characterized by specific patterns called 'waveforms' (or 'components'), which are elicited around 50–1000 ms starting from the onset of the stimulus and show positive (P) and negative (N) oscillatory amplitudes (i.e., voltage deflections). For instance, P100, N100, P200, P300, N400, P600 (or P1, N1, P2, and so on) are the principal components elicited during language processing starting from sound perception to semantic and syntactic operations. So, this technique gives millisecond-by-millisecond indices of brain functions and therefore provides excellent temporal resolution (Luck 2005).

2.2 The phonetic-phonological brain: acquisition and mapping auditory principles

The sensitivity to speech inputs in humans is very early. It seems that begins in the womb, when the auditory system of the fetus is matured and becomes attuned to a variety of features of the surrounding auditory environment (Partanen et al.

2013). In the first year of life, a clear perceptual transition from all the possible (universal) learning options to language-specific learning options emerges. Before 6–8 months of age, infants seem able to discriminate all the contrasts phonetically relevant in any of the world's languages; by 12 months their discrimination sensitivity is warped by native phonemes while the perceptual sensitivity for non-native phonemes gradually declines (Werker & Tees 2005; Kuhl et al. 2006). According to Werker & Tees (1984), a recent neurophysiological study suggested that this cerebral reorganization around native categories is already formed at 6 months of age and may reflect a continuous process of neural commitment towards the first language categories (Ortiz-Mantilla et al. 2013).

The reshaping of the perceptual space in infants according to the phonetic properties of the mother tongue implies that constant computational processes on the signal are encoded online into abstract discrete representations of sounds by means of probabilistic and statistical operations computed by the brain on the acoustic signal (Kuhl 2004). A consequent hypothesis is that the acoustic-phonetic structures map directly onto clusters of neurons within the auditory cortex thanks to the specific sensitivity of nerve cells to the spectral properties of sounds: i.e., the so-called *tonotopic principle* (Romani et al. 1982). This coding of acoustic frequencies in different sites of auditory cortex is ensured by a selective activation process that begins early in the cochlear neurons regularly positioned along the basilar membrane (Moerel et al. 2014; Saenz, Langers 2014). Then, the neural signals emitted by cochlear neurons are transmitted in the brainstem and preserved up to the auditory cortex from the primary auditory cortex (A1) to the superior temporal gyrus (STG) and the superior temporal sulcus (STS) (Da Costa et al. 2011; Talavage et al. 2004). While pre-cortical processing seems to be common to all sounds, speech-specificity appears to arise at the cortex (Scott & Johnsrude 2003). Like retinotopy in vision, tonotopy is one of the most accepted models of cortical organization of the auditory pathway (Moerel et al. 2014) as also showed by studies on animals (Kaas & Hackett 2000; Rauschecker & Tian 2000; Mesgarani et al. 2008). Thus, from a linguistic perspective, speech-specific processing in the auditory cortex may be based on the *phonemotopy principle*.

In addition to the topographical separation of sounds of different frequencies, it has been suggested that latency of evoked responses may be a supplementary dimension for object encoding in the auditory system. Roberts & Poeppel (1996) demonstrated that there is a frequency dependence of latencies separate from stimulus intensity. Furthermore, recent animal data has shown that the precision of temporally based neural representations declines from periphery to the cortical regions entailing different encoding strategies for slow and fast acoustic modulations (Wang 2007). Thus, the temporal code may represent the ability of some pools of neurons to discharge at a particular phase of the structure of sounds (Zatorre & Belin 2001; Boemio et al. 2005). This temporal mechanism of auditory encoding is known as the *tonochrony principle*. That is, the latency of auditory evoked components appears to be sensitive to some stimulus properties; this suggests that the mechanism of tonochronic encoding might augment or supplement the tonotopic strategy in the frequency range critical to human speech (*phonemochrony*) (Roberts et al. 2000).

2.3 Event-related potentials, and event-related magnetic fields components for phonetic-phonological investigations

The auditory component widely investigated is N1, with its magnetic counterpart N1m, and mismatch negativity (MMN), with its magnetic counterpart MMNm. N1/N1m is a negative peak between 70 and 150 ms after the onset of an auditory stimulus (cf. Fig. 2) that appears to be involved in the basic processing of speech sounds in auditory cortices (Woods 1995). It seems that the amplitudes and the latencies of the N1/N1m are relevant markers reflecting the cortical encoding of acoustic features of incoming speech sounds. The source location of the N1/N1m responses along the auditory planes seems to be driven by the spectral properties that are linguistically salient, e.g., the F1/F2 ratio for vowels, or the place of articulation for consonants, and then it may represent a good tool to investigate auditory cognitive processes.

MMN/MMNm is a component temporally subsequent to the N1/N1m (cf. Fig. 2), automatically and preattentively elicited by an acoustic change or by a rule violation between 150 and 250 ms post-stimulus onset (Näätänen 2001). Contrary to the N1/N1m, it is generated in a passive oddball paradigm, where subjects listen to frequent (standard) stimuli interspersed with infrequent (deviant) stimuli and attend to a secondary task (e.g. watching a silent movie). MMN/MMNm is visible by subtracting standard responses from deviant responses to the same acoustic stimuli: its amplitude seems to be directly correlated with the discriminability of the two stimuli involving both acoustic change-detection processes and phoneme-specific processes (Sussman et al. 2013). This component has been exploited to investigate (i) the categorical representation of phonemes in the subjects' mother tongue (e.g., Näätänen et al. 1997); (ii) if the acoustic signal is mapped onto lexical representations through different levels of featural representation: in this case, N1m and MMNm have also been used together (Scharinger et al. 2011b; 2012), and (iii) if phonemic representations may eventually develop during second language acquisition (Grimaldi et al. 2014, and the literature therein).

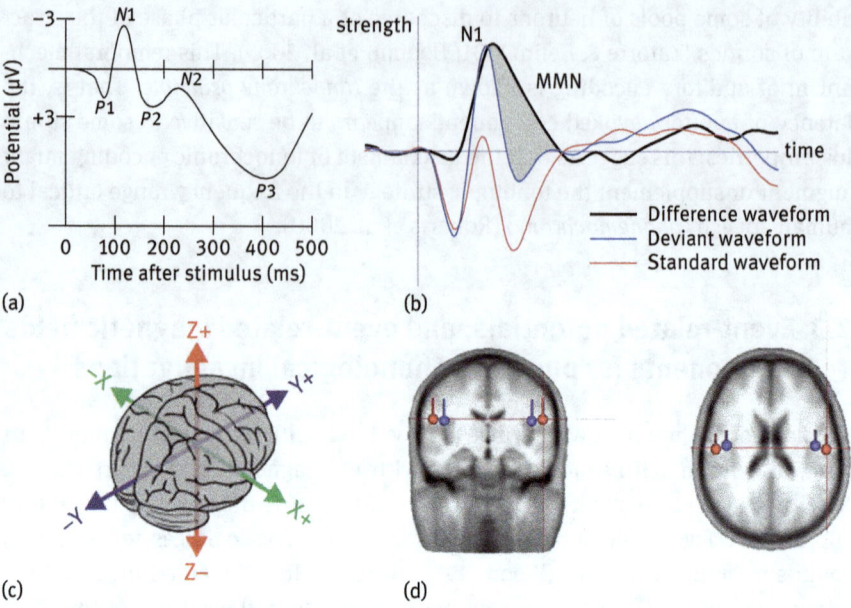

Fig. 2: (a) Representation of the auditory N1 wave evoked from EEG to an auditory stimulus. The peak around 100 ms post-stimulus onset, measured in microvolts (µV) is evidenced (adapted from Lageman et al. 2012). (b) ERP waveforms evoked at a frontal scalp location by the standard and deviant sounds superimposed on the difference waveform in which the ERP to the standard has been subtracted from that to the deviant. The MMN appears as an enlarged negativity to the deviant sound as compared with the standard sound, following the N1 peak. Adapted from (Brattico 2006). (c) The 3D space within the brain along the classical Talairach coordinates: the direction of x axis is from left to right, that of y axis to the front, and the z axis thus points up. (d) Average location and orientation of the equivalent current dipole sources fitted in the bilateral auditory cortical areas. Adapted from Cirelli et al. (2014).

As the signals measured on the scalp surface do not directly indicate the location of the active neurons in the brain, when interpreting EEG and MEG data, one has to solve the so-called *inverse problem*: that is, the deduction of the source currents responsible for the externally fields measured on the scalp (Hallez et al. 2007). It is possible to simulate the neural activity by means of a dipolar model (Malmivuo et al. 1997). Dipoles are created by post-synaptic potentials of many single neurons oriented in the same direction and firing synchronously in response to the same event. Under stimulation, the dipoles from the individual neurons sum solving in a single equivalent current dipole (ECD) that seems to be the best approximation of auditory evoked potentials observed by sensors on the scalp. Location, orientation, and magnitude of the assumed ECDs provide information about the behavior of the activity under investigation (Luck 2005). The ECD can be described as a point located in a 3D space within the brain along the classical Talairach coordinates that represent the center of simultaneously active neural sources (Sanei & Chambers 2013): i.e., *x* (lateral-medial), *y* (anterior-posterior), and z (inferior-superior) axes (cf. Fig. 2).

Do the available findings support a direct link between linguistic and neurophysiological primitives? That is, can tonotopy and tonochrony (as mirrored in N1m/N1 patterns) explain the properties of the phoneme computations and representations in terms of distinctive features within the auditory cortex?

2.3.1 Amplitudes for vowels and consonants

From a general point of view, it has been shown that N1/N1m responses evoked by non-speech tokens differ from those recorded with the speech tokens, which show stronger amplitude and longer latency. However, no indication of different underlying neural representations of speech sounds were found (Eulitz et al. 1995; Diesch et al. 1996; Poeppel et al. 1997; Swink & Stuart 2012). Subsequent works focusing on vowels discrimination tasks suggest that their representation is mainly guided by the spectral relations of frequencies rather than by abstract, phonological relevant features. As already showed for animals (Ohl & Scheich 1997), vowels with large F2-F1 distance (e.g., [i], [u]) elicited larger amplitudes than vowels with close F2-F1 formants peaks (e.g., [a]) (Diesch & Luce 1997; 2000; Obleser et al. 2003a; Shestakova et al. 2004) (cf. Fig. 1). These data have been interpreted at the light of the inhibition principle (Shamma 1985a: 1985b) according to which there exists a vowel-specific reduction of neuronal activity that depends on the vowel formant distance F2-F1 and that may be topographically organized along isofrequency contours.

All these previous studies used synthetic stimuli. When natural and large sets of vowels are compared, indications of phoneme distinction resulted broadly associated to the processing of featural variables. Scharinger et al. (2011a) and Grimaldi et al. (2016) investigated the entire Turkish and Salento vowel systems respectively. Turkish vowel system symmetrically distinguishes between high/non-high ([i, ɯ, y, u]/[ɛ, ɑ, œ, ɔ]), unrounded front/back ([i, ɛ]/[ɯ, ɑ]) and rounded front/back ([y, œ]/[u, ɔ]) vowels, while the Salento system is characterize by five vowels, i.e., [i, ɛ, a, ɔ, u], where [i, u] are high and [ɛ, a, ɔ] are non-high vowels. Both studies found that high vowels elicited larger amplitude than non-high vowels showing a categorical effect for phonological patterns. However, this result is also compatible with acoustic properties of speech sounds, as high vowels are significantly characterized by low F1 values, while low vowels by high F1 values (but see Monahan & Idsardi 2010, where a correlation of N1m with

F1/F3 ratio is suggested). Note that Scharinger et al. (2011a) applied a mixed model statistical approach, testing whether the N1m complex was better accounted for by acoustic gradient predictors (acoustic model) or by distinctive features oppositions (feature model): interestingly, the feature model fitted the data better than the acoustic model suggesting that the processing of a vowel system may be relied on the abstract representation of articulatory plans and acoustic outputs, i.e., the binary opposition of distinctive features.

As for consonants, the data are scarce. Stable evidence pertains only to stops segments: stops ([b, p, d, t, g, k]) produce higher amplitudes than non-stop counterparts ([f], [r], [m], [r], [s]) (Gage et al. 1998). Also, the N1m amplitudes seem to vary as a function of the onset of the speech sounds with a higher amplitude for labial [ba] than alveolar [da] as compared to velar [ga] in both hemispheres. The overall difference in amplitude to stops vs. non-stops may be attributed to the acoustic differences in the onset dynamics of these two classes of stimuli. At the same time, it seems that N1m amplitude is sensitive to place of articulation. Within the class of stop consonants, the N1m peak amplitude resulted also sensitive to the feature Voicing. As revealed by Obleser et al. (2006), only intelligible voiced consonants ([d], [g]) yielded the stronger N1m amplitudes than their unvoiced counterparts ([t], [k]) did.

2.3.2 Latencies for vowels and consonants

The N1m latency appears to be mainly related to the F1: i.e., high F1 values (e.g., [a] and [æ]) evoke shorter latency than low F1 values (e.g., [i] and [u]) (Diesch et al. 1996; Poeppel et al. 1997; Eulitz et al. 1995; Obleser et al. 2003a). Yet, works focusing on entire phonological systems highlight that the N1m/N1 changes seem related to the abstract processing of phonological features, although still tentatively: back vowels (e.g., [a, o, ɔ u]) peaked later than the front vowels (e.g., [e, ɛ, ø, i]) (Obleser et al. 2004a; 2004b; Grimaldi et al. 2016).

The mapping rules seem to proceed in a different way when testing the large set of the Turkish vowel system (Scharinger et al. 2011a). This study found that back vowels (e.g., [u]) were earlier than front vowels (e.g., [y]), and that the features Height and Round affected the timing neuronal strategies resulting in later responses to high (e.g., [i]) than non-high (e.g., [ɑ]) vowels and in faster N1m to unrounded vowels (e.g. [ɯ]) than to the rounded counterparts (e.g., [u]).

The N1m latency was also found to be involved for point of articulation, Voice and the Back in naturally spoken syllables: the velar-back rounded CV syllable [go] elicited a later response than labial ([bø]), alveolar ([dø]), velar ([gø]) with front rounded vowel (Obleser et al. 2003b) confirming the critical role of point of articulation for temporal coding in human speech recognition (Roberts et al. 2000; Gage et al. 2002; Obleser et al. 2004b). According to the authors, this suggests that the assimilatory effect of a back vowel is very influential on a back consonant like [g]. Also, it has been observed that the N1m to isolated alveolar consonants [d] and [t] peaked earlier than responses to velar consonants [g] and [k], and voiced consonants [d] and [g] peaked later as compared to voiceless consonants [t] and [k] (Obleser et al. 2006). The authors, thus, proposed that the latency changes are mainly driven by the spectral (Place, spectral peak of [d-t] versus [g-k]) and temporal (Voicing, voice onset time, [d-g] versus [t-k]) features of the stimuli.

2.3.3 Source generators for vowels and consonants

The dipole approach for modeling the N1m patterns and observing the spatial arrangement into the brain assumes that the sound salient features for the phonological encoding drive the displacement of the N1m generators, which define specific arrangements (maps) on the cortical sheet. There are two perspectives of analysis concerning the spatial arrangement of speech sounds into the brain: the first observes the absolute distance of dipole generators in the cortical space (the auditory cortex in our case), the second calculates these distances relatively to a 3D space considering the anterior-posterior, lateral-medial, and inferior-superior Talairach axes (cf. Section 2, Fig. 1).

In line with the amplitude and latency findings, the absolute Euclidean distances between the representational centers of vowels reveal that the most dissimilar vowels in the F2-F1 space ([a-i]) tend to generate larger cortical distances than the most similar ones ([e-i]) (Obleser et al. 2003a; Mäkelä et al. 2003; Shestakova et al. 2004). However, some studies reported that vowels differing in only one place feature (front vowels [e]-[i] and front–rounded vowels [ø]-[y]) were closer than vowels maximally different for two or more features ([e]-[i] vs. back–rounded [o]-[u]) (Obleser et al. 2004b; see also Scharinger et al. 2011a).

The abstract representation of vowels emerges also for the relative distances along the Talairach axes. The N1m dipoles appear dependent on both spectro-temporal cues and phonetic features. The lateral-medial axis showed medial locations for vowels with F1 high frequencies (that is, low vowels) (Diesch & Luce 1997). Eulitz et al. (2004) found that the German vowel [i] with large spectral F2-F1 distance, was more medial than vowels with close formants peaks (e.g., [a]). Further studies described a broad cortical vowel distinction according to different phonological patterns. Obleser et al. (2004a) observed that the German back vowel [o] was lateral to the front vowel [ø]. On their part, Scharinger et al.

(2011a) demonstrated that the dipole movements were more affected by phonological features than by acoustic properties and found a gradient for Round along this plane: i.e., rounded vowels ([y, œ, u, ɔ]) were at more lateral positions than unrounded vowels ([i, ɛ, ɯ, ɑ]).

The anterior-posterior plane seems responsive to the F1 and F2 values associated with Height and PoA. High vowels (e.g., [ɪ] or [u]), with low F1, elicited a dipole that was located more anterior to the dipole of non-high vowels (a, [ɛ], [æ]), with high F1 values (Mäkelä et al. 2003; Scharinger et al. 2012). Also, the anterior-posterior plane seems correlated with the F2 values directly dependent by the Place phonological feature: back vowels (e.g., [ɯ, ɑ, u, ɔ]) appeared at more posterior locations than front vowels (e.g., [i, e ɛ, y, œ]) (Obleser et al. 2004b; Scharinger et al. 2011a). As for consonants, fricative response was more posterior, on average, than the plosive, the vowel and the nasal response sources (Kuriki et al. 1995). Obleser et al. (2003b) found that the differences in N1m source location were dependent on the point of articulation of the vowel but independent of the different syllable onsets: the front vowel [ø] elicited activity anterior to dorsal vowel [o]. Furthermore, the intelligibility alveolar [d] and [t] were more anterior than velar [k] and [g] irrespective of the voicing feature of the stimuli (Obleser et al. 2006). When labial and coronal consonants were compared (as in the couple [awa]-[aja] and [ava]-[aʒa] respectively) labials elicited dipoles with more anterior locations than coronals (Scharinger et al. 2011b). This spatial location was independent of manner of articulation: anterior–posterior locations did not differ between [w] and [v] or [j] and [ʒ]. A statistical model comparison showed that although the F2-F1 ratio was the best predictor for an acoustic model, a model built on the additional fixed effect place (labial/coronal) provided a better fit to the location data along the anterior/posterior axis. This might be interpreted as evidence for top-down categorical effects on the acoustically driven dipole location in auditory cortex.

Few studies reported significant results along the inferior-superior axis. Generally, low vowels resulted in superior location than high vowels (Shestakova et al. 2004; Eulitz et al. 2004; Obleser et al. 2003a). Conversely, Scharinger et al. (2012) revealed that the dipoles for the high [ɪ] were approximately 7mm more superior to the dipoles for the low [æ], whereas the locations between [ɪ] and [ɛ] and between [ɛ] and [æ] did not differ. Finally, Scharinger and colleagues (2011a) revealed a Round effect on the dipole locations, so that rounded vowels, which are acoustically marked by low F2 frequencies, were located at more inferior locations than dipoles to non-round vowels. However, when this effect was investigated for Front and Back vowels separately, the authors stated that the F1 and the related Height effects were, once again, the guiding rules for the cortical segregation within Front vowels only. For what concerns consonants, Obleser et al.

(2006) showed that front consonants (e.g., [d, t]) have a more superior location than back counterparts ([k, g]).

2.3.4 The MMNm/MMN

On the other side of the issue, also the MMNm/MMN studies offered important contributions on the understanding of categorical perception. Perception of vowels or VOT contrasts in the across-category conditions elicit MMNm/MMN amplitudes only for those segments having a contrastive role in the phonological system of listeners (e.g., Näätänen et al. 1997; Sharma & Dorman 2000). These results suggest that the MMNm/MMN is sensitive to the phonetic-phonological category distributions of the subjects' native language (see Winkler et al. 1999; Grimaldi et al. 2014 for sensitivity to second language categories). Also, studies on categorical discrimination (generally on consonant continua differing in the duration of VOT) highlighted that listeners are able to perceptually group acoustic distinct tokens together to form a category. When listeners perceive a token from the other side of the category boundary, a change is detected as indexed by MMN (e.g., Sharma & Dorman, 1999; Phillips et al. 2000).

Phonemes used to contrastively distinguish lexical meaning may generate non-contrastive variants (i.e., allophones) that regularly appear in specific contexts because of the influence of adjacent vowels or consonants. Kazanina et al. (2006) used a multiple-token design with acoustic varying tokens for each of the stimuli to analyze the sound pair [t–d], which has allophonic status in Korean ([d] occurs between voiced sounds and [t] elsewhere) and a phonemic status in Russian. The results revealed an MMNm response for the Russian listeners but no response for the Korean listeners. The authors concluded that the phonemic representations, but not the allophonic ones, are computed from speech. These data, however, refer to VOT distinctions: what happens when vowels allophonic pairs generated by phonological processes are investigated? Miglietta, Grimaldi & Calabrese (2013) found different MMN patterns. They studied the allophonic variant generated by a phonological process (i.e., metaphony) characterizing southern Salento varieties that raises the stressed low-mid front vowel [ɛ] to its high-mid counterpart [e] when followed by the unstressed high vowel [i]. MMNs were elicited for both the allophonic and phonemic conditions, but a shorter latency was observed for the phonemic vowel pair suggesting a rapid access to contrastive sound properties for the phonological patterns. Yet, the discrimination of the allophonic contrast indicates that also allophones – generated by specific rules of the grammar – are part of the knowledge of speakers and then of their memory representations. Thus, according to Calabrese (2012), the auditory cortex may have two 'modes' of perceiving speech: phonological perception (faster as it picks out from deeper language knowledge) and phonetic perception (slower as it refers to low-level acoustic properties only).

Finally, studies investigating whether phonemic representations in the lexicon are underspecified for non-contrastive distinctive features values in the language systems (Section 4.4) showed that MMNm/MMN are elicited only when the standard stimulus is fully specified for a distinctive feature while the deviant stimulus not (e.g., Eulitz et al., 2004; Scharinger et al., 2012). This is because a fully specified vowel (for instance for Height) in standard position should generate a strong expectation regarding tongue height specification that might be violated if the deviant to this standard sequence is an underspecified segment (for instance, a mid-vowel). This finding suggests that the MMNm/MMN may index more than just physical properties of the stimulus. However, Mitterer et al. (2003, 2006) found a symmetric MMN: a labial as deviant and a putatively underspecified alveolar as standard elicited the same MMN as the alveolar deviant with the specified labial standard. The same results were obtained by Bonte et al. (2005) with fricatives. Finally, evidence for underspecified features was not successively confirmed for labio-velar and palatal glides labial and palato-alveolar fricatives ([awa]-[aja] and [ava]-[aʒa]) (Scharinger et al. 2011b).

2.4 The event related oscillatory rhythms perspective

Although the ERP approach has opened an important window on the time course and the neural basis of speech and language processing, more than 100 years after the initial discovery of EEG activity, researchers are turning back to reconsider another aspect of EEG, that is the event-related oscillations. This is because an increasing number of researchers began to realize that an ERP only represents a certain part of the event-related EEG signal. Actually, there is another aspect of extreme interest for the study of cognitive functions: the event-related fluctuations in rhythmic, oscillatory EEG/MEG activity. This view, indeed, might provide a new window on the dynamics of the coupling and uncoupling of functional networks involved in cognitive processing (Varela et al., 2001). In fact, substantial literature now indicates that some ERP features may arise from changes in the dynamics of ongoing EEG rhythms/oscillations of different frequency bands that reflect ongoing sensory and/or cognitive processes (Başar et al. 2001; Buzsáki 2006). More precisely, the EEG oscillations that are measured in a resting state become organized, amplified, and/or coupled during cognitive processes. It has been argued that ERP does not simply emerge from evoked, latency–fixed polarity responses that are additive to and independent of ongoing EEG (Sauseng et al.

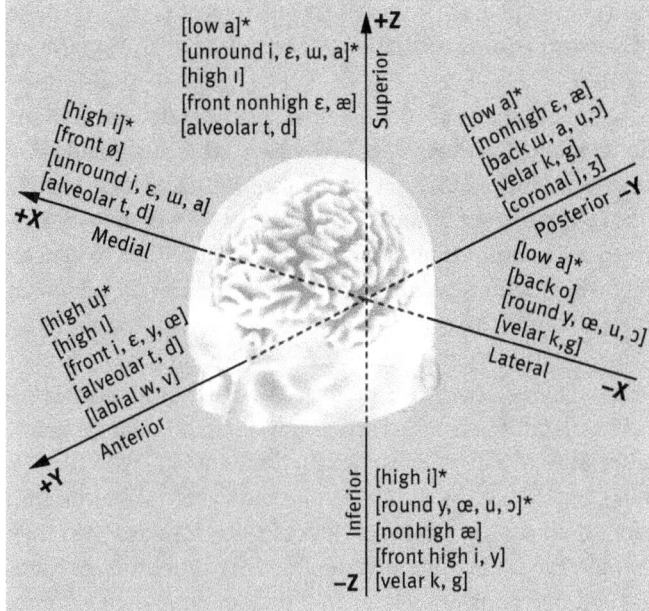

Fig. 3: Graphical representation of the main trends emerging from the N1m ECD analysis along the Talairach three-dimensional spaces slicing human brain in lateral-medial (x), anterior-posterior (y), and inferior-superior axis (z). The symbol (*) indicates that the topographical gradient was explained in terms of acoustics effects rather than of featural variables (adapted from Manca, Grimaldi 2016).

2007): instead, evidence suggests that early ERP components are generated by a superposition of ongoing EEG oscillations that reset their phases in response to sensory input: i.e., the external or internal stimuli generating cognitive activities. Therefore, event-related oscillations, further than to have the time-locked EEG information, permits the retrieval of non-phase locked EEG information related to the cognitive activity induced by the stimulus (cf. Fig. 4(a) and (c)).

Within this perspective, ongoing cerebral activity can no longer be thought of as just relatively random background noise (the non-phase EEG activity), but as a whole containing crucial information on the dynamical activity of neural networks: thus, the EEG and ERP are the same neuronal event, as the ERP is generated because of stimulus-evoked phase perturbations in the ongoing EEG. A fundamental feature of the phase-resetting hypothesis is that following the presentation of a stimulus, the phases of ongoing EEG rhythms are shifted to lock to the stimulus. From this, it follows that during pre-stimulus intervals, the distribution of the phase at each EEG frequency would be random, whereas upon stimulus presentation, the phases would be set (or reset) to specific values (for each frequency). The resetting of the phases causes an ERP waveform to appear in the average in the form of an event-related oscillation (Makeig et al. 2002; Penny et al. 2002; Klimesch et al. 2004).

Unlike ERP (based on the analysis of components), event-related oscillations are based on the time-frequency analyses (e.g. Gross 2014). One such method is wavelet analysis. The general idea is that not all relevant EEG activity is strictly phase-locked (or evoked) to the event of interest (Buszáki 2006). Obviously, this activity shortly before stimulus onset is mostly not visible in ERPs due to cancellation; nevertheless, this pre-stimulus baseline activity may have a crucial impact on the observed ERPs (Klimesch 2011). Time-frequency analyses enable us to determine the presence of oscillatory patterns in different frequency bands over time. Thus, with wavelet analyses, it can be established whether oscillatory activity in a specific frequency band, often expressed in power (squared amplitude), increases or decreases relative to a certain event, as represented in Fig. 4(b).

The importance in considering the non-phase locked event-related oscillations consists in the fact that, contrary to phase-locked responses as ERPs, they reflect the extent to which the underlying neuronal activity synchronizes. Synchronization and de-synchronization are related to the coupling and uncoupling of functional networks in cortical and subcortical areas of the brain (Varela et al. 2001; Bastiaansen, Mazaheri & Jensen 2012). This aspect, of course, is related to how different types of information, which are stored in different parts of the network, are integrated during computational and representational processes. Importantly, elements pertaining to one and the same functional network are identifiable as such by the fact that they fire synchronously at a given frequency (cf. Fig. 4). This frequency specificity allows the same neuron (or neuronal pool) to participate at different times in different representations. Hence, synchronous oscillations in a wide range of frequencies are considered to play a crucial role in linking areas that are part of the same functional network. Importantly, in addition to recruiting all the relevant network elements, oscillatory neuronal synchrony serves to bind together the information represented in the different elements (Gray et al. 1989).

In brief, the ERP approach is based on time domain analysis and wants to know: when do things (amplitudes and latencies) happen? The oscillatory approach is based on Frequency domain (spectral) analysis (Fourier analysis), analyzes magnitudes and frequencies of wave (renouncing to time information), and wants to know: when do which frequencies occur and when their power increases/decreases? That is, the ERP perspective treats peaks and troughs as single events, while the oscillatory approach as separate entities.

Also, recent findings suggest that ERP components and oscillatory rhythms represent complementary measures of the neural processing underlying high-level

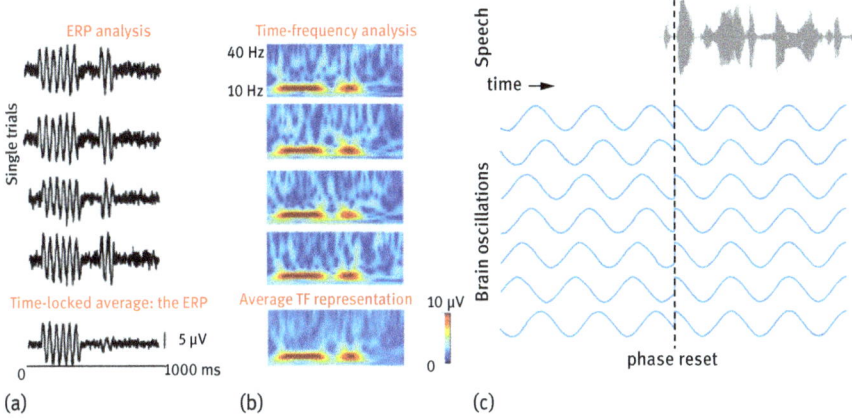

Fig. 4: Simulated EEG data illustrating the difference between phase-locked (evoked) activity and non-phase-locked (induced) activity. (a): Single-trial EEG time courses showing two consecutive event-related responses (an amplitude increase at 10 Hz). The first response is phase-locked with respect to the reference time-point (t=0), and as a result this evoked response is adequately represented in the average ERP. The second response is time-locked, but not phase-locked to t=0, and as a result this induced response is largely lost in the average ERP. (b): time-frequency (TF) representations of each single trial, with red colors coding for the amplitude increase at 10 Hz. Crucially, the average TF representation contains both the phase-locked and the non-phase-locked responses. Adapted from Bastiaansen, Mazaheri & Jensen (2012). (c) Illustration of the phase of ongoing neural oscillations being reset by an external stimulus. Prior to the stimulus event the phases of the oscillations are random, but following the stimulus they are aligned. All the figures (a), (b) and (c) are adapted from Pelle & Davis (2012).

cognitive processing: the extent at which they capture same aspects of language processing is at the moment unclear (Wang 2010). Actually, neural oscillations in the low delta-theta ranges and high beta-gamma ranges have been shown to temporally correlate with different speech and categorial processes (including lexical processing) (Kösem, van Wassenhove 2017).

2.4.1 The event related oscillatory rhythms data

The idea being investigating oscillatory rhythms is that endogenous fluctuations in neural excitability can be controlled by the brain so that they may be entrained (synchronized) with external rhythmic (and predictable) inputs as speech sounds (Zoefel, VanRullen 2015). In fact, the frequency of the speech envelope – roughly defined as the sum of energy across sound frequencies at a given point in time – is relatively stable between 2 and 8 Hz and phases of low phonetic information rhythmically alternate with phases of high phonetic information. It seems that there is a remarkable correspondence between average durations of speech units and the frequency ranges of cortical oscillations: phonetic properties (duration of 20–50 ms) are associated with gamma (>50 Hz) and beta (15–30 Hz) oscillations; syllables, and words (mean duration of 250 ms) with theta (4–8 Hz) oscillations; sequences of syllables and words embedded within a prosodic phrase (500–2000 ms) with delta oscillations (<3 Hz) (Ghitza 2011). In brief, there would exist a principled relation between the time scales present in speech and the time constants underlying neuronal cortical oscillations that is both a reflection of and the means by which the brain converts speech rhythms into phonemes (Giraud, Poeppel 2012). The same question posited for ERPs components arises: is the oscillatory rhythms entrainment a generic processing of acoustic patterns or is it informative of specific categorial processing in speech? (see Kösem, van Wassenhove 2017 for a critical review).

High-frequency gamma rhythms are involved in speech perception. A recent ECoG study succeeded at reconstructing the original speech input (series of words and pseudowords) by using a combination of linear and nonlinear methods to decode neural responses from high-gamma (70–150 Hz) activity recorded in auditory cortical regions. The decoded speech representations allowed readout and identification of individual words directly from brain activity during single trial sound presentations (Pasley et al. 2012). Mesgarani et al. (2014) analyzed the same high gamma cortical surface field potentials, which correlate with neuronal spiking, while participants listened to English natural speech samples (500 sentences spoken by 400 people) and the neural answers were recorded with ECoG. Most speech-responsive sites were found in posterior and middle STG. Neural responses showed distributed spatiotemporal patterns evoked during listening in line with different subsets phonetic-phonological patterns. Thus, the ECoG electrodes collocated in the auditory cortex divide STG sites into two distinct spatial gradients: obstruent- and sonorant-selective neural sites. The obstruent-selective group resulted divided into two subgroups: plosive and fricative electrodes. Among plosive electrodes, some were responsive to all plosives, whereas others were selective to place of articulation (dorsal /g/ and /k/ versus coronal /d/ and /t/ versus labial /p/ and /b/) and voicing (separating voiced /b/, /d/, and /g/ from unvoiced /p/, /t/, and /k/). Fricative-selective electrodes showed weak, overlapping selectivity to coronal plosives (/d/ and /t/). Sonorant selective cortical sites, in contrast, were partitioned into four partially overlapping groups: low-back vowels, low-front vowels, high-front vowels, and nasals. Although very interesting, this neural mapping showed just a selective response to subsets of phonemes. Also, the authors found selectivity for some higher-order acoustic parameters, such as examples of nonlinear, spatial encoding of VOT, which could have important implications for the categorical representation of this temporal cue.

Furthermore, they observed a joint differential encoding of F1 and F2 at single cortical sites, suggesting evidence of spectral integration processing.

Interestingly, high-gamma oscillations play a crucial role also in speech production. Bouchard et al. (2013) found that these rhythms are generated in the ventral sensory motor cortex – a cortical region that controls the vocal articulators – during the production of American English vowels and consonants. Populations of neurons in this cortex showed convergent and divergent dynamics during the production of different phonetic features. The dynamics of individual phonemes were superimposed on a slower oscillation that characterizes the transition between consonants and vowels. Although trajectories were found to originate or terminate in different regions, they consistently pass through the same (target) region of the state-space for shared phonetic features. Consonants and vowels occupy distinct regions of the cortical state-space. Large state-space distances between consonant and vowel representations may explain why it is more common in speech errors to substitute consonants with one another, and vowels with vowels, but very rarely consonants with vowels or vowels with consonants (that is, in 'slips of the tongue'). A recent study, Rapela (2016), confirmed this view by showing that rhythmic speech production (i.e., sequence of syllables) modulates the power of high-gamma oscillations over the ventral sensory motor cortex and the power of beta oscillations over the auditory cortex (due to the auditory feedback necessary control acoustic-articulatory outputs). He found significant coupling between the phase of brain oscillations at the frequency of speech production and their amplitude in the high-gamma range (i.e., phase-amplitude coupling). Furthermore, the data showed that brain oscillations at the frequency of speech production were organized as traveling waves and synchronized to the rhythm of speech production.

Additional evidence suggests that high frequency activity tags the timing of abstract linguistic speech units and structures (Kösem & van Wassenhove 2017). For instance, high-frequency activity has been shown to reflect the result of top-down word parsing: high-frequency oscillatory power dynamics systematically delineated the boundaries of perceived monosyllabic words in ambiguous speech streams (Kösem et al. 2016). High-frequency activity also represented, concurrently with delta oscillations, the segmentation of longer abstract linguistic structures (phrases and sentences) in continuous speech (Ding et al., 2016).

Di Liberto, O'Sullivan, Lalor (2015) performed an interesting EEG experiment in order to provide evidence of the neural indexing of the categorical perception of phonemes using series of natural sentences. They adopted a cross-validation approach to quantify how well each speech representation related to the neural data testing five speech representations: (1) broadband amplitude envelope; (2) spectrogram; (3) time-aligned sequence of phonemes; (4) time-aligned sequence of phonetic features (according to Chomsky & Halle 1968); and

(5) a combination of time-aligned phonetic features and spectrogram. Crucially, the combined time-aligned phonetic features and spectrogram model of representation outperformed all other models principally in the theta but also in the delta bands. Within latencies of 150–200 ms vowels and consonants resulted neurally mapped on hierarchical clusters according to different acoustic-articulatory features. As the experimental subjects were exposed to sequences of natural sentences (derived from a professional audio-book version of a popular mid-20th century American work of fiction), one can suppose that theta oscillations are involved in phonological discretization processes, while delta in suprasegmental processing.

Accordingly, theta (3–8 Hz) oscillations are also recruited during phonemic restoration (Riecke et al. 2012; Sunami et al. 2013; Strauß et al. 2014). It has been showed that theta oscillations may be involved in the identifications of consonants in syllables ([da], [ga]) matching the different temporal onset delays in natural audiovisual speech between mouth movements and speech sounds (Ten Oever & Sack 2015; see also Kösem et al. 2016).

From a general point of view, delta oscillations have been associated with the processing of non-speech-specific attentional and predictive modulations of auditory processing (Kösem et al. 2016), but they do not serve the same purpose as theta oscillations. Recent findings suggest that they can play a crucial role in parsing speech units in the acoustic signal (Buiatti et al. 2009). According to Ghitza (2011) this rhythm plays an important role in prosodic parsing, which pertains to sequences of syllables and words, hence tapping contextual effects: as such, the delta oscillator may interact with the theta, beta, and gamma oscillators in a top-down fashion. Recently, Ding et al. (2016) observed that delta frequency corresponded to the syntactic complexity of the heard speech signal. Series of phrases constituted of two monosyllabic words were associated with a neural entrainment at 2 Hz, and sentences composed of four monosyllabic words induced a delta response at 1 Hz. These data suggest that delta oscillations could also be involved in the combination (or unification) of word units into a longer and more abstract linguistic structure, that is in the full range of hierarchical linguistic structures from syllables to phrases and sentences. Along these lines, Murphy (2016) proposes a revolutionary theory of neurolinguistics, proposing that nested oscillations execute elementary linguistic computations involved in phrase structure building. Murphy's theory goes considerably beyond existing models, and it will be of interest for future research whether causal-explanatory power can also be attributed to nested oscillations with respect to the phonological system.

In brief, nested low theta and high gamma frequency activity may be associated with the output of phonetic-phonological processing, while delta phase resetting and entrainment may reflect the combinatorial processes underlying sentence unification, including phrase level prosody processing.

It is important to note that it is impossible to assign a single function to a given type of oscillatory activity (Başar et al. 2001). It is thus unlikely that, for instance, theta has a single role in language processing. In fact, theta's role and its varying patterns of coherence as a function of task demands may be better seen in its relationship to beta and gamma (and the same thing is true for the other oscillatory rhythms). It is arguable that the same oscillatory rhythms play different roles in speech and language processing (as in other cognitive processes) with simultaneous changes in the coherence patterns in the different frequency ranges. Actually, theta rhythms seem involved also in retrieving lexical semantic information and controlling processes with multiple items; on the other hand, gamma-band neuronal synchronization is involved in sentence-level semantic unification; alpha phase acts not only in decisional weighting, but also in semantic orientation, in creative thinking, and lexical decisions; beta synchronization serves to bind distributed sets of neurons into a coherent representation of (memorized) contents during language processing, and, in particular, building syntactic structures (cf. Grimaldi in press for a detailed discussion).

3 What does neurophysiological data tell us?

Cumulatively, the reviewed N1m/N1 studies suggest that the acoustic-articulatory patterns of speech sounds affect amplitudes, latencies and the spatial arrangement of neural sources. However, finding a ubiquitous system for speech-specific processing in line with the phonological features hypothesis is difficult. When we look at the data, it is hard to disambiguate between N1m/N1 evidence suggesting pure acoustic patterns and those indicating abstract phonological features. Solid evidence is that the acoustic distance between the first two formants of vowels is preserved in the auditory cortex and is directly detectable in sensor and source data (as found in the mammalian auditory cortex). This implies neuronal sensitivity interactions between spectral components during vowel discrimination that does not necessarily require separate formant representations (in the sense of feature extraction).

At the same time, these data coexist with further findings suggesting that acoustic-articulatory properties are affected by top-down features processing such as Height, Place and Round (this seems true also for Voice and Place for consonants), as showed by amplitudes, latencies and Talairach spatial coordinates in the auditory cortex. Note, however, that also when an entire vowel space of a language (Turkish) has been investigated (Scharinger et al. 2011) and evidence for the spatial arrangements of neural sources according to distinctive features seem strong, it is very difficult to disentangle the effect of acoustic parameters (F1, F2, F3) from that of distinctive features processing and representation in neural maps. In fact, the comparison of the source locations suggests that the auditory spatial encoding scheme is based both on acoustic bottom-up and top-down phonological information, and only a sophisticated statistical analysis of the data led to suggest that the continuous acoustic parameters per se do not warrant the understanding of abstract featural representation. But, again, it remains unclear how the correlation between acoustic parameters (e.g., F1) and feature patterns (tongue height) are eventually processed in different neural dimensions in perceiving sounds of speech.

To sum up, while the N1m/N1 findings show that the electrophysiological sensitivity to the properties of the stimuli is not exclusively correlated with their physical attributes, but rather with top-down processes associated with phonological categories, they are not so strong to preclude purely acoustic explanations of the auditory activity involved in speech processing: the amplitude data are not sufficient to prove a correlation with phonological patterns and the latency results appear contradictory (cf. Section 4). For example, while Obleser et al. (2004a, 2004b) and Grimaldi et al. (2016) showed that back vowels peaked later than non-back vowels, Scharinger et al. (2011a) revealed the reverse pattern. Finally, only one study on consonants has obtained strong evidence of latency modulations for Place and Voice (Obleser et al., 2006). Although it seems that latencies are probably correlated also with Height and Round features (Scharinger et al. 2011), it is difficult to establish to what extent the activity involved in speech encoding reflects merely mechanisms of spectro-temporal information extraction or rather of top-down processes related to phonological computations.

On the other side of the issue, also the MMNm/MMN studies seem to support this view. While many studies have provided neural evidence for categorical (and then abstract) representations of speech sounds and that distinctive features may be the neural signature of perception mechanisms, others suggest that also sensory inputs guide speech computation and representation. A crucial data for this perspective is represented by the fact that allophones generated by a phonological process (that is, a rule of the grammar) elicited the same MMN of phonemes (with the later characterized by an early neural answer): this suggests that both acoustic and abstract modes are immanent in the mapping of auditory inputs into higher perceptual representations and that they are related to memory processes (i.e., the listeners' knowledge of the phonological system).

In principle, this difficulty in showing the abstract representation of speech sounds in terms of neural processing may be due to different factors, as the nature of the stimuli, the experimental procedures developed, etc. However, I suggest that the constant joined effect of acoustic parameters and phonological processing in neural maps representation may reveal important properties of the phonetics-phonology relationship rather than showing the limits of these studies.

The oscillatory approach permits us to address this issue from another perspective and to clarify the phonetics-phonology relationship from a new viewpoint. The available data (not yet extensive) suggest a neural multidimensional feature space for speech perception and production encoding and not precise unit boundaries for each speech sound feature (cf. Mesgarani et al. 2014 and Bouchard et al. 2013). This flexible encoding of neural patterns may account for coarticulation and temporal overlap over phonemes. Thus, responses to group of acoustic parameters show a neural selectivity for specific phonetic features dynamically encoded by oscillatory rhythms: this selectivity emerges from combined neural tuning to multiple acoustic parameters that delimit phonetic contrasts. If we assume that the auditory system has evolutionally become tuned to the complex acoustic signal rhythmically produced by vocal apparatus, it is possible to hypothesize that neural oscillation patterns reflect the patterns of decoded speech (Giraud, Poeppel 2012). In other words, the input signal generates phase resetting of the intrinsic oscillation in auditory cortex in line with the spectro-temporal properties of speech stimuli (Schroeder & Lakatos 2009). As gamma oscillations have a period of approximately 25 ms, they may provide 10–15-ms window for integrating spectrotemporal information (low spiking rate) followed by a 10–15-ms window for propagating the output (high spiking rate). However, because the average length of a phoneme is about 50 ms, a 10–15-ms window might be too short for integrating this information (Arnal, Poeppel & Giraud 2016). Accordingly, thanks to computational models of gamma oscillations, it has been suggested that a 50-ms phoneme could be correctly processed with two/three gamma cycles (Borgers et al. 2005; Shamir et al. 2009).

So, the temporally limited capacity of gamma oscillations to integrate information over time possibly imposes a lower limit to the phoneme length. On the other hand, the average length of syllables is approximately 150–300 ms: because the theta band (4–8 Hz) falls around the mean syllabic rate of speech (~ 5 Hz), the phase of theta-band activity likely tracks syllabic-level features of speech. In short, it is arguable that the auditory cortex uses gamma oscillations to integrate the speech auditory stream at the phonemic timescale, and theta oscillations to signal syllable boundaries and orchestrate gamma activity (Ghitza 2012; Arnal, Poeppel, Giraud 2016). The gamma and theta bands, which concurrently process stimulus information, lie in a nesting relation such that the phase of theta shapes the properties (amplitude, and possibly phase) of gamma bands.

4 A preliminary proposal to explain bottom-up and top-down processes

4.1 Analog and digital processing of speech sounds

How the data until now discussed can explain the classical linguistic assumption that, starting from the acoustic signal, the phonetics properties are analyzed online and decoded into abstract representations (distinctive features)? That is, how neural data can explain the notion that speech perception is discrete (categorical) (Repp 1984; Scott & Evans 2010; Liebenthal & Bernstein 2017; see also Van Rullen & Koch 2003)? It is well known that categorical perception relates to the way in which a continuous sequence of equal physical changes in a stimulus is perceived and represented as different categories of stimuli. According to Giraud & Poeppel (2012)'s model, an incoming speech signal generates the neuronal (spiking) activity in the form of oscillatory rhythms (note that spike, or action potential, is a neuron discharged signal in response to stimuli, generally called synapse). The activity in the gamma band has a tightly coupled relation to spike trains, regulating spike patterns. Finally, neuronal excitability is modulated such that acoustic structure of the input is aligned with neuronal excitability. By this hypothesis, the theta and gamma oscillations act (i) by discretizing (sampling) the input spike trains to generate elementary units of the appropriate temporal granularity for subsequent processing and (ii) by creating packages of spike trains and excitability cycles.

Giraud & Poeppel (2012) argue that a functional consequence of the modulation of low and high pyramidal neurons by theta and gamma oscillators is the organization of spike timing and the ensuing discretization of the cortical output. Spike discretization serves to present the stimulus in discrete chunks (segments) from which many different types of computations can be performed thanks to a principled relation between the time scales present in speech and the time constants underlying neuronal cortical oscillations. Ultimately, the process permits phonological abstraction, generating discrete representations that make contact with spatially distributed phonemic and syllable representations underlying recognition (Giraud & Poeppel 2012: 3). This view, as clearly suggested by Arnal, Giraud & Poeppel (2016: 466), presupposes that the continuous stream of natural speech is analyzed online and decoded by discontinuous, separable modes in the auditory cortex (i.e.,neural spikes) in a sort of binary code: for each oscillatory cycle, output neurons may fire or not fire, which constitutes a binary code reflecting the shape of the speech envelope (Giraud & Poeppel 2012: 4).

However, as observed by Obleser, Herrmann & Henry (2012), the time scales present in speech cross functional boundaries between oscillatory bands in the human brain. Furthermore, while there are studies suggesting that synaptic activity onto pyramidal neurons (for instance in the hippocampus) is altered in discrete steps (Petersen et al. 1998; O'Connor et al. 2005), other studies show that a property of synapses is to change continuously, also for what concerns memory processes (Tanaka et al. 2008; see also Chaudhuri & Fiete 2016; Sjöström & Gerstner 2017). Although a longstanding tradition has hypothesized that information in a spike train is digitally (i.e. discreetly) encoded by the number of spikes in a given time interval, other empirical and theoretical perspectives suggest that information can also be encoded in the precise timings between single spikes as they arrive, namely through analog encoding (Rieke et al. 1999). Recently, Mochizuki & Shinomoto (2014) confirmed this perspective showing that fractions of neurons in subcortical regions (e.g. thalamic nuclei) exhibit digital patterns while cortical regions (e.g., primary visual cortex and middle temporal area) exhibit analog patterns. Therefore, it seems that both analog and digital forms are used by neurons to encode that is sent to and from the brain.

4.2 From spectro-temporal states to neurophysiological states through analog and digital spike-trains

I hypothesize that speech discretization is not due only to rhythmic packages of spike trains as resulted by the precise alignment of acoustic structure with neuronal excitability. Instead, discretization and phonological abstraction are the result of a continuous process which converts physical states into other physical states. I hypothesize that the *spectro-temporal states* are continuously converted into the *neurophysiological states* so that properties of the former states undergo changes interacting with the latter states until a new equilibrium is reached: such equilibrium is represented by synapses spatially distributed within the auditory cortex by means synchronized activities of oscillatory rhythms. At the production level, the inverse dynamical and continuous conversion happens: i.e., the neurophysiological states are converted into the spectrotemporal states through the same principle (here, however, I will restrict my discussion at the perception level only).

Why might the cortical brain use continuous process to convert the spectrotemporal states into the neurophysiological states rather than into well-separated discrete states? Two steps are needed to encode a continuous variable in a set of well-separated discrete stable states in some other coding dimension: (i) discretizing, and then (ii) choosing how to map such discrete values. In general, there is no metric-preserving mapping and the complexity of such encoding process is considerable. Conversely, the values of a continuous variable can be naturally and continuously mapped onto (quasi-)continuous states, preserving metric relationships between different values of the variable. The encoding is relatively simple, as the selection of a different storage state for a different value is based on the change in the variable value (cf. Chaudhuri & Fiete 2016).

I suggest that a continuous process is better suitable for learning and memory processes. Mapping spectro-acoustic variable onto a continuous multiple of matching neural states can preserve much more information useful for computational and memory processes. With a neural representation that preserves the information of the external variable input, it becomes possible, given an input with spectro-temporal variable patterns, to directly update the neural states according to the values of the external variables. For instance, when a learner is exposed to a linguistic system he/she does not only have to acquire which sounds represent phonemic categories but also to acquire the rules which generate allophonic variants in the appropriate environments (i.e., phonological processes) (cf. Miglietta, Grimaldi & Calabrese 2013). As we have seen in Section 3, a clear perceptual transition from the universal learning options to language-specific learning options emerge very early in infants: this view is compatible with a model of phonology in which the acquisition of phonemic categories parallel occurs with the learning of phonetic (allophonic) distribution patterns and their relationships. Moreover, a subsequent process is required to map the abstract representation of speech sound onto concepts, so as to generate lexical items, labelling, morphological computations, and Spell-Out transfer operations to the conceptual-intentional and sensory-motor interfaces, and ultimately to have a coherent representation of sentences. This process must be necessarily continuous, probably controlled by theta-gamma, alpha-gamma-beta and gamma-beta-theta nested oscillations (see Grimaldi in press).

The process that convert spectro-temporal states into neurophysiological states starts from the cochlea response where different frequencies reflect spectro-temporal properties of vowels and consonants, and continue through the auditory pathways where these frequencies are progressively converted into oscillatory rhythm in the auditory cortex creating nested neural oscillatory states resulting in distinctive features representations. As in the cochlea a tonotopic coding of acoustic frequencies is ensured by the selective activation of the cochlear neurons regularly positioned along the basilar membrane (Moerel et al. 2014; Saenz & Langers 2014), also the auditory cortex ensures a spatiotemporal mechanism as a tool to discretize speech sounds (the so-called tonotopic principle: Romani et al. 1982). In production, auditory and motor cortices integrate their activity through the oscillatory rhythms in order to produce the acoustic output.

I hypothesize that, from the cochlea, speech sounds activate a preliminary spectrotemporal computation in the auditory thalamus, or medial geniculate body (cf. Bartlett 2013). Here, the first conversion of spectrotemporal states in neurophysiological states begins, and neurons encode the signal in digital form, so as to phase-lock to speech envelope modulating theta oscillations. In this state, phonetic categories are broadly mapped. After reset, theta oscillations generate a nested modulation of gamma oscillations in the primary auditory cortex where neurons begin to decode the signal into continuous (analog) linguistically-relevant categories. Finally, the last neurophysiological state takes place in secondary auditory areas (superior temporal gyrus, Brodmann area 22), where invariant properties of phonetic categories (i.e., distinctive features) are mapped leading to abstract representation through analog and spatially distributed gamma oscillations (cf. Fig. 5).

I assume that, at the end of the process, phonological segments (and then categorical processes) take the form of continuous neural states represented by nested cortical oscillatory rhythms spatially distributed in the auditory cortex (as suggested by Bouchard et al. 2013; Mesgarani et al. 2014). Within this perspective, distinctive features (i.e., the relevant representational linguistic primitives) are

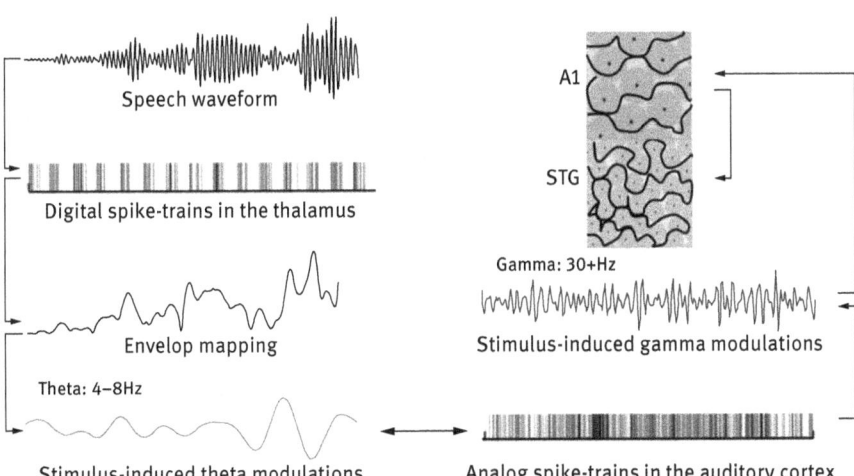

Fig. 5: A model of speech perception based on digital and analog spike-trains processing that convert spectro-temporal states within neurophysiological states. Acoustic stimuli induced digital spike-trains in the thalamus (medial geniculate body) and theta oscillations are modulated to map speech envelop. Theta oscillations are coupled with gamma oscillations and analog spike-trains decode broad phonetic categories within the primary auditory cortex (A1) and invariant properties of phonetic categories (distinctive features) within the superior temporal gyrus (STG, Brodmann area 22).

represented by both spatially local and distributed neural selectivity (Mesgarani et al. 2014; Di Liberto et al. 2015). So, the abstract representation of distinctive feature is reached when nested theta and gamma bands (and probably also beta bands: cf. Ghitza 2011) reach the maximum power within the appropriate auditory space tonotopically deputed to transform the peculiar properties of a speech stimulus into discrete neural states (i.e., distinctive features). While Giraud & Poeppel (2012) see the spatially distributed phonemic and syllabic representations as a consequence of discrete chunks generated by spike trains, I suggest that discretization processes emerge at the cortical level when different neurophysiological states result spatially distributed within the secondary auditory cortex, without the need for the alignment of acoustic structure of the input with neuronal excitability. Therefore, the binary properties of distinctive features that permit polar oppositions is neurally instantiated in the tonotopic presence or absence of appropriate neurophysiological states within the secondary auditory cortex. In brief, discretization and categorization consist in dynamical neurophysiological states tonotopically distributed.

This idea is in line with fMRI, MEG, EEG and ECoG studies which showed that the auditory areas are characterized by a hierarchical layout highly specialized in analyzing different aspects of the signal: the primary auditory cortex (A1) seems engaged in the acoustic processing of the signal – where broad properties of speech sound or phonetic cues for landmarks serving to identify phoneme boundaries are computed (Stevens 2002) – while the superior temporal gyrus and the superior temporal sulcus work smoothly for encoding the acoustic patterns onto phonological features (Scott & Johnsrude 2003; Price 2012; Manca & Grimaldi 2016; Santoro et al. 2014). Thus, it seems that speech discretization is a dynamical process where transient changes from the physical spectro-temporal states to neurophysiological states generate categorial perception.

Ultimately, the discrete neural states here proposed are not static: as we have seen in Section 2, an important characteristic of oscillatory rhythms is the temporal (dynamical) way in which they are constantly nested inside other through synchronization and desynchronization processes. Such characteristic is suitable for further computational processes required to reach adequate representations of the other levels of language (lexical, syntactic, etc.), which, in turn, will be realized thanks to subsequent neural states and continuous nesting of further oscillatory bands (see Grimaldi in press). At the end, the traditional multilevel properties of language (phones, phonemes, syllables, words, syntax, etc.) hypothesized by linguistics may be seen as neural states dynamically and spatially changing in the time and resulted by online computation and representations.

In conclusion, within a neurobiological perspective the classical distinction between bottom-up processes (phonetics) reflecting acoustic differences and top-down (phonology) processes reflecting distinctive features extraction should be reinterpreted as a continuous process involving different physical states (spectro-temporal states and neurophysiological states) where a phase transition indicates a progressive changes in structure and a consequent changes in properties, so that the properties of the former states are converted in the properties of the latter states, as it happens for states of matter. With a crucial difference: changes in structure and in properties from the spectro-temporal states to the neurophysiological states generates abstract representations of speech sounds.

Acknowledgments: I wish to thank two anonymous reviewers for their useful comments on the first version of the manuscript that have permitted me to improve the work.

References

Archangeli, Diana & Douglas Pulleyblank. 1994. *Grounded phonology*. Cambridge, MA: MIT Press.
Arnal, Luc, David Poeppel & Anne-Lise Giraud. 2016. A neurophysiological perspective on speech processing in "the neurobiology of language". In Gregory Hickok & Steven L. Small, *Neurobiology of Language*, 463–478. Amsterdam: Elsevier.
Bartlett, Edward L. 2013. The organization and physiology of the auditory thalamus and its role in processing acoustic features important for speech perception. *Brain & Language* 126. 29–48.
Başar, Erol, Canan Başar-Erogluc, Sirel Karakaş & Martin Schürmann. 2001. Gamma, alpha, delta, and theta oscillations govern cognitive processes. *International Journal of Psychophysiology* 39. 241–248.
Bastiaansen, Marcel, Ali Mazaheri & Ole Jensen. 2012. Beyond ERPs: Oscillatory neuronal dynamics. In Emily S. Kappenman & Steven J. Luck (eds.), *The Oxford handbook of event-related potential components*, 1–21. Oxford: Oxford University Press.
Blumstein, S. 1991. The relation between phonetics and phonology. *Phonetica* 48. 108–119.
Boemio, Anthony, Stephen Fromm, Allen Braun & David Poeppel. 2005. Hierarchical and asymmetric temporal sensitivity in human auditory cortices. *Nature neuroscience* 8. 389–395.
Borgers, Christoph, Steven Epstein & Nancy J. Kopell. 2005. Background gamma rhythmicity and attention in cortical local circuits: a computational study. *Proceedings of National Academy of Science* 102. 7002–7007.
Bouchard, Kristofer E., Nima Mesgarani, Keith Johnson & Edward F. Chang. 2012. Functional organization of human sensorimotor cortex for speech articulation. *Nature* 495. 327–334.

Brattico, Elvira. 2006. *Cortical processing of musical pitch as reflected by behavioural and electrophysiological evidence*. Helsinki: Yliopistopaino.
Bromberger, Sylvain, Morris Halle. 1986. On the relationship of phonology and phonetics: Comments on B. Lindblom 'On the origin and purpose of discreteness and invariance in sound patterns'. In Joseph S. Perkell, Dennis H. Klat (eds.), *Invariance and variability in speech processes*, 510–520. Hillsdale, NJ: Lawrence Erlbaum Associates.
Buzsáki, Gyorgy 2006. *Rhythms of the brain*. Oxford: Oxford University Press.
Calabrese, Andrea 2012. Auditory representations and phonological illusions: A linguist's perspective on the neurophysiological bases of speech perception. *Journal of Neurolinguistics*, 25(5). 355–381.
Carterette, E. C., C. Shipley, and J. S. Buchwald. 1984. On synthesizing animal speech: The case of the cat. In Geoff Bristow (ed.), *Electronic speech synthesis: Techniques, technology, and applications*, 292–302, New York: McGraw-Hill.
Chomsky, Noam & Morris Halle. 1968. *The sound patterns of English*. New York: Harper & Row.
Cirelli, Laura K., Dan Bosnyak, Fiona C. Manning, Christina Spinelli, Celine Marie, Fujioka Takako, et al. 2014. Beat-induced fluctuations in auditory cortical beta-band activity: Using EEG to measure age-related changes. *Frontiers in psychology* 5. doi: 10.3389/fpsyg.2014.00742.
Da Costa, Sandra, Wietske van der Zwaag, Jose P. Marques, Richard S. Frackowiak, Stephanie Clarke & Melissa Saenz. 2011. Human primary auditory cortex follows the shape of Heschl's gyrus. *The Journal of Neuroscience* 31. 14067–14075.
Darwin, Charles 1871. *The descent of man, and selection in relation to sex*. London: John Murray.
Di Liberto, Giovanni M., James A. O'Sullivan & Edmund C. Lalor. 2015. Low-frequency cortical entrainment to speech reflects phoneme level processing. *Current Biology* 25(19). 2457–2465.
Diesch, Eugen & Thomas Luce. 1997. Magnetic fields elicited by tones and vowel formants reveal tonotopy and nonlinear summation of cortical activation. *Psychophysiology* 34. 501–510.
Diesch, Eugen & Thomas Luce. 2000. Topographic and temporal indices of vowel spectral envelope extraction in the human auditory cortex. *Journal of cognitive neuroscience* 12(5). 878–893.
Diesch, Eugen, Carsten Eulitz, Scott Hampson & Bernhard Ross. 1996. The neurotopography of vowels as mirrored by evoked magnetic field measurements. *Brain Language* 53. 143–168.
Ding, Nai, Lucia Melloni, Hang Zhang, Xing Tian & David Poeppel. 2016. Cortical tracking of hierarchical linguistic structures in connected speech. *Nature Neuroscience* 19(1). 158–164. doi:10.1038/nn.4186
Durand, Jacques & Bernard Laks. 2002. Phonology, phonetics and cognition. In Jacques Durand & Laks Bernard (eds.), *Phonetics, phonology and cognition*, 10–50. Oxford: Oxford University Press.
Edelman, Gerald M. & Giulio Tononi. 2000. *A universe of consciousness. How matter becomes imagination*. New York: Basic Books.
Eulitz, Carsten, Eugen Diesch, Christoph Pantev, Steven Hampson & Thomas Elbert. 1995. Magnetic and electric brain activity evoked by the processing of tone and vowel stimuli. *The Journal of neuroscience* 1. 2748–2755.
Eulitz, Carsten, Jonas Obleser & Aditi Lahiri. 2004. Intra-subject replication of brain magnetic activity during the processing of speech sounds. *Cognitive brain research* 19. 82–91.
Fitch, W. Tecumseh. 2010. *The evolution of language*. New York: Cambridge University Press.

Fujisaki, H. & T. Kawashima. 1969. On the nodes and mechanisms of speech perception. *Annual Report of the Engineering Research Institute* 28. 67–73. Faculty of Engineering of Tokyo.

Fujisaki, H. & T. Kawashima. 1970. Some experiments on speech perception and a model for the perceptual mechanism. *Annual Report of the Engineering Research Institute* 29. 207–214. Faculty of Engineering of Tokyo.

Gage, Nicole, Timothy P. L. Roberts & Gregory Hickok. 2006. Temporal resolution properties of human auditory cortex: Reflections in the neuromagnetic auditory evoked M100 component. *Brain Research* 1069(1). 166–171.

Ghitza, Oded. 2011. Linking speech perception and neurophysiology: speech decoding guided by cascaded oscillators locked to the input rhythm. *Frontiers in Psychology* 2. 130.

Giraud, Anne-Lise & David Poeppel. 2012. Cortical oscillations and speech processing: emerging computational principles and operations. *Nature Neuroscience* 15. 511–517.

Gray, Charles M., Andreas K. Engel, Peter König & Wolf Singer. 1990. Stimulus-dependent neuronal oscillations in cat visual cortex: receptive field properties and feature dependence. *European Journal of Neuroscience* 2. 607–619.

Grimaldi, Mirko, Anna Dora Manca, Francesco Sigona & Francesco Di Russo. 2016. Electroencephalographic evidence of vowels computation and representation in human auditory cortex. In Anna Maria Di Sciullo (ed.), *Biolinguistics investigations on the language faculty*, 79–100. Amsterdam/Philadelphia: Benjamins.

Grimaldi, Mirko, Bianca Sisinni, Barbara Gili Fivela, Sara Invitto, Donatella Resta, Paavo Alku & Elvira Brattico. 2014. Assimilation of L2 vowels to L1 phonemes governs L2 learning in adulthood: A behavioral and ERP study. *Frontiers in human neuroscience* 8.

Grimaldi, Mirko. In press. From brain noise to syntactic structures: A formal proposal within the oscillatory rhythms perspective. In Ludovico Franco & Paolo Lorusso (eds.), *Linguistic variation: Structure and interpretation – A Festschrift in Honour of M. Rita Manzini in occasion of her 60th birthday*. Boston/Berlin: De Gruyter Mouton.

Halle, Morris. 2002. *From memory to speech and back: Papers on phonetics and phonology 1954–2002*. Berlin: Mouton de Gruyter.

Hallez, Hans, Bart Vanrumste, Roberta Grech, Joseph Muscat, Wima De Clercq, Anneleen Vergult, et al. 2007. Review on solving the forward problem in EEG source analysis. *Journal of neuroengineering and rehabilitation* 4.1. 1–29.

Hulst, H.G. van der. 2013. The discoverers of the phoneme. In Keith Allen (ed.), *Oxford handbook of the history of linguistics*, 167–191. Oxford: Oxford University Press.

Jakobson, Roman & Linda R. Waugh. 1979. *The sound shape of language*. (11th edn.) Brighton Sussex: Harvester Press.

Jakobson, Roman, Gunner Fant & Morris Halle. 1952. *Preliminaries to speech analysis*. Cambridge, MA: MIT Press.

Kaas, Jon & Troy A. Hackett. 2000. Subdivisions of auditory cortex and processing streams in primates. *Proceedings of the National Academy of Sciences of the United States of America* 97. 11793–11799.

Kazanina, Nina, Colin Phillips & Willima J. Idsardi. 2006. The influence of meaning on the perception of speech sounds. *Proceedings of the National Academy of Sciences of the United States of America* 103(30). 1138–1186.

Keating, Path A. 1991. On phonetics / phonology interaction. *Phonetica* 48. 221–222.

Klimesch, Wolfgang. 2011. Evoked alpha and early access to the knowledge system: the P1 inhibition timing hypothesis. *Brain Research* 1408. 52–71.

Klimesch, Wolfgang, Bärbel Schack, Manuel Schabus, Michael Doppelmayr, Walter Gruber, Paul Sauseng. 2004. Phase-locked alpha and theta oscillations generate the P1-N1 complex and are related to memory performance. *Cognitive Brain Research* 19. 302–316.

Kösem, Aanne, Anahita Basira, Leila Azizi & Virginia van Wassenhove. 2016. High frequency neural activity predicts word parsing in ambiguous speech streams. *Journal of Neurophysiology* 116. 2497–2512.

Kösem, Anne & Virginie van Wassenhove. 2017. Distinct contributions of low- and high-frequency neural oscillations to speech comprehension. *Language, Cognition and Neuroscience* 32(5). 536–544. doi:10.1080/23273798.2016.1238495

Kuhl, Patricia K. & James D. Miller. 1978. Speech perception by the chinchilla: Identification functions for synthetic VOT stimuli. *Journal of the Acoustical Society of America* 63. 905–917.

Kuhl, Patricia K. 2004. Early language acquisition: Cracking the speech code. *Nature reviews neuroscience* 5(11). 831–843.

Kuhl, Patricia K., Erika Stevens, Akiko Hayashi, Toshisada Deguchi, Shigeru Kiritani & Paul Iverson. 2006. Infants show a facilitation effect for native language phonetic perception between 6 and 12 months. *Developmental Science* 9(2). F13–F21.

Kuriki, S., Y. Okita, Y. Hirata 1995. Source analysis of magnetic field responses from the human auditory cortex elicited by short speech sounds. *Experimental brain research* 104(1). 144–152.

Lagemann, Lothar, Hidehiko Okamoto, Henning Teismann, Christo Pantev. 2012. Involuntary monitoring of sound signals in noise is reflected in the human auditory evoked n1m response. *Plos One* 7(2). e31634.

Leonard, Matthew K., Edward F. Chang. 2016. Direct cortical neurophysiology of speech perception. In Gregory Hickok & Steven L. Small, *Neurobiology of language*, 479–489, Amsterdam: Elsevier.

Liebenthal, Einat & Lynne E. Bernstein (eds.). 2017. *Neural mechanisms of perceptual categorizationas precursors to speech perception. Frontiers in neuroscience.* Lausanne: Frontiers Media.

Lindblom, Bjhorn. 1986. On the origin and purpose of discreteness and invariance in sound patterns. In Joseph S. Perkell & Dennis H. Klat (eds.), *Invariance and variability in speech processes*, 493–510. Hillsdale, NJ: Lawrence Erlbaum Associates.

Lu, Thomas, Li Liang, Xiaoquin Wang. 2001. Temporal and rate representations of time-varying signals in the auditory cortex of awake primates. *Nature Neuroscience* 4. 1131–1138.

Luck, Steve J. 2005. *An introduction to the event-related potential technique.* Cambridge MA: MIT press.

Makeig, Scott, Monte Westerfield, Tzyy-Ping Jung, Sonia Enghoff, John Townsend, Eric Courchesne, Terry J. Sejnowski. 2002. Dynamic brain sources of visual evoked responses. *Science* 295. 690–694.

Mäkelä, Anna Mari, Paavo Alku & Hannu Tiitinen. 2003. The auditory N1m reveals the left-hemispheric representation of vowel identity in humans. *Neuroscience Letters* 353. 111–114.

Malmivuo, Jaakko, Veikko Suihko & Hannu Eskola. 1997. Sensitivity distributions of EEG and MEG measurements. *IEEE Transactions on Biomedical Engineering* 44. 196–208.

Manca, Anna Dora & Mirko Grimaldi. 2016. Vowels and consonants in the brain: Evidence from magnetoencephalographic studies on the n1m in normal-hearing listeners. *Frontiers in Psychology* 7.1413.

Mesgarani, Nima, Stephen V. David, Jonathan B. Fritz & Shihab A. Shamma. 2008. Phoneme representation and classification in primary auditory cortex. *The Journal of the Acoustical Society of America* 123(2). 899–909.

Mesgarani, Nima, Connie Cheung, Keith Chang & Edward F. Johnson. 2014. Phonetic feature encoding in human superior temporal Gyrus. *Science* 343. 1006–1010.

Miglietta, Sandra, Mirko Grimaldi & Andrea Calabrese. 2013. Conditioned allophony in speech perception: An ERP study. *Brain & Language* 126. 285–290.

Mitterer, H. 2007. Behavior reflects the (degree of) reality of phonological features in the brain as well. *ICPhS XVI*. 127–130. Saarbrücken, 6–10 August 2007.

Mochizuki, Yasuhiro, Shigeru Shinomoto. 2014. Analog and digital codes in the brain. *Physical Review E*. 89(2).

Moerel, Michelle, Federico De Martino & Elia Formisano. 2014. An anatomical and functional topography of human auditory cortical areas. *Frontiers in neuroscience* 8.

Murphy, Elliot. 2016. A theta-gamma neural code for feature set composition with phase-entrained delta nestings. *University College London Working Papers in Linguistics* (UCLWPL). 1–22.

Näätänen, Risto. 2001. The perception of speech sounds by the human brain as reflected by the mismatch negativity (MMN) and its magnetic equivalent (MMNm). *Psychophysiology* 38. 1–21.

Näätänen, Risto, Anne Lehtokoski, Mietta Lennes, Marie Cheour, Minna Huotilainen et al. 1997. Language-specific phoneme representations revealed by electric and magnetic brain responses. *Nature* 385. 432–434.

Nelson, D. A. and P. Marler. 1989. Categorical perception of a natural stimulus continuum: Birdsong. *Science* 244, 976–978.

O'Connor, Daniel H., Gayle M. Wittenberg & Samuel S-H. Wang. 2005. Graded bidirectional synaptic plasticity is composed of switch-like unitary events. *Proceedings of National Academy of Sciences U.S.A* 102. 9679–9684.

Obleser, Jonas, Thomas Elbert, Aditi Lahiri & Carsten Eulitz. 2003a. Cortical representation of vowels reflects acoustic dissimilarity determined by formant frequencies. *Cognitive Brain Research* 15. 207–213.

Obleser, Jonas, Aditi Lahiri & Carsten Eulitz. 2003b. Auditory-evoked magnetic field codes place of articulation in timing and topography around 100 milliseconds post syllable onset. *Neuroimage* 20. 1839–1847.

Obleser, Jonas, Thomas Elbert & Carsten Eulitz. 2004a. Attentional influences on functional mapping of speech sounds in human auditory cortex. *BMC neuroscience* 5(24).

Obleser, Jonas, Björn Herrmann & Molly J. Henry. 2012. Neural oscillations in speech: don't be enslaved by the envelope. *Frontiers in Human Neurosciences* 6.

Obleser, Jonas, Aditi Lahiri & Carsten Eulitz. 2004b. Magnetic brain response mirrors extraction of phonological features from spoken vowels. *Journal of Cognitive Neuroscience* 16. 31–39.

Obleser, Jonas, Sophie Skott & Carsten Eulitz. 2006. Now you hear it, now you don't: transient traces of consonants and their nonspeech analogues in the human brain. *Cerebral Cortex* 16. 1069–1076.

Ohala, John. 1990. There is no interface between phonology and phonetics: a personal view. in *Journal of Phonetics* 18. 153–171.

Ohl, Frank W. & Henning Scheich. 1997. Orderly cortical representation of vowels based on formant interaction. *Proceedings of the National Academy of Sciences* 94. 9440–9444.

Ohl, Frank W. & Henning Scheich. 2005. Learning-induced plasticity in animal and human auditory cortex, *Current Opinion in Neurobiology* 15. 470–477.

Ortiz-Mantilla, Silvia, Jarmo A., Hämäläinen, Gabriella Musacchia & April A. Benasich. 2013. Enhancement of gamma oscillations indicates preferential processing of native over foreign phonemic contrasts in infants. *The Journal of Neuroscience* 33(48). 18746–18754.

Partanen, Eino, Teija Kujala, Liitola Risto, Auli Näätänen, Anke Sambeth & Minna Huotilainen. 2013. Learning-induced neural plasticity of speech processing before birth. *Proceedings of the National Academy of Sciences* 110(37). 15145–15150.

Pasley, Brian N., Stephen V. David, Nima Mesgarani, Adeen Flinker, Shihab A. Shamma, Nathan E. Crone, Robert T. Knight & Edward F. Chang. 2012. Reconstructing speech from human auditory cortex. *Plos Biology* 10(1). e1001251.

Peelle, Jonathan E. & Matthew H. Davis. 2012. Neural oscillations carry speech rhythm through to comprehension. *Frontiers in psychology* 3. 320.

Penny, Will D., Stefan J. Kiebel, James M. Kilner, Michael D. Rugg. 2002. Event-related brain dynamics. *Trends in Neuroscience* 25. 387–389.

Petersen, Carl, Robert C. Malenka, Roger Nicoll & John Hopfield. 1998. All-or-none potentiation of ca3-ca1 synapses. *Proceedings of National Academy of Sciences U.S.A* 95. 4732–4737.

Phillips, Colin, Thomas Pellathy, Alec Marantz, Elron Yellin, Kenneth Wexler, David Poeppel et al. 2000. Auditory cortex accesses phonological categories: An MEG mismatch study. *Journal of Cognitive Neuroscience* 12 (6). 1038–1055.

Phillips, Colin. 2000. Levels of representation in the electrophysiology of speech perception. *Cognitive Science* 25. 711–731.

Pierrehumbert, Janet. 1990. Phonological and phonetic representations. *Journal of Phonetics* 18. 375–394.

Pisoni, David B. 1975. The role of auditory short-term memory in discrimination consonants and vowels. *Memory & Cognition* 3. 7–18.

Poeppel, David & Gregory Hickok. 2015. Electromagnetic recording of the auditory system. *The Human Auditory System: Fundamental Organization and Clinical Disorders* 129. 245–255.

Poeppel, David, William J. Idsardi & Virginia van Wassenhov. 2008. Speech perception at the interface of neurobiology and linguistics. *Philosophical Transactions of the Royal Society, Biological Sciences* 363. 1071–1086.

Poeppel, David, Colin Phillips, Elron Yellin, Howard A., Rowley, Timothy P. Roberts & Alec Marantz. 1997. Processing of vowels in supratemporal auditory cortex. *Neuroscience Letters* 221. 145–148.

Price, Cathy. J. 2012. A review and synthesis of the first 20 years of PET and fMRI studies of heard speech, spoken language and reading. *Neuroimage* 62. 816–847.

Rapela, Joaquín. 2016. Entrainment of traveling waves to rhythmic motor acts. *arXiv Quantitative Biology – Neurons and Cognition* 206.

Rauschecker, Josef P. & Biao. Tian. 2000. Mechanisms and streams for processing of "what" and "where" in auditory cortex. *Proceedings of the National Academy of Sciences* 97. 11800–11806.

Rieke, Fred, William Bialek, Rob. de Ruyter van Stevenick. 1999. *Spikes: exploring the neural code*. Cambridge, MA: MIT Press.

Repp, Bruno H. 1984. Categorical perception: Issues, methods, findings. *Speech and Language: Advance in Basic Research and Practice* 10. 243–335.

Riecke, Lars, Mieke Vanbussel, Lars Hausfeld, Deniz Başkent, Elisa Formisano & Fabrizio Esposito. 2012. Hearing an illusory vowel in noise: Suppression of auditory cortical activity. *The Journal of Neuroscience* 32(23). 8024–8034.
Rishidev, Chaudhuri & Fiete Ila. 2016. Computational principles of memory. *Nature Neuroscience Review* 19(3). 394–403.
Roberts, Timothy P. & David Poeppel. 1996. Latency of auditory evoked M100 as a function of tone frequency. *Neuro Report* 7. 1138–1140.
Roberts, Timothy P., Paul Ferrari, Steven M. Stufflebeam & David Poeppel 2000. Latency of the auditory evoked neuromagnetic field components: Stimulus dependence and insights toward perception. *Journal of Clinical Neurophysiology* 17. 114–129.
Romani, Gian Luca, Samuel J. Williamson & Lloyd Kaufman. 1982. Tonotopic organization of the human auditory cortex. *Science* 216. 1339–1340.
Saenz, Melissa & Dave R. M. Langers. 2014. Tonotopic mapping of human auditory cortex. *Hearing Research* 307. 42–52.
Sanei, Saeid & Jonathan A. Chambers. 2013. *EEG source location in EEG signal processing*. New York: John Wiley and Sons.
Santoro, Roberta, Michelle Moerel, Federico De Martino, Rainer Goebel, Kamil Ugurbil, Essa Yacoub & Elisa Formisano. 2014. Encoding of natural sounds at multiple spectral and temporal resolutions in the human auditory cortex. *PLoS Computational Biology* 10.
Sauseng, Paul, Wolfang Klimesch, Walter R. Gruber, Simon Hanslmayr, Roman Freunberger & Michael Doppelmayr. 2007. Are event-related potential components generated by phase resetting of brain oscillations? A critical discussion. *Neuroscience* 146(4). 1435–1444.
Scharinger, Mathias, William J. Idsardi & Samantha Poe. 2011a. A comprehensive three-dimensional cortical map of vowel space. *Journal of Cognitive Neuroscience* 23. 3972–3982.
Scharinger, Mathias, Jennifer Merickel, Joshua Riley & William J. Idsardi. 2011b. Neuromagnetic evidence for a featural distinction of English consonants: Sensor-and source-space data. *Brain and language* 116(2). 71–82.
Scharinger, Mathias, Phillip J. Monahan & William J. Idsardi. 2012. Asymmetries in the processing of vowel height. *Journal of Speech, Language, and Hearing Research* 55(3). 903–918.
Schroeder, Charles E. & Peter Lakatos. 2009. Low-frequency neuronal oscillations as instruments of sensory selection. *Trends in Neurosciences* 32. 9–18.
Scott, Sophie K. & Samuel Evans. 2010. Categorizing speech. *Nature Neuroscience* 13(11). 1304–1306.
Scott, Sophie K. & Ingrid S. Johnsrude. 2003. The neuroanatomical and functional organization of speech perception. *Trends in neurosciences* 26. 100–107.
Shamir, Maoz, Oded Ghitza, Steven Epstein & Nancy Kopell. 2009. Representation of time-varying stimuli by a network exhibiting oscillations on a faster time scale. *PLoS Computationla Biology* 5. e1000370.
Shamma, Shihab A. 1985a. Speech processing in the auditory system I: The representation of speech sounds in the responses of the auditory nerve. *The Journal of the Acoustical Society of America* 78(5). 1612–1621.
Shamma, Shihab A. 1985b. Speech processing in the auditory system II: The representation of speech sounds in the responses of the auditory nerve. *The Journal of the Acoustical Society of America* 78(5). 1622–1632.

Sharma, Anu & Michael F. Dorman. 1999. Cortical auditory evoked potential correlates of categorical perception of voice-onset time. *Journal of the Acoustical Society of America* 106 (2). 1078–1083.

Shestakova, Anna, Elvira Brattico, Alexei Soloviev, Vasily Klucharev & Minna Huotilainen. 2004. Orderly cortical representation of vowel categories presented by multiple exemplars. *Brain Cognitive Research* 21. 342–350.

Sjöström, Jesper & Wulfram Gerstner. Spike-timing dependent plasticity. 2017. Henry Markram, Wulfram Gerstner & Per Jesper Sjöström (eds.), *Spike-timing-dependent plasticity: A comprehensive overview*, 35–44. Frontiers Computational Neuroscience.

Stevens, Kenneth N. & Morris Halle. 1967. Remarks on analysis by synthesis and distinctive features. In Weiant Wathen-Dunn (ed.), *Models for the perception of speech and visual form*, 88–102. Cambridge: MA: MIT Press.

Stevens, Kenneth N. 2002. Toward a model for lexical access based on acoustic landmarks and distinctive features. *Journal of Acoustical Society of America* 111. 1872–1891.

Strauß, Antje, Sonia A. Kotz, Mathias Scharinger & Jonas Obleser. 2014. Alpha and theta brain oscillations index dissociable processes in spoken word recognition. *NeuroImage* 97. 387–395.

Sunami, Kishico, Akira Ishii, Sakurako Takano, Hidefuni Yamamoto, Tetsuhi Sakashita, Masaaka Tanaka & Hideo Yamane. 2013. Neural mechanisms of phonemic restoration for speech comprehension revealed by magnetoencephalography. *Brain Research* 1537. 164–173.

Sussman, Elise S., Suan Chen, Jonathan Sussman-Fort & Elisabeth Dinces. 2013. The five myths of MMN: Redefining how to use MMN in basic and clinical research. *Brain Topography* 25. 553–564.

Swink, Shannon & Andrew Stuart. 2012. Auditory long latency responses to tonal and speech stimuli. *Journal of Speech, language, and Hearing research* 55(2). 447–459.

Talavage, Thomas M., Martin I. Sereno, Jennifer R. Melcher, Patrik J. Ledden, Bruce R. Rosen & Anders M. Dale. 2004. Tonotopic organization in human auditory cortex revealed by progressions of frequency sensitivity. *Journal of neurophysiology* 91. 1282–1296.

Tanaka, Jun-ichi, Yoshihiro Horiike, Masanori Matsuzaki, Takashi Miyazaki, Graham C. Ellis-Davies & Haruo Kasai. 2008. Protein synthesis and neurotrophin-dependent structural plasticity of single dendritic spines. *Science* 319. 1683–1687.

Ten Oever, Sanne & Alexander T. Sack. 2015. Oscillatory phase shapes syllable perception. *Proceedings of the National Academy of Sciences of the United States of America* 112(52). 15833–15837.

Teuber, Hans-Lucas. 1967. Lacunae and Research Approaches to Them: I. In Clark H. Millikan & Francis L. Darley, *Brain Mechanisms Underlying Speech and Language*, 204–216. York: New MIT Press.

VanRullen, Rufin & Christof Koch. 2003. Is perception discrete or continuous? *Trends in Cognitive Neuroscience* 7(5). 207–213.

Varela, Francisco, Jean-Philippe Lachaux, Eugenio Rodriguez & Jacques Martinerie. 2001. The brain web: phase synchronization and large-scale integration. *Nature Review Neuroscience* 2. 229–239.

Wang, Xiao-Jing. 2010. Neurophysiological and computational principles of cortical rhythms in cognition. *Physiological Review* 90. 1195–1268.

Wang, Xiaoqin. 2007. Neural coding strategies in auditory cortex. *Hearing Research* 229. 81–93.

Werker, Janet F. & Richard C. Tees. 1984. Cross-language speech perception: evidence for perceptual reorganization during the first year of life. *Infant Behavior and Development* 7. 49–63.

Werker, Janet F. & Richard C. Tees. 2005. Speech perception as a window for understanding plasticity and commitment in language systems of the brain. *Developmental Psychobiology* 46(3). 233–251.

Winkler, Istvan, Teija Kujala, Hhannu Tiitinen, Päivi Sivonen, Paavo Alku, [...], Risto Näätänen. 1999. Brain responses reveal the learning of foreign language phonemes. *Psychophysiology* 36. 638–642.

Woods, David L. 1995. The component structure of the N 1 wave of the human auditory evoked potential. *Electroencephalography and Clinical Neurophysiology-Supplements Only* 44. 102–109.

Zatorre Robert J. & Pascal Belin. 2001. Spectral and temporal processing in human auditory cortex. *Cerebral cortex* 11. 946–953.

Zoefel, Benedikt & Rufin VanRullen. 2015. The role of high-level processes for oscillatory phase entrainment to speech sound. *Frontiers in Human Neuroscience* 9: 651.

Zoloth, S. R., M. R. Petersen, M. D. Beecher, S. Green, P. Marler, D. B. Moody & W. C. Stebbins. 1979. Species-specific perceptual processing of vocal sounds by monkeys, *Science* 204. 870–872.

Harry van der Hulst
Metaphony with unary elements

1 Introduction

In this article,[1] I analyze several vowel harmony systems, generally referred to as metaphony. These systems (which come in many different varieties; see below) have been described or analyzed in terms of binary features, either using the feature [±high] (Walker 2005) or [±ATR] (Calabrese 2011) or in terms of unary features. In the latter case some authors have supported the use of unary features (Maiden 1991; Canalis 2016; d'Alessandro & van Oostendorp 2016), while others have argued against their use (Kaze 1991). In this article, I adopt the use of unary elements, such as the 'AIU' system that has been proposed in Dependency Phonology (Anderson & Ewen 1987), Government Phonology (Kaye, Lowenstamm & Vergnaud 1985), with some modifications that have been proposed in Radical CV Phonology (van der Hulst 2005, in prep.; van der Hulst & van de Weijer, to appear).

My main goal is not to motivate in general that unary features are preferred over binary features. Rather, given that we use unary elements, I investigate which set of such features is required and how metaphony is best formally represented. Kaze (1991) has argued that an 'AIU' system fails to provide an adequate analysis of metaphony, based on the argument that in such a system it is not immediately obvious how one can account for processes that are triggered by high vowels (such as [i] and [u]), arguing that the 'AIU' system is unable to treat high vowels as a natural class of vowels that share the property 'high'. Similar objections have been raised in Clements & Hume (1995). Staun (2003), making reference to discussions of other processes that seemingly require access to a feature [high] in dependency-based analyses, remarks that "[I]n each such account the notion of a negated component, in particular negated |a| has played a central part. [...] despite the claims of both Clements and Hume and Kaze, a unique specification of high vowels is perfectly possible within the dependency-based model, viz. as |~a|". Clearly, there is a 'risk' in appealing to (the spreading of) negated elements when one advocated for a unary feature system. Here I will take a different route. Whatever the merits (and dangers) of using negated elements, the adoption of a unary system does by no means imply a necessary commitment to the 'AIU' set, without any other features. Indeed, Anderson and Ewen (1987), as well as

---

[1] This article uses material from chapter 6 in van der Hulst (2018a). I am grateful for two anonymous reviewers or their very useful comments.

Kaye, Lowenstamm and Vergnaud (1985), propose additional features. The set of features in binary or unary systems can vary, depending on various considerations, both empirical and theoretical. The choice between binarism or unarism does not depend on the analysis of specific processes. As discussed in Kaye (1988) and van der Hulst (2016a), postulating a unary system is by and large the null hypothesis, since, keeping the set of feature 'names' constant, treating these 'names' as unary features leads to a more restricted theory; it only allows for half the number of natural classes and processes. Additionally, a unary system provides a head-on answer to the problem of markedness that was 'noted' in chapter 9 of Chomsky & Halle (1968). For these reasons, my point of departure is to explore the consequences of a unary approach which, then, requires a specific choice of unary features. While the 'AIU' set of features is well-founded and widely used, my own work has pursued a theory of features which derives the actual set of features from several general factors, which are partly grounded in the phonetic substance that features capture, and partly in cognitive principles of categorization of the phonetic substance. In section 2 I will outline this model, called Radical CV Phonology (RcvP), that adheres to these considerations. A specific consequence of this theory is that the set of features contains a feature that roughly refers to the notion 'high'. In section 3, I will then explore how in this model metaphony processes can be handled. Given the enormous variety of metaphony systems, it will not be possible to do justice to all reported systems. The data that I will analyze are all drawn from Calabrese (2011). As shown there, in various Romance dialects metaphony is morphologized. Such case can perhaps best be accounted for in terms of lexically listed allomorphs. The focus in the present article is on metaphony that relies on phonological conditions only which I assume is the case in at least some of the dialects that Calabrese discusses.

2 The framework

Radical CV Phonology[2] (RcvP for short, van der Hulst (1995), (2015a), (2015b), (in prep.); van der Hulst & van de Weijer (to appear) is a version of Dependency Phonology (DP; Anderson & Ewen 1987).[3] This model adopts the following principles:

---

[2] See van der Hulst (2018a, chapter 2) for details concerning the model summarized in this section.
[3] The present state of RcvP differs somewhat from van der Hulst (2005), making use of a discussion of this proposal in Anderson (2011b), who, in his turn, adopts some aspects of van der Hulst (2005), thus modifying some of the proposals in Anderson and Ewen (1987).

(1) Fundamental principles of my proposal

   a. Phonological primes are unary (they are called *elements*), organized into classes[4]
   b. There are only two elements: |C| and |V| which occur in all classes
   c. Element specification is *minimal*
   d. Vowel harmony involves the *licensing* of *variable* elements in nuclei, with licensers typically being vowels in adjacent nuclei that contain a licensed instance of the relevant element
   e. A variable element is phonetically interpreted only if it is licensed
   f. Licensing is strictly *local*

In (2) we represent the full RcvP geometry:

(2) The 'geometry' of elements in Radical cv Phonology[5]

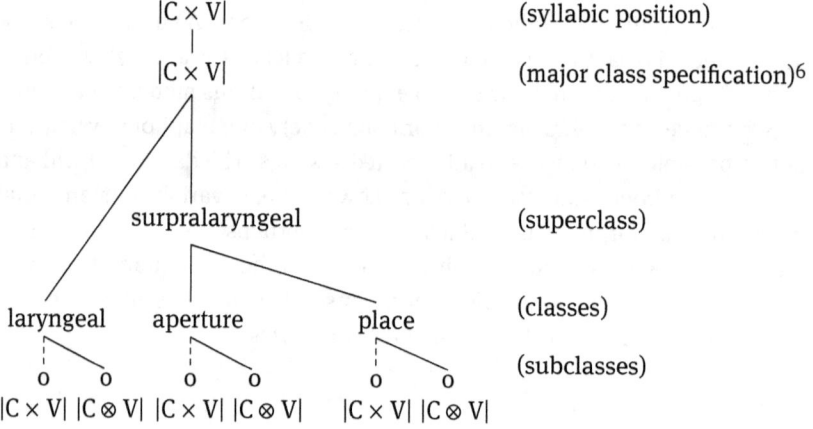

---

[4] The idea to acknowledge element classes occurs in the earliest version of Dependency Phonology (e.g., see Anderson & Jones 1974). The same idea later led to versions of what was called 'feature geometry' (see Clements 1985).

[5] This geometry deviates somewhat from the one adopted in Anderson & Ewen (1987) and bears a close resemblance to the original geometry that was proposed in Clements (1985). In van der Hulst (in prep.) this model is compared to other models with which it shares certain properties.

[6] It is assumed here that the major class specifications and syllabic positions, although both characterized as C/V structure are distinct; see van der Hulst (in prep.) and van der Hulst and van de Weijer (to appear) for possible motivation and discussion.

The various labels for the classes are for convenience only and have no formal status in RcvP. Each unit in the structure can be defined in purely structural terms. The elements |C| and |V| are also strictly formal units, which, depending on their place in the segmental structure, correlate with specific phonetic properties. Additionally, their interpretation is also dependent on the major class specification and the syllabic position of the entire segmental structure. This means that both elements have several different (albeit related) interpretations (on this see (5) below).

How is segmental phonological complexity encoded in this model? Within a head class, an element can occur alone or in combination. In (2), the symbol 'x' means that elements *can* combine and enter into a dependency relation. This allows for a four-way distinction, given here in two notations:

(3) a. C   C   V   V
                | |
                V   C
    b. {C}   {C;V}   {V;C}[7]   {V}

The two elements can furthermore occur in a secondary (dependent) subclass,[8] where, however, element combinations are *typically* not allowed[9] (which is indicated by the symbol '⊗' in 2). This, in principle, allows the following list of representations for each class, where the lower case symbols represent the secondary occurrence of the element:

(4)   {C}   {C;V}   {V;C}   {V}
       {{C}c}   {{C;V}c}   {{V;C}c}   {{V}c}
       {{C}v}   {{C;V}v}   {{V;C}v}   {{V}v}

In van der Hulst (2015b), it is proposed that the limitation of the set of elements to two units per class can be seen as resulting from a basic principle of categorization (rooted in categorical perception), called the Opponent Principle which creates

---

7 DP uses 'x;y' to indicate that x is the head and y is the dependent. Underlining, used in Government Phonology, is an alternative notation to indicate headedness.
8 This distinction is also adopted in Anderson (2011a, volume 3).
9 In van der Hulst (in prep.) I motivate this, referring to the fact that in a dependency approach it is 'natural' for dependent to display fewer structural options than heads; see Harris (1990) and Dresher & van der Hulst (1998).

perceptually maximally opposed categories.[10] Assuming that each subclass in (4) correlates with a 'phonetic dimension', |C| and |V| correlate with (and phonologize) maximally opposed phonetic categories ('polar opposites') within such a dimension. While the elements are strictly formal, cognitive units, they do correlate with phonetic events (or phonetic categories, covering a subrange of the relevant phonetic dimension). In fact, we can think of elements as (subconscious) cognitive percepts and proprioceps that correlate with phonetic events/categories.[11] The relation between formal units such as elements and phonetic events is referred as Phonetic Interpretation (PI), which embodies a set of interpretation functions (see 5). Naturally, since the elements |C| and |V| occur in all classes, these elements correlate with a wide variety of phonetic interpretations. Additionally, interpretation is dependent on syllabic position and major class specification:

(5) Phonetic Interpretation Functions for elements in head classes

PI (|Man: C|, head class, consonant, onset) = [[stop]]
PI (|Man: C|, head class, vowel, nucleus) = [[high]]

PI (|Man: V|, head class, consonant, onset) = [[fricative]]
PI (|Man: V|, head class, vowel, nucleus) = [[low]]

PI (|Place: C|, head class, consonant, onset) = [[palatal]]
PI (|Place: C|, head class, vowel, nucleus) = [[front]]

PI (|Place: V|, head class, consonant, onset) = [[labial]]
PI (|Place: V|, head class, vowel, nucleus) = [[round]]

PI (|Lar: C|, head class, consonant, onset) = [[fortis]]
PI (|Lar: C|, head class, vowel, nucleus) = [[high tone]]

PI (|Lar: V|, head class, consonant, onset) = [[voiced]]
PI (|Lar: V|, head class, vowel, nucleus) = [[low tone]]

I refer to van der Hulst (in prep.) for a complete discussion and motivation of all the interpretations.

---

10 A question that could be asked is why the Opponent Principle does not enforce four phonetic spaces rather than three. This is because the emergence of categories is also dependent on the phonetic substance which, in specific cases, does not allow for a four-way distinction. This is discussed in van der Hulst (in prep.), where it is also shown that there are only three major class categories (obstruents, sonorant consonants and vowels).
11 I assume that elements have both an acoustic correlate (a percept) and an articulatory plan (a proprioceept).

In this article, I will only be concerned with the aperture class. While the primary subclass indicates aperture differences in the oral cavity, the secondary subclass allows activation of the other cavities, i.e. the nasal and pharyngeal ones. As a shorthand, I will use the common AIU labels (with less common labels such as ∀ and P), here with the C/V 'nature' added as a subscript (which I will not continue to add):

(6) Aperture

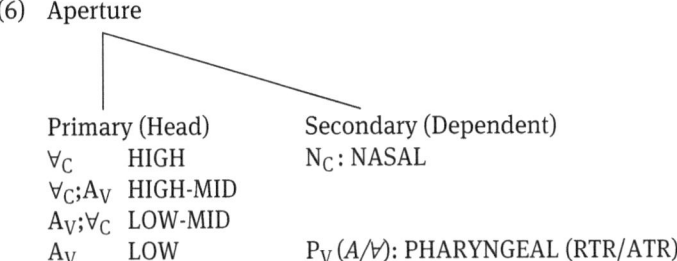

Primary (Head)   Secondary (Dependent)
∀$_C$ HIGH   N$_C$: NASAL
∀$_C$;A$_V$ HIGH-MID
A$_V$;∀$_C$ LOW-MID
A$_V$ LOW   P$_V$ (*A/∀*): PHARYNGEAL (RTR/ATR)

Note that the Opponent Principle 'enforces' a polar counterpart to |A|, symbolized as |∀|, which together creates four degrees of aperture. There are two secondary elements, |N| and |P|, both referring to activation of an extra resonating cavity. The secondary P-element refers to activation of the pharyngeal cavity, which can take two forms: expansion (ATR, indicated with |*∀*|) or contraction (indicated with |*A*|). I regard these two option as different phonetic *implementations* of the same phonetic *interpretation* (which is simply [[pharyngeal]]) to explain why they cannot both occur contrastively in the same language. In a sense, these two different phonetic realizations of the pharyngeal cavity element display a C/V split in the phonetic domain.[12]

Minimal specification, (1c), is achieved by following an algorithm proposed in Dresher (2009), the *Successive Division Algorithm* (SDA).[13] This algorithm uses a specific ranking of the elements which I derive from (7), by assigning a grid mark to each head position[14]:

---

12 My use of italic |*∀*| and |*A*| is motivated by the fact that their phonetic interpretation is near-identical to that of the primary elements |∀| and |A|.
13 This algorithm is similar to the notion of 'Recursive Splitting' (following the Opponent Principle) in RcvP (see van der Hulst 2005: 195).
14 While elements within class nodes can enter in dependency relations with either one being a possible head, both the |A| element and the |U| elements are 'natural heads' in nuclear position. This is because the nuclear position is a V-position which thus favors V-type elements. I do not include a relative ranking for laryngeal elements here, nor a ranking of laryngeal elements with respect to manner and place elements. See van der Hulst (in prep.) for details on these various matters.

(7) a.

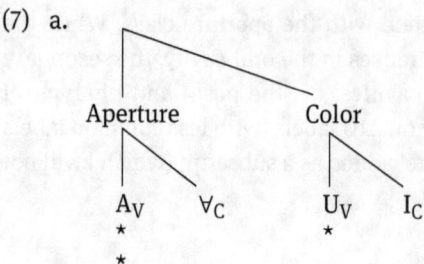

b. Ranking: $A_V > U_V > I_C / \forall_C > \{N_C, P_V\}$

(7b) also assumes that primary elements come before secondary elements (for which I do not postulate a relative ranking). The equal ranking of |∀| and |I| allows for 'free' variation. However, I will assume that |I|, which denotes a more *salient* phonetic event, takes precedence over |∀|, unless this element is non-distinctive (as in Finnish where [i] and [e] are so-called neutral vowels). In section 3 I will explain how the SDA in conjunction with the element ranking in (7b) accounts for *a minimal, redundancy-free representation* of vowel systems.

(1d) presents a crucial innovation of the RcvP account of vowel harmony. The motivation for using the variable notation is that it allows a distinction between invariant 'negative' vowels (i.e. vowels that lack the harmonic element) in *disharmonic roots* and *non-alternating affix vowels* on the one hand, and alternating vowels on the other. Thus, the model allows the following three-way distinction (where 'ε' stands for 'any element'):

(8) a.   ε   b. (ε)   c.   –
         X   X   X

a = invariant ε (*positive vowel*)
b = alternating vowel, element must be licensed to get interpreted
c = invariant non-ε (*negative vowel*)

This distinction parallels the distinction between [+F], [0F] and [-F] in a binary system.[15] While (8) allows a three-way distinction in how vowels in the lexicon are represented with respect to a given element, this proposal does not undermine the unary nature of the elements. Contrast *in the vowel system* is only expressed

---

15 Inkelas (1995) exploits this three-way difference in a binary system for much the same purpose that I exploit the three-way distinction in (8).

through presence or absence of an element. The variable notation encodes that certain vowels *as part of specific morphemes* have a dual character in displaying an alternation between presence and absence of the element. The notation '(ε)' simply means that for the relevant vowel it is undecided *in the lexicon* whether it will surface with or without the element in question.[16]

One potential difference between the present proposal and comparable three-way distinction in a binary system is that the notation in (8) suggests that the two 'marked values' of element |ε| are effectively (8a) ('|ε| is definitely present') and (8b) ('|ε| is potentially present, contingent on licensing'), while (8c) ('|ε| is definitely absent') is unmarked.

(1e) is derived from approaches to vowel harmony in *Government Phonology* (GP; Kaye, Lowenstamm & Vergnaud 1985; Harris & Lindsey 1995; Ritter 1995; Charette & Göksel 1998, among others). In the present model (1e) implies that variable elements that are not licensed remain 'silent'. The notion of licensing has been widely referenced as playing a role in phonological generalizations (see e.g. Walker 2010). In my account of vowel harmony, the key type of licensing will be *lateral licensing*[17] along phonological 'tiers'. I will assume that the default setting for licensing directionality is 'bidirectional'. This is necessary for both root-control systems that have both harmonic prefixes and suffixes and for dominant-recessive systems.[18]

(1f), locality, is a central theme in the discussion of vowel harmony (if not of all linguistic relations). The notion of locality has been used in different ways even within the study of vowel harmony. While virtually all accounts of vowel harmony appeal to some notion of locality, frameworks differ in important details of defining the relationship or in dealing with apparent violations of locality. I will adopt a *strict* interpretation of locality, which avoids mechanisms such 'discontinuous association' or 'feature/element insertion' to account for apparent violations. I emphasize that, for me, locality does *not* mean establishing a relation between two entities that are 'as close as possible' (as proposed in Nevins 2010), but rather between elements that are adjacent with reference to the nuclear tier (*nuclear locality*).[19] Languages that display vowel harmony for some element 'ε' are subject to a constraint of the general format in (9):

---

[16] This notation does not mean 'floating', as in autosegmental models, which is used for different purposes.
[17] In van der Hulst (2018a) I also make use of another kind of licensing called *positional licensing*.
[18] In van der Hulst (2018a: chapter 4), I propose that licensers must be head elements. This refers to the head status of elements within a class.
[19] To account for some cases of expected 'transparency' I will also invoke *bridge locality*, in which case the locality requirement for licensing is satisfied on an element tier that differs from

(9) All units X in domain D must be positive or negative for element |ɛ|

In the usual case X=nucleus, but X can also be another element (when we are dealing with bridge locality). The constraint in (9) is satisfied by specifying alternating vowels with the variable element, which automatically triggers the licensing relation. Vowel harmony is thus *not* the result of a (repair) rule that fills in or changes segmental structure.

A key aspect of my approach to vowel harmony (mentioned for its key importance in the study of vowel harmony, although it is not at issue in this article) is that vowels that refuse to alternate, and as such either block harmony or are (seemingly) 'ignored' by it, should not simply be designated as 'opaque' or 'transparent' on a language-specific basis. In fact, following a proposal made by van der Hulst & Smith (1986), the behavior of non-alternating vowels is largely predictable from their element structure (which depends on the structure of the vowel system). So-called 'transparent' behavior is possible when a vowel is *compatible* with the harmonic element. Thus, a vowel [i] can behave as 'transparent' in a palatal system because it is compatible with the presence of the palatal element |I|. As such, this vowel could carry the harmonic element.[20] On the other hand, vowels that are *incompatible* with the harmonic element, such as a non-advanced [a] in advanced tongue root (ATR) systems are predicted to be opaque, because the licensing relation cannot ignore or 'skip' an intervening vowel, as per strict locality.[21]

The proposed elements allow the following vowel distinctions in terms of primary elements, with in the top row the ATR difference shown for high vowels. Of course, ATR can also apply to mid-vowels and low vowels, which is not shown here; when ATR applies to mid-vowels, there is likely to be only one mid aperture degree. I refer to van der Hulst (2018a,b) for detailed discussion of the complementarity of ATR and aperture with reference to mid-vowels.[22]

---

the harmonic tier (such cases fall under the rubric of 'parasitic harmony', as first described in Steriade (1981), but form a special subclass of this rubric).

20 However, such vowels can also act opaquely. In fact, there are four different ways in which a vowel such as [i] can behave in palatal harmony systems, following an important typological study of harmony on Balto-Finnic languages by Kiparsky & Pajusalu (2003). Importantly, none of the four types violate strict locality. See van der Hulst (2018a: chapter 4).

21 Apparent counterexamples to the expected opacity of incompatible vowels can be explained in terms of allowing locality to be defined with reference to another element tier (i.e. in terms of bridge locality). See van der Hulst (2018a: chapter 3). A special case of apparent non-locality is discussed toward the end of this article.

22 This complementarity is dependent on the structure of the overall vowel system as shown in Casali (2003, 2008).

(10)

	I	IU	-	UI	U
|V_C| + |V|	i	y	ɨ	ʉ	u
|V_C|	I (>i)²³	Y	ɪ	ʊ	ʊ (>u)
|V_C;A_V|	e	ø	ʌ	ɘ	o
|A_V;V_C|	ɛ	œ	ɐ	æ	ɔ
|A_V|	æ	ɶ	a	ɑ	ɒ

Kaze (1991) focuses on metaphony in Italian with the specific purpose of showing that 'AIU' models are inadequate. He states that the problem with these models is that there is no equivalent to the feature [+high], which appears to be needed for raising. I will show that RcvP, having adopted the element |V|, does not 'solve' this issue since this element is *not* an exclusive property of high vowels, being present in all non-low vowels. However, it will be shown here that the model can account for the various types of metaphony in spite of this.

In section 3, following Calabrese (2011), I will discuss two possible analyses of the most common metaphony patterns. The first one mirrors the analysis of Calabrese who used the feature [±ATR], which in RcvP correlates with secondary |V|. Due to the particular properties of the RCVP system of elements, this approach necessitates a dual analysis of mid vowels. I will then suggest a second type of analysis which uses a mechanism of *stress-driven element copy* and conclude that this analysis is superior to the first analysis within the context of the unary feature model that is assumed here.

3 Metaphony in Italian dialects

3.1 Representative examples

Calabrese (2011) provides a comprehensive overview of metaphony in Italian dialects.²⁴ Metaphony selects stressed vowels are targets. Calabrese notes that in all

---

23 In the absence of an ATR distinction the vowels in this row would be phonetically advanced due to 'enhancement'.
24 There are numerous descriptions and analyses of metaphony in Romance languages: Blayblock (1965); Calabrese (1985); Frigeni (2003); Kaze (1989, 1991); Zetterstrand (1996); Maiden

cases there is raising of high mid stressed [e, o] to [i, u]. The target is thus in a stressed syllable and the trigger is a following *unstressed high vowel*. Low mid vowels ([ɛ, ɔ]) are targets only in certain dialects, and these vowels then raise (to [e, o]) or, more commonly, diphthongize. In this case, the precise nature of the diphthongs varies depending on the dialect ([je], [jɛ], [iə], [ia] and [wo], [wɔ], [uə], [ua]). Calabrese regards the difference between high and low mid vowels in terms of [±ATR] and I will follow him in this respect in the first analysis of the data. In this first RcvP account, I will use the P_V-element (or $|∀|$ for short) as the active element, which corresponds to an ATR interpretation. The following three cases represent three possible outcomes of metaphony for low mid vowels, while in all three high mid vowels raise to high:

(11) The dialect of Calvello (Gioscio 1985)
Metaphonic alternations: [e o] → [i u]; [ɛ ɔ] → [je wo]
a. [+ATR] [e o]

		singular	plural	
	masc	súlu	súli	'alone'
	fem	sóla	sóle	
		kavróne	kavrúni	'charcoal'
		mése	mísi	'month'
		vérde	vírdi	'green'

b. [–ATR] [ɛ ɔ]

	masc	vjékkju	vjékkji	'old'
	fem	vékkja	vékkje	

(12) The dialect of Servigliano (Camilli 1929)
Metaphonic alternations: [e o] → [i u]; [ɛ ɔ] → [e o]
a. [+ATR] [e o]

		singular	plural	
	masc	kúrtu	kúrti	'short'
	fem	kórta	kórte	
		fjóre	fjúri	'flower'
		bótte	bútti	'barrel'
		vérde	vírdi	'green'

(1986, 1991); Walker (2011). Here I will base myself on some representative examples that are discussed in Calabrese (2011). Kaze (1989) is based on a study of 90 dialects in which he distinguishes four different types of harmony.

b. [−ATR] [ɛ ɔ]

		singular	plural	
masc		véccu	vécci	'old'
fem		vécca	vécce	
masc		pjóttsu	pjótsi	'slow'
fem		pjóttsa	pjótse	

(13) The dialect of Grado (Walker 2005)
Metaphonic alternations: [e o] → [i u]; no metaphony for [ɛ ɔ]
a. [+ATR] [e o]

	singular	plural	
masc	véro	víri	'true'
masc	róso	rúsi	'red'
masc	fjór	fjúri	'flower'
fem	amór	amúri	'love'

b. [−ATR] [ɛ ɔ]

	singular	plural	
masc	mɔ́rto	mɔ́rti	'dead'
fem	mɔ́rta	mɔ́rte	

In several southern dialects, low mid vowels, like the high mid [e o], are raised to high [i u]. This could either be the result of monophthongization of the diphthongs ([ɛ ɔ] → [je wo] → [i u]) or, as argued in Calabrese (1985, 1998), be a direct outcome of raising:

(14) The dialect of Foggia (Valente 1975)

móßßa	múßßu	'soft FEM SG/MASC SG'
kjéna	kjínu	'full FEM SG/MASC SG'
péte	píti	'foot SG/PL'
grɔ́sa	grússu	'big FEM SG/MASC SG'

Additional variations occur as well. In some dialects, the low vowel [a] can also be raised, becoming [ɛ], [e] or a diphthong [je, jɛ]. In the Teramo dialect of the Abruzzo region, *all* vowels become high: vowels [e ɛ a] raise to [i] and [o ɔ] raise to [u] in a metaphonic context. In some dialects the trigger [u] has lowered to [o]. This change could occur before metaphony started (dialects in which only [i] triggers raising), or after, in which case raising before [o] (<[u]) is derivationally opaque. The change could also take place after raising of high mid vowels but before raising of low mid vowels. In such dialects, metaphony of the high mid vowels is triggered by both [i] and [o] (<[u]) but low mid vowels only by [i].[25] In many Italian dialects, further changes, such as reduction to schwa, deletion, or raising, have affected final vowels, leading to morphologization of raising. Another cause of derivational opacity occurs when high mid vowels become low mid resulting in low mid vowels having two phonological behaviors in many southern dialects.

3.2 Formal analysis

In this section I will explore two alternative analyses of the data presented in the previous section. The difference lies in the analysis of the 'high mid' vowels [e] and [o]. From studies of African seven-vowel systems it is well-known that seven-vowel systems can either display a distinction between two high series (2H) or between two mid series (1H) (Casali 2003, 2008). Casali (2003: 326 ff.) devotes considerable attention to the fact that the difference between 2H systems with one series of mid vowels and 1H systems may be difficult to establish.

(15) a. 2H-system   b. 1H-system
         i   u   i   u
         ɪ   ʊ   e   o
         ɛ   ɔ   ɛ   ɔ
           a   a

Indeed, Casali cites cases in which a single language has been analyzed both ways by different linguists or even by the same linguist. Casali (2003, 2008) has shown that 2H and 1H system differ in terms of the dominance of [+ATR] or [-ATR]. In 2H system [+ATR] is dominant, while [-ATR] is dominant in 1H systems. In van der Hulst (2018a) I show how the dominance of [+ATR] in 2H systems is due to the fact that the ATR element |ɣ| is necessarily activated. 1H systems in this account distinguish the two series of mid vowels in terms of A-headedness.

---

[25] This raises a potential problem for the approach in which [o] is the phonetic interpretation of [u] because this would then also necessarily have to attribute the raising of [−ATR] vowels to phonetic interpretation.

3.2.1 Metaphony in terms of ATR-dominance

If we analyze the Italian seven-vowel system in terms of two high series (as in 15a), the effect of raising can be analyzed as ATR harmony. This implies that that phonetic [e] and [o] are analyzed as bare [ɪ] {I} and [ʊ] {U} with a variable ATR-element. Adopting this choice, let us see how the licensing approach can derive the various types of dialects. In (16a) I show the specification of a seven-vowel system with two high series and one mid series following the SDA and the element ranking in (16b):

(16) A seven-vowel system (aɛɔiuɪʊ)

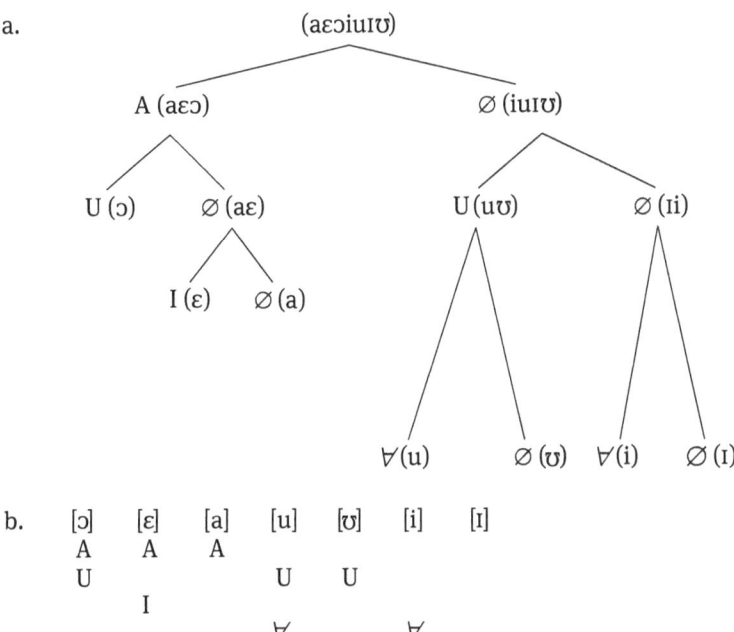

In terms of this analysis of the vowel system, metaphony in the Servigliano dialect is accounted for as the licensing of variable ATR on stressed vowels by the ATR element of unstressed vowels:

(17) The dialect of Servigliano (Camilli 1929)
Metaphonic alternations: [e o] → [i u]; [ɛ ɔ] → [e o]
Interpretation: [ɪ ʊ] → [i u] in raising context, elsewhere [ɪ ʊ] (18a)
[ɛ ɔ] → [e o] (18b)

With this analysis of the vowel system, metaphony brings about the following changes:

(18) a. [ɪ]   [ʊ] > [i]   [u]   b. [ɛ]   [ɔ] > [e]   [o]
                                       A   A   A   A
         U   U   U   U   U   U
                                       I
         (Ʉ)   (Ʉ)   Ʉ   Ʉ   (Ʉ)   (Ʉ) Ʉ   Ʉ

In this analysis, [ɪ]/[ʊ] (when not raised) and [e]/[o] (the product of raising [ɛ] and [ɔ]) must merge into phonetic [e]/[o] due to phonetic *implementation*.[26] In dialects in which [a] also raises to [ɛ], [a] is provided with the variable harmonic element in which case {A Ʉ} receives the same phonetic interpretation as {AI}.[27]

In the dialect of Calvello, raising of low mid vowels leads to diphthongization:

(19) The dialect of Calvello (Gioscio 1985)
Metaphonic alternations: [e o] → [i u]; [ɛ ɔ] → [je wo]
Interpretation: [ɪ ʊ] → [i u] in raising context, elsewhere [e o]
                [ɛ ɔ] → [je wo]

Following Calabrese (2011) I will assume that the diphthongal output of raising low mid vowels is the result of a process of 'breaking':

(20) Breaking
     {I/UA Ʉ}   →   {I/U} + {I/UA Ʉ}
                   [j/w]   [e/o]

In the dialect of Grado, raising does not affect low mid vowels:

(21) The dialect of Grado (Walker 2005)
Metaphonic alternations: [e o] → [i u]; no metaphony for [ɛ ɔ]
Interpretation: [ɪ ʊ] → [i u] in raising context, elsewhere [e o]
                [ɛ ɔ] do not have variable (Ʉ)

Finally, in the dialect of Foggia, all raised vowels end up as [i] and [u]:

---

26 In van der Hulst (2017, 2018a) I motivate that such phonetic merger is always *monotonic*, i.e. it can 'add' phonetic properties not rooted in a specified element, but it cannot ignore an element that is specified.
27 Technically, this means that raising of [a] is not structure preserving in that it delivers an output that is not a contrastive vowel.

(22) The dialect of Foggia (Valente 1975)
Metaphonic alternations: [e o] → [i u]; [ɛ ɔ] → [i u]
Interpretation: [ɪ ʊ] → [i u] in raising context, elsewhere [e o]
[ɛ ɔ] → [i u]

When the output for raising [ɛ ɔ], unexpectedly, yields [i u], this can be interpreted, following Calabrese's idea, as a simplification of the breaking output:

(23) Breaking plus Simplification
{I/UA|∀|} → {I/U} + {I/UA|∀|} → {I/U|∀|}
              [j/w]   [e/o]   [e/o]

While the preceding analysis is possible and consistent, it is perhaps not satisfactory, because of the need to represent high mid vowels in terms of two distinct structures. While RcvP does not forbid this kind of phonological ambiguity (see van der Hulst 2016c), I will explore a different analysis in the next section that attributes metaphony to activity of the primary element |∀|. This analysis avoids phonological ambiguity (which arguably makes it simpler) and it also acknowledges the role of stress, which the previous analysis ignored.

3.2.2 Metaphony in terms of HIGH-dominance

Analyzing the seven-vowel systems as a 1H system leads to the following result:

(24) Seven-vowel system (iueoɛɔa)

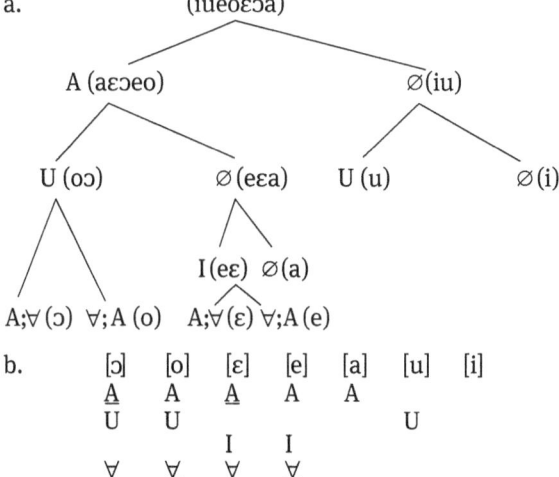

In this case, there is no reason to activate the secondary ATR-element. The distinction between the mid vowels can be made in terms of headedness, which requires specification of the ∀-element. While African tongue root system that have a 1H vowel system display dominance of [-ATR], which is formally represented in terms of A-headedness "agreement", Italian metaphony takes a different (in some sense, an opposite) route, namely licensing of the ∀-element. The choice between analyzing the harmony as in terms of A-activity or ∀-activity is dependent on which vowels (high mid or low mid) occur in the absence of a harmony trigger. In African systems, the default is high mid, showing that low mid is the result of harmony (i.e. licensing), but in the Italian cases the default is the lower mid vowel, or when the alternation is between [e]/[o] and [i]/[u] (as in the dialect of Grado; 13), the mid vowels as in the feminine singular *amor* 'love'. This shows that the non-raised vowels are the default. Raising is what happens in a specific context, namely when [i] or [u] are following. Thus, while in African 1H systems the alternation between high-mid and low-mid vowels shows dominance of the low mid vowels (indicated by the arrow in (25) on the left), metaphony involves dominance of the high vowels [i] and [u] (as indicated by the arrows on the right):

(25)   [i]   [u] ↑
        [e]   [o] ↑
     ↓ [ɛ]   [ɔ] ↑

I will now develop an analysis of metaphony which appeals to the ∀-element as the active element. This analysis will make crucial reference to the role of stress.

It has been suggested that the cause for metaphony is that vowels in unstressed position 'weaken' and that this results in the need for licensing. This notion of the need to license elements in the unstressed position is also present in Walker's (2011) account of metaphony. However, by giving stressed vowels the role of licensers, we do not account for the fact that the stressed vowels need to raise. In a sense, stressed vowels always act as licensers for following unstressed vowels, if these vowels form a 'trochaic foot'. Another angle on metaphony is that raising is a direct result of transferring a height feature from the unstressed vowel to the stressed vowel. This notion of transfer is also applied in analyses of umlaut in Germanic languages, where the frontness of unstressed vowels is transferred to the preceding stressed vowel, often followed, in a diachronic sense, by loss of frontness in the unstressed vowels.[28] In the analysis developed here we could say that

---

28 After such loss, the frontness of stressed vowels will either be captured in term of a morphologically conditioned rule, or be attributed to a floating feature.

the height element in unstressed vowels becomes variable (as a formal expression of their reduction), which then necessitates an increase in the preponderance of this same element in the stressed vowels. However, to account for all three possible instances of raising, increasing preponderance *must* be formally implemented in terms of *adding* the |∀|-element (especially when the target of raising is a low vowel which does not contain this element). However, a theory that allows addition of elements runs the danger of being too powerful, unless element addition is somehow constrained. We could therefore propose that elements can only be added if needed to license a variable element. This means that the added element must be identical to the variable element. Alternatively, we could think of the metaphony process as an 'attraction' by the stressed vowel of the ∀-element of the unstressed vowels; this approach avoids the notion of 'just adding' an element. Attraction could be formalized as a copying of this element, or, literally, as a case of movement. In this case we could construe the variable elements on the unstressed vowels as a 'trace' that needs to be licensed, although, strictly speaking, an attraction analysis does not require that the element on the high vowels become variable. The effect of attracting a copy of the ∀-element to stressed vowels triggers a convention called **resolution**, which was already proposed in Anderson & Jones (1974):

(26)　A　>　A̲B　>　AB̲　>　B
　　　　Add B　　Add B　　Add B

In the case at hand, this schema applies as follows:

(27)　Add ∀ to A　　=>　A;∀　(low becomes low mid)
　　　Add ∀ to A;∀　=>　∀;A　(low mid vowel becomes high mid; loss of A-headedness)
　　　Add ∀ to ∀;A　=>　∀　(high mid vowel becomes high; loss of |A|)

This schema allows the representation of processes that involve the apparent deletion of elements in a very specific circumstance, namely when the element is 'pushed out' by an increase in preponderance of the antagonistic element that it combines with. It can be applied both to the vowel-related shifts (e.g. the Great Vowel Shift in the history of English), to consonant-related phenomena such as lenition or, as in our case, to step-wise raising:

(28)　a.　(　V　　　　　V　)$_F$
　　　　　　e/o > i/u　　i/u

```
          {∀;A}          {∀}
          {∀;A+∀}        (∀)   copying/movement of the ∀-element
          {∀}      »     (∀)   resolution: loss of |A|

    b. (  V              V   )_F
          ɛ/ɔ > e/o      i/u
          {A;∀}          {∀}
          {A;∀+∀}        (∀)   copying/movement of the ∀-element
          {∀;A}    »     (∀)   resolution: loss of A-headedness

    c. (  V              V   )_F
          a > ɛ          i/u
          {A}            {∀}
          {A +∀}         (∀)   copying/movement of the ∀-element
          {A;∀}    »     (∀)   resolution: no change
```

The likelihood of copying/movement of ∀ follows the following ranking:

(29) e/o > ɛ/ɔ > a

This ranking show that addition of |∀| is increasingly dispreferred in proportion to the preponderance of the |A| element in the recipient.

In (30) and (31) I illustrate raising of mid vowels and breaking of low mid vowels, respectively (data from the dialect of Calvello in 11):

```
(30) a.  só  lu      só  lu          sú  lu
         A           A
         U   U       U   U           U   U
         ∀   ∀       ∀∀  (∀)         ∀ » (∀)
                     copying         resolution and licensing

     b.  vjɛ́kkju     vjɛ́kkju                vjékkju
         A           A                      A
             U           U                  U
         ∀   ∀       ∀∀  (∀)         ∀ » (∀)
                     copying         resolution and licensing
```

The emergence of diphthongs is the result of a different kind of resolution. The added element does not fuse, but gets its own realization as a glide:

(31) [ɛ]   [ɔ]   >   [je] [wo]
      A   A   A   A
      I   U   I   U
      ∀∀   ∀∀   ∀∀   ∀∀

In conclusion, metaphony can be formally represented in terms of '∀-attraction' by a recipient stressed nuclei, which leads to variability of the element in the source. While the latter step is not crucial to account for raising, it does capture the 'intuition that the need to be licensed is part of the process. Both the attraction (or movement) of the harmonic element by the stressed syllable and the variability of the harmonic element variable in unstressed syllables are two sides of the same coin. The formalization of '∀-attraction' as the addition of the ∀-element triggers the resolution convention which accounts for the raising effect. Attraction harmony can be seen as a natural consequence of the strengthening of a stressed vowel and a concomitant weakening of an unstressed vowel within a foot. This alternative to the ATR-analysis does justice to the fact that stress-induced harmony has traditionally been considered to be distinct from non-stress-induced harmony. The present proposal provides a theoretical basis for this traditional view, placing metaphony in a broader class of harmonies that have been variously referred to as umlaut, mutation or affection (see Majors 1998; van der Hulst, 2018a: chapter 6; Mascaró 2016).

So far I have not discussed locality aspects of metaphony. Can the stressed vowel and the source vowel be separated by a third, non-participating vowel? Hualde (1989) discusses a relevant example. In the Lena Bable dialect of Spanish, a final high vowel causes raising of a stressed vowel. Stressed [a, e, o] raise to [e, i, u], respectively, as shown in (32a). As shown by the data in (32b), the vowel [a] is transparent to harmony when it intervenes between the final vowel and the stressed antepenultimate vowel:

(32) Lena Bable Spanish height harmony
 a. stressed vowel target:
   gétu   'cat' m.sg.   (cf. gátos m.pl.)
   nínu   'child' m.sg.   (cf. nénos m.pl.)
   kúku   'worm' m.sg.   (cf. kókos m.pl.)

 b. unstressed vowel:
   burwíbanu   'wild strawberry' m.sg.   (cf. burwébanos)
   kékabu   'wreck' m.sg.   (cf. kakabos)

The fact that the post-stress [a] can be skipped might mean that the locality for licensing is, or can be, defined at the level of foot heads, if we stick to strictly binary feet, which would mean that licensing is not local at the first nuclear projection, but rather at a second nuclear projection.

(33)   N   »   N
        (N   N)_F (N)_F
         ∀   (∀)
         ké   ka   bu
      (cf. se   ka   só)

As shown in Walker (2011), the vowel [a], while never blocking metaphony, may or may not be affected. This raises the question of how we account for cases in which the vowel is affected. It seems to me that the explanation for interveners to be affected must be attributed to a low level co-articulatory effect.

4 Discussion and conclusions

Metaphony has been analyzed as an instance of stress-induced vowel harmony. Metaphony involves the attraction of properties of following unstressed vowels by stressed vowels. This leads, at the same time, to strengthening of the stressed syllable and weakening of the unstressed syllable, thus enhancing the contrast in two ways. Both the attraction (or movement) of the harmonic element by the stressed syllable and the variability of the harmonic element variable in unstressed syllables are two sides of the same coin. The formalization of '∀-attraction' as the addition of the ∀-element triggers the resolution convention which accounts for the raising effect. Since metaphony is clearly stress-related, it would be almost perverse to disregard stress as an important factor in this process. In fact, following an important proposal in Van Coetsem, McCormick & Hendricks (1981), McCormick (1982) and Van Coetsem (1996), I assume that this is precisely what distinguishes metaphony (and umlaut) from vowel harmony proper. In van Coetsem's theory, umlaut (and, I will assume, metaphony) occurs in languages with 'strong' (often lexical) stress, whereas (non-stress related) vowel harmony is more typical of language with 'weak', typically predictable stress. A correlation of this type has been noted in many typological studies (see van der Hulst (2016b) for an overview).

The use of a 'high' |∀|-element in RcvP allows an analysis of metaphony (and, more generally raising processes) to make reference to this element. There is no direct reference to the A-element in raising processes (although there will be in 'lowering' processes in African languages), which gets removed from high mid vowels due to a general resolution convention. Unary analyses of metaphony that use models without a high element have either been restricted to cases of metaphony that only involve fronting (see Canalis (2016), who also appeals to the resolution notion in order to 'get rid of the A-element' in some cases) or they have postulated A-deletion Maiden (1986, 1991) or use of a negated element (Staun 2003). It seems to me that both deletion and negated elements should be avoided at all cost. D'Alessandro and van Oostendorp (2016) propose an original method to 'get rid' of the A-element. Rather than using deletion, they analyze metaphony in terms of an inserted mora that 'eats' or absorbs the A-element. They provide some independent evidence for the appearance of the A-element outside the stressed vowels.

The preceding formal account of metaphony makes explicit use of stress-driven |∀|-attraction (or movement) which causes an extra 'insertion' of |∀| into the stressed vowels which then has three different consequences: simply adding |∀|, demoting the |A|-element to non-head status and pushing out the A-element. While these are seemingly three different responses, I maintain that all three constitute natural formal consequences of |∀|-addition in a system that does not allow multiple occurrence of the same element,[29] as such formally expressing the increase in preponderance of an element. I fully realize that the array of data that I have used to illustrate this type of analysis does not do justice to the full array of metaphony cases in Romance dialects. This means that further work needs to be done to test the account presented here.

References

Anderson, John M. 2011a. *The substance of language*. [Three volumes]. Oxford: Oxford University Press.
Anderson, John M. 2011b. *The substance of language, Volume III: Phonology-syntax analogies*. Oxford: Oxford University Press.
Anderson, John M. & Colin J. Ewen. 1987. *Principles of dependency phonology* (Cambridge Studies in Linguistics 47). Cambridge: Cambridge University Press.
Anderson, John M. & Charles Jones. 1974. Three theses concerning phonological representations. *Journal of Linguistics* 10. 1–26.
Blayblock, Curtis. 1965. Hispanic metaphony. *Romance philology* 18. 253–71.

---

[29] Here the expression 'the same element' refers to the occurrence of the basic C- or V-element in the same structural position. By disallowing multiple occurrences of the same element, RcvP (as well as DP and GP) distinguish themselves from the element theory proposed in Schane (1984).

Calabrese, Andrea. 1985. Metaphony in Salentino. *Rivista di Grammatica Generativa* 9–10, 1–141.
Calabrese, Andrea. 1998. Metaphony revisited. *Rivista di Linguistica* 10, 7–68.
Calabrese, Andrea. 2011. Metaphony in Romance. In Marc van Oostendorp, Colin J. Ewen, Elizabeth Hume & Keren Rice (eds.), *The Blackwell companion to phonology*, 2632–2661. Malden, MA and Oxford: Wiley-Blackwell.
Camilli, Amerindo. 1929. Il dialetto di Servigliano. *Archivum Romanicum* 13. 220–71.
Canalis, Stefano. 2016. Metaphony in the Ticino Canton and phonological features. In Francesc Torres-Tamarit, Kathrin Linke & Marc van Oostendorp (eds.), *Approaches to metaphony in the languages of Italy*, 127–46. Berlin: De Gruyter Mouton.
Casali, Roderic F. 2003. [ATR] value asymmetries and underlying vowel inventory structure in Niger-Congo and Nilo-Saharan. *Linguistic Typology* 7. 307–82.
Casali, Roderic F. 2008. ATR harmony in African languages. *Language and Linguistics Compass* 2(3). 496–549.
Charette, Monik & Asli Göksel. 1998. Licensing constraints and vowel harmony in Turkic languages. In Eugeniusz Cyran (ed.), *Structure and interpretation: Studies in Phonology, Volume 4*. 65–89. Lublin: PASE.
Chomsky, Noam & Morris Halle. 1968. *The sound pattern of English* (Studies in Language). New York: Harper and Row.
Clements, George N. 1985. The geometry of phonological features. *Phonology* 2. 225–52.
Clements, George N. & Elisabeth Hume. 1995. The internal organization of speech sounds. In John Goldsmith (ed.), *The handbook of phonological theory*, 245–306. Oxford: Basil Blackwell.
d'Alessandro, Roberta & Marc van Oostendorp. 2016. Abruzzese metaphony and the |A| eater. In Francesc Torres-Tamarit, Kathrin Linke & Marc van Oostendorp (eds.), *Approaches to metaphony in the languages of Italy*, 349–68. Berlin: De Gruyter Mouton.
Dresher, B. Elan. 2009. *The contrastive hierarchy in phonology* (Cambridge studies in linguistics 121). Cambridge: Cambridge University Press.
Dresher, B. Elan & Harry van der Hulst. 1998. Head-dependent asymmetries in phonology. *Phonology* 15. 317–52.
Frigeni, Chiara. 2003. Metaphony in Campidanian Sardinian: A domain-based analysis. *Toronto Working Papers in Linguistics* 20. 63–91.
Gioscio, Joseph. 1985. *Il dialetto Lucano di Calvello*. Stuttgart: Steiner.
Harris, John. 1990. Segmental complexity and phonological government. *Phonology* 7(2). 255–300.
Harris, John & Geoff Lindsey. 1995. The elements for phonological representation. In Jacques Durand & Francis Katamba (eds.), *Frontiers of phonology: Atoms, structures, derivations*, 34–79. London: Longman.
Hualde, José I. 1989. Autosegmental and metrical spreading in the vowel-harmony systems of northwestern Spain. *Linguistics* 27(5). 773–806.
Inkelas, Sharon. 1995. The consequences of optimization for underspecification. *Proceedings of the North East Linguistic Society (NELS)* 25. 287–302.
Kaye, Jonathan. 1988. The phonologist's dilemma: A game-theoretic approach to phonological debate. *GLOW Newsletter* 21. 16–9.
Kaye, Jonathan, Jean Lowenstamm & Jean-Roger Vergnaud. 1985. The internal structure of phonological elements: A theory of charm and government. *Phonology Yearbook* 2. 305–28.
Kaze, Jefferey W. 1989. *Metaphony in Spanish and Italian dialects revisited*. University of Illinois PhD dissertation.

Kaze, Jefferey W. 1991. Metaphony and two models for the description of vowel systems. *Phonology* 8(1). 163–70.
Kiparsky, Paul & Karl Pajusalu. 2003. Towards a typology of disharmony. *The Linguistic Review* 20(2–4). 217–41.
Maiden, Martin. 1986. *Metaphony and the Italian dialects: A study in morphologisation*. Cambridge University PhD dissertation.
Maiden, Martin. 1991. *Interactive morphonology: Metaphony in Italy*. London: Routledge.
Majors, Tivoli. 1998. *Stress-dependent harmony*. University of Texas PhD dissertation.
Mascaró, Joan. 2016. On the typology of metaphony/stress dependent harmony. In Francesc Torres-Tamarit, Kathrin Linke & Marc van Oostendorp (eds.), *Approaches to metaphony in the languages of Italy*, 259–76. Berlin: De Gruyter Mouton.
McCormick, Susan M. 1982. *Vowel harmony and umlaut: Implications for a typology of accent*. Cornell University PhD dissertation.
Nevins, Andrew. 2010. *Locality in vowel harmony*. Cambridge, MA: MIT Press.
Ritter, Nancy A. 1995. *The role of Universal Grammar in phonology: A Government Phonology approach to Hungarian*. New York University PhD dissertation.
Schane, Sanford A. 1984. The fundamentals of Particle Phonology. *Phonology Yearbook* 1. 129–55.
Staun, Jørgen. 2003. On vocalic feature hierarchisation. *Language Sciences* 25. 111–58.
Steriade, Donca. 1981. Parameters of metrical vowel harmony rules. MIT manuscript.
Valente, Vincenzo. 1975. *Puglia*. Pisa: Pacini.
Van Coetsem, Frans. 1996. *Towards a typology of lexical accent: Stress accent and pitch accent in a renewed perspective*. Heidelberg: Carl Winter.
Van Coetsem, Frans, Susan M. McCormick & Ronald Hendricks. 1981. Accent typology and sound change. *Lingua* 53. 295–315.
van der Hulst, Harry. 1995. Radical CV Phonology: The categorial gesture. In Jacques Durand & Francis Katamba (eds.), *Frontiers of phonology: Atoms, structures, derivations*, 80–116. London: Longman.
van der Hulst, Harry. 2005. The molecular structure of phonological segments. In Phil Carr, Jacques Durand & Colin J. Ewen (eds.), *Headhood, elements, specification and contrastivity*, 193–234. Amsterdam and Philadelphia: John Benjamins.
van der Hulst, Harry. 2015a. The laryngeal class in RcvP and voice phenomena in Dutch. In Johanneke Caspers et al. (eds.), *Above and beyond the segments*, 323–49. Amsterdam and Philadelphia: John Benjamins.
van der Hulst, Harry. 2015b. The opponent principle in RcvP: Binarity in a unary system. In Eric Raimy & Charles Cairns (eds.), *The segment in phonetics and phonology*, 149–79. London: Wiley-Blackwell.
van der Hulst, Harry. 2016a. Monovalent 'features' in phonology. *Language and Linguistics Compass* 10(2). 83–102.
van der Hulst, Harry. 2016b. *Vowel harmony* (Oxford Research Encyclopedia of Linguistics). http://linguistics.oxfordre.com/view/10.1093/acrefore/9780199384655.001.0001/acrefore-9780199384655-e-38.
van der Hulst, Harry. 2016c. Phonological ambiguity. *Theoretical Linguistics* 41(1–2): 79–87.
van der Hulst, Harry. 2017. A representational account of vowel harmony in terms of variable elements and licensing. In Harry van der Hulst & Anikó Liptak (eds.), *The structure of Hungarian. Proceedings of the 12th International Conference on the Structure of Hungarian*, 95–133. Amsterdam and Philadelphia: John Benjamins.

van der Hulst, Harry. 2018a. *Asymmetries in vowel harmony – A representational account*. Oxford: Oxford University Press.

van der Hulst, Harry. 2018b. Deconstructing tongue root harmony systems. In Geoff Lindsey & Andrew Nevins (eds.), *Sonic signatures*, 73–99. Amsterdam and Philadelphia: John Benjamins.

van der Hulst, Harry. in prep. Principles of Radical CV Phonology. University of Connecticut manuscript.

van der Hulst, Harry & Norval Smith. 1986. On neutral vowels. In Koen Bogers, Harry van der Hulst & Norval Smith (eds.), *The phonological representation of suprasegmentals*, 233–79. Dordrecht: Foris.

van der Hulst, Harry & Jeroen van de Weijer. to appear. Phonological complexity: A Radical CV Phonology perspective. In Harry van der Hulst & Roger Böhm (eds.), *Substance-based grammar – The (ongoing) work of John Anderson*. Amsterdam and Philadelphia: John Benjamins.

Walker, Rachel. 2005. Weak triggers in vowel harmony. *Natural Language & Linguistic Theory* 23(4). 917–89.

Walker, Rachel. 2010. Nonmyopic harmony and the nature of derivations. *Linguistic Inquiry* 41. 169–79.

Walker, Rachel. 2011. *Vowel patterns in language*. Cambridge: Cambridge University Press.

Zetterstrand, Sylvia. 1996. Scalar effects in Italian metaphony. In Estela Treviño & José Lema (eds.), *Theoretical analyses on Romance languages*, 351–60. Amsterdam and Philadelphia: John Benjamins.

Elizabeth J. Pyatt
Many sons of *Aodh*: Tracing multiple outcomes of the Scottish and Irish clan name *MacAoidh/Ó hAodha*

1 Introduction

The Old Irish patronymic *Mac Áeda* /mak ajða/ 'son of Áedh' evolved into the family name *MacAodha/MacAoidh/Ó hAodha* by the Classical period and was then adapted into English with a relatively high number of vowel realizations including /e/ (*Hayes, O'Hea, MacKay* U.S.), /i/ (*McKee, McKie, MacGhee*), /u/ (*Hughes, McCue*), /ɔj/ (*McCoy*) and /aj/ (*MacKay*, Scotland). This chapter will trace the development of these variations to certain regions within Scotland and Ireland, but also show that the variety of outcomes is due to multiple repairs of the back unrounded vowels /ə:/ or /ɯ:/ which happens in different regions and eras.

Section 2 of this chapter will describe the evolution of modern Irish and Scottish Gaelic from the Goedelic Celtic language Old Irish. Section 3 discusses the etymology of *Aodh* and tracks how different versions of the family names evolved within Irish and Scottish Gaelic. Section 4 reviews common Goedelic phonological issues such as palatalization before moving on to documenting different English phonological outcomes of *Aodh* and the *Aodh* family names. Section 5 discusses multiple English realizations of *MacAodha/MacAoidh*. Section 6 summarizes the evolution of the back unrounded vowels in the Goedelic languages, and Section 7 ends with some discussion of the challenges and benefits of working with phonological variations within family names.

2 Goedelic Celtic languages

2.1 Stages of "Irish"

The bulk of the data in this article comes from the Goedelic (a.k.a. "Goidelic" or "Gaelic") branch of the Indo–European Celtic family which is represented by the modern languages Irish, Scottish Gaelic and the revived language Manx (Thurneysen 1980: 1–2; Stifter 2006: 1).[1] Historically, Celticists identify the

---

[1] The other modern Celtic languages, Welsh, Breton and Cornish, are part of the Brythonic branch. Additional ancient Celtic languages such as Gaulish are indirectly related to Goedelic and Brythonic Celtic.

https://doi.org/10.1515/9781501506734-005

following linguistic stages within the Goedelic branch (MacEoin 1993; Doyle 2015: 3–4).

(1) Stages of Goedelic Celtic languages

Stage	Dates
Primitive/Ogham	5th–7th centuries AD
Old Irish (incl. Archaic)	7th–10th centuries
Middle Irish	10th–12th centuries
Classical Gaelic ("Early Modern Irish")	13th–17th centuries
Irish/Scottish Gaelic/Manx	17th centuries – present

The earliest attested stage of this family is Primitive Irish, represented by funerary monuments inscriptions in the Ogham script (McManus 1991: 51; Thurneysen 1980: 9–11). During this period, groups of Goedelic language speakers are established in Northern Scotland (Gillies 1993; MacBain 1911) and the Isle of Man (Broderick 1993), where Ogham inscriptions can be found (McManus 1991).

The next attested stages are Old Irish and Middle Irish. Old Irish is first attested in the 7th centuries, but primarily found in manuscripts circa the 8th century A.D. Most Old Irish material comes from Old Irish glosses and notes to Latin Biblical manuscripts written in Irish monasteries (Thurneysen 1980: 4–7). At this stage, there is a relatively consistent grammar that can be reconstructed although there are some variations attested.

Documents from the following stage of Middle Irish (10th – 12th centuries) show changes in morphology, spelling and syntax representing features found in later stages of the Goedelic languages. However, this stage is also marked with orthographic variation across documents (Mac Gearailt 1992; Breatnach 1994; O'Rahilly 1926), a possible indication that dialectal features were emerging. Generally the changes generally show the evolution from Old Irish to later stages of Irish, but some documents such as the *Book of Deer* with Middle Irish from the 12th century may show the emergence of dialectal features (Ó Maolalaigh 2008).

The next stage, Classical Gaelic or Early Modern Irish (13th–18th centuries), is a written standard which was used in both Ireland and Scotland (McManus 1996; Ó Baoill 2010). It is not until the 18th–19th centuries that differentiated written forms of what is now Modern Irish, Scottish Gaelic and Manx are established (Doyle 2015: 141–157; Ó Baoill 2010; Broderick 1993). It is important to note that dialectal features such as the presence of back unrounded vowels, can cross national borders (Hickey 2011: 240).

2.2 Transition to English in Goedelic language territories

The spread of English into Ireland, Scotland and the Island of Man took place over a period of centuries. Due to the military and cultural influence of different English or Scots forces, Goedelic languages lost their political dominance in the 12th century AD in Scotland (Gillies 1993; Ó Baoill 2010), 14th century in the Isle of Man (Broderick 1993) and by the early 17th century in Ireland (Doyle 2015: 17–41).² However, the majority of the population in these areas were still speaking a Goedelic language as of 1700 in the Scottish Highlands (Gillies 1993), the Isle of Man (Broderick 1993) and Ireland outside of Dublin (Doyle 2015: 66). By 1900, the majority of speakers had switched to speaking English with Irish and Scottish Gaelic being spoken primarily in rural areas along the northern and western coasts (MacKinnon 1993; Doyle 2015: 166).

At the same time, many inhabitants from Scotland and later Ireland emigrated to different parts of the British Empire including North America (18th–19th centuries), Australia (19th century), New Zealand (19th century) and elsewhere. Although the original emigrants may have been proficient in a Celtic language, social conditions in these areas generally required rudimentary proficiency in English for most speakers. As a generalization, their descendants became monolingual English speakers with no surviving Goedelic speaking communities except for the Scottish Gaelic community of Nova Scotia and the Atlantic Provinces of Canada of approximately 1600 active Gaelic speakers (Statistics Canada 2015).

2.3 Dating borrowings

Dating borrowings is important when considering the interactions between Goedelic and English phonology in Anglicized forms of Goedelic names and other vocabulary items. For instance, whether a word was borrowed before or after the Great English vowel shift (ca. 15th–16th centuries, Baugh & Cable 2013: 196–197; Barber 1997: 105–109) impacts how a vowel will be realized in Modern English. The Goedelic communities have been in close contact with different Anglo–Scots language communities for at least a millennium, so as might be expected, there

---

2 The diagnostic I am using for the end of political dominance is when the noble class had switched away from Goedelic. In Scotland, the Lowlands aristocracy had switched to Scots even being absorbed into the future United Kingdom (Gillies 1993). In Ireland, there was an Anglo–Norman conquest in the 12th century, but for a period of time, the Anglo-Norman rulers adopted Irish (Doyle 2015: 15–17) and only later switched to English.

are borrowings from a Goedelic language into English from multiple periods. Examples of borrowings from both before and after the Great English Vowel Shift can be seen below in (2a) and (2b):

(2) a. Borrowings pre English vowel shift
  i. *Neil* /nil/ (E) personal name < *Néil* /nʲeːlʲ/ (Ir)
     Original Irish /eː/ has shifted to /i/ in English
  ii. *Niall* /najəl/ (E) personal name < *Niall* /nʲəlˠ/ (Ir)
     Original Irish /iː/ has shifted to /aj/ in English
  iii. *Tyrone* /tajron/ (E) place name < *Tír Eoghain* /tʲiːrʲ oːɣən/ (Ir)
     Original Irish /iː/ has shifted to /aj/ in English
  iv. *Brady* /bredi/ (E) family name < *Ó Brádaigh* /braːdiyʲ/ (Ir)
     Original Irish /aː/ has shifted to /e/ in English
 b. Borrowings post English vowel shift
  v. *Colleen* /kalin/ (E) personal name < *cáilín* /kalʲiːnʲ/ 'girl' (Ir)
  vi. *Sheila* /ʃilə/ (E) < *sile* /ʃilə/ 'she' (Ir)
  vii. *Clery* /kleri/ (E) < *Ó Cléirigh* /kʲlʲeːrʲiː/ (family name) (Ir)

When discussing Irish and Scottish Gaelic family names tracking parallel developments in English and Scots is important to keep in mind.

3 The name *Aodh* and clan names

3.1 Etymology of *Aodh*

The Classical Gaelic name *Aodh* is commonly derived from Old Irish *Aéd* /ajð/ meaning 'fire, eye' (MacKillop 2006: 3), a meaning preserved in Modern Irish *aodh* 'inflammation' (Ó Dónaill 1977). Old Irish a*éd* is in turn derived from the Proto-Celtic **ajdʰu–* 'fire', a neuter u–stem noun (Koch 2006: 17) which is cognate with Old English *ad* 'funeral pyre' Welsh *aidd* /ajð/ 'zeal, ardor', Latin *aedes* 'hearth, house' and Greek *αἶθος* 'fire, burning heat' (OED Online 2016). Koch (2006: 17) also connects this form to the Gaulish tribal name *Aedui*.

The name *Aéd* and later *Aodh* was commonly used as a male personal name in the Old Irish through Classical Gaelic periods (MacKillop 2006: 3–4; O'Brien 2000–2007). MacKillop notes that a version of the name is attested for over twenty saints, multiple kings and chieftans and multiple figures from traditional Irish folklore. Two later historical Irish rulers named *Aodh* include *Aodh Mór Ó Neill*/ Hugh "The Great" O'Neill (1550–1616), the 2nd Earl of Tyrone and *Aodh Ruadh*

Ó Domhnaill/Hugh Roe O'Donnell/Red Hugh II (1572–1602), two leaders of the Tyrone Rebellion against the English powers in Ireland (Canny 2008; Silke 2006).

3.2 Goedelic clan name variants with *Aodh*

Many Irish and Scottish family names are based on an original patronymic pattern in which either *Mac/Mc* (originally 'son of') or *Ó* (from Old Irish *ua* 'descendant of') is attached to a genitive form of a personal name (MacKillop 2006: 280–281, 370; McManus 1991: 51–52, 108–111).[3] An example of a patronymic use of *mac* is *(C)onst(antín) mac Aéda* (Constantine II of Scotland, d. 952), the son of King Aéd (Broun 2004), where *Aéda* is the genitive form of *Aéd* (eDil 2017). As a generalization, Anglicized family names with *O'* are found primarily in Ireland while family names with *Mac* are found in both Ireland, particularly the Ulster region, and Scotland (MacLysaught 1972: 16–17; Matheson 1894: 15). It should be further noted that since *Aodh* was so commonly found as a name, it is generally assumed that not all clans named after *Aodh* are derived from the same ancestor (Woulfe 1923).[4]

Before being borrowed into English, the Goedelic clan names using *Aodh* showed morphological variations depending on their regional dialect. First, some families used the *Mac* marker while others used the *Ó* marker, and this marker triggers an /h/ insertion mutation (Christian Brothers 1993: 6) which causes an /h/ to be inserted when the following word begins with a vowel.[5] This leads to variants *Mac Aodha* (3a) and *Ó hAodha* (3b). Note that both forms use the genitive form *Aodha* which is directly descended from the Old Irish u–stem genitive form *Aéda*.

In some dialects though, particularly in Scotland, *Aodh* was reclassified into the more common o–stem/1st declension (Thurneysen 1980: 196) and the genitive became *Aoidh*, where – *idh* represents a palatalized voiced fricative. Combined

---

3 Mac is derived from Proto–Celtic *makkʷos 'son' and is found as MAQI in Ogham inscriptions (and is cognate *mab* 'son' in Welsh and the other Brythonic languages (McManus 1991: 109–111). In Welsh, *mab* (or *ab*) was also used to form patronymc names like *Llywelyn ap Iorwerth* (Llewellyn Fawr, the son of Iowerth) (MacKillop 1998: 276). The Old Irish form *ua* is also found in Ogham inscriptions as AVI (McManus 1991: 109–111).
4 McManus (1991: 111) notes that *Mac/MAQI* names could refer to a divine founder of a *tuath* or a human ancestor while *Ua/AVI* names were more likely to only refer to a human ancestor. It appears that this distinction was later lost.
5 See Pyatt (1997: 48–52, 136–140) for arguments that this rule is a mutation and not a phonologically based insertion of a hiatus consonant between two vowels.

with *Mac* and *Ó* this leads to the third and fourth variants *Mac Aoidh* (3c) and the fairly rare *Ó hAoidh* (3d).[6]

(3) Summary of Goedelic clan with *Aodh*

Declension	With *Mac* 'son'	With *Ó* 'descendant'
u–stem (original)	a. *Mac Aodha*	b. *Ó hAodha*
o–stem (change)	c. *Mac Aoidh*	d. *Ó hAoidh*

The presence of the multiple variants does affect how forms are borrowed into English. For instance, if a family is using an *Ó hAodha/Ó hAoidh* form, the Anglicized form will likely include an /h/ (e.g. *O'Hea*). Some forms like *Hayes, Hay, Hughes* preserve the /h/ but drop the prefix *Ó (O')*. Further, as will be explained in section 5, if *Aoidh* is the basis of the Anglicization, the Goedelic form may include a rising diphthong ending with /j/, but generally not if the form is *Aodha*.

4 Some Middle Irish phonological changes

4.1 Change of Old Irish /ð/ to /ɣ/ (to Ø)

A phonological change affecting the phonological evolution of Old Irish *Aéd* to Classical Gaelic *Aodh* was the merger of the interdental fricative /ð/ to the voiced velar fricative /ɣ/. Celticists generally date this change to the Middle Irish period when "misspellings" of *d(h)* versus *g(h)* suggest there was a merger in progress (Breatnach 1994). However, the orthographic distinction between *dh* and *gh* was preserved in Classical Gaelic as well as Modern Irish and Scottish Gaelic spelling. In English borrowings, this voiced velar fricative is almost always deleted in the clan name since English has never had a phonemic /ɣ/ (that is, English has always had a feature cooccurence constraint of *[DOR, –son, +cont, +voice].[7]

---

[6] The only source claiming a family name derived from *Ó hAoidh* is O'Kane (1998) which derives *Hoy* from *Ó hAoidh*. However, other sources like Woulfe (1923) derive *Hoy* from *Ó hEochaidh*.
[7] Note that Modern English treats the Goedelic voiceless velar fricative differently. For instance, Scottish Gaelic *loch* /lʲox/ is borrowed into English with final /x/ changed to /k/. Similarly the Irish family name *(Ó) hUallacháin* /huəlʲəxəɲ́/ becomes English *Houlihan* with the internal /x/ changed to /h/.

4.2 Palatalized /ɣ/ and glides

Another phonological element of the modern Goedelic languages is the development of contrastive palatalized versus non-palatalized consonants which was also firmly established in the Middle Irish period (Ní Chíosáin 1991: 7–8; Gillies 1993; Mac Eoin 1993; Broderick 1993). In both Irish and Scottish Gaelic, the vowel letters "e,i" can indicate that an adjacent consonant is palatalized (Cʲ), while "a,o,u" may indicate an non-palatalized consonant (C).[8] Some examples of the palatal contrast in Irish are listed below. Examples of contrastive palatalization can be seen in (4).

(4) Phonemic palatalized consonants in Irish (Ní Chíosáin & Padgett 2012: 190; Mac Eoin 1993: 106)
  a. *scál* 'phantom/giant' /skaːl/ [skɔːl]   vs. *scáil* 'shadow' /skaːlʲ/ [skɔːlʲ]
  b. *cat* /kat/ 'cat'   vs. *cait* /katʲ/ [katʲ]~[katɕ] 'cats'
  c. *bád* /baːd/ [bˠɔːd] 'boat.nom'   vs. *báid* /baːdʲ/ [bɔːdʲ] 'boat.gen'
  d. *bó* 'cow' /boː/ [bˠoː]   vs. *beo* 'alive' [bʲoː]

Recall from section 3.2 that by the Classical Gaelic period, the clan name could be either *Mac/Ó Aodha* with non palatal /ɣ/ or *Mac/Ó Aoidh* with final palatal /ɣʲ/ depending on the dialect. In fact though, in all three modern languages, palatal /ɣʲ/ surfaces as the palatal glide [j], at least in post-vocalic position (Ní Chíosáin 1991: 155, Gillies 1993, Broderick 1993) as seen in the examples below (5).

(5) Palatal /ɣʲ/ to glide [j]
  a. **Irish** (Ní Chíosáin 1991: 212, 31)
    inseoidh 'tell.fut' /inʲʃoːɣʲ/ as [inʃoːj]
    do-dhéanta 'impossible' /do-ɣʲeːntə/ as [do-jeːntə]
  b. **Scottish Gaelic** (Gillies 1993: 155, Bosch 2010: 268)
    a chaoidh 'forever' /ə xɯːɣʲ/ as [ə xəi]
    laoigh 'calf.gen' /lˠɯːɣʲ/ as [lˠɣʊiː]

In some cases glide formation rule may help distinguish borrowings from *MacAoidh* with final [j] from *MacAaodha/Ó hAodha*.

---

8 Manx orthography switched to a form closer to English orthography and does not visually indicate palatalization.

4.3 Monophthongization of Old Irish *aé*

The orthography of Modern Irish and Scottish Gaelic both contain the digraph *ao* used in the family name *Mac Aoidh/Mac Aodha/Ó hAodh*. Depending on the language and dialect, this digraph usually represents a long vowel and can be pronounced as [ɯː,ə:,iː,eː,ɑi] depending on the dialect (Borgstrøm 1940; Ladefoged & Turk 1998; Bosch 2013; Dorian 1978; Hickey 2011: 260–262). The distribution of variant pronunciations of *ao* by region is shown in (6).[9]

(6) Regional pronunciation of digraph *ao*
    a. Irish South   [eː–] (*ao* [eː–] slightly back of [eː] *é*)
    b. Irish Southeast   [eː]~[ɑi]
    c. Irish Standard/West   [iː]~[ɯː]
    d. Irish North (Ulster)   [ɯː]
    e. Scottish Gaelic North [ɯː]
    f. Scottish Gaelic South [əː]

Note that even for dialects like Standard Irish in which the vowel of *ao* is described as a high front long /iː/, many sources also describe the phonetics as more "retracted" (i.e. [ɨ]) rather than the [iː] for the vowel spelled as *í* (Mac Eoin 1993; Hickey 2011: 239–241). The same is true for dialects with *ao* as /eː/ where the phonetic value is a slightly backed mid vowel ([eː–]) (Mac Eoin 1993; Hickey 2011: 239–241). Synchronically, *ao* can act as the front vowel which comes after a velarized consonant (vs. *í/é* which usually comes after a palatalized consonant) and so Mac Eoin and Hickey assume that the phonetic retraction of *ao* is a synchronic result of interactions with the palatalization/velarization feature of Irish consonants. However, it is also possible that the centralized value is due to the historical origin of this vowel as a back unrounded vowel as found in other dialects.

In terms of phonological change, the path from Old Irish diphthong to the later long vowel is not entirely clear, but all sources agree that by Middle Irish, the diphthong had become monophthongized as some sort of unrounded mid vowel (Hickey 2011: 360; Jackson: 1972: 133–134; Breatnach 1994; McManus 1994; Shaw 1968). Following Jackson and McManus, I assume that Old Irish diphthong

---

[9] It should be noted that *ao* [ɯː] is considered to be a phoneme in Scottish Gaelic (Bosch 2010), but in Donegal Irish, Hickey (2011: 240–241) considers both [ɯː] and central [ɨ] to be allophones of /iː/ which occur after non-palatal consonants. When considering foreign language borrowings, either analysis works since adaptations are based more on surface phonetic cues.

spelled *áe* monophthongized as a mid, back and unrounded or only slightly rounded vowel which I transcribe as /ə:/. A more detailed discussion of this change will be seen in Section 6.

5 Clan Name Anglicizations

5.1 Methodological Notes

This section will review different phonetic outcomes for Anglicized versions of *Ó hAodha/Mac Aodha/Mac Aoidh* and discuss what the probable dialectal forms and vowels that would produce the English outcomes. Based on the evidence from both genealogical records and phonology, it would appear that most forms date from the Classical Gaelic (ca. 1500–1800) period or later. Attestations from Middle Irish will be discussed in Section 6.

When working with the origins of family names, it is important to ensure that data about a family name is properly documented and not derived from family mythology. Another complication is that the spelling of family names can be fluid and include vowel changes. For instance, one family in Virginia and Maryland had records under both *McKay* and *McCoy* (Good 1976). Finally, families did move between regions and could have retained a particular Anglicized form of a last name (Matheson 1894: 20).

Despite these complications, it is possible to detect some regional patterns for certain names and that the original phonetic value of *ao* in *Aodha/Aoidh* might be deduced. For instance, Woulfe (1923) and MacLysaught (1972: 176, 185–6) notes the *ó hAodha* name was typically Anglicized as *Hayes* /heyz/ in the South, where *ao* as [e:] is common but *Hughes* /hjuz/ in the North where *ao* is usually [ɯ:] or [i:].

5.2 "Southern" vs. "Northern" *ao*

For the purposes of describing outcomes of Irish/Scottish Gaelic *ao* into English, I make distinction between Southern (Munster) Irish where *ao* is usually pronounced as the mid front vowel [e:] and forms further north (Connaught/Ulster/Scotland) where *ao* is pronounced as a high vowel [i:/ɯ:] in Connaught/Ulster/Northern Scottish Gaelic) or /ə:/ in southern Scottish Gaelic.

In reference to Ulster, the distinction between southern and northern Irish is also useful for political and cultural reasons. As noted earlier in this paper, the

Goedelic languages came to the Highlands of Scotland in the pre Old Irish period, likely from the Ulster region in Northern Ireland. Cultural connections between Goedelic speaking communities in Ireland and Scotland were maintained at least through the beginning of the Classical Gaelic period, again with Ulster as a point of connection with western Scotland.

However, several events in 15th–16th century complicate the matter further. First both the English and Scottish churches shifted away from following papal authority in Rome to become identified as Protestant (with multiple sects), while Ireland remained Catholic. Second was that England developed a colonization program in Ulster starting in the early 1600s (Doyle 2015: 63–68). As a result, a group of families from Scotland with Scottish Gaelic family names settled in Ulster. Some may have been speaking Scottish Gaelic, but the majority were Lowlands Scots speakers, with the result that Ulster Scots is a recognized minority language in Northern Ireland, with approximately 35,000 active native speakers as of the 2011 Census (Northern Ireland Statistics and Research Agency, 2015).[10]

Thus, when discussing what I call "northern forms", it's important to distinguish multiple populations – indigenous Irish families of Ulster and Connaught, Scottish Gaelic immigrants to Ulster and Scottish Gaelic families in Scotland, and emigrants outside of Britain who could be anyone of the three previously mentioned groups (7).

(7) Populations with Goedelic family names
    a. Families indigenous to Ireland
    b. Families indigenous to Scotland
    c. Scottish families in Ulster (typically speaking English or Scots)
    d. Any family from 6(a–c) who emigrated from Ireland or Scotland

Whether a family identifies as Protestant or Catholic is of some use in determining ethnicity, although it is possible for families to change religions. In Ireland, most remaining Irish speakers identify themselves as Catholic and indigenous Irish (McCoy 1997).[11] That is, there is no recognized Scottish Gaelic speaking community in Northern Ireland even though some grammatical features may be found in both Ulster Irish and Scottish Gaelic.

---

10 There were about 97,000 active Irish speakers in Northern Ireland in the same period.
11 Interestingly though, some Protestants of Northern Ireland are taking Irish classes as a way to learn more about indigenous Irish cultures (McCoy 1997).

5.3 Ó hAodha variants with English /e/

Anglicizations of Ó hAodha with /e/ are commonly found, particularly in the South. They include *Hayes* /hez/ in multiple locations and *O'Hea* in Cork in the South (MacLysaught 1972: 176; Woulfe 1923). For these variants, I assume that they point to a variant of Ó hAodha pronounced as /oː heːðə/ > /oː heɣə/ > /oː heː/ which becomes /o he/ *O'Hea* in Modern English.

Collins (1946) traces the history of the *O'Hea* family in Cork and the Ross diocese in Southern Ireland. The name Ó hAodha appears as *O Hethe* in Anglo-Norman legal documents from Cork in 1295 (*Royry O Hethe*) and ca. 1298–1299 (*Thomas O Hethe*). Two separate papal letters from 1433, in reference to Ross Ireland mention a *Dermid o heda* and a *Nicholas o heda*. In 1549, another papal letter refers to *Dermit o Hega*, a canon of Ross, and then *Donatus Ohega*, a monk, is referenced in 1469. By 1559, *Maurice O'Hea* (likely /o heː/ at that stage of English) has been named the Bishop of Ross (8).[12]

(8) Attestestions of Ó hAodha from Cork/Ross region (Collins 1946)
    a. 1295   Roryry O Hethe
    b. 1298–99   Thomas O Hethe
    c. 1433   Dermid o heda, Nicholas o heda
    d. 1549   Dermit o Hega
    e. 1469   Donatus Ohega
    f. 1559   Maurice O'Hea

Hayes /heyz/ with the English surname suffix –s is a more common outcome for Ó hAodha in this region (Woulfe 1923; MacLysaught 1972: 176). In addition to these forms, Hickey (2011: 356) mentions place names *Killea* [kɪleː] (*Cille Aodha* 'Aodh's church') from Waterford Ireland, *Killmokea* (*Cille Mhic Aodha* 'Mac Aodha's church') in Wexford[13] and *Coolea* [kuːlʲ eː] (*Cúil Aodha* 'Aodha's corner') in the Cork Gaeltacht (9).

(9) *Aodha* place names with /e/ (Hickey 2011: 356–358)
    a. *Killea* /kɪleː/ < *Cille Aodha* 'Aodh's church' (Waterford, Munster)

---

[12] In the medieval period (before ca 1500), I assume that the use of *th* in French, Latin or English documents listing Irish/Scottish Gaelic names is a representation of Irish *dh* which could have been /ð/ in the earliest documents. Sometimes *d* is also used for Irish *dh*.
[13] Hickey (2011) notes that English *ea* was pronounced as /e/ in Hiberno English through the 19th century. In contrast *ee* was a typical Anglicized spelling of Irish /iː/.

b. *Killmokea* < *Cille Mhic Aodha* 'Mac Aodha's church' (Wexford, S. Leinster)
c. *Cúil Aodha* [kuːlʲeː] 'Aodha's corner' (Cork Gaeltacht, Munster)

These follow the general pattern that *ao* place names in Munster and South Leinster are pronounced as [eː] while those from North Leinster, Connaught and Ulster are often pronounced with a high vowel (Hickey 2011: 351–358). As with *O'Hea*, I assume that *Hayes* /hez/ was adapted directly from an Irish /eː/ and as explained in Section 6, this Southern Irish /eː/ is a result of a change from earlier /əː/ in Middle Irish. Because the vowel did not shift to /i/ in English, I assume they date to after the English Great Vowel Shift.

5.4 Variants with English /i/

There are several Anglicized variants of *MacAodha* with Modern English /i/ including *McKee/McKie* /məki/, *Kee* /ki/ and *Eason* /i/+–*son* (Woulfe 1923; MacLysaught 1972: 185). Another relatively well documented groiup include the *McGhees* /məgi/ of *Balmaghie* (from *Baile MacAodha* 'McGhee Town') in southwestern Scotland as well as Irish *McGee's* /məgi/ in Protestant Ulster and Westmeath, Leinster in central Ireland (Woulfe 1923; Black 1974: 182–3; M'Kie 1906). There also two McGee place names in eastern Ulster in Northern Ireland: *Ballymagee* (*Baile Mhic Aodha*), a town and *Islandmagee* (*Oileán Mhic Aodha*), a peninsula just north of Belfast (10).[14]

(10) *Aodha* place names with /i/ (Hickey 2011: 354; M'Kie 1906)
  a. *Ballymagee* /bælıməgi/ < *Baile Mhic Aodha* 'MacAodha town' (Ulster, Ireland)
  b. *Islandmagee* /ajlnænd–məgi/ < *Oileán Mhic Aodha* 'MacAodha isle' (Ulster)
  c. *Cloonee* /kluni/ < *Cluain Aodha* 'Aodh's pasture' (Meath, N. Leinster, Ireland)
  d. *Balmaghee* /bælməgi/ < *Baile Mac Aoidh* 'MacAodha town' (Dumfries, Scotland)

Forms 10 (a–c) from Irish follow the generalization that *ao* place names in northern regions are often realized with /iː/ in Irish. In Standard Modern Irish, based

---

14 The placename *Islandmagee* is prefixed by English *Island*. Its official Irish name has the Irish word *Oiléan* 'island'.

on the Connaught dialect, *ao* is phonemically /iː/ although typically a little further back phonetically than the /iː/ spelled *í*. If these families originated from Connaught, an analysis where English /i/ was a direct borrowing of Connaught /iː/ would be plausible.

However, since many of these forms come from Ulster and Scotland where *ao* is phonetically [ɯː], it is possible that the English /i/ represents a repaired form of a high back unrounded vowel in these cases. That is, since English disallows *[+high, −round, +back], one repair option is to change the [+back] value to [−back] (11).

(11) Delinking repair [ɯː] to [iː]
 [+back] → [−back] / [_____ +high, −round]

Because no other local European language (i.e. English, Scots, Norse, Welsh or French) has phonemic /ɯː/, there is no orthographic convention to distinguish [iː] from [ɯː]. Therefore it is possible that some Anglicized spellings of *Aodh* with English *i* or *y* could represent a represent an adaptation of either Irish [iː] or [ɯː] depending on which dialect the family name came from.

Another option besides a direct borrowing from Goedelic [iː] or [ɯː] is that the English /i/ represents a Goedelic mid vowel which was borrowed into English before the Great Vowel Shift which changes Early Modern English [eː] to [iː]. The Great Vowel Shift takes place in several stages, but the dating of the shift [eː] to [iː] in English and Scots is dated to the mid–late 15th century (Baugh & Cable 2013: 196–197; Barber 1997: 105–109; Macafee & Aitken 2002). That would mean that the shift of the Middle Irish mid vowel to a higher vowel would not have happened in this region until after the late 15th centry.

As noted in the previous section, it is generally assumed that Old Irish *áe* initially changed to a mid vowel monophthong in Middle Irish, but in the North, this vowel was further raised to a high vowel. Shaw (1968) shows that the mid vowel monopthong from Old Irish *oé/aé* was shifting to a high vowel starting in the 13th century in some areas. Examples from documents of that era showing the change include *dine* (later *daoine* 'people') and *scilud* (later *scaoileadh* 'loosening, undoing').

One family with a fairly long written record are the *McGhees* (M'Gies) and *McKees* (M'Kies) of Balmaghie (originally *Balmakethe*) from the Dumfries & Galloway region (Shaw 1892–3; M'Kie 1906). Since they are from the south, one could posit that their dialect of Scottish Gaelic had preserved a mid vowel for *ao*, which was borrowed into English as /eː/ and then raised to /iː/ due to the Great Vowel Shift. Yet, the distribution of the modern *MacGee/MacKee* places in Ireland of *Ballymagee/Islandmagee* (near Belfast on the west coast of the Irish Sea) and

Dumfries Scotland (nearest to the east coast of Irish Sea) suggests a single dialectal form.[15] In addition, both the Scottish *Maghees* and Irish *McGees* represent an unusual instance where the /k/ of *mac* can be changed to voiced /g/.

One of the earliest attestations from 1296 is *Gilmyhel Mac Eth* (*del counte de Dunfres* 'from Dumfries county') as recorded in the Ragman Rolls which lists noblemen of Scotland swearing fealty to the English king Edward I (M'Kie 1906).[16] At this stage, the vowel is written as a mid vowel. By the the early 15th century, the high vowel was being used in *Gilbert M'Gy of Balmage* (1426). A listing of attested forms is found in (12).

(12) Attestations of *Mac Aodh* from Balmagee (M'Kie 1906; MacKay 1906: 347–350)
  a. early 12th Balmakethe (town)
  b. 1296   Gilmyhel Mac Eth (del counte de Dunfres)
  c. 1339   Michael Macge
  d. 1426   Gilbert M'Gy, Lord of Balmage
  e. 1460   Gilbert M'Gy of Balmagy
  f. 1587   Alexandro Makghie

The transition from the *e* spelling to the *y* spelling appears to be in the early 15th century which may be a little earlier than the English Great Vowel shift. Similarly, a papal letter from 1433 mentions *Odo Mac Idh, (Aodh mac Aoidh)*, a bishop of Argyll, Scotland (MacDonald 2013). It should be noted that the same person was documented as *Odo Mayg* (1408) and *Adain Mocaid* (1408). Based on this data, it appears to be the case that the raising in Goedelic happened before the adaptation of the name into English. Therefore I am currently assuming that English /i/ is an adaptation of a Goedelic high vowel, probably probably [ɯ:] in Ulster and Scotland which was repaired to /i:/ at some stage in English.

Another *MacAoidh* family in Galloway is *Mc'Kie* /məki/ who lived in Larg and Minnigaff at various times. In this case, the family appears to use the *e* spelling until a much later time as in the list below – specifically (13):

(13) Attestations of *Mac Aodha* from Larg (MacKay 1906: 353)
  a. 1529   Patrick Makge
  b. 1598   Patrick Makkie

---

15 A MacGhee (*MacAoidh*) branch was also deeded the Rhins of Islay in the Irish Sea north of Ireland (MacKay 1906).
16 The document dates from a time when Norman French was still the official language of England.

In this case, the vowel raising may be due to the Great Vowel Shift in English. Alternatively, the 1529 *e* may represent an archaic spelling for a phonetic high vowel.

5.5 Variants with English /u/

In Section 5.3, we have seen probable instances of original Goedelic [ɯː] becoming /i/ in English as a delinking repair of [+back] in the combination of *[+back, −round]. Another delinking repair for /ɯ/ could be to change [−round] to [+round] resulting in the high back round vowel /u/. As with /i/, it appears that there are cases where Irish or Scottish Gaelic *ao* is Anglicized as /u/ (14).

(14) Delinking repair [ɯː] to /u/
      [−round] → [+round] / [_____ +high, +back]

As previously mentioned in Section 3.1, the name *Hugh* is a common English substitution for the personal name *Aodh* in Ireland (MacLysaught 1972: 185–186; Hickey 2011: 261). Examples of prominent Irish men named *Aodh/Hugh* include *Aodh Mór Ó Neill/Hugh "The Great" O'Neill* (1550–1616), and *Aodh Ruadh Ó Domhnaill/Hugh Roe O'Donnell/Red Hugh II* (1572–1602).[17] In a similar vein, in the northern part of Ireland, *McHughes* is a common Anglicization of of *MacAodha* (MacLysaught 1972: 185–186; Woulfe 1923). McLysaught notes that a notable branch of the MacHughes was found in County Clare in Connaught. An early person referred to by this surname was Malachy MacHugh (Mac Aedha) (1313–1348), archbishop of Tuam (Kelly 1907). MacLysaught (1999: 68) mentions that *McHughes* could also be rendered as *McCoo* /u/ which was later spelled *McCue* /məkju/, both of which make the English phonetic value of [u] clearer.

The English personal name *Hugh* was borrowed from Norman French and is etymologically of Germanic origin (Hanks, Hardcastle & Hodges 2006) The same root is also found in *Hugo* and *Ugo* (Italian). The modern English pronunciation /hju/ points to an earlier high front rounded /y/ in Norman French and earlier stages of English, but always a rounded vowel. In English, /y/ as a phoneme was lost in London English by 1400 (Barber 1976: 104; Smith 1999: 102), so that by the 15th century, I assume that the *Hugh* would would be pronounced with a /u/. Even at earlier /y/ stages though, the vowel of *Hugh* would have been [+high, +round].

---

[17] For Scotland, McKay (1906) argues that *Hugh* is not the usual equivalent of *Aodh*, but rather *Odo* (in Latin) or *I/Iye* in other cases.

Ideally, other clearer cases of Irish *ao* being borrowed as English /u/ should be attested and examples can be found. One is the family *Ó Maonaigh* 'wealthy' which is Anglicized as *Mooney* /muni/ (Woulfe 1923; MacLysaught 1972: 227–228). One branch of this family hails from *Ballymooney* 'Mooney Town' in central Ireland west of Dublin near Offaly and another from an adjacent county. Additional variants include *Meeney* /mini/ in County Sligo, Connaught (home to *Ballymeeny*) and *Mainey* /meni/ in Munster in Southern Ireland (15).

(15) Distribution of *Ó Maonaigh* variant Anglicizations (MacLysaught 1972: 227–228)
   a. *Mooney* /muni/ Offaly, Meath (Central Ireland)
   b. *Meeney* /mini/ County Sligo (Connaught)
   c. *Mainey* /meni/ Munster

Hickey (2011: 353) further mentions the Ulster place name *Liscloon* /lɪsklun/ from Irish *Lios Claon* 'sloping ring fort' and McManus (1994) also gives these examples of *ao* sometimes being spelled as *ú* [u:] – *cúnach* for *caonach* 'moss' and *iomlúid* for *iomlaoid* 'change, exchange'. Finally, Irish surnames beginning with *Maol* 'bald, dedicated to a saint' are Anglicized as *Mul*– with families distributed all across Ireland (MacLysaught 1999: 224–229; 1972: 232–234). These include *Mulpatrick, Mulpeters, Mulberry, Mulcahy, Muldoon, Mulgrew, Mullholland* and several others.[18]

5.6 Variants with English /ɔj/

One of the two outcomes of *MacAoidh* with a falling diphthong is *McCoy* /məkɔj/, with the other being *MacKay* pronounced as /məkaj/.[19] According to MacLysaught (1972: 97), the McCoys were primarily a Scots–Irish family, possibly first coming in as foreign mercenaries from the Islay islands, which would have been near the same territory as the Scottish *McGhies* of *Balmaghie* (Dumfries).[20] On the other hand some genealogies suggest that some families in the

---

[18] In the reverse, some older [ui] are spelled ao in later languages. A notable case is Old Irish *druí* 'druid/wizard' (Thurneysen 1980: 206) becomes *draoi* in Modern Irish and Scottish Gaelic (MacBain 1911).
[19] MacLysaught (1999) and Woulfe (1923) both derive *McCoy* from *MacAodha*, but given the phonology of *McCoy*, an origin from *MacAoidh* which also gives *MacKay* seems more plausible.
[20] MacKay (1906) includes a 1408 Gaelic charter from the Macdonalds giving the island of Islay to the *Magaodh* family headed by *Bhrian Bhicaire Mhagaodh*.

Strathnaver region of the Highlands also used a pronunciation like McCoy (McCoy 1904: 17).

Some North American McCoy genealogies (Good 1976; McKoy 1955: 8–9) also convey that the *McCoy* spelling sometimes arose after family had come to North America. That is, a *MacKay* of one generation might decide to switch to *McCoy*. McKoy (1955: 9) in particular records a family account that an *Alexander McKay* changed the name to *McKoy* because it was a more accurate version of the actual pronunciation in the English spelling system.

Phonologically, the English outcome of [ɔj] suggests that the Gaelic form had some sort of back unrounded vowel. If it were [iː] or [eː], one would expect [iː,eː] or possibly [aj] post English Vowel Shift from Early Modern English [iː]. This form is another instances of an Anglicized form with a repaired back unrounded vowel from a Goedelic language.

As with the other variants, there are multiple possible paths to McCoy. If the form was originally *MacAoidh* /məkɯːɣʲ/ with Ulster [ɯː] for *ao*, then we can assume that /ɣʲ/ became [j] phonetically. This would result in either a Goedelic diphthong [ɯːj] or perhaps [uːj] (per Bosch 2010) or [əːi] (per Gillies 1993). None of these are phonemic in English, but could be plausible repaired as English /ɔj/. For [əːj] to [ɔj], the repair would preserve the glide [j] and backness of the main vowel but change [−round] to [+round]. For [uj] to [ɔj], the [+high, +round] vowel would become [−high, +round]. For [ɯːj] to [ɔj], both the height and the roundness of the vowel are changed (16).

(16) Possible repairs to English /ɔj/
 a. *[uj] to [ɔj]: [+high] → [−high] / ___j
 b. *[əj] to [ɔj]: [−round] → [+round] / ___j
 c. *[ɯj] to [ɔj]: [+high, −round] → [−high, +round] /___j

In addition to *McCoy*, a handful of other Irish family surnames from Ulster with *aoi* are Anglicized as /ɔj/ (17).

(17) Additional Family Names with aoi as /ɔj/ (MacLysaught 1972: 1999)
 a. *Boyle* (*Ó Baoighill*) Donegal, Ulster (MacLysaught)
 b. *Boylan* (*Ó Baoigheallàin*) Monoghan, Ulster
 c. *Boyne* < *MacBoyheen* (*Mac Baoithin*), Leitrim, Ulster[21]

---

[21] This *Boyne* is different from the *Boyne* River derived from Irish *Bóinn* < *Boann*, an Irish river goddess.

Hickey (2011: 352–353) also notes that some place names with *maol* 'bare' are Anglicized as *Moyle*. Interestingly, both names are from the south where *ao* is normally [eː] (18).²²

(18) *Maol* Place Names with *ao* as /ɔj/ (Hickey 2011: 352–353)
 a. *Rathmoylan* < *Ráth Maoláin* 'Fort of the bare hill', Waterford
 b. *Bally Moyle* < *Baile Maol*, 'Bare town' Wicklow, S. Leinster

These examples show that the /ɔj/ outcomes of *ao* are not unique to *McCoy*. They are however, the least likely to be found in Scotland. For instance, *McCoys* appear to be mostly found in Northern Ireland and the United States (Forbears, 2012–2016).

5.7 *MacKay*: /aj/ vs. /e/

One of the more prominent Anglicizations of *MacAoidh* is *MacKay*, also spelled *McKay* and sometimes *MacCay/McCay*. For this spelling, there are currently two pronunciations in use in the English speaking domain: either /aj/ or /e/ depending on the family. For example *MacKay*, Australia, named after John MacKay of Inverness, tends to be pronounced as /məkaj/, but some also argue for /məke/ (Mackay Historical Society 2012).²³ In contrast, the U.S. pronunciation tends to be /məke/ as in former American sportcaster Jim McKay /məke/ (actually born Jim McManus).

These differences appear to originate in Scotland itself where multiple *MacAoidh* families could be found (MacKay 1906: 4–5). In Section 5.3, this paper discussed the MacGhies /i/ of Balmaghie in Dumfries. Another prominent branch comes from the Strathnaver region of Northern Scotland where the Chief of Clan MacKay is Lord Reay (MacKay 1906: 35–236). In that region, the /aj/ pronunciation is found.²⁴ However MacKay (1906: 360–362) also mentions another branch

---

22 This /ɔj/ could be the result of a fission repair from an earlier mid central unrounded vowel such as /ʌː/. That is an original [+back, −round] vowel /ʌː/ could have been split into a [+back, +round] and [−back] segment.
23 My mother Constance McCay of Pennsylvania used /e/, but was told by a Scotswoman that /aj/ was correct in Scotland. However, a video from the Strathnaver Museum about MacKay Country uses [əj] with a Scottish accent (https://www.youtube.com/watch?v=CuhbdIPNPL0, 0:45) while James MacKay, Baron MacKay of Clasfern is referred to as /məkaj/ in RP British.
24 Another Scottish family name in which *ao* becomes English /aj/ is *MacIntyre* /mækɪntajər/ from Gaelic *Mac an tSaoir*. This name also becomes Anglicized as *Mac Ateer* /ətir/ in Ulster (Lysaught 1999: 8).

in the Kintyre peninsula and the island of Islay in Western Scotland, and in that family, *MacAoidh* may have been Anglicized with /e/, but perhaps also as McCoy with /oj/.²⁵

The Strathnaver region is located on the northern coast of Scotland where Scottish Gaelic *ao* is pronounced as /ɯː/. By 1415 and until the early 18th century, many documents mentioning the Strathnaver *MacAoidhs* used *McKy* with a high vowel (19). It was not until the early 18th century that the *Mackay* spelling was commonly used (19k–l).

(19) Strathnaver MacAoidhs (MacKay 1906: 375–451)
  a. 1415   *Y McKy*
  b. 1496   *Y McKy* of Straithnauer/ Odo (Aodh) *Mcky de Straithnauer*
             Bilingual Latin/Scots
  c. 1517   *Y Mckye*
  d. 1518   *Johnne McKy*
  e. 1548   *Y Makky de Far*
  f. 1608   *Hugo* (Hugh) *McKy Forbes* (via James VI court), Latin
  g. 1639   Letter signed by
             Jo Mky of Dilrett, William Macky of Bighouse,
             D. Reay /rei/ and *Jo. McKeay*
  h. 1655   *Hugh MacKey of Dilred*
  i. 1665   Letter signed by
             Ja. MacKay, William MacKy
  j. 1681   *Murdo MacKy* (Carnach)
  k. 1733   *James Mackay*
  l. 1745   *Hugh Mackay* of Reay Estate

Note further though that variations from the Highlands were used by the 17th century. For instance, one 1639 letter from the MacAoidh clans was signed by a *Mky of Dilrett*, a *Macky of Bighouse* and a *McKeay* (19g). Another mentions the *MacKeys of Dilred* (19h). In the Highlands, it seems that Anglicized forms remained in flux until more recent eras.

---

25 In MacKay's geneology, the Strathnaver *MacKays* becomes its own branch in the early 13th century, but posits that earlier generations were in Galloway, Scotland which is home to the *McGhies* (*MacAodha*). Thus these two families are sometimes considered connected but also distinct. MacKay (1906: 27) also connects the MacKays to an *Aéd*, Earl of Moray whose family was in opposition to that era's ruling family of Scotland.

One could posit that /aj/ is the result of the an early shift of *ao* to /iː/ which became /aj/ as the Great English Vowel Shift. Yet the different variations, even in the Highlands, suggest that /aj/ may be a direct outcome of Scottish Gaelic /ɯːj/. This is a repair similar to /ɯːj/ to /ɔːj/, but this repair to /aj/ features the only English phonemic [+back, −round vowel] (20).

(20) [ɯːj] to /aj/ Repair
      [−low] → [+low] /____j

Documents mentioning the Kintyre *MacAoidhs* tend to use different Anglicizations such as *M'Cay, M'Cei* and *McCay* which suggest an /e/ form (21). This region is also where the *McCoys* and other Scottish emigres to Ulster might have come from. That could explain the generalization that *MacKay* is pronounced as /e/ in areas such as the United States.

(21) Kintyre MacAoidh (MacKay 1906: 360–362, 370–418)
    a.   1329   Gilchrist MacYmar M'Cay
    b.   1408   Aodh M'Cei
    c.   1542   Ewir McCay Mor
    d.   1615   Donald M'Cay

Unlike *Hayes* and *O'Hea*, it appears unlikely that *MacKay* with /e/ represents a preservation of an original Scottish Gaelic /eː/. Based on the regional position between Ulster and the Highlands, I assume that this region also had a back unrounded vowel for *ao* – either high [ɯː] or mid [əː]. This is further confirmed by genealogies in which *MacKay* alternates with *McCoy*. If the Scottish Gaelic or Scots form had been /eː/, the Anglicization to *MacKay* /e/ would be expected to be more consistent.

The vowel though could be either /ɯː/ or the central /əː/ more common in southern Gaelic dialects.[26] A /əː/ could plausibly be repaired to /eː/ in a delinking rule of [+back] to [−back]. However the presence of /i/ Anglicized forms in Ulster (Magee) and Dumfries (Maghie) suggests that *ao* may have been /ɯː/ in Kintyre also. In that case, the /e/ could be the result of a negation repair changing a [+high, +back, −round] vowel to a [−high, −back, −round] vowel (22).

---

[26] East Sutherland Gaelic in northeastern Scotland is a Scottish Gaelic dialect with phonemic /əː/ instead of /ɯː/ (Dorian 1978).

(22) Possible paths to Anglicized *MacKay* with /e/
    a. Negation Repair of /ɯː/
       [+back, +high] → [−back, −high] / [____ −round]
    b. Delinking Repair of /əː/
       [+back] → [−back] / [____ −round]

In Calabrese's framework (2005: 279–299), the negation repair addresses a feature co-occurrence restriction *[αF, βG] with a repair that results in changing both values to the opposite (i.e. [−αF, −βG]). Although not very common, it can be found in different languages such as Okpe (changing *[+high, −ATR] */ɪ,ʊ/ to surface [−high, +ATR] /e,o/ vowels), Welsh in the historical merger of Middle Welsh /y/ ([−back, +round]) to central unrounded /ɨ/ ([+back, −round]) and other languages.

This is the final phonological outcome that will be discussed for the Anglicizations of the *Aodh* surname. However it should be mentioned that *ao* can result in a low vowel in English, particularly when it comes before a coronal sonorant. These include the name *Angus* /æŋɡəs/ from Old Irish *Oengus*, *Aonghus* (Irish/Scottish Gaelic), the Scottish name *Malcolm* /mælkəm/ from Middle Irish *Máel Coluim* 'follower of St. Columba' and the Irish family name Malone /malon/ from *(Ó) Maoileoin* 'follower of St. John' (MacLysaught 1999). These changes are rarely mentioned when discussing English borrowings with *ao*, but are worth a future investigation.

6 Middle Irish to Classical Gaelic

6.1 Summary of family name data

The phonological outcomes for the different Goedelic *Aodh* surname borrowings into English can generally be predicted from regional origins of the family (23).

(23) Summary of *Aodh* outcomes
    a. Munster/S. Leinster (*ao*=[eː])
       /e/: Hayes, O'Hea
    b. Ulster/Scotland (*ao*=[ɯː])
       /i/: Maghie, Magee, McKee, Mackie, Makky, MacKey (Ulster/Scotland)
       /u/: McCoo, McCue, Hughes (Ulster)
       /ɔj/: McCoy (Ulster)
       /aj/: MacKay (Highlands Scotland)
       /e/: MacKay (West Scotland, Ulster)

Families originating from the southern half of Ireland where *ao* is [e:] have outcomes with /e/ in English while families originating from Ulster and Scotland where *ao* is back unrounded /ɯ:/ or possibly /ə:/ have English surnames with variable vowels and diphthongs which can all be explained as repairs of back unrounded vowels (*[−back, −round, −low]). Similar patterns can be found for other family and place names in Ireland. Interestingly though there are family names with *ao* which do break the regional mold. One case is the southern Irish family *O'Keefe* /kif/ from original *Ó Caoimh* /ki:v/ with English /i/ instead of /e/.[27]

6.2 Old Irish diphthong merger

An issue not yet addressed in this paper is the exact mechanism deriving Old Irish /aj/ to a later Middle Irish mid vowel spelled *e* which becomes *ao* with the multiple dialectal variations. Within Old Irish, there was an initial merger of /oj/ (*ói/óe*) and /aj/ (*aé/aí*) (Thurneysen 1980: 42–43). Thurneysen gives an example of the *aos* 'people' (Modern Irish) being spelled in Old Irish as *aés/aís* (both spellings) and *óes/óis* in the same document. This suggests that the diphthong might have been phonetically a value in between [oj] and [aj] such as [ɒj] with a central low round vowel or perhaps even [əj] with a schwa which monophthongizes to [ə:].

6.3 Middle Irish monophthongization

Eventually this diphthong changes to a monophthongized mid vowel spelled *e* in most documents from the Middle Irish era. Similarly, Old Irish /aw/ *áu/áo* becomes monophthongized as /o:/ *ó* (Thurneysen 1980: 44) and other Old Irish vowel–vowel sequences simplify to monophthongs in Middle Irish (Breatnach 1994). That is, the change of *ói/óe*, *aé/aí* to *e* is part of a larger monophthongization process.

For attestation of Middle Irish *e* from Old Irish *ae*, a particularly relevant case comes from the Middle Irish document *Book of Deer* written in Scotland with the Middle Irish coming from approximately the 12th century. In that document, the *MacAodha* family name is attested as both *mac Éda* and *mac Æd*

---

[27] Since this family was politically prominent, It is possible that *O'Caoimh* was Anglicized early enough to go through the Great Vowel Shift. However, it is a testament to how a family name can diverge from more expected phonological outcomes.

(Jackson 1972: 30, 32). Additional examples of how the name was transcribed in the 12th–13th centuries are given below (24).

(24) Late Middle Irish attestations of *Aodh*
    a. 12th cent   Mac Éda, Mac Æd (Book of Deer)
    b. early 12th   Balmakethe (town)
    c. 1262   Eth (Pipe Rolls, O'Rahilly 1926)
    b. 1296   Gilmyhel Mac Eth del counte de Dunfres (*McGhee*)
    c. 1295   Roryry O Hethe (*O'Hea*)
    d. 1298–99   Thomas O Hethe (*O'Hea*)

In addition, borrowings of this vowel into other languages is usually spelled as *e*. Thurneysen (1980: 42) gives the example of *Melpatrekr* (< *Máil Patric* 'follower of Patrick' later the family name *Mulpatrick*) recorded in the Icelandic document *Landnámabók*. In French, *e* is also used for this sound as in *Leys/Leis* for the Irish place name *Laoighis*, *Of(f)elan* for the family name *Uí Faoláin (Phelan/Whelan)* (O'Rahilly 1926).[28] Additional examples from the Book of Deer with the historical *áe* diphthong are compiled in Jackson (1973: 133–134). They include *Mal-* 'follower of' (< *Máel*) as in *Mal-Brigte* 'follower of Brigid' as well as *Moilbrigte*. In addition, the Scottish title *mormaer* /mormajr/ is written as *mormaer, mormer* and *mormær*.

Based on evidence from the later languages, Jackson (1972: 133–134) and McManus (1994) propose that this mid vowel is not [e], but a "retracted" mid vowel which Jackson (1972: 133–134) identifies as "slightly rounded" [ɤ:] and McManus as [ə:]. The assumption is that *e* is the closest approximation of the sound that the scribes could find in the Western European Latin alphabet. It should be noted that some like O'Rahilly (1926) and Hickey (2011: 360) assume that this *e* is /e:/ which may be phonetically retracted to [e:-] because it comes after a velarized consonant. In this scenario, this vowel raises to a high vowel in some dialects and may become more extremely retracted as in [ɯ:] as in the Ulster/Scottish Gaelic dialects.

For this paper, I assume that the initial change is to a sound which is a mid unrounded vowel further back than /e:/ and a distinct phoneme. I transcribe this vowel as [ə:] but I would not rule it being as far back as a [ɤ:] or [ʌ:]. One reason to assume that [ə:] is different from [e:] in Middle Irish is that only [ə:] *ao* raises

---

28 Exceptions are some spellings of Irish words with *Mael/Maol*. Thurneysen mentions that Old English documents which spell the Scottish Gaelic name *Malcolm* as *Mælcolm*. O'Rahilly also cites French *Omalori* and *Malethin/Molethin* for *Ó Maoil Doraidh* and *Ó Maoil Sheachlainn*.

to a high vowel [ɯ:, i:] in the northern dialects. In contrast, Old Irish *é* [e:] does NOT become [i:] or [ɯ:] in the northern dialects, but remains as /e:/ or becomes some other sound (25).

(25) Sample outcomes of Old Irish *é*
    a. *én* [e:n] 'bird' (OI)   >   *éan* [e:n] (Ir), *eun* [e:n]~[ian] (SG) (**ín* /i:nʲ/)
    b. *cét* [kʲe:d] '100' (OI)   >   *céad* [kʲe:d] (Ir), *ceud* [kʲe:d]~[kʲiad] (SG)
    c. *féin* [fʲe:nʲ] 'self' (OI)   >   *féin* [fʲe:nʲ] (Ir), *fèin* [fʲe:nʲ] (SG)

Another argument for an original central vowel is the occasional diphthongization found in southern place names with *Maol* 'bare' such as *Rathmoylan* < *Ráth Maoláin* 'Fort of the bare hill', Waterford and *Bally Moyle* < *Baile Maol*, 'Bare town' Wicklow, S. Leinster. Per section 5.5, these changes are consistent with the repair of a phonetically central vowel rather than a phonetically front vowel.[29]

Although the monophthongization of /aj/ to /e:/ is seen in other languages like Late Latin, pre-Sanskrit Indic, and Koine Greek among others, the change to /ə:/ is less common. As a generalization back unrounded vowels are more marked so their formation is less expected. However, the merger of Old Irish /ai/ and /oi/ suggests that this diphthong was phonetically further back in comparison to the /aj/ of Latin and Sanskrit. Therefore the a change [ə:] preserves the backness of the original diphthong while changing the [+low] vowel to a [−low] vowel.

Once [ə:] is formed, I do assume that in the Southern dialects it is fronted to [e:–] and reanalyzed as a /e:/ in a similar type delinking repair seen in *MacK/e/y* (section 5.6) (26). In the northern dialects, I also assume that in many cases, the /ə:/ raises to a high vowel, either [ɯ:] or [ɨ] depending on the dialect, but in Connaught, this vowel is further fronted and reanalyzed as an /i:/.

(26) Devleopments of Middle Irish [ə:]
    1. [ə:] to [e:] (Southern Ireland)
        a. [ə:] to English [ɔj] in *Moyle* < *Maol* place names
        b. [ə:] to English [a] (particularly before coronal sonorants)
    2. [ə:] to [ɯ:], most Northern dialects.
        a. [ɯ:] to [i:] (Connaught)
        b. i.   [ɯ:] to English [u] (Ulster)
           ii.   [ɯ:j] to [u:j] to English [ɔj] (Ulster)
           iii.   [ɯ:] to English [i:] (Ulster/ W. Scotland)

---

[29] Thanks to an anonymous reviewer for this comment.

One variation not discussed is the occurrence of [əː] in some modern southern Scottish Gaelic dialects such as East Sutherland Gaelic. One possibility is that this represents a preservation of the original mid central vowel. However this dialect, although "southern" in comparison to other Scottish Gaelic dialects is still definitely within the Highlands, much further north than locations such as Dumfries suggesting that this /əː/ is a relatively recent repair of /ɯː/. Further research is needed to determine the origin of this vowel.

7 Sociolinguistic observations

This paper began with the observation that there is a relatively large number of phonological outcomes for the Irish and Scottish Gaelic surnames with the element *Aodh* in English, many of which can be derived from the back unrounded vowel of /ɯː/ found in several dialects of Irish and Scottish Gaelic. Others can be traced back to dialectal outcomes in Irish of a Middle Irish back unrounded central vowel /əː/ which were directly adapted into English. A common question in linguistics is whether all sound changes can be predicted or whether some may be the result of one or more equally possible repair outcomes which are normalized within a particular linguistic community as Calabrese (2005: 136–137) suggests.

Examining family names provides unique opportunities to observe phonological outcomes in English–Goedelic contact situations. Due to the cultural and political dominance of English there are relatively few loan words from any Goedelic language into Standard English despite centuries of contact with Ireland and Scotland. Similarly, there are comparatively fewer written records of dialectal forms of Goedelic, particularly in Scotland. On the other hand, there are larger numbers of Goedelic place name and personal/family names adapted into English that can be examined.

Family names in particular can be a window into how contact situations from region to region. Because the contact between the English/Scots communities and the Goedelic communities was so widespread, the grammars in contact would have changed in different communities. That is the grammar of Southern Irish would have been different from Scottish Gaelic, and similarly, the grammar of Scots in Lowlands Scots would have been different from any speaker from England, particularly from the capital of London in Southern England.

In some cases, outcomes of a family name may represent particularly small communities where an outcome could differ from the larger community norm. Consider that in Ulster (Northern Ireland), one can find *McGees* (/i/), *Kee* (/i/), *McKee* (/i/), *McCoys* (/ɔj/) and *McCays* (/e/) all living in the region. Some variations represent emigration from other Goedelic areas, but they also represent the idea that families can follow norms slightly different from others in the community. Although the repair patterns for the *Aodh* family names generally conform with expected regional norms, it is interesting to see the complexity of interactions within the Ulster and Western Scotland regional areas that could use additional investigation.

Doublet names in Scotland and Ireland are not unusual. In this paper we have encountered *Whelan/Phelan* from *Ó Faoláin* (MacLysaught 1972: 245–246), and *Mainey/Meaney/Mooney* from *Ó Maonaigh* from Ireland as well as *MacIntyre/Mac Ateer* from *Mac an tSaoir*, another pair from Scotland and Ireland (Woulfe 1923; MacLysaught 1999: 8). In other languages such as Spanish, one can find doublets such as *Hernandez/Fernandez*.

On a personal note, it is always amazing to see how modern political borders obscured past cultural connections. The linguistic data suggests that Western Scotland and Ulster had close connections at one point, but later events have placed the people there at cultural odds. It's clear to me now that the people of northern Scotland and Ireland had a connection in culture and language that has been lost, but perhaps could be found again.

References

Barber, Charles. 1997. *Early Modern English*. Edinburgh: Edinburgh University Press.
Baugh Albert C. & Thomas Cable. 2013. *A history of the English language*. London: Routledge.
Black, Anderson J. 1974. *Your Irish ancestors*. Secaucus, NJ: Castle Books.
Bosch, Anna S. 2010. Phonology in Modern Gaelic. In Moray Watson and Michelle Macleod (eds.), *The Edinburgh companion to the Gaelic language*, 262–282. Edinburgh: University of Edinburgh Press.
Borgstrøm, Carl H. 1940. *A linguistic survey of the Gaelic dialects of Scotland Vol 1: The dialects of the Outer Hebrides* Oslo: Oslo University Press.
Breatnach, Liam. 1994. An Mhean-Ghaeilge [Middle Irish]. In McKone, Kim R. *Stair na Gaeilge* [Story of Irish]. 221–261. Maig Nuad [Maynooth]: Roinn na Sean-Ghaeilge, Coláiste Phádraig. [Department of Old Irish, St. Patrick's College].
Broderick, George. 1993. Manx. In Martin J. Ball & James Fife. *The Celtic languages*, 228–287. London: Routledge.
Broun, Dauvit. 2004. Constantine II (d. 952). In David Dannadine, *Oxford dictionary of national biography, online edition*. Oxford: Oxford University Press. http://www.oxforddnb.com/view/article/6115. (accessed 19 December 2016)
Calabrese, Andrea. 2005. *Markedness and economy in a derivational model of phonology*. (Studies in Generative Grammar 80). Berlin & New York: Mouton de Gruyter.
Canny, Nicholas. 2008. Hugh O'Neill, second earl of Tyrone (c.1550–1616). In David Dannadine, *Oxford dictionary of national biography, online edition*. Oxford: Oxford University Press. http://www.oxforddnb.com/view/article/20775 (accessed 21 December 2016).

Christian Brothers. 1990. *New Irish grammar (English and Irish Edition)*. Dublin: C.J. Fallon.
Collins, John T. 1946. Genealogy of the the O'Hea family of South West Cork from ca 1295 AD. *Journal of the Cork Historical and Archaeological Society*. Vol. LI, No. 174. 97–107. https://durrushistory.wordpress.com/2014/08/16/the-kings-writ-runs-in-west-cork-from-1298-a-d-sheriff-in-cork-paid-36-15-4d-for-having-the-ings- peace-by-mathew-richard-thomas-barett-richard-son-of-william-barett-junior-basilia-barett-loc/ (accessed 22 December 2016).
Dorian, Nancy C. 1978. *East Sutherland Gaelic: the dialect of the Brora, Golspie, and Embo fishing communities*. Dublin: Dublin Institute for Advanced Studies.
Doughtie, Beatrice Mackey. 1957. *The Mackeys (variously spelled) and allied families*. Decatur, GA: Bowen Press. http://hdl.handle.net/2027/wu.89061966214 (accessed 28 December 2016).
Doyle, Aidan. 2015. *A history of the Irish language*. Oxford: Oxford University Press.
Fife, James. 1993. Introduction: Historical Aspects. In Martin J. Ball and James Fife. *The Celtic languages, 1–25*. London: Routledge.
Forbears. 2012–2016. *Forbears genealogy resources online*. http://forebears.co.uk (accessed 1–29 December 2016).
Gillies, William 1993. Scottish Gaelic. In Martin J. Ball and James Fife. *The Celtic languages*, 145–227. London: Routledge.
Good, Rebecca H. 1976. The McKays … In Warren for a long time. *The Winchester Evening Star*. Monday 5 July 1976. http://www.robertmackayclan.com/rmc/rmcmem/5jul1976.html (accessed 22 December 2016).
Hanks Patrick, Richard Coates & Peter McClure. 2017. *The Oxford dictionary of family names in Britain and Ireland,* first edition. Oxford: Oxford University Press. https://books.google.com/books?id=0AyDDQAAQBAJ&pg=PA1790&lpg=PA1790&dq=mccoy+macaoidh&source=bl&ots=iwxuSZFvQI&sig=TrqDWyH8U3jjLr5z2DPXGbjPdog&hl=en&sa=X&ved=0ahUKEwjwn-bvypXRAhVo2oMKHSgyAeoQ6AEIVjAI#v=onepage&q=mccoy%20macaoidh&f=false (accessed 27 December 2016).
Hanks, Patrick, Kate Hardcastle & Flavia Hodges. 2006. *A dictionary of first names, second edition*. Oxford: Oxford University Press. http://www.oxfordreference.com (accessed 11 July 2016).
Hickey, Raymond. 2011. *The dialects of Irish: Study of a changing landscape*. Berlin: Mouton de Gruyter.
Kelly, J.J. 1907. Episcopal succession in the diocese of Elphin during the Reformation period. *The Irish Ecclesiastical Record* 21 (XXI). 459–485.
Koch, John T. 2006. *Celtic culture: A historical encyclopedia, vol 1*. Santa Barbara: ABC–CLIO.
Jackson, Kenneth H. 1972. *The Gaelic notes in the book of deer*. Cambridge: Cambridge University Press.
Ladefoged, Peter & Alice Turk. 1998. Phonetic structures of Scottish Gaelic. *Journal of the International Phonetic Association* 28. 1–41.
Lewis, Henry & Holger Pedersen. 1989. *A concise comparative Celtic grammar, 3rd edition*. Göttingen: Vandenhoeck & Ruprecht.
Macafee, Caroline & A. J. Aitken. 2002. A history of Scots to 1700. *A dictionary of the older Scottish tongue online* vol. XII, xxix–clvii. http://www.dsl.ac.uk/about-scots/history-of-scots/ (accessed 25 December 2016).
MacBain, Alexander. 1982 [1911]. *An etymology dictionary of the Gaelic language*. Glasgow: Gairm. http://www.ceantar.org/Dicts/MB2/ (accessed 27 June 2017).

McCarthy, John J. & Alan Prince. 1995. Faithfulness and reduplicative identity. *University of Massachusetts Occasional Papers in Linguistics* 18. 249–384. Amherst, MA: GLSA Publications.

MacDonald, Iain G. 2013. *Clerics and clansmen: The Diocese of Argyll between the Twelfth and Sixteenth Centuries*. Leiden: Brill.

Mac Eoin, Gearóid. 1993. Irish. In Ball, Martin J. and James Fife. *The Celtic languages*, 101–144. London: Routledge.

Mac Gearailt, Uáitéar. 1992. The language of some late Middle Irish texts in the book of Leinster. *Studica Hibernica* 26. 167–216.

MacKay, Angus 1906. *The book of Mackay* Edinburgh: Norman MacLeod. http://hdl.handle.net/2027/hvd.32044090387168 (accessed 16 July 2016).

MacKay Historical Society and Museum. 2009–2012. Mac "Eye" or Mac "A". http://www.mackay-history.org/research/maceye/maceye_or_macka.html (accessed 29 December 2016).

MacKinnon, Kenneth. 1993. Scottish Gaelic today: social history and contemporary status. In Martin J. Ball & James Fife. *The Celtic languages*, 491–535. London: Routledge.

McKoy, Henry Bacon. 1955. *The McKoy family of North Carolina and other ancestors including Ancrum, Berry, Halling, Hasell and Usher*. Greenville, SC: Keys Printing Company. http://hdl.handle.net/2027/wu.89061966115 (accessed 28 December 2016).

MacLeod, Michelle. 2010. Language in society: 1800 to the modern day. In Moray Watson & Michelle MacLeod. *The Edinburgh companion to the Gaelic language*, 1–21. Edinburgh: The University of Edinburgh Press.

MacLysaught, Edward. 1972. *Irish families: their names, arms and origins*, 3rd edition. New York: Crown Publishers.

MacLysaught, Edward. 1999. *The surnames of Ireland*, 6th edition. Kildare: Irish Academic Press.

Maddieson, Ian. 1984. *Patterns of sounds*. Cambridge: Cambridge University Press.

Matheson, Robert E. 1894. *Special report on surnames in Ireland*. Dublin: Alexander Thom & Co, for Her Majesty's Stationery Office. https://archive.org/details/cu31924029805540 (accessed 21 December 2016).

McCone, Kim. 1994. *Stair na Gaeilge* [Story of Irish]. Maig Nuad [Maynooth]: Roinn na Sean-Ghaeilge, Coláiste Phádraig [Department of Old Irish, St. Patrick's College].

McCoy, Gordon. 1997. Protestant learners of Irish in Northern Ireland. In Aodán Mac Póilin, *The Irish language in Northern Ireland*, 131–170. Belfast: ULTACH Trust.

McCoy, Lycurgus. 1904. *William McCoy and his descendants; a genealogical history of the family of William McCoy, one of the Scotch families coming to America before the revolutionary war, who died in Kentucky about the year 1818. Also a history of the family of Alexander McCoy, a Scotchman who served through the revolutionary war, and died in Ohio in the year 1829*. Battle Creek, MI (self-published).

McManus, Damian. 1991. *A guide to Ogham*. Maynooth: An Sagart.

McManus, Damian. 1994. An Nua-Ghaeilge Chlasaiceah [Classical Gaelic]. In Kim R. McKone, *Stair na Gaeilge* [Story of Irish], 335–445. Maig Nuad [Maynooth]: Roinn na Sean-Ghaeilge, Coláiste Phádraig. [Department of Old Irish, St. Patrick's College].

McManus, Damian. 1996. Classical Modern Irish. In Kim R. McCone & Katharine Simms. *Progress in Medieval Irish studies*, 165–187. Maynooth: Department of Old Irish, St. Patrick's College.

M'Kie, Norman J. 1906. The M'Ghies of Balmaghie. *The Celtic Monthly* 14. 151–154.

Ní Chíosáin, Máire. 1991. *Topics in the phonology of Irish*. University of Massachusetts, Amherst, PhD dissertation.

Ní Chíosáin, Máire & Jaye Padgett. 2012. An acoustic and perceptual study of Connemara Irish palatalization. *Journal of the International Phonetic Association* 42(2). 171–191.

Nilsen, Kenneth E. 2010. A Ghàidhig an Canada: Scottish Gaelic in Canada. In Moray Watson & Michelle MacLeod, *The Edinburgh companion to the Gaelic Language,* 90–107. Edinburgh: The University of Edinburgh Press.

Northern Ireland Statistics and Research Agency. 2015. Census 2011: Knowledge of Irish: KS209NI (Settlement 2015). http://www.ninis2.nisra.gov.uk/public/PivotGrid.aspx?ds=6655&lh=74&yn=2011&sk=136 &sn=Census%202011&yearfilter=2037 (accessed 31 Dec 2016)

O'Brien, Kathleen M. 2000–2007. Masculine given names index of names: *Áed/Aodh.* in *Index of Names in Irish Annals.* http://medievalscotland.org/kmo/AnnalsIndex/Masculine/Aed.shtml (accessed 19 September 2016).

Ó Baoill, Colm. 2010. A history of Gaelic to 1800. In Moray Watson & Michelle MacLeod, *The Edinburgh companion to the Gaelic Language,* 1–21. Edinburgh: The University of Edinburgh Press.

Ó Dónail, Niall (ed.). 1977. *Foclóir Gaeilg–Béarla.* Dublin: An Gum.

Ó Maolalaigh, Roibeard. 2008. The Scotticisation of Gaelic: a reassessment of the language and orthography of the Gaelic notes in the Book of Deer. In Katharine Forsyth, *Studies on the Book of Deer*, 179–249. Dublin: Four Courts Press: Dublin.

O'Rahilly Thomas F. 1926. Notes on Middle–Irish pronunciation. *Hermathena* 20(44). 152–195.

O'Kane Willie. 1998. Surnames of County Monoghan. *Irish Roots Magazine* 2. 12–13.

Oxford University Press. 2016. † ad, n.1. *OED (Oxford English Dictionary Online.* December 2016. Oxford: Oxford University Press. http://www.oed.com.ezaccess.libraries.psu.edu/view/Entry/2047?rskey=gd08Gm&result=8&isAdvanced=false (accessed 19 December 2017).

Pyatt, Elizabeth J. 1997. *An integrated model of the syntax and phonology of Celtic mutation.* Harvard University Ph.D dissertation.

Royal Irish Academy. 2013. áed. In *eDIL (electronic dictionary of the Irish language).* http://www.dil.ie/613 (accessed 24 June 2017).

Shaw, James. 1892–3. Surnames of Kirkcudbrightshire. *The Transactions and Journal of Proceedings of the Dumfriesshire and Galloway Natural History & Antiquarian Society* 9. 45–53.

Shaw, John. 1968. L'Evolution de 'Vieil–Irlandais *ae, oe, ai, oi*' dans les dialectes gaeliques [The evolution of Old Irish *ae, oe, ai, oi*' in the Goedelic dialects.] *Études Celtiques* 12. 147–156.

Silke, John J. 2006. O'Donnell, Hugh, lord of Tyrconnell (1572–1602) In David Dannadine, *Oxford dictionary of national biography, online edition.* Oxford: Oxford University Press http://www.oxforddnb.com/view/article/20554 (accessed 21 December 2016).

Smith, Jeremy J. 1999. *Essentials of Early English.* London: Routledge.

Statistics Canada/Statistique Canada. 2015. 2011 Census of Canada: Topic–based tabulations, Detailed Mother Tongue http://www12.statcan.gc.ca/census-recensement/2011/dp-pd/tbt-tt/Rp-eng.cfm?TABID=4&LANG=E&A=R&APATH=3&DETAIL=0&DIM=0&FL=A&FREE=0 &GC=01&GL=-1&GID=1098735&GK=1&GRP=1&O=D&PID=103415&PRID=0&PTYPE=10195 5&S=0&SHOWALL=0&SUB=0&Temporal=2011&THEME=90&VID=0&VNAMEE=& VNAMEF=&D1=0&D2=0&D3=0&D4=0&D5=0&D6=0(accessed 21 December 2016).

Stifter, David. 2006. *Sengoidelc: Old Irish for beginners.* Syracuse: Syracuse University Press.

Thurneysen, Rudolf. 1944, 1990. *A grammar of Old Irish*. Dublin: Dublin Institute for Advanced Studies.
Welch, Robert 2000, 2003. *The concise Oxford companion to Irish literature*. Oxford: Oxford University Press.
Woulfe, Patrick 1923. *Sloinnte Gaedheal is Gall: Irish names and surnames* http://www.libraryireland.com/Names.php (accessed on 16 July 2016).

Part II: *Issues* in Morpho-Phonology

Jonathan David Bobaljik
Disharmony and decay
Itelmen vowel harmony in the 20th century

1 Introduction

The Chukotko-Kamchatkan (CK) languages have a characteristic dominant-recessive, bi-directional vowel-harmony process, in which both roots and affixes alternate: an underlying recessive vowel alternates with its dominant counterpart, if there is a dominant element elsewhere in the word. Itelmen [itl], whose status in the CK group is still debated, shows vowel alternations that appear to be the remnants of the standard CK harmony system, such as in (1):

(1) a. **isx**   **esx**-anke
     'father'   'father-DAT'
   b. k-**siŋ**-qzu-kne'n   **seŋ**-zo-z-in
     'PRT-fly-ASP-PRT.PL'   'fly-NDIR-PRES-3SG'

I have two goals in this paper. First, I will attempt to establish that a harmony system essentially of the CK sort was robustly active in Itelmen as recently as a century ago, drawing on an analysis of Itelmen texts collected at the beginning of the 20th century. In this, I concur with other authors who argue that the harmony system was all but lost over approximately three generations, remaining in vestigial form as a morphologized ablaut system affecting some (but by no means all) roots and affixes (Volodin, 1976; Asinovskij & Volodin, 1987).[1]

The second goal is to ask why the harmony system collapsed in such a short span of time. In keeping with current events, I blame Russian influence. Specifically, I suggest that the sudden and drastic decline of harmony was a result of language contact – an influx of disharmonic loanwords, primarily from Russian (although also possibly from neighbouring Koryak *a*-dialects). More narrowly, I

---

[1] The system attested in 1910 was very similar to the general CK pattern, but is not identical, notably, as Volodin stresses, in the apparent absence of *e~a* alternations in verbal roots. The question of the origin of the system is therefore related to the question of whether Itelmen is a divergent member of the CK family, or a distinct language whose many shared grammatical properties are the result of extended language contact (the latter is the view held by Volodin). While I tend towards an account of the similarities in terms of a common ancestor, the focus of this paper is an understanding of the change in Itelmen across the 20th century, for which the question of the original (pre-1910) nature and source of the Itelmen harmony system does not need to be resolved.

report here on a preliminary attempt to characterize this effect quantitatively, comparing texts collected by W. Jochelson in 1910–1911 (Worth, 1961) to texts collected in 1993–1994, and making use of the general approach to rule learnability proposed in Yang (2016). The leading idea is as follows: the learner of Itelmen (or of any CK language) is faced with vowel alternations in some, but not all morphemes, and must decide whether these alternations are governed by a general phonological rule, or are simply listed variants (equivalently, the output of 'minor' phonological rules) that must be learned as such and listed as lexically-specific alternations. For Itelmen, any rule that is to be posited will have some number of exceptions. Yang's approach offers a formula for calculating the robustness of any given phonological rule, a measure of the proportion of exceptions in a corpus with some quantifiable number of opportunities for the rule to apply. Yang posits a specific threshold which constitutes the number of exceptions to a given rule that can be tolerated while still maintaining a productive grammatical rule. With some (I hope plausible) assumptions about how to calculate this for Itelmen vowel harmony, I demonstrate here over a preliminary sample that the number of harmony exceptions falls below Yang's Threshold in 1910, but vastly exceeds the threshold by 1994. Over that time period, the number of Russian loans in Itelmen texts increased substantially, plausibly to a sufficient extent to have rendered the harmony rule unlearnable.

Before discussing the quantitative evidence, I first introduce the standard Chukotkan harmony pattern. I then provide a close analysis of a sample of the texts collected by W. Jochelson in 1910–1911. While there is clear evidence of vowel alternations in these texts, there are also significant numbers of apparently disharmonic forms. When examined more carefully, many of the apparent exceptions in the old texts are best seen as artifacts of the transcription used in that source. Once idiosyncracies of transcription are controlled for, the vowel harmony rule turns out to be learnable, under Yang's formula, in the 1910 texts. Applying the same criteria to a text collected in the 1990s, we find that the vowel harmony system had become unlearnable by that time, consistent with the main hypothesis that Itelmen has indeed lost (productive) vowel harmony.

2 Vowel harmony in Chukotko-Kamchatkan

Itelmen constitutes the Kamchatkan branch of the Chukotko-Kamchatkan family. Three hundred years ago, at the time of first European contact, there were (at least) three distinct Itelmen languages, together spoken by somewhere between 10–25,000 speakers across the southern half of the Kamchatka peninsula (Volodin, 2003, 27). By the early 20th century, the Itelmen-speaking population had been decimated, with only the Western Itelmen language spoken in two dialect groups covering eight villages on the Okhotsk coast. As of 2017, the language is spoken natively and fluidly by fewer than five elderly members of the community. The Chukotkan branch of the family includes Chukchi, Koryak, Kerek and Alutor, the former two comprising multiple dialects and having a few thousand native speakers.

Of interest in this paper is the vowel harmony system, shared in one form or another by most of the modern languages and therefore generally reconstructed for the proto-language (Muravyova, 1979; Fortescue, 2005). The system is a dominant-recessive system. The Proto-Chukotkan vowel inventory is reconstructed as in (2), see (Muravyova, 1979; Fortescue, 2005), with some variation among authors regarding specifics of vowel quality.

(2) Proto-Chukotkan vowel inventory

recessive	i	u	ε
dominant	e	o	a
transparent	ə		

Non-schwa vowels in a morpheme, and indeed in a word, will be either all dominant, or all recessive (schwa, whether underlying or epenthetic, may occur with either set). Dominant vowels undergo no alternations, but recessive vowels change to their corresponding dominant counterparts if any morpheme in the same word has dominant vowels. Kenstowicz (1979) suggests that this may be an ATR harmony system, that is spreading of [-ATR] (i.e., root retraction), although various questions (especially of phonetic detail) are left unresolved (see in particular Krause, 1979; Calabrese, 1988 for discussion). I take no stand here on the actual feature involved and simply use a diacritic [±D] as a stand-in for whatever phonological feature turns out to be accurate. Thus, the following loose characterization of the vowel harmony rule will suffice for the purposes of this paper:

(3) $V^{[-D]} \rightarrow V^{[+D]} / [\:\{... \_, (V)^{[+D]} ...\}\:]_\omega$

2.1 Vowel harmony in Chukchi: the ideal pattern

The Chukchi vowel harmony system, well discussed in the literature (Bogoras, 1922; Skorik, 1961; Krause, 1979; Kenstowicz, 1979; Calabrese, 1988; Dunn, 1999), presents a fairly conservative example which thus serves as a convenient point of departure to illustrate (3).

The Chukchi vowel inventory is given in (4). The vowels are divided into three pairs, each pair having a recessive and dominant member. The ambivalent status of *e* will be discussed shortly. In addition, there is a schwa, which is normally (but not always, see below) neutral and transparent to vowel harmony, undergoing no change in harmony contexts but not blocking the application of harmony across it.

(4)   Chukchi vowel inventory

recessive	i	u	e_1
dominant	e_2	o	a
transparent		ə	

Other than schwa, a given Chukchi word normally contains only dominant or only recessive vowels. A dominant vowel in any morpheme causes all recessive vowels elsewhere in the word to be replaced by their dominant counterparts, as dictated by (3).

The examples in (5) show the alternation in affix vowels, controlled by the root. Affixes with a recessive vowel surface as such with recessive roots, but the dominant alternants are used with roots containing dominant vowels.

(5)   Root controls affix (prefix and suffix)

-(n)u DESIG   recessive: /milute/ 'rabbit'   milute-**nu**
                               /tutlik/ 'snipe'   tutlik-**u**
                   dominant: /wopqa/ 'moose'   wopqa-**no**
                               /orw/ 'sled'   orw-**o**

(ɣ(e))-...-(t)e INSTR recessive: /milute/ 'rabbit'   **ɣe**-milute-**te**
                                   /kupre/ 'net'   **ɣe**-kupre-**te**
                       dominant: /wala/ 'knife'   wala-**ta**
                                   /rərka/ 'knife'   **ɣa**-rərka-**ta**

The inverse pattern is shown in (6). Here, the roots alternate, surfacing with dominant vowels when the affix contains a dominant vowel, and with recessive vowels otherwise.[2]

---

[2] It has been claimed that there are quite generally no dominant prefixes in vowel harmony systems (see e.g., Baković, 2000, 228; see Moskal, 2015 for exceptions and discussion). Bogoras (1922) and (Skorik, 1977, 325) both claim that there are dominant prefixes in Chukchi. However I suspect that the items they identify are independent roots, suggesting an analysis of these forms as root-root compounds, rather than prefixes. The comitative in (6) is (descriptively)

(6) Affix controls root ROOT   ABS   COMITATIVE /ɣ(a)-...-ma/
                         /milute/ 'rabbit' milute-t ɣa-**melota**-ma
                         /titi/ 'needle'   titi-ŋə   ɣa-**tete**-ma
                         /rʔew/ 'whale'   rʔew   ɣa-**rʔaw**-ma
                         /ləle/ 'eye'   ləle-t   ɣa-**lola**-ma

Showing a typologically rare pattern, compounding (incorporation) structures show vowel harmony applying in combinations of two roots, with a dominant vowel in one root triggering lowering of a recessive vowel in another, regardless of direction (7):

(7) Root-Root interaction (incorporation)
    ROOT   PREDICATE FORM   INCORPORATED   ROOT 2 GLOSS
    /teŋ/ 'good'   nə-teŋ-qin   **taŋ**-kawkaw   /kawkaw/ 'zwieback'
                                       taŋ-čotčot   /čotčot/ 'pillow'
    /om/ 'warm'   n-om-qen   om-**peŋpeŋ**   /piŋpiŋ/ 'ash'

2.2 Morphologization of harmony

Although the discussion above represents the basic Chukotkan system, there are a few respects in which the actual surface system of Chukchi deviates from the idealized system just outlined.

First, as noted in (4), there are two phonologically distinct /e/ vowels, one dominant, the other recessive. Recessive /e/ undergoes harmony and becomes [a], as shown in (8a), where the trigger is the comitative circumfix seen in (6). By contrast, the word for 'road' has a dominant /e/ which undergoes no alternation but itself triggers the alternation, in this case forcing an alternation on the incorporated adjective (just as in (7) above):

(8) a. /rʔew/ 'whale' → ɣa-**rʔaw**-ma COMITATIVE
    b. /rʔet/ 'road' → **taŋ**-rʔet 'good road'

---

circumfixal, and appears to contain a dominant vowel in the prefixal portion. The prefixal portion can instead be analyzed as the same (recessive) element as in the instrumental ɣ(e)-...-(t)e in (5). The trigger for harmony on this view would be the dominant vowel in the suffix, -ma.

While distinct in terms of their phonological behaviour, there are conflicting views in the literature as to whether dominant and recessive /e/ are phonetically distinct. Bogoras (1922), Skorik (1961, 22ff), and Asinovskij & Volodin (1987) report that the two /e/ vowels are distinct, while Mel'nikov (1948, 209), Fortescue (1998, 128), Dunn (1999) dispute this; for example, Dunn (1999, 48) states unequivocally: "there is no phonetic difference between" dominant and recessive [e].[3] It may well be the case that the system requires diacritic marking of two distinct underlying /e/ vowels, as in (4).

A diacritic is needed in Chukchi in any event (and indeed in all Chukotko-Kamchatkan languages with vowel harmony) to account for morphemes that contain no full vowels and have only schwa (whether epenthetic or underlying) or no vowel at all. Some of these trigger harmony as if they contained a dominant vowel, while others do not (Krause, 1979, 13–14; Muravyova, 1979, 138–141). For example, the affixes in (9) have only schwa or no vowel at all, but trigger harmony alternations in the roots they attach to:

(9)		AFFIX	ROOT	SUFFIXED FORM
	a.	-ɣtə	/milute/	**melota**-ɣtə 'to the rabbit'
	b.	-jpə	/titi/	**tete**-jpə 'from the needle'
	c.	-tk-	/utt/	**ott**-ə-tk-ən 'crown of a tree'
	d.	-lɣən	/milute/	**melota**-l-ɣ-ən 'rabbit (singulative)'

Further contrasting pairs with schwa-containing roots are given in (10). In each pair, the first member fails to trigger harmony on a recessive suffix, while the second member triggers harmony on the same suffix.

(10)	a.		GLOSS	ROOT	INFINITIVE
		i.	sleep	/jəlq/	jəlq-**et**-ək
		ii.	dark	/pəlm/	pəlm-**at**-ək
	b.		GLOSS	ROOT	ADJECTIVE
		i.	old	/ənpə/	n-ənpə-**qin**
		ii.	dark	/pəlm/	nə-pəlm-**qen**

---

[3] A related question is whether the vowels that are the output of the harmony rule are phonetically the same as underlyingly dominant vowels. Here too, reports diverge, with Skorik (1961) claiming that the derived dominant vowels are phonetically distinct from underlyingly dominant ones, and Bogoras (1922) and Dunn (1999) disagreeing. Calabrese (1988) sees the conflicting descriptions as evidence of dialect differences. The issue is clearly relevant to the proper understanding of the rule in (3). See also Kenstowicz (1979) and Krause (1979).

Examples of purely consonantal roots (i.e., roots with no underlying vowel at all) are given in (11). Those in group a. fail to trigger harmony, while those in group b. trigger vowel harmony, illustrated with the preterite circumfix.

(11)
     ROOT PRETERITE GLOSS
 a. i. /ŋt/ ɣe-nt-ə-**lin** 'he has cut off'
  ii. /rɣ/ ɣe-rɣ-ə-**lin** 'he has dug, scratched'
 b. i. /tm/ ɣa-nm-ə-**len** 'he has killed'
  ii. /tw/ ɣa-tw-ə-**len** 'he has said'
  iii. /rw/ ɣa-rw-ə-**len** 'he has split'

Calabrese (1988) proposes that Chukchi may treat [-ATR] (i.e., [+D]) as a (diacritic) property of morphemes and not of vowels as such, interpreting (3) as applying at the morpheme tier, rather than the vowel tier. On this view, Chukchi would have only three full vowels underlyingly (rather than the three pairs in (4)), which undergo alternations according to whether they occur in a [+ATR] or [-ATR] environment. The morphological diacritic approach, of course, deals with the facts in (9)–(11) quite readily (compare the root markers of Lightner, 1965 and related work).

Whether we adopt such a proposal or not, what is important is that the evidence in (9)–(11) shows that diacritic marking is needed – the vowel harmony system is not entirely phonologically transparent. Nevertheless, it is internally consistent: the diacritic value of a morpheme cannot conflict with the value of the vowels in a word, yielding disharmonic words. Morphemes containing {i,u} are unambiguously recessive and will always undergo harmony alternations. Morphemes containing {a,o} are unambiguously dominant and will trigger harmony alternations on recessive morphemes. Morphemes containing only e and/or schwa or no vowels at all are ambiguous, and require diacritic marking (though the former may in fact be phonetically distinguished in some dialects).[4]

---

[4] There are two instances where apparent surface disharmony is tolerated, both noted in Krause (1979). In the vocative only, a stressed schwa may be pronounced [o], with this pronunciation having no effect on harmony, see (i). There is also an optional rule rounding schwa to [u] before /w/. This segment may occur in a dominant environment and does not undergo a further change to [o]; see (ii). The existence of these forms is not widely commented on in the literature, but is potentially relevant to the question of how tolerant a productive rule may be to surface exceptions, taken up later in this paper.
i. ə́ → ó : túmɣ-ət 'friend-PL' vs. tumɣ-ót 'O friends!' (Krause, 1979, 59)
ii. ə → u / _w : ətləwjot ~ ətluwjot 'grandchildren' (Krause, 1979, 116)

2.3 Postscript: the rest of Chukotkan

South of Chukchi, the vowel harmony patterns are less pristine, a fact that is relevant since Itelmen has been in extended contact with Koryak, rather than Chukchi. In some Koryak and Alutor dialects, recessive *e* (<*ɛ) and (dominant) *a* have partially merged (Stebnickij, 1934; Muravyova, 1979, cf. Bogoras, 1917, 1922). This has led to a curious two-part harmony system, as described by Muravyova (1979); Abramovitz (2015): merged *a* may be described as 'weakly dominant'; it does not affect recessive vowels {*i,u*}, allowing for words that have both *a* and *i* on the surface. However, weakly dominant *a* does trigger a limited harmony rule changing recessive *e* to *a*. The examples in (12) illustrate: *a*-dialect *kali* 'write' corresponds to Chukchi *keli*. In the (a) example, /e/ lowers to [a] under the influence of the weakly dominant /a/ in *kali*, but the /i/ remains unaffected. Addition of a truly dominant morpheme, such as -*jo* in (12b) lowers the /i/ to [e]. More curiously, just as a morpheme with no dominant vowels may be diacritically marked as dominant, so too may morphemes with no dominant vowels be diacritically specified as weakly dominant, as in (12c) from (Muravyova, 1979, 148), and confirmed by Rafael Abramovitz (pc and Abramovitz, 2015):

(12) a. /kali/ 'write' + -te   kali-**ta**
     b. /kali/ 'write' + -jo + -te   **kale**-jo-**ta**
     c. /quqlu/ 'make a hole' + ɣe-....-lin   **ɣa**-quqlu-lin

Muravyova (1979) notes that some dialects with the *e/a*-merger have gone even further. According to her description, Vyvenka Alutor has seen a merger of all dominant-recessive pairs, and has been reorganized as having a simple three-vowel inventory *i-u-a* with no harmony (but an innovative length contrast in the initial syllables).

3 Itelmen: quantifying the decay of a rule

In broad strokes, Itelmen is like Chukchi in the phonological aspects that are relevant to the current discussion. The basic vowel inventory is the same as that in Chukchi, as given in (13) (see also Volodin, 1976, 43).[5]

---

[5] Volodin does not recognize schwa as a phoneme, suggesting that many instances of schwa are epenthetic (on which see also Bobaljik, 1998), while the remainder are highly reduced instances of other vowel phonemes, particularly in closed syllables with consonant clusters. Volodin's orthography contrasts reduced and full vowels, but he explicitly treats only the full vowels as pho-

(13) Itelmen vowel inventory

recessive	i	u	e_1
dominant	e_2	o	a
transparent		ə	

Likewise, in terms of the alternations attested, Itelmen vowel harmony conforms to the Chukotko-Kamchatkan type: recessive vowels become their dominant counterparts in words with dominant vowels.[6] The question that will occupy the remainder of this paper is a difference not in the phonological aspects of the vowel harmony process in Itelmen, but rather its pervasiveness in Itelmen grammar, and the striking change in the robustness with which alternations and exceptions are attested in materials over the course of three generations from 1910–1994.

The hypothesis I advance here is that Itelmen vowel harmony was (essentially) a productive process at the start of the 20th century and was effectively lost by the century's end. Qualitatively, this is relatively uncontroversial. Among the limited group of scholars who have considered the matter, there is a general consensus that Itelmen had a productive set of vowel harmony alternations, noted by Bogoras (1922) and visible in the texts recorded in 1910–1911, and that the contemporary language has a few alternating forms, but far less than it had a century ago. Writing about material he collected in the 1960s and 1970s, the preeminent Itelmen scholar A.P. Volodin already noted that the vowel harmony system (then still productive in nominal morphology) was losing ground in the verb:

> Harmony is most inconsistently maintained in the finite verb. If the cases with the affixes -a(ł) (which never controls [harmony]) and -(xk)miŋ (which never undergoes [harmony]) are put aside, it should be established that even the affixes represented by harmonic variants -kičen ~ -kečan, -kinen ~ -kenan et al. obey the demands of harmony in comparatively rare cases. Most often, the alternation does not take place: tmaʔłkičen 'I played' (should have been: tmaʔłkečan), tk'ołkičen 'I came' (should have been: tk'ołkečan), etc. The examples given above of harmonically regular verb forms look rather like exceptions. (Volodin, 1976, 46)

---

nemes. Bogoras (1922) gives an inventory with 22 vowels, although his contemporary Jochelson recognizes only 5; on which see below.
6 Although there are also some i~a alternations (Volodin, 1976, 43), as noted in n. 12 below.

Nevertheless, despite the substantial agreement on the broad pattern, the more interesting question I wish to pursue here is whether a quantitative evaluation can shed any light on the change, in particular, whether the type of approach to productivity pursued by Yang would show a critical change over this period. This section presents a preliminary investigation along these lines.

Note that the material from both periods (Jochelson's texts from 1910–1911, and mine from 1993–1996) have a mix of harmony-consistent alternating forms, and apparently disharmonic failures to alternate.

3.1 Contemporary Itelmen: 1993–1996

In the contemporary material, examples such as (14) and (15) show expected alternations. In (14), independently established recessive vowels *(i,u,e)* in roots change to their dominant counterparts *(e,o,a)* in the presence of a dominant suffix.

(14)
ROOT	HARMONY FORM	GLOSS	SOURCE
ki(j)	**ke**-xʔal	river-ABLATIVE	A13
isx	**esx**-anke	father-DATIVE	MimKp:2
kist	**kest**-ank	house-DATIVE	Tilval:3
kuke-	(x)an-**koka**-zo-nen	3.IRR-cook-ITER-3>3SG	SP 47

In (15), we see the same alternation in an affix, triggered by a dominant root[7]:

(15)
AFFIX	ALTERNATING FORMS	GLOSS	SOURCE
-enk	isx-**enk**	father-LOCATIVE	Tilval:2
	laχsχ-**ank**	mother-LOCATIVE	Tilval:2

Yet alongside these alternations, most affixes with recessive vowels fail to alternate:

---

7 The locative suffix *-enk~-ank* is recessive across Itelmen dialects. The related dative suffix is dominant wherever harmony-like alternations are attested. In the Khairjuzovo-Kovran dialect cluster, the dative is *-(an)ke*, as in *esx-anke* in (14). In the Sedanka-Tigil dialect group, the dative surfaces as *-(an)k* (e.g., *kest-ank*) thus creating a minimal pair with the locative in terms of their dominant/recessive behaviour. In Sedanka-Tigil, the dative also surfaces as diacritically dominant *-ŋ* (a borrowing from Koryak) or as *-ankəŋ*, combining the Itelmen and Koryak endings.

(16) AFFIX W/ DOMINANT ROOT   GLOSS   SOURCE
     -qzu   k-čača-**qzu**-knen PRT-cry-ASP-PRT   AS:1
     -βum   q-oms-**qzu**-βum-sx 2.IRR-leave-ASP-1.OBJ-2PL AS:1
     -in   k'oɬ-**in**   come-3SG   S3:3
     -kičen n-alχt-**kiče?n**   1PL-spend.day-1PL   RasDan:50
     -kiɬχ elβant-zo-**kiɬχ**   fish-ITER-NML   SP 22

Likewise, most affixes with dominant vowels fail to trigger harmony:

(17) AFFIX W/ RECESSIVE ROOT   GLOSS   SOURCE
     -kaq   **siŋ**-kaq   fly-NEG.PRT AS:1
     -aɬ   **qetit**-aɬ-sx   freeze-FUT-2PL AS:1
     -čaχ   **jimsx**-čaχ   woman-DIM   Tilval:1
     -laχ   **ulʲu**-lʲaχ   little-ADJ   Tilval:1

Some roots fail to harmonize, even with affixes which do trigger alternations on other roots:

(18) esxɬin **esxɬin**-x?al   place.name-ABLATIVE Tn:40
     kist   % **kist**-anke   house-DATIVE   (variation)

And there are numerous internally disharmonic morphemes:

(19) zlatumx   sibling
     muza, tuza   1PL, 2PL PRON
     sinaŋewt, qusɬnaqu   names (mythical figures) < Kor.
     niqa   quick(ly) < Kor. ?
     oxotiɬ-   hunt < Russian

3.2 Itelmen in 1910

At first blush, a similar ambivalence characterizes Jochelson's material, and to some extent that collected by Jochelson's contemporary, Waldemar Bogoras.[8]

---

[8] Bogoras (1922) specifically reports that the C-K vowel harmony system affects "almost all the vowels" (678) in Itelmen, yet his own examples include forms that appear to be disharmonic (even on the same page where he asserts vowel harmony applies), such as *k'ölkmin* 'he has come' (678), *tsünülotıjk* 'I live in the woods' (679), etc. (*i,ü* recessive, *o,ö* dominant). In contrast to Jochelson's 5-vowel orthography, Bogoras gave 22 vowels for Itelmen.

The examples in this section are presented in Jochelson's orthography, which raises various issues to which we return below.

Examples such as (20) and (21) show expected alternations. In (20), independently established recessive vowels *(i,u)* in roots change to their dominant counterparts *(e,o)* in the presence of a dominant suffix.

(20)　isx 'father'　　**isx**-enk (LOC)　**esx**-anke (DAT)　　　　　K2.1
　　　kuke-'cook'　**kuke**-ki (INFIN)　**koke**-zo-xc (ITER-IMP)[9]　K2.27, 38

In (21), we see the same alternations in affixes, triggered by a dominant root:

(21)　-enk LOC　　　　　isx-**enk**　　　　stó-al-**ank**　　　K2.1, 5
　　　　　　　　　　　　　　　　　　　　xonograf-**ank**　　K2.3
　　　-lax ADJ[10]　　　cíneŋ-**lex**　　　caca-**lax**　　　K2.10, 35
　　　　　　　　　　　íw-**lex**　　　　ás-**lax**　　　　K2.11, 4
　　　-(g)in 3SUBJ　　 íɬ-**gin**　　　　ɬale-z-**en**　　　K2.2, 5
　　　-kicen 1SUBJ　　t-pilgetí-z-**kicen**　t-són-**kecan**　K2.1, 2
　　　　　　　　　　　n-ɬxi-**kicen**　　n-ánta-**kecan**　K2.3

While it appears that far more affixes undergo harmony in 1910 than in 1993, even in the older material, some affixes with recessive vowels apparently fail to undergo harmony:

(22)　AFFIX　W/ DOMINANT　　　　GLOSS　　　　　　　　　　SOURCE
　　　　　　ROOT
　　　-ŋin　　hán-txal-**ŋin**　　　　　3.IRR-eat-3PL(>3)　　　　K2.1
　　　-in　　k-tifsa-xk-**in**　　　　　CND-raise-II->2SG　　　　K2.1
　　　-min-　txál-a-s-**min**-sx　　　　eat-DESID-PRES-1OBJ-2PL.　K2.4
　　　　　　　　　　　　　　　　　　　SUBJ

And some affixes with strong vowels fail to trigger harmony:

---

[9] Note that *e* seems not to alternate here; compare to the corresponding contemporary example above.
[10] Volodin doubts that this affix alternated in Jochelson's time, despite these forms. See Volodin (1976, 76 n.25).

(23)	AFFIX	W/ RECESSIVE ROOT	GLOSS	SOURCE
	-ał	**čki**-ał-**ki**	find-FUT-INFIN	K2.39
		cf. **čke**-kaz	find-INFIN	K2.22 etc.
				(-kaz dominant)
		nú-ał-keq	eat-FUT-NEG	K2.23
		ił-ał-c	go-FUT-2SG	K2.5
	-maŋ	q-**téfsi**-xk-maŋ	IMP-raise-II->1SG	K2.1

Some roots fail to harmonize, even with affixes which do trigger alternations on other roots (cf. (20))[11]:

(24) lexsx **lexsx**-anke mother-DATIVE K2.1, 9

And there are numerous internally disharmonic morphemes:

(25) silatumx   older sister
      muza, tuza   1PL, 2PL PRON
      sinaŋewt, kuskłíaqu names (mythical figures)
      qula   other
      mozit   is.able < Russian

3.3 The Jochelson-Danilov orthography

The examples above were presented in the previous section in the transcription used in Jochelson's material (Worth, 1961, 1969), about which a number of remarks are in order before we proceed to a count.

The Jochelson collection comprises 41 texts of varying length (conventionally numbered K2.1, K2.2, etc.), in total 277 pages (including translations) in the published version (Worth, 1969), collected in Kamchatka in 1910–1911. The majority are from the southern (Khairjuzovo) dialect, with a few from the northern (Sedanka) variety. There are hints that the texts were transcribed by a native Itelmen speaker working as a guide and assistant to Jochelson, probably one A.M. Danilov (see Bobaljik & Koester, 1999). Worth (1969) compiled a dictionary from the texts, which serves also as a partial concordance, listing all distinct wordforms. The dictionary, including headwords and examples, has 4,285 wordforms

---

[11] The vowel in *lexsx* is not dominant, cf. vocative *lexsx-e* rather than *lexsx-a* and discussion at (38) below.

(tokens). Of these, 861 (20%) are on the face of it violations of vowel harmony, containing at least one unambiguously dominant vowel {o,a} and at least one unambiguously recessive vowel {i,u}. (Since e may be either dominant or recessive, it was excluded from this count.)

Closer scrutiny of the texts shows that it would be misleading to conclude that this represents the actual number of disharmonic forms, for a few reasons.

Notably, more than 40% of these exceptions (371 of the 861 exceptions) involve an *a* between a uvular and a sonorant (including /z/), in a word with otherwise recessive vowels, as in the following:

(26) a. ksunɬqazúknen
 b. qazíɬqazuknen
 c. kúneŋtqazuknen
 d. kkelqazúknen

The "a" here is undoubtedly excrescent: a brief, but audible release of the uvular stop before the following voiced segment. Contemporary transcriptions, such as Volodin (1976) and my own notes, do not indicate this as a vowel, and it is not consciously perceived by speakers as such (although it is still audible as a transitory element). Contemporary transcriptions corresponding to (26a-b) are given in (27).

(27) a. k-sunɬ-qazú-knen   Jochelson
 k-sunɬ-qzu-knen   Contemporary
 PRT-live-ASP-PRT
 'He lived.'
 b. qazíɬ-qazu-knen   Jochelson
 [k]-qziɬ-qzu-knen   Contemporary
 PRT-get.ready-ASP-PRT
 'He got ready.'

In this context, it is worth noting that Jochelson (or Danilov) frequently indicates an accent on the vowel immediately following this excrescent vowel, as in three of the four examples above. There is no interpretation of stress in Itelmen for which this would make sense, but we can presumably understand it as indicating the relative perceptual contrast between an excrescent and adjacent full vowel.

Many of the excrescent vowels, as in the examples in (26), appear in the aspectual morpheme /-qzu-/. In the 1910 texts, this morpheme behaves regularly as concerns vowel harmony, if one ignores the excrescent vowel, alternating between -*qazu*- and -*qazo*-, as in (28). These examples all show vowel harmony behaving as expected not just with the aspectual morpheme, but with subsequent inflectional suffixes as well, once the excrescent *a* is factored out.[12]

(28) RECESSIVE ROOT   DOMINANT ROOT
    k-sunɬ-**qazú-knen**   k-wetat-**qazó-knan**
    k-txzi-**qazú-knen**   k-xaimanto-**qazó-knan**
    min-sxezí-**qazu**-sx   k-swatał-**qazó-knan**
    k-tmpɬ-**qazú-in**   k-tpal-zo-**qazo-án**

Two other characteristics of the transcription scheme result in apparent disharmony, where there probably was none. Many examples of orthographic "i" in 1910, especially those adjacent to another vowel, are undoubtedly glides /j/, and thus not subject to the harmony process:

(29) Jochelson: a(y)iwa   káitatān   csalai   brawoi
    contemporary: aʔjuβʔaj   k'-ajtat-an   tsal-aj   braβ-oj
                brains   herded   fox-AUG   good < Russian

In addition, Jochelson-Danilov uses a five-vowel transcription system. Many vowels written with full vowel characters in 1910 correspond to schwa in the contemporary language, which has (at least) five full vowels plus schwa.[13] Some examples are given in (30):

(30) Jochelson: ína   kima   kantxigaan
    Contemporary (S): ənna   kəmma   k-əntxa-(ʔ)an[14]
                        3SG.PRON 1SG.PRON PRT-forget-TR.PRT

It is implausible that the discrepancy represents a change – reduction from full vowels to schwa – over the last century. Schwa is a prominent part of the vowel inventory in all of the Chukotko-Kamchatkan languages, and for some of the items

---

12 The "i" in *xaimanto-* is a glide, not subject to harmony; see below. In general, harmony alternations in Chukotko-Kamchatkan pair *i~e* or *e~a*. There is a small number of alternations in Itelmen which instead pair *i~a*. The alternation *-in~-an* for the transitive participle (in the last line of (28)) is one such example, and is preserved to some extent in the modern language. The cognate ending shows an *e~a* alternation in the Chukotkan languages, perhaps suggesting that *i~a* arises as a means to avoid the neutralization that would result from the *e-a* merger in some Koryak dialects.
13 The distribution of schwa is largely, but not entirely, predictable. See Bobaljik (1998)
14 Jochelson's "g" = [γ] was preserved in inflectional morphology in the speech of the speakers who consulted for Volodin (1976), although few traces remained in the 1990s.

in (30), the schwa is consistently present in the cognates in the other Chukotkan languages, e.g., Chukchi 3SG.EMPH/REFL ənan, 1SG yəm, strongly suggesting that these words did not have full vowels in the previous generation in Itelmen, and that this is indeed an artifact of the notation.[15]

In addition to the systematic factors just indicated, there is some measure of internal inconsistency in the Jocheslon-Danilov transcriptions, as there is in all subsequent corpora of any substantial size. Presumably, we may recognize some measure of noise introduced by transcriber error and other factors.[16]

Factoring out excrescent *a*, glides, and presumed schwas leaves us nevertheless with a residue of items which appear to be disharmonic, many consistently so across multiple occurrences in the texts, making transcriber error unlikely. Some examples are given here. Those in (31) are probably loan words from Russian, or from Koryak *a*-dialects (recall from above that the *a*-dialects of Koryak and Alutor have seen recessive *e* merge with *a*; this recessive *a* does not undergo harmony and triggers only *e* →*a*, but leaves *i,u* unaffected):

(31) docista   < Russian: dočista 'clean / everything'
      mozit   < Russian   možet 'is.able'
      ilyá   < Russian   ilja (name)
      sinaŋewt   < Koryak   jiniaŋawɣut (name, mythological figure)
                             (s : j is regular)
      kuskɬíaqu < Koryak   qujqinjaqu (name, mythological figure)

But there are also disharmonic words that are less obviously[17] loanwords, such as those in (32):

---

[15] More so than the considerations above, identifying a particular vowel in the Jochelson-Danilov transcriptions as schwa requires some measure of guesswork, both since there is some variation in the contemporary language, and in some cases, since the corresponding contemporary form is not readily identifiable. In addition to my own field notes, I have made use of Volodin & Khaloimova (1989) and the modern edition of Jochelson's tales, as edited by K. N. Khaloimova (Khaloimova et al., 2014).

[16] From personal experience, I can attest to blurry boundaries in the vowel space, for example between *i* and *e*, or *e* and *a*, leading to uncertainty especially among non-native transcribers, but even among native speakers aiding in editing and transcribing.

[17] Where there are apparent cognates, as in the first person plural pronoun, it is of course difficult to determine whether these are loanwords, or true cognates representing a common ancestor. Since I will not be excluding loanwords in the counts, settling this challenging point is not necessary.

(32) muza   1PL.PRON   cf. Koryak *muri*
    qulán   'other'   cf. Koryak *qul(i), qullu*, also Kerek *qula*[18]
    awi   'crab'   cf. Koryak *avi*
    akiká   INTERJ (Hot!)

Finally, of particular note is the FUTURE/DESIDERATIVE suffix -*a⥷*, which is inert to harmony both in the 1910 material and in contemporary forms, and which curiously has no known cognate in Chukotkan. Examples of this affix failing to trigger harmony were given in (23); an additional minimal pair with a recessive and dominant root (with harmony applying across the future affix) are given in (33):

(33) RECESSIVE ROOT   DOMINANT ROOT
      t-łxiln-ář-**kicen**   ta-wetat-al-**kecan**
      1SG-stop-FUT-1SG (K2.1)   1SG-work-FUT-1SG (K2.30)

In sum, while there are surface disharmonic forms in the Jochelson texts, they are not nearly as pervasive as a superficial count of vowels as written might suggest. Taking account of the various important quirks of the Jochelson-Danilov transcription, we may proceed to a quantitative evaluation of samples of Itelmen from the beginning and end of the 20th century.

4 Counting harmony

At both the beginning and the end of the 20th century, the Itelmen child was faced with ambivalent evidence for the harmony rule in (34), where [D] is [-ATR] or whatever feature it is that relates pairs of dominant and recessive vowels, and the rule is read without regard to linear order: a recessive vowel is changed to its dominant counterpart in a word with a dominant vowel.

(34) $V^{[-D]} \rightarrow V^{[+D]} / [\{... \_\_, V^{[+D]} ...\}]_\omega$

At both time periods, some vowels alternated, but some did not, and in both periods, there were superficial exceptions to harmony – words that on the surface contain a mix of dominant and recessive vowels. By all accounts, (34)

---

18 From Fortescue (2005).

(or something similar) was acquired as a productive rule by speakers who lived a century ago, but not acquired by the current generation of speakers. Why?

4.1 Tolerating exceptions: Yang's threshold

Yang (2016) proposes a means to determine whether a rule is learnable in the face of exceptions. Intuitively, what Yang proposes is a measure of the threshold of permissible exceptions – the cut-off point for deciding whether the proper analysis is to posit a rule, with some exceptions, or whether it is more appropriate to simply list the alternating forms lexically. Specifically, (Yang, 2016, 64) proposes the Tolerance Principle in (35), which defines the cut-off point for the learnability of a rule[19]:

(35) *Tolerance Principle*
Let R be a rule applicable to N items, of which e are exceptions. R is productive iff:
$e \leq \theta_N$, where $\theta_N := \dfrac{N}{\ln(N)}$

In this formula, N is the number of opportunities for the rule to apply (instances where the structural description is met), and e is the number of exceptions. The formula counts types, not tokens and thus a few high-frequency exceptions will not undermine an otherwise productive rule. In Yang's analysis, the regular past tense inflection of English (add *-ed*) is productive, despite the existence of exceptions, but to a first approximation, irregular forms must be learned on an item-by-item basis, despite subregularities.

Table 1 reports the results for a count from this perspective for the first text from Jochelson's collection, and the first text from my collection. The first line of the table is the total number of distinct words in each text. This line counts types, not tokens, and is not lemmatized (since a given root may combine with dominant or recessive inflectional affixes). N counts the number of words (types) whose underlying representation contains at least one unambiguously

---

[19] The following discussion is not meant to necessarily endorse the idea of a sharp dividing line between productive and non-productive rules, but to ask whether it is possible in principle to quantitatively characterize such a divide in a way that makes sense of the Itelmen change. I am sympathetic, in principle, to the idea that a more articulated model might assume that learners consider multiple potential rules, with weighted probabilities (as in Albright & Hayes, 2003), and that there may be a gray area near the threshold.

Table 1: Yang's measure of productivity for vowel harmony in two Itelmen texts.

	K2.1 (1910)	Angaqe (1994)
words	242	229
N	49	42
e	11	37
Yang's Threshold θ_N	13	11
Productive ($e \leq \theta_N$)?	Y	N

dominant element and at least one unambiguously recessive element. e counts the number of these which fail to resolve the harmony conflict and remain disharmonic on the surface.[20] Unsegmentable interjections (*akika(x)!* 'Ouch! [for something hot]') and (probably borrowed) proper names *(Sinaŋewt, Ilyá)* are excluded, on the grounds that it is not uncommon for these to fall outside the regular phonology.[21]

---

[20] A reviewer raises the question of whether this is the correct choice for N, asking whether N should in-clude all polysyllabic words, including those which are underlyingly harmonic. Clearly, this would increase N (and thereby also θ_N) in Table 1, without increasing e, and would thus affect the key calculation. If I have understood correctly, the reviewer's suggestion asks a different question from Yang's. The reviewer's suggested approach to N asks about surface distribution: to what extent is the set of surface forms consistent with the constraint in (i) (a ban on words containing a mix of dominant and recessive vowels, i.e., the constraint corresponding to the rule in (34)):

(i) *[{... $V^{[-D]}$, $V^{[+D]}$ ...}]ω

An approach along these lines is taken by Harrison et al., 2002; Dras & Harrison, 2003—see fn. 30 for some discussion. My understanding of Yang's calculation, and thus the approach to N taken in the text, is narrower. It asks how often the rule in (34) applies *in contexts in which it could apply*. The assumption is that evidence for a rule comes only from alternations in which the rule actually applies. Just as words with only a single (full) vowel provide no evidence for whether there is a harmony rule (although they trivially satisfy (i)), words with underlyingly harmonic vowel combinations do not distinguish between a grammar that has a harmony rule (or constraint) and one which lacks such a rule, and are thus not counted as instances of N. In a fuller treatment of this material I hope to explore in more detail the consequences of differing assumptions for the model, but must leave this for future work.

[21] The corresponding figures with names and interjections included are: K2.1: $N = 54$, $e = 16$, $\theta_N = 14$ and Angaqe: $N = 45$, $e = 40$, $\theta_N = 12$. While there is still a substantial difference between the two time periods, on this way of counting, the exceptions to the harmony system would fall slightly above the threshold even in 1910. I provisionally take this to be an artifact of counting words, rather than morphemes: the single disharmonic name *Sinaŋéwt* shows up in three

By Yang's criterion, vowel harmony was learnable as a productive rule in 1910, and unlearnable three generations later (assuming that these results scale up to the larger corpus). The two texts are roughly the same size, and contain comparable values for N (and thus for Yang's Threshold θ_N), but differ drastically in their values for e–the number of surface exceptions to harmony. Even allowing for some degree of transcriber error in identifying vowels in the *Angaqe* text, the number of exceptions there exceeds the threshold by a factor of three.

While this result provides quantitative support for the initial hypothesis that vowel harmony was productive in 1910 and has been lost recently, there are various qualifications worth making in understanding the numbers.[22] In the next paragraphs, I discuss some of the practical choices that went into the count, acknowledging that at each point, different choices could have been made, perhaps leading to different results.

The first point to note is that I have, for the purposes of this pilot study, followed Yang in counting word-types in the texts. For Yang's examples, such as the English past tense or the German plural suffixes, the combinations of interest are bi-morphemic words. For each English verb root (or stem) there is in the general case one word which constitutes the past tense of that verb. Thus words (types) are a convenient proxy for morpheme combinations that do or do not trigger a specific rule. But Itelmen words, in particular verbs, are significantly more complex, often multi-morphemic. The form in (36) (from the representative 1994 text in the table) has three vowels in five morphemes, and on the surface is an exception to vowel harmony. By counting words, this word adds one each to the value of N (the harmony rule could have applied) and e (an exception).

(36) q'-oms-qzu-βum-sx
     2.IRR-leave-ASP-1SG.OBJ-2PL.SUBJ
     'You (should) leave me.' (AS)

---

different word-types in this short text; this name alone effectively makes the difference between productive and non-productive results in this small sample.

22 There is also, as a reviewer notes, an important question of what productivity means in general and how we establish it. Since there are morphologically-specified exceptions to harmony in all attested Chukotko-Kamchatkan languages, one might wonder if it is ever accurate to call the process productive. Table 1 documents a substantial change in the degree of harmony-like alternations in Itelmen words, which (as we will see below) correlates with the rise of Russian loans over the same time period, many of which are disharmonic. Yang's theory provides an explanatory mechanism for understanding this correlation in terms of the loss of productivity — the eventual unlearnability of a previously learnable productive rule. It is, however, true that no systematic *wug*-test was conducted at any point over the history of Itelmen, and is infeasible now.

On the other hand, there are two morphemes with recessive vowels in this word, neither of which changes. One could instead have counted morphemes or vowels, but this greatly increases the complexity of the exercise. If we count morphemes (or vowels), should (36) count as two exceptions, since two recessive vowels fail to undergo the rule, or one, since the single dominant vowel fails to act as a trigger? The task is even more complex with pairs like the following, from the same text:

(37) a. seŋ-zo-z-in   b. k-siŋ-qzu-kne'n
     fly-NDIR-PRES-3SG   PRT-fly-ASP-PRT.PL

The root /siŋ/ 'fly' (seen as such in (37b)) surfaces as *seŋ* in (37a) under the influence of dominant *-zo* (a derivational morpheme that derives the non-directed meaning 'fly around' from 'fly'). Thus harmony has applied in this form, but at the same time, it remains a surface violation, since the inflectional suffix *-in* retains its recessive vowel. By counting words, (37a) counts as an exception, despite the harmony alternation in the root. Note that this increases the proportion of $e : N$, making it harder for a productive rule to be detected as such.

Another way in which counting words under-counts N is that a word that shows multiple instances of the harmony rule applying (such as *k-caqał-**qzo-knan**</k-caqał-**qzu-knen**/) will contribute only one N to the sum. By under-counting harmony rule application in this way, we are, if anything, setting Yang's Threshold too low, and thus we can be that much more confident in a positive result for productive harmony.

On the other hand, counting word-types, rather than morpheme types, runs the risk of allowing high frequency morphemes to have an inordinately large effect of the outcome. But this cuts both ways. The most frequent morphemes[23] in Jochelson's K2.1 text include the aspectual morpheme *-qzu*, which alternates with *-qzo*, and the future morpheme *-ał* which, as noted above, fails to trigger harmony as it should.

Establishing the value for N requires a determination of the underlying representation of each form in the texts. Each word in each text was segmented by hand into constituent morphemes, and its UR was determined as accurately as possible by comparing to other occurrences of the same morpheme. This is not always trivial, and is a source of possible inaccuracies, in particular in cases where a given morpheme is infrequent. The treatment of surface *e* is particularly tricky. Two words from K2.1 are given in (38); each is bi-morphemic and both contain 2 instances of the vowel *e* (and no other vowels):

---

23 I.e., those that occur in the most distinct word types.

(38) Surface: a. lexsx-e   b. sen-ke
    UR: /lexsx-e/   /sin-(an)ke/
    gloss: mother-voc   woods-DAT/ALL
                'O mother!'   'Into the woods.'
    source: K2.1   K2.1

Surface *e* may correspond to any of: (i) dominant /e/, (ii) underlying /i/ after the application of harmony, (iii) recessive /e/ in a non-harmony context, or (iv) an exceptional, non-alternating, but also non-dominant /e/. As it happens, (38) shows all four. Starting with (38b), the (bound) root for 'forest, woods' is /sin/, seen in its recessive form in *sin-k* 'forest-LOC'; in (38b), the vowel has changed under the influence of the dative/allative suffix *-(an)ke*. This suffix has a long and short form, and the short form *-ke* is a reliable harmony trigger, as in *ŋon-ke* 'here-ALL' < *ŋun* 'here'. In (38a), the vocative suffix /-e/ is recessive and alternates with [-a] after a dominant stem, as in *la:ŋé-sg-a* 'girl-PL-VOC'. This could suggest that *e* in the root *lexsx* 'mother' is also recessive, however, this root fails to alternate in the Jochelson texts, and stays as *e* before dominant affixes, as in *lexsx-anke* 'mother-DAT.'[24]

As these examples indicate, recovering the underlying form is not always a simple matter. Surface *e* is compatible both with dominant and with recessive contexts, and some amount of analysis is required to identify both the action of harmony (as in *sen-ke*) and apparent exceptions (such as inert, non-alternating, non-triggering *lexsx*). For practical reasons then, underlying representations of morphemes were counted as unambiguously recessive if either (i) they contain {i,u} or, if their vowel is *e* and they demonstrably alternate with *a* in the corpus (such as vocative *-e~-a*, participial *-knen~-knan*). Likewise, unambiguously dominant forms are those with {a,o}, or those which clearly behave as such (such as the short dative allomorph *-ke*, as in (38)).

Although setting aside non-alternating *e* in this matter may reduce the accuracy of the counts, another interpretation of this is that the phonology of vowel harmony in 1910 was already somewhat different from the general Chukotkan pattern. Rather than a division of all vowels into recessive and dominant pairs, perhaps already in 1910, it was better to think of a recessive series i, u, e_1, a dominant series a, o, and a neutral series $e_2, ə$. On this view, there is no 'dominant *e*'; the apparent dominant behaviour of the short dative/allative *-ke* is then attributed to a morpheme-level diacritic, rather than the vowel itself. Note in this context that the dative is a dominant affix also in Chukchi and Koryak, where it has no full

---

24 In contemporary materials, the attested form is *laχsx* or *laχsχ*.

vowel and must be marked with a diacritic: Chukchi *nenenə* 'child', *nanan-ytə* 'child-DAT' (Kurebito, 2012, 182), Koryak: *milute-k* 'hare-LOC', *melota-ŋ* 'hare-DAT' (Abramovitz, 2015, 3). From this perspective, the behaviour of *lexsx* is not in any way exceptional, and it is right to therefore exclude it from the count, as I have done.

Here, one could consider again the view of Chukotkan vowel harmony in Calabrese (1988) in which the feature [+D] in the vowel harmony rule (34) is always a morpheme-level diacritic. From this perspective, exceptions above are not exceptions to the vowel harmony rule as such, but rather to the generalizations that regulate the assignment of the diacritic [+D]. In addition to lexically-specific marking of [+D] for certain morphemes (required in any event for dominant morphemes with no full vowels), there would be a rule that assigns the diacritic [+D] to any morpheme that contains /a/ or /o/:

(39) $\mu \to \mu^{[+D]}/[\ldots \{a, o\} \ldots]_\mu$

The (older) Chukchi analog of this rule would have included dominant *e* (assuming it was at some point phonetically distinguishable from recessive *ɛ*) in the context for assigning the [+D] diacritic.

Despite these qualifications, it is not seriously in doubt that there has been a qualitative change in whatever vowel-alternation processes Itelmen has, and that this change has been significant over the course of the 20th century. Even with many sources of uncertainty, the major finding reported here is that Yang's Tolerance Principle appears to quantitatively bear out the hypothesis that there was a productive process of vowel harmony operative in 1910, and that there no longer is.

4.2 Russian loans

The previous sections tentatively establish that there has been a substantive change in the vowel harmony pattern in Itelmen over the course of the 20th century, but the numbers alone do not provide any indication of the causal mechanism involved. The loss of vowel harmony is presumably an effect of language shift, a product of the declining spheres of influence of Itelmen. Russian subjugation of Kamchatka began in the 18th century, and continued throughout both the tsarist and Soviet periods. As the numbers in (40) show, not only was the ethnically Itelmen population decimated, but the number of Itelmen people who retained Itelmen as their native language contracted substantially:

(40) Demographics

	ca. 1700	1926	1994	2001	Sources
ethnic	10–25,000	3,414	1,141		Stebnickij (1934); Volodin (1976)
speakers		all	803	<80	<40 Koester & Bobaljik (1994)

By the time of Jochelson's expedition in 1910–1911, Itelmen was spoken only in 8 villages on the remote Okhotsk Coast. The Soviet period saw further drastic decline: schools were established, and children were prohibited from speaking Itelmen, in some case forcibly removed to boarding schools. Itelmen villages were razed and Itelmen speakers forcibly resettled. By 2017, a veritable handful of fluent, native speakers remain.[25]

Language shift alone does not explain the loss of harmony. I offer here the hypothesis that a more specific mechanism was the large influx of disharmonic Russian loanwords into the quotidien vocabulary. Although Table 1 shows that harmony was productive in 1910, it was only marginally so – the number of exceptions was only just below Yang's Threshold. Consider in this light the counts in (41). This table counts the number of Russian loan words in the entire Jochelson corpus as compared to two selected texts from 1994:

(41) Loan rates (Russian words / Total words) [lexeme types]:

CORPUS	# lexemes	russian	loan rate	notes
1910 – Jochelson	1546	130	8.4%	entire corpus
1994 – Tilval	243	48	20%	youngest fluent generation
1994 – KL	279	50	18%	youngest fluent generation

The number of Russian loans more than doubled. Although I do not have a count at this time of what percentage of Russian loans are disharmonic, it can be observed that it would take only a few to push the number of exceptions over Yang's Threshold.

Russian loans represented 8% of the vocabulary in 1910 and as much as 18–20% by 1994. For a text comparable to K2.1, we would expect to find perhaps

---

[25] There is room for differences in the criteria, but there are currently fewer than 5 speakers for whom Itelmen was their first language, and who continue to speak it fluidly.

15–20 more Russian loans in 1994 than in 1910.[26] Even if a mere 3 wordforms among these loans were disharmonic (and did not 'displace' equally disharmonic wordforms), the rate of exceptions would surpass Yang's Threshold and make the critical change from a learnable to an unlearnable rule. While a missing variable in this back-of-the-envelope calculation is the actual percentage of the Russian loanword vocabulary that is disharmonic in Itelmen, the result just mentioned is that it would be enough if only roughly 1 in 5 to 1 in 7 Russian loans are like those in (42) (all attested in the 1993–1994 texts) having at least one *a,o* and least one *i,u*:

(42) a. bumag(a?) 'paper'
 b. babu-čχ 'grandmother/old.woman-DIM'
 c. izmennoj 'betrayed'[27]
 d. oxotił- 'hunt' (k-oxotił-qzu-knen 'PRT-hunt-ASP-PRT')
 e. natjanut 'draw' (a bowstring)

By no means does this conclusively establish that Russian loans were the proverbial camel's-back-breaking straw, but I suggest that the figures above establish a clear quantitative case for the plausibility of the scenario entertained here. From the numbers, we have seen that the number of exceptions to vowel harmony in Itelmen in 1910 was perilously close to the critical threshold beyond which the rule could no longer be learned; a mere handful of disharmonic loans would be enough to push the harmony process over that cut-off. We know that many Russian loans are disharmonic, and we know that the rate of Russian loans occurring in the texts increased substantially over the relevant period.

If this hypothesis is on the right track, it also has implications (as a reviewer observes) for how lexical stratification and productivity interact. In theory, one could imagine that the Russian loans constitute a distinct lexical stratum or co-phonology, (cf. Ito & Mester, 1999) and that the harmony rule is limited to the native stratum. Yang recognizes that rules that may seem non-productive over the whole language may emerge as productive in discrete sub-domains. If learners were to have entertained the hypothesis that the harmony rule is limited to the

---

26 The text K2.1 has 242 word (types), but this count includes different inflected forms of the same lexeme; where the figures in (ii) count lexemes. Using the same criteria, K2.1 has approximately 175 lexemes. If 8% were Russian loans in 1910, these would number 14 lexemes; where we would expect 31-35 loanword lexemes under the 1994 loanword rate.
27 Borrowed Russian adjectives in Itelmen tend to be borrowed with the fixed adjectival suffix *-oj* regardless of the suffix formative in Russian.

native stratum, they may discount un- or partially-assimilated Russian loans as being irrelevant to the productivity of the rule. In Bobaljik (2006) I argued that the Itelmen lexicon is indeed stratified, and that reduplication is limited to the core stratum, which is distinguished by a number of other properties, while the non-native vocabulary spans a variety of strata. However, there is evidence that harmony extended to the stratum or strata containing Russian loans inasmuch as they do (or did) participate in harmony, at least as triggers – borrowed roots with dominant vowels do occur with the dominant versions of alternating affixes, as shown in (43)[28]:

(43) a. kápusta-ʔaʔn 'cabbage-ATTRIB.PL' < Russian *kapústa* 'cabbage'
   stol-ank 'table-LOC' < Russian *stol* 'table'
   b. k-swatał-**qazó-knan** 'PRT-WOO-ASP-PRT' < Russian *svatat'* 'woo'
   Nówoi-gód-ank 'New-Year-LOC' < Russian *Novyj God* 'New Year'

Evidently, lexical stratification as such does not necessarily prevent loanwords from being taken into consideration in the computation of the productivity of a rule. A related conclusion is drawn in Dresher & Lahiri (2015) who offer an analysis of the influence of Romance loanwords on English stress, also couched in terms of Yang's Threshold. Their analysis of English differs somewhat from the tentative hypothesis I have advanced here, for example, in that it is not the absolute number of Romance loans with a non-English stress-pattern that matters, but rather the evidence for stress-shifting latinate affixes that affects the learnability of the stress rules differentially over the history of English. But their account shares with the one offered here, and indeed with any account that pins phonological change on the influence of loanwords, the view that lexical stratification does not automatically exclude loanword strata from the computation of Yang's Threshold.

5 Beyond Itelmen: disharmony in a broader context

Before closing, I offer a final speculation. Other languages have seen an influx of foreign, disharmonic loans, and yet retain vowel harmony systems. Turkish is a widely discussed case in point (Clements & Sezer 1982). Why should the outcome be different in different languages? After all, Yang's Tolerance Principle regards

---

[28] The a. examples are from my fieldwork, and the b. examples from Jochelson's first two texts.

the proportion of exceptions in (a corpus representative of) the Primary Linguistic Data available to the child settling on their grammar. I speculate here that one critical difference is in the nature of the harmony process itself, and thus the rule to which Yang's learnability calculation applies.

Turkish vowel harmony is illustrated in (44)–(45) (examples from Kabak, 2011, which offers an overview). The basic harmony system is that vowels agree in [backness] with the immediately preceding vowel (as in (44)), and high vowels agree moreover in roundness (as in (45)).

(44) a. dal-**lar-ɯn** branch-PL-GEN 'of branches'
     b. jer-**ler-in** place-PL-GEN 'of places'

(45) a. boyn-**un** 'neck-2SG.POSS'
     b. gøɥs-**yn** 'breast-2SG.POSS'
     c. aln-**ɯn** 'forehead-2SG.POSS'
     d. vakt-**in** 'time-2SG.POSS'

There is, however, a notably large inventory of disharmonic roots, many of which are loanwwords from Arabic and from European languages (Clements & Sezer, 1982; Kabak, 2011):

(46) kitab 'book', siroz 'cirrhosis', garip 'strange', polis 'police', butik 'boutique', pilot 'pilot'

For the sake of argument, let's assume the number of disharmonic roots in Turkish is comparable to Itelmen. So why has this inventory not brought down the harmony system in Turkish?

As various authors have noted, the generalizations about Turkish are of two types. Affixes undergo alternations: essentially every suffix in Turkish has multiple surface allomorphs, and thus there is a motivation for a phonological harmony rule governing these alternations. But roots in Turkish do not undergo alternations. To the extent there are generalizations about the distribution of vowels in Turkish roots, these are Morpheme Structure Constraints (MSCs, see Kiparsky, 1973), static generalizations about lexical items which are not the result of a phonological rule. One way of approaching this (Clements & Sezer, 1982) is to posit that affix vowels are unspecified for backness and roundness, while roots, learned directly as such from the output, are fully specified. The harmony rule on this perspective is a feature-filling rule. Whatever technical implementation is chosen, assimilating 'disharmonic' loanwords into Turkish for the most part is then a matter of updating the lexicon. The feature-filling harmony rule is unaffected by roots that do not conform to the historically motivated MSCs. Indeed, whether a root is disharmonic or not, the final vowel of the root typically spreads its backness (and, to high vowels, roundness) rightwards, as in (47), participating in the productive part of the harmony system:

(47) a. kitab-**un** book-GEN
b. siroz-**un** cirrhosis-GEN

In other words, because Turkish vowel harmony is directional, and thus root-controlled (since Turkish is a suffixing language), apparently disharmonic roots can be easily integrated into the phonological system of Turkish, without affecting the phonological rule that governs alternations (and thus without jeopardizing its learnablity).[29]

Chukotko-Kamchatkan is crucially different from Turkic in this regards. In Chukotko-Kamchatkan, harmony operates in both directions and roots, as well as affixes, undergo alternations. A borrowed 'disharmonic' root in Turkish is, as we have seen, not only not a violation of the productive (rule-governed) part of harmony, it participates fully in that system, in light of the underlying representation of its final vowel. By contrast, a disharmonic root in Chukotko-Kamchatkan truly is an exception – no matter how it interacts with affixes, it will either contain an apparently dominant vowel that fails to act as a harmony trigger, or it will contain a recessive vowel that fails to act as harmony undergoer. This line of reasoning offers a straightforward account of why the Itelmen harmony system would be more vulnerable to decay under influence of loanwords than a root-controlled system would be. What remains to be shown is that this hunch scales up. Various languages with root-controlled systems are known to have lost harmony (see for example, Harrison et al., 2002; Dras & Harrison, 2003 on some Turkic languages, also Estonian), and Chukchi, by all accounts, has retained the bi-directional dominant-recessive system, despite undergoing language shift towards Russian and thus incorporating Russian loans (see Dunn, 1999).

An approach such as Yang's gives us a potential tool with which to investigate these differences systematically.[30] The conjecture just given is that the effects of

---

29 There are also a few disharmonic suffixes in Turkish, but the key contrast with Itelmen is in the role of roots in the harmony system.
30 Harrison et al. (2002); Dras & Harrison (2003) provide a different quantitative approach to the learnability of vowel harmony, with specific attention to variation across Turkic. In a nutshell, their approach counts the relative frequencies of each vowel in a corpus of data, and calculates from this the expected distribution of combinations of vowels in pollysyllabic words. In the simple case, if there are two equal groups of vowels (dominant and recessive) that could be combined freely, then 50% of bisyllabic words should be 'disharmonic', containing one vowel

disharmonic roots will be more pernicious in bi-directional, root-affecting systems than in systems of root-controlled spreading. But the force of the exceptions is relative to the overall robustness of the evidence for the rule. Independent of the Russian loans, all of Chukotko-Kamchatkan vowel harmony has some unpredictable aspects that require a diacritic mark (such as the dominant morphemes that lack a full vowel). And within Chukotko-Kamchatkan, Itelmen, much more than Chukchi, evidences other surface exceptions to the harmony system: the ambivalent behaviour of *e*, reflexes of the *a-e* merger from neighbouring Koryak *a*-dialects, and indigenous, harmony-violating morphemes, such as the harmony-inert future -*ał*. It strikes me then, as not out of the question that a careful, quantitative comparative analysis from the perspective taken here may turn out to be able to characterize the finer distinctions in the preservation or decay of vowel harmony under language contact, and to support or refute the conjecture offered here, that bi-directional systems in which roots alternate will be more vulnerable in language shift than root-controlled, directional harmony.

Acknowledgments: Above all I am grateful to the many speakers of Itelmen who have shared their language with me in Kovran, Tigil, and Sedanka (Kamchatka, Russia) since 1993. The text analyzed in detail in section 4.1 was recorded in Tigil in 1994, as told by the late Tatiana N. Bragina, and transcribed with the generous help of Ludmila E. Pravdoshina. This paper has had a long gestation. I am glad to be able to contribute it to this volume, in recognition of many stimulating and enjoyable discussions with Andrea Calabrese over the years we have been friends and colleagues, including conversations about some of the material here. In addition to Andrea's feedback, I have benefited from discussions at various points with Rafael Abramovitz, Jeff Bernath, Michael Krauss, Irina Monich, Andrew Nevins, †Aleksandr P. Volodin, Susi Wurmbrand, Charles Yang, and audiences at the LSA (1995), McGill University, the University of Connecticut, and the Workshop on the

---

from each group. If, however, recessive vowels were significantly more frequent to start with, then the basic statistical computation would yield a higher proportion of apparently 'harmonic' words, in which all vowels are recessive, just because most vowel tokens are recessive. Harrison et al. (2002) identify a harmony process as learnable if the distribution of vowels in multi-vocalic words is more harmonic than would be expected from combining the baseline frequencies of the individual vowels. Under their system, even contemporary Itelmen has vowel harmony, evidently a false result. Although I leave demonstration of this to a more fuller presentation at a later date, the source of the inadequacy of the Harrison et al. model lies in the effect of alternations. Any vowel alternation will skew the attested combinations of vowels away from baseline chance and the system has no way to distinguish between a productive phonological rule and morphologized, listed ablaut-like alternations.

Division of Labour between Morphology and Phonology at the Meertens Institute (2009). I also thank two anonymous referees for their valuable comments. For assistance with various text counts, I thank Ksenia Bogomolets and Irina Monich. Errors are, of course, my own responsibility. Funding for portions of the research reported here was provided by the National Council for Soviet and East European Research (PI: D. Koester), and NSF BCS-1065038 and BCS-1263535.

Abbreviations: The following abbreviations are used here:

ADJ	adjective	ALL	allative	ASP	aspect
ATTRIB	attributive	AUG	augmentative	CND	conditional
DAT	dative/allative	DESID	desiderative	DESIG	designative
DIM	diminutive	FUT	future	II	class II
IMP	imperative	INFIN	infinitive	INSTR	instrumental
INTERJ	interjection	IRR	irrealis	ITER	iterative
KOR	Koryak	LOC	locative	NDIR	non-directed (motion)
NEG	negative	NML	nominalizer	OBJ	object
PL	plural	PRES	present	PRON	pronoun
PRT	participle	SG	singular	SUBJ	subject
TR	transitive	VOC	vocative	#>#	subject > object (agreement)

Example sources K2.*n* refer to the texts collected by Jochelson following the text numbering format in Worth (1961); among the 1993–94 sources, AS is the text *Angaqe Sisike*.

References

Abramovitz, Rafael. 2015. Morphologically conditioned restrictions on vowel distribution in Koryak. Handout from MIT Phonology Circle.

Albright, Adam & Bruce Hayes. 2003. Rules vs. analogy in English past tenses: a computational/experimental study. *Cognition* 119–161.

Asinovskij, Aleksandr S. & Aleksandr P. Volodin. 1987. The typology of vocalic structures of the word in Chukchi-Kamchatkan languages. In Tamaz Gamkrelidze (ed.), *Proceedings of the eleventh international congress of phonetic sciences*, 362–364. Tallinn: Academy of Sciences of the Estonian SSR.

Baković, Eric. 2000. *Harmony, dominance and control*. New Brunswick, NJ: Rutgers University dissertation.

Bobaljik, Jonathan David. 1998. Mostly predictable: Cyclicity and the distribution of schwa in itelmen. In Vida Samiian (ed.), *Proceedings of the western conference on linguistics (1996)*, vol. 9, 14–28. Fresno: CSU.

Bobaljik, Jonathan David. 2006. Itelmen reduplication: Edge-in association and lexical stratification. *Journal of Linguistics* 42. 1–23.

Bobaljik, Jonathan David & David Koester. 1999. The first Itelmen author? *SSILA Newsletter* 17(4). 5–6.

Bogoras, Waldemar. 1917. *Koryak texts*. Leyden: E. J. Brill.

Bogoras, Waldemar. 1922. Chukchee. In Franz Boas (ed.), *Handbook of american indian languages*, 631–903. Washington: Government Printing Office.

Calabrese, Andrea. 1988. *Towards a theory of phonological alphabets*: MIT dissertation.

Clements, George N. & Engin Sezer. 1982. Vowel and consonant disharmony in turkish. In Harry van der Hulst & Norval Smith (eds.), *The structure of phonological representations*, 213–255. Dordrecht: Foris.

Dras, Mark & K. David Harrison. 2003. Emergent behavior in phonological pattern change. In Russell K Standish, Mark A. Bedau & Hussein A. Abbass (eds.), *Artificial life*, vol. VIII, 390–393. MIT Press.

Dresher, B. Elan & Aditi Lahiri. 2015. Romance loanwords and stress shift in English: A quantitative approach. Talk presented at the Second Edinburgh Symposium on Historical Phonology, University of Edinburgh, 3–4 December 2015.

Dunn, Michael. 1999. *A grammar of Chukchi*: Australian National University dissertation.

Fortescue, Michael. 1998. *Language relations across Bering Strait*. London: Cassell.

Fortescue, Michael. 2005. *Comparative chukotko-kamchatkan dictionary*. Berlin: Mouton de Gruyter.

Harrison, K. David, Mark Dras & Berk Kapicioglu. 2002. Agent-based modeling of the evolution of vowel harmony. In *Proceedings of NELS 32*, 217–236.

Ito, Junko & Armin Mester. 1999. The phonological lexicon. In Natsuko Tsujimura (ed.), *The handbook of Japanese linguistics*, 62–100. Blackwell.

Kabak, Bariş. 2011. Turkish vowel harmony. In Marc van Oostendorp, Colin J. Ewen, Elizabeth Hume & Keren Rice (eds.), *The Blackwell companion to phonology*, 2831–2854. Oxford: Blackwell.

Kenstowicz, Michael. 1979. Chukchee vowel harmony and epenthesis. In Paul R. Clyne, William F. Hanks & Carol L. Hofbauer (eds.), *Papers from "the elements," a parasession*, 402–412. Chicago: Chicago Linguistics Society.

Khaloimova, Klavdia N., Michael Dürr & Erich Kasten. 2014. Ительменские сказки собранные В.И. Иохельсоном в 1910–1911 гг. Fürstenberg, Germany: Kulturstiftung Sibirien.

Kiparsky, Paul. 1973. Phonological representations. In Osamu Fujimura (ed.), *Three dimensions of linguistic theory*, 3–136. Tokyo: Taikusha.

Koester, David & Jonathan David Bobaljik. 1994. Minority language, cultural revival and native rights in Russia: The Itel'men language as a case study. *NCSEER Working Papers*.

Krause, Scott. 1979. *Topics in Chukchee phonology and morphology*. Urbana-Champaign, IL: University of Illinois dissertation.

Kurebito, Tokusu. 2012. An outline of valency-reducing operations in Chukchi. In Wataru Nakamura & Ritsuko Kikusawa (eds.), *Objectivization and subjectivization: A typology of voice systems*, vol. 77 Senri Ethnological Studies, 177–189.

Lightner, Theodore M. 1965. On the description of vowel and consonant harmony. *Word* 19. 376–387.

Mel'nikov, G. I. 1948. Фонемы чукотского языка. *Язык и мышление* 11. 208–229.

Moskal, Beata. 2015. *Domains on the border: between morphology and phonology*. Storrs, CT: University of Connecticut Ph.d. dissertation.

Muravyova, Irina A. 1979. *Сопоставительное исследование морфонологии чукотского, корякского и алюторского языков*. Moscow: Moscow State University dissertation.
Skorik, Piotr Ja. 1961. *Грамматика чукотского языка*, vol. 1. Moscow: Izdatel'stvo akademii nauk SSSR.
Skorik, Piotr Ja. 1977. *Грамматика чукотского языка, часть II: глагол, наречие, служебные слова*. Leningrad: Nauka.
Stebnickij, S. N. 1934. Ительменский язык. In G. N. Prokof'ev, E. A. Kreinovich & Ja. P. Al'kor (eds.), *Языки и письменность народов севера*, 85–104. Moscow: Gos. Uchpedgiz.
Volodin, Aleksandr P. 1976. *Ительменский язык*. Moscow: Nauka.
Volodin, Aleksandr P. 2003. *Ительмены*. Saint Petersburg: Drofa.
Volodin, Aleksandr P. & Klavdia N. Khaloimova. 1989. *Словарь ительменско-русский и русско-ительменский*. Leningrad: Prosveshchenie.
Worth, Dean S. 1961. *Kamchadal texts collected by W. Jochelson*. Berlin: Mouton.
Worth, Dean S. 1969. *Dictionary of Western Kamchadal*. Berkeley: University of California Press.
Yang, Charles. 2016. *The price of linguistic productivity*. Cambridge: MIT Press.

David Embick and Kobey Shwayder
Deriving morphophonological (mis)applications

Etenim quaedam foedera exstant, ut Cenomanorum, Insubrium, Helvetiorum, Iapydum, non nullorum item ex Gallia barbarorum, quorum in foederibus exceptum est ne quis eorum a nobis civis recipiatur. Quod si exceptio facit ne liceat, ubi non sit exceptum, ibi necesse est licere.

Cicero, *Pro L. Cornelio Balbo Oratio*

*****

A proposition of SPE *that has received relatively little attention, but gains notable support from the stress facts discussed below, is that rules may have lexically marked exceptions. We wrote that*

> ...not infrequently an individual lexical item is exceptional in that it alone fails to undergo a given phonological rule or, alternatively, in that it is subject to some phonological rule...The natural way to reflect such exceptional behavior in the grammar is to associate with such lexical items diacritic features referring to particular rules... (SPE, 374)

Halle, 1998:541

1 Introduction: Morphophonology and exceptionality

By *morphophonology* in the narrow sense, we refer to alternations that are (i) not obviously part of the "normal" phonology of a language, but (ii) which effect changes that can be defined in terms of the phonology, in ways that (iii) relate to the presence of particular morphemes, or morphological features. The main analytical challenge posed by such alternations is that most theories of grammar provide (at least) two ways in which they could be analyzed, each of which has independent motivation. On the one hand, morphophonological alternations could be handled by phonological rules (or their equivalent); i.e. they could be treated as part of the phonological grammar, broadly construed so as to include contact with morphology. On the other hand, morphophonological alternations could be treated as (suppletive) contextual allomorphy, such that one alternant is not actually related to the other phonologically; instead, both alternants are stored, and employed in the appropriate contexts. Since both the phonological grammar and the need to store at least some suppletive allomorphs are essential parts of most linguistic theories, the status of morphophonological alternations raises what we call the Fundamental Question of Morphophonology (FQM): *Are morphophonological alternations the result of phonological rules, or do they result from the storage in memory of distinct allomorphs?*

Part of the interest of the FQM is its generalizability. Though centered on details of form, it implicates questions of much more general interest; in particular, the tension between "derivation by rule" (or its equivalent) on the one hand, versus "storage" on the other. The high-profile "past tense debate" in the experimental domain is – whatever one might conclude about the positions taken, and the conclusions reached – testimony to the importance that questions of computation versus storage have for the scientific study of language, with perhaps broader implications as well.

Terminologically, we will refer to theories that take the former option as *morphophonologically dynamic* (MPD) theories, since they involve phonological changes effected in ways that involve morphological triggers or targets, or more broadly, they treat morphophonology without memorized alternants. The latter type of theory will be referred to as involving Stem Storage (SS), since (in the typical case) it involves storing multiple distinct stems for the same Root.

Although we will touch on the FQM at various points below, our main goal in this paper is to explore another aspect of morphophonology – specifically, the conditions under which such alternations apply, do not apply, and misapply (over- or underapply), to work towards a general theory of morphophonological application.

The theory of morphophonology starts with the observation that a defining aspect of such alternations is their *exceptionality* when viewed next to "normal" phonology. This exceptionality can take different forms. One form involves the nature of the alternation itself. Some morphophonological alternations involve changes in a single environment whose phonological properties might be difficult to state in terms of a single rule, or changes (sometimes classified as "mutations") that appear bizarre or unexpected from the perspective of (a particular theory's) priors about phonological naturalness.

A second type of exceptionality – the one that is of interest to us here – concerns the conditions under which morphophonological alternations apply. Morphophonological alternations of the typical type are exceptional in that they are either (i) triggered by certain morphemes, often for no apparent reason when viewed from the perspective of the (synchronic) phonology, (ii) apply to certain morphemes and not to others, again for reasons that do not appear to be phonological in nature; or (iii) show both property (i) and property (ii).[1]

---

[1] The qualification concerning *apparent* phonological motivations in (i–ii) is motivated by the possibility of phonological representations with e.g. floating features; see §5.

Exceptionality of the type just mentioned is, for the most part, what produces the FQM. From the perspective of many different theories, the exceptionality of an alternation is a sufficient condition for classifying it: any form that is exceptional in any way is stored as an unanalyzed whole. In the framework that is adopted here, on the other hand, exceptionality is not in and of itself evidence for storage. Rather, exceptions are an important part of the (morpho)phonological grammar, and one of the goals of the theory is to characterize the conditions (in terms of locality in different representations, or cyclic domains, and so on) under which exceptionality may or may not be found.

Part of the argument that we will develop is that at least some types of exceptional behavior require a morpheme to be seen as a particular morpheme, and not simply as a phonological representation. Thus, the theory of exceptional behavior is a subpart of a more general theory of the conditions under which morphemes may affect each other's form; this general theory is, for lack of a better term, what could be called the theory of *morphophonology in the broad sense*. Along these lines, the approach that we develop here is an outgrowth of an approach to contextual allomorphy (Embick 2010a) that hypothesizes that both syntactic (=phase theoretic) and PF-specific (see below) locality conditions interact to produce the conditions under which allomorphy may be found. To the extent that our approach is on the right track, we should expect exceptional behavior in morphophonology as (narrowly) defined above to be constrained by the same factors implicated in the study of contextual allomorphy: in particular, by different types of locality – phase cyclic, linear, and phonological – that appear to play an important role in morphophonology broadly construed.

We will begin our discussion by outlining a specific approach to morphophonological interactions (§2), and by systematizing and illustrating a number of predictions that it makes about exceptional behavior (§3). The discussion of these sections is in part illustrative, and in part meant to provide an impetus for further investigation: in a number of domains, the theory makes specific predictions about morphophonological interactions that have not been connected with specific case studies, and our hope is that by making these predictions explicit we will be able to move inquiry in productive directions.

Following this overview, we turn in §4 to a look at Umlaut in Standard German, where a number of the factors considered in §§2-3 interact in complex ways. While Umlaut has been touched on at various points in the literature assuming the general architecture that we adopt here, it turns out on a close inspection to have a number of important properties whose analysis implicates several ongoing areas of active theoretical research; our discussion highlights these, and suggests several areas for further investigation. Following this, §5 synthesizes the main theoretical points from preceding sections, and makes pertinent comparisons with alternative approaches to morphophonology, including those framed in "affixless" theories of morphology, and those employing floating features and other purely phonological devices; we also discuss some of the broader prospects for stem storage theories, making reference to examples examined earlier in the paper. §6 offers general conclusions.

2 An approach to morphophonology

The approach that we develop here is based on the idea that different types of locality constraints apply in morphophonology broadly construed; some of these are syntactic, deriving from phase theory; some are more "morphological", in that they are stated in terms of morphemes, and their relations; and others are more "phonological", and are stated in terms of phonological representations. Building on the outlines of Embick (2010a), this set of assumptions is developed in works by Embick (2010b, 2012, 2014), Calabrese (2012, 2013a, 2013b, 2015, 2016), Ingason (2016), Petrosino (2018), and others; its most developed phonological form is Shwayder (2015) (see also Shwayder 2017, on which our analysis of Umlaut in §4 is built).

Our work is centered on research intuitions that derive from *generative* approaches to the study of grammar, and on the idea that – speaking informally – memorization of alternants is sometimes necessary, but dispreferred relative to rules (or their equivalent) whenever possible. In the particular domain that we investigate here, this assumption comes close to what is called *Full Decomposition* in Embick (2015); for obvious reasons, this idea has manifestations in both the theoretical and experimental domains (see e.g. Stockall and Marantz 2006).

For the types of morphophonology that we investigate here, we have been at pains in other works to stress the point that, whatever one might make of conceptual arguments, the reasons for deciding between more memory-oriented and more rule-centered theories (SS and MPD of §1) must ultimately be empirical. Before turning to the details of (grammar-related) evidence about how morphophonological alternations work, we would like to outline in one paragraph one of the reasons that we assume a generative perspective.

Put simply, we believe that *a priori*, there is very little reason to think that alternants should not be memorized as much as possible. Memory is clearly vast – human beings certainly have the capacity to memorize a large number of irregular forms, and it would be unsurprising if they were able to memorize alternate "stems" for thousands of Roots (although, of course, it would be important to identify which memory system(s) could do this). Thus, it is always possible to fall back on a position in which much morphophonology involves memorizing alternants, and deploying them in the proper contexts. Given that memory is so vast and that memorizing alternants is clearly an option, our view is that any evidence that speakers are *not* memorizing forms should be given special priority. If the language system broadly construed could in principle memorize this information but does not, then it is presumably because of the architecture. And, we believe that there is sufficient evidence from both the theoretical and experimental sides to suggest that even "irregular" alternations of various types do not involve storage of alternants, even if evidence from these domains has not been synthesized.

Intuitions like the one outlined above are, of course, productive to the extent that they generate empirical hypotheses. From this point on most of the rest of the paper we will concentrate on an approach and its predictions, with some additional discussion of larger claims appearing again in §5.3.

The predictions that we will examine in the sections to come center on the locality of morphophonological interactions. As a first step, we adopt the assumption that an important difference derives from the types of information that are referred to in the statement of an alternation: that is, whether the alternation applies only to morphologically defined targets or to phonologically defined targets; the triggers of such alternations can be either morphological or phonological as well, yielding (1):

(1) Trigger/Target classification of alternations

	P-Targets	M-Targets
P-Triggers	1	2
M-Triggers	3	4

The Type 1 interactions are purely phonological rules – they apply when their structural descriptions met. These are thus "exceptionless" phonological changes, of the type schematized in (2):

(2) $A \rightarrow B / X\_Y$

A rule of this type applies when the phonological conditioning environment that it specifies (in this case, the sequence XAY) is met. The information that the rule refers to is only phonological in nature. Though exceptionless, these rules need not be surface true, in spite of being purely phonological; they could over- or underapply, in ways attributable (in some theories, anyway) to opacity produced by rule ordering, for example.

Alternations of Types 2 and 3 have morphologically-specified targets and triggers respectively. The defining property of these rules is that they mix morphologically- and phonologically-defined information: that is, morphological triggers with phonological targets, or vice versa. As a cover term, we will sometimes refer to these two together as *MP* rules or alternations, taking their "hybrid" nature into account.

Spanish diphthongization is a Type 2 rule according to this classification. Diphthongization applies to certain vowels only when they are stressed, to change /e/ to /ie/ and /o/ to /ue/. However, whether diphthongization applies to a particular Root is something that has to be memorized; so, for instance, in *pensar* 'to think', the Root is subject to this change, so that the 1s present form is *pienso*; but e.g. *tensar* 'to make tense' does not diphthongize (cp. 1s present *tenso*). In sum, while the trigger is defined phonologically, the target of the change appears to be defined morphologically, in the sense that some morphemes undergo the change in the relevant phonological environment, whereas others do not.

Conversely, Type 3 alternations are triggered by particular morphemes but apply to phonologically defined targets. The metaphony reported in the Italo-Romance variety of Ischia shows this property, as shown in (3), which also shows Standard Italian for purposes of comparison. It can be seen that in the second person singular, the agreement morpheme in these verbs is realized as schwa (just as it is in the first and third person singular forms). Certain stressed vowels in the syllable preceding this morpheme undergo metaphonic raising; in these examples, we see /a/ to /ɛ/ (underlined) in the 2s forms, as opposed to the 1s and 3s which show /a/:

(3) Metaphony triggered by AGR (Maiden 1991:159); *cant/kand* 'sing'

	Standard Italian		*Ischia, Campania*	
	present	**imperfect**	**present**	**imperfect**
1sg	canto	cantavo	kandə	kandavə
2sg	canti	cantavi	**kɛndə**	**kandɛvə**
3sg	canta	cantava	kandə	kandavə

In short, for both Type 2 and Type 3, one member of the alternation is defined phonologically and the other morphologically. For this reason, rules of these types are *prima facie* amenable to treatments that employ (relatively) "abstract" phonological representations; e.g. different underlying representations for the Roots that do and do not undergo diphthongization (see e.g. Harris 1985), or by positing a floating [+high] autosegment with 2s Agr (but not with the other singular agreement morphemes) in the Ischia variety. For present purposes, we acknowledge that this type of analysis is possible for many MP alternations; we will continue to refer to these processes as having morphologically-defined triggers and targets in the discussion of the next two sections, though, putting off further discussion of what might adjudicate between morphophonological and "purely" phonological accounts until §5.

Type 4 alternations are both triggered by specific morphemes (or features) and restricted to apply to certain morphemes and not others. Many of the alternations seen in e.g. the English past tense are of this type. The specific trigger T[+past] is responsible for changes to specific hosts, in ways that make reference to morphological identity, not phonology: e.g. *think, thought, drink, drank*. In examples of this type, there are two morpheme-specific pieces of information at play. The first concerns the identity of the Root: e.g. √THINK does not behave like √DRINK. The second concerns the specific identity of the trigger: while one type of change is triggered by the past tense morpheme, it is sometimes the case that a different change is triggered by the participial morpheme, so that, for example √SING has past tense *sang* and participle *sung*. Thus, unlike the MP alternations of Types 2 and 3, neither the trigger nor the target are defined phonologically – both must be identified as particular morphemes. For this reason, we employ the term *MM* ("Morpheme/Morpheme") for Type 4 alternations. It will be assumed that while MM-rules are activated when two morphemes are concatenated, they are still possible phonological rules: that is to say, they obey phonological locality and so on.[2]

The idea that MM alternations occur under concatenation implicates some additional assumptions about when morphemes can interact. The structure of a past tense verb is shown in (4):

(4) Past tense verb

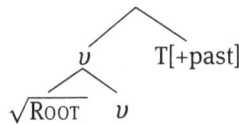

---

2 We remain neutral as to how many rules are required to effect the relevant changes (see e.g. Halle and Mohanan 1982 for a "reductionist" view). Considerations of this type might be important in weighing evidence for and against stem suppletion. Note as well that when we identify a process as having morphologically-defined targets, we do not wish to imply that there are no "phonological neighborhoods" that cover the undergoers; there often are. While these neighborhoods are important to language acquirers, and how they construct lists (or other ways of specifying undergoers), the point is that the alternation cannot be defined phonologically *in toto*.

In this structure, a verbalizing head v appears structurally between the Root and Tense. This head is sometimes realized overtly, e.g. in *color*-**ize** or *dark*-**en**. Irregular past tense (and participle) forms are found only when there is no overt realization of v. Embick (2003, 2010a, 2010b) hypothesizes that (certain) morphemes are *pruned* – that is, eliminated from a representation. In the particular example of the past tense, pruning v has the effect that the Root and T[+past] are concatenated $\sqrt{\text{Root}} \frown \text{T[+past]}$, so that these two morphemes can see each other for allomorphic purposes.

A main point of interest in classifying alternations according to their trigger and target properties is that it becomes possible to connect this part of morphophonology with more general properties of the theory of allomorphy. Based on the theory of contextual allomorphy advanced in Embick (2010a), which proposes that morphemes must be concatenated (=linearly adjacent) in order to see each other for the purposes of Vocabulary Insertion, we have been exploring the more general claim that *any* interaction in which two morphemes must be identified as morphemes requires linear adjacency; this is advanced as the Morpheme Interaction Conjecture in Embick (2010b, 2012):[3]

(5) **Morpheme Interaction Conjecture:** PF Interactions in which two morphemes are referred to as morphemes occur only under linear adjacency (concatenation).

According to the MIC, there are two primary expectations concerning MM and MP processes, each of which will figure in our discussion of exceptionality in the following sections.

The first prediction is that MP rules, which mix morphological and phonological information, should be able to show "morpheme skipping" effects, where the target and the trigger of the alternation have a morpheme intervening linearly between them. In fact, the example of metaphony from Ischia above in (3) contains an illustration of this very effect. While the 2s Ischia verb in the "present" column of shows metaphony affecting the vowel of the Root $\sqrt{\text{KAND}}$, in the imperfect 2s metaphony applies to the theme vowel -*a*, which is separated from the trigger of metaphony – 2s Agr – by the past tense morpheme, whose exponent is -v:

---

[3] For some additional discussion of the MIC, see Smith et al. (2016), where it is argued that pronouns are a counterexample to it; and, for a suggestion as to why pronouns (as opposed to lexical nouns) might be "special" in the relevant way that allows MIC to be retained, see Akkuş & Bezrukov (2016).

(6) kand -a   -v   -ə   → kandɛvə
    sing TH TNS Agr.2s

Several other MP processes have been shown to exhibit this type of "phonologically-defined" locality as well; see the works cited above for additional examples, as well as §3.1 below. We note that while phonological locality is clearly implicated in examples of this type, morphological representations are also crucial, in at least the following sense: morphemes that trigger phonological changes are the *locus* of the phonological effect (Embick 2013), and thus define the position from which the phonological operation applies. So, for example, the reason that the theme vowel undergoes metaphony in (6), and not the stem vowel, is that the trigger of metaphony is the 2s Agr morpheme: this trigger is linearly closer to the vowel of the Theme, and it is thus this vowel that is phonologically raised. Thus, even though phonological interactions may "skip" morphemes, in the way illustrated above, they are constrained by the morphological representation.

The second prediction is that MM rules should *not* apply when there is a morpheme intervening linearly between the trigger and the target; that is, such alternations should exhibit morphologically-defined locality, which we take to require concatenation. Since this prediction is part of the more general theory of exceptionality that is the topic of §3, we illustrate it there.

Before we proceed to illustrations, a final note is in order concerning terminology. While we will often refer to a particular rule *R* as being an MM rule, or an MP rule, this phrasing should be taken as shorthand for "rule R is triggered in an MM (or MP) way". As will become clear as the discussion proceeds, and in §4 in particular, it is possible that the same rule *R* may be activated in both the MP and MM ways, depending on which targets and triggers are involved. Under these circumstances, it is clearly inappropriate to refer to a rule as having MM or MP properties.

3 Application and exceptional behavior

The theory that we have outlined in the preceding section talks about rules that apply in ways that respect either morphologically defined locality, which we take to involve concatenation of morphemes, or phonological locality, which implicates phonological representations. In addition, it has been hypothesized that phase cycles (Chomsky 2000, 2001) constrain interactions in ways discussed in Embick (2010a); see below.

With these proposals at hand, we now look at three different situations in which (already exceptional) morphophonological rules do not apply. First, the different types of locality constraints implicated in the difference between MP and MM processes predict non-application of rules under different kinds of *intervention*. Second, phase cycles predict a further type of effect, in which an MM rule fails to apply because of *cyclic inactivity*. Finally, we examine something that we call *exceptional switching*, in which an MP rule is deactivated by a local morpheme. In summary:[4]

INTERVENTION: Under certain circumstances, material that intervenes linearly between a trigger and a target will preclude an alternation from taking place. In the case of MP alternations, which may skip morphemes, the relevant intervention is in terms of phonological representations; in the case of MM rules, it is morphological intervention that is at issue.

CYCLIC INACTIVITY: MM rules will not apply when the trigger and the target cannot see each other as morphemes in the same phase cycle (cp. "Readjustment activity hypothesis" of Embick 2010a).

EXCEPTIONAL SWITCHING: MP rules that are turned (ON) by particular morphemes may be exceptionally switched (OFF) by morphemes that are concatenated with them. In the type of case that we will see twice in this paper, an MP rule R is turned (ON) by a morpheme [X], and typically applies. However, a specific set of Roots or morphemes that is potentially subject to R fails to undergo the rule. Exceptional switching requires two morphemes to interact as morphemes; hence, exceptional switching is predicted to happen under linear adjacency.

We illustrate these predictions in subsequent sections. The emphasis in §3.1 and §3.2 is on providing synthesized looks at some of the locality based part of the theory, with the goal of showing how patterns of exceptionality require something like the distinction between MP and MM rules, and the theory of phases that has been developed as part of the theory of contextual allomorphy.

The discussion of §3.3 on exceptional switching is more exploratory in nature, and is meant to highlight some fine-grained predictions that have not been articulated in detail; it also provides a foundation for understanding some of the complexities of German Umlaut that are addressed in §4.

---

[4] Our focus on these types of (mis)application is motivated by a particular set of concerns and is not meant to be exhaustive. There are certainly other types, arising from e.g. phonological cyclicity (not the same as phase cyclicity; Embick 2014, Shwayder 2015). See Myler (2015) for a pertinent discussion of Spanish diphthongization.

3.1 (Linear) intervention

Here we illustrate two different types of intervention effect that are expected given the difference between MP and MM alternations. For MP, it is expected that while morphemes might intervene between triggers and targets, such rules will show phonological locality that is determined by the position of the triggering morpheme. Thus, only relevant phonological material intervening between a trigger and a potential target will cause the rule to not apply. For MM rules, which are subject to morphological locality, the prediction is that any morphemes intervening between the trigger and target will prevent the application of the rule.

3.1.1 MP: Icelandic Umlaut

Ingason (2014, 2016) and Wood (2015) argue that Icelandic *u*-Umlaut (a → ö) is an MP rule, triggered by certain suffixes. As such, it is expected to exhibit phonologically-defined locality. To illustrate this point, consider (7), where *u*-Umlaut is triggered by certain nominal inflectional morphemes, boldfaced below; as can be seen in (7b), *u*-Umlaut affects a Root across an overt intervening suffix:

(7) Icelandic Umlaut: Phonological locality
    a. rak-ur 'moist-masc.nom.sg'
         rök-**Ø** 'moist-fem.nom.sg'
    b. dan-sk-ur 'Dan-ish-masc.nom.sg'
         dön-sk-**Ø** 'Dan-ish-fem.nom.sg'

While *u*-Umlaut is able to skip intervening morphemes, it is only able to do so provided that its phonologically-defined locality conditions are met. In particular, if an affix containing a non-umlauting vowel appears between the Root and the MP trigger, it is expected that *u*-Umlaut should not occur. Ingason (2016) provides a particularly clear example of this effect with the Icelandic word for 'Assamese', *assam*, which variably takes *-sk* (as in 7b) and *-ísk* adjectival exponents. With the former, Umlaut occurs, whereas with the latter, it does not:

(8) 'Assamese', in Icelandic
    a. assam-sk-ur (masculine nominative singular)
         assöm-sk-Ø (feminine nominative singular)
    b. assam-ísk-ur (masculine nominative singular)
         assam-ísk-Ø (feminine nominative singular)

In the second example in (8b), the *u*-Umlaut trigger fails to have an effect on *assam*, due to the *phonological* intervention of a non-umlauting vowel in the nationality suffix; when this vowel is not present, as in the (8a) variant, Umlaut takes place. That is, *u*-Umlaut can skip morphemes, but not relevant phonemes.

As we discussed earlier in this section, there are two components that are required for the analysis of the effect. The first concerns the *u*-Umlaut rule, which, as an MP-rule, obeys phonological locality. The second is morphological: although phonologically defined, the locality of Umlaut requires an analysis in which the trigger of Umlaut *is in the position of the triggering morpheme*. Otherwise – i.e. if the umlaut trigger did not have a morphologically defined locus – the absence of *u*-Umlaut in (8b) would be unexpected (or at least, it would have to be stipulated). The latter point might seem trivial in the context of the current discussion, but assumes greater importance when we consider that many morphological theories dispense with morphemes, and are hence unable to state this kind of restriction in a straightforward way (see Embick 2013, and §5.1).

3.1.2 MM: Icelandic verbs

Wood (2015) and Ingason (2016) provide valuable discussion of linear intervention effects in Icelandic verb alternations, highlighting the importance of the MM versus MP distinction as we have outlined it above.

As a starting point, consider the transitive forms of the verb $\sqrt{\text{BROT}}$ 'break' in (9). $\sqrt{\text{BROT}}$ is a *strong* verb that shows changes to vowel quality (Ablaut) characteristic of such verbs in Germanic (as opposed to *weak* verbs, which do not exhibit these changes).

(9) Transitive forms of $\sqrt{\text{BROT}}$ 'break'

	Indicative		Subjunctive	
	present	*past*	*present*	*past*
1s	brýt-Ø	braut-Ø	brjót-i	bryt-i
2s	brýt-ur	braut-st	brjót-ir	bryt-ir
3s	brýt-ur	braut-Ø	brjót-i	bryt-i
1p	brjót-um	brut-um	brjót-um	bryt-um
2p	brjót-ið	brut-uð	brjót-ið	bryt-uð
3p	brjót-a	brut-u	brjót-i	bryt-u

There are several things going on in the forms in (9), including what Wood and Ingason treat as rules triggered by Tense and having effects on specific (Root) targets whose identity must be memorized – the defining properties of MM rules.

Strikingly, all of the stem allomorphy exhibited in (9) disappears when √BROT appears in an intransitive form in which an overt morpheme -*n* appears between the Root and the Tense morpheme, as can be seen in comparing (10) with (9):

(10) Intransitive forms of √BROT 'break'

	Indicative		*Subjunctive*	
	present	*past*	*present*	*past*
1s	brot-n-a	brot-n-að-i	brot-n-i	brot-n-að-i
2s	brot-n-ar	brot-n-að-ir	brot-n-ir	brot-n-að-ir
3s	brot-n-ar	brot-n-að-i	brot-n-i	brot-n-að-i
1p	brot-n-um	brot-n-uð-um	brot-n-um	brot-n-uð-um
2p	brot-n-ið	brot-n-uð-uð	brot-n-ið	brot-n-uð-uð
3p	brot-n-a	brot-n-uð-u	brot-n-i	brot-n-uð-u

The overt -*n* exponent in intransitives prevents the vowel-changing Roots and Tense from being linearly adjacent, with the result that the MM changes that apply in the transitive are not found. There is, moreover, a symmetrical effect in the realization of the past tense morpheme T[+past]. In the transitives in (9), this morpheme does not have an overt realization. In one way of analyzing this, the T[+past] morpheme shows a -Ø contextual allomorph in the context of √BROT and other Roots. In the intransitives in -*n*, on the other hand, both the indicative and subjunctive pasts show -ð exponents for T[+past]: its default form (cf. Wood 2015). Thus, in the same way that -*n* intervenes between the Root and Tense for the purposes of MM rules, it also intervenes for contextual allomorphy of T[+past], as expected under the MIC.[5]

Wood (2015:126) makes the important observation that there is one exception to the exceptional non-application of exceptional rules in these verb forms: u-Umlaut, discussed above as an MP rule, continues to apply in intransitives with overt -*n*, as shown in (11) for the verb √BAT 'improve' (umlaut triggers are boldfaced):

(11) Umlaut in √BAT (indicative forms)

	present	**past**
1s	bat-n-a	bat-n-aði
2s	bat-n-ar	bat-n-aðir
3s	bat-n-ar	bat-n-aði
1p	böt-n-**um**	böt-n-**u**ð-um
2p	bat-n-ið	böt-n-**u**ð-uð
3p	bat-n-a	böt-n-**u**ð-u

---

5 In these comments we abstract away from the vowels accompanying -ð, and some additional questions about allomorphy for agreement suffixes.

This is, as noted earlier, what is expected if MP rules follow phonological and not morphological locality.

In sum, we see in this case study the different locality conditions that apply to MM versus MP alternations, as highlighted by the different patters of exceptionality that ablaut and umlaut show with morphological interveners.[6]

3.1.3 MM: Italian *passato remoto*

Calabrese's (2012, 2013a, 2013b, 2015) discussion of the Italian *passato remoto* contains a number of components that resonate with the discussion of Icelandic stem alternations immediately above. Verbs that show irregularity in this tense, like those in (12a-d), show different patterns that are systematically

---

[6] A reviewer points that there is at least one type of stem change in Icelandic strong verbs that raises an additional set of questions about MM/MP rules and their locality conditions. Some strong verbs, like the one see in in (9), are not solely Tense/Mood sensitive, but are also sensitive to number (e.g., indicative pres sg *brýt-*, pl *brjót-*; past sg *braut-*, pl *brut-*). In fact, this type of verb shows several stem changes, as can be seen from the fact that in the indicative, there are four different stem forms for the combinations [±past] and [±plural]. This is a potential problem for an MM analysis because for at least some of the relevant changes (those in the past indicative singular in particular), information from three distinct morphemes – the Root (strong or weak), Tense ([±past]), and Number ([±plural]) is evidently required. Linearly, these morphemes appear as Root-Tense-Agr (assuming that v is pruned). While both the Root and Agr morphemes are concatenated with Tense, the Root and Agr morphemes are not concatenated with each other; and, apparently, the features of the Agr morpheme are inducing changes on the form of the Root.

Several properties of the Agr-driven changes call for detailed study (cf. Árnason 2011, Gussmann 2011). First, the phonological changes associated with Agr are complex. One of them, *i-umlaut*, can be stated as a fronting rule phonologically (cf. its application in deriving the present indicative singulars from the stem form seen in the present indicative plurals). However, it remains to be seen whether another set of changes, affecting singular forms in the past indicative, can be accounted for with a single rule.

Second, in terms of locality, Agr-driven stem changes appear to skip the past tense morpheme, since they affect the Root. This is not expected of MM processes. However, the application of Agr-driven rules crucially refers to features of the intervening Tense morpheme. That is, [-pl] stem changes are different for indicative present and indicative past. This suggests to us that while [±plural] is certainly implicated in the relevant changes, the locus of the effect is the *Tense* morpheme, much as is seen in the patterns discussed in the main text. On the face of it, this could be analyzed by having rules with a locus in Tense turned (ON) when Agr bears specific features where, crucially, the effects of the rules are seen on the Root. Such a proposal would have implications for how to understand the MM/MP distinction, in ways that warrant careful study. Though we are unable to go further into the matter here, the analysis of the full set of effects associated with Tense and Agr is an important topic for further investigation.

correlated with person and number: in particular, the 1sg, 3sg, and 3pl forms show a number of changes to the stem that are not found in the other person number combinations; for purposes of comparison and contrast, a regular verb is shown in (12e):

(12) Some verbs in the Italian *passato remoto*

		inf.	*1sg*	2sg	*3sg*	1pl	2pl	*3pl*
(a)	'come'	venire	vénni	venísti	vénne	venímmo	veníste	vénnero
(b)	'move'	mwovere	móssi	mwovesti	mósse	mwovémmo	mwovéste	móssero
(c)	'put'	mettere	mísi	mettésti	míse	mettémmo	mettéste	mísero
(d)	'see'	vedere	vídi	vedésti	víde	vedémmo	vedéste	vídero
(e)	'fear'	temere	teméi	temésti	temé	temémmo	teméste	temérono

The Root-specific stem changes here are correlated with two other effects: first, they are found only in athematic forms; and, second, some of these forms (b,c) show an overt -*s* exponent of tense in the stem-changing forms – unlike the regular passato remoto, where T[+past] has a -Ø exponent.[7]

Calabrese's insight is that the interesting allomorphic effects in the passato remoto are found in athematic verb forms (forms lacking a theme vowel immediately after the Root), and that they are found there because it is in such forms that the verb Root and the past tense morpheme are concatenated. Putting to the side the exact statement of how the verbs in question lose their theme vowel, the relevant representations are those in (13):

(13) Linear order for verbs:
    a. **Thematic:** Root-TH-Tense-Agr
    b. **Athematic:** Root-Tense-Agr

In these linear orders, the correlation between irregular tense allomorphy and the stem changing processes follows from how MM locality works. When the TH position intervenes between the Root and Tense, there are (i) no MM processes triggered by Tense that affect the Root, and (ii) no Root conditioned allomorphy of Tense, as predicted by the MIC.

---

[7] For example, according to Calabrese's analysis, (12b) shows the -*s* exponent of Tense in the 1sg, 3sg, and 3pl, (e.g. 1sg *muov-s-i*) with subsequent assimilation of the stem-final /v/ to yield /ss/.

3.1.4 MM: The Kashaya decrement rule

Kashaya, a Southwestern Pomo language of California, has a process called the *decrement* in Oswalt (1961), by which a laryngeal increment (a /ʔ/ or /h/ linked with the following consonant, see Buckley 1994) is deleted in certain morphologically-defined environments. The triggers of the decrement rule are heterogeneous both phonologically and morphologically, as shown in (14):

(14) Some triggers for the decrement (Buckley 1994:288–297)
    a. Directional suffixes (some not all): *-ibic* 'up, away', *-aq* 'out hence', *-ala* 'down', *-ay* 'against', etc.
    b. Plural act allomorphs (most not all): *-t*, infixing *-t-*, *-w*, *ʔta*, *-Ø*, *-aq*, *-ataq*, etc.
    c. Derivational suffix *-t* forming verbs from nouns and adjectives
    d. Nominal locative suffix *-·*
    e. 3sg. possessor prefix of kinship nouns *miya·-*

In (15) are examples of the decrement applying with two different allomorphs of the plural act morpheme, *-aq* and *-t*; for clarity, these triggers are boldfaced, and the target of decrement is underlined (note that there are some other phonological processes reflected in the outputs; what is important is that the underlined segments are deleted):

(15) Decrement with Pl.Act.
    a. ba-   <u>h</u>cʰital   **-aq**   -ʔ → bacʰita;laʔ
        PFX:MOUTH √STRING PL.ACT ABS
        'string together meat (plural) to make jerky'
        (Compare *bahcʰitalʔ* 'string together meat (singular) to make jerky')
    b. mu-   <u>ʔ</u>k'a   **-t**   -ʔ → muk'aʔ
        PFX:ENERGY √CRACK PL.ACT ABS
        'crack (plural) with heat'
        (Compare *muʔk'aw* 'crack (singular) with heat')

As noted above, the decrement rule is morphologically-triggered since there is nothing phonological that unifies the triggering morphemes in a way that would produce the deletion in question. In addition to this, the decrement rule targets a specific set of morphemes; other morphemes do not undergo the process (Buckley 1994, p.302), as illustrated in (16), which employs the same Plural Act suffixes seen above:

(16) Failure to Decrement with Pl.Act.
    a. di-   ʔk'ol -aq   -ʔ   → diʔk'olaʔ
       PFX:GRAVITY √CUT PL.ACT ABS.
       'cut off parts (plural); prune (trees)'

    b. da-   ʔcʰa -t   -ʔ   → daʔcʰaʔ
       PFX:HANDS √STOP PL.ACT ABS.
       '(falling forward) land on extended arms (plural)'

As expected given its morphologically-defined triggers and targets, the decrement rule obeys morphological locality. If a morpheme intervenes between the trigger and the target, it does not apply. In (17), the intervening movement morpheme realized as -*w* blocks decrement between the directional morpheme trigger -*ay* 'against' and the root; when the -*w* is not present, the Root is subject to decrement, as shown in (17b):

(17) Intervening /-w/ MOVEMENT suffix   (Buckley 1994:296)
    a. mihca   -w   -ay   -ʔ   → *mihcaway*'
       √TOSS MVMT DIR:AGAINST ABS
       'toss to someone (pl)'

    b. mihca   -ay   -ʔ   → *micay*'
       √TOSS DIR:AGAINST ABS
       'toss...'

The idea that the intervention effect is morphological – and not phonological – is important for identifying the decrement as an MM process. In both the examples in which decrement applies like (15) and in examples where it does not like (17), there are several phonological segments intervening between the trigger morpheme and the target of deletion (for a formulation of the rule, see Buckley 1994). The difference is that in the latter cases, there is a morpheme intervening between the trigger and the target, whereas in the former there is not. Thus, we are able to rule out a possible analysis according to which decrement is an MP rule that is (ON) by default with the triggers listed above. If this analysis were correct, we would not expect to find the morphological intervention effect (compare the MP alternations seen to skip morphemes in the Ischia variety (§2) and in Icelandic Umlaut (§3.1.1)).

3.2 Phase-cyclic effects

By definition, MM rules require two morphemes to see each other *as morphemes*. In the approach that we have adopted here, visibility as a particular morpheme is also affected by phase cyclicity. The version of phase theory adopted here is developed for PF purposes in Embick 2010a, 2014 and Shwayder 2015, building on and connecting with Chomsky (2000, 2001), Marvin (2002), Marantz (2001, 2007), Embick and Marantz (2008), Newell (2008), and related work. In summary form, we take the view that certain morphemes cease to be identifiable as morphemes when they become inactive in terms of phase theory; this is stated in the ACTIVITY COROLLARY in (18):[8]

(18) ACTIVITY COROLLARY (AC): In $[[\ldots x]\ldots y]$, x and y cyclic, the complement of x is not *active* in the PF cycle in which y is spelled out. (Embick 2010a)

Putting to the side the specific mechanics that produce (18), the prediction that the ACTIVITY COROLLARY makes for MM rules is that in category-changing derivations, where a $\sqrt{\text{ROOT}}$ is first categorized by x, then changed to category y ($[[\sqrt{\text{ROOT}}\ x]\ y]$), an MM rule triggered by y (or material outside of y) cannot apply to the Root, because the Root is not visible as a morpheme when y is spelled out.[9]

By way of illustrating one of the scenarios relevant to this prediction, consider fricative voicing (FV) in English, which is triggered by the plural morpheme, as well as by the verbalizer υ:

(19) Fricative voicing
    a.   wol*f*, wol*v*-es /f/∼/v/
           pa*th*, pa*th*-s /θ/∼/ð/
           hou*s*e, hou*s*-es /s/∼/z/
    b.   shel*f*, to shel*v*e /f/∼/v/
           ba*th*, to ba*th*e /θ/∼/ð/
           hou*s*e, to hou*s*e /s/∼/z/

---

[8] The qualification "cease to be identifiable *as morphemes*" leaves open the possibility that cyclically inactive elements may have phonological representations that can be affected in various ways; see Embick (2014) for discussion and some specific proposals.

[9] This view assumes that "typical" derivational exponents realize category-defining heads (*n*, *v*, *a*,...), and that these heads define phase domains. Different assumptions about this and related issues concerning Roots have led to different predictions concerning (for the most part) phonological behavior; see, for example, Lowenstamm (2015b) and Creemers et al. (2017).

This process has MM properties: it is triggered by specific morphemes ([+pl] and v),[10] and it applies only to some Roots, and not to others that are phonologically identical to the undergoers (e.g. there is no voicing in plurals like *gulfs*, *deaths*, or *excuses*). The last example illustrates the further point that some Roots undergo voicing in one environment, but not another: the verb *to excuse* takes the voiced allomorph, unlike the plural noun *excuses*. As further illustration of this point, consider *one leaf, two leaves*; but *leaf through a book*; *one wolf, two wolves*, but *wolf down some food*. The trigger and target specificity of FV suggests that it is an MM rule.[11]

Most relevant for our immediate purposes is that with the verbal trigger it is possible to prevent FV from applying by introducing a cyclic boundary between the trigger and the target. This point is illustrated with the root $\sqrt{\text{HOUSE}}$ in Marantz (2013). In its Root verbalization [$\sqrt{\text{HOUSE}}$ v], the voiced allomorph appears. However, like other English nouns (preferably concrete), [$\sqrt{\text{HOUSE}}$ n] denominal verb, whose meaning is something like 'provide with noun':

(20) table those rooms =provide those rooms with tables
room those houses =provide those houses with rooms
house those lots =provide those lots with houses

In the last example here, where the noun *house* is verbalized, it is the voiceless allomorph that surfaces. This is the effect that is predicted by the phase theory: when the Root is not visible to the v morpheme, FV does not occur.[12]

---

[10] Possibly some nominal morphemes trigger the process as well: consider *housing* and *shelving* (unless there is a v in these that is responsible).

[11] If, for example, the verb *to leaf* were denominal [[$\sqrt{\text{LEAF}}$ n] v], but e.g. *to house* were Root-derived [$\sqrt{\text{HOUSE}}$ v], the voicing difference between these two could be explained in terms of phase theory. However, there is little reason to believe that this structural difference should be posited for this pair. Along these lines, Borer (2013) discusses at length why derivations like [[$\sqrt{\text{ROOT}}$ n] v] (with v not realized phonologically) might be ruled out in general.

Our view is that the clearest case of verbalization involving a noun is found with the "provide with" interpretation discussed in (20) in the main text.

[12] Relatedly, Root verbalization to *shelve the book* means to 'put the book on a shelf', or, idiosyncratically, to put the book 'on the back burner'; on the other hand, to *shelf a wall* means to 'put a shelf or shelves on a wall'. It might be possible to produce the voiced alternant with the latter (locatum) interpretation, as pointed out to us by a reviewer. This would suggest both denominal and Root-based derivations of locatum meanings, a matter that could be studied in greater detail. However, our judgment is that in a scenario in which shelves are put into a room for some reason, but not mounted on a wall, along the lines of (20), it is the voiceless allomorph that surfaces (*We need to shelf two more rooms*).

There is more that could be said here about the structure underlying verbalizations– like *house* with the voiceless allomorph. As noted in Fn. 11, there might not be [[√ROOT n] v] derivation productively in English. On this point, we agree with the spirit (though not necessarily the letter) of Borer (2013). Concerning the specifics of the derivations in (20), it is possible that the derivation of *to house* with this meaning involve additional structure (beyond just n and v), including perhaps a head expressing a "prepositional" meaning. What is crucial for our purposes is that when there is a denominal verb formation, the Root and the triggering v morpheme are not active as morphemes in the same cycle; and, when this happens, there is no fricative voicing, as predicted by the version of phase theory we have adopted.[13]

---

[13] By way of providing a preview for §3.3 and for §4.2 in the analysis of Umlaut, we note that there are in principle two ways of talking about the "Root-specific" aspect of FV. The first (and most obvious) is that the presence of a specified ('+') Root next to one of the trigger morphemes turns FV (ON):

(i) Root+ ⌢ TRIGGER ⇒ FV (ON)

A second way of conceiving of the trigger/target relation, much less obvious given the facts of English under consideration, would be to hold that the triggers in question "default" to activating FV, so that the non-undergoers are specified ('–') as turning off the rule:

(ii) a TRIGGER ⇒ FV (ON)
      b Root– ⌢ TRIGGER ⇒ FV (OFF)

This latter way of analyzing the MM effect, with Root-triggered exceptionality to an MP rule, may appear counterintuitive, but it is able to account for the "basic" facts about fricative voicing like those considered in (19). Interestingly, though, it makes incorrect predictions about the consequences of introducing a cyclic boundary between the trigger and target like in (20). Under the analysis in (ii), the default setting of FV would be (ON) for [+pl] and v, such that FV has to be turned (OFF) when these morphemes are concatenated with particular sets of Roots. If the Roots are not visible as Roots due to phase inactivity, the prediction is that FV should be (ON), so that voicing is found across the board for such denominal verbs: even for Roots that never show FV with [+pl] and v. That is, (ii) predicts overapplication of FV, contrary to fact:

(iii) mouse (/s/, */z/) the room =provide the room with mice
       mammoth (/θ/, */ð/) the exhibit =provide the exhibit with mammoths
       smurf (/f/, */v/) the kids =provide the kids with smurfs

However, the first approach (i), with FV turned on under concatenation, does not make these incorrect predictions.

The general point is that *over*application across phase boundaries would provide important evidence about how triggering works; see §4.2.3.

3.3 Exceptional switching

Finally, we arrive at the topic of exceptions to exceptional behavior. In many cases, being an exception to an exception amounts to being unremarkable. Halle (1998) observes something to this effect in his analysis of English stress, where exceptions, though not the norm, are also not uncommon (emphasis ours):

> To reinforce the point that rules may have lexical exceptions, I note that the majority of suffixed adjectives such as those in (8b) are subject to RLR Edge marking. As shown in (12a), however, adjectives in *-ic* generally are not. Since the suffix *-ic* makes a light rime, the Main Stress Rule assigns penultimate stress to these adjectives. However, in a handful of such adjectives – of which a few are listed in (12b) – RLR Edge Marking does apply. *The latter are thus exceptions to exceptions; that is, they are regular.* (1998:550)

For the types of morphophonology that we are interested in here, the exceptionality that is of interest involves (i) an MP trigger that can be (ii) turned off under concatenation with a particular set of morphemes. In part, our interest in this kind of effect stems from what we will say about German Umlaut in §4. Here, we will examine a case that appears to have something like the correct properties, and which connects to other predictions of interest in a few ways. While there are alternatives to the analysis that we arrive at, and while some of the key empirical predictions deriving from this analysis have not been tested, it is our hope that the line of reasoning that is found in this part of the discussion will provide a useful focus for additional research on this and related questions.

The Arpinate variety of Italo-Romance (Calabrese 1998; Parodi 1892; Torres-Tamarit and Linke 2016) shows metaphonic changes that are triggered morphologically. This case of metaphony is phonologically opaque, in that the exponent of the triggers is *-ə* due to many of the (final/post-tonic) vowels in this variety having been reduced (cp. the Ischia variety in §2). It is also non-uniform phonologically, in that it can produce both mid-vowel raising and diphthongization, as well as the raising of /a/ (called "hypermetaphony" in Maiden 1991) with verbs.

Nominal inflection in Arpinate is shown schematically in (21), where the boldfaced cells are metaphony triggers:

(21) Arpinate noun inflection

class	singular	plural
I (fem.)	-a	**-ə**
II (masc.)	-ə	**-ə**
III (fem./masc.)	-ə	-ə

So, for example, adjectives which alternate between Class I and II (in feminine and masculine, respectively) show metaphony in the masculine singular and plural but not in the feminine plural, despite the desinence being realized as /-ə/ for all three categories:

(22) Class I/II adjectives

	gender	singular	plural	
(a)	f	sól-a	sól-ə	'alone'
	m	súl-ə	súl-ə	
	f	bón-a	bón-ə	'good'
	m	bwón-ə	bwón-ə	
(b)	f	nér-a	nér-ə	'black'
	m	nír-ə	nír-ə	
	f	vékkj-a	vékkj-ə	'old'
	m	vjékkj-ə	vjékkj-ə	

As can be seen in these examples, metaphony in this variety has two different effects, raising and diphthongization, reflecting the difference between [±ATR] mid-vowels (/e,ɛ/, /o,ɔ/).

Interestingly, there are some lexical exceptions to metaphony. Certain Class III nominals fail to show metaphony in the plural (Parodi 1892).

(23) Class III nouns

(a) Normal metaphony in:

sg.	pl.	gloss
kɔr-ə	kwor-ə	'heart'
fjor-ə	fjur-ə	'flower'
mes-ə	mis-ə	'month'

(b) but not in:

sg.	pl.	gloss
mont-ə	mont-ə	'mountain'
pont-ə	pont-ə	'bridge'
peʃ-ə	peʃ-ə	'fish'

The situation in Arpinate calls for an analysis with at least two components: first, there are certain morphemes that are triggers for metaphony; and second, certain Roots are specified to turn this process off.

We take the morphemes that trigger metaphony to be MP triggers (we use features like [II] and [III] here for convenience; there might be better ways of encoding these classes):[14]

(24) Metaphony: (ON) with [II], [III,+pl], ...

The precise form of the metaphony rule (better, rules) is a question that has been examined extensively in Calabrese's work, most recently in Calabrese (2016). Putting aside the formal phonological details of these processes, the two different outcomes (raising for /o,e/, diphthongization for /ɔ,ɛ/) are activated when metaphony is (ON).

This process is "exceptional" in the sense that it is triggered morphologically, and not phonologically. We take it to be MP because it appears that the triggering morphemes are triggers by default. That is, they produce a metaphony environment, except in the case of a limited set of exceptions: those in (23b). In principle it would be possible to take the exceptionality of these Roots as evidence for metaphony being an MM rule. While such an analysis is able to account for the facts that we have access to (it is not clear from the available descriptions whether morpheme-skipping metaphony happens in Arpinate), it is somewhat forced given that the trigger morphemes are triggers across the board, with a limited set of listed exceptions. For this reason, our analysis treats metaphony as turned (ON) with the [III,+pl] morpheme whenever it occurs.[15] Then, to account for the exceptionality seen in (23b), the rule is locally turned (OFF) when this morpheme is concatenated with a particular list of Roots. As a result, the Roots in question are exceptions to exceptions, and nothing happens to them in the plural environment.

In summary, we have advanced the idea that Arpinate metaphony is an MP process triggered by certain morphemes; the rule can be exceptionally turned (OFF) when those morphemes are concatenated with particular Roots. In principle, this behavior could be handled with MM activation as we have defined it. In making the exceptional switching proposal, we have two differences from MM in mind.

First, the MP+exceptional switching versus MM treatment produces different expectations concerning the productivity of the metaphonic process. All else equal, the MP analysis predicts that metaphony should apply with nonce Roots affixed with [III,+pl], whereas the MM treatment does not necessarily make

---

14 Other metaphony triggers – e.g. [+2] Agr – would be included in this list as well; as noted above, metaphony in the verbal system (but not in nouns) raises /a/ in addition to the mid vowels.
15 Since metaphony occurs with class II masculines as well, there could be a more general statement here about the triggering in plural forms.

this prediction. As indicated by the *all else equal* qualification, other factors (including but not limited to phonological neighborhood effects, Fn. 2) complicate the predictions concerning productivity. See also the comments at the end of this section, and in §4.

Second, our analysis predicts that exceptional switching requires concatenation between the trigger and the morpheme that turns the trigger off, because these two morphemes need to see each other as morphemes. Schematically, where $\sqrt{\text{ROOT}}^-$ stands for the list of Roots that turn (OFF) an MP rule turned (ON) by X, and M is a linearly intervening morpheme, the configuration of interest is shown in (25):

(25) $\sqrt{\text{ROOT}}^-$-M-X

That is, assuming that M creates a phonological environment in which the MP rule triggered by X could target the Root, the prediction is that the Root could not turn the MP rule off because it is not local to the trigger.

Although we do not have data to (dis)confirm this additional prediction in Arpinate study, the prediction is a strong one, and thus worth highlighting for future work.

Finally, we note that in this particular case study, the exceptional switching is relatively simple, in that there is a single list of Roots that are unaffected by a metaphony trigger. In our analysis of Umlaut in §4, it will be shown that exceptional switching might sometimes become entangled with more varied relations between triggers and potential targets, producing surface patterns of considerable complexity.

3.4 Summary

In this section we have looked at a number of different alternations, both MP and MM, in terms of our classification in §2, and we have looked at a number of predictions concerning when these (exceptional) processes should have exceptions.

Broadly speaking, there are two main points that arise from this survey and synthesis. The first is that something like the distinction between MP and MM rules is required, as there appear to be systematically different patterns of application among morphophonological alternations broadly construed. We have pursued the hypothesis that MP alternations require phonological locality (and thus may skip morphemes), whereas MM alternations require concatenation of morphemes, bringing them under the MIC.

The second focus of this section was on two additional types of application effects, involving phase cyclic boundaries and exceptional switching. Our hope is that highlighting the predictions that the theory produces in these domains will provide an impetus for further investigations along these lines. Finally, in addition to extending the theoretical dimension of the discussion, these phenomena play an important role in understanding the complex behaviors of German Umlaut, to which we now turn.

4 Some properties of German Umlaut

In this section we develop an analysis of the alternation called *Umlaut* in (Standard High) German. Descriptively, Umlaut is a vowel fronting process, whose effects (represented orthographically by V̈) are shown in (26):

(26) Umlaut Examples

Vowels		Examples	
/uː/	/yː/	Huhn	Hühn-er
/ʊ/	/ʏ/	dumm	dümm-lich
/oː/	/øː/	hoch	höch-st
/ɔ/	/œ/	Holz	hölz-ern
/a/	/ɛː/	Europa	europä-isch
/a/	/ɛ/	Stand	ständ-ig
/aʊ/	/ɔʏ/	sauf	Säuf-er

While originally a phonological alternation triggered by a suffixal front vowel or glide, Umlaut is clearly morphophonological in contemporary German, in the sense that the phonemes that originally triggered it no longer are present in the triggering affixes.[16] In addition to this trigger behavior, Umlaut is (for the most part) sensitive to particular targets: for example, Umlaut triggered by 3s verb inflection applies to the verb *laufen* 'to run' to yield *läuft*, but not to e.g. *kaufen* 'to buy', which has 3s *kauft*. The "mixed" character of Umlaut – a phonological change that is associated with sets of morphologically defined triggers and targets – has been at the center of an intense discussion of the boundaries between morphology and phonology (see e.g. Wiese 1996b for a concise statement and review of the literature).

---

[16] This is a standard description of how Umlaut has been "morphologized"; it might be possible to posit, with e.g. Lieber (1987), a floating [-bk] autosegment with Umlaut-triggering affixes. See §5 for discussion.

Our goals for this section are to analyze Umlaut within the framework that we have outlined and illustrated in §§2-3. The main direction of the discussion is an argument to the effect that while Umlaut has many *prima facie* MM properties, there are some indications that Umlaut might be activated as an MP rule as well. After developing this main point, we will point to a number of fine-grained details in the study of Umlaut that could provide the basis for future work.

4.1 The analysis in outline

As noted above, Umlaut is triggered by a number of different morphemes. A non-exhaustive list, chosen to emphasize the syntacticosemantic heterogeneity of the triggers, is given in (27):[17]

(27) Umlaut: Morphosyntactic environments (not exhaustive)
    a. Verb forms: *fahr-en* 'drive' infinitive, *fähr-t* 3s pres.
    b. Noun plurals: *Huhn* 'hen', *Hühn-er* 'hens'
    c. Diminutives: *Glocke* 'bell', *Glöck-chen* 'bell-Dim.'
    d. Adjective formation: *Europa* 'Europe', *europä-isch* 'European'
    e. Comparatives: *lang* 'long', *läng-er* 'longer'

As has been amply noted in the literature, most of the Umlaut triggers have targets that they do not apply to; these have to be specified on a case-by-case basis for individual trigger/target pairs, in the sense that a single Root can undergo Umlaut in some of the environments in (27), but not others. An illustration of this effect is shown for plurals with *-e* and adjectives with *-ig* in (45) (cf. Wurzel 1970; Janda 1998):

(28) Trigger-Target pair specificity for umlaut in nouns

Singular	Plural	Adjective in *-ig*	Glosses
Harz	Harz-e	harz-ig	'resin-resins-resinous'
Tag	Tag-e	**täg-ig**	'day-days-days.long'
Saft	**Säft-e**	saft-ig	'juice-juices-juicy'
Macht	**Mächt-e**	**mächt-ig**	'power-powers-powerful'

---

[17] We are speaking of the triggers as morphemes, not the exponents of these morphemes. There are some reasons to think that one could look into this part of Umlaut in more detail. For example, *-s* plurals never trigger Umlaut, whereas *-er* plurals apparently always do (Lowenstamm 2012, 2015a). See §4.2 for some related comments.

While almost all Umlaut triggers must be specified to apply to some Roots and not others, there is also one context in which Umlaut is exceptionless: when it is triggered by "true" diminutives, realized in Standard German as -*chen*.

Building on what has been discussed in prior sections, there must be at least three components to the analysis of Umlaut:
1. **Phonology:** The first is a phonological rule, abbreviated $\mathring{R}$; this rule effects the phonological changes called *Umlaut*.
2. **Triggers:** The rule $\mathring{R}$ is activated by certain morphemes – i.e. those in (27); but
3. **Targets:** Certain Roots (or morphemes) do not undergo $\mathring{R}$ in the presence of the Triggering morphemes.

As far as the phonology goes, we have little to say as long as there is a single rule that effects Umlaut. As for specifics (see Wiese 1996a, 1996b for discussion), it could be that this "rule" is written so as to front a vowel in the context of a trigger:

(29) V →[-bk]/__<Trigger>

Or, it could be that the process is actually bipartite:

(30) Implementing Umlaut in 2 steps
    a.   Insert [-bk] to the left of the phonological exponent (if any) of the morpheme that triggers Umlaut;
    b.   Associate [-bk] to the left.

For the purposes of what we will concentrate on here, either one of these treatments works (though, of course, we leave open the possibility that there might be ways of distinguishing them that are not known at present). What is crucial for our purposes is that there is a single Umlaut rule that is activated under a complex set of circumstances.

As illustrated above, the type of exceptionality that is seen with Umlaut needs to make reference to both Triggers and Targets. For this reason, it looks *prima facie* like an MM rule; that is:[18]

(31) Target ⌢ Trigger → $\mathring{R}$ (ON)

---

[18] Later in this section we will consider the possibility that Umlaut could be MP triggered (by at least certain morphemes), and exceptionally switched (OFF) (recall the discussion of Arpinate in §3.3).

More concretely, the grammar of German would, on an MM analysis, contain a series of statements specifying a trigger and a target, such that Umlaut would be turned (ON) under concatenation of certain pairs; for example, with reference to (28):[19]

(32) √TAG⌢ [a,-ig] → Ř (ON)
√SAFT ⌢ [+pl,-e] → Ř (ON)
√MACHT ⌢ [a,-ig], [+pl,-e] → Ř (ON)
⋮

Listing pairs of morphemes like this, and specifying certain pairs as turning Umlaut (ON), is inelegant; but as far as we can determine, *something* along these lines must play a role in any analysis of the phenomenon. The reason for this is that particular Roots do not undergo Umlaut in every possible Umlaut environment; rather, the information required to set Ř correctly comes from trigger/target pairs.

A consequence of this kind of "sporadic" application to a given Root is that it is not possible to appeal to different underlying forms for surface-identical vowels, depending on whether they undergo umlaut or not. This point requires some unpacking.

In outline, and considering e.g. *täg-ig* versus *saft-ig*, one idea is that the vowel of √TAG would be specified phonologically in such a way as to undergo Umlaut, but the vowel of √SAFT would be specified so that this did not happen.[20]

If we looked only at one possible trigger – adjectives with *-ig* – this type of solution might appear promising.[21] However, while this kind of analysis is able

---

[19] In this way of encoding things, we are being intentionally vague about whether the Umlaut trigger is the morpheme (defined in terms of synsem features) or its exponent. Some additional comments on this point are advanced below.

[20] Some comparative considerations are useful here, since a kind of "underlying phonological difference" solution appears promising for certain types of alterations. For example, as we noted earlier in this paper, Spanish diphthongization is a typical morphophonological alternation, in the sense that it applies to some Roots (e.g. *pensar*, 'to think', with 1s *pienso*, but not others e.g. *tensar*, 1s *tenso*). Building on the idea that diphthongization applies to stressed vowels, Harris (1985) proposes that the underlying phonological representations of Roots that undergo diphthongization are different from those that do not: the former have two timing slots, the latter one. This difference – neutralized on the surface when the vowels in question are not stressed – works in conjunction with a number of other rules to produce diphthongization under stress with the Roots that have two timing slots underlyingly, and no change with the Roots that have a single timing slot.

[21] For example, Wiese (1996b) puts a floating [+front] feature in the URs of Roots that undergo Umlaut; more recently, Scharinger (2009) proposes something along these lines as well.

to account for the $\sqrt{\text{SAFT}}$ versus $\sqrt{\text{TAG}}$ difference with -*ig* adjectives, it does not account for the fact that $\sqrt{\text{SAFT}}$ *does*, in fact, undergo Umlaut in the plural (*Säfte*), while $\sqrt{\text{TAG}}$ does not (*Tage*). If underlying phonological specification determined Umlaut behavior of Roots, then a particular Root should either umlaut with all triggers, or never umlaut; but this is not what happens. In short, because the same Root may or may not undergo Umlaut depending on which Umlaut trigger it appears with, some statement of trigger/target pairs along the lines of (32) is needed.[22,23]

As an interim summary, it appears that a basic treatment of Umlaut is possible in which the rule $\ddot{R}$ is triggered under concatenation of triggers/targets pairs, making this look like an MM alternation.

4.2 MM versus MP

Building on the results of the preceding subsection, we now look at a further set of phenomena which, taken collectively, suggest that there is much to be said about Umlaut, and that, in particular, there might be evidence for an MP treatment of Umlaut with certain morphemes.

As a first step, we note that there is one primary reason for taking Umlaut to be an MM rule: its trigger/target specificity. There are then two further things to consider. The first is to ask, given the illustrations of intervention effects of different types in §3, whether there is converging evidence for this treatment of Umlaut when we examine its locality properties. With this in mind, we examine an argument that Umlaut shows "morpheme-skipping" in §4.2.1.

The second part of the discussion looks at one case where Umlaut shows MP properties, at least as far as trigger/target relations are concerned – diminutives (§4.2.4). After examining additional points of interest involving apparent

---

[22] Regarding the structure of trigger/target interactions, it is unknown to us whether there are meaningful patterns in terms of how Roots behave when considered in all possible Umlaut environments. That is, subsets of the data like (28) clearly show that for the two morphemes considered there, all four possible Root Umlaut behaviors are found. But this does not mean that all four types are equally common in the language. There could be a number of correlations relating trigger behaviors that would be revealed by a quantitative study of the vocabulary, leading to generalizations that would be relevant both to language acquisition and language change. See Wurzel 1970 for an attempt to create implicational relationships between Umlaut triggers, although we note that he allows exceptions to his implications.

[23] An alternative to encoding Umlaut phonological in targets is to encode it in triggers, by specifying their exponents with a floating [-bk] feature, for example (this is done in Lieber's work). See §5 for some discussion of this kind of approach.

overapplication of Umlaut in compounds (§4.2.3) and the challenges presented by *-er* Nominals (§4.2.4), we provide in §4.3 a summary of why further investigation of Umlaut in terms of MM/MP is needed.

4.2.1 Locality: The Konjunktiv II (past subjunctive)

Kiparsky (1996) argues that Umlaut can skip morphemes, based on his take on the "Konjunktiv II" (past subjunctive) verb forms in German. Briefly, the argument is based on verbs like *brauchen* 'to need', which has the forms shown in (33):

(33) brauchen 'need'; 1s forms
  present: brauche
  preterite: brauchte
  past subjunctive: bräuchte

On Kiparsky's analysis, the past subjunctive is *bräuch-t-e*, where *-t* is an exponent of Tense (also found in the preterite), and *-e* an agreement morpheme that triggers Umlaut. If *-e* (or the morpheme it realizes) were indeed the trigger of Umlaut, this would be clear evidence for the MP status of the rule, since the trigger and target (the Root) are separated by an intervening Tense morpheme.

However, a closer look at the past subjunctive shows that it is not actually agreement that triggers Umlaut. There is thus no evidence in these forms that Umlaut skips morphemes, as would be expected from an MP rule.

Some additional facts are important in developing this argument. The past subjunctive form shows four patterns. For weak verbs (34a), it is formed with *-t*, like the preterite. The majority of strong verbs (34b) show past subjunctives that are the Umlauted versions of the preterite. The preterite itself shows a set of vowel changes called *Ablaut*, so that past subjunctives are derived by applying Umlaut to the output of Ablaut (cf. Wiese 1996a). In addition, a subset of strong verbs (34c) show vowel forms that are not the Umlaut derivatives of the Ablauted preterite form. Finally, there is a "mixed" type (34d) to which *brauchen* belongs, with both the *-t* seen in the weak verbs, along with Umlaut (forms cited in first person singular):[24]

---

[24] For some speakers of German, the Konjunktiv II is reported to be archaic, or, at least, not frequent in day-to-day usage (this is particularly true of the (c) type). For our purposes, this is immaterial, as the behavior of Umlaut seen in these verb forms were clearly active and not archaic in a recent form of the language.

(34) Past subjunctive forms

	present	preterite	past subj,	gloss
a.	sage	sagte	sagte	'play'
	loben	lobte	lobte	'praise'
	suchen	suchte	suchte	'look for'
b.	komme	kam	käme	'come'
	sehe	sah	sähe	'see'
	fahre	fuhr	führe	'drive'
c.	stehe	stand	stünde	'stand'
	sterbe	starb	stürbe	'die'
	verderbe	verdarb	verdürbe	'spoil'
	werfe	warf	würfe	'throw'
d.	brauche	brauchte	bräuchte	'need'
	bringe	brachte	brächte	'bring'
	denke	dachte	dächte	'think'
	weiss	wusste	wüsste	'know'

There are some different types of generalizations at play in these patterns. For example, the verbs that show Ablaut – those in (34b,c) – also show a -Ø exponent of Tense, not the -t seen elsewhere. Moreover, all of these verbs show Umlaut in the past subjunctive. However, while Umlaut occurs with some of the verbs showing -t for Tense like those in (34d), for the much larger class of weak verbs in (34a), Umlaut is not found. If Umlaut were able to skip morphemes, then in our terms it would be an MP rule; as such, it would not be sensitive to specific Roots over an intervening overt tense morpheme: either all -t past subjunctives should show Umlaut, or all should not, contrary to fact.

This line of reasoning suggests that Agr is not the trigger for Umlaut in the past subjunctive. There are further observations that support this claim. For illustration, consider the inflection of *kommen* 'to come' in (35):

(35) Some forms of *kommen*

	present	preterite	present subj.	past subj.
1s	komme	kam	komme	käme
2s	kommst	kamst	kommest	kämest
3s	kommt	kam	komme	käme
1p	kommen	kamen	kommen	kämen
2p	kommt	kamt	kommet	kämet
3p	kommen	kamen	kommen	kämen

The agreement exponents in the present subjunctive are identical to the agreement that is found in the past subjunctive (and different from agreement in the indicative);[25] but there is no Umlaut in the present subjunctive. We take this to show that Agr is not the Umlaut trigger in the past subjunctive. Similarly, the preterite shows the stem alternant that is found in the past subjunctive, but does not show Umlaut. This shows that T[+past] is not the Umlaut trigger. The most transparent interpretation of these observations is that neither [+subj], nor T[+past], nor Agr in the subjunctive is individually an Umlaut trigger; rather, it is the features T[+past,+subj] together that trigger it.

Our analysis of the forms (34) is based on the structure in (36), where [+past] and [+subj] features occur on the same morpheme (which is labelled T(ense), but could be called T/M for "Tense/Mood"):

(36)   Structure for past subjunctive

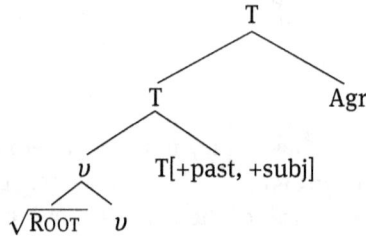

There are three aspects of the analysis to be unpacked:
- First, the morpheme T[+past,+subj] shows allomorphy between -*t* and -Ø in the past subjunctive (in fact, exactly as it does in the preterite).
- Second, T[+past] triggers Ablaut (and other changes) on certain verb Roots, in a way characteristic of MM rules. Ablaut will be viewed here abstractly; that is, as a set of rules that are triggered when a particular class of Roots is local to an Ablaut trigger. What we mean by the "abstract" treatment of this diacritic is that it actually stands proxy for a set of different phonological changes, whose properties and interrelations could be examined in their own right. Although the question of which patterns of Ablaut are triggered in the preterite and participle forms are of some interest, they do not play a role in our analysis here.

---

25 Wiese (1996a:127) suggests that the schwa (orthographic e) that appears in the final syllable of the subjunctive forms is inserted to satisfy a morphophonological requirement specific to that mood. The status of this vowel— in particular whether it might be an exponent of a morpheme— is worth looking into further, but is beyond the scope of the present discussion.

– Third, the morpheme T[+past,+subj] is an Umlaut trigger. In the linear representation derived from (36), the Root is concatenated with the Tense morpheme; this allows for Roots to affect whether or not Umlaut applies.[26] For the verbs of type (34b), the output of Ablaut is subjected to Umlaut (cf. Wiese 1996b). (The (34c) type verbs are more complicated than this; see below).

Starting with Tense allomorphy, we posit the Vocabulary Items in (37). These are underspecified, so that the same exponent is inserted in both the preterite T[+past], and the past subjunctive T[+past,+subj]. LIST1 here contains all the verbs that take a -Ø:

(37) T[+past] ↔ -Ø/LIST1 __
      T[+past] ↔ -t

For the second component of the analysis, there needs to be a set of MM rules that effect the vowel changes seen in (34b-d) (Ablaut, at least for (b-c), along with the additional changes seen in e.g. *bringen*, with preterite *brach-t-e*). As noted earlier, these MM rules could be implemented in different ways, but we will abstract away from details here. What is important for our purposes are two additional points, which comprise the third bullet above: first, the fact that Umlaut follows Ablaut for the (34b) class; and second, the behavior of the (34c) class, where the past subjunctive is *not* the umlauted preterite (but is nevertheless a front vowel).

In the simpler case, the (34b) class, the correct results are produced if Ablaut precedes Umlaut in a theory with rule ordering (cf. Wiese 1996a). In order to function properly, this analysis requires that the trigger of Ablaut, the [+past] feature, not be "used up" or "discharged" when Ablaut applies. This is because [+past] must also be referred to when Umlaut is triggered subsequently; that is (and including only these two rules):

(38) Ablaut/Umlaut
    a. Ablaut: Triggered by T[+past]
    b. Umlaut: Triggered by T[+past,+subjunctive]

Although not frequently discussed, having a single feature trigger more than one (MP or MM) rule must be part of theories that employ morphologically-triggered phonological changes. For instance, if we approach alternations like *think ~ thought*

---

[26] Note that this approach assumes that the υ morpheme is pruned from the representation, so that the √ROOT is adjacent to the past tense morpheme; cf. §2.

morphophonologically (as the result of MM rules), then there are at least two changes effected (assuming that the underling form is like the one that surfaces in the non-past *think*): one to the vocalism, and one to the coda (details depend on further assumptions, since, of course, a number of different assumptions could be made about the phonological underlying representation of the Root).[27]

The idea that features can trigger more than one morphophonological rule provides a way of handling the (34c) class, where the past subjunctive is not the umlauted preterite. Here, we hypothesize that there is an Ablaut rule for these Roots that is triggered by T[+past,+subj] together, in addition to the Ablaut rule triggered by T[+past] alone. This part of the analysis is schematized in (39), where LIST^c stands for the Roots of type (34c):

(39) Ablaut rules for type (34c)
    a. LIST^c⌒ T[+past,+subj] ⇒ Ablaut /e/ → /u/ (ON)
    b. LIST^c⌒ T[+past] ⇒ Ablaut /e/ → /a/ (ON)

In a past subjunctive, the more specific (39a) applies; in a preterite, (39b).

Note that although the first rule (39a) is more specific than (39b), something further must be said about why both do not apply, given that we have found that the same features may activate more than one morphophonological rule. The most obvious thing to say is that (39a) bleeds (39b), by virtue of the phonological change that it effects.

Subsequently, the Umlaut rule, which is activated by T[+past,+subj], applies to the output of Ablaut. This produces umlauted *stünde*, *stürbe*, and so on.

In summary, the past subjunctive forms do not provide an argument for "morpheme skipping" in Umlaut, although they do reveal a great deal about the ways in which Umlaut is triggered, and how it relates to other alternations. Concerning the general question of morphologically non-local Umlaut, there is one more case that we have identified as being a possible instance; this involves diminutives, to which we turn now.

4.2.2 Exceptionless Triggering in Diminutives

In this and the following section we look at two phenomena that suggest that in some cases Umlaut has MP properties. The first is based on an observation made

---

[27] For an application in English – and a version of what form a complete reduction of morphophonology to individual rules might look like – see Halle & Mohanan (1985).

in numerous works: while Umlaut shows numerous Root-specific exceptions with many triggers, it always applies with Diminutives (cf. Wurzel 1970; Lieber 1980; Wiese 1996b).[28]

(40) Regularity of Umlaut for *-chen* and *-lein* (Wiese 1996a)

Glöck-chen 'bell-Dim.' Fräu-lein 'miss' (woman-Dim.)
Hünd-chen 'dog-Dim.' Häus-lein 'house-Dim.'
Melön-chen 'melon-Dim.' Lämp-lein 'lamp-Dim.'
Büs-chen 'bus-Dim.' Männ-lein 'man-Dim.'
Natiön-chen 'nation-Dim.' Gärt-lein 'garden-Dim.'
Prögrämm-chen 'program-Dim.' Löch-lein 'hole-Dim.'

The exceptionless application of Umlaut with [+dim] is striking when considered in the context of the complex patterns of morpheme-specific exceptions that characterize this process with other triggers. In particular it focuses attention on the question of whether Umlaut with diminutives is MM or MP.

Beginning with an MM approach, the exceptionlessness of [+dim] triggering could certainly be stated. It would simply have to be the case that every morpheme that appears adjacent to the diminutive morpheme turns Umlaut (ON). Although it is possible to formulate an MM rule with this property, the move seems forced, since what we are observing is that Umlaut does not have morphologically-defined targets with [+dim]. (Moreover this approach might have difficulties with locality – see below).

On the face of it, it looks like diminutives provide evidence for an MP treatment of Umlaut, as stated in (41) (cf. Shwayder 2015):

(41) [+dim] ⇒ $\ddot{R}$ (ON)

Along these lines, there appears to be at least some corroborating evidence that Umlaut has MP properties in diminutives from locality. The Root *fahr*, which surfaces as the verb *fahren* 'drive' that is seen at various points above, forms the Root nominal *Fahr-t* 'trip', with the exponent *-t* of *n*. From this noun, a diminutive can be formed, and, crucially, it shows Umlaut: *Fähr-t-chen* 'little trip'. Assuming

---

[28] There are examples with *-chen*, the typical diminutive suffix in Standard German, and no Umlaut: e.g. *Hundchen*, from *Hund* 'dog'. However, these are not semantically diminutives; rather, they are a type of hypocoristic that is semantically distinguishable from a true diminutive. Thus, *Hundchen* means something like 'dog' and conveys endearment, whereas Umlauted *Hündchen* also exists in the language, and means 'dog.diminutive'; see Ott (2011) for a recent discussion.

that *Fahr-t* is in fact bi-morphemic, as we have shown here, this is an example in which Umlaut skips a morpheme, as expected with MP.[29]

While an improvement over an MM analysis for the reasons noted above, (41) raises a number of questions when we consider the possibility of an analysis involving exceptional switching (§3.3). Note that this sort of analysis could posit an MP application of Umlaut e.g. for [a,-ig] that Umlaut is (ON), but switched off when that morpheme is concatenated with certain Roots. While it would be possible to hold to the MM analysis and state that there are simply no Roots or morphemes that turn Umlaut (OFF) for [+dim], a more interesting analysis would be based on the idea that diminutive exceptionlessness arises for *systematic* reasons: ideally, having to do with the structure of diminutives. For example (and not committing ourselves to details of any particular analysis), Ott's (2011) paper cited above argues at length that the structure in which diminutives are derived differs in crucial ways from more "garden variety" affixation structures that involve head adjunction. Of particular interest would be structures in which there is a head intervening linearly between a Root (or other Umlaut target) and the diminutive morpheme, as this head would prevent the target from being local to the trigger, precluding exceptional switching. While we cannot examine this issue in detail here, we believe that an important avenue for future investigation, since it highlights the question of how closely the morphophonology follows the morphosyntax.

In summary, the fact that there are no exceptions to Umlaut with diminutives suggests that – at least for [+dim] – the rule is triggered in an MP way. While there is more to be investigated concerning the possible structural basis for this exceptionlessness behavior, we have now at least one piece of evidence against treating Umlaut as MM across the board.

4.2.3 Overapplication in compounds

Lowenstamm (2012, 2015a) presents an analysis of Umlaut in which the sporadic trigger/target properties of the rule are derivative of differences in phase-cyclic structure. While, in our view, the account does not generalize in the ways that Lowenstamm envisions (see below), it contains as a subpart a core set of insights about

---

[29] We raise the point about whether or not decomposition is necessary here because of other examples that appear to show the same *-t*, but which might no longer be decomposed in the contemporary language. For example, *machen* 'do, make' is the source of the noun *Macht* 'power', but the latter might not have the *-t* realizing a morpheme (i.e. there might be a Root $\sqrt{\text{MACHT}}$ distinct from the source of *machen*).

the behavior of compounds which, in the context of the current discussion, provide further evidence that Umlaut might (sometimes) be MP triggered. At the very least, it provides the motivation for a more detailed look at compounds (cf. also Wiese 1996a).

The basic proposal made by Lowenstamm is similar in many ways to one discussed in §3.2 above, where we noted that phase cyclic derivation could produce situations in which two morphemes could not see each other as morphemes due to cyclic spell out. In particular, Lowenstamm proposes that an Umlaut trigger may only affect a target when the two are in the same phase cyclic domain. Illustrating with the contrast between *männlich* 'masculine', from *Mann* 'man', and *amtlich* 'official', from *Amt* 'office', he argues that the Umlaut difference results from the former being a Root adjective [√MANN *a*], while the latter is denominal [[√AMT *n*] *a*]. In the Root adjective, the Umlaut trigger and target are in the same phase cyclic domain, and Umlaut applies; in the denominal adjective, the *a* head and the Root are separated cyclically, such that Umlaut does not apply.

This account might work for the examples with *-lich* just mentioned; it would be useful to have corroborating evidence (whether semantic or phonological) that *amtlich* is denominal and *männlich* is not, since the argument hinges crucially on this point. Beyond this, our view is that while there is clearly something to Lowenstamm's insight about phases, there are some instances of sporadic application to which a phase-based approach will not extend. For example, Umlaut is triggered by 3rd person Agr in the present tense, to yield 3s *läuf-t* for *laufen* 'to run'; however, other verbs, such as *kaufen* 'to buy', show no Umlaut in this context: 3s *kauf-t*. There does not appear to be any evidence in favor of there being a cyclic boundary between Agr and the Root in the latter case. The same reasoning applies with other Umlaut triggers; for example, the comparative of *kurz* 'short' is *kürz-er*, but *stolz* 'proud' shows *stolz-er*. It thus appears that while being in different phase domains might prevent Umlaut from applying, something remains to be said about why it can either apply or not when the trigger and target are within the same phase domain.[30]

Lowenstamm's discussion highlights another important behavior of Umlaut – apparent *overapplication* of the process in compounds, an effect noted in passing in Wiese (1996a). The observation is that a Root that is not umlauted on its own shows Umlaut in (at least certain) compounds, as shown in (42):

(42) a. Blut 'blood'; blut-ig 'bloody'
    Voll-blut 'pure blood'; Voll-blüt-ig 'pure blooded'

---

[30] Lowenstamm suggests that both umlauted and un-umlauted variants are derived by the grammar under certain circumstances, with the choice of which is produced being the result of another system; see Fn. 31)

b. Mut 'courage'; mut-ig 'brave'
   Groß-mut 'magnanimity'; groß-müt-ig 'magnanimous'

Although based on only a preliminary investigation that is restricted to adjectives with -*ig*, it appears that this effect might prove to be important for distinguishing between MM and MP analyses of Umlaut. What we have in mind is as follows. It is possible that the exponent -*ig* is inserted into adjective heads that are Root attached ([√Root *a*], as in *blut-ig*, *mut-ig*, and probably the examples in (28)), and also into a denominal structure, with the meaning "possessed of the noun" (cp. Nevins and Myler 2014). The latter structure is shown in (43):

(43) Structure for *vollblütig*

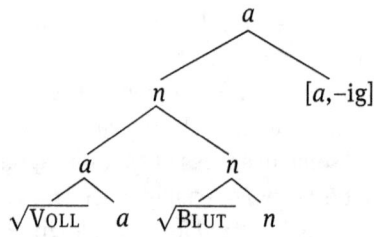

In (43), there is a cyclic boundary between the trigger of Umlaut [*a*,-ig] and the Root that it targets. If Umlaut is MP triggered by [*a*,-ig], it would follow that it should overapply in this environment, because √Blut would not be visible as a morpheme to exceptionally switch the rule (OFF). On the other hand, an approach with Umlaut switched (ON) as an MM rule would predict no Umlaut in this structure.

While promising, there are some complications to this story that remain to be investigated systematically. For one, it is quite possible that there are other ways of deriving an -*ig* affixed compound – for example, as a compound adjective, in which the *a* head realized as -*ig* is Root attached:

(44) Root-attached -*ig*

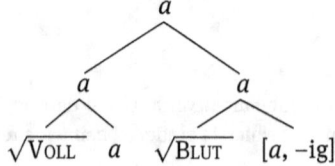

Here, we would expect Umlaut to behave exactly as it does with [√BLUT *a*], since there is no cyclic boundary between trigger and target. As it turns out, speakers we have consulted have produced complex reactions, such that *vollblutig* is perhaps grammatical, but strongly dispreferred, perhaps because of a competition for use effect of a type that is not infrequent in derivational morphology (Embick and Marantz 2008; Embick 2016).

A further complication, noted by Lowenstamm, is that some of the compounds in question have idiomatic interpretations; for example, from *Rotze* 'snot' and *Nase* 'nose', there exists *rotznäsig* 'bratty'(='snot nosed'), and also, apparently *rotznasig* 'with a snotty nose'. At least one speaker we have consulted accepts for *blau* 'blue' and *Auge* 'eye' the form *blauaugig* 'blue eyed in the typical human iris sense', and interprets *blauäugig* as idiomatic 'naïve', as well as 'having blue eyes in an atypical sense' (the latter being for, e.g. an eye painted completely blue on a statue).

Clearly, there are a number of factors at play here, including but not limited to dialect effects, variation in the sociolinguistic sense, idiomaticity, and competition for use. As a way of structuring a closer look at these phenomena, we note by way of concluding that the effects of interest for distinguishing MP from MM can be stated in the following predictions, derived from the discussion of §3.2:

Cyclic prediction 1: If Umlaut is an MM rule that must be switched (ON) under concatenation of a trigger and a target, Umlaut will underapply in compounds when there is a cyclic boundary between the trigger and the target.

Cyclic prediction 2: If Umlaut is an MP rule that is (ON) by default with its triggers, then the process should overapply in compounds when there is a cyclic boundary between the trigger and the target, because the cyclic boundary prevents the rule from being exceptionally switched (OFF).

Overall, compounds appear to provide some indication that Umlaut might be MP, not MM for [*a*,- ig]; at the very least, they suggest a domain in which further investigation could look closely at how morphophonology relates to cyclic structure.

4.2.4 A question about -er nominals

Nominal forms in -*er* – which we abbreviate as N-er – present a particular challenge to the analysis of Umlaut. Many of the nouns in question are referred to as *agent(ive) nouns*, a term we will not employ for reasons to be discussed below.

Some N-er forms are shown in (45):

(45) Trigger-Target pair specificity for Umlaut

infinitive	3s present	-er nominal	glosses
mal-en	mal-t	Mal-er	'paint-paints-painter'
back-en	back-t	**Bäck-er**	'bake-bakes-baker'
fahr-en	**fähr-t**	Fahr-er	'drive-drives-driver'
trag-en	**träg-t**	**Träg-er**	'carry-carries-carrier'

The question raised by Umlaut patterns in N-er is one of cyclic visibility: briefly, if nominals like those in (45) are deverbal $[[[\sqrt{\text{ROOT}}\ v]...]n]$ (the ... stands in for e.g. Voice and other morphemes that have been posited in agentive nominals), then they should, it would seem, all behave identically with respect to Umlaut. The reason for this is trigger/target visibility, as defined by the phase-cyclic part of the theory. The $\sqrt{\text{ROOT}}$ target and the n morpheme that triggers Umlaut are not active in the same phase cycle according to the definitions adopted above. Thus, it appears that either there should always be Umlaut (if $\ddot{R}$ is MP (ON) for the n realized as -er), or it should always be off (if $\ddot{R}$ is an MM rule).

As we noted at the beginning of this section, we are being careful to avoid referring to all of nouns in question as "agentive nominals" – there appear to be a number of different structures in which -er realizes a nominalizing head, and not all of these are necessarily deverbal (cf. Alexiadou and Schäfer 2008, 2010). Schematically, what is at issue is whether or not presence or absence of Umlaut in a particular derivative can be correlated with the presence or absence of a verbalizing v head between the n head realized as -er and the Root that is the target of Umlaut, since this would produce different phase-locality conditions between trigger and target:

(46) Phase locality:
Root and n active together: $[\sqrt{\text{ROOT}} ... n]$
Root and n not active together: $[[\sqrt{\text{ROOT}}\ v] ... n]$

An ideal scenario would be one in which these or other structural differences had direct consequences for morphophonology. Along these lines, for example, Ingason & Sigurðsson (2015) show that two types of agent nominals in Icelandic exhibit morphophonological differences that derive from the presence of a verbalizing head in one type, but not the other.

To the extent that the phonological differences (Umlaut or not) could be made to correlate with cyclic structure that is motivated by other considerations (syntactic or semantic), there would be converging evidence for the version of the theory that we have adopted here. In addition, such a correlation would help to distinguish between the MM and MP analyses we have developed above. If Umlaut never applied in (46b), there would be evidence for MM; if Umlaut "overapplied" in this context (as with compounds), there would be further evidence for MP Umlaut.

At present it is not clear whether a more detailed study of *-er* nominals will be able to reduce Umlaut differences to differences in cyclic structure. If no such correlations between structure and Umlaut be found, there are important implications for phase theory, or for the treatment of Umlaut's target-sensitivity, or both. We leave a detailed examination of this question for future work.[31]

4.3 Concluding remarks

Our analysis of Umlaut starts with the idea that there is a single phonological rule $\ddot{R}$ that is activated by a number of distinct morphemes. It is important, for reasons discussed below, that there be a unified phonological analysis of the alternation, and our treatment provides this directly (*contra* Wurzel 1970; Anderson 1992). With respect to how Umlaut is activated, things are more interesting. On the one hand, the complex patterns of trigger/target behaviors, in which the same Root may or may not undergo Umlaut depending on which trigger it is next to, suggest that Umlaut is an MM rule, with triggers and targets identified as particular morphemes. We provided a working analysis in §4.1 along these lines. On the other hand, data from diminutives and compounds suggests Umlaut that is sometimes an MP rule, while our overview of *-er* Nominals suggests that there is more to be studied about Umlaut and phase structure.

---

[31] As far as the Umlaut part of this question is concerned, it is worth noting that both Lieber (1980, 1987) and Lowenstamm (2012, 2015) explicitly propose that the grammar of German generates both umlauted and unumlauted forms for potential undergoers, leaving the determination of which is employed to another system – presumably language use. The move is reminiscent of the "Potential Lexicon" posited in Halle (1973), revisited more recently in Embick (2016).

While it appears to be the case that alternations decided "at the level of use" might not be subject to the locality properties that are posited for grammatical derivations – see Tamminga et al. (2016) for extensive discussion – it is not clear to us at present whether there is evidence that this is what is happening with Umlaut. Along these lines, experimental evidence would be valuable; see e.g. Scharinger et al. (2010) for a study that speaks to the types of questions raised in this note.

One possible response to the observations about "overapplication" and exceptionless Umlaut in diminutives would be to say that the Umlaut rule is triggered in different ways by different morphemes (i.e. some are MM and some are MP). However, a plausible analysis which unifies the properties of both Umlaut behaviors can be derived with the tools that we have developed in §§2-3. Recall in our discussion of metaphonic changes in Arpinate (§3.3) that while certain morphemes trigger metaphony for most of the Roots that are possible targets, there are a few exceptional Roots that do not undergo any change. We analyzed this effect with what we called "exceptional switching": under concatenation, as an MM effect, a particular set of Roots turns an MP-triggered rule (OFF).

Umlaut could be treated in essentially the same way, an idea that is investigated in depth in Shwayder (2017) (cf. also Wurzel 1970). There are two components to this analysis:

(47) Outline of a theory of Exceptional Switching for MP Umlaut
 a. The morphemes that trigger MP Umlaut are set to $\ddot{R}$ (ON)
 b. Under concatenation, Roots may turn the (ON) setting of certain triggers to (OFF)

The difference between this exceptional switching analysis and the MM analysis presented above is subtle. In the MM analysis, we said that Umlaut is turned (ON) when e.g. $\sqrt{\text{SAFT}}$ is concatenated with [+pl], but not when it is next to [a,-ig] (unlike e.g. $\sqrt{\text{MACHT}}$). The analysis in (47) says that Umlaut is (ON) when the trigger morphemes are present in a derivation; but, it can be deactivated when the trigger is adjacent to a Root that exceptionally switches it (OFF).

In simple cases, both the MM and exceptional switching analyses can derive the correct results. In more complex cases, like those examined in §4.2, we pointed that even though "non-local" Umlaut is not robustly attested (§4.2.1), there are some cases of overapplication, suggesting that – for at least those triggers – Umlaut behaves like an MP process, one that is exceptionally switched (OFF) by certain Roots. Importantly, this conclusion is restricted to particular morphemes, like the head realized as -*ig* where Umlaut overapplies. For other morphemes, e.g. the 2s and 3s agreement morphemes that trigger Umlaut for certain verbs in the present tense, we have found no such overapplication; for these morphemes, an MP analysis is less obvious.

Taken together, these findings suggest, as noted earlier, that the single Umlaut rule is activated in both MM and MP ways. If this approach is on the right track, evidence from other domains could be sought, since the difference between MP

Umlaut "(ON) by default" and MM Umlaut effectively "(OFF) by default" might be detectable in acquisition data or in experimental findings.[32]

We hope that although this part of the investigation is more exploratory and less decisive than some other case studies that we have engaged in, it will provide structure to further investigation of both Umlaut and other morphophonological patterns.

5 Discussion

Our main goals in this paper fall into two parts. First, in §§2-3, we outlined an approach to morphophonological alternations, one that invokes phonological locality, morphological locality (=linear adjacency), and phases. The case studies brought together in §3 provide evidence for the MP versus MM distinction that is centered on phonological and morphological locality respectively; and, in addition, illustrate phase-cyclic and exceptional switching effects that add further directions for empirical investigation. The main goal of the second part of the paper, §4, is the extension of this approach to an examination of Umlaut in Standard German. Our main argument in that section is that Umlaut looks *prima facie* like an MM rule; but there are several avenues for further investigation suggesting, first, that at least some Umlaut triggers are MP; and second, that there are puzzles with how Umlaut interacts with phase theory that warrant careful study.

The discussion of this section compares some key properties of our approach with some alternative ways of treating morphophonology.

5.1 On the identity of exponents and rules

A basic dichotomy in morphology exists between theories that employ discrete morphemes, like the one adopted here, and theories that eliminate pieces in favor of "word formation rules" or the like, as most definitively argued for in Anderson (1992).

The phenomena analyzed in this paper highlight the importance of grounding morphophonology in a piece-based theory. As discussed elsewhere, affixless theories have a basic difficulty in accounting for what Embick (2013) calls morphophonological *loci*: abstractly, the observation that such alternations behave as if they originate in a position where a morpheme would be posited in a theory with morphemes. So, for

---

32 E.g., of the type that is invoked in discussions of *productivity*, although this is often more complex than much of the literature would suggest.

example, where a morpheme-based theory might say that a Root is affixed with morphemes -X, -Y, -Z, in an affixless theory the Root is combined with features [±X] etc., and rewritten by word-formation rules referring to these features; the output of these rules is given as phonological /XYZ/ in (48), to emphasize that they are not pieces):

(48) a. Morpheme-based theory

$$\sqrt{\text{Root}} - X - Y - Z$$

b. Affixless theory

$$\sqrt{\text{Root}} \begin{bmatrix} \pm X \\ \pm Y \\ \pm Z \end{bmatrix} - (\text{Word Formation Rules}) \rightarrow /\text{RootXYZ}/$$

A theory that employs representations like (48b) does not provide a straightforward way of analyzing the intervention effects that are discussed in §3.1. Those examples show MM changes that are prevented from occurring when a morpheme intervenes between the trigger and the target of the change. Crucially, because the intervention effects are defined morphologically, and not phonologically, they cannot be stated directly in a theory that does not employ morphemes in the first place.[33,34]

A second important point of comparison with affixless theories comes into contact with the analysis of Umlaut. One aspect of Umlaut that is emphasized in Embick and Halle (2005) is its "disjunctive" set of triggers. For an exponent – i.e. a phonological representation /XYZ/ inserted into a morpheme – the set of environments that have nothing in common syntacticosemantically would be treated as homophony, with multiple distinct Vocabulary Items that each happen to possess /XYZ/ as their exponent.

An important generalization is missed if Umlaut is treated in this way: *there is a single phonological rule at play, in all of the different environments in which it applies*. Having a different rule for each of the Umlaut triggers, where each of these rules effects exactly the same change, misses the generalization that at a phonological level of analysis, exactly the same change is effected.

---

[33] One possibility would be to use stored stems, effectively suppletion. This approach is deployed for *sing/sang* type alternations in Anderson (1992), but makes incorrect predictions about the "double-marking" of forms that are discussed in Halle and Marantz (1993). For more on stem storage, see also §5.3.

[34] The same sort of considerations apply with MP rules, where an amorphous theory does not have a natural way of stating the locus of the effect (although of course it could be stipulated). See Embick (2013) for discussion.

As it turns out, proponents of affixless theories like Anderson (1992) have argued that there are multiple rules of Umlaut. In order to see why this is the case, it is necessary to examine a more general set of issues that connects with the specific points considered above.

Within a theory that is centered on morphemes, it is possible to appeal to a general set of principles concerning the differences between piece-based realization on the one-hand versus morphophonological readjustment on the other. In the specific form that is implicated by Umlaut, (49) does this:

(49) **Piece/process asymmetry**
  a. When identical exponents are inserted by Vocabulary Items that are specified for feature sets that do not overlap, there is *homophony*; but
  b. A single same phonological rule can be triggered by morphemes that do not overlap at all in feature content (and still be the same phonological rule).

It is important to emphasize that this is but one of the differences between pieces and processes that plays a role in the approach adopted here; another, which is central to the discussion of blocking, is that piece-based realization appears to block the insertion of other pieces, but pieces do not block processes, or vice versa (Halle and Marantz 1993, reviewed in Embick 2015).

Formulating something like (49) is not possible in theory without affixes. As a result, such theories have difficulties stating the "unity of process" of Umlaut phonologically. Anderson (1992), which builds on earlier work on Umlaut, is clear on this point. His theory denies the existence of morphophonology in the "narrow" sense: there are either purely phonological rules, or purely morphological rules. In an amorphous theory, *all* of the morphology is treated with morphologically conditioned phonological rules (=Word Formation Rules).[35]

There is no reason, it would seem, to admit "morpho**phono**logically conditioned phonological rules" as well; how could these be distinguished in effect from WFRs, whose sole function is to effect phonological changes when triggered morphologically?[36]

---

[35] Things are more complicated for this if one assumes, like Anderson does, that derivational morphology involves pieces, whereas inflectional morphology does not, since Umlaut triggers appear to be of both types. We abstract away from this further complication here.

[36] Anderson in fact suggests that there might be different locality conditions for phonological rules and WFRs– "...we might find that a rule which in its original, purely phonological form only applied to potential 'foci' immediately adjacent to its 'determinant' would later, when mor-

The WFRs in Anderson's approach are required to make reference to a single set of features for application, much as stated in our discussion of formal identity above. But, because there can be no distinction made along the lines of (49), there must be as many "Umlaut rules" as there are triggers for Umlaut. Anderson approaches this point by talking about Umlaut as a phonological rule that, due to diachronic changes, has been restricted to morphologically-defined environments: "...if a change were morphologized so as to apply in a number of distinct morphological categories instead of in a unitary phonological environment, this would result in its formal fragmentation into a number of distinct rules, insofar as there is no single property that unifies the categories involved" (1992:345). After suggesting that rules like German Umlaut are specifically of the type that involve 'rule fragmentation', Anderson appeals to historical idiosyncrasies as evidence for the existence of multiple Umlaut rules; his conclusion is that idiosyncrasy "...is exactly what is predicted if ... morphologization involves replacement of a phonological environment by a morphological one (rather than mere adding morphological conditions to phonological ones)." (1992:344-5).

The problem with this line of reasoning is that to the extent that there are idiosyncrasies with Umlaut, they are not phonological in nature; rather, all of the idiosyncrasies have to do with whether or not a particular Root undergoes Umlaut in the presence of a particular trigger. Once it is determined whether or not Umlaut applies, there is no idiosyncrasy at all in what the rule does: it effects the same phonological changes across the board. A theory that is incapable of stating that this pattern is the result of a single phonological rule is missing an obvious generalization.[37]

5.2 Phonology + Vocabulary Insertion only

As noted in §4, one possible approach to Umlaut would be to build a purely phonological cause of fronting into the affixes that trigger it; Lieber (1992) (adapting

---

phologized, come to apply to multiple 'foci', not all of which satisfied an adjacency condition" (1992:45). This point has not been developed in detail, however.

[37] It is conceivable that the particular approach advanced in Anderson's (1992) might employ stem storage as well as multiple distinct Umlaut rules. As noted Fn. 33, for inflectional irregularities like that seen in e.g. the English past tense (*sing, sang* etc.), Anderson appeals to an analysis in terms of "stem sets" in which *sang* competes with *sing* (and *sung, song*) to express the features [SING +V +past]. If *sing* and *sang* are treated as different stored stems of the same lexical item, why not do the same for umlauted and un-umlauted stems? Anderson does not discuss this issue. The most obvious answer is that it is because Umlaut frequently cooccurs with (does not block) an affix, precisely the situation that Anderson's theory of stem storage is designed to avoid. See Embick (2015) for general discussion.

Lieber 1987), for example, posits a floating [-bk] feature with Umlaut triggers.[38] Two things are required for this analysis to work. First, the grammar must contain the pairs of Vocabulary Items listed in (50), for all of the morphemes that trigger Umlaut. In the two Vocabulary Items, the first is the Umlauting allomorph, and the second does not cause Umlaut; the first is shown with a LIST, which represents the Umlaut undergoers for that particular morpheme:[39]

(50) Pairs of Vocabulary Items
  a. [-1, -2] ↔ -$^{[-bk]}$t/LIST
     [-1, -2] ↔ -t
  b. [+pl]   ↔ -$^{[-bk]}$er/LIST
     [+pl]   ↔ -er
  c. [+pl]   ↔ -$^{[-bk]}$e/LIST
     [+pl]   ↔ -e
  d. [a]   ↔ -$^{[-bk]}$ig/LIST
     [a]   ↔ -ig
  e. ⋮

Along with these Vocabulary Items, the LISTs come into play in specifying which allomorphs are selected by particular Roots. Effectively, this analysis treats Umlaut as deriving from a form of contextual allomorphy, with some attendant action in the phonology to handle the autosegment. The allomorphic aspect of this analysis is important for two reasons. First, it means that this type of approach, like the one that we presented in §4, makes extensive use of lists; it is not better or worse as far as this goes. The second point concerns locality. If MM rules and contextual allomorphy both respect concatenation, locality alone will not distinguish the analysis in (50) from an analysis that makes use of an MM-rule for Umlaut.

The analysis in (50) generates the facts that have been considered to this point. Moreover, it employs only Vocabulary Insertion plus phonology, phonology that does not make reference to morphology. While the analysis is thus restrictive in terms of what it employs, it derives the facts with some violence to the intuition that grammars minimize the storage of morphemes: each of the pairs in (50) consists of two suppletive allomorphs, phonologically identical except for the presence of [-bk]

---

38 Lieber (1992) uses underspecification of vowels, such that only [-bk] is specified underlyingly. This removes the need to delink [+bk] features when Umlaut occurs.
39 Lieber does not address the fact that the same Root may Umlaut in some environments, but not is others. Our allomorphic solution in (50) is what we assume an analysis like a [-bk] in exponents would need to employ.

in one of them. This seems like the kind of situation that should be avoided when possible, even in approaches that are liberal with respect to memorization (cf. §2).

One side of the theoretical tension that occupies the last paragraph is based on the intuition that Vocabulary Insertion and "normal" phonology should be used to analyze what we refer to as morphophonology. What is the motivation for this intuition? Aside from "standard" parsimony (e.g. Lieber 1987, or, more recently, Bye and Svenonius 2012), it appears to be based on the idea that phonology should not "see" morphology (in the way that is required for morphological triggering or targeting to be stated), or vice versa.

In our view, a number of developments in morphophonology (broadly construed) suggest that the reasons for adopting this idea are quite limited. For instance, the existence of phonologically conditioned suppletive allomorphy, studied extensively in Paster (2006) and Embick (2010a) because of what it reveals about morphology/phonology interactions, provides evidence that phonological representations are visible to the (morphological) operation of Vocabulary Insertion. In the other direction, Vocabulary Insertion – a basic part of any realizational theory, in some form – requires that a morpheme be visible to an operation that provides it with its phonological content. It is difficult to see how this fundamental association of form with feature content complies with the claim that phonology does not see morphological representations. It could be that establishing basic sound/meaning connections is not as "phonological" as, for example, effecting the changes that are associated with phonological rules or their equivalent. As far as this latter point goes, we note that one of the most productive research programs in morphophonology, Lexical Morphology and Phonology (Kiparsky 1982 and related work), continues to be of interest precisely because of how morphology and phonology see each other in the theory, and because of how the theory is at pains to explain how the exceptional behavior of certain morphemes must be understood in ways that connect with broader architectural questions.

In summary, our intuition, based on observations like those immediately above, is that there is no clear reason at present to completely disallow morphological information from being referred to in the phonology. Intuitions aside, it is difficult to come up with empirical predictions that clearly differentiate theories with morpheme reference from theories without it. Part of the reason for this stems from similarities between the approaches. For example, our MP rules apply under phonological conditions of locality; as such, they are amenable to treatments in which the phonological effect is built into a Vocabulary Item (or into the target of the change). Similarly, our MM rules are (by hypothesis) restricted to apply under the same conditions as contextual allomorphy. Thus, where our theory would say that a rule is switched (ON) when a target X is concatenated with a trigger Y, an alternative without morpheme-reference could say that X selects for an allomorph of Y that contains an autosegment that effects the change.[40] Ultimately, it is possible that some of the fine-grained predictions deriving from phase cycles or from exceptional switching might be important here, but we do not have any case studies that speak to these issues at present.

In short, there are alternatives to the approach that we have developed here, alternatives in which only Vocabulary Items and phonological operations are used, with no phonological rules that have particular triggers and targets identified morphologically. Approaches of this type are able to analyze complex phenomena like Umlaut, albeit with accidents of the Vocabulary that look unacceptable from the perspective of many types of theories.

It is not entirely clear at present how to separate the empirical predictions of the two approaches, even though they look superficially quite different; we take the development of pertinent predictions to be an important task for future work on this part of the grammar.

5.3 Stem Storage

Finally, we come to the Fundamental Question of Morphophonology: Stem Storage (SS) or not (what we have called MPD). In this and related work, we have explored an MPD view, based on a position that is called *Full Decomposition*: the idea that all complex forms are derived, whether they are morphophonologically regular or not. Theories incorporating this view include Chomsky & Halle (1968), and more recently Distributed Morphology (Halle and Marantz 1993; for the generative part, see Embick and Marantz 2008; for Full Decomposition, Embick 2015, and the connections to experimental work in Embick and Marantz 2005 and Stockall and Marantz 2006). Full Decomposition is certainly the minority view when the language sciences as a whole are considered, and it is very likely a minority view within theoretical linguistics as well.

It is important to note that Full Decomposition holds that complex forms (e.g. "past tense verbs") are decomposed *morphosyntactically* into multiple morphemes (in the approach adopted here, something like $[[\sqrt{\text{ROOT}}\upsilon]\ T[+past]]$). It leaves open the possibility that the sound form that is heard – e.g. *sang* for the past tense of *sing* – is stored in memory. Thus, the kind of theory that we adopt could employ SS for certain alternations, and, in fact, many approaches both similar and different to the one we assume here use SS for (at least some)

---

[40] Or that a "changed" stem allomorph is selected in the context of the relevant morpheme; recall the comments on Anderson (1992), and see the next subsection.

irregular alternations. When SS is employed, morphophonology is reduced to Vocabulary Insertion *without* phonology – i.e., to suppletion.[41]

With this in mind, and taking into account the importance of FQM, we examine some of the aspects of the phenomena considered above in terms of MPD versus SS. The first place to look is at Umlaut. Here, there are some parallels with our discussion in §5.1. Umlaut is "irregular" in terms of having (apparently) morphological triggers, and in terms of its target/trigger relations. Treating Umlaut with SS would require memorizing umlauted and non-umlauted variants of a large part of the Vocabulary: *Form1* and *Förm2* for most (or many) Roots of the language.[42] Then, the correct stem form would have to be chosen in the context of "Umlaut triggers", in a way that would be encoded in lists: e.g. for $\sqrt{\text{SAFT}}$ the umlauted stem would be selected in the context of [+pl] but not [a,-ig], and so on. For most of what needs to be said about Umlaut, this could probably be encoded with contextual allomorphy as it is currently understood.[43] While this analysis could produce the correct distribution of forms, it is open to the sorts of objections identified in §5.1: in particular, since the two stored stems for all of these Roots would be related directly in a way that reduces to alternations in [±bk], this analysis is like the one in (50) in that it appears to miss a clear generalization (perhaps to a greater extent, since there would be more memorized pairs of stem forms in an SS theory than there would be pairs of Vocabulary Items in the analysis summarized in (50)).

Moving beyond Umlaut, the general question at issue is what kinds of empirical evidence could be adduced to decide between MPD and SS. As discussed elsewhere (cf. Embick 2010b, 2012), one question to ask is whether morphophonological alternations show the same trigger/target locality conditions as contextual allomorphy. To the extent that they do not, that is a clear reason for not treating them as suppletion; to the extent that they do, locality-based arguments alone cannot be decisive, and evidence must be sought elsewhere. It appears that there are some morphophonological phenomena that look like they do not share locality properties with suppletive contextual allomorphy, and others that do. This observation is, in a sense, a (re)statement of part of the MP/MM distinction that is motivated in §§2-3, since MM is predicted (by the MIC) to share locality properties with contextual allomorphy, whereas MP alternations are expected to

---

[41] There are, of course, hybrid views, with Vocabulary Insertion plus normal phonology for some alternations and SS for others; Bye and Svenonius 2012, for example.

[42] It would not have to be all Roots, since some would not appear in environments in which Umlaut is triggered due to independent reasons, having to do with Root distribution.

[43] The qualification to 'probably' is for the phenomena considered in §§4.2.2–4.2.4; MP Umlaut would (by hypothesis) have different locality conditions from contextual allomorphy.

behave differently. By way of example, consider Ischia metaphony, from §2. The Root √KAND is "irregularly" affected by 2s agreement, to produce kɛnd- ə. This fact alone could be treated as suppletion, if the language had competing stem allomorphs kand and kɛnd for √KAND, as encoded in (51):

(51) √KAND ↔ kɛnd
      √KAND ↔ kand

However, the effects of 2s Agr skip a morpheme, as seen in past tense forms like kand-ɛ-v-ə, where metaphony from the schwa skips the past tense morpheme with exponent -v. If, as hypothesized, contextual allomorphy requires concatenation, then this shows that the effects of 2s Agr cannot be treated as suppletive allomorphy, since a morpheme intervenes between the theme vowel and the agreement morpheme.[44]

On the other hand, some alternations do not show any intervening morphemes between the trigger and the target. In the English past tense, for example, the alternation between *sing* and *sang* could be treated as the result of an MM rule (or rules) applying under concatenation of the Root and T[+past]; or it could be treated along the lines of (51), with *sang* inserted for √SING in the context of T[+past], and *sing* in the present tense. The Root and Tense are adjacent, making it impossible to draw strong conclusions based on locality conditions alone.

The upshot of this line of reasoning is that it might not be possible to determine on the basis of locality or "stem distribution" patterns alone whether MPD or SS is correct. Naturally, the argument depends on a particular set of assumptions about the locality conditions for contextual allomorphy, which may or may not turn out to be correct. We have argued elsewhere (see in particular Embick 2010b) that this area of research is one in which theoretical and experimental (psycho- and neuro-linguistic) approaches must be brought into closer contact, as it is possible that converging evidence from these domains will be required to determine how grammars encode stem alternations that could in principle be analyzed with either MP or SS. In this larger project, grammatical theories of the type that we have developed here are in part generating hypotheses that can guide a wide range of experimental projects, along the lines discussed in works such as Marantz (2005), Poeppel & Embick (2005), and Embick & Poeppel (2015).

---

[44] For additional arguments along these lines where it is the actual "stem" (and not a theme vowel) that is affected, see Embick (2010b, 2012).

6 Conclusion

The analysis of morphophonological alternations is controversial because there are in principle different ways of analyzing them: phonological rules, phonological rules that make reference to morphemes (or features, or diacritics), and suppletive contextual allomorphy. In practice, and despite there sometimes being rather different guiding intuitions behind approaches that advocate different analyses, it has proven difficult to distinguish analytical options empirically.

The theory outlined in §2 and illustrated further in §3 involves three different types of locality, defined phonologically, morphologically, and in terms of phase-cycles. Part of the claim that we are defending here is that something like these components is required for analyzing morphophonology in the broad sense, as revealed by the complex set of conditions under which morphophonological alternations apply and, crucially, fail to apply even though they "might have". These tools were then deployed in an analysis of German Umlaut in §4, one that we hope raises a number of questions for further research, in addition to illustrating some of the key components of the theory outlined in the earlier sections.

One of the themes that should emerge clearly from the discussion of §5 is that the research programs that are actively investigating morphophonology are starting from very different priors, and are often linked closely to very different and often diametrically opposed conceptual viewpoints. While we believe it is important to highlight connections with guiding intuitions, much of the focus above has been on ways of trying to find differences in empirical predictions between theories.

By way of offering a general conclusion, there is one aspect of the type of approach presented here that we believe requires further comment. Our theory employs locality conditions of different types. On the one hand, it appeals to phase cyclic domains, which are defined by the way in which syntactic computations operate. On the other hand, it also employs interface-parochial conditions of morphological and phonological locality, which derive from the requirement that PF linearize the hierarchical representations that are produced by syntactic derivations. In its most abstract form, this kind of theory says that the surface complexity of morphophonology is not the result of a single system whose locality properties explain everything; rather, it is the result of "deep" syntactic principles *interacting* with interface-specific types of locality. It might be objected (on conceptual level) that this type of theory is "too rich" ontologically to be correct. Our view is that it is a substantial empirical finding that complex morphophonological phenomena are the product of a sequence of systems interacting, and that while specific formulations of the relevant kinds of locality might change, the core insight that an interaction is responsible for attested patterns must be retained.

In another type of context, this finding could be related to discoveries about the properties of other cognitive systems; but that will have to wait for another occasion.

Acknowledgments: We are delighted to be able to contribute a paper to this volume in honor of Andrea Calabrese. One of the pleasures in reading Andrea's work is that there is always a comprehensive analysis, with a minimum of hand-waving about details. This kind of approach is manifested in this paper in an adjacent way – in many of our case studies, phenomena that are, at a first glance, apparently quite 'well-behaved' turn out to be more complex on closer examination. Moreover, some of these complexities do not yield obvious solutions. We hope that by presenting and illustrating a particular framework, and identifying open questions that arise along the way, attention will be focused on the kinds of important interface questions that are addressed in Andrea's work.

Thanks to Akiva Bacovcin, Ava Creemers, Anton Ingason, Beatrice Santorini, and Florian Schwarz for discussion of theoretical contents, answering our questions on a number of topics, and reading earlier drafts. Comments from two reviewers have helped us a great deal as well. Finally, special thanks to the editors for organizing the volume, and for being patient.

References

Akkuş, Faruk & Nikita Bezrukov. 2016. Saving NAH in Armenian and Ingush. University of Pennsylvania.
Alexiadou, Artemis & Florian Schäfer. 2008. Instrumental -er nominals revisited. In Kevin Ryan (ed.), *Online proceedings of WCCFL XXVII (poster session)*, 10–19. UCLA.
Alexiadou, Artemis & Florian Schäfer. 2010. On the syntax of episodic vs. dispositional -er nominals. In Artemis Alexiadou & Monika Rathert (eds.), *The syntax of nominalizations across languages and frameworks*, 9–38. Berlin/New York: Mouton de Gruyter.
Anderson, Stephen. 1992. *Amorphous morphology*. Cambridge: Cambridge University Press.
Árnason, Kristján. 2011. *The phonology of Icelandic and Faroese*. Oxford University Press.
Borer, Hagit. 2013. *Taking form*, vol. 3 of *Structuring Sense*. Oxford: Oxford University Press.
Buckley, Eugene. 1994. *Theoretical aspects of Kashaya phonology and morphology*. Stanford: CSLI.
Bye, Patrik & Peter Svenonius. 2012. Non-concatenative morphology as epiphenomenon. In Jochen Trommer (ed.), *The morphology and phonology of exponence*, Oxford: Oxford University Press.
Calabrese, Andrea. 1985. Metaphony in Salentino. *Rivista di grammatica generativa* 9-10. 3–140.
Calabrese, Andrea. 1998. Metaphony revisited. *Rivista di Linguistica* 10(1). 7–68.
Calabrese, Andrea. 2012. Allomorphy in the Italian Passato Remoto: A Distributed Morphology analysis. In *Language and information society*, 1–75. Sogang University, Korea.

Calabrese, Andrea. 2013a. The irregular forms of the Italian "passato remoto": a synchronic and diachronic analysis. In Sergio Baauw, Frank Drijkoningen, Luisa Meroni & Manuela Pinto (eds.), *Romance languages and linguistic theory 2011: Selected papers from 'Going Romance' Utrecht 2011*, 17–58. John Benjamins.

Calabrese, Andrea. 2013b. New arguments for a classical generative analysis of an old problem: The irregular forms of the Italian *passato remoto*. University of Connecticut.

Calabrese, Andrea. 2015. Locality effects in Italian verbal morphology. In Elisa Di Domenico, Cornelia Hamann & Simona Matteini (eds.), *Structures, strategies, and beyond: Studies in honour of Adriana Belletti*, 97–134. John Benjamins.

Calabrese, Andrea. 2016. On the morphophonology of metaphonic alternations in Altamurano. In Fancesc Torres-Tamarit, Kathrin Linke & Marc van Oostendorp (eds.), *Approaches to metaphony in the languages of Italy*, 89–126. Berlin: De Gruyter.

Chomsky, Noam. 2000. Minimalist inquiries: The framework. In Roger Martin, David Michaels & Juan Uriagereka (eds.), *Step by step: Essays on minimalist syntax in honor of Howard Lasnik*, 89–156. MIT Press.

Chomsky, Noam. 2001. Derivation by phase. In Michael Kenstowicz (ed.), *Ken Hale: A life in language*, 1–52. Cambridge, MA: MIT Press.

Chomsky, Noam & Morris Halle. 1968. *The sound pattern of English*. New York: Harper and Row.

Creemers, Ava, Jan Don & Paula Fenger. 2017. Some affixes are roots, others are heads. *Natural Language and Linguistic Theory* 36(1). 45–84.

Embick, David. 2003. Locality, listedness, and morphological identity. *Studia Linguistica* 57(3). 143–169.

Embick, David. 2010a. *Localism versus globalism in morphology and phonology*. Cambridge, MA: MIT Press.

Embick, David. 2010b. Stem alternations and stem distributions. University of Pennsylvania.

Embick, David. 2012. Contextual conditions on stem alternations: Illustrations from the Spanish conjugation. In Irene Franco, Sara Lusini & Andrés Saab (eds.), *Romance languages and linguistic theory 2010*, 21–40. Amsterdam/Philadelphia: John Benjamins.

Embick, David. 2013. Morphemes and morphophonological loci. In Alec Marantz & Ora Matushansky (eds.), *Distributed Morphology Today: Morphemes for Morris Halle*, 151–166. Cambridge, MA: MIT Press.

Embick, David. 2014. Phase cycles, ϕ-cycles, and phonological (in)activity. In S. Bendjaballah, M. Lahrouchi, N. Faust & N. Lampitelli (eds.), *The form of structure, the structure of forms: Essays in honor of Jean Lowenstamm*, 270–286. John Benjamins.

Embick, David. 2015. *The morpheme: A theoretical introduction*. Boston and Berlin: Gruyter.

Embick, David. 2016. Approaching *polymorphy*. Handout of a talk series given at the Sociedad Argentina de Análisis Filosófico (SADAF), Buenos Aires, Argentina.

Embick, David & Morris Halle. 2005. On the status of *stems* in morphological theory. In T. Geerts & H. Jacobs (eds.), *Proceedings of Going Romance 2003*, 59–88. Amsterdam/Philadelphia: John Benjamins.

Embick, David & Alec Marantz. 2005. Cognitive neuroscience and the English past tense: Comments on the paper by Ullman et al. *Brain and Language* 93. 243–247.

Embick, David & Alec Marantz. 2008. Architecture and blocking. *Linguistic Inquiry* 39(1). 1–53.

Embick, David & David Poeppel. 2015. Towards a computational(ist) neurobiology of language: *correlational*, *integrated*, and *explanatory* neurolinguistics. *Language, Cognition, and Neuroscience* 30(4). 357–366.

Gussmann, Edmund. 2011. Getting your head around: the vowel system of Modern Icelandic. *Folia Scandinavica Posnaniensia* 12. 71–90.
Halle, Morris. 1973. Prolegomena to a theory of word formation. *Linguistic Inquiry* 4(1). 3–16.
Halle, Morris. 1998. The stress of English words 1968–1998. *Linguistic Inquiry* 29(4). 539–568.
Halle, Morris & Alec Marantz. 1993. Distributed Morphology and the pieces of inflection. In Kenneth Hale & Samuel Jay Keyser (eds.), *The view from building 20: Essays in linguistics in honor of Sylvain Bromberger*, 111–176. Cambridge, MA: MIT Press.
Halle, Morris & K. P. Mohanan. 1985. Segmental phonology of Modern English. *Linguistic Inquiry* 16(1). 57–116.
Harris, James W. 1985. Spanish diphthongization and stress: A paradox resolved. *Phonology Yearbook* 2. 31–45.
Ingason, Anton Karl. 2014. Icelandic umlaut as morpheme-specific phonology. In *Proceedings of Phonology 2013*.
Ingason, Anton Karl. 2016. *Realizing morphemes in the Icelandic noun phrase*: University of Pennsylvania dissertation.
Ingason, Anton Karl & Einar Freyr Sigurðsson. 2015. Phase locality in Distributed Morphology and two types of Icelandic agent nominals. In *Proceedings of NELS 45*, vol. 2, 45–58. Amherst, MA: GLSA.
Janda, Richard. 1998. German umlaut: Morpholexical all the way down. *Rivista di Linguistica* 19(1). 165–234.
Kiparsky, Paul. 1982. Lexical morphology and phonology. In Linguistic Society of Korea (ed.), *Linguistics in the morning calm: Selected essays from SICOL-1981*, Seoul: Hanshin.
Kiparsky, Paul. 1996. Allomorphy or morphophonology? In Rajendra Singh & Richard Desrochers (eds.), *Trubetzkoy's orphan*, 13–31. Amsterdam/Philadelphia: John Benjamins.
Lieber, Rochelle. 1980. *The organization of the lexicon*. MIT dissertation.
Lieber, Rochelle. 1987. *An integrated theory of autosegmental processes*. Albany: State University of New York Press.
Lieber, Rochelle. 1992. *Deconstructing morphology*. Chicago: University of Chicago Press.
Lowenstamm, Jean. 2012. German umlaut, an outline of a minimalist account. Université Paris 7.
Lowenstamm, Jean. 2015a. A brief paper on German umlaut. In *Proceedings of IATL 2014*, 69–82. MITWPL.
Lowenstamm, Jean. 2015b. Derivational affixes as roots: Phasal spell-out meets English stress shift. In Artemis Alexiadou, Hagit Borer & Florian Schäfer (eds.), *The syntax of roots and the roots of syntax*, 230–259. Oxford: Oxford University Press.
Maiden, Martin. 1991. *Interactive morphology: Metaphony in Italy*. London and New York: Routledge.
Marantz, Alec. 2001. Words and things. MIT.
Marantz, Alec. 2005. Generative linguistics within the cognitive neuroscience of language. *Linguistic Review* 22. 429–445.
Marantz, Alec. 2007. Phases and words. In S. H. Choe et al (ed.), *Phases in the theory of grammar*, Seoul: Dong In Publisher.
Marantz, Alec. 2013. Locality domains for contextual allomorphy across the interfaces. In Ora Matushansky & Alec Marantz (eds.), *Distributed Morphology today: Morphemes for Morris Halle*, Cambridge, MA: MIT Press.
Marvin, Tatjana. 2002. *Topics in the stress and syntax of words*. MIT dissertation.
Myler, Neil. 2015. Stem storage? not proven: A reply to Bermúdez-Otero 2013. *Linguistic Inquiry* 46(1). 173–186.

Nevins, Andrew & Neil Myler. 2014. A brown-eyed girl. In Carson T. Schütze & Linnaea Stockall (eds.), *Connectedness: Papers by and for Sarah VanWagenen*, vol. 18, 243–257. UCLA Working Papers in Linguistics.

Newell, Heather. 2008. *Aspects of the morphology and phonology of phases*: McGill University dissertation.

Oswalt, Robert L. 1961. *A Kashaya grammar (Southwestern Pomo)*: U.C. Berkeley dissertation.

Ott, Dennis. 2011. Diminutive-formation in German: Spelling out the classifier analysis. *Journal of Comparative Germanic Linguistics* 14. 1–46.

Parodi, Ernesto. 1892. Il dialetto di Arpino. *Archivo Glottologico Italiano* 13. 299–308.

Paster, Mary. 2006. *Phonological conditions on affixation*: University of California at Berkeley dissertation.

Petrosino, Roberto. 2018. On the necessity of morpho-phonology. University of Connecticut.

Poeppel, David & David Embick. 2005. Defining the relation between linguistics and neuroscience. In Ann Cutler (ed.), *Twenty-first century psycholinguistics: Four cornerstones*, Lawrence Erlbaum.

Scharinger, Mathias. 2009. Minimal representation of alternating vowels. *Lingua* 119(10). 1414–1425.

Scharinger, Mathias, Aditi Lahiri & Carsten Eulitz. 2010. Mismatch negativity effects of alternating vowels in morphologically complex word forms. *Journal of Neurolinguistics* 23(4). 383–399.

Shwayder, Kobey. 2015. *Words and subwords: Phonology in a piece-based syntactic morphology*: University of Pennsylvania dissertation.

Shwayder, Kobey. 2017. Morphophonological rules and readjustments: A case study in German umlaut. University of Pennsylvania.

Smith, Peter W., Beata Moskal, Ting Xu, Jungmin Kang & Jonathan D. Bobaljik. 2016. Case and number suppletion in pronouns. Frankfurt, Syracuse, and UConn.

Stockall, Linnea & Alec Marantz. 2006. A single-route, full decomposition model of morphological complexity: MEG evidence. *Mental Lexicon* 1(1). 85–123.

Tamminga, Meredith, Laurel MacKenzie & David Embick. 2016. The dynamics of variation in individuals. *Language Variation* 16(2). 300–336.

Torres-Tamarit, Francesc & Kathrin Linke. 2016. Opaque vowel merger-metaphony interactions. In Kathrin Linke & Marc van Oostendorp (eds.), *Approaches to metaphony in the languages of Italy*. Berlin/Boston: Gruyter.

Wiese, Richard. 1996a. Phonological versus morphological rules: On German umlaut and ablaut. *Journal of Linguistics* 32(1). 113–135.

Wiese, Richard. 1996b. *The phonology of German*. Oxford University Press.

Wood, Jim. 2015. *Icelandic morphosyntax and argument structure*. Springer.

Wurzel, Wolfgang. 1970. *Studien zur deutschen Lautstruktur* (Studia Grammatica VIII). Berlin: Akademie Verlag.

Irina Monich
Distribution of falling tones in Mabaan

1 Introduction

This article examines the tonal inventory of Mabaan, a Nilotic language described in a series of articles by Andersen (1992, 1999, 2006). According to Andersen (1992), the syllable in Mabaan may be associated with a high, low, a falling or a rising tonal contour. The nature of the rising tone will be completely left out of discussion, since it occurs only on non-initial syllables in specific morphological constructions, and is virtually absent in content words outside of those contexts. In this article, I focus on the falling tone, especially the falling tone on the root, with the intention to show that its distribution is largely predictable based on phonological and morphological factors.

The vowel system of Mabaan, as established by Andersen (1992), is shown in Figure 1. There are 11 monophthongs and 4 diphthongs. Each monophthong and diphthong comes as a phonemic pair contrasting in length. Here I use Andersen's convention of showing length of a diphthong by doubling the first grapheme.

With the exception of personal names, every content word in Mabaan is minimally disyllabic, consisting of a root and at least one suffix. I will distinguish between three types of affixes: those containing a full vowel (i.e. a vowel other than ʌ), monoconsonantal affixes, and those consisting of a reduced vowel (i.e. ʌ). The distinction between full vowels and ʌ is made in Andersen (2006), where the suffixal ʌ is called a "variable" vowel due to the fact that it is changed to e or dropped in non pre-pausal environments. As I will argue here, unlike suffixes containing full vowels, the suffix -ʌ is toneless, which, together with its tendency to elide, further supports the notion that it is phonologically reduced.

What follows is a brief description of the distribution of tones on the root based on the data in Andersen (1999, 2006). The system of rules proposed here will be based on those data only, as it accounts only for those morphological structures that are amply documented in Andersen (1999, 2006). However, tonal contour in some morphological structures that are possible in Mabaan will remain unaccounted due to the sparseness of data in regards to such constructions. I will address the counterexamples briefly after the analysis is presented and, whenever possible, suggest pathways to possible solution of such cases.

Note: The research presented here is funded by the Arts & Humanities Research Council (UK) under grant AH/L011824/1 ('Morphological Complexity in Nuer').

https://doi.org/10.1515/9781501506734-008

```
i, ii                              u, uu
  e, ee                           ie, iie
    ɛ, ɛɛ    ʌ, ʌʌ    ɔ, ɔɔ      iɛ, iiɛ    uʌ, uuʌ
            a, aa                            ua, uua
         Monophthongs                    Diphthongs
```

Figure 8.1: Mabaan vowel system.

2 Data

In disyllabic words containing a reduced vocalic suffix – ʌ the tone of the root is either high or falling. If the tone of the root is falling, the suffix is always low; if the tone of the root is high, the suffix may be high or low. These possible patterns are illustrated in (1).

(1) t̪îen-g-ʌ̀   'breast.PL'
    t̪íen-n-ʌ́   'breast.SG'
    ɲʌ̂ʌk-ʌ̀   'louse.PL'
    kâak-c-ʌ̀   'chair.SG'
    lɛ́ŋ-ɲ-ʌ́   'tooth.SG'
    lɛ̂k-ʌ̀   'tooth.PL'
    ʔám-ʌ́   'food.SG'
    lɛ́p-ʌ́   'tongue.PL'
    wáŋ-ʌ́   'eye.SG'
    tɔ́ɔl-ʌ́   'girl.SG'
    kɔ̂t̪-k-ʌ̀   'boat.PL'
    yûum-ʌ̀   'rope for fishing.SG'
    yûp-k-ʌ̀   'rope for fishing.PL'
    bɔ̂g-g-ʌ̀   'arm.PL'
    guʌ́t̪-ʌ́   'untie:AP-1SG'
    bʌ̂ʌt̪-ʌ̀   'follow:AP-1SG'
    gɔ́k- ʌ̀   'say:AP-1SG'

In verbs containing a derivational suffix consisting of a single consonant, the tone of the root may be low, as in (2), or falling, as in (3), independently of the length of the syllable. Andersen (1992) makes it clear that if the falling tone is followed by a high tone in the next syllable, the fall is not as deep as when it is followed by a low syllable, and the subsequent high tone is downstepped. However, this seems to be a matter of a phonetic implementation of the fall in the context of the following high tone, and thus is not significant for the present discussion, which focuses on phonological aspects of the falling tone.

(2) a. ḍɔ̂ɔj-j-ɛ́
'put:CP-PAST:3PL:3'
'they put (thither)'
b. lùul-j-ɛ́
take-CF-PAST:3PL:3
'they took (somewhere)'

(3) a. jîɛp-c-én
beat-CF-NMLZ
'beating thither'
b. wiîɛc-c-ɛ́
sweep-CF-PAST:3PL:3
'They swept (something)'

In roots before a suffix containing a full vowel all three tones are possible. However, the high tone and the falling tone are in complementary distribution depending on the phonological identity of the root and on the tonal value of the following affix. The falling tone is found on the root before a suffix containing a full vowel, if the root syllable ends in a long vowel or a nasal, and the following suffix is high-toned. This pattern illustrated in (4a). If the root syllable does not end in a long vowel or a nasal, the tone of the root is high before a high-toned suffix containing a full vowel, as shown in (4b). Before low-toned suffixes containing a full vowel, the tone of the root vowel is high, as shown in (4c).

(4) a. t̪ɔ̂ɔ-rɔ́n   'donkey.SG'
ŋêɛr-án   'rib.SG'
lîŋ-ɲán   'bead.SG'
bêɛ-nán   'skin.SG'
lâŋɲ-án   'fly.SG'
t̪âan-ɛ́   'push:PAST-3PL:3'
cîiem-ɛ́   'carry on one's head:PAST-3PL:3'
b. wiiɛ́c-cán   'broom.SG'
ciiɛ́g-gɔ́n   'thief.SG'
káal-gɔ́n   'bachelor.SG'

	piéj-ɛ	'weed:PAST-3PL:3'
	déj-ɛ̂	'thresh:PAST-3PL:3'
c.	ʈɔ́p-à	'knife.SG'
	ʔɔ́ɔl-à	'snail.SG'

The high and falling tones on the root before suffixes containing full vowels in (4) contrast with the low tone on the root, as illustrated in (5).

(5) ɲʌʌk-cán 'louse.SG'
     jìɛb-ɛ̂   'beat:PAST-3PL:3'

One set of nouns that I will avoid discussing here, is represented by the nouns in (6).

(6) ɟîik-én   'rubbish.PL'
     kùc-én   'bag.PL'
     gɔ̀ɔb-gén 'scar.PL'
     kʌ́l-èn   'sheep.PL'
     ʔʌ̂ʌm-ḓén 'food.PL'
     kʌ́k-én   'chair.PL'
     kɛ́ɛ-gén   'child.PL'

All these nouns contain a suffix which ends in -en. There are reasons to believe that the vowel contained in this suffix is an instance of the 'variable' ʌ. Andersen (2006) states that in the dialect of Mabaan described in his publications, 'variable' ʌ is either elided or realized as /e/ in non-prepausal environments. Moreover, he points out that in a different dialect of Mabaan the 'variable' ʌ corresponds to /u/ and alternates between *i* and zero in non-prepausal contexts. This seems to be a dialect similar to the one documented by Blench (2006). In the Mabaan dictionary compiled by Blench, nominal forms corresponding to Andersen's ʌ-final forms, end in a vowel transcribed as *o*, while –*en*-final plurals end in –*in*. For example, the noun *kɛɛgén* 'children', found in Andersen (2006) corresponds to *kɛɛgin* in Blench's dictionary.

The suffix –*en* is also used as a nominalizer with derived verbs (with non-derived verbs -*n*-ʌ sequence is used). For example, the gerund of a basic transitive verb 'beat' is *jíɛm-m-ʌ̂*, while the gerund of a corresponding centrifugal verb is *jîɛp-c-én*. Therefore, it seems likely that the nouns in (4) involve additional non-segmental morphology which may interfere with tone. In fact, some of the nouns show changes in the quality of the stem vowel: for example, the singular of 'sheep' is *kâl-ŋ-ʌ̀*, but the plural of 'sheep' is *kʌ́l-èn*, with a

[+ATR] vowel in the root. Considering the uncertainties associated with the morphological composition of nouns containing this suffix, I will leave them out of discussion.

3 Account

Focusing on the data in (1–4), I propose to account for the distribution of the falling tone in Mabaan, while assuming a tonal inventory of only two lexical tones L and H. The most important feature of Mabaan tonal system which I am proposing here, is that tonal autosegments are associated to syllables from right to left. Lexically specified tonal autosegments link to the last mora of the syllable and then spread towards the beginning of the syllable (the TBU is mora). Tonal association in a sample structure is shown in (7). The motivation for assuming that tonal assignment proceeds from right to left will be offered further on in the article.

(7) a.   C μ μ C C μ   C μ μ C C μ   C μ μ C C μ
             T_1 T_2 → T_1 T_2 → T_1 T_2

All suffixes containing vowels other than ʌ (and in some instances e, as explained below) are specified for tone. If the tone of the suffix and the tone of the stem are both H, the Obligatory Contour Principle (OCP) (Odden, 1986) is observed, whenever possible. First, the H-tone of the suffix is associated, then the H tone of the root. If the syllable formed by the root ends in a long vowel or a sonorant (with some complication for liquids to be noted below), instead of being associated to the last mora of the stem, the lexical H of the root is associated to the mora before it. The skipped mora can act as a "buffer" between the two H-tones in observation of the OCP. This mora (if it is linked to a sonorant or a vowel) is then assigned an L-tone forming a falling tone with the preceding H. Examples deriving a falling tone due to the OCP between the root and the suffix are shown in (8).[1]

---

[1] Due to the convention adopted in the Nilotic literature of indicating length by means of doubling the vowel grapheme, in all examples each mora is associated to an individual grapheme of a long vowel instead of being multiply associated to the root vowel, as is customary in phonological literature.

(8) a. tɔɔ. rɔn → tɔɔ. rɔn → tɔ ɔ. rɔn
       H_Lex H_Lex   H_Lex H_Lex   H_Lex L H_Lex

   b. liŋ.ɲan → liŋ.ɲan → li ŋ.ɲan
       H_Lex H_Lex   H_Lex H_Lex   H_Lex L H_Lex

If the root syllable is short (i.e. it contains a short vowel and no coda), the OCP is violated, as shown in (9):

(9) dé. jɛ → dé. jɛ
     H_Lex H_Lex   H_Lex H_Lex

Interestingly, as illustrated in (10), non-sonorant codas, although ineligible to be associated with tonal autosegments, still count towards moraic weigh of a syllable and can act as a 'buffer' between two H-tones for the purpose of the OCP.

(10) wiiɛc. can → wiiɛc. can → wiiɛc. can
      H_Lex H_Lex   H_Lex H_Lex   H_Lex H_Lex

There is not a lot of examples of sonorant non-nasal codas in such structures (for various phonotactic reasons), but it seems that liquids in the syllable coda pattern with non-nasals after long vowels but with nasals after short vowels. In other words, after long vowels /l/ and /r/ act as a buffer between the H-tone of the root and the H-tone of the suffix without themselves being associated with an L-tone, i.e. káal-gɔ́n 'bachelor.SG' and lúuʌr-kɛ̂ 'take:AP:INSTR-PAST:3PL:3'. But after short vowels, liquids not only offer a mora to prevent adjacency between two H-tones but are also associated with an L-tone, yielding the falling tone on the root, i.e. *kêl-tán* 'star.PL' and *ʔîr-kɛ́* 'pull:AP:INSTR-PAST:3PL:3'. There exist other examples documenting both patterns.

Of course, if a suffix is lexically low toned, as in (11), the lexical H of the root is associated in a straightforward fashion to the rightmost mora of the root, and then spread to the preceding mora, it there is one.

(11) ʔɔɔ.la   ʔɔɔ.   la   ʔɔɔ.   la
       → | | →   \| |
      H_Lex L_Lex   H_Lex L_Lex   H_Lex L_Lex

We can thus account for the distribution of high vs falling tones in forms with suffixes containing full vowels, exemplified in (2) and (3). The appearance of the falling tone in these wordforms is due to the OCP triggered by the proximity of two H-tones: one of the root and one of the suffix. Such structures make it clear that a falling tone may be produced by means of tonal insertion, where an autosegment that is not originally present in the tonal structure of a form, is inserted and linked to a mora that would otherwise be left toneless.

The tonal patterns of disyllabic words ending in -ʌ are harder to account for. My basic assumption in regards to these items is that the suffix -ʌ is phonologically deficient. One of the manifestations of its deficiency is that it is unspecified for tone. Due to the leftward direction of tonal association in Mabaan, the tonal value that is associated to this affix is the autosegment that the root is lexically specified for. Whichever its value, L or H, it links to the first available toneless syllable proceeding from the right. The root is then associated with an H, regardless of its original tonal specification, and this H is realized as a high tone over monomoraic syllables and as a falling tone over dimoraic syllables.

This analysis can be expressed formally as follows. Assuming right to left association of tonal autosegments to TBUs, the lexical tone of the root associates to the suffix -ʌ due to it being unspecified for tone. If the lexical tone of the root is H, the H associates to the final -ʌ and spreads to all moras of the preceding syllable from right to left, as shown in (12a) and (12b). Note that unlike in combinations of two syllables linked to two distinct H-tones, which have to obey the OCP in dimoraic syllables (i.e. structures in (8)), spread H-tones do not become falling over long syllables.

(12) a. ʔa.mʌ   ʔa. mʌ   ʔa.mʌ
              → | →   ⸌⸍
         H_Lex   H_Lex   H_Lex
    b.   tɔɔ.lʌ   tɔɔ.lʌ   tɔɔ.lʌ
              → | →   ⸌⸍
         H_Lex   H_Lex   H_Lex

If the lexical tone of the root is L, it is associated to the vocalic suffix -ʌ, and an H-tone is inserted before it, providing the root with tonal material. If the root contains a single mora, as in (13), nothing else needs to be said.

(13) gɔk-ʌ   gɔk-ʌ   gɔk-ʌ
           → | → | |
      L_Lex   L_Lex   H L_Lex

However, in dimoraic roots (those containing long vowels or sonorant codas) the tone resulting from the insertion of an H-tone is falling. Unlike lexical tones which are associated to TBUs right to left, the tonal autosegments which are *inserted* into the structure link to the first available mora progressing from the left, and do not automatically spread to other moras. In dimoraic roots this leaves the second mora of the root unassociated to tonal material, but, as made clear by the earlier discussion of forms with tonally specified affixes, the mechanism for supplying such moras with tonal material is already available in the language: an L-tone is inserted after H and associated to the second mora of the root. The resulting configuration is shown in (14).

(14) yuum-ʌ   yuum-ʌ   yuum-ʌ   yuum-ʌ
          → | → | | → || |
     L_Lex   L_Lex   H L_Lex   HL L_Lex

Not all examples of falling tones in (1) can be accounted for at this point. Lexical items containing non-nasal consonantal suffixes, such as *kɔ̂t̪-k-ʌ̀*, are not covered by the analysis as presented so far but they will be revisited shortly.

There are two pieces of evidence that support the claim made here that the tone found on the vocalic affix -ʌ is actually the lexical tone of the root.

First of all, this point of the account is supported by the data from a closely related language Jumjum. Although in terms of segmental content, Jumjum words are almost identical to their Mabaan cognates, tonal patterns in Jumjum and Mabaan cognates are very different. The significant fact is that the tone that appears on the affix -ʌ in disyllabic singular nouns in Mabaan, is identical to the tone that appears on the root in Jumjum cognates.[2] Not all such nouns have the suffix -ʌ in Jumjum, but when they do, the tonal value of the suffix is the opposite to that of the root. Relevant Mabaan and Jumjum cognates are shown in (15), citing Jumjum data from Andersen (2006).

(15)

Mabaan	Jumjum	
jâan-ʌ̀	jàan	'bull.SG'
dúaŋ-ʌ́	dɔ́ŋ	'back.SG'
lɛ́ŋ-ɲ-ʌ́	lɛ́ŋ-ɲ-ʌ̀	'tooth.SG'
t̪íen-n-ʌ́	t̪íen-n-ʌ̀	'breast.SG'
lɛ́m-m-ʌ́	lɛ́m-m-ʌ̀	'tongue.SG
tîen-n-ʌ̀	tìn-n-ʌ́	'witch-doctor.SG'
kûm-m-ʌ̀	kùm-m-ú	'egg.SG'
yâŋ-ŋ-ʌ̀	yàŋ-ŋ-ʌ́	'meat.SG'

The second argument in favour of the analysis that shifts the lexical tone of the root to the underlyingly toneless suffix, comes from 1sg antipassive forms which also have the 'variable' suffix -ʌ and which follow the same pattern as nouns ending in -ʌ. The tone of the 1sg antipassive suffix is high or low, depending on the tonal class of the verb, as illustrated in (16), while the verbal stem itself is high or falling (in long stems, if followed by a low suffix). Rather than concluding that 1sg morpheme has variable tone, it is better to posit that the tonal autosegment that originates as part of the lexical specification of the antipassive stem, associates to the vowel of the suffix.

(16) guʌ́t̪-ʌ́   'untie.AP-1SG'
     bʌ̂ʌt̪-ʌ̀   'follow.AP-1SG'

The phonological deficiency of the suffix -ʌ (whether it is a nominal suffix or a verbal inflectional suffix) is therefore expressed in several properties: it tends to be elided, and it is the only affix containing a vowel that is unspecified for tone. It may therefore be claimed that the tonal shift from root to the affix in this case is due to affix attrition, i.e. a phenomenon whereby an affix loses some or all of its phonological properties. While it may be reversely claimed that the variable -ʌ

---

[2] Only singular nouns are considered for this purpose because formation of plural forms interferes with tonal content of the root in some way. While in singular disyllabic forms in Jumjum only two tonal patterns seem to be possible: L-H or H-L (i.e. lexical tone followed by the polar tone of the suffix), in plural forms, all combinations of L and H tones are possible.

is due to epenthesis, two factors make it unlikely. First of all, the suffix -ʌ occurs in words that have simple codas (for example, ʔâam-ʌ̀), which seem to be an unlikely environment to trigger epenthesis. Incidentally, the corresponding words in Jumjum consist of a root only, without the vocalic suffix. Rather than positing that epenthesis took place in Mabaan even after simple codas, it is more probable that the final vowel -ʌ is a reflex of some old affix (or of several collapsed affixes) which was completely lost in Jumjum after stems ending in a single consonant but retained after consonantal clusters. Moreover, at least in one instance the "variable" ʌ is not just a vowel at the end of a word, but an exponent of a specific morpheme, i.e. 1sg antipassive inflection.[3] The fact that in the case of 1sg morpheme the phonological deficiency of the "variable" ʌ *must* be a result of affix attrition makes it more likely that that is the case for all other instances of this vowel.

Whether the "variable" ʌ is a reflex of some reduced vocalic affix or a result of epenthesis is in a way beside the point, since whatever the case may be, its particular behaviour in regards to the tone shift is due to affix attrition one way or the other. When we compare nominal forms in Mabaan to their cognates in Mayak (which is considered to be a more conservative representative of the Burun subbranch in Andersen 2006), we observe that the consonantal singulative and plural suffixes in Mabaan correspond to –VC suffixes in Mayak. Some cognate pairs from the two languages are shown in (17).

(17) | **Mayak** | **Mabaan** | |
|---|---|---|
| ʔaam-at̪ | ʔâam-ʌ̀ | 'left hand.Sg' |
| t̪in-it̪ | t̪ién-n-ʌ́ | 'breast.Sg' |
| yɪɪð-ak | jíid̪-g-ʌ́ | 'well.Pl' |
| kɪɪð-ɪn | kêɛd-g-ʌ̀ | 'guinea-fowl.Pl' |
| guɣ-iɲ | gôk-k-ʌ̀ | 'dog.PL' |
| kʌɣ-it̪ | kʌ́g-g-ʌ́ | 'snake.PL' |
| tid̪-ʌt̪ | tiên-n-ʌ̀ | 'witch-doctor.SG' |
| rim-at̪ | yîm-m-ʌ̀ | 'blood.SG' |
| ʔɪn-at̪ | ʔîn-t̪-ʌ̀ | 'hand' |
| win-it̪ | wién-t̪-ʌ́ | 'rope' |

As Andersen (2006) argues, the nasal suffix in singular forms and, at least in some cases, the velar suffix in plural forms, is actually a secondary development

---

[3] Since Andersen does not provide examples of non-antipassive 1sg forms, it is impossible to say whether -ʌ is a general 1sg inflection or specifically the one used with the antipassive verb.

in Mabaan, and may even be remnants of definite articles. Importantly, the original number affixes, still seen in Mayak, have undergone attrition in Mabaan. Andersen illustrates the process of attrition undergone by the original singulative affix in the noun wʌ́n-n-ʌ́ 'buttock.Sg' as shown in (18).

(18) *wʌt̪-Vt̪-n- >*wʌt̪ -Vn-n- >*wʌt̪ -Vn- >*wʌt̪-n- > wʌ́n-n-ʌ́

Absence of full, and thus tonally specified, vowels in affixes in the position after the root is chiefly responsible for the rightward shift of the lexical tone. Whether the reduced vowel that attracts the lexical tone in the synchronic grammar emerged due to epenthesis or can be traced to some atrophied affix – a secondary definiteness marker or an old Nilotic affix completely lost in Mayak – is immaterial.

Now we can tackle forms containing consonantal non-nasal suffixes, illustrated in (2) and (3), and the remainder of ʌ-final items in (1). We can account for the facts if we assume that these suffixes have segmental structure – VC- where V is an empty V-slot. The V-slot does not have tonal specifications, not being a full vowel, and is similar to the 'variable' ʌ in that respect. Unlike the 'variable' ʌ, however, the empty V-slot lacks segmental material, and is skipped during the initial association of tonal material. Nevertheless, later in the derivation, a filter against toneless V-slots is activated, and the empty syllabic nucleus is associated with a tonal autosegment. The missing tonal value is supplied the same way as it has been done every time so far in this analysis: with reference to the lexical tone of the root, either an autosegment is inserted which creates a falling tone between the tone of the root and the tone of the affix, as illustrated in (19a), or, if that is impossible, the lexical tone of the root spreads to the following toneless V-slot, as illustrated in (19b). Since in the surface output the empty V-slots remain without segmental content, the L-tones associated with them are not deleted but re-associated to the root. Consequently, the low tone in such structures is found in contrast with a falling tone.

(19) (For the sake of clarity, the details of tonal association in the full-vowel suffix have been simplified).
   a. jiɛp-(V)c-en   jiɛp-(V)c-en   jiɛp-(V)c-en   jiɛp-c-en
      H_{Lex} H_{Lex} H_{Lex} H_{Lex} H_{Lex} L H_{Lex} H_{Lex} L H_{Lex}
   b. ŋɔɔr-(V)k-ɛ   ŋɔɔr-(V)k-ɛ   ŋɔɔr-(V)k-ɛ   ŋɔɔr-k-ɛ
      L_{Lex} H_{Lex} L_{Lex} H_{Lex} L_{Lex} H_{Lex} L_{Lex} H_{Lex}

The same analysis applies to the remainder of ʌ-final nouns in (1) which could not be accounted for at the earlier stages of this analysis. All examples where the falling tone is found on short vowels, contain a non-nasal consonantal suffix before the final low-toned -ʌ. Assuming that these suffixes, unlike the nasal suffix, contain an empty V-slot which is associated with an L-tone at one point in derivation, we can derive the falling tone on the root by analogy with (19a).

(20) yup-(V)k-ʌ   yup-(V)k-ʌ   yup-(V)k-ʌ   yup-(V)k-ʌ   yup-k-ʌ
          → | → | | → | | | →   \ |
     L$_{Lex}$ L$_{Lex}$ H   L$_{Lex}$ H L   L$_{Lex}$ H L L$_{Lex}$

Note that in nouns where the final -ʌ is high-toned, the high tone spreads from the final suffix to the root. Consequently, there is no L-tone inserted into the structure in such cases. The lexical tone, which is primarily linked to the 'variable' ʌ, spreads to the empty V-slot, as shown in (21).

(21) kʌg-g-ʌ   kʌg-(V)g-ʌ   kʌg-(V)g-ʌ   kʌg-(V)g-ʌ   kʌg-g-ʌ
          → | →   ⌟   →   ⌟   →   ⌟
     H$_{Lex}$ H$_{Lex}$ H$_{Lex}$ H$_{Lex}$ H$_{Lex}$

We have successfully accounted for the data in (1–4). However, there is a handful of items that resist this account. These items are listed in (22).

(22) a. kâwwɔ̂   'your (pl) sisters'
     b. bɔ̂ggɛ   'his arms'
     c. lúuʌt-t-ê   'take.AP-PAST-3'
     d. kuuádàn   'jump:MULT:3SG'
     e. jɔ̂gdɛ́   'kick:MULT:FUT:2PL:3'
     f. jɔ̂gdɛ́   'kick:FUT:3SG:3'
     g. jɔ̂gdɛ̀   'kick:FUT:2PL:3'
     h. kâatân   'bite:FUT:3PL:3'
     i. duuʌ̀ŋkân   'grasshopper.PL'

I cannot venture here into fully explaining what is going on with these items, since there is not enough data to go on. However, a few suggestions can be made.

The items in (22) fall into several categories. The easiest category to deal with are the two possessive items in (22a) and (22b). The non-possessive forms of these nouns – bɔ̂g-g-ʌ 'arm.PL' and kâw-w-ʌ 'sister.PL' – are produced in accordance to the principles laid out here. Significantly, the 'variable' ʌ is missing when the noun is affixed with a possessive suffix. This is not surprising, since one of the characteristics of this suffix is that it may be elided. Note that the tone of the root is unaffected by the elision of the suffix in the case of these two nouns. This is likewise to be expected, since both H and L autosegments found on the root in these nouns are products of insertion. When the 'variable' ʌ is elided in these forms, the tonal content of the root is not affected. By contrast, the possessive forms of the noun kʌ́w-ʌ́ 'sister.PL', which is lexically high-toned according to the present analysis, have a low tone on the stem: kʌ̀w-wɔ́ 'your (pl) sister' and kʌ̀w-wɔ́ 'my sister'. This is consistent with the proposal made here that in ʌ-final forms the lexical tone spreads to the root from the suffix. Elision of the 'variable' ʌ in possessive forms of high-toned nouns results in deletion of the lexical H-tone associated to this suffix and consequently in the absence of the H-tone on the root (we can consider the L-tone on the root to be a 'default' tone that associates to toneless TBUs when no other strategy is available).

The tonal contour of the past antipassive form in (22c) at first seems impossible to account for. Since the tone of the root is high instead of falling, it appears that the presence of a consonantal affix does not trigger L-insertion. By itself it would not be problematic, as we could simply propose that the structure of the past suffix does not involve an empty vocalic nucleus. However, taken together with the rest of the past antipassive forms found in Andersen (1999), it is clear that this explanation does not work. As illustrated in (23), 3rd person past tense forms of other antipassives *do* have a falling tone on the root – a fact that suggests that the past suffix does trigger L-insertion.

(23) lúuʌt-t-ê   'take.AP-PAST-3'
      wêɛc-c-è   'sweep:AP-PAST-3'
      ʔʌ̂t-t-è   'pull.AP-PAST-3'
      wên-n-è   'tie.AP-PAST-3'
      ʔên-n-è   'mold.AP-PAST-3'

I believe that the key to the puzzle of the past antipassive forms is the identity of the form-final vowel. Remember that *e* is another variant of the 'variable' ʌ suffix in the dialect described in Andersen (1996), and arguments have been offered earlier in this article for treating the vowel of the plural suffix *-en* as another instance of this phonologically deficient vowel. Assuming that *-e* in the antipassive forms is another instance of a phonologically reduced affix, we can observe that tonal patterns in 3rd person past tense antipassives are the same ones found in ʌ-final forms, i.e. a high tone on the root followed by a high tone on the suffix, or a falling/high tone on the root followed by a low tone on the suffix. If the phonologically deficient (i.e. toneless) vowel –e attracts lexical tone of the antipassive stem, the forms in (23) are all derived in the manner identical to those in (20) and (21).

Another category of exceptions in regards to the derivation of the tone in the root is made up by future and multiplicative verbs, i.e. (22d-g). The exact morphological make-up of these verbs is unclear based on the data in Andersen (1992, 1999, 2006). The future tense is presumably a recent innovation in Mabaan, since a future suffix is absent even in a closely related Jumjum, where future tense is expressed by means of a particle *bi* rather than by morphological means. Resorting to speculation, it is possible that future markers in Mabaan are cliticized auxiliaries, just like the possessive markers are, and that they interact differently with the root in terms of tone.

The multiplicative forms likewise need to be understood better. Multiplicative stem contains a non-segmental multiplicative suffix but the phonological effects of this suffix cannot be established based on the available Mabaan data. It should be noted however, that in related languages the multiplicative affix is non-consonantal (for example -*i*- in Surkum; Andersen 2009), and thus should be expected to interact with phonological properties of the root, including its tonal properties, in a manner different from consonantal derivational suffixes.

Finally, it is not clear why in some nouns the tone of the suffix is falling (21d,h,i). It is not coincidental perhaps, however, that all such suffixes end in -*n*. As Andersen (2006) notes, in plural forms a consonantal plural suffix is followed by a 'variable' ʌ, unless it is suffix –*n*. The plural –*n*- is always attached in such cases after another suffix, containing a vowel. It is therefore possible that some *n*-final forms end in -ʌ underlyingly but delete the final vowel in all forms that are longer than two syllables. Of course, having a 'variable' ʌ in the underlying form of the word would greatly impact the way that the tonal material is associated, due to the progressive shift of the tonal material that this article proposes. It is an interesting question which I cannot answer at this point. Having no other examples of falling tones in suffixes but the three examples in (22), I leave the question of what causes the falling tone in these contexts to future research.

Setting aside the few patterns in (22) which require further data and investigation, we are able to account for the distribution of falling tones in Mabaan assuming a tonal inventory of only two tonemes: L and H. The falling tone emerges in situations where the phonological structure contains one or more TBUs unassociated to tonal material. Such situations arise in three morphological contexts: when a dimoraic H-toned root is followed by an H-toned suffix, when a dimoraic L-toned root is followed by a 'variable' ʌ suffix, and when an H-toned root is followed by a non-nasal consonantal suffix. Appearance of the falling tone in all these cases is due to the general strategy adopted by Mabaan that whenever a TBU lacks tonal material, a tonal autosegment is inserted with such value that the combination of the existing tone and the inserted tone (no matter their relative order) results in a falling contour. If such insertion is not possible, an existing tone spreads to the toneless TBU (no matter which direction). It appears that the value of the inserted tonal autosegment is chosen in relation to a preceding existing tonal autosegment, unless there is no such tone, in which case the value of the inserted tonal autosegment is chosen in relation to the following tonal autosegment.

The three principles of tonal association established for Mabaan are summarized below.
1. Tonal autosegments are associated to syllables right to left.
2. Contour is preferred to spreading.
3. The only permitted tonal contour is HL.

The last two principles in combination state that if a TBU associated with a tonal autosegment is preceded or followed by a toneless TBU, insertion of an opposite-valued tonal element and associating it to the toneless TBU will be favoured over tonal spreading to the toneless TBU. However, this principle is constrained by another which disallows rising tones. Consequently, in a configuration where a toneless TBU *precedes* a TBU associated to a lexical tone, the following two patterns will result: if the lexical tone is L, an H will be inserted before it, yielding a falling tone as in (24b); if, on the other hand, the lexical tone is H, the toneless TBU will be associated to tonal material through tonal spreading, as in (24a), yielding a flat high tone.

(24) a. V V   V V   b. V V   V V
          →   →
         H_{Lex} H_{Lex} L_{Lex} H L_{Lex}

When the TBU associated with a tonal element is *followed* by a toneless TBU, if the lexical tone is H, an L-tone is inserted after it, yielding a falling tone, as in (25a). If the lexical tone is L, the lexical tone spreads to the following toneless TBU (since rising tones are not permitted), yielding a low flat tone, as in (25b).

(25) a. V V   V V   b. V V   V V
          →   →
         H_{Lex} H_{Lex} L L_{Lex} L_{Lex}

While generation of structures involving progressive tonal spreading and tonal insertion, such as shown in (25), may not be surprising, regressive application of the same principles, as shown in (24), is more unique. This could be an innovation introduced in Mabaan due to affix attrition, as described earlier in this article.

It is clear that affix attrition played an important role in the emergence of the falling tone in Mabaan. One type of a reduced suffix contains a phonologically deficient vowel ʌ. It is unspecified for tone and is subject to elision in non-prepausal positions but has a segmental nucleus (prior to elision) and therefore attracts tonal material that should properly precede it. Another type of a reduced suffix is of a phonological form –VC, where V is a segmentally empty nucleus. Suffixes of this form most likely contained a reduced vowel at some point which was then further reduced to an empty V-slot. Comparative data collaborates suggestion that these suffixes originally contained vowels: in languages such as Mayak and Surkum, suffixes corresponding to the consonantal suffixes in Mabaan have a –CVC or –VC segmental structure.[4] Moreover, in the synchronic grammar of Mabaan, some consonantal suffixes are associated with changes in the quality of root vowels. This fact is consistent with analysing consonantal affixes as being structurally -(V)C, as such analysis provides a nucleus to which floating vocalic features may be associated prior to docking onto the root. Note that when the floating L-tone re-associates to the root following deletion of the empty vocalic nucleus in structures such as (19a) and (20), its behaviour parallels that of the floating vocalic features.

We may presume that appearance of falling tones on long syllables has always been demanded by the OCP considerations (a universal principle) in Mabaan. Insertion of an L-tone between two H-tones which otherwise would be adjacent is a commonly encountered strategy in languages of the world. However, appearance of reduced affixes and their ambiguity in regards to tone – i.e. the fact that, on one hand, they contain vowels that are phonologically deficient and thus not lexically specified for tone but on the other still function as valid TBUs – engendered new environments where falling tones could emerge through tonal insertion, in accordance with the already existing principles.

4 Conclusions

Although more work remains to be done to explain a few exceptional patterns, this article provides a first step towards a two-tone analysis of the tonal system of

---

[4] For example, in Surkum the benefactive suffix –(C)ic while the antipassive suffix is –(C)ɪ (Andersen 2009).

Mabaan. The account proposes that Mabaan has a number of permissible tonal structures/melodies, and that in various morphological and phonological environments the tonal material is associated to TBUs in a way that avoids generating tonal melodies which are not part of this set. The rules that govern application of various tonal processes, such as tonal insertion or tonal spreading, are not stated with reference to specific morphological/phonological environments. All tonal processes apply as a natural outcome of universal constraints on tonal association (i.e. OCP, constraints against tonal crowding and multiply linked tones, etc.) and language-specific constraints on possible tonal melodies (i.e. no rising tone).

Perhaps one of the more striking features of the account is the implication that Mabaan has undergone a diachronic shift towards left-to-right direction in tonal association, which appears to have been triggered by attrition of segmental affixes. As a result of this shift, the lexical tone of the root, often surfaces on the phonologically reduced vowel of the suffix, rather than the root vowel itself. This phenomenon may be of interest to those researchers who are looking at the impact that morphological changes have on tonal systems. Additionally, in regards to this diachronic development, Mabaan may provide an intriguing point of comparison with other Nilotic languages, where deterioration of segmental suffixes was even more complete than it has been in Mabaan, i.e. languages of the Nuer-Dinka group.

References

Andersen, Torben. 1990. Vowel length in Western Nilotic languages. *Acta Linguistica Hafniensia* 22. 5–26.
Andersen, Torben. 1992. Aspects of Mabaan tonology. *Journal of African Languages and Linguistics* 13. 183–204.
Andersen, Torben. 1999. Consonant alternation and verbal morphology in Mayak (Northern Burun). *Afrika und Ubersee* 82. 65–97.
Andersen, Torben. 1999. Vowel harmony and vowel alternation in Mayak (Western Nilotic). *Studies in African Linguistics* 28. 1–29.
Andersen, Torben. 1999. Vowel quality alternation in Mabaan and its Western Nilotic history. *Journal of African Languages and Linguistics* 20. 97–120.
Andersen, Torben. 2004. Jumjum Phonology. *Studies in African Linguistics* 33(2). 133–162.
Andersen, Torben. 2006. Layers of number inflection in Mabaan. *Journal of African Languages and Linguistics* 27. 1–27.
Andersen, Torben. 2009. Verbal suffixes and suffix reduction in Surkum and other Northern Burun languages: Interaction with focus. *Journal of African Languages and Linguistics* 30. 147–196.
Blench, Roger. 2006. Mabaan dictionary. http://www.rogerblench.info/Language/NiloSaharan/Nilotic/Mabaan%20dictionary%20Unicode.pdf
Odden, David. 1986. On the role of the Obligatory Contour Principle in phonological theory. *Language* 62. 353–383.

J. Joseph Perry and Bert Vaux
Vedic Sanskrit accentuation and readjustment rules

1 Readjustment in morphological theory

This paper is a contribution to a debate which has arisen concerning the necessity of *readjustment*, i.e. phonological processes sensitive to morphological information, as a device for implementing allomorphic alternations, the question being whether readjustment is necessary as such, or whether these alternations can be accounted for by a combination of listed allomorphs and regular phonology. We show that, given a piece-based morphological framework such as Distributed Morphology, an accurate description of the phonology of accent in Vedic Sanskrit requires readjustment or a close analogue; listed allomorphs do not suffice to capture the observed facts. We also discuss ways in which these readjustment rules may be constrained, observing that they require a degree of derivational articulation, and that they may not be readily segregated from those phonological processes lacking morphological conditioning.

Readjustment rules are a device in Distributed Morphology (Halle and Marantz 1993) to capture morphologically conditioned alternations in the phonological form of items, and to account for phenomena such as *extended exponence*, whereby the presence of a morphosyntactic feature may be simultaneously signalled in two places (e.g. in a stem as well as in a suffix). The type of phenomenon which readjustment rules are invoked to account for is well exemplified by stem alternations in English irregular verbs (see e.g. Embick and Halle 2005). For instance, an example like *brought*, taken to be derived from initial exponents *bring + ed*, might involve two readjustment operations applying to the stem (deletion of the final consonant sequence and alteration of the vowel), and a third applying to the affix (devoicing of the consonant). As the example of *ringed* (i.e. encircled) shows, none of these operations can be taken to apply automatically in the relevant phonological environment. Rather the alternations depend on their morphological context.

(1) a) (n)C → ø / [v __] T_{PST}, where √ = √*think*, √*bring*, √*teach*, ...
    b) V → /ɔː/ / [v __] T_{PST}, where √ = √*buy*, √*bring*, √*fight*, ...
    c) /d/ → /t/ / √ [T_{PST} __], where √ = √*dream*, √*bring*, √*send*, ...

As (1) shows, readjustment is conventionally formalised in terms of traditional phonological rewrite rules, but with a morphological environment. However,

https://doi.org/10.1515/9781501506734-009

we can speak more broadly about 'readjustment' in the abstract to talk about cases where phonological statements are relativised to particular morphological environments, including not just rules of the type in (1) but also, for example, morpheme specific constraints or constraint rankings in an OT framework (e.g. Anttila 2002; Inkelas 1998; Orgun 1996; Pater 2000 among many others). While we will generally cast readjustment rules in a form similar to (1), we believe the conclusions reached here can plausibly be extended to various piece-based frameworks beyond conventional Distributed Morphology.

Readjustment has properties which seem to render it (all things being equal) an undesirable feature of a morphological theory. Left unconstrained, readjustment rules are exceptionally powerful. There is nothing to stop them from providing arbitrary lexical exceptions to phonological derivations, rendering individual phonological analyses within a given model effectively unfalsifiable. Bermúdez-Otero (2012) states this most forcefully when he says that readjustment rules "utterly destroy the empirical content of morphological and phonological hypotheses".[1] What is more, in most cases where readjustment rules have been proposed, they are not easily shown to be necessary. Distributed Morphology allows the operation of Vocabulary Insertion (which yields the initial exponents of lexical items) to be conditioned by surrounding morphological environments – a possibility which is required by the existence of *suppletive* alternations such as that between English *go* and *went*. In principle, there is no reason why the alternations accounted for by readjustment could not be dealt with by assuming an individual Vocabulary Item for each alternant. The sorts of Vocabulary Items which would be required for the example of *brought* are given in (2).

(2) a) $\sqrt{bring} \leftrightarrow /\text{brɪŋ}/$
    b) $\sqrt{bring} \leftrightarrow /\text{brɔ:}/ \; / \_\_T_{PST}$
    c) $T_{PST} \leftrightarrow /d/$
    d) $T_{PST} \leftrightarrow /t/ \; / \; \sqrt{\_\_}$, where $\sqrt{} = \sqrt{bring}, \sqrt{dream}, \ldots$

Because Vocabulary Insertion may only occur once at a given node, at a very early stage of the morphophonological computation, a model making use only of

---

[1] As Embick points out in his review of this paper, this may be something of an overstatement: while in general readjustment rules can provide exceptions to phonological generalisations in particular forms, all other phonological generalisations will be expected to hold in the forms in question, as illustrated by Halle's (1998) discussion of English accentuation – the grammar with the fewest possible exceptions will be preferred. Nonetheless, a theory with unconstrained readjustment rules still allows us to construct grammars with an arbitrary number of exceptions; if we wish to constrain the hypothesis space open to learners, this seems to be problematic.

suppletive allomorphy does not have the undesirable effects on the falsifiability of phonological analyses which readjustment has.

Another issue with readjustment, observed in particular by Bermúdez-Otero (2012), is that it constitutes a violation of *modularity*. It involves the manipulation of phonological forms by operations which lie outside phonology (or, alternatively, the visibility to the phonology of features which are non-phonological in nature). Bermúdez-Otero proposes the *Morph Integrity Hypothesis*, given in (3).

(3) *Morph Integrity Hypothesis* (Bermúdez-Otero 2012: 46)
Morphological operations do not alter the syntactic specifications or phonological content of morphs.

On the other hand, conceptual arguments be made in favour of a theory incorporating readjustment (see in particular Embick and Halle 2005). Most notably, readjustment ensures that it is possible to maximise generalisations over classes of lexical items, rather than having each allomorph individually memorised – in this way, readjustment allows a language learner to optimise memory usage. Both this argument and the modularity argument against readjustment seem to rely on particular hypotheses of how the language faculty functions. In our view, our aim should be to make use of empirical data to decide which (if any) of these hypotheses is correct: it does not seem to be possible to decide between them *a priori*. This echoes a point made by Calabrese (2015), who aims to show that metaphonic alternations in Altamurano (an Italian dialect of Apulia) are due to readjustment ('Morphophonological (MP) Rules', in his terminology) rather than listed allomorphy or regular phonology – he observes that arguments advanced on the basis of modularity against the possibility of readjustment are 'ideological' rather than empirical. Whatever conceptual objections (or advantages) there are to readjustment, conceptual arguments must fall by the wayside if the data contradicts their conclusions.

Various authors (see e.g. Embick 2010; Bobaljik 2012; Moskal 2015; Bobaljik and Harley 2017; Harley, Tubino and Haugen 2017) have suggested that incontrovertibly listed allomorphs are subject to certain locality conditions; another mechanism, for which readjustment is an obvious candidate, is then required in order to account for instances of allomorphy which obey different locality conditions. Such arguments are indeed suggestive, but not watertight – the data observed is still compatible with a model with unconstrained suppletive allomorphy and no readjustment, even if such a model does not explain the cross-linguistic patterns observed entirely satisfactorily. These arguments are also potentially subject to disproof by counterexample – they rely on the locality conditions in question being the correct ones.

Setting metatheoretical questions aside, then, the key empirical question is whether there are any phenomena under a piece-based morphological framework such as Distributed Morphology which require the use of readjustment operations as opposed to suppletion. If there are not, then the conceptual concerns just outlined may well suffice to exclude readjustment from such a theory of morphology. This question is considered by Haugen (2016), who finds that the previous arguments for the necessity of readjustment in various languages, such as Hiaki (Harley and Tubino Blanco 2013) and Sye (Frampton 2009), do not stand up to scrutiny. What this chapter attempts to show is that the behaviour of Vedic accentuation and its interaction with ablaut require readjustment within a piece-based morphological framework such as Distributed Morphology. This entails that the Morph Integrity Hypothesis in (3) cannot be taken to be correct in such a theory, at least in its strongest form. The implications of this are discussed in Section 4.

Section 2 of this chapter sets out the relevant accentual facts for Vedic Sanskrit, and the phonological analysis of these facts. Section 3 discusses instances in Vedic where these analyses do not seem on the surface to be adequate, and shows that these anomalous cases seem to require some sort of Readjustment operation. Finally, in section 4, we discuss the implications that the necessity of readjustment, and the particular case we observe in Vedic, has for morphophonological theory, noting that the process in question requires a degree of derivational structure in the phonology, and must be interleaved with at least some phonological processes which are not morphologically conditioned.

2 Vedic Sanskrit accentuation and ablaut

In this section we briefly review some facts concerning the Vedic Sanskrit language, the texts from which the examples here are drawn, and the nature of its accentual and ablaut systems. Drawing primarily on Kiparsky's (2010a) account of Indo-European accent, we introduce an analysis of accentuation and its interaction with ablaut in Vedic, before turning to the problematic forms of interest in the next section.

2.1 Vedic Sanskrit

The language discussed here is the language of the *R̥gveda*, a collection of hymns which is the oldest of the four *Vedas*, a group of Hindu scriptures dating to the first and second millennia BCE. Jamison and Brereton (2014: 5) date the composition of the Ṛgveda to the period 1400–1000 BCE. The first manuscript of the text, however, dates to the 14th century CE, more than two millennia later (Jamison and Brereton 2014:18). Despite this large interval, the text is generally considered to have been transmitted with a high degree of accuracy.

Vedic Sanskrit is an Indo-European language of the Indo-Iranian branch, and plausibly the most morphologically conservative recorded Indo-European language. Like other conservative Indo-European languages, it possesses a complex, highly fusional morphological system. It is also relatively conservative from a phonological perspective – it preserves the three-way contrast between stops (voiceless, voiced, voiced aspirated) postulated for Proto-Indo-European, as well as innovating a fourth category of stop (voiceless aspirates). It also preserves the non-nasal syllabic consonants of IE.[2]

Most importantly here, Vedic plausibly preserves the Indo-European accentual system more closely than any other recorded case – a fact which can be surmised, for example, from the correspondence between the position of Vedic accent and the application of Verner's law in Germanic.[3]

We will give a brief overview of the source of the accentual generalisations discussed here. The Vedic texts do not record accent as such. Rather, in manuscripts and critical editions, various pitch features are indicated, from which the placement of the accent can be deduced, as illustrated in (4). Specifically, a fall in pitch, known as *svarita* ('sounded'), and which generally follows the accented syllable,[4] is indicated through a short vertical line above the syllable in question, and a low pitch before the accented syllable, known as *sannatara* ('more depressed'), is indicated with a horizontal line below the syllable. These can both be seen, for example, in the word पुरोहितं (*puróhitaṃ*, 'foremost, priest') in (4). The high-pitched, accented syllable (known as *udātta* 'raised') is not marked, nor are the mid-toned (*ekaśruti* 'monotone') syllables following the post-accentual fall.[5]

---

[2] We make use of IAST transliteration for the segments of Sanskrit. A few relevant features may benefit from being highlighted briefly. We use a macron to indicate length (so that *i* is short and *ī* is long). The retroflex series is indicated with a dot under a coronal consonant (so that *t* is dental but *ṭ* is retroflex), and syllabic consonants are indicated with a ring below (so that *ṛ* is a syllabic rhotic).

[3] For example, the PIE *t becomes Germanic /d/ pre-tonically and /θ/ elsewhere. So Old English *mōdor* 'mother' corresponds to Vedic *mātā́*, and OE *brōþor* 'brother' corresponds to *bhrā́tā*.

[4] *Svarita* may also appear as a result of *sandhi* processes, e.g. when two vowels in hiatus are coalesced, if the first is accented and the second unaccented. This is known as 'independent' *svarita*.

[5] Both *ekaśruti* and *sannatara* syllables are traditionally considered variants of a category *anudātta* 'not raised'. For further discussion see Monier-Williams (1857), Whitney (1879), MacDonnell (1916).

To give an impression of how the original transcription functions, consider the first line of the *Ṛgveda* – here we give the *devanāgari* transcription (line 1) together with a Latin transliteration (line 2). Unconventionally, we give a one-to-one transliteration of the accentual marks in the *devanāgari* text, transliterating the *sanattara* (low) here as a grave accent and the *svarita* (fall) as a circumflex. Line 2 also includes *external sandhi* effects (sound changes which occur at word boundaries). In the word breakdown in the third line, we neglect external sandhi and (as elsewhere in this paper) make use of conventional accentual transliteration, which only marks accented syllables – an *udātta* (high pitch) syllable receives an acute accent and the independent svarita (i.e. secondary fall) is marked with a grave accent. Other syllables are left unmarked.

(4) अग्निमीळे पुरोहितं यज्ञस्य
 àgnimîḷe pùrohîtaṃ yàjñasyâ
 agní-m īḷ-e puróhita-m yajñá-sya
 agni-ACC.SG praise-MID.PRS.1SG foremost-M.ACC.SG sacrifice-GEN.SG

देवमृत्विजम्
dèvamṛ̀tvijâm
devá-m ṛtvíj-am
god-ACC.SG priest-ACC.SG

"Agni do I invoke – the one placed to the fore, god and priest of sacrifices [. . .]" (translation from Jamison and Brereton 2014)

The sentence in (4) reflects a few properties of the Sanskrit accentual system. For instance, while there is generally a one-to-one correspondence between word and accent, this is not always the case – in particular, finite main verbs (such as *īḷe* here) are unaccented, as are nouns in the vocative case. It is also possible for a word to have multiple accents – certain compounds (particularly *dvandva* compounds, which have the interpretation of coordinated nouns) exemplify this, as discussed by Kiparsky (1982 [1984], 2010b).

The main phonological phenomenon apart from accent which will be of interest to us here is *ablaut*. Sanskrit syllables (like reconstructed PIE syllables) can be classified into various *grades*. We must posit a *reduced grade* (or zero-grade), which contains no low vowels, a *full grade* (Skt. *guṇa*), which contains a short low vowel or light diphthong, and a *lengthened grade* (Skt. *vṛddhi*), which contains a long low vowel or a heavy diphthong. The term 'ablaut' describes the alternation among these grades. This alternation is illustrated using forms of the root *kar*- 'do' below:

(5) Ablaut grades of the root kar- ($\sqrt{do}$)
    Reduced Grade   kr̥-ta-   'done'
    Full Grade   kar-man-   'action, *karma*'
    Lengthened Grade   kār-ya-   '[thing] to be done'

Traditionally, the reduced grade was taken to basic in most cases, and the other grades were derived from the reduced-grade form. It is, however, simpler to assume that the full grade is underlying in all cases – this allows us to fully generalise the operation (*samprasāraṇa*) posited by traditional Sanskrit grammarians which transformed full-grade forms into reduced-grade forms.[6]

The interaction of accent and ablaut will be key to the discussion which follows – we will not be very concerned with the alternation between full and lengthened grades, but we will make extensive use of Kiparsky's (2010a) proposal that the alternation between full and reduced grades is due to the presence of an immediately following accent. This will be discussed further in the next few sections.

One topic which is of great interest, but which will not be discussed here, is the difference between the Sanskrit accentual system as it relates to nominals and as it relates to (finite) verbs. we will focus here on the *nominal* system,[7] but an extensive discussion of the verbal system is provided in Perry (2016).

2.2 Monosyllabic stems

The next two subsections will review the facts of nominal accentuation in Vedic, essentially following the analysis of Kiparsky (2010a) and previous work (in particular Kiparsky and Halle 1977; Kiparsky 1982 [1984]).

Monosyllabic nominal stems in Vedic can be divided into two categories – namely, those with *mobile* accent and those with *fixed* accent. In the case of the

---

[6] The reason this rule was originally required was that full-grade low vowels could appear on either side of a root semivowel, so that we have both *svap-a-ti* '(s/he) sleeps' and *joṣ-a-ti* (=*javṣ-a-ti*) '(s/he) rejoices'. To distinguish these, Sanskrit grammarians supposed that the former (but not the latter) took the full grade *svap-* as its basic form, and that cases where it appeared in the reduced grade (e.g. the past passive participle *sup-ta-*) were derived through *samprasāraṇa*. Here we generalise it to all roots, and rid the analysis of the operations which strengthen syllables to full grade.

[7] Noting that the nominal system also subsumes the inflection of adjectives and participles.

former, accent may appear (depending on the form) either on the stem or on the following gender/number/case ending. For the latter, accent always falls on the stem. This can be seen by comparing forms of the stem *pad-* 'foot', which is a mobile stem, and *gav-* 'bull', which is a fixed stem. We give a selection of inflected forms of these stems in (6).

(6)
	gav- 'cow'	*pad-* 'foot'
Accusative Singular	gáv-am	pā́d-am
Nominative Dual	gáv-ā	pā́d-ā
Dative Singular	gáv-e	pad-é
Instrumental Plural	gó-bhis	pad-bhís

As we can see from (6), each of the forms of *gav-* has stress on the stem. While this is also true of the accusative singular and nominative dual forms of *pad-*, the accent falls on the ending in the dative singular and instrumental plural. Traditionally, the forms with stem-accent are called 'strong' and the forms with accent on the endings 'weak'.

In order to capture the distinction between fixed and mobile stems in a piece-based way, Kiparsky and Halle (1977) propose that fixed stems are underlyingly accented, but that mobile stems are not. Similarly, they suppose that the endings of weak forms are underlyingly accented, but that the endings of strong forms are not. In combination with the *Basic Accentual Principle*, quoted in (7), these assumptions capture the different behaviour of the two types of stems (and two types of endings) in a straightforward way.

(7) *Basic Accentual Principle (BAP)* (as originally formulated by Kiparsky and Halle 1977: 209)
If a word has more than one [underlyingly] accented vowel, the first of these gets the word accent. If a word has no [underlyingly] accented vowel, the first vowel gets the word accent.

Clearly, whatever endings the accented stem *gáv-* is attached to, (7) will mean that, as the stem always possesses the leftmost underlying accent in the word, the stem is always accented on the surface, as we see in (6). When the unaccented stem *pad-* is attached to an accented suffix, the suffix will bear the leftmost underlying accent in the word, and will bear the surface accent. If an unaccented suffix is attached to *pad-*, there is no underlyingly accented syllable in the word, and the surface accent falls on the leftmost syllable (i.e. the stem), giving the patterns we see in (6).

(8) Application of BAP[8]

Input	Output
gáv + é	gáv-e
gáv + am	gáv-am
pad + é	pad-é
pad + am	pád-am

This applies unproblematically for the vast majority of monosyllabic noun stems.

2.3 Polysyllabic stems

There seems to be a similar division between fixed and mobile polysyllabic nominal stems. This can be seen by considering a selection of inflected forms of the words *hotar-* 'priest' and *pitar-* 'father'. These include the forms which will constitute one of the main points of interest in this chapter, namely the genitive plural.

(9)	*hotar-* 'priest'	*pitar-* 'father'
Accusative Singular	hótār-am	pitár-am
Instrumental Plural	hótr̥-bhis	pitr̥-bhis
Instrumental Singular	hótr-ā	pitr-ā́
Genitive Plural	hótr̥-ṇām	pitr̥-ṇā́m

In many ways, the facts in (9) look very much like those in (6). Accent remains on the stem throughout the paradigm of *hotar-*, but shifts to the ending in certain forms of *pitar-*. There are certain differences, however. Most importantly, the particular forms which display accentual shift from monosyllabic stems are different to those which show the same shift in polysyllabic stems. For example, the instrumental plural (marked with the suffix *-bhis*) shows accentual mobility for *pad-*, but not for *pitar-*. A second fact which requires some modification of the account so far is the difference in the placement of accent in mobile polysyllabic stems when compared with monosyllabic stems. The Basic Accentual Principle (7) predicts that when an accent falls on a mobile (i.e. underlyingly unaccented) stem such as *pitar-*, the accent should be placed on the leftmost syllable of the word and stem, but this is not what we see – rather we see an accent on the final syllable of the stem: *pitár-am*, not **pítar-am*.

---

[8] In the output column, we give the surface form, which may have undergone processes such as vowel lengthening in addition to the BAP.

To capture this second observation, Kiparsky (2010a) supposes that these stems are assigned a final accent at an early stage, according to a rule which he calls *Oxytone*.⁹

(10) *Oxytone Rule* (Kiparsky 2010a)
Accent the rightmost syllable of an inflectional stem.

Suppose that we adopt an analysis which takes these accentual generalisations to be expressed in terms of ordered rules.¹⁰ If we further suppose that the rules implementing the BAP follow Oxytone, we are then required to explain why we see any mobility at all – why does the accent assigned to *pitar-* by Oxytone not simply act as an underlying accent and remain fixed in all cases? The answer given by Kiparsky comes from the interaction of accentuation, ablaut and syllabification. The account given also explains the difference between monosyllabic and polysyllabic stems in terms of mobility-triggering affixes.

Kiparsky observes that a particularly regular environment for zero-grade ablaut (i.e. reduction of a syllable from its underlying full grade to its reduced grade) is the position before an underlying accent. It is this ablaut process which is responsible for the stem alternations in *hotar-* and *pitar-*. We give a semi-formal definition of the relevant operation below:

(11) A → ∅ / [$_\sigma$ . . .___. . .] ó, where A is an ablauting vowel.¹¹

---

9 Alternatively, we could assume these accents to be underlying, but this would miss the generalisation that no mobile stems involve anything like our hypothetical **pítar-am*, and that (as Kiparsky observes) compounds of unaccented roots undergo the Oxytone rule – e.g. *tri-* 'three'+ *vr̥t-* 'turning' → *trivŕ̥t-* 'threefold'.
10 This is the approach we will generally take throughout this paper, in part because analyses of the data in terms of ordered rules are relatively easy to formulate, but recastings of our analyses in other frameworks can be easily imagined. The conclusions we reach do not rely on a rule-based phonological framework.
11 Although most instances of *a* undergo ablaut in this position, not all do. We consequently posit /A/ on the analogy of the abstract yer phonemes of Lightner's (1965) analysis (and many subsequent analyses) of Russian, which undergo a deletion process to which other segments are not subject, otherwise being lowered so that they are identical to other surface vowels. Alternatively, we could say that the rule here is a morphologically sensitive readjustment rule, and that /A/ should simply be taken to be /a/ in the relevant morphological contexts. Since the aim of this paper is to argue for the necessity of readjustment rules, however, to assume this would be begging the question.

Ablaut interacts with the (re)syllabification of the relevant word. If the final consonant of a stem is followed by a vowel-initial suffix, that consonant is (re)syllabified as the onset of the following syllable.

(12) C [$_\sigma$ → [$_\sigma$ C / ___V

In the case of a reduced syllable where the final consonant is a sonorant, resyllabification of a final consonant as the onset of a final syllable bleeds a process whereby the coda of the reduced syllable is resyllabified as its nucleus.

(13)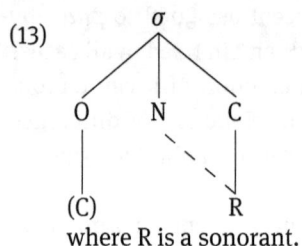

where R is a sonorant.

Unless there is an alternative candidate for a nucleus (e.g. in the onset of the syllable), the syllable is rendered defective, lacking a nucleus, and consequently cannot bear an accent. The relevant accent is eliminated, and the surface word accent consequently appears elsewhere. This is what Kiparsky (2010a) calls *Secondary Mobility* – it is this interaction, he supposes, that accounts for the mobility of *pitar-*. This also accounts for a regularity in the data – every ending which triggers accentual mobility in monosyllables, but not in polysyllables, is C-initial, and so would not be expected to trigger Secondary Mobility, since they do not provide the environment required for (12) to apply.

We illustrate the way this analysis proceeds in various forms of *pitar-* in (14):

(14) *Secondary Mobility in polysyllables*

Acc. Sg.	Ins. Sg.	Ins. Pl.	
pitAr-am	pitAr-ā́	pitAr-bhís	(Input)
pitÁr-am	pitÁr-ā́	pitÁr-bhís	(Oxytone, 10)
pitár-am	pi'tr-ā́	pi'tr-bhís	(Ablaut, 11)
pitá.r-am	pi't.r-ā́	pi'tr-bhís	(Onset, 12)
–	–	pitŕ̯-bhís	(Nucleus, 13)
–	pit.r-ā́	–	(Defective Accent Deletion)
pitár-am	pitr-ā́	pitŕ̯-bhis	(BAP, Output)

As we can see, this derives the correct forms. In *pitár-am*, the ending is unaccented and does not trigger ablaut. The stem remains in its full grade and the final syllable retains its nucleus. The accent falls on that nucleus straightforwardly through the BAP. In *pitr-ä́*, the ending is underlyingly accented, and as such triggers ablaut in the preceding syllable. The Onset rule resyllabifies /r/, an alternative candidate for the stem-final nucleus, as the onset of the following syllable. The stem-final syllable, being left without a nucleus, may no longer bear accent, so the lexical accent is deleted. When the BAP applies, the only remaining accent is on the ending, which therefore receives the surface accent. In *pitŕ̥-bhis*, the ending is accented, and ablaut removes the nucleus, but the Onset rule does not apply. This means that /r/ may be resyllabified as the nucleus of the stem-final syllable – because the syllable is then not defective, it retains its accent. When the BAP applies, the word contains two accents, and selects the leftmost (i.e. the stem accent) as the surface accent.

There is a single cell in the nominal paradigm, however, where this analysis does not obtain the right result: namely the genitive plural, marked with the suffix *-nām*. This accent is C-initial, but nonetheless triggers accentual mobility, so that we see *pitr̥̄-nā́m*, not **pi'tr̥̄-nām*.[12] C-initial suffixes should not trigger the resyllabification process in (12), and consequently should not permit Secondary Mobility. The predicted (and incorrect) derivation is shown in (15), which proceeds in a manner exactly parallel to *pitŕ̥-bhis* above.

(15) *Incorrect derivation of genitive plural form*
    pitAr-nám   (Input)
    pitÁr-nám   (Oxytone)
    pi'tr-nám   (Ablaut)
    –   (Onset)
    pitŕ̥-nám   (Nucleus)
    –   (Defective Accent Deletion)
    pitr̥̄́-nám   (Lengthening)
    pitr̥̄́-ṇām   (BAP, Retroflexion, Output)

The anomalous behaviour of this form requires explanation, and we turn to this in the next section.

---

[12] The retroflexion of /n/ here is a regular process following /r/ (whether syllabic or not). The lengthening we observe is morpheme specific, but could presumably be accounted for without using a readjustment rule by assuming that the suffix contains a floating mora or similar device.

3 Anomalous accentuation: A case for readjustment

This section discusses two main instances where Secondary Mobility, as discussed above and by Kiparsky (2010a), does not recover the correct accentuation – these are the genitive plural, discussed briefly above, and the case forms of the present participle. We propose an analysis of these forms making use of readjustment, and show that alternative analyses fail to capture the facts.

3.1 The genitive plural

As mentioned at the end of the previous section, the accentuation of forms containing the genitive plural ending *-nām* is anomalous. Although it is an ending which is C-initial, and consequently should not trigger accentual mobility in polysyllabic stems, we actually see that it usually does trigger accentual mobility. Kiparsky makes note of this problem, and suggests that *-nām* is a *dominant* suffix: that is to say, a suffix which triggers the deletion of other accents in the word. But this cannot be the case, since there are many cases where *-nām* does not cause mobility – one example is the form *hótr̥-ṇām*, where the initial syllable retains its accent, as it does with the putatively recessive desinence *-bhís*. More cases of this type will be discussed later in this subsection and in section 3.3.

Kiparsky does, however, provide a hint to what we believe is the correct analysis. Specifically, he observes that the *-nām* suffix is an innovation of the Indo-Iranian family (of which Sanskrit is a member) – other Indo-European languages show a vowel-initial suffix in this position. The accentual pattern we observe, then, is a result of suffix in question historically beginning with a vowel – in which case it is expected to trigger accentual mobility.

How are we to recast this historical observation in terms of a synchronic analysis? As it turns out, Sanskrit itself shows allomorphy between *-nām* and a vowel initial suffix *-ām*. The alternant *-nām* appears after non-nasal sonorants (with certain exceptions, mostly in monosyllables), and the alternant *-ām* elsewhere. In the absence of readjustment rules (or some analogue thereof), we must assume (if this is really allomorphy, rather than a phonological process) that *-nām* and *ām* are in competition as exponents of genitive plural features – that is, there is no derivational relationship between the two. But a derivational relationship is precisely what we need to encode the fact that *-nām* acts accentually as if it is a V-intial ending. If the allomorphy is suppletive, we expect the C-initial form to be inserted at the stage of Vocabulary Insertion (or equivalent), before phonological rules involving the suffix apply. This means we have a derivation identical to that we see if there was no allomorphy at all. That is, a derivation along the lines of (16), giving the incorrect output

(16) Incorrect derivation assuming suppletive allomorphy[13]
    pitAr-{ā́m, nā́m}   (Input)
    pitÁr-{ā́m, nā́m}   (Oxytone)
    pitAr-nā́m   (Allomorph Selection)
    pi'tr-nā́m   (Ablaut)
    –   (Onset)
    pitṙ̥-nā́m   (Nucleus)
    –   (Defective Accent Deletion)
    pitṙ̥́-nā́m   (Lengthening)
    pitṙ̥́-nām   (BAP, Retroflexion, Output)

To obtain the correct result, we must insert *-ām* as the initial exponent, assign accent on that basis, and only then insert /n/ before the suffix. Again, if we assume that readjustment rules do not exist, the most plausible analysis which permits this sort of derivational relationship would be to suppose that the /n/ acts as a phonological hiatus-breaker, intervening between two (semi)vocalic elements. The issue here is that /n/ is not always inserted in this phonological environment. Take the instrumental suffix *-ā*: phonologically speaking, there is no reason to expect this ending to act differently to the suffix *-ām* in creating a hiatus environment. But we never see the insertion of /n/ before this suffix – we see *pitr̥-ā*, not **pitr̥-ṇā́*. The insertion of /n/ seems to be sensitive to the morphological identity of the ending. One approach which has been taken to deal with morphologically specific insertion rules of this sort has been to assume what Zimmermann (2016) calls a 'mono-representational' analysis of allomorphy, where two allomorphs are derived from a single underlying representation. Typically this involves material (segmental or otherwise) which is present in the underlying representation without being attached to a node necessary for its realisation, leading to its being unrealised if not later associated by a phonological process.[14] In the present case, rather than two allomorphs *-ām* and *-nām*, we would posit a single underlying form for both, with a floating *n* which remains unrealised in most instances. The

---

[13] Here assuming allomorph selection as late as possible in the derivation – it can be supposed to follow Oxytone, which applies only to the stem and is not sensitive to properties of the affix, but must precede Ablaut, which crucially relies on accentual properties of the affix.
[14] For recent analyses along these lines see in particular Trommer (2011), Bye and Svenonius (2012), who focus on affixation of floating subsegmental elements, and Scheer (2016), who focuses on floating segments.

representation of the genitive plural suffix -*(n)ām*, then, would be something like the following (abstracting away from subsyllabic structure):

(17)
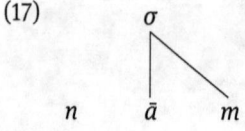

*

This too yields incorrect results, however. We would expect the floating *n* segment to be syllabified as the onset of the final, suffixal syllable in preference to the more distant *r*, meaning that, again, we would not expect accent shift – the derivation would proceed along more or less the same lines as (15) and (16), as shown in (18).

(18) *Incorrect derivation using monorepresentational analysis*[15]
    pitAr-⟨n⟩ám̃   (Input)
    pitÁr-⟨n⟩ám̃   (Oxytone)
    pi'tr-⟨n⟩ám̃   (Ablaut)
    pi'tr-nám̃   (Onset)
    pitr̥-nám̃   (Nucleus)
    –   (Defective Accent Deletion)
    pitr̥̄-nám̃   (Lengthening)
    pitr̥̄-nám̃   (BAP, Retroflexion, Output)

To obtain the correct results, it seems that we must assume *n* to be entirely absent from the representation when the Onset resyllabification rule applies, before being inserted by a morphologically specific process.

To summarise, the relationship between -*ām* and -*nām* must be derivational in nature (i.e. not suppletive), and must be conditioned by morphological properties. This kind of relationship is exactly what readjustment rules encode. That is to say, the behaviour of the Sanskrit genitive plural seems to require readjustment. The proposed rule is given in (19):

(19) $\emptyset \rightarrow /n/ \: / \: \begin{bmatrix} +\text{son} \\ +\text{cont} \end{bmatrix} \underline{\quad} K_{[+\text{gen}, +\text{pl}]}$

---

[15] Here the floating segment is enclosed by triangular brackets ⟨ ⟩.

This rule, it must be supposed, applies after the operations resulting in Secondary Mobility, but before a late resyllabification rule which reassociates a coda sonorant with a preceding nucleus. The derivation of *pitṝ-ṇā́m* is given in (20), with readjustment rule (19) in bold.

(20) Successful derivation using Readjustment Rule
    pitAr-ā́m   (Input)
    pitÅr-ā́m   (Oxytone)
    pi'tr-ā́m   (Ablaut)
    pi't.r-ā́m   (Onset)
    –   (Nucleus)
    pit.r-ā́m   (Defective Accent Deletion)
    pit.r-nā́m   (**n-Insertion**, 19)
    pitṛ-nā́m   (Late Resyllabification)
    pitṝ-nā́m   (Lengthening)
    pitṝ-ṇā́m   (BAP, Retroflexion, Output)

This derivation behaves in exactly the same way as *pitr-ā́* up to the deletion of accents in defective syllables. After the stem-final accent is deleted in this way, the n-insertion readjustment rule applies, followed by the 'late resyllabification' operation (or operations) above, which associate the inserted /n/ with the onset of the word-final syllable and the stem-final /r/ with the final nucleus of the stem.

What this analysis predicts is that in all polysyllabic stems where we have Secondary Mobility as a result of Ablaut and resyllabification, *-nām* should attract accent. In other polysyllabic stems, where Secondary Mobility does not apply, we predict that accent before *-nām* should remain stable. This distinguishes the approach here from Kiparsky's identification of *-nām* as a 'dominant' affix (discussed further at the end of this section), which predicts that *-nām* should trigger accent shift in all stems.

Other ablauting stems which take *-nām* in their genitive plural do indeed seem to show mobility. For instance, we see *kavī-nā́m* 'poet-GEN.PL', with mobile accent. And indeed this is an ablauting stem of the sort we expect to undergo accentual mobility (although the ablaut pattern is somewhat more complex than that obeyed by r-stems), as we can see from the nominative plural of the word for poet, which displays full grade and retains its accent: *kaváy-as*.

Now consider stems like *nadī-* 'river'. These have the genitive plural ending *-nām*, but we do not see accentual mobility: we have *nadī́-nām*, not **nadī-nā́m*.

And indeed, as predicted, we *do not* see ablaut alternation in this stem: the nominative plural is *nadíy-as* (> *nadyàs*), not *nadáyas.[16]

(21) nadī-ā́m   (Input)
    nadī́-ā́m   (Oxytone)
    –   (Ablaut)
    nadí-yā́m   (Onset)
    nadī́-nā́m   (**n-insertion**)
    nadī́-nām   (BAP, Output)

The final syllable of the stem *nadī-* remains in its reduced grade (albeit with lengthening) throughout its paradigm, presumably because the underlying form of the stem lacks /a/. Another set of stems of interest will be those which show full grade throughout their paradigm. One example of such a class is the set of *thematic* stems – those which form their stem by combining a root (or sometimes a derived form) with a theme vowel *-a-*. This /a/ is non-ablauting, and so we expect these forms to always retain their accent when combined with the genitive plural suffix *-nām*. This is indeed what we see – for instance, the genitive plural of the thematic stem *deva-* is *devā́-nām*, not **devā-nā́m*.

(22) deva-ā́m   (Input)
    devá-ā́m   (Oxytone)
    –   (Ablaut)
    –   (Onset)
    devá-nā́m   (**n-insertion**)
    devá-nā́m   (Lengthening)
    devá-nām   (BAP, Output)

In conclusion, the distribution of accentual mobility triggered by the Genitive Plural marker *-nām* is exactly what we would expect if the marker in question triggered secondary mobility in exactly the same way as V-initial markers, and not

---

16 The surface form of the nominative plural here (*nadyàs*) is *syncopated*. That this is a relatively late process is indicated by the independent *svarita* which appears here rather than the secondary mobility we see with ablauting stems. This suggests that the syncope follows pitch-accent assignment – independent *svarita* elsewhere tends to result from post-lexical sandhi processes. Not all stems in -*ī* behave in exactly the way that *nadī-* does. So-called *devī* stems, while they do not show accent shift in the genitive plural, do undergo relatively early syncope and consequent secondary accent shift. The point, however, is that this shift does not result from ablaut – i.e. it is possible to order the relevant process after n-insertion.

what we would expect if we took it to be accentually 'dominant'. This is straightforwardly captured by positing a readjustment rule which inserts an *n* before the initial exponent -*ām*, a rule which applies after secondary mobility has taken place. In what follows, we will consider other cases where a similar readjustment rule resolves problems in the distribution of Vedic accent.

3.2 Participles

If formed from an unaccented verb stem, the Vedic present participle[17] shows mobility identical to that of ablauting nouns ending in a sonorant, discussed in the previous section. What makes this unexpected is a) that the present participle appears to underlyingly end in a consonant cluster, not a single consonant – so that resyllabification would not be expected to render a syllable defective and b) that the present participle, even in its ablauting forms, always displays a full vowel in the final syllable of its stem.

The accentuation of the present participial forms (the participial ending followed by case/number markers), as they appear when attached to an unaccented verbal base, is illustrated in the table below:

(23) *Declension and accentuation of present participle (with unaccented base)*

	Singular	Dual	Plural
Nominative	-án	-ánt-ā	-ánt-as
Accusative	-ánt-am		-at-ás
Instrumental	-at-ā́		-ád-bhis
Dative	-at-é	-ád-bhyām	-ád-bhyas
Ablative	-at-ás		
Genitive		-at-ós	-at-ā́m
Locative	-at-í		-át-su

As will be observed, the accent of the participle shifts to the ending if and only if that ending is both accented[18] and V-initial. This is exactly the pattern we

---

[17] Or more precisely, non-perfect participial forms, including so-called aorist participles as well as present participles proper. These inflect with the same suffix, but a different stem; the difference between present and aorist participles is not relevant here, and we will use the term 'present participle' loosely to refer to both.

[18] Cases with unaccented endings are the nominative and accusative singular and dual, and the Nominative plural.

expect from the application of Secondary Mobility, as outlined in the previous section. But the Secondary Mobility effect cannot be straightforwardly derived here, as it can for a sonorant-final stem. Recall that Secondary Mobility was a consequence of resyllabification of a final consonant creating a defective syllable in an ablauted form. Here, ablauted forms of the stem-final syllable preceding a V-initial suffix and those preceding C-initial suffixes do not differ. In both cases, the syllable contains a filled nucleus – consider locative plural *-át-su* and locative singular *-at-í*. Even if we resyllabify the stem-final consonant /t/ as the onset of the following syllable, /n/ is still present in the stem-final syllable, and may be resyllabified as the nucleus when ablaut applies.[19] This being the case, we should expect fixed accent on the participial ending.

We can observe that the nominative singular form of the participle lacks the final /t/ of the participial ending. This is not surprising, since Sanskrit forbids word-final consonant clusters in general. It does, however, give us a hint to the solution to our problem. Suppose that the nominative singular, being the most frequent form, has also been reanalysed as the underlying form – i.e. as the initially inserted exponent of the present participle. As was the case with the genitive plural ending, we require a derivational relationship between participial endings *-an-* and *-ant-*: competition between these exponents at the point of insertion simply fails to give us the relevant accentual facts. Suppose, then that a readjustment rule (shown in (24)) inserts /t/ after the participial ending following Secondary Mobility, but before the late resyllabification process which we posited for the genitive plural, above.

(24) n → nt / [Wd [Ptcp$_{[-perf]}$ . . . ___] X], where X is any phonological material.[20]

This must be a readjustment rule rather than a phonological rule as it does not apply in all morphological environments – for example, there are plentiful examples of n-stemmed nouns like *naman-* 'name' or *rājan-* 'king', which never display the /t/ we see here. The rule in (24), applying after Secondary Mobility, produces exactly the forms we see in (3.2). Derivations of some relevant participial forms of the verb root *śuc-* 'to shine' are shown below:

---

19 This syllabic /n/ is realised on the surface as *a*. That this represents a resyllabification of /n/ is indicated by the fact that surface *n* alternates with *a* in exactly the same contexts as surface *r* alternates with *r̥*. Alternative analyses of alternations such as that observed here between *-ant* and *-at* can be imagined, but this makes no substantive difference to the argument here: whatever the analysis adopted, the presence of the final /t/ would be expected to block accent shift.
20 A slightly broader environment may be necessary here – exactly the same facts we observe in participles hold for the proprietive adjectival endings *-an(t)*, *-man(t)* and *-van(t)*. The only difference in these cases is that the nominative singular form shows lengthening (e.g. *mahān* 'great', **mahan*).

(25) *Participial forms and Secondary Mobility*

Nom. Pl.	Gen. Sg.	Ins. Pl.	
śuc-An-as	śuc-An-ás	śuc-An-bhis	(Input)
śuc-Án-as	śuc-Án-ás	śuc-Án-bhís	(Oxytone)
śuc-án-as	śu'c-n-ás	śu'c-n-bhís	(Ablaut)
śuc-á.n-as	śu'c-.n-ás	śu'c-n-.bhís	(Onset)
śuc-án-as	–	śuc-n̥-bhís	(Nucleus)
–	śuc-n-ás	–	(Defective Accent Deletion)
śuc-ánt-as	śuc-nt-ás	śuc-n̥t-bhís	(**t-insertion**, 24)
–	śuc-n̥t-ás	–	(Late Resyllabification)
–	śuc-at-ás	śuc-át-bhís	(n̥-vocalisation)
–	–	śuc-ád-bhís	(Voice Assimilation)
śuc-ánt-as	śuc-at-ás	śuc-ád-bhis	(BAP, Output)

Again, we see that a readjustment rule (in bold here), applying after Secondary Mobility, gives us the right result.

It may be instructive to compare this case to the perfect participle, which does not show accentual mobility. As with the present participle, the nominative singular form is sonorant-final. We might expect that it, too, would serve as a trigger for reanalysis, and that the perfect participle would undergo similar Secondary Mobility, but this is not what we see – instead we see fixed accent on the participial ending. The relevant forms are given in (26).[21]

(26) *Declension and acentuation of perfect participle*

	Singular	Dual	Plural
Nominative	-vā́n	-vā́ṃs-ā	-vā́ṃs-as
Accusative	-vā́ṃs-am		-úṣ-as
Instrumental	-úṣ-ā		-vád-bhis
Dative	-úṣ-e	(-vád-bhyām)	(-vád-bhyas)
Ablative	-úṣ-as		
Genitive		(-úṣ-os)	-úṣ-ām
Locative	(-úṣ-i)		(-vát-su)

It might be reasonable to attribute the failure of reanalysis in this case to the more complex allomorphy of the perfect participle. Abstracting away from superficial

---

21 The forms in parentheses here are unattested in the Ṛgveda, but rather are inferred from the corresponding Classical Sanskrit forms.

differences caused by processes like voicing assimilation, the present participle has three forms: *-an*, *-ant-* and *-at-*. Deriving the last two forms from the first is a relatively simple matter of applying the independently motivated process of ablaut, in addition to the t-insertion process of (24). The perfect participle, on the other hand, has four forms which differ non-trivially: *-vān*, *-vāṃs-*, *-vat-* and *-uṣ-*. Deriving a form such as *-uṣ-* from *-vān* is a much less transparent process than deriving *-at-* from *-an*, and so reanalysis of the Nom. Sg. as underlying here may be disfavoured.

To conclude, we can see that the accentuation of the genitive plural is not the only accentual phenomenon in Vedic which motivates readjustment, and that the paradigm of the Present Participle provides further support for the necessity of readjustment. We now turn to discuss possible analyses of these phenomena which do not require readjustment, showing how these analyses are (in various ways) inadequate to account for the data we see.

3.3 Alternatives

As was mentioned in section 3.1, Kiparsky (2010a) proposes that the genitive plural *-nām* is a dominant suffix. We dismissed this in rather short order, and it may be worth examining the proposal in a little more detail, to show why it cannot account for the phenomena we observe.

The dominant suffixes are a set of affixes in Sanskrit which produce forms other than those which would be expected from the Basic Accentual Principle (7) alone – they apparently trigger the deletion of lexical accents. Kiparsky (1982 [1984]) divides these into three categories – dominant accented suffixes, which remove lexical accents in preceding material, but are accented themselves (e.g. the past passive participle suffix *-ta*: *kár* 'do' + *ta* → *kr̥-tá-*), dominant *preaccenting* suffixes, which cause the accent to surface on the preceding syllable (e.g. the nominaliser *-tā*: *púruṣa* + *tā* → *puruṣá-tā*), and dominant *unaccented* suffixes, which remove lexical accents, but are not themselves accented, so that the BAP assigns initial accent (e.g. the comparative suffix *-iyaṃs*: *prati-cyáv-* 'moving towards' → *práti-cyav-iyaṃs-* 'moving more [ardently] towards'). Affixes which do not trigger accent deletion are called *recessive* affixes.

Because 'dominance' is a morphologically specific property which triggers accentual effects, it might reasonably be supposed to be a result of readjustment. This is not necessarily the case, however: Halle and Vergnaud (1987), for example, building on Kiparsky (1982 [1984]), propose an analysis whereby accentual dominance is a consequence of phonological cyclicity. In their analysis dominant suffixes are cyclic (unlike recessive suffixes), and the accentual derivation is erased each cycle. While there is reason to believe that this analysis does not suffice, at least in a Distributed Morphology framework (see Perry 2016), we can assume for the time being that some mechanism other than readjustment is responsible for accentual dominance.

Is it possible, then, to treat the genitive plural marker *-nām* as an dominant suffix? We can show straight away that it is not, by observing that it may attach to fixed-accent stems without removing their accent, so that we see *hótr̥-ṇām* 'of the priests', never **hotr̥-ṇā́m*. But what of a more 'locally' dominant affix? I.e. one which deaccents only the syllable immediately preceding it? One can imagine various ways of achieving this without explicitly invoking readjustment – for example, perhaps the suffix is associated with some sort of floating low tone, which triggers deletion of a preceding high.

This solution, too, is inadequate, as we can see from forms like *devā́-nām* 'of the gods' and *nadī́-nām* 'of the rivers' (**devā-nā́m, *nadī-nā́m*). Clearly, not all instances of *-nām* trigger deletion of the preceding accent. As a last-ditch attempt, we might say that there are different allomorphs of *-nām* – some which are 'locally dominant' in the relevant sense, and some which are not, and that these allomorphs are selected by different stems.

This solution, however, is undesirable for various reasons – besides the fact that it must posit two separate allomorphs (which must also be suppletive, forming entirely different vocabulary entries, given that we are not assuming the existence of readjustment rules) that are identical on the surface,[22] we then entirely lose the generalisation that we observe accent shift after ablauting syllables, but not elsewhere: the differing behaviour of *nadī́-nām* 'of the rivers' and *kavī-nā́m* 'of the poets' must simply be stipulated.

Finally, this analysis is of no help at all when we turn to the accentual behaviour of participles. While readjustment allows us to account for the anomalous accentuation of participles along much the same lines as the accentuation of the genitive plural (albeit with a different rule), the idea of local dominance cannot easily explain the behaviour of participles – we would have to assume that all V-initial accented suffixes were locally dominant in the relevant sense when attached to a participle. That is to say, all vowel-initial suffixes would have two suppletive allomorphs: one which triggers deletion of a preceding accent, and one which does not. Furthermore, each of the former set of allomorphs must

---

[22] This is, in principle, permissible even in a framework where we assume a constraint along the lines of Embick's (2003) *Avoid Accidental Homophony*. This hypothetical analysis would take these forms not to be precisely homophonous, but with a floating feature which distinguishes them. The question of how the relevant representations are acquired given their surface identity remains, however.

occur only in one environment – after the participles in question.²³ While this system is in principle permitted by a framework such as Distributed Morphology, it provides us with no explanation whatsoever of the phonological regularities we see in the data.

Perhaps, though, the explanation for configurations like these lies outside the synchronic linguistic system of these languages. Although the proposed synchronic system, making use of allomorphically conditioned locally dominant affixes, does not give us an explanation for any of the observed regularities in the system, it may be that an *amphichronic* approach to this problem (in the sense of Kiparsky 2006, Bermúdez-Otero 2013) is necessary – that is to say, the explanation for the present system lies in its historical development. This could plausibly be argued for the case of the genitive plural, where the insertion of /n/ before the genitive affix is an innovation. However, we run into problems when we consider participles. Here the forms with /t/ are conservative – the loss of /t/ in the nominative singular is a result of phonological simplification of a word-final cluster. The participial forms with accent shift, in other words, have never had a sonorant at the end of their stem. That is, there has never been a historical configuration which we would expect to yield Secondary Mobility in the phonology – meaning that an amphichronic approach does not provide any more explanation than the synchronic system just discussed.

4 Conclusion: Restraining readjustment

We have argued that readjustment rules, or some close analogue, must be responsible for phenomena which condition the distribution of Vedic accent, so long as we analyse it in a piece-based, compositional way. It seems likely that Vedic is not the only case where readjustment is required in this way – readjustment is required by any process where we have two phonologically similar allomorphs X and Y, with a phonological process expected to be triggered by allomorph X and not allomorph Y, but where the process in question does in fact apply in the environment of both allomorphs. Any case where we have a process triggered by vowel-initial syllables but not by consonant-initial syllables, for instance, but where this process emerges before a consonant-initial allomorph of an otherwise vowel-initial morpheme, will require a readjustment-based analysis. As Embick

---

23 Even the genitive plural, for which we have independently proposed this allomorphy, must have a unique allomorph following the relevant participle. This is because the form of the allomorph in question is *-ām*, while the form which is 'locally dominant' in other cases is *-nām*.

observes in his review of this chapter, morphologically specific operations inserting consonants in hiatus position are not particularly rare in the languages of the world.[24] This may well be a productive domain in which to find further examples of the sort of phenomenon discussed here.

The question is, where do we go from here? The conceptual objections to readjustment – that it makes it difficult to formulate testable phonological analyses, and that it constitutes a violation of strict modularity, remain. What, then, are we to conclude from their apparent necessity, in spite of these arguments?

One obvious tack starts by observing that the conclusion that readjustment rules are necessary is only forced upon us if we insist on a piece-based analysis of Vedic morphology and accent. Perhaps what we should conclude from the result here, then, is that a piece-based analysis is untenable, and that we should instead pursue a paradigmatic approach to accent (and ablaut), one in which we simply state, for instance, that it is a property of the genitive plural cell that accent is borne on the ending in the relevant set of nouns, or that the set of stems ending in -*nt* displays accent on the ending in V-initial 'weak' forms.[25] It is not within the scope of this chapter to discuss the merits of a paradigmatic approach as opposed to the piece-based approach we have been assuming, but it is worth noting that, in any case, we are forced to assume that phonological properties (including, but not limited to, accent placement) can be conditioned by morphological considerations – paradigmatic approaches, then, do not seem to represent an improvement as far as modularity is concerned.

If we do not abandon the piece-based approach, we must accept that some readjustment is necessary. But that is not to say, of course, that we must allow unconstrained readjustment rules to apply throughout the phonological derivation. One useful feature of cases like the Vedic accentual system, where readjustment can be shown to be a necessity, is that they allow us to test which restrictions on the operations in question may hold. There are two ways in which we can constrain readjustment rules – by constraining their form, and by constraining their interactions with other components of the phonological derivation. We will briefly discuss some possible constraints of the latter type.

One constraint on readjustment that the Vedic data is compatible with is proposed by Embick (2010). He supposes that readjustment is cyclic, and that

---

24 e.g. in Turkish the 3rd person possessive marker and accusative marker both have a V-initial allomorph /i/ which appears after consonants, but after vowels these markers surface as /si/ and /ji/, respectively.
25 That is, those which we analyse as having underlyingly accented endings.

the morphological trigger must share a cycle with a (morphologically specified) target.[26]

(27) *Readjustment Activity Hypothesis* (Embick 2010: 101)
A readjustment rule triggered by a morpheme X can effect a Root- or morpheme-specific change only when X and the Root/functional head are in the same PF cycle.

If we identify the PF cycle with the syntactic Spellout cycle or phase domain (Chomsky 2000), or indeed a slightly larger domain (following Embick, who takes a phonological spellout cycle to constitute not only a syntactic phase domain, but also all heads lying between that domain and the next phase head), this condition is readily satisfied: the case marker lies within the maximal nominal projection, which can plausibly be taken to constitute a phase domain (as assumed by e.g. Svenonius 2004; Bošković 2005, 2013 among others).[27]

On the other hand, one constrained model of readjustment with which the data here are not straightforwardly compatible is a monostratal OT model which implements readjustment using morphologically indexed constraints (e.g. the model adopted by Pater 2000). Recall that in order to capture the accentual facts, we require a derivational relationship between the initially inserted allomorph *-ām* and the derived allomorph *-nām*. And not only this: *n*-insertion counterbleeds accent shift, which means that the insertion of the initial exponent must apply at a different stage to readjustment. This, of course, presents the same issues to a monostratal OT model as any other instance of counterbleeding, and so readjustment cannot apply as part of such a computation.

---

26 Embick in his review of this chapter suggests that this could be tested by investigating category-changing morphology; unfortunately this is not possible using the Vedic phenomona under discussion. One case of category changing morphology which does participate in the phenomenon here is the participial marker, which attaches to a verb stem and creates a nominal form. But since the outermost categorial head will generally be taken to share a cyclic domain with a following case marker (since it lies outside the phase domain that it heads – see next paragraph), its behaviour is not informative. The ideal test-case might involve zero-derivation from an already-categorised item, where the behaviour of the inner categoriser with respect to readjustment would test this hypothesis, but this case does not seem to arise straightforwardly in Vedic.
27 This is one reason to reject Halle and Vergnaud's (1987) analysis of accentual dominance as a consequence of 'cyclic' affixation: case markers do not trigger deletion as dominant affixes do, but are plausibly taken to share a phonological cycle with the noun to which they are attached. Halle and Vergnaud assume that the cyclic/non-cyclic distinction is entirely diacritic, but if we assume any non-arbitrary correlation between the syntactic and phonological cycle, their account cannot be retained.

Apart from cyclicity, what possible constraints on readjustment are permitted in a derivational model? One broad notion that we might expect to be adhered to is that readjustment rules are 'early', in that they precede straightforwardly phonological rules, even where those rules take place in the same cycle. This, of course, recalls the restriction of morpheme-specific phonological rules to the lexicon in Lexical Phonology models (Mohanan 1982). And indeed we see that the readjustment rules here are preceded and followed by other morpheme-specific processes, such as ablaut, or the lengthening triggered by the genitive plural, making it plausible that there is a readjustment 'block' which precedes other phonological operations. Issues remain, however – interleaved within this block are rules which are not obviously conditioned by morphological structure. The most obvious of these are the rules which resyllabify items, whether as onsets or as nuclei, but also the Oxytone rule which seems to apply without exception.[28] This would not be an issue in a Lexical Phonology framework, where we can analyse morphology-sensitive readjustment operations and the interleaved phonological rules alike as lexical phonological rules, albeit with morphological indexing in the former. In any framework such as Distributed Morphology which dispenses with a generative lexicon, however, these considerations take on more importance. In order to retain the notion of an readjustment 'block', we could distinguish between phonological rules, and readjustment rules which happen not to have any morphological conditioning. Unless we have a principled way to distinguish the former from the latter, however, this is no different from assuming that phonological rules may be freely interleaved with readjustment operations.

One tempting way retain some notion of a readjustment block would distinguish between *structure-building* and *structure-changing* operations. Syllabification operations may be taken to exemplify the former, and Oxytone might also plausibly be taken to constitute a metrical structure-building operation. Then we could allow structure-building to be interleaved with readjustment rules, but not structure-changing operations.[29] This, in combination with the cyclicity condition

---

28 A *prima facie* exception can be found in verbs with *athematic presents*. These display accentual mobility even with C-initial suffixes, suggesting that there is no Oxytone accent present. However, the ablaut patterns here indicate the presence of Oxytone accent, suggesting that it is indeed inserted early, but removed by a later (morphologically specific) process. This seems to be confirmed by the behaviour of reduplicating verbs, where the distinction between C-initial suffixes and V-initial suffixes is visible in the direction of mobility (so that from the root *bhar* we see 1pl *bi~bhr̥-más* but 3pl *bí~bhr-ati*). This does not seem readily explicable without some sort of secondary mobility triggered by the V-initial suffix, which would be unmotivated unless Oxytone accent was assigned.

29 Cf. the distinction between structure-building and structure-changing assumed by Kiparsky (1982), who assumes that structure-building is not subject to the Strict Cyclicity Condition (and

above, would at least present some constraint on the phenomena for which readjustment is to be posited.

These and other constraints on readjustment must be considered if we are to retain a theory of (morpho)phonology which permits us to develop falsifiable analyses of phonology. The essential point demonstrated by the case of Vedic accentuation, however, is that some kind of Readjustment, however it is to be constrained, is forced upon us by piece-based analyses of morphophonological processes.

Acknowledgments: We thought it appropriate to contribute a piece combining empirical and theoretical work spanning Sanskrit phonology, morphology, and syntax, given the second author's fond memories of Andrea's inspirational ability to navigate these complex waters in his own research and teaching. It was in fact Andrea who first made the second author aware of the theoretical importance and potential of the Sanskrit stress system when he was Andrea's graduate student in the early 1990s. This paper is a development of a conference paper entitled "Allomorphy, Morphophonology and Opacity in the Accentuation of the Vedic Noun", given by the first author at the second Edinburgh Symposium on Historical Phonology (ESHP). Thanks are due to members of the ESHP2 audience (in particular Ricardo Bermúdez-Otero) and members of the Cambridge Experimental Phonetics and Phonology research cluster for their helpful comments and questions. Thanks also to an anonymous reviewer and the onymous David Embick for their suggestions. All errors are, of course, our own.

References

Anttila, Arto. 2002. Morphologically conditioned phonological alternations. *Natural Language and Linguistic Theory* 20(1). 1–42.

Bermudez-Otero, Ricardo. 2012. The architecture of grammar and the division of labour in exponence. In Jochen Trommer (ed.), *The morphology and phonology of exponence*, Oxford: Oxford University Press.

---

consequently does not display derived environment effects), while structure-changing rules are subject to the SCC and may not apply in non-derived environments. This allows underived stems to be metrified in English, for example. Halle and Mohanan (1985) suppose that the BAP in Vedic is a structure-changing operation, since some metrical information seems to be specified underlyingly in the language. If we follow them in assuming that there is a distinction between *accent* (concrete tonal specifications) and *stress* (abstract prominence), however, we can suppose that only the former is encoded in the UR, allowing at least some metrical processes to be treated as structure-building.

Bermudez-Otero, Ricardo. 2013. Amphichronic explanation and the life cycle of phono-logical processes. In Patrick Honeybone & Joseph Salmons (eds.), *The Oxford handbook of historical phonology*, Oxford: Oxford University Press.
Bobaljik, Jonathan. 2012. *Universals in comparative morphology*. Cambridge, MA: MIT Press.
Bobaljik, Jonathan & Heidi Harley. 2017. Suppletion is local: Evidence from Hiaki. In Heather Newell, Máire Noonan, Glyne Piggott & Lisa Travis (eds.), *The structure of words at the interfaces*, Oxford: Oxford University Press.
Boškovic, Željko. 2005. On the locality of left branch extraction and the structure of NP. *Studia Linguistica* 59(1). 1–45.
Boškovic, Željko. 2012. Phases beyond clauses. In Lilla Schürcks, Anastasia Giannakidou & Urtzi Etxeberria (eds.), *The nominal structure in Slavic and beyond*, Berlin: De Gruyter Mouton.
Bye, Patrik & Peter Svenonius. 2012. Exponence, phonology and non-concatenative morphology. In Jochen Trommer (ed.), *The morphology and phonology of exponence*, Oxford: Oxford University Press.
Calabrese, Andrea. 2015. On the morphophonology of metaphonic alternations in altamurano. In Fransesc Torres-Tamarit, Kathrin Linke & Marc van Oostendorp (eds.), *Approaches to metaphony in the languages of Italy,* Berlin: De Gruyter Mouton.
Chomsky, Noam. 2000. Minimalist inquiries: The framework. In Roger Martin, David Michaels & Juan Uriagereka (eds.), *Step by step*, Cambridge, MA: MIT Press.
Embick, David. 2003. Locality, listedness and morphological identity. *Studia Linguistica* 57(3). 143–169.
Embick, David. 2010. *Localism versus Globalism in Morphology and Phonology*. Cambridge, MA: MIT Press
Embick, David & Morris Halle. 2005. On the status of stems in morphological theory. In Twan Geerts, Ivo van Ginneken & Haike Jacobs (eds.), *Romance languages and linguistic theory 2003*, Amsterdam: John Benjamins. 2003, Amsterdam: John Benjamins.
Frampton, John. 2009. *Distributed reduplication*. Cambridge, MA: MIT Press.
Halle, Morris. 1998. The stress of English words 1968–1998. *Linguistic Inquiry* 29(4). 539–568.
Halle, Morris & Alec Marantz. 1993. Distributed morphology and the pieces of inflection. In Kenneth L. Hale & Samuel Jay Keyser (eds.), *The view from building 20*, Cambridge, MA: MIT Press.
Halle, Morris & K. P. Mohanan. 1985. Segmental phonology of modern English. *Linguistic Inquiry* 16(1). 57–116.
Halle, Morris & Jean-Roger Vergnaud. 1987. *An essay on stress*. Cambridge, MA: MIT Press.
Harley, Heidi & Mercedes Tubino Blanco. 2013. Cycles, vocabulary items and stem forms in Hiaki. In Alec Marantz & Ora Matushansky (eds.), *Distributed morphology today*, Cambridge, MA: MIT Press.
Harley, Heidi, Mercedes Tubino & Jason D. Haugen. 2017. Locality conditions on suppletive verbs in Hiaki. In Vera Gribanova & Stephanie S. Shih (eds.), *The morphosyntax-phonology connection*, Oxford: Oxford University Press.
Haugen, Jason D. 2016. Readjustment: Rejected? In Daniel Siddiqi & Heidi Harley (eds.), *Morphological metatheory*, Cambridge, MA: MIT Press.
Inkelas, Sharon. 1998. Segmental phonology of modern English. *Yearbook of Morphology* 1997. 121–155.
Jamison, Stephanie W. & Joel P. Brereton. 1987. *The Rigveda*. Oxford: Oxford University Press.

Kiparsky, Paul. 1982. The lexical phonology of Vedic accent. Ms. [partially published as Kiparsky, Paul. 1984. A Compositional Approach to Vedic Word Accent. In S.D. Joshi (ed.) *Amṛadhārā*. Delhi: Ajanta Publications.].

Kiparsky, Paul. 2006. The amphichronic program vs. evolutionary phonology. *Theoretical Linguistics* 32(2). 217–236.

Kiparsky, Paul. 2010a. Compositional vs. paradigmatic approaches to accent and ablaut. In Stephanie W. Jamison, H. Craig Melchert & Bert Vine (eds.), *Proceedings of the 21st annual UCLA Indo-European linguistics conference*, Bremen: Hempen.

Kiparsky, Paul. 2010b. Dvandvas, blocking and the associative: The bumpy ride from phrase to word. *Language* 86(2). 301–331.

Lightner, Theodore. 1965. *Segmental phonology of modern standard Russian*: MIT dissertation.

MacDonnell, Anthony A. 1916. *A Vedic grammar for students*: Motilal Banarsidass.

Mohanan, K. P. 1982. *Lexical phonology*: MIT dissertation.

Monier-Williams, Monier. 1857. *A practical grammar of the Sanskrit language*. Oxford: Oxford University Press.

Moskal, Beata. 2015. Limits on allomorphy: A case study in nominal suppletion. *Linguistic Inquiry* 46(2). 363–376.

Orgun, Orhan. 1996. *Sign-based morphology and phonology with special attention to Optimality Theory*: UC Berkeley dissertation.

Pater, Joe. 2000. Non-uniformity in English secondary stress: the role of ranked and lexically specific constraints *Phonology* 17(2). 237–274.

Perry, J. Joseph. 2016. *Tone and prosodic constituency in Gyalsumdo*: University of Cambridge dissertation.

Scheer, Tobias. 2016. Melody-free syntax and phonologically conditioned allomorphy. *Morphology* 26(3–4). 341–378.

Svenonius, Peter. 2004. On the edge. In David Adger, Cécile de Cat & George Tsoulas (eds.), *Peripheries: Syntactic edges and their effects*, Dordrecht: Kluwer.

Trommer, Jochen. 2011. Phonological aspects of Western Nilotic mutation morphology. University of Leipzig Habilitation Thesis.

Whitney, William Dwight. 1879. *A Sanskrit grammar*. Gotha: Breitkopf & Hartel.

Zimermann, Eva. 2016. The power of a single representation: Morphological tone and allomorphy. *Morphology* 26(3–4). 269–294.

Roberto Petrosino
Allomorphy of Italian determiners at the morphology-phonology interface

> *Ad Andrea.*
> καί σε τοσοῦτον ἔθηκα θεοῖς ἐπιείκελ' Ἀχιλλεῦ,
> ἐκ θυμοῦ φιλέων, ἐπεὶ οὐκ ἐθέλεσκες ἅμ' ἄλλῳ
> οὔτ' ἐς δαῖτ' ἰέναι οὔτ' ἐν μεγάροισι πάσασθαι,
> πρίν γ' ὅτε δή ς' ἐπ' ἐμοῖσιν ἐγὼ γουνέσσι καθίσσας
> ὄψου τ' ἄσαιμι προταμὼν καὶ οἶνον ἐπισχών.
> πολλάκι μοι κατέδευσας ἐπὶ στήθεσσι χιτῶνα
> οἴνου ἀποβλύζων ἐν νηπιέῃ ἀλεγεινῇ.
> *Il.* IX, 485ff.

1 Introduction

There is no consensus on how to properly treat morpho-phonologically conditioned alternations, namely alternations that are sensitive to both morpho-syntactic and phonological information. In *morpho-phonological accounts*, they are accounted for via application of morphologically-conditioned phonological OPERATIONS (e.g., *readjustment rules*: Embick & Halle 2005). In *listing accounts*, they are LISTED as lexical independent entries (among others, Haugen & Siddiqi 2013).

This paper deals with the allomorphic distributions of the Standard Italian (henceforth, SI, to distinguish it from the other Italo-Romance varieties) determiners, which constitute a relevant case to such a hotly debated issue. Contra previous accounts, and in line with Calabrese's recent work (a.o., Calabrese 2016, 2018), this paper argues for a model that makes use of language-wide morpho-phonological operations to account for these alternations. I show that this model is able to explain the allomorphic micro-variation of determiners detectable in the entire Italo-Romance area.

Note: Many thanks to Jonathan Bobaljik, Andrea Calabrese, Christos Christopoulos, Harry van der Hulst, and Andrew Nevins for their valuable feedback. All errors remain my own.

https://doi.org/10.1515/9781501506734-010

The discussion unfolds as follows. In section 2, I present the data from the Italian definite determiner and in section 3, I propose a morpho-phonological account for it. The discussion then turns to other SI determiners and pre-nominal adjectives in section 4. In section 5, I review a recent listing account for the definite determiner (Artés 2013); in taking stock of both accounts, I ultimately argue that the morpho-phonological account proposed is to be preferred as being effortlessly able to account for the inter- and intra-dialectal variation of determiners. Section 6 concludes the paper.

2 The SI definite determiner

The SI definite determiner presents alternations that are dependent on both the morpho-syntactic (i.e., ϕ-features) and phonological (i.e., the syllabic structure) properties of the following host.[1]

First, the singular form of the determiner is realized as *l* before a vowel, regardless of gender.

(1) l   [i]dea   (2) l   [i]ndice
    D.FSG idea.FSG   D.MSG index.MSG
    'the idea'   'the index'

The plural forms are instead *le* for the feminine, and *ʎi* for the masculine.[2]

---

[1] In all the examples below, alternants are followed by nouns for illustration purposes only. The same forms are found when the clitic host is not a noun.

[2] An interesting asymmetry concerns diphthong-initial hosts. Typically, the vowel of the definite determiner is deleted in the singular, and preserved in the plural, rather like what happens before vowel-initial hosts (a):

	[−FEM]			[−FEM]	
a.	l [aw]mento ~ ʎi [aw]menti	'the increase(s)'	l [aw]la ~ le [aw]le	'the room(s)'
b.	lo [ja]to ~ ʎi [ja]ti	'the hiatus(es)'	la [jo]lla ~ le [jo]lle	'the boat(s)'

However, words like *whiskey* [wiski] or *web* [wɛb] select the pair *il~i*, instead of the expected pair *l~ʎi*. This is arguably due to the fact that the back glide [w] is syllabified as a consonant.

A similar phenomenon happens with hosts that begins with the front glide [j] (b). In such cases, vowel deletion does not apply, and the form of the determiner is the same as that found before extended-syllable-initial hosts (see data in the following pages). Due to page restrictions I will not deal with these cases, as they are not relevant to the purposes of the paper.

(3) le   [i]dee   (4) ʎi   [i]ndici
    D.FPL idea.FPL   D.MPL index.MPL
    'the ideas'   'the indices'

Second, before consonants, the feminine forms of the determiner are *la ~ le*, in the singular and plural respectively.

(5) a. la   [k]asa   (6) a. la   [st]anza
       D.FSG home.FSG   D.FSG room.FSG
       'the home'   'the room'
    b. le   [k]ase   b. le   [st]anze
       D.FPL home.FPL   D.FPL room.FPL
       'the homes'   'the rooms'

Unlike the feminine forms, the masculine forms alternate. They surface as *il ~ i* before hosts as in (7), and as *lo ~ ʎi* before hosts as in (8).

(7) a. il   [k]orso   b. i   [k]orsi
       D.MSG course.MSG   D.MPL course.MPL
       'the course'   'the courses'

(8) a. lo   [ʃʃ]emo   b. ʎi   [ʃʃ]emi
       D.MSG fool.MSG   D.MPL fool.MPL
       'the fool'   'the fools'

Formally speaking, the pair *lo ~ ʎi* shows up before an extended syllabic structure consisting of an extra σ-tier (see Vaux & Wolfe 2009 and references therein) and occupied by one of the following phonological segments:

1. [+anterior] fricative /s/ (traditionally called '*spurious s*'):

(9)
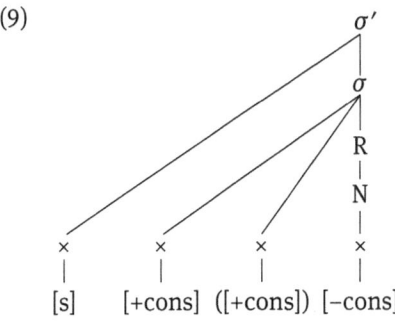

2. [+anterior, +distributed] fricatives (i.e., [ʃ, ɲ]; (10)) and affricates (i.e, [ts, dz]; (11)), which are always geminated in Italian:

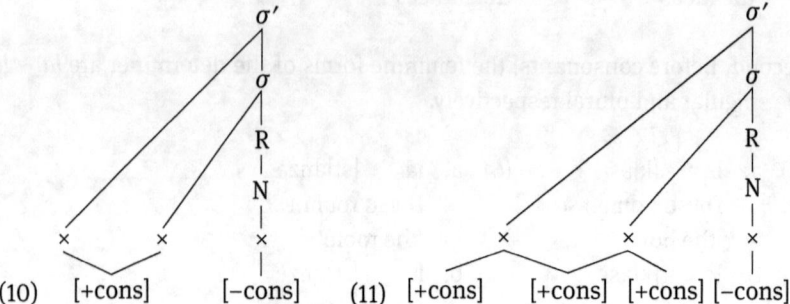

3. Greek-derived consonantal clusters (such as [pn-], [ps-], [ks-]):

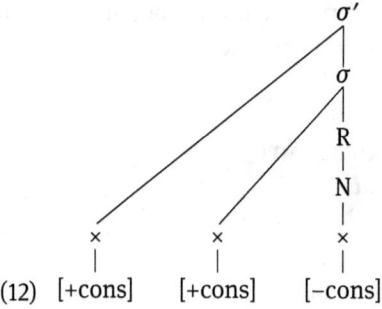

Table 1 below summarizes all of the forms of the determiner. Some other relevant examples follow in Table 2.

Table 1: Forms of the SI definite determiner.

	[−FEM]		[+FEM]	
	[−PL]	[+PL]	[−PL]	[+PL]
_ [σ	il	i	la	le
_ [σ'	lo	ʎi		
_ [V	l		l	

Table 2: Some examples of the forms of the SI definite determiner.

C-initial feminine hosts

la [p]orta ~ le [p]orte   'D door(s)'   la [dz]anzara ~ le [dz]anzare 'D mosquito(es)'
la [s]alsa ~ le [s]alse   'D sauce(s)'   la [st]atzione ~ le [st]azioni 'D station(s)'

Table 2: (*Continued*)

C-initial masculine hosts				
core-syllable-initial hosts			extended-syllable-initial hosts	
il [k]ane ~ i [k]ani	'D dog(s)'		lo [st]ruzzo ~ ʎi [st]ruzzi	'D ostrich(es)'
il [tr]eno ~ i [tr]eni	'D train(s)'		lo [ps]icologo ~ ʎi [ps]icologi	'D psychologist(s)'
V-initial hosts				
masculine			feminine	
l [o]rko ~ ʎi [o]rki	'D ogre(s)'		l [ɔ]ka ~ le [ɔ]ke	'D goose/geese'

3 Morpho-phonological analysis

The analysis I propose assumes the main tenets of *Distributed Morphology* (henceforth, DM; Halle & Marantz 1993, 1994). In this framework, syntactic properties are realized with phonological segments (called *exponents*) through the process of *Vocabulary Insertion* (henceforth, VI). In the wake of the long-standing debate on the appropriate treatment of morpho-phonological alternations (see sec. 1), I argue that the allomorphic distribution just seen may be accounted for by a series of language-specific, but language-wide morpho-phonological operations.

The derivation goes through as follows. At Spell-Out, the structure (13) has a complex internal structure consisting at least of the root, the category-defining head n, and a ϕ_n-head in which number and gender features are specified. Such morpho-syntactic features are assumed to percolate onto the ϕ_D head via Concord. VI applies as formalized in (14), where the exponent of the definite determiner is argued to be /l/.

(13)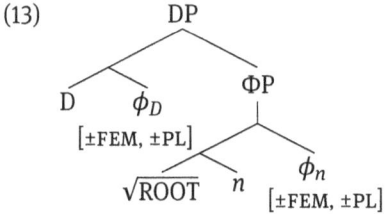

(14) *Vocabulary Items*:
    a. $D_{[+\text{DEF}]} \leftrightarrow l$
    b. $[+\text{PL}, +\text{FEM}] \leftrightarrow e \,/\, \_\,]_{\phi_D}$
    c. $[+\text{PL}, -\text{FEM}] \leftrightarrow i \,/\, \_\,]_{\phi_D}$
    d. $[-\text{PL}, +\text{FEM}] \leftrightarrow a \,/\, \_\,]_{\phi_D}$
    e. $[-\text{PL}, -\text{FEM}] \leftrightarrow o \,/\, \_\,]_{\phi_D}$

Once the appropriate Vocabulary Items are inserted, post-syntactic operations may apply (Embick & Noyer 2001). After cliticizing onto its host (signaled by ⊕ below), the definite determiner may undergo a series of morpho-phonological operations in the appropriate environment.

Cross-boundary hiatus is generally repaired by vowel deletion:[3]

(15) *hiatus*:
$$\begin{array}{c} N \\ | \\ x \\ | \\ \text{[–cons]} \end{array} \rightarrow \emptyset\ /\ \_\oplus\quad \begin{array}{c} N \\ | \\ x \\ | \\ \text{[–cons]} \end{array}]_{[-\text{PL}]}$$

The operation above applies before vowel-initial hosts carrying the unmarked value for number, but does not apply in plural forms. Sample derivations follow in Table 3.

Table 3: Sample derivations of the definite determiner before vowel-initial hosts.

	/l-o ⊕ amore/	/l-a ⊕ ɔka/	/l-e ⊕ ɔke/
hiatus	l_amore	l_ɔka	–
SR	[la.mo.re]	[lɔ.ka]	[le.ɔ.ke]

When cliticizing onto a core-syllable-initial host, the masculine singular form of the definite determiner undergoes an operation of truncation (*troncamento*):

(16) *troncamento*:
$$\begin{array}{c} N \\ | \\ x \\ | \\ \text{[–cons]} \end{array} \rightarrow \emptyset\ /\ \_\_\oplus\quad \begin{array}{c} \\ \\ x \\ | \\ \text{[+cons]} \end{array} \begin{array}{c} \sigma \\ | \\ R \\ | \\ N \\ | \\ x \\ | \\ \text{[–cons]} \end{array}]_{[-\text{FEM},\ -\text{PL}]}$$

In spite of its idiosyncrasy, *troncamento* (16) expresses the weakness of the unmarked feature bundle [-FEM, -PL], which is widely attested in Romance.[4]

---

3 For ease of illustration, all the operations in this paper will be formalized as rules, but some should be formalized as resulting from the interplay of filters and repairs. For example (15) should be more correctly formalized as the filter in (i), in which cross-boundary vocalic segments are dispreferred in Italian. When violated, the constraint above triggers application of a vowel deletion rule (ii).

(i) * $\begin{array}{c} x \\ | \\ \text{[–cons]} \end{array}$) ⊕ ($\begin{array}{c} x \\ | \\ \text{[–cons]} \end{array}$ (ii) $\begin{array}{c} x \\ | \\ \text{[–cons]} \end{array} \rightarrow \emptyset\ /\ \_\ ]_{[-\text{PL}]}$

4 As we will see below, *troncamento* turns out to play a crucial role in the micro-parametric variation of Italo-Romance determiners (see section 4 and appendices).

Once (16) applies, resyllabification fails, as the lateral is left unsyllabified e.g.,: *[lkane]. Therefore, a post-cyclic epenthesis rule applies:[5]

(17) *epenthesis:* $\emptyset \rightarrow \begin{bmatrix} -\text{cons} \\ +\text{high} \\ -\text{back} \end{bmatrix} / \_ \times$ where × is unsyllabified

Relevant derivations follow in Table 4.

Table 4: Sample derivations of the definite determiner before masculine hosts.

	/l-o ⊕ kane)/	/l-o ⊕ studente/
troncamento	l_kane	–
epenthesis	ilkane	–
SR	[il.ka.ne]	[los.tu.den.te]

Within Romance, two other examples are worthy of note. First, in Spanish the definite determiner displays a similar behavior if we compare the singular forms of masculine and feminine nouns:

(i) a. el   gat-o   (ii) a. l-a   βanðer-a
        D.MSG cat-MSG   D-FSG flag-FSG
        'the cat'   'the flag'
    b. l-o-s   gat-o-s   b. l-a-s   βanðer-a-s
        D-M-PL cat-M-PL   D-F-PL flag-F-PL
        'the cats'   'the flags'

The absence of asymmetry between simple-consonant initiality and complex-consonant initiality is neutralized due to co-occurring language-specific constraints on the syllabic structure.

Second, French œ-*dropping* operates on the masculine singular, and interacts with *liaison* (Dell 1980; Tranel 1987):

(iii) a. l-[œ]   pεr   (iv) a. l   ami
          D-MSG father.M.SG   D.SG friend.SG
          'the father'   'the friend'
      b. l-e   pεr   b. l-e-z   ami
          D-MPL father.M.PL   D-M/F-PL friend.PL
          'the fathers'   'the friends'

[5] Akin to the hiatus resolution rule above, this operation should more correctly be formalized as the result of rule (i) repairing the violation of constraint (ii):

(i) $\emptyset \rightarrow \begin{bmatrix} -\text{cons} \\ +\text{high} \\ -\text{back} \end{bmatrix} / \_ \times$ (ii) *× where × unsyllabified

Note in the table above that none of the relevant operations apply before an extended syllable as in *[st]udente*. Here, resyllabification proceeds smoothly, as the appendix of the host-initial syllable is resyllabified as rhyme of the preceding syllabic unit, as shown below:

(18)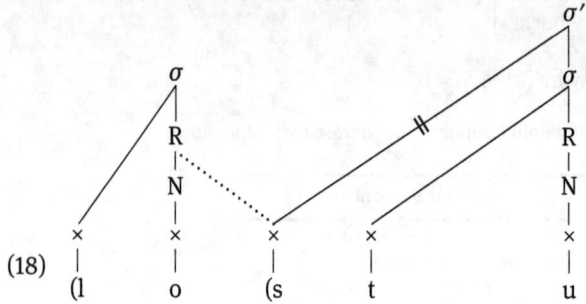

The plural masculine allomorphs of the definite determiner show a similar patterning. The determiner surfaces as *i* before core-syllable-initial hosts, and as *Ai* before extended-syllable-initial hosts. I argue that the underlying form of the masculine plural determiner – i.e., /l-i/ – undergoes the same processes as the singular form, with the addition of the following palatalization rule:

(19) *l-palatalization:* $/l/ \rightarrow \begin{bmatrix} -\text{ant} \\ +\text{distr} \end{bmatrix} / \_ \begin{bmatrix} -\text{cons} \\ +\text{high} \\ -\text{back} \end{bmatrix}]D_{[+\text{PL}]}$

As we will see in the next section, further evidence for this rule comes from the fact that *l*-final roots of demonstratives (e.g., *quell*- 'that') and adjectives (e.g., *bell*- 'beautiful') undergo the same process.

Before core-syllable-initial hosts, the determiner undergoes *troncamento* (16) and then epenthesis (17). At this point, geminated palatal onsets are deleted in open syllables:

(20) *palatal deletion:*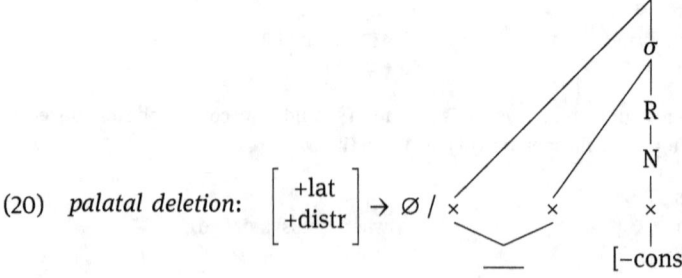

Some relevant derivations follow in Table 5.

Table 5: Sample derivations for the plural forms of the SI definite determiner.

	a. /l-i ⊕ kani/	b. /l-i ⊕ studenti/
lat. palatalization	ʎikani	ʎistudenti
troncamento	–	–
epenthesis	–	–
palatal deletion	ikani	–
SR	[i.ka.ni]	[ʎis.stu.den.ti]

3.1 Definite prepositions

Further support for the analysis above comes from the contracted forms of prepositions with the definite determiner. The relevant forms are given in Table 6.[6]

Table 6: Definite prepositions in SI.

	[−FEM]					[+FEM]		
	[−PL]			[+PL]		[−PL]		[+PL]
	σ	σ'	V	σ	σ', V	C	V	C, V
of + D	del	dello	dell	dei	degli	della	dell	delle
at + D	al	allo	all	ai	agli	alla	all	alle
from + D	dal	dallo	dall	dai	dagli	dalla	dall	dalle
in¹ + D	nel	nello	nell	nei	negli	nello	nell	nelle
on + D	sul	sullo	sull	sui	sugli	sullo	sull	sulle

Note:
1 An interesting case is the preposition *in* 'in, at'. It has the form *ne-* when attached to the definite determiner, therefore a suppletive form */ni-/* in clitic clusters seems to be the best solution. This type of special case does not weaken the analysis sketched above, which allows for suppletion and morpho-phonology to be both at play in allomorphy.

---

[6] The prepositions *per* 'for, through' and *tra/fra* 'among, between' are set aside here. They never fuse with the definite determiner: *per il, per lo, tra/fra il, tra/fra lo* are grammatical, whereas **pel, *pello, *tral, *trallo* are archaic forms. This may be due to the fact that two liquids are forbidden across morphological boundaries in Italian. The preposition *con* 'with' is also set aside, as contracted and non-contracted forms are equally grammatical.

The definite forms of prepositions can be easily explained with the account given above. After the determiner cliticizes onto its host, the preposition cyclically cliticizes onto the DP, and undergoes the appropriate morpho-phonological adjustments. First, it undergoes vowel lowering (22), similarly to what happens in clitic clusters:[7]

(21) [−cons] → [−high] / _ ⊕ CL . . .   where $CL_{<-\omega>}$ is a clitic unit

Hiatus resolution (15) then applies; note that *troncamento* (16) does not apply, as prepositions do not carry any ϕ-specification. For example, the definite forms of the prepositions *di* 'of' and *a* 'to, for' are derived as in Tables 7 and 8:

Table 7: Sample derivations of definite prepositions (I).

		/l-o ⊕ kane/	/l-i ⊕ kani/	/l-i ⊕ studenti/
cycle 1	lat. pal.	–	ʎikani	ʎistudenti
	troncamento	l_kane	–	–
	palatal deletion	–	ikani	–
cycle 2		/di ⊕ lkane/	/di ⊕ ikani/	/di ⊕ ʎistudenti/
	v. lowering	delkane	/deikani/	/deʎistudenti/
	hiatus res.	–	–	–
	other rules	–	–	deʎʎistudenti
	SR	[del.ka.ne]	[dei.ka.ni]	[deʎ.ʎis.tu.den.ti]

Table 8: Sample derivations of definite prepositions (II).

		/l-o ⊕ kane/	/l-i ⊕ kani/
cycle 1	lat. pal.	–	ʎikani
	troncamento	l_kane	–
	palatal deletion	–	ikani
cycle 2		/a ⊕ lkane/	/a ⊕ ikani/
	v. lowering	–	–
	hiatus res.	–	–
	SR	[al.ka.ne]	[ai.ka.ni]

---

[7] For example:

(i) a. *Mi*   ha   *mandato*   una   *lettera.*
       CL.1SG.DAT   AUX.3SG   send.MSG   D.FSG   letter.FSG
       '(S/he) sent me a letter'
    b. *Me*   *l'*   ha   *mandata.*
       CL.1SG.DAT   CL.3MSG.ACC   AUX.3SG   send.FSG
       '(S/he) sent it to me.'

In the next section, I show that the allomorphic distribution of the other SI determiners (indefinite and demonstratives) and pre-nominal adjectives provides additional support for the morpho-phonological account proposed above.

4 Widening the allomorphic spectrum

The indefinite determiner has a two-way alternation. The allomorph *un* surfaces before vowels:

(22) a. un idɛa b. un inditʃe
     D.FSG idea   D.MSG index
     'an idea'   'an index'

It is always *una* before feminine consonant-initial hosts (23c, d). Before masculine consonant-initial hosts, it either shows up as *uno* (23a) or *un* (23b), akin to the definite determiner.

(23) a. uno   [ʃʃ]emo   c. una   [k]asa
        D.MSG foolMSG   D.FSG home.FSG
        'uno fool'   'a home'
     b. un   [k]orso   d. una   [st]anza
        D.MSG course.MSG   D.FSG room.FSG
        'a course'   'a room'

Table 9 summarizes the forms.

Table 9: Forms of the SI indefinite determiner.

	[−FEM]	[+FEM]
_ N [σ	un	una
_ N [σ'	uno	
_ N [V		un

The SI demonstrative *quello* [kʷello] 'that' (24) shows the by-now usual patterning.[8]

(24) *quello* 'that/those'
    a. quell [i]dea   ~ quelle [i]dee
        D.FSG idea.FSG   D.FPL Idea.FPL
        'that (those) idea(s)'
    b. quell [i]ndice   ~ queʎʎi [i]ndici
        D.MSG index.MSG   D.MPL index.MPL
        'that (those) index/indices'
    c. quello [ʃʃ]emo   ~ queʎʎi [ʃʃ]emi
        D.MSG fool.MSG   D.MPL fool.MPL
        'that (those) fool(s)'
    d. quel [k]orso   ~ quei [k]orsi
        D.MSG course.MSG   D.MPL course.MPL
        'that (those) course(s)'
    e. quella [k]asa   ~ quelle [k]ase
        D.FSG home.FSG   D.FPL home.FPL
        'that (those) home(s)'
    f. quella [k]orso   ~ quelle [st]anze
        D.FSG room.FSG   D.FPL room.FPL
        'that (those) room(s)'

The form *quell* occurs before vowel-initial hosts (23a, b); the forms *quel* ~ *quei* and *quello* ~ *queʎʎi* occur before simple-consonant-initial (23c) and complex-consonant-initial (23d) masculine hosts, respectively; the feminine forms *quella* ~ *quelle* do not show any allomorphy (23e, f).

Finally, adjectives occurring in pre-nominal position show similar alternations. For example, the final vowel of the adjectives *buono* 'good' (25) and *bello* 'beautiful' (26) is only deleted before vowel-initial, and masculine singular core-syllable-initial hosts – the two morpho-phonological environments we have seen SI determiners are sensitive to:

---

[8] I will not deal with the distal demonstratives *codesto* [kodesto] 'that' and *questo* [kʷesto] 'this', as they do not undergo *troncamento*. I argue that this is due to *phonological blocking*, which arises when an operation leads to a series of illicit configurations that the system is not able to repair anyhow. As extensively shown in Calabrese (2005), in such cases the system licenses the input as is, thus tolerating eventual violations of active constraints in the language.

(25) *buono* 'good'
    a. buon   [i]dea   ~ buone   [i]dee
        good.FSG idea.FSG   good.FPL idea.FPL
        'good idea(s)'
    b. buon   [i]ndice ~ buoni   [i]ndici
        good.MSG index.MSG   good.MPL index.MPL
        'good index/indices'
    c. buono   [ʃʃ]emo ~ buoni   [ʃʃ]emi
        good.MSG fool.MSG   good.MPL fool.MPL
        'good fool(s)'
    d. buon   [k]orso ~ buoni   [k]orsi
        good.MSG course.MSG good.MPL course.MPL
        'good course(s)'
    e. buona   [k]asa   ~ buone   [k]ase
        good.FSG home.FSG   good.FPL home.FPL
        'good home(s)'
    f. buona   [st]anza ~ buone   [st]anze
        good.FSG room.FSG   good.FPL room.FPL
        'good room(s)'

(26) *bello* 'beautiful'
    a. bell   [i]dea   ~ belle   [i]dee
        beautiful.FSG idea.FSG   beautiful.FPL idea.FPL
        'beautiful idea(s)'
    b. bell   [i]ndice   ~ beʎʎi   [i]ndici
        beautiful.MSG index.MSG   beautiful.MPL index.MPL
        'beautiful index/indices'
    c. bello   [ʃʃ]emo   ~ beʎʎi   [ʃʃ]emi
        beautiful.MSG fool.MSG   beautiful.MPL fool.MPL
        'beautiful fool(s)'
    d. bel   [k]orso   ~ bei   [k]orsi
        beautiful.MSG course.MSG beautiful.MPL course.MPL
        'beautiful course(s)'
    e. bella   [k]asa   ~ belle   [k]ase
        beautiful.FSG home.FSG   beautiful.FPL home.FPL
        'beautiful home(s)'
    f. bella   [st]anza   ~ belle   [st]anze
        beautiful.FSG room.FSG   beautiful.FPL room.FPL
        'beautiful room(s)'

The adjective *grande* 'big' may optionally show vowel-final dropping in the same morpho-phonological contexts just seen: before vowels (regardless of gender) (27a, b), and before core syllable (in the masculine singular) (27d); in the latter case, the alveolar stop [d] drops too.

(27) *grande* 'big'[9]
    a. grand(e) [i]dea   ~ grandi [i]dee
        big.FSG   idea.FSG   big.FPL idea.FPL
        'big idea(s)'
    b. grand(e) [i]nditʃe   ~ grandi [i]nditʃi
        big.MSG   index.MSG   big.MPL index .MPL
        'big index/indices'
    c. grande   [ʃʃ]emo   ~ grandi [ʃʃ]emi
        big.MSG   fool.MSG   big.MPL fool.MPL
        'big fool(s)'

---

9 The optionality of such operations is possibly connected to the fact that *grande* is a second-class adjective in which gender marking is neutralized, and only number is morphologically realized via the pair *-e* ~ *-i*. Speakers also reported a slight, but clear dichotomy between truncated and non-truncated forms. For example:

(i) a. È   un   grande   maestro.
        BE.3SG D.MSG big.MSG   master
    b. È   un   gran   maestro.
        BE.3SG D.MSG big.MSG   master

Speakers seem to agree that the non-truncated form (ia) is preferred in contexts where the interpretation of the adjective is speaker-oriented (the speaker has a strong feeling of affection for him, because e.g. he taught the speaker many things), whereas the truncated form (ib) is used when the interpretation of the adjective is subject-oriented ("as an expert, he is great"). These two interpretive possibilities are compatible with Cinque et al. (1994)'s proposal of assuming two NP-preceding adjectival heads, one carrying the speaker-oriented interpretation and the other carrying the subject-oriented interpretation (see also Jackendoff 1972):

(ii). $[_{DP} D \ldots [_{XP} AP_{sp.or} [_{YP} AP_{subj.or} [_{NP} N \ldots]]]]$ (Cinque et al. 1994)

The association between the presence/absence of truncation and the subject/speaker-oriented interpretation would then be syntactically motivated, in line with the tenets of both cartography and DM approaches. Future research is advisable in this regard.

d. gran(de) [k]orso ∼ grandi [k]orsi
   big.MSG course.MSG   big.MPL course.MPL
   'big course(s)'
e. grande [k]asa ∼ grandi [k]ase
   big.FSG home.FSG   big.FPL home.FPL
   'big home(s)'
f. grande [st]anza ∼ grandi [st]anze
   big.FSG room.FSG   big.FPL room.FPL
   'big room(s)'

"Epithetic" adjectives such as *santo* 'saint' undergo similar morpho-phonological changes before proper nouns.[10] As usual, the final vowel of the adjective only drops before vowel-initial proper nouns (28ai, bi) and masculine singular core-syllable-initial proper nouns (28bii), but never elsewhere (28aiii, bii-iii).

(28) *Santo* 'saint'
   a. [−FEM]   b. [+FEM]
   (i) sant(*o)   [a]ntonio   (i) sant(*a)   [i]laria
        saint.MSG Anthony   saint.FSG   Hilary
        'Saint Anthony'   'Saint Hilary'
   (ii) san(*to)   [p]asquale (ii) santa   [t]eresa
        saint.MSG Pasquale   saint.FSG   Theresa
        'Saint Timothy'   'Saint Theresa'

---

10 Besides, other epithetic adjectives – such as *frate* 'brother' and *suora* 'sister' – always surface in their truncated form, regardless of gender and of the noun-initial syllabic structure:

(i) a. fra(*te)   Antonio   (ii) a. suor(*a)   Ilaria
       brother.MSG Anthony   sister.MSG Hilary
       'brother Anthony'   'sister Hilary'
    b. fra(*te)   Pasquale   b. suor(*a)   Teresa
       brother.MSG Pasquale   sister.MSG Theresa
       'brother Timothy'   'sister Theresa'
    c. fra(*te)   Stefano   c. suor(*a)   Stefania
       brother.MSG Stephen   sister.MSG Stephanie
       'brother Stephen'   'sister Stephanie'

Unlike 'saint' alternants, these should be considered fossilized forms, which have lost any sensitivity to the current morpho-phonological environment.

(iii) san*(to) [st]efano (iii) santa [st]efania
saint.MSG Stephen saint.MSG Stephanie
'Saint Stephen' 'Saint Stephanie'

The morpho-phonological account presented above can explain the above alternations quite effortlessly. Assume the following vocabulary items:

(29) *Vocabulary Items*
  a. $D_{[-DEF]}$ ↔ un   d. √BEAUTIFUL ↔ bell
  b. $D_{[+DISTAL]}$ ↔ kʷell e. √BIG ↔ gran
  c. √GOOD ↔ bwon   f. √SAINT ↔ sant

Once gender and number have appropriately been realized in compliance with VI (14), hiatus (15) and *troncamento* (16). Relevant derivations follow in Table 10–11 below.

Table 10: Sample derivations of indefinite and distal determiners.

	/un-o ⊕ kane/	/kʷell-o ⊕ kane/	/kʷell-i ⊕ studenti/
lat. pal.	–	–	kʷeʎʎistudenti
troncamento	un_kane	kʷel_kane	–
SR	[un.ka.ne]	[kʷel.ka.ne]	[kʷeʎ.ʎis.tu.den.ti]

Table 11: Sample derivations of pre-nominal adjectives.

	/bwon-o ⊕ kane/	/bell-o ⊕ kane/	/bell-i ⊕ studenti/
lat. pal.	–	–	beʎʎi studenti
troncamento	bwon_kane	bel_kane	–
epenthesis	–	–	–
SR	[bwon.ka.ne]	[bel.ka.ne]	[beʎ.ʎis.tu.den.ti]

The analysis needs just one minor refinement for 'saint' before core-syllable-initial proper nouns – e.g., *san(*to) Pasquale*. In this form, I assume that, after the final vowel drops due to *troncamento*, the preceding obstruent drops in compliance with a rule that deletes obstruents in triconsonantal clusters.[11]

(30) *obstruent deletion*: [–son] → ∅ [+cons] _ [+cons]

Table 12: Sample derivations of pre-nominal adjectives.

	/sant-o ⊕ antonio/	/sant-o ⊕ pasquale/	/sant-o ⊕ stefano/
hiatus	sant_antonio	–	–
troncamento	–	sant_pasquale	–
obstruent deletion	–	san_pasquale	–
SR	[san.tan.to.nio]	[san.pas.qua.le]	[san.tos.te.fa.no]

In the next section, I turn to reviewing a listing account that has recently been proposed for some of the alternations of the SI definite determiner. As we will see, such an account ultimately ends up (i) assuming multiple alternations for each of the determiners and pre-nominal adjective, and therefore (ii) overlooking the consistent generalization that all determiners and pre-nominal adjectives undergo the same morpho-phonological operations.

5 Is morpho-phonology actually indispensable?

In the previous section, I argued that the rule of *troncamento* (16) is the only responsible factor for the alternations in SI determiners. Such a rule, though general, idiosyncratically mashes up morphological and phonological alphabets. Is this theoretically reasonable? Listing accounts hold that it is not, and that the morphological and the phonological modules must be kept separate. By way of considering a listing account for SI determiners, this section explores the consequences of such an approach, and ultimately highlights some of its major drawbacks when dealing with the allomorphic alternations at hand.

---

[11] This operation should more correctly be formalized as the result of rule (i) triggered by the violation of the constraint (ii):

(i) [–son]→ ∅   (ii) *[–son]/ [+cons] _ [+cons]

Among several listing accounts that have previously been proposed for the allomorphy of SI definite determiner (for a review, see Garrapa 2011), Artés (2013) is a recent attempt.[12] Under the assumption that the phonological module cannot make use of morphological information, Artés (2013) proposes that for SI definite determiner two exponents are selected in the unmarked masculine singular:

(31) *Vocabulary Insertion*
    a. $D_{[+DEF]} \leftrightarrow l$
    b. $[FEM] \leftrightarrow a$
    c. $[\ \ ] \leftrightarrow \{o > \emptyset\}$

In (31c), both entries – *o* and *ø* – are sent off to PF in the order formalized via the operator '>', which prioritizes the former exponent over the latter (Bonet et al. 2007).[13] At this point, the optimal candidate is chosen by virtue of the interplay of the following constraints:[14]

(32) a. *S<small>YLL</small>S<small>TRUC</small>: Constraint cluster governing the idiosyncratic structural requirements of Italian.
      (i) *C<small>OMPLEX</small>: No complex syllable margins (Prince & Smolensky 1993).
      (ii) S<small>ON</small>S<small>EQ</small>: Complex onsets rise in sonority, and complex codas fall in sonority (cf. Clements 1990).
      (iii) S<small>YLL</small>C<small>ONTACT</small>: If C_1 and C_2 are adjacent non-tautosyllabic consonants, C_1 must have higher or equal sonority to and C_2.
    b. O<small>NSET</small>: Every syllable must have an onset.
    c. O-C<small>ONTIGUITY</small>: The portion of S_2 standing in correspondence forms a contiguous string (McCarthy & Prince 1995).

---

12 I will not discuss other possible analyses such as those involving floating features. These analyses essentially handle morpho-phonological alternations akin to other listing accounts, and therefore are here considered as such.

13 The exponent /o/ is assumed to be less marked than /Ø/ in line with Cardinaletti & Repetti (2008; *morphological epenthesis*). I put aside the issue as to why this might be the case, since it is not relevant to the purposes of the discussion.

14 It is worth pointing out that the use of OT constraints in such accounts is fairly common, although not crucial for the current argument. If anything, it is a theoretical consequence of the assumption that phonology must be morphology-free, hence *"natural"*. I will not be able to address this issue here, but suffices it to say that there is compelling evidence that phonology cannot be just natural (see, for example, Anderson 1981).

d. PRIORITY: Respect lexical priority (ordering) of allomorphs. Given an input containing allomorphs m_1, m_2, m_n, and a candidate containing m_i' in correspondence with m_i, the constraint assigns as many violations marks as the depth of the ordering between m_n and the highest dominating morph(s) (Bonet et al. 2007).

Before vowel-initial hosts, the candidate faithful to the input is selected.[15]

Tableau 13: Selection of the singular masculine allomorph before V-initial hosts.

/l-{o > ∅}inditʃe/	O-Contiguity	Dep	Onset	Priority
☞ a. linditʃe				*
b. i̱linditʃe		*	*	*
c. loinditʃe			*	*
d. li̱inditʃe	*		*	*

Before hosts beginning with an extended syllable, *SYLLSTRUCT is violated as many times as two phonological segments are illicitly adjacent to each other. Here, PRIORITY is crucial for the desired output [lostruttso] to win over the candidate [li̱struttso]:

Tableau 14: Selection of the singular masculine allomorph before extended-syllable-initial hosts.

/l-{o > ø}struttso/	*SyllStuct	O-Contiguity	Dep	Onset	Priority
a. lstruttso	***				*
b. i̱lstruttso	***		*	*	*
☞ c. lostruttso	**			*	
d. li̱struttso	**	*		*	*

Problems arise before core-syllable-initial hosts. In such cases, an additional constraint RESPECT must be assumed for [i̱lkane] to win over [lokane].

(32) e. RESPECT: Respect idiosyncratic lexical specification.

---

15 In the tableaux below, epenthetic phonological segments are underlined.

Tableau 15: Selection of the singular masculine allomorph before core-syllable-initial hosts.

/l-{o > Ø} kane/	*SYLLSTRUCT	O-CONTIGUITY	DEP	RESPECT	ONSET	PRIORITY
a. lkane	*					*
☞ b. ilkane			*		*	*
c. lokane				*		
d. likane		*	*			*

It is unclear what these "lexical specifications" are, and, more importantly, how they could be evaluated in an OT module that is assumed to be completely separated from the other modules of grammar.[16]

Another point is worth making here. Artés (2013)'s analysis, as well as any other listing account, holds that syntactic operations are not involved in the allomorph selection, which is exclusive prerogative of phonology. The assumption, however, seems to be contradicted in the example below:

(33) a. Ieri   lessi   un   paper   corto...
       yesterday read.PFV.1SG DET.MSG paper.MSG short.MSG
       'Yesteday I read a short paper...
    b. ... oggi   ne   leggo   uno   –   lungo.
       today NE.CL read.PRES.1SG DET.MSG ~~paper.MSG~~ long.MSG
       Today I read a long one.'

---

16 Due to page limitations, I just point out here that a similar effect arises when looking at plurals. Recall that *i* and *ʎi* are the plural forms corresponding to the singular forms *il* and *lo*, respectively. Therefore, is it tempting to posit a PRIORITY-relationship between the two plural forms similarly to (31):

(i) [+PL] ⟷ {ʎi > i}

In the tableau below, notice that RESPECT is again the only thing that prevents the system from being in a tie that would otherwise be hard to break.

/l-{ʎi> i}kani/	RESPECT	ONSET	PRIORITY
☞ a. ikani			*
b. ʎikani	*	*	

Besides, the nature of such constraints as RESPECT and PRIORITY is rather opaque: on the one hand, they look like faithfulness constraints, as militating against candidates not sticking to the ordering defined in the lexicon; on the other hand, they also look like markedness constraints, since they force selection of a lexical entry over another.

Above, the indefinite determiner surfaces as *uno* even though is linearly followed by the core-syllable-initial adjective *lungo* (33b). An account like Artés (2013)'s, in which the phonology and the morphology are not allowed to interact, would instead mispredict that the allomorph *un* is the optimal one as the determiner is linearly adjacent to the core-syllable-initial adjective *lungo*. A viable option would be to constrain the VI procedure in the morpho-syntactic module with some ad-hoc formalism that unreasonably overloads the grammar. Such an endemic adoption of "rampant" solutions is reminiscent of what listing accounts themselves argue against.

In a morpho-phonological analysis, no further adjustment is needed. Assuming that NP-ellipsis applies at Spell-Out (Saab & Lipták 2016), the determiner in (33b) latches onto an already elided element, which lacks phonological content, and therefore does not trigger *troncamento*.

5.1 Afterthoughts on *rampant* morpho-phonology

It is evident that my analysis implies a lesser degree of theory-internal complexity compared to such a listing account as Artés (2013)'s: the entire allomorphic spectrum of SI determiners and pre-nominal adjectives is effortlessly accounted for thanks to one idiosyncratic, but language-wide morpho-phonological operation of *troncamento* (16).

The theoretical feasibility of such an account gains even more support when looking at the allomorphic variation of determiners in Italo-Romance (henceforth, IR). For the current purposes let us look at the definite determiner (the data for the other determiners and pre-nominal adjectives are available in the Appendices at the end of the paper).

By looking at the forms in Table 16, it is intuitively unreasonable to list all alternants of each IR variety as independent suppletive entries. It is actually even more unreasonable if we look at the diatopic variation of IR determiners, which quite consistently reveals that allomorphy of determiners shows up only in conjunction with *troncamento*: indeed, northern and central varieties show a proliferation of alternations for determiners and a generalized use of truncation operations, whereas southern varieties lack both. My morpho-phonological account can easily explain this correlation just by assuming that application of the *troncamento* rule (16) may be micro-parametrically deactivated. Listing accounts instead prefer a proliferation of independent lexical entries (for each determiner, for each variety) over morpho-phonological operations that appear to be at play over the entire macro-linguistic area.

Table 16: Micro-parametric variation of the definite determiner in Italo-Romance.

	[−FEM]						[+FEM]			
	_[σ]		_[σ']		_[V]		_[C]		_[V]	
	[−PL]	[+PL]	[−PL]	[+PL]	[−PL]	[+PL]	[−PL]	[+PL]	[−PL]	[+PL]
Lombardia & Triveneto	il		il					(r)e		
	al		al		l		la	le		e
	el	i	e(l)	(l)i		i			l	
	ol		ol					i		i
	ul/ur		u(l)		ul/ur		ra	e		e
Piemonte	al		(l)u				(l)a	(l)e		(l)e
Liguria	u									
Emilia Romagna	al	i	al	i		l	la			al/li
Marche			(l)o		l					l
Tuscany	i(l)		lo	(ʎ)i	l, ʎi					(l)e
Rome and central area	er		o	i		l	a	e		
Southern varieties[1]	lu	li	lu	li	lu/l	li/l	la	le	la/l	le/l

Note:
1 The Neapolitan definite determiner shows special forms (see A.3) that surface differently from the forms in the other nearby varieties. The analysis for these forms goes beyond the purposes of this paper, so it will not be dealt with here (see Petrosino 2018 for further discussion).

Suppletion (i.e., in our terms, listing) is dogmatically endorsed as the only possible source for morpho-phonological alternations in the name of the *autonomy of morphology* (Baudouin de Courtenay 1972). In this view, "rampant" readjustment rules are the devil to cast out, since they dangerously mash morphology and phonology together (Bermúdez-Otero 2012). This is a precise theoretical choice that forces one to wobble on a narrow rope it is easy to fall from, as we have seen above.

Allomorphy is a very multi-faceted phenomenon, and both devices – LISTS and OPERATIONS – are equally able to account for it (Aronoff 2012). Abstracting away from ideological beliefs on the issue, what is actually needed is an evaluation metrics able to assess what is the most appropriate device for the alternation at hand. Here I refer to Kiparsky (1996)'s characterization of allomorphic alternations:

(34) *Evaluation metrics for allomorphic alternations*
   a. Suppletive alternations:
      (i)   are idiosyncratic;
      (ii) may involve more than one segment;
      (iii) obey morphological locality conditions;
      (iv) occur before (morpho-)phonological processes.
   b. Morpho-phonological alternations:
      (i)   are general (not item-specific);
      (ii) involve a single segment;
      (iii) observe phonological locality conditions;
      (iv) occur after suppletive alternations (i.e., after VI).
                                         (adapted from Kiparsky (1996))

In the previous section I showed that the alternations involved SI determiners (i) are general, as they arise not only for determiners but also for pre-nominal adjectives; (ii) involve a single segment – namely, deletion of the vocalic suffix; (iii) observe phonological adjacency, as they occur in a specific phonological context; and finally, (iv) must occur after VI of the appropriate entries. Treating these alternations as suppletive means treating them as completely arbitrary, and overlooks general morpho-phonological operations.

6 Conclusions

In contrast with previous accounts, this paper argued that the alternations of the SI definite determiner can be accounted for a few language-wide morpho-phonological operations. I showed that the operations of hiatus resolution and *troncamento* substantially contribute to the alternations involving SI determiners as well as pre-nominal adjectives. These operations gain further theoretical support when we extend our analysis to the allomorphy of determiners in non-standard IR varieties (see Appendices for further data). Analysis of the diatopic variation also reveals a correlation between the existence of alternations in the D-domain and *troncamento*: varieties that have no truncated forms show no alternations at all. Such a strong correlation would be completely overlooked in an account in which morphology and phonology are not allowed to interact. On the other hand, it effortlessly falls out under the morpho-phonological account proposed here by assuming a micro-parametric deactivation of the operation of *troncamento*.

Ultimately, this paper offers new insights concerning the long-standing debate on the nature of allomorphic alternations, and provides evidence in favor of a framework in which both suppletion *and* morpho-phonology may be used in accounting for allomorphy. Forbidding morpho-phonology *in toto* leads to disregarding robust generalizations at the interface between morphology and phonology. In doing this we fail twice: as theoreticians, we fail to provide reliable models to analyze data with; as scientists, we fail to generalize over consistently co-occurring phenomena.

A Allomorphy of the definite determiner in Italo-Romance

A.1 Northern varieties

The definite determiner shows a huge degree of variation in northern varieties, as the table below shows:

Table 17: Micro-parametric variation of the definite determiner in northern varieties of Italo-Romance.

	[−FEM]						[+FEM]			
	_ [σ		_ [σ'		_ [V		_ [C		_ [V	
	[−PL]	[+PL]	[−PL]	[+PL]	[−PL]	[+PL]	[−PL]	[+PL]	[−PL]	[+PL]
Lombardia & Triveneto	il	i	il	(l)i	l	i	la	(r)e	l	e
	al		al					le		
	el		e(l)							
	ol		ol					i		i
	ul/ur		u(l)		ul/ur		ra	e		e
Piemonte	al	i	(l)u	i	l	i	(l)a	(l)e	l	(l)e
Liguria	u									
Emilia Romagna	al		al							al/li
Marche			(l)o				la			l
Tuscany	i(l)		lo		(ʎ)i		l, ʎi			(l)e

In Table 17 above, most of the forms – i.e., the feminine singular and plural, and the masculine plural – look alike. Only the masculine singular form varies in the vowel preceding the lateral. All dialects but Florentine (i.e., SI) preserve the form *Vl* (with *V* being a language-specific vowel), regardless of whether or not a syllabic appendix occurs noun-initially.

(35) a. Introbio (Lombardia, LC):
el pa 'the father'; el staɲ 'the pond'
b. Prosito (Ticino, Switzerland):
al pa; al staɲ
c. Arcumeggia (Lombardia, VA):
ur pa; u(l) staɲ

This type of reduction in allomorphic complexity may be due to differences in syllable structure; e.g., it may be due to the fact that these dialects allow complex codas such as [ls]/[rs].

A few micro-varieties have a single form for all masculine singular hosts, regardless of the noun-initial context:

(36) Arcumeggia (Lombardia, VA):
ur orts 'the bear'; ur amis 'the friend'; ur iɱfern 'the hell'

Exceptionally, Veneziano, the dialect spoken in Venice, has preserved sensitivity to the following host-initial syllable structure: as shown in (37) the lateral drops before a extended-syllable-initial host.

(37) Venice (Veneto, VE):
el papa 'the father'; e staɲo 'the pond'

When moving to the borders with France (in the regions of Piemonte and Liguria), an epenthetic vowel (whose phonetic nature slightly changes diatopically) is always inserted before extended-syllable-initial hosts; this means that the form that should surface in such contexts (i.e., *lo*) never does:

(38) Corio (Piemonte, TO):
al pare 'the father'; l *a*-staɲ 'the pond'

Finally, varieties spoken Liguria have all the lateral dropped, similarly to what we will see in Neapolitan (see below, sec. A.3):

(39) Genoa (Liguria, GE):
u pwè 'the father'; u staɲu 'the pond'

Going south, while dialects of Emilia Romagna and Marche fairly uniformly select *al*, most Tuscan dialects are quite different from Florentine (i.e., SI) in the treatment of the masculine singular determiner. Here, the lateral of the masculine singular uniformly assimilates with the following host-initial core syllable (Table 18a); with vowel-initial nouns the masculine plural form usually has the suffixal vowel dropped (Table 18b), instead of the SI palatalized lateral. The form *lo* surfaces with extended-syllable-initial hosts (Table 18c).

Table 18: Forms of a Tuscan varies as compared to SI.

	Radda (Toscana, SI)	cf. SI	gloss
a.	i kkane	il kane	'the dog (m. sg.)'
b.	l agi	ʎi agi	'the needles (m. pl.)'
c.	l ɔke	le ɔke	'the geese (f. pl.)'
d.		lo staɲɲo	'the pond (m. sg.)'

A.2 Central dialects

The nature of the initial syllable of the following host also causes allomorphy on the definite determiner in Romanesco, the variety of Italian spoken in Rome (Loporcaro 1991), as shown in Table 19 below.

Table 19: Forms of the SI definite determiner in Romanesco.

	[−FEM]		[+FEM]	
	[−pl]	[+pl]	[−pl]	[+pl]
_ [σ	er	i:	a:	e:
_ [σ'	o:			
_ [V̀	l			
_ [V	ɸ [V:			

Before core-syllable-initial masculine singular hosts, the determiner has the form *er*, similar to the forms detected in standard Italian and northern varieties (sec. A.1). The presence of [r] instead of [l] is due to the fact that Romanesco laterals commonly rhoticize in coda position. When followed by any other consonant-initial hosts, the determiner shows a lengthened form of the ɸ-marking vowel. Before vowel-initial hosts, the surface form depends on the stress position. If stress is on the initial syllable of the host, the determiner surfaces as *l*; otherwise, the host-initial vowel gets lengthened (Table 20).

Table 20: Some relevant examples of the forms of the definite determiner in Romanesco.

σ'-initial hosts	σ-initial hosts	stressed-V-initial hosts	unstressed-V-initial hosts
o: stupido 'the fool (m.sg)'	er kane 'the dog (m. sg)'	lɛrba 'the grass (f. sg.)'	a:mika 'the friend (f. sg.)'
a: stupida 'the fool (d.sg)'	a: piskella 'the girl (f. sg.)'	lɔke 'the goose (f. pl.)'	a:mike 'the friends (f. pl.)'
i: stupidi 'the fools (m.pl.)'	i: kani 'the dogs (m. pl.)'	l urtimo 'the last (m. sg.)'	e:ddʒittsjano 'the Egyptian (m. sg.)'
e: stupide 'the fools (f.pl.)'	e: piskelle 'the girls (f. pl.)'	l ortsi 'the bears (f. pl.)'	e:eddʒittsjani 'the Egyptians (m. pl.)'

A.3 Southern dialects

Southern dialects show a rather minimal allomorphic distribution (Table 21):

Table 21: Forms of the definite determiner in southern varieties.

	[−FEM]		[+FEM]	
	[−PL]	[+PL]	[−PL]	[+PL]
_ [C	lu	li	la	le
_ [V	lu, l		la, l	

We can distinguish two sub-groups. The first sub-group does not show allomorphy on determiners at all. Table 22 below shows some example from Salentino:

Table 22: Some examples of the forms of the definite determiner in the first sub-group of southern varieties.

C-initial feminine nouns				
la [p]orta ~ le [p]orte	'D door(s)'	la [dz]anzara ~ le [dz]anzare		'D mosquito(es)'

C-initial masculine nouns				
lu [k]ane ~ li [k]ani	'D dog(s)'	lu [str]utzze ~ li [str]uzzi		'D ostrich(es)'

V-initial nouns				
masculine			feminine	
l [o]rko ~ l [o]rki	'D ogre(s)'	l [ɔ]ka ~ le [ɔ]ke		'D goose/geese'

The second sub-group of varieties shows a certain degree of allomorphy that has a different morpho-phonological scope from *troncamento* (16); Neapolitan, the dialect spoken in Campania, is its main representative (Ledgeway 2009).

Table 23: Forms of the definite determiner in Neapolitan (roots are underlined).

	[−FEM]				[+FEM]		
	[−PL]	[+PL]	gloss		[−PL]	[+PL]	gloss
_ [C	o	e			a	e[CC]	
a.	o tavələ	e tavələ	'the table(s)'	a'.	a tavələ	e ttavələ	'the board(s)'
b.	o pɛrə	e p*je*rə	'the foot(s)'	b'.	a sɛddʒə	e ssɛddʒə	'the chair(s)'
_ [V		l				l	əll
c.	l ɔccjə	l w*o*ccjə	'the eye(s)'	c'.	l oɲɲə	əll oɲɲə	'the nail(s)'

When preceding consonant-initial hosts, the determiner surfaces as *o* in the masculine singular, *a* or in the feminine singular, and *e* in the plural. Additionally, plural feminine hosts have the initial segment geminated (in the table above, in bold).[17] When preceding vowel-initial nouns, the definite determiner surfaces as *l*. In plurals, *l* is geminated and preceded by *ə*.

B Allomorphy of the indefinite determiner

The indefinite determiner is sensitive to the same morpho-phonological environments as the definite determiner: in northern and central varieties it has the suffixal vowel deleted before core-syllable-initial singular masculine, and vowel-initial hosts. In southern varieties it is only subject to vowel elision.

However, there is less variation in the underlying form of the indefinite determiner, which contrasts with the wide variety of realizations of the definite determiner. Unlike the latter, the former just has the back vowel /u/ dropped in some varieties, but its exponence seems to be quite stable across dialects (Table 24).

---

17 Plural masculine nouns with a stressed mid vowel instead undergo metaphony (in Table 23, in italic). Note that, unlike initial consonant gemination in feminine plural nouns, this phenomenon occurs independently of the presence of the determiner. For an analysis, see Calabrese (2011, 2016).

Table 24: Forms of the indefinite determiner in Italo-Romance.

	[−FEM]			[+FEM]	
	_ [σ	_ [σ′	_ [V	_ [C	_ [V
North	un	un(o)	un	(u)na	(u)n
Center	un	no	n	na	n
South	(u)nu	nu	n	(u)na	(u)n

C Allomorphy of demonstratives and pre-nominal adjectives

While northern dialects display the same distribution of forms for demonstratives and pre-nominal adjectives that we have seen for standard Italian (see sec. 4), southern dialects do not show any other morpho-phonological phenomenon undergone by demonstrative and pre-nominal adjectives than hiatus resolution (15). As an example of such lack of variation, the forms below are taken from Neapolitan.

(40) *killə* 'that/those'
  a. kell   [i]deə   ~ kell   [i]deə
     D.FSG idea.FSG   D.FPL idea.FPL
     'that (those) idea(s)'
  b. kill   [i]ndiʃə   ~ kill   [i]ndiʃə
     D.MSG index.MSG   D.MPL index.MPL
     'that (those) index/indices'
  c. killu   [ʃʃ]emə   ~ killi   [ʃʃjemə
     D.MSG fool.MSG   D.MPL fool.MPL
     'that (those) fool(s)'
  d. killu   [k]orsə   ~ killi   [k]ursə
     D.MSG course.MSG   D.MPL course.MPPL
     'that (those) course(s)'
  e. kella   [k]asə   ~ kelli   [kk]asə
     D.FSG home.FSG   D.FPL home.FPL
     'that (those) home(s)'
  f. kella   [st]anzə   ~ kelli   [st]anzə
     D.FSG room.FSG   D.FPL room.FPL
     'that (those) room(s)'

What the data above shows is that the same morpho-phonological strategies that Neapolitan has for marking the plural on the definite determiner are active for demonstratives too: in the masculine plural, the front mid vowel gets metaphonized [40b, c, d]; in the feminine plural, the noun-initial consonant gets geminated (40e). Hiatus (15) seems to be forbidden at all times (40a, b), where no truncation phenomena seem to affect southern dialects at all.

Similarly, the epithetic adjective *santu* 'saint' shows no alternation. Compare the following forms with the corresponding SI forms in (28a)–(28b):

(41) *santə* 'saint'
    a. [-FEM]
        (i)   sant(*u)   Andoniə
              saint.MSG   Anthony
              'Saint Anthony'
        (ii)   santu   Timoteə
              saint.MSG   Timothy
              'Saint Timothy'
        (iii) santu   Stefənə
              saint.MSG   Stephen
              'Saint Stephen'

    b. [-FEM]
        (i)   sant(*a)   Ilariə
              saint.FSG   Hilary
              'Saint Hilary'
        (ii)   santa   Təresə
              saint.FSG   Theresa
              'Saint Theresa'
        (ii)   santa   Stəfaniə
              saint.FSG   Stephanie
              'Saint Stephanie'

References

Anderson, Stephen R. 1981. Why phonology isn't "natural". *Linguistic Inquiry* 12(4). 493–539.
Aronoff, Mark. 2012. Morphological stems: What William of Ockham really said. *Word Structure* 5. 28–51.
Artés, Eduard. 2013. Morphological epenthesis in Romance: A case of Lexical Conservativism. Poster presented at the 39th Incontro di Grammatica Generativa, Modena and Reggio Emilia, February 2013.
Bermúdez-Otero, Ricardo. 2012. The architecture of grammar and the division of labour in exponence. *The Morphology and Phonology of Exponence* 41. 8–83.
Bonet, Eulàlia, Maria-Rosa Lloret & Joan Mascaró. 2007. Allomorph selection and lexical preferences: Two case studies. *Lingua* 117(6). 903–927.
Calabrese, Andrea. 2005. *Markedness and economy in a derivation model of phonology*. Berlin/New York: Mouton de Gruyter.
Calabrese, Andrea. 2011. Metaphony in romance. In M. van Oostendorp, C. J. Ewen, E. Hume & K. Rice (eds.), *The Blackwell companion to phonology*. Malden, MA: Wiley-Blackwell.
Calabrese, Andrea. 2016. On the morphophonology of metaphonic alternations in Altamurano. In Francesc Torres-Tamarit, Kathrin Linke & Marc van Oostendorp (eds.), *Approaches to metaphony in the languages of Italy*, 89–126. Berlin: Mouton de Gruyter.
Calabrese, Andrea. 2018. *Essays in morpho-phonology*. Ms.: University of Connecticut.

Cardinaletti, A. & L. Repetti. 2008. The phonology and syntax of preverbal and postverbal subject clitics in northern italian dialects. *Linguistic Inquiry* 39(4). 523–563.
Cinque, Guglielmo et al. 1994. On the evidence for partial N-movement in the romance DP. In G. Cinque & R. S. Kayne (eds.), *Paths towards universal grammar*, 85–110. Washington, DC: Georgetown University Press.
Clements, George N. 1990. The role of the sonority cycle in core syllabification. In K. Kingston & M. E. Beckman (eds.), *Papers in laboratory phonology*, vol. 1, 283–333. Cambridge University Press.
Baudouin de Courtenay, Jan. 1972. An attempt at a theory of phonetic alternations. In Edward Stankiewicz (ed.), *A Baudouin De Courtenay anthology: The beginnings of structural linguistics*, 144–212. First published (1895), *Versuch einer Theorie phonetischer Alternationen: ein Kapitel aus der Psychophonetik*. Strassburg: Trübner.
Dell, François. 1980. *Generative phonology and French phonology*. Cambridge: Cambridge University Press.
Embick, David & Rolf Noyer (2001). Movement operations after syntax. In: *Linguistic inquiry 32.4*, pp. 555–595.
Embick, David & Morris Halle. 2005. On the status of *stems* in morphophological theory. In Twan Geerts Geerts, Ivo van Ginneken & Haike Jacobs (eds.), *Romance Language and Linguistic Theory 2003. Selected paper from 'Going Romance' 2003*, Amsterdam/Philadephia: John Benjamins.
Garrapa, Luigia. 2011. *Vowel elision in florentine italian*. Konstanz: Universität Konstanz dissertation.
Halle, Morris & Alec Marantz. 1993. Distributed morphology and the pieces of inflection. In K. Hale & S. J. Keyser (eds.), *The view from building 20: Essays in linguistics in honor of sylvain bromberger*, 111–176. Cambridge, MA: MIT Press.
Halle, Morris & Alec Marantz. 1994. Some key features of distributed morphology. *MIT Working Papers in Linguistics* 21. 275–288.
Haugen, Jason D. & Daniel Siddiqi. 2013. Roots and the derivation. *Linguistic Inquiry* 44(3). 493–517.
Jackendoff, Ray. 1972. *Semantic interpretation in generative grammar*. Cambridge, MA: MIT Press.
Kiparsky, Paul. 1996. Allomorphy or morphophonology? In Rejandra Singh (ed.), *Trubetzkoy's orphan. Proceedings of the montréal roundtable of morphophonology: Contemporary responses*, Amsterdam: Benjamins.
Ledgeway, Adam. 2009. *Grammatica diacronica del dialetto napoletano*, vol. 350 Beihefte zur Zeitschrift für Romanische Philologie Band. Tübingen: Max Niemeyer Verlag.
Loporcaro, Michele. 1991. Compensatory lengthening in romanesco. In P. M. Bertinetto, M. Kenstowicz & M. Loporcaro (eds.), *Certamen phonologicum ii*, 279–307. Torino: Rosenberg & Sellier.
McCarthy, J. J. & A. Prince. 1995. Faithfulness and reduplicative identity. In Jill Beckman, Laura Walsh Dickey & Suzanne Urbanczyk (eds.), *Papers in optimality theory. University of massachusetts occasional papers*, vol. 18, 249–384. Amherst, MA: Graduate Linguistic Student Association.
Petrosino, Roberto. 2018. *On the necessity of morpho-phonology*. Ms.:University of Connecticut.

Saab, Andrés & Anikó Lipták. 2016. Movement and deletion after syntax: Licensing by inflection reconsidered. *Studia Linguistica* 70(1). 66–108.
Tranel, Bernard. 1987. *The sounds of French. An introduction*. Cambridge, UK: Cambridge University Press.
Vaux, Bert & Andrew Wolfe. 2009. The appendix. In E. Raimy & C. E. Cairns (eds.), *Contemporary views on architecture and representations in phonology*, 261–304. Cambridge, MA: The MIT Press.

Part III: *Issues* in the Morpho-Syntax

Paola Benincà, Mariachiara Berizzi, Laura Vanelli
Diachronic and synchronic aspects in the expression of temporal distance in the past: A process of grammaticalization in Italian compared with other Romance languages and English

1 Introduction

In this work, we will observe the characteristics of some expressions used to localize an event in time, giving the measure of the temporal distance.[1] We will concentrate in particular on the deictic localization in the past, which in Italian is expressed with the particle *fa* (homophonous of the 3rd sg. of the verb *fare* 'it does, it makes'), preceded by the measure of time span. *Fa* is necessarily deictic, since it localizes the event with respect to the Utterance Time (UT).

(1) a. *Gianni arrivò / è arrivato / *arriverà / *arrivava / due ore fa.*
    'G. arrived / has arrived / *will arrive / *arrived (impf.) two hours ago.'
   b. *Gianni arrivò / è arrivato / arriverà / arrivava due ore prima.*
    'G. arrived / has arrived / will arrive / arrived (impf.) two hours before.'

As shown by these examples, *fa* has necessarily a deictic interpretation: the point of reference for the localization of the event in the past is the time of utterance (UT), and consequently the verb expressing the event has to be in the past perfective (simple past or present perfect, also depending on the variety of Italian). The adverbial preposition *prima* 'before', instead, chooses the point of reference from the immediate or recoverable context.

We will show that the forms used in Modern Italian can be interestingly compared with Old Italian, Spanish, other Romance varieties, and English. Moreover, a comparison with the parallel expressions of spatial distance can also be interestingly developed, as recent works on the relationships between the localization in time and in space already suggest.

---

[1] With fond admiration and gratitude, we dedicate this work to Andrea, for his fascinating and inspiring contribution to phonological and morphological research.
For the concerns of the Italian academy, Laura Vanelli is responsible for section 1–4, Paola Benincà for section 5–6.1, 7 and Mariachiara Berizzi for section 6.2.

https://doi.org/10.1515/9781501506734-011

In section 2 we present a description and a syntactic interpretation of the constructions expressing the temporal distance in Modern Italian. In section 3 we illustrate the differences with modern Spanish and in section 4 the parallel differences with respect to Old Italian. On the basis of this comparison, in 4.1 we outline a description of the diachronic evolution of the construction in Italian. In sect. 5 we will compare structures with the same value which use the verb *essere* 'to be' instead of *fa / fare*, and will compare the conclusions reached on the basis of Italian and Spanish with forms attested for some Italian dialects. The structure of temporal distance expressions can be fruitfully compared with that of space distance; we will deal with this aspect in section 6, proposing a cartographic description of the construction, which can account for the parallelisms and the differences that we have illustrated.

Throughout the analysis we will compare the deictic expressions of the temporal distance with the anaphoric parallel, dwelling in particular in 5.2 upon *prima* 'before', in order to shed some light on the specific properties of the two semantic areas.

2 The expression of temporal distance in the past in Modern Italian

In Modern Italian the temporal distance between an event and a point set *before* in the temporal sequence is indicated mostly by two distinct elements, *fa* and *prima*, both preceded by an expression indicating a measure of time (TMeas): *tre giorni fa / prima* 'three days ago / before'; *due mesi fa / prima* 'two months ago / before'; *mezz'ora fa / prima* 'half an hour ago / before'. Notice that the terms 'day, month, hour, etc.' are used purely as unities of temporal measurement and not in their "calendric" value. Examples:

(2) a. *Sergio è tornato a Padova il 13 giugno. Io invece tre giorni fa.*
 'S. has come back to Padua the 13 of June. I instead three days ago.'
 b. *Sergio è tornato a Padova il 13 giugno. Io invece tre giorni prima.*
 'S. has come back to Padua the 13 of June. I instead three days before.'
 c. *Sergio tornerà a Padova il 13 giugno. Io invece tre giorni prima.*
 'S. will come back to Padua the 13 of June. I instead three days before.'

As in the English translation, the date of the speaker's arrival in Padua can be deduced from the information provided in (2b) and (2c), but in (2a) the localisation of the speaker's arrival requires another information, namely the time of utterance (UT), which is the point of reference.

With both *fa* and *prima* the event is localised a certain measure of time before a point of reference, but when *prima* is used, the point of reference is recoverable directly or indirectly from the context, with *fa*, instead, it coincides with UT, the time of utterance. For this reason, even used in a future context, *fa* can only refer to the past with respect to the UT, and thus a sentence like (3) is ungrammatical:

(3) *Sergio tornerà a Padova il 13 giugno. *Io invece tre giorni fa.*
 'S. will come back to Padua the 13 of June. I instead three days ago.'

This amounts to saying that a temporal expression followed by *fa* is intrinsically deictic, since the time is measured having the UT as point of reference, while *prima* is intrinsically anaphoric, as it measures the time starting from a moment explicitly or implicitly provided in the context.

2.1 A syntactic description

After having outlined the semantic and pragmatic properties of the temporal expressions with *prima* and *fa*, we analyse them from the syntactic point of view. In a functional-relational perspective, the two expressions are circumstantial complements; they have the same function as, for example, an Adverb like *ieri* 'yesterday', a Prepositional Phrase (PP) like *in maggio* 'in May', a Sentence (S) like *quando ci sono state le elezioni* 'when elections took place'.

Let us consider first the case of XP + *prima* 'before', a phrase whose head is *prima*. This element belongs to the class of adverbial (or secondary, improper, polysyllabic) prepositions, like *dopo* 'after', *davanti* 'in front of', *dietro* 'behind, after', *sopra* 'above, on', *sotto* 'under, below', etc. (see Rizzi 2001, Salvi 2013: 6.2). Etymologically, *prima* also derives from a preposition, since it is the superlative form of the Latin preposition *prae* 'in front of'. The prepositions of this class express a localisation in time or space with respect to an overt or recoverable point of reference; they do not require an overt complement NP or PP – differently from primary (or proper) prepositions, like *di* 'of', *a* 'to', *da* 'from, by', etc.

Examples (4) show that proper prepositions cannot omit their complements, while examples (5) show that adverbial prepositions can:

(4) a. *Vengo da *(Torino).*
  'I come from Turin.'
  b. *Mario sta andando a *(Torino).*
  'M. is going to Turin.'
(5) a. *E' partita (mezz'ora) dopo / prima di colazione.*
  'He left (half an hour) after / before breakfast.'

a'. *Io partirò (mezz'ora) dopo / prima.*
   'I will leave (half an hour) after / before.'
b. *L'albero si trova (dieci metri) dietro / davanti (al)la casa.*
   'The tree is (10 metres) behind / before the house.'
b'. *Il cancello è (dieci metri) davanti /dietro.*
   'The gate is (10 metres) before / behind.'
c. *La valigia è* sopra / sotto *(al)l'armadio.*
   'The suit-case is over / under / above / below the wardrobe.'
c'. *La borsa l'ho messa* sopra / sotto.
   'The handbag I put over / under / above / below.'

The elements we are considering are inherently relational, in the sense that they contribute to indicate a position in time or space with respect to a specific point of reference, which can be present in the sentence as an overt complement (as in (5a), (5b), and (5c)), or recoverable from the immediate context (as in (5a'), (5b') and (5c')). The measure of the temporal or spatial distance is also optional, as shown in the examples above.

The formula TMeas + *prima* comes within the syntactic type that we have just described, as it realises two of the options open to prepositional adverbs: the TMeas is given but the point of reference is anaphorically recoverable from the context. We can also have the other options: the point of reference is present, the TMeas is not:

(6) *L'ho vista (un'ora)* prima *delle otto.*
    'I have seen her (one hour) before eight o' clock.'

We can now compare what we have seen so far with the characteristics of the parallel temporal expression with *fa,* which shares some properties with *prima*:
a) it is invariable;
b) it is intrinsically relational;
c) it is preceded by a phrase containing a temporal measure.

Differently from *prima, fa* has the following properties:
d) it can only be deictic, and thus it has a unique implicit point of reference, namely the UT, which cannot be modified with the insertion of other points of reference; *L'ho vista un'ora fa delle otto* 'I have seen her one hour ago eight';
e) moreover, *fa* requires the expression of the measure of time, which is instead optional with *prima*, as in the following contrast: *L'ho vista prima* 'I have seen her before' / *L'ho vista fa* 'I have seen her ago';
f) finally, *fa* is homophonous with the 3rd sg. person of the verb *fare* 'to do, to make'.

In what follows, we will resume some of the aspects that we have touched in this section. Let us now compare Modern Italian with Spanish and Old Italian with respect to this construction. These languages show that homophony hinted at in f) between *fa* and the verb *fare* 'to make' is not accidental, since *fa* in these Romance varieties heads a sentential structure and has a verbal behaviour. These verbal properties have undergone a process of impoverishment in Modern Italian.

3 A comparison with Spanish

In Spanish two constructions are used to indicate temporal distance, and both use the verb *hacer* 'make, do'. The following data are taken from Bosque and Demonte (1999: II, 48.3).

In the first construction *hace* appears in a circumstantial complement, as in Italian:

(7) a. *Lo conocí* hace un año.
 'I met him it-makes one year (= one year ago)'.
 b. *El presidente dimitió* hace dos días.
 'The president resigned it-makes two days (= two days ago).'

Differently from Italian, though,
a) *hace* precedes the temporal measure;
b) as will be shown below, *hace* is not a frozen expression, as in Italian, but a form of the verb *hacer*, and can be inflected for tense and mood (see (8));
c) the verb *hacer* in this construction can only be in the 3rd sg., even when the temporal measure is in the plural (as *dos días* in (7b)). The temporal measure cannot be the subject of *hacer* but presumably the direct object.

Hace, as *fa*, requires that the measure of time has – as point of reference – the UT, it is then deictic, but this depends on the fact that *hace* is a verb in the present indicative, a tense that requires deictic interpretation. As a consequence, if *hacer* is in a different tense, the indication of the temporal distance is not deictic anymore, but anaphoric:

(8) a. *Se habían casado en Las Vegas* hacía dos años.
 'They had married in Las Vegas it-made two years (= two years before).'
 b. *Lo conocí ayer* hizo un año.
 'I met him yesterday it-made one year (= it was one year yesterday).'

In the second Spanish construction, the verb *hacer* is the head of a sentence (expressing the time measure) whose sentential complement introduced by *que* 'that' describes the event localised in the past time:

(9) a. Hace un año *que lo conocí*.
'It-makes one year that I met him (= I met him one year ago)'.
b. Hacía un año *que se abía ido*.
'It-made one year that he had gone (= he had gone one year before).'

In this construction too, the either deictic or anaphoric value of the temporal expression depends on the verb tense: with the present indicative, the point of reference is the time of utterance, with the other tenses it is recoverable from the context.

4 The expression of the temporal distance in the past in Old Italian

The description that we are going to present is based on Florentine texts going from the 13th to the 15th century; in some cases we also had a look at texts of the 15th century.[2] The description and the analysis of the construction, in its synchronic and diachronic aspects, have been developed and widened in Vanelli (2002a, 2002b, 2010), limitedly to texts of 13th and early 14th century, and in Benincà and Vanelli (2014).[3]

From all these texts it emerges that Old Italian had various possible constructions. Some cases seem to correspond to Modern Italian (examples (10) are of the 14th century, examples (11) of the 15th century):

(10) a. *In Roma (...) fu un giovane*, poco tempo fa (Boccaccio, *Decameron*, p. 357).
'In Rome (...) was a young man, a short time ago.'
b. *a Giogoli, presso a Firenze*, poco tempo fa, *fu un piovano* (F. Sacchetti, *Trecentonovelle*, CXVIII).
'in G., near to Florence, a short time ago, was a parish priest.'

---

[2] Data come from the data-base of the *Opera del Vocabolario Italiano* http://gattoweb.ovi.cnr.it3, which collects vernacular texts of Italy until 1375. For documents of 14th and 15th we used the data-base of CIBID, *Biblioteca Italiana Digitale*.
[3] Franco (2012) analyses some aspects of the same construction, basing on a limited set of data. His descriptive and theoretical conclusions, despite similarity, differ in fact from ours; we will not discuss his points in the present work.

(11) a. *Morì Giovanni della Luna*, tre di fa (Macinghi Strozzi, *Lettere*, XXXI).
'Died G. d. L. three days ago.'
b. *migliorato del male che ebbe* duo mesi fa (Macinghi Strozzi, *Lettere*, LXIII).
'recovered from illness that he-had two months ago.'
c. *ch'io n'ho la sentenza* uno anno fa *o più* (*Novella del grasso legnaiolo*).
'that I of-it. I-have the judgement one year ago or more.'

Beside this version of the construction, which is the same as that of Modern Italian, we find, in particular in older texts, other constructions with the same value, where *fa* appears, but a) the syntax is different and b) *fa* is clearly the 3rd sg. form of the present indicative of the verb *fare* 'to make'. We find in fact two different versions, similar to the ones we have seen above for Spanish, as appears from the examples in (12) and (13):

(12) a. *il figliuolo mio, che morì* già fa XIII anni (*Leggenda aurea*, p. A354).
'the my son, who died already it-makes thirteen years (= who died thirteen years ago).'
b. *sì com'egli fecero*, ora fa tre anni (*Deca prima di Tito Livio*, p. a176).
'so as they did now it-makes three years (as they did three years ago).'
c. *più che re che portasse corona* già fa mille e più anni (G. Villani, *Cronica*, p.f025).
'more than king who wear crown already it-makes thousand and more years (= since thousand years or more).'
d. *no l'arai a sì buono mercato come l'aresti auto* già fa uno mese (Macinghi Strozzi, *Lettere*, II).
'you will not have it at such a good price as you would have had it already it-makes one month (= one month ago).'
e. *È vero che*, or fa un anno, *n'avevo voglia* (Macinghi Strozzi, *Lettere*, II aggiunta).
'It-is true that, now it-makes one year (= one year ago), I wanted it.'

(13) a. *Oi nobile intelletto*, oggi fa l'anno *che nel ciel salisti* (Dante, *Vita Nuova*, 34, 11, pp. 13–14).
'Oh noble mind, today it-makes the year that to the heaven you ascended.'
b. *Tristano*, oggi fa XXVI giorni, *che lo re Marco entrò negli borghi della Gioiosa Guardia* (*Tavola Ritonda*, cap. 123, p. 478).
'Tristan, today it-makes twenty six days that (= twenty six days ago) the king Mark entered the villages of the Gioiosa Guardia.'

c. *e fa ora di questo mese anni sette [che]*[4] *ti partisti* (Macinghi Strozzi, *Lettere*, XI).
'and it-makes now in this month years seven (that) you left (= you left seven years ago).'

The two constructions are parallel to that of Spanish, as shown in examples (12), where the phrase with *fa* is a circumstantial complement of the sentence (as the Spanish cases seen in (7)), while in the examples (13) the phrase containing *fa* is a main sentence governing as its complement the sentence introduced by the complementizer which expresses the event localised in time (as the Spanish examples in (9)). Moreover, as in Spanish and differently from Modern Italian, *fa* precedes the temporal expression. The natural conclusion is that *fa*, as in Spanish, is a proper verb in these kinds of constructions. Notice that the verb *fare* is always in the 3rd sg. person, and then does not agree in number with the measure of time. The verb can be considered an impersonal verb, with the measure of time as a kind of non-argumental object, with an inherent accusative Case (see, among others, Corver 2009). The construction can be compared with other constructions with *fare*, such as *fa caldo* 'it makes hot (= it is hot)', *fa brutto tempo* 'it makes bad weather (=it is bad weather)' (see Boccaccio, *Dec.* V, 4: *O figliuola mia, che caldo fa egli?* 'O my girl, how hot makes it? (=how hot is it?')). In other cases *fare* governs a measure term, such as *Quanto fa?* 'How much makes it? (= How much is it?)', *Fa trenta euro* 'It is thirty euros'. *Fare* appears also in arithmetical expressions, as in *venti più dieci fa trenta* 'twenty and ten makes / is thirty', *tre volte cinque fa quindici* 'three times five makes / is fifteen'.

From a semantic point of view, in these expressions *fa* means *compiere* 'to complete' (as *hacer* in Spanish), similarly to what happens in other contexts, as for example in *Gianni ha fatto dodici anni in dicembre* 'G. has completed twelve years in December, is now twenty years old'.

A property which is found only in Old Italian is the obligatory presence of deictic adverbs *ora* 'now', *oggi* 'today', *già* 'already'[5]; these adverbs integrate and

---

[4] The complementizer is omitted, a typical phenomenon of 15th C Florentine, which for a short period expanded also in other varieties (cf. Scorretti 1981).

[5] In some contexts these adverbs can only be deictic, but both *già* 'already' and even *ora* 'now' can be anaphoric.

For *ora* the context that triggers the anaphoric interpretation is a sort of 'free indirect speech', attested all along the history of Italian. The following examples are taken from the *Grande Dizionario della Lingua Italiana*, s. *ora*:

i. *Chi porìa mai (...) dicer del sangue e delle piaghe (...) ch'i ora vidi?* (Dante, *Inferno*, 28, 3).
'Who could ever say about the blood and the wounds that I now saw?'

reinforce the deictic interpretation of the temporal expressions, primarily provided by the present tense of *fare*. Notice that in Modern Italian *fa* is incompatible with deictic adverbs:

(14)   *Carlo è partito* (*oggi / *ora) *tre giorni fa.*
       'C. has left (*today / *now) three days ago.'

Since we have hypothesised that *fa* in Old Italian is still a full verb, we expect to find cases where *fare* has other tenses and non-deictic points of reference. We found a few clear examples as the following (in (15a) *fare* is the head of a main clause, in (15b) *fare* is the head of a circumstantial complement):

(15)   a.   e a dì 7 di questo [mese] fece anni tre *[che] si partì di qua* (Macinghi Strozzi, *Lettere*, p. 34).
            'and on the day 7 of this month it-made years three that he-left from here.'
       b.   Martedì fece otto giorni *[che] prese la medicina* (Rucellai, *Lettere*, p. 99).
            'Tuesday it-made eight days (that) she-took the medicine.'

In Old Italian other structures are used to express the temporal distance, where we find the same deictic adverbs *oggi* 'today', *ora* 'now', *già* 'already' accompany an inflected form of the verb *essere* 'to be'; in these constructions the temporal phrase is the subject, as the rigorous agreement with the verb indicates. In (16a) the temporal expression is the main sentence, in the other examples the temporal expressions are circumstantial complements:

(16)   a.   oggi sono due giorni, *che tutto il mondo fu privato di cotal padre* (D. Cavalca, *Vita*, 6, 13).
            'today are two days that (= two days ago) all the world was deprived of such a father.'
       b.   *Io, misera me*, già sono otto anni, *t'ho più che la mia vita amato* (Boccaccio, *Dec.*, 3, 6, 33).
            'I poor me, already are eight years (= eight years ago) you.have more than my life loved (= I loved you...).'

---

   ii.   Quella lontananza (...) le parve ora una disposizione della provvidenza (A. Manzoni, *Pr. Sp.* 24).
         'That remoteness her seemed now a provision of Providence.'
   iii. Ora anche i suonatori tacquero (D. Buzzati, *Deserto Tart.*, I, 197).
         'Now even the players silenced themselves.'

c. già sono più mesi, *varie maniere di scuse ho trovate* (Boccaccio, *Fiammetta*, 2, 4).
already are several months (= several months ago) various manners of excuses I-have found.'

d. *se coloro che partiro d'esta vita* già sono mille anni *tornassero alle loro cittadi* (Dante, *Convivio*, 5, 22).
'If those who left from this life already are thousand years (= thousand years ago) could come back to their towns.'

4.1 The transition to the new construction

We have seen above, examples (10), that the first examples of the modern construction with *fa* (TMeas + *fa*) are quite early, dated from the end of the 14th century. On the other hand, the constructions exemplified in (12) and (13), which are to be considered – chronologically and structurally – preceding the construction where *fa* appears to be functionally impoverished, continue to be used till the end of the 15th century; in some authors the old and the new structures survive together, as shown in the following examples from the letters of Alessandra Macinghi Strozzi (some of them already quoted above):

(17) a. *e fa ora di questo mese anni sette [che] ti partisti* (Macinghi Strozzi, *Lettere*, XI).
'and it-makes in this month years seven that you left.'

b. *e a dì 7 di questo [mese] fece anni tre [che] si parti di qua* (Macinghi Strozzi, *Lettere*, p. 34).
'and on the day 7 of this month it-made years three that he-left from here.'

c. *È vero che, or fa un anno, n'avevo voglia* (Macinghi Strozzi, *Lettere*, II aggiunta).
'It is true that, now it-makes one year (= one year ago), I wanted it.'

d. *Morì Giovanni della Luna, tre dì fa* (Macinghi Strozzi, *Lettere*, XXXI).
'Died G. d. L. three days ago.'

In the following example by Franco Sacchetti we have a sort of minimal pair:

(18) a. *Che facevi tu oggi fa otto dì a quest'ora?* (F. Sacchetti, *Trecentonovelle*, CLI).
'What were you doing today it-makes eight days (= eight days ago) at this time?'

b. *Io salai un porco forse otto dì fa* (F. Sacchetti, *Trecentonovelle*, CCXIV).
'I salted a pork perhaps eight days ago.'

In the 16th century the new construction had completely substituted the older ones, and in the texts of this period we find only examples like the following, taken from Machiavelli:

(19) a. *Chi conobbe Nicomaco* uno anno fa (...) *ne debbe restare maravigliato* (*Clizia*, I, sc. IV).
'Who knew N. one year ago (...) by-him has to be amazed.'
     b. *andò per certe sua faccende*, uno anno fa, *in Francia* (*Mandragola*, III, sc. IV).
'he-went for certain matters one year ago.'
     c. *Ma vegnamo a quello che è seguito* poco tempo fa (*Il principe*, XII).
'But let us move to what followed a short time ago.'

Let us now observe the changes that the old constructions met in their transition to the new one. First of all, the constructions where *fare* was the head of a main sentence disappear (only *essere* and copular verbs maintain this function). The modern construction appears then to develop from the circumstantial structure, in which on the other hand we notice some changes. In particular:

a) the deictic adverbs *oggi* 'today', *ora* 'now', *già* 'already', which explicitly indicated the UT as point of reference, disappear, leaving to the verbal morphology of the present indicative the deictic function, as is the case in modern Spanish.

b) *fa* is undergoing a gradual process of impoverishment leading to a change of category. Presumably the verbal status of *fa* was maintained for a long while, as shown in the following passage from Boccaccio's *Decameron*. Notice that in the whole Decameron, where the passage is taken from, only the 'new' structure is used:

(20) rispose «*Io non so, ma egli era pur* poco fa *qui dinanzi a noi.*» Disse Bruno: «*Ben* che fa poco! *a me par egli esser certo che egli è ora a casa a desinare*» (p. 518).
'he replied «I don't know, but he was just little (= a short [time] ago) here in front of us.» Said Bruno: «Well that it-makes little (= a short time)! It seems to me that he is now at home to dinner!»'

The first instance has the 'modern' usage of *fa*, but Bruno in his reply uses *fa* with the old structure, where *fa* is the head of a subordinate sentence, introduced by the complementiser *che* 'that', as a fully verbal form; consistently with the old structure, *fa* precedes the temporal expression.

c) in the new structure, *fa* follows the temporal expression, as do other adverbial prepositions in temporal expressions indicating a temporal distance with respect to a point of reference; we are referring to adverbial prepositions, as *(d)avanti* 'before', *addietro* 'behind', etc., exemplified in (21) (see also Vanelli 2010: 1268 ff., and for prepositions in Old Italian, Andreose 2010: cap. 18):

(21) a. *quel medesimo exemplo della ragione che noi aven detta* poco davanti (Brunetto Latini, *Rettorica*, p. 134, rr. 3–5).
'that same example of the reason that we have said short before (= a short while ago).'
b. *tu mi ti mostrasti* poco avanti *così lieta* (Boccaccio, *Filocolo*, libro 2, cap. 48, par. 5).
'you yourself.to-me- showed short before so happy'
c. *e questi d[anari] ebi da la tavola* due die dinanzi (*Libro di Lapo Riccomanni*, 518, r.17).
'and these monies I-had from the table two days before.'
d. *perciò che v'era stato* sett'anni addietro *un'altra volta* (P. Pieri, *Cronica*, 14, rr. 6–8).
'because he it.had been seven years before once again.'
e. *L'anno* dappresso *furono fatti consoli Marco Geganio Macerino e Tito Quinzio Capitolino* (*Deca prima di Tito Livio*, p. 57, rr. 2).
'The year after M. G. M. and T. Q. C. were created consuls.'

d) Finally, through the process of grammaticalization *fa* acquired a new status of functional element; it is fixed in its exclusively deictic value and assumes its position after the temporal measure; in this way, it became parallel to the other temporal expressions followed by an adverbial preposition that indicate the temporal distance (in the past, in the future, or with respect to any temporal point of reference). The reordering of elements is then the result of the grammaticalization process: *fa* assumes the position that its new status requires.

We could also conclude that *fa* is not anymore a verb at all but another adverbial preposition; we will see below, though, that possibly *fa* has preserved a feature from its preceding verbal status, and this is precisely the obligatory activation of the deictic point of reference.

5 Structures of temporal measure with *essere* 'to be'

Alongside with *fare*, a time measure in the past can be expressed with the verb 'to be', with a parallel structure (see Vanelli 2010: 1275). The examples in (16) and (22) are found in Old Italian and are still grammatical – in a formal style – in Modern Italian.

(22) a. Or sono [già] LXX anni. (Anon., *Leggenda Aurea*).
'Now are already 70 years.'
b. Oggi sono due giorni *che tutto il mondo fu privato di cotal padre* (D. Cavalca, *Vita di Ilarione*, 6, 13).
'Today are two days that all the world was deprived of such a father.'
c. *per ciò che* sono anni *che nacque...* (Boccaccio, *Esposizioni Comedia*, c. I,ii, par. *167, 89)
'and because that are years that he-was-born (= because he was born years ago).'

In Modern Italian we have the following possibilities, the same that we observed in Old Italian with *fare*:

(23) a. [(Adv) *sono/erano* MeasT] *che* Sentence
(Oggi) sono / (ieri) erano due giorni *che Mario è / era partito*.
'Today are / yesterday were two days that M. has left.'
b. Sentence *che* [(Adv) *sono / erano* MeasT]
Mario è / era partito che sono / erano due giorni
'M. has / was left that are / were two days.'

As we have seen with *fare > fa*, also *ora sono* 'now are' underwent a process of grammaticalization, and *orsono* or *or sono*[6] behaves as an adverbial preposition; just like *fa*, the temporal measure has to precede the 'preposition' and gets obligatorily deictic interpretation. While the deictic adverb disappears when *fa* undergoes grammaticalization, with the verb *to be* the deictic adverb *or(a)* 'now' becomes part of the new form The possible structures are the following two: the formula in square brackets is an Adverbial Phrase, a circumstantial complement:

(24) a. [TMeas *orsono*] Sentence   [Due giorni or sono] *Mario è partito*
'[Two days now are] M. has left.'
b. Sentence [TMeas *orsono*]   M. *è partito* [due giorni or sono]
'M. has left [two days now are] (= M. (has) left two days ago).'

When the deictic adverb *ora* 'now' incorporates into the verb 'be', the verb must appear inflected in the 3rd pl. person of the present indicative; the time measure has to be in the plural, showing that at some level the time measure

---

[6] There is not agreement about the orthographically correct alternative. Notice that none of the many Italian dictionaries that we have checked records a lemma *or sono / orsono*.

is the subject of 'to be'. As we have suggested for *fa*, it appears that the new, grammaticalized form has preserved some features of the verb, not only the deixis (reinforced by the adverb), but also personal agreement: Even though the expression is not commonly used in the colloquial style, the grammaticality judgments are very clear:

(25) a. *Un anno * un mese * orsono*
'One year / one month now are'
b. *Due anni / due mesi orsono*
'Two years / two months now are'

Orsono as well shows that, even though it seems a frozen structure, it maintains some morpho-syntactic properties active, thus the TMeas has to be consistent with number features of the verb, namely the 3rd pl. person. Notice that *fa* and *orsono* are the only temporal expressions that are exclusively deictic.

[TMeas *orsono*] and [TMeas *fa*] are adverbial complements, whose position in sentence structure will be tentatively defined below, in sect. 6.

Notice that the expressions we are considering are specific for time distance, and can be applied to spatial distance only as metaphors. It would be interesting to further investigate similarities and differences between spatial deixis, which refers to the place where the speaker is physically located, and temporal deixis, which is linked to the point in time when the speech act takes place.

5.1 Other Romance varieties

If we observe how other Romance varieties express the temporal distance in the past, we find that constructions that characterised Old Italian and have disappeared in Modern Italian, survive in various Italian dialects, so that we find – synchronically distributed in the geographical space – the diachronic stages that have been proposed above for Italian. To a great extent, these findings confirm the reconstruction that we have proposed.

We will observe predications expressing the temporal distance that use *essere* 'to be', *avere* 'to have', and *fare* 'to do'. The data are drawn from two maps of the AIS: VII 1265 *(hanno cominciato) otto giorni fa*, 'they began eight days ago', and VIII 1646 *l'anno scorso* 'one year ago, last year'. We comment just a few of the numerous variants that appear in the two maps of AIS, those that are more directly relevant for our discussion.

The verb 'to be' can be used to mean 'eight days ago', with the following possibilities, which we report in Italian as typified forms:

(26) a. *che è / sono già otto giorni* (Northern and Central Italy)
'that is / are already eight days'
b. *già sono otto giorni* (Central Italy)
'already are eight days'
c. *è bell'e otto giorni* (pt. 275 Bozzolo, MN; pt. 286 Castiglione d'Adda)
'is well and eight days'[7]

The verb *avere* 'to have' can be used with existential value, as in:

(27) *ha otto giorni* (Sicily, Central Italy)
'has eight days (= there are eight days / eight days ago)'

Sardinian, using *fa*, presents both orders: TMeas–fa *and* fa-TMeas; the latter corresponds to the Old Italian order (see above examples (12) and (13)):

(28) a. (*da*) *otto giorni fa*
'(since) eight days it-makes'
b. *fa otto giorni*
'it-makes eight days'

In a number of Sardinian localities, spread mainly in central and southern parts of the island, the correspondent of *fa* appears in a very interesting morphological form, which can contribute to enlighten the value of *fa* in Italian and other Italian dialects:

(29) a. *otto dies fàeðe* (pt. 959 Baunei)
'eight days it-makes'
b. *fàiði òttu dis* (pt. 941 Milis)
'it-makes eight days'

In Italian and Italian dialects *fa* seems reduced to a pure verbal root, with the status of particle, but it is formally identical with the 3rd person singular of present indicative. Italian, as many Romance variants, is then ambiguous as for the status of the particle *fa*, which can be represented by a pure root, or derive from a functional reinterpretation of the 3rd person singular. These Sardinian varieties show that, both in initial and final position – corresponding respectively to Modern Italian (28a) and Old Italian (28b) – the element corresponding to *fa* is not the pure root but a fully inflected form of 3rd singular

---

[7] The formula *bell'e* lit. 'beautiful and' is a periphrasis for 'already'.

of present indicative (< FACIT). This observation confirms the hypothesis that modern *fa* has preserved at least some features of the old deictic present indicative form.

For 'last year, one year ago', in a narrow area on the borders between northern Puglia Campania and Abruzzo, we find another example clearly corresponding to Old Italian:

(30) *mo fa l'anno*
      'now it-makes the year'

For what concerns the Case assigned by the verb *fare* to the measure of time, the comparison with Old Romance provides further hints, in particular Old French, which has maintained till quite late morphological Case distinctions. From Old French we get evidence that existential *avoir* assigns accusative Case to its internal argument, including the measure of time (cf. (27)). This is consistent with the observation made above on Old Italian and Modern Italian with respect to the lack of agreement between the verb *fare* e the noun expressing the measure of time. Presumably, the verb *fare* in these constructions assigns accusative Case in Old Italian as in Old French.

Earlier than in Italian (end of 13th century), in Old French the elements undergo a reordering of elements, with *fare* after the measure of time, as in the following example, which is interesting also because it expresses a 'decurrential' value, which has not been acquired in Modern Italian:

(31) trois jours a, *ne dormi* (*Adenet le roi*, fine XIII sec.).
      'three daysACC ago, not I-slept (= I haven't slept since three days ago).'

This structure is impossible in Italian and has disappeared in French. In colloquial French we find a variant, lost in Italian, where *fare* is still a verb, as it takes tense markers different from present indicative (as in Spanish):

(32) ça fasait dix ans *que j'habitais là* (Freddi 1997: 224).
      'it made ten years that I lived there (= I had been living there for ten years).'

Notice that agreement again shows that the temporal measure is not the subject of *fare* but, presumably, the object.

Looking at the Romance area as a whole, we can see the alternative structures present in different points in time and space as variants of a unique structure which variably undergoes processes grammaticalization, movement, coalescence.

But let us go back briefly to another adverbial preposition that is linked to the temporal distance in the past, namely *prima*, 'before', introduced above in comparison with *fa* as its non-deictic counterpart.

5.2 Some specific characteristics of *prima* 'before'

Resuming some observations on *prima* made above, we recall that while *fa* can only have a deictic point of reference, *prima* can have various possibilities, including the deictic interpretation. The latter is admitted – with some restrictions on tense– only if the temporal distance is not quantified:

(33) a. Prima *Mario mi ha dato la sua risposta.*
      'Before M. has given me his answer.'
   b. *Poco prima *mi ha dato la sua risposta.*
      'Short before M. has given me his answer.'
   c. Poco fa *Mario mi ha dato la sua risposta.* (Cf. Poco prima *mi aveva dato...*)
      'A short [time] ago M. has given me his answer.' (Cf. 'Short before he had given...')

In (33a) *prima* localizes the event either before an event recoverable from the context (anaphoric interpretation), or before the UT (deictic interpretation); moreover, in this case, the event has to be localised inside the minimal temporal unit in which the sentence is produced; the relevant temporal unit can be morning, afternoon, evening, night, in some contexts also month or year. For example, if sentence (33a) is pronounced at 4 pm, the sentence is felicitous if the event has happened within the same afternoon, while, if it happened before dinner, the correct expression is *stamattina* 'this morning'. Only when the event happens at the border between two units the interpretation can be more flexible.

Probably the interpretation is indirectly linked to the present tense of the auxiliary, as one can see observing the behaviour of speakers of varieties of Italian that distinguish simple past from present perfect. In these varieties it is impossible to use the absolute *prima* with a simple past. The following example is ungrammatical for a Neapolitan speaker with deictic interpretation of *prima*:

(34) *Prima *Mario disse che verrà.*
     'Before M. said that he will come.'

Notice that if *prima* is accompanied by a measure of time, even vague as *poco* 'a little' it is obligatorily interpreted as 'short before a moment X different from the UT'.

In this case, the tense can be the future or the pluperfect, but not the present perfect, as we said above:[8]

---

[8] These constraints are not active when the point of reference is not expressed but recoverable from the context:
   (i) D: *Quando lo vedesti*, prima o dopo di avermi incontrato?
       Q: 'When did you see him, before or after having met me?'

(35) a. Poco prima *Mario aveva dato la sua risposta*.
'Short before M. had given his answer.'
b. Poco prima *Mario darà la sua risposta*.
'Short before M. will give his answer.'

In this case we can hypothesise that the locative nature of *prima* 'before' comes into play. We have seen above that *prima* 'before' is etymologically a superlative form of the Latin preposition *prae* 'in front of'. *Fa*, instead, being the result of the grammaticalization of a verb, has not the axial component that characterises locatives, and then it can only be deictic. In itself, *fa* marks a point in the time line which necessarily coincides with the UT, and it selects past to orient the direction of the line where the moment of the event is determined. The TMeas has to be necessarily expressed with *fa*, as we have seen. If *fa* is still in part a verb, we can conclude that its object must be expressed, and this object is the TMeas, as we suggested above.

Differently from *fa*, *prima* does not require the presence of a temporal measure, but the presence / absence of the temporal measure conditions the semantic interpretations. If the TMeas is expressed (*tre giorni* 'three days', *poco* 'short'), the only available interpretation is axial and thus anaphoric, while if the TMeas is not expressed, with the past tense, the deictic interpretation is also available. (*Ho mangiato prima* 'I ate before').

In conclusion, while *prima* 'before' can have different temporal links, depending on the context, *fa* and *orsono* can only be deictic; this can be related to the fact that these elements are the result of the grammaticalization of present indicative verbal forms and inherited deictic features from the respective verbs.

6 Localization of temporal expressions in the structure

Based on what we have observed and discussed so far concerning the constructions that express temporal distance, we will try to outline a hypothesis on the syntactic structure of these constructions and the dedicated positions of the elements in the temporal PP. Assuming as a starting point a universally understood

---

(ii) R.: *Lo vidi* prima (*scilicet* di averti incontrato).
A: 'I saw him before (*scilicet* having met me)'

analogy between time and space,⁹ we will discuss the possibility to apply the highly detailed structure of locative PP as proposed by Cinque (2010) to the temporal PP. In order to widen the empirical – and consequently theoretical – basis, we will introduce English in our comparison, since much of the analyses of the Spatial PP are based on this language.

6.1 Localization in the sentence

If we focus on the expressions with *fa*, we notice that *tre anni fa* 'three years ago' has two possible non-marked positions: on the left (*Tre anni fa è partito per l'America* 'Three years ago he left to America'), and on the right (*È partito per l'America tre anni fa*, 'He left to America three years ago'). The pre-verbal position is ambiguous though, as we can see if we add a pre-verbal subject (*Mario tre anni fa è partito per l'America* 'Mario left to America three years ago' / *Tre anni fa Mario è partito per l'America* 'Three years ago Mario left to America').

In order to localize the exact position, we will observe the position of the adverbial locution in Paduan, a dialect with subject clitics.

In Paduan subject clitics are mandatory if the subject position is not occupied by a lexical (or abstract) subject; when a lexical subject is present, as in (36a), they seem to be optional; but again, they are mandatory if the lexical subject is obligatorily left dislocated due to the presence of certain types of arguments that appear between the lexical subject and the verb, as in (36b) and (36c):

(36) a. *Mario (l) me dize tuto.*
 'M. (he) to-me tells everything.'
 b. *Mario, mì, *(l) me dize tuto.*
 'M., to-me he says everything'.
 c. *Mario, casa sua, *(l) ghe ndarà doman.*
 'M. home his subj.cl. loc.cl. will go tomorrow.'
 d. *Mario doman (el) torna casa.*
 'M. tomorrow subj.cl. returns home.'
 e. *Mario geri (el) ze partìo presto.*
 'M. yesterday subj.cl. is left soon.'

---

9 Among many others, we refer to Haspelmath (1997, p.1): "Human languages again and again express temporal and spatial notions in a similar way. This phenomenon is so widespread in different languages across the world and in different parts of the vocabulary, that we have to conclude that space and time are linked to each other in human thinking as well". Analyses of many different languages have shown that representation of time depends on representation of space.

Notice that in both (36b, c) and (36d, e) the subject is not adjacent to the verb; in (36b) and (36c), though, the lexical subject is separated from the verb by an argument that, being copied by a clitic, is necessarily left dislocated; thus, the lexical subject, appearing on its left, is forced to be itself left dislocated, and consequently copied by a clitic. In (36d) and (36e) a temporal adverb is found between the subject and the verb, and is not necessarily copied by a clitic; this means that the temporal adverb is not necessarily left dislocated but can be hosted in a dedicated functional position between nominative subject and verb agreement

The area in which *fa* is located leads to think that the grammaticalization of the verb *fare*, which is now considered as a 'particle', is strictly connected to the exclusively deictic function that it has acquired. As we have already stated above, though *fa* is not fully a verb anymore, it has kept the deictic feature of the original verbal form as part of its inventory of semantic and functional features. Similarly, the frozen expression *orsono* maintains the feature Plural, which obligatorily selects a plural TMeas.

6.2 Order of the elements in the temporal and spatial distance phrase

To sum up, everything points to the fact that the grammaticalization of *fa* and *orsono* is connected to deixis: both expressions become exclusively deictic.

In order to go beyond the descriptive approach we have adopted so far and account for the given structures and their relations, it is necessary to develop a complex hypothesis, similar to the hypothesis proposed for locative PPs with functional and adverbial prepositions among other elements. The locative PP, as proposed by the cartographic approach, hosts not only prepositions but also adverbs, particles and spatial locutions.

As a first step towards a more detailed hypothesis of the temporal PP, we will see how the structure of the spatial PP can be applied to the temporal PP and what the structural differences are between the two phrases, if there are any.

In order to do so, we start by observing at a closer sight the spatial PP. The idea that the spatial PP presents a sophisticated structure with a number of functional projections above the lexical projection of P has been gradually outlined by Riemsdijk (1990). Koopman (2000), den Dikken (2006) and Tortora (2005, 2006, 2008), among others, contributed significantly to the identification of dedicated projections hosted in the locative PP in Dutch and Italian. On the basis of much cross-linguistic evidence, the inner structure of spatial PP has been further refined by Cinque (2010) and Svenonius (2010). The proposal of Cinque (2010) in (41) presents a highly detailed, bipartite structure. In this structure we can identify a 'higher functional portion' and a 'lower lexical portion'. The higher portion of this structure is the functional area of the PP where directionality and stativity are encoded. More precisely, directionality is encoded in PPdir, and stativity is encoded in PPstat.

In the lower portion we have a NPPlace whose head hosts a null PLACE and whose specifier hosts the 'Ground', that is to say the object that represents the reference point for all higher modifiers. The NPPlace itself is hosted in a DPPlace, which has also a highly detailed structure. In DPPlace a series of projections can be found hosting several types of modifiers of Ground, among them, AxPartP, a projection that hosts 'axial prepositions' (Jackendoff 1996, Svenonius 2006) that is, prepositions 'which define a place by projecting vectors on one of the possible axes (*sopra* 'above', *sotto* 'under', *dietro* 'behind', etc.), which depart from the object that provides the reference point in Ground:

(37) [PPdir [PPstat AT [DPPlace [DegP right [ModeDirP diagonally [AbsViewP north/south [RelViewP up/down [RelViewP *in / out* [DeicticP *here / there* [AxPartP [PP P [NPPlace Ground [PLACE]...]

The first part of the present work has often referred to the analogy between time and space, which is treated in literature. In his study on the conceptualization of time, Martin Haspelmath (1997) takes into consideration 53 languages, and, interestingly, shows very clearly that the possibility to express time by means of spatial elements can be considered universal, being unrestricted neither from a genetic nor a typological point of view. On the contrary, the possibility to express space by means of temporal elements which are not derived from spatial elements is not attested, except for some rather controversial cases.

In this regard, Roy and Svenonius (2008) observe that a crucial difference between space and time is the switch from three dimensions to one. Roy and Svenonius (2008) also show that complex temporal prepositions have the same structure of the complex spatial prepositions, sharing three fundamental parts of the structure: Place (PPstat in Cinque 2010), AxPartP and KP (Case).

Haspelmath (1997) had already observed that while space is tri-dimensional, time can be described as mono-dimensional; moreover – if we consider that, taken two non-coincident points on the temporal line, one necessarily comes 'before' and the other comes 'after', time is also unidirectional. In addition to this, time spans can undergo quantitative evaluations – they can be longer or shorter, they can thus be measured.

In this framework, Berizzi and Rossi (2013) analyze a verbal tense of Hiberno English known as *after*-perfect, in a spatial perspective adopting the structure proposed by Cinque (2010). The *after*-perfect is made up of a tensed form of the verb *to be*, the preposition *after* and a lexical verb in the *-ing* form.

Unsurprisingly, several temporal prepositions in English are used also in locative contexts (cf. *at home / at midnight; on the table / on Monday; in the garden / in (the) Summer*, etc.). In the case of *after*, it is the etymology itself that confirms the exquisitely spatial nature: *after* derives from Old English æfter, a compound of *of/af* 'off' designating origin (cf. Latin *ab*, Greek *apo-*) and the IE comparative element *-TER. Thus, *after* originally means 'more away than, further off than', (cf. also the *Old English Dictionary* s. *after*).

In order to adopt a highly detailed structure also for the temporal PP, similar to the structure proposed by Cinque (2010) for the spatial PP, Berizzi and Rossi (2013) propose that the temporal preposition *after* defines a portion of the temporal line in relation to a specific moment, an event or a time span. In (38a), for example, *after* defines a portion of the temporal line that is placed after the specific moment / event represented by *Christmas, the party*, and *midnight*. These events, which are syntactically the complement of the preposition *after*, are hosted in Ground, while *after* is one of the modifiers of Ground, and more precisely, an axial modifier hosted in AxPartP, as can be seen in (38b):

(38) a. *We met after Christmas / the party / midnight*
 b. *We met* [PPdir [PPstat AT [DPplace [AxPartP after AxPart° [PP P° [NPplace *Christmas*, etc. [PLACE/TIME]

As seen at the beginning of the present work, the expressions of temporal distance of anteriority in Italian, that is to say, those expressions with *fa* and *prima* in which a quantified element is present, show interesting differences.

In the case of *fa* the reference time, that is the Ground, corresponds to the UT, and the element is thus to be considered deictic, while in the case of *prima*, the Ground does not coincide with the UT, but is represented by a temporal event, recoverable from the linguistic context, ('half an hour before lunch') and the expression is therefore to be considered anaphoric.

In the light of these considerations, a finely detailed structure of the spatial/temporal PP permits us to interpret quantified temporal elements such as *three days / two months / half an hour* as purely 'metric' expressions hosted in the Spec of DegP, a projection in which elements expressing 'measure' are usually located (as *ten meters* in the spatial PP *ten meters behind the house*). The deictic particle *fa* is hosted in DeicticP (cf. (39a)), the projection dedicated to deictic elements, as *qua* ('here') in the spatial PP *qua sotto al tavolo* 'here under the table'; the anaphoric element *prima* is hosted in the Spec of AxPArtP (cf. (39b)), as *dopo* 'after' in *ci siamo incontrati dopo Natale* 'we met after Christmas':

(39) a. [PPdir [PPstat AT [DPPlace [DegP *three days*, etc. [DeicticP fa [AxPartP [PP P
[NPPlace Ground 'UT' [TIME]...]
b. [PPdir [PPstat AT [DPPlace [DegP *three days* etc.[DeicticP [AxPartP prima [PP P [NPPlace Ground 'event' [TIME]...]

Interestingly, at a first glance, the structure of the spatial PP does not seem to be entirely transferrable to the temporal PP. Consider the following contrast:

(40) a. *mezzo metro qua sotto*
'half a meter here under'
b. **tre giorni fa prima*
'*three days ago before'

In the spatial PP in (40a) the deictic element *qua* can be followed by the axial *sotto* 'under', while in the temporal PP in (40b) the deictic element *fa* cannot be followed by the axial *prima*.

This asymmetry might be related to Haspelmath's (1997) observation that time is not only mono-dimensional, but also unidirectional, differently from space. If we think of space as a temporal line with a single direction, that is a single vector, the insertion of the deictic element *fa* would permit to orient the vector towards the past, so that the lower part containing the axial specification would become unavailable. The result is that the Ground could not be axially defined. This constraint is not active in the spatial PP, due to the fact that Space has at least other two dimensions that can be axially defined, also in presence of a deictic element, as in *qui dietro al tavolo* 'here behind the table', *qua sopra* 'over here', etc. The temporal PP instead, being time mono-dimensional and unidirectional, cannot exploit this possibility. An apparent counter-example to this conclusion on temporal PP comes from the observation that the sentence (40b) becomes fully acceptable if the event modified by the axial is found in Ground, as in (41):

(41) *otto giorni fa prima della tua partenza*
'three days ago before your departure'

Apparently, the sentence contains two different objects of reference, that is to say two Grounds: the TMeas for *fa* 'ago', and the event *la tua partenza* 'your departure' for *prima* 'before'. Probably, a more detailed and rich structure is needed to represent the intuition that *prima della tua partenza* in (41) is a further specification of the event, similar to a structurally external adposition to the phrase.¹⁰

Many other aspects must be left to future investigation, such as the role of the higher part of the temporal PP, the same functional part that encodes directionality and stativity in the locative PP. We can suppose that in the temporal PP this is the same area in which directionality and presumably information concerning future and past are encoded.

Future deixis, for example, raises a number of specific problems compared to past deixis. In the case of deixis expressed by *tra/fra* 'in' and *entro* 'by' followed by an elements of temporal measure, we observe that the only possible order is DeicticP-DegP (*tra tre giorni, entro tre giorni*), the opposite order displayed by past deixis with *fa* as in *tre giorni fa*, DegP-DeicticP. Both with *tra* and *entro* we have a quantified time span in DegP (*tre giorni*) which represents the object of reference. The initial moment of the time span corresponds in both cases to the UT, but with *tra* the event is supposed to take place in a moment that coincides with the final moment of the time span, while with *entro* the event is expected to take place at any moment within the time span.

Considering that the prepositions *tra / fra* and *entro* seem to act as axial modifiers, it is not clear what element is responsible for the interpretation of future deixis and more generally how we can account for the asymmetry between past and future deixis. The time span that is selected in the interpretation of future deixis seems to be a crucial aspect if we consider the cases in which *dopo* 'after' occurs without expression of measure. In *mangio dopo*, for example, *dopo* selects that portion of temporal line that comes after the Ground, that is after UT, but the portion of the temporal line is not a half-line that tends to infinity: the event must take place within a specific time space, which can be the morning, the afternoon, or the day (as we have seen above for *prima* 'before').

An interesting element that might contribute to a sophisticated representation of the temporal PP is the deictic *ago* in English (*three years ago*). Similarly to *fa*, *ago* derives from the grammaticalization of a verb, the Old English verb *go*, more precisely the participle form *agan, agone* 'left, gone'.

---

10 It must be underlined that we have used an 'event noun' like *partenza* "departure" in the formula in (41), but the same structure can appear with non-eventive nouns, such as *Pasqua, compleanno, maggio*:

(i) *Otto giorni fa prima di Pasqua / del tuo compleanno*
    'three days ago before Easter / your birthday, May'

We do not have, then, consistent reasons to hypothesize here restrictions on conjunctions under the event semantics, as suggested by a reviewer.

Undoubtedly, the prefix *a-* of the verbal forms *a-gan* / *a-gone* is diachronically connected to a spatial element found in several Germanic languages. If we look at the example in (42), we notice that *ago* precedes – and does not follow as in modern English – the measure of time:

42) *It was ago fif ȝer Þat he was last þer* (c1330 Guy of Warwick: *Oxford English Dictionary* s. *ago*).
 'It was ago five years that he was last there.'

Further research is needed in order to establish a correspondence between the order *ago* – TMeas and the occurrence of *ago* in non-deictic contexts, as we have seen is the case for *fa* in Old Italian and Spanish.

Differently from *fa*, *ago* admits a non-strictly deictic interpretation, as shown by the examples in (43), where *ago* has an anaphoric point of reference:

(43) a. *She'd retired about eighteen months ago* (W. Trevor, *Mathilda's England*, London: Penguin 1995, p. 57).
 b. *in a green avenue where a duel was rumored to have been fought many deem years ago* (V. Nabokov, *Speak, Memory*, London: Penguin 1998, p. 149).

Examples like these are not numerous, but very natural, as confirmed by various native speakers, who judged these sentences fully acceptable.

7 Conclusions

In this paper we have compared the locutions used to express temporal distance in the past as they appear in some Romance languages and dialects and in English, including some aspects of the old stages of these languages. Comparing minimally different elements and their detailed properties we aimed at a deeper understanding of the structures analyzed and a more abstract description of the functions of the elements involved.

Our analysis has shown that the presence of deictic or anaphoric features accounts for the different behaviour of the locutions. Temporal measure locutions are inherently relational; they provide a measure of time that must refer to points of reference, which can be either recoverable from the context or coinciding with the Utterance Time.

We have compared synchronic Romance data and data from Old Romance languages, first of all Old Italian. We have shown that modern Spanish has preserved the old construction, and is exactly parallel to Old Italian. In Old Italian and in Modern Spanish, the expressions that provide the temporal measure in the past are dependent clauses headed by a fully verbal form of the "make" (*fare, hacer*, etc.) or the "be" type (*ora è, orsono,* etc.); the verbal inflection depends on the tense of the main clause, and agrees with the number of time units used to localize the event in the past. In modern Italian, and other Romance varieties, the head of the expression seems to be a frozen particle, resulting from a grammaticalisation process of the original verb, as in Italian *fa, orsono*. At first sight, it seems that the particle is just a sort of 'place holder' which triggers a deictic relationship with the time of the event. But at a closer examination, one has to conclude that the particle has deictic features which derive from the older verbal form. Then, the process of grammaticalisation that affected the verbal forms, has not deleted the present indicative feature, which becomes the point of reference of temporal measure.

The grammaticalization process is strictly connected with a fixation of the surface order of *fa* etc. with respect to the TMeas: in Old Italian, and in Modern Spanish, the TMeas follows *fa, (or)sono*, while in Modern Italian it precedes it. The same happens in English: the TMeas follows the parallel form *ago* in Old English, and it precedes it in Modern English.

The comparison with English, whose temporal expressions and their diachronic evolutions are largely parallel to the Romance ones, also provides a basis for a further development of the analysis of these structures. We have tried to determine the position of their elements in the functional structure of a temporal PP, which seems to mimic the locative PP, as has been hypothesized within different frameworks. Interestingly, what seems to emerge is that the locative nature of many temporal adverbials plays a relevant role in the organization of the temporal space and consequently in the availability of different interpretations (deictic / anaphoric).

The idea of a precise correspondence between the two dimensions – spatial and temporal – is undoubtedly attractive, but many crucial aspects remain currently unclear and are thus left to future research.

In conclusion, an aspect that we like to underline is something that was clear to the dialectologists of the 19th–20th Century: synchronic data, the distribution in the space of variants of a given linguistic form or construction, represent in the space the stages that the forms have passed through in their diachronic evolution, and the two dimensions enlighten each other.

References

Andreose, Alvise. 2010. Il sintagma preposizionale. In Giampaolo Salvi & Lorenzo Renzi (eds.), *Grammatica dell'italiano antico*, 617—714. Bologna: Il Mulino.
Benincà, Paola & Laura Vanelli. 2014. *Settecento anni fa non si diceva così*. L'espressione della distanza temporale nel passato in italiano antico e moderno. In Paul Danler & Christine Konecny (eds.), *Dall'architettura della lingua italiana all'architettura linguistica dell'Italia*, 23–44. Frankfurt am Main: Peter Lang.
Berizzi, Mariachiara, & Silvia Rossi. 2013. The syntax of the After Perfect in Hiberno-English. In Catrin S. Rhys, Pavel Iosad, & Alison Henry (eds.), *Minority languages, microvariation, minimalism and meaning* (Proceedings of the Irish Network in Formal Linguistics), 53–70. Newcastle upon Tyne: Cambridge Scholars.
Bosque, Ignacio & Violeta Demonte. 1999. *Gramatica Ddescriptiva de la lengua española*. Madrid: Editorial Espasa.
Brugè Laura & Avellina Suñer. 2010. La cartografía de las partículas temporales complejas antes y después. In Alicia Avellana (ed.), *Actas del V Encuentro de Gramática Generativa*, 1. 153—172. Editorial Universitaria del Comahue.
Cinque, Guglielmo. 1999. *Adverbs and functional heads*. New York and Oxford: Oxford University Press.
Cinque, Guglielmo. 2010. Introduction. In Guglielmo Cinque & Luigi Rizzi (eds.), *Mapping spatial PPs*, 3–25. New York & Oxford: Oxford University Press.
Corver, Norbert F. M. 2009. Getting the (syntactic) measure of measure phrases. *The Linguistic Review* 26, 67–134. http://norbert.abelcorver.com/wp-content/uploads/2010/10/TLRCOR-VERMeasurePhrase.pdf
den Dikken, Marcel. 2006. On the functional structure of locative and directional PPs. CUNY manuscript.
Franco, Ludovico. 2012. Movement triggers and the etiology of grammaticalization: the case of Italian postposition *fa*. *Sintagma* 24. 65–83 http://www.sintagma.udl.cat/export/sites/Sintagma/documents/articles_24/franco.pdf
Freddi, Lucia. 1997. *La struttura della frase nel francese popolare. I costrutti marcati all'inizio*. Padova: Università di Padova, Tesi di Laurea.
Haspelmath, Martin. 1997. *From space to time. Temporal adverbials in the world's languages* (Lincom Studies in Theoretical Linguistics). Munich & Newcastle: Lincom Europa.
Jackendoff, Ray. 1996. The architecture of the linguistic-spatial interface. In Paul Bloom, Mary A. Peterson, Lynn Nadel & Mary F. Garrett (eds.), *Language and space*, 1–30. Cambridge, MA: MIT Press.
Koopman, Hilda. 2000. Prepositions, postpositions, circumpositions, and particles. In Hilda Koopman, (ed.), *The syntax of specifiers and heads*, 204–260. London: Routledge.
van Riemsdijk, Henk. 1990. Functional prepositions. In Harm Pinkster & Inge Genée (eds.), *Unity in diversity. Festschrift for Simon Dik*, 229–242. Dordrecht: Foris.
Rizzi, Luigi. 2001. Il sintagma preposizionale. In Lorenzo Renzi, Giampaolo Salvi & Anna Cardinaletti (eds.), *Grande grammatica italiana di consultazione*, I, 521–545. Bologna: Il Mulino.
Roy, Isabelle & Peter Svenonius. 2008. Complex prepositions. http://ling.auf.net/lingbuzz/000850

Salvi, Giampaolo. 2013. *Le parti del discorso*. Roma: Carocci editore.

Scorretti, Mauro. 1981. Complementizer ellipsis in 15th Century Italian. *Journal of Italian Linguistics* 6 (1). 35–47.

Svenonius, Peter. 2006. The emergence of axial parts. In Peter Svenonius & Marina Pantcheva (eds.), *Adpositions*, 49–77. [Working Papers in Linguistics Special issue 33(1)]. Nordlyd: Tromsø. www.hum.uit.no/mra/papers/pdf/Svenonius06AxParts.pdf

Svenonius, Peter. 2010. Spatial P in English. In Guglielmo Cinque & Luigi Rizzi (eds.), *Mapping spatial PPs*, 127–160. New York & Oxford: Oxford University Press.

Tortora, Christina. 2005. The preposition's preposition in Italian: evidence for boundedness of space. In Randall Gess & Edward J. Rubin (eds.), *Theoretical and experimental approaches to Romance linguistics*, 307–327. Amsterdam: John Benjamins.

Tortora, Christina. 2006. On the aspect of space: The case of PLACE in Italian and Spanish. In Nicoletta Penello & Diego Pescarini (eds.), *Atti dell'undicesima giornata di dialettologia* (Quaderni di lavoro ASIS 5), 50–69. Padova: Consiglio Nazionale delle Ricerche. http://asis-cnr.unipd.it/ql-5.it.html

Tortora, Christina. 2008. Aspect inside PLACE PPs. In Anna Asbury, Jakub Dotlačil, Berit Gehrke & Rick Nouwen (eds.), *The syntax and semantics of spatial P.*, 273–301. Amsterdam: John Benjamins.

Vanelli, Laura. 2001. La deissi. In Lorenzo Renzi, Giampaolo Salvi & Anna Cardinaletti (eds.), *Grande grammatica italiana di consultazione* III, 261–350. Bologna: Il Mulino.

Vanelli, Laura. 2002a. Alcune espressioni temporali in italiano antico. In Gian Luigi Beccaria & Carla Marello (eds.), *La parola al testo. Scritti per Bice Mortara Garavelli*, 463–479. Alessandria: Edizioni dell'Orso.

Vanelli, Laura. 2002b. Oggi fa l'anno che nel ciel salisti: l'espressione della distanza temporale nel passato in italiano antico. *Verbum* 4 (2). 36–376.

Vanelli, Laura. 2010. La deissi. In Giampaolo Salvi & Lorenzo Renzi (eds.), *Grammatica dell'italiano antico* II, 1247–1288. Bologna: Il Mulino.

M. Rita Manzini and Leonardo M. Savoia
N inflections and their interpretation: Neuter -*o* and plural -*a* in Italian varieties

1 Introduction: A framework syntactic theory for N

This article is placed within the syntactic framework of Chomsky (1995, 2000, 2001, 2013). We assume that the same basic computational mechanisms underlie syntax and morphology, as in Distributed Morphology (DM, Halle and Marantz 1993). However, we assume that there is no separate Morphological Structure component in the sense of Halle and Marantz (1993: 114–115 ff.), capable of rearranging the syntax prior to vocabulary insertion. In other words, the syntax projects structures from actual lexical items – and no operations not licenced by a minimalist syntax (e.g. Impoverishment) can take place before lexical insertion. This stance is generally deemed to be too strong – but see Kayne (2010), Manzini and Savoia (2007, 2011) for arguments that it is quite sufficient (and necessary) to account for significant portions of the morphosyntax of Romance languages, for instance mesoclisis. Arregi and Nevins (2017) have recently labelled this theoretical position as the 'syntactic Occam's razor'.

The morphemic analysis of Indo-European nouns (Halle and Vaux 1998; Calabrese 1998b, 2008) individuates three components. The first component is a root, which following Marantz (1997) is category-less. The root is followed by a vocalic morpheme, which encodes gender and/or number and/or inflection class. A third slot may be available, specialized for number and/or case. For instance, Latin *rosarum* 'of the roses' can be decomposed as *ros-a-rum*, i.e. the root *ros-*, the inflectional class vowel *-a-* and the plural genitive *-(r)um* suffix; Spanish *libros* 'books' is formed by the root *libr-* followed by the thematic vowel *-o-* and by the number inflection -*s*.

The consensus in the literature (Picallo 2008; cf. Déchaine et al. 2014 on Bantu nominal classes, Fassi Fehri 2015 on Arabic) is that at least two functional projections are needed – corresponding roughly to gender and number. In homage to the cross-linguistic comparison with Bantu languages (and possibly with Chinese classifiers, Crisma et al. 2011), the lower category is often labelled Class.[1]

---

[1] The similarity holds despite the fact that most Romance languages have just two sex-based classes while Bantu languages typically have a dozen or more classes, based not only on sex and animacy but also on size, shape etc. In the words of Déchaine et al's (2014:19): "By definition, the lower bound of an N-class partition is two. But there is no upper bound. This is because class

https://doi.org/10.1515/9781501506734-012

The higher category is Num, as illustrated in (1) (alternatively, Carstens 2008 treats Bantu nominal classes as genders).²

(1)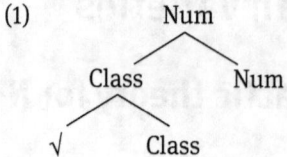

A variant on the schema in (1) takes Class to identify with Marantz's (1997) nominalizing category *n* (Kihm 2005; Ferrari Bridgers 2008; Kramer 2014, 2015). However even scholars who embrace *n* do not necessarily agree on this point; for instance, Déchaine et al. place *n* lower than Class (or NAsp in their terms). Furthermore, though we adopted the traditional Class/gender vs. Number categorization in (1), Borer (2005) identifies number with Div (count) property falling within the set of classifiers. Déchaine et al. (2014) incorporate this conclusion in their structure for N(P), by assuming that Class is a field of categories including at least two projections, for sortal Class elements (gender) and for count/mass Class elements (number). In any event, at least two different positions appear to be needed.

Following Higginbotham (1985), the category-less root is interpreted as a predicate. The predicate represented by the root in turn has one open argument place (the R-role, Williams 1994), which is ultimately bound by a D/Q operator. Gender (and number) specifications, and in general classifiers, restrict the argument *x* open at the predicate. Specifically, Percus (2011) entertains the possibility of a conjunctive semantics for the (root, gender) pair.

Extra complexity arises in Indo-European languages from the fact that there is no one-to-one mapping between the content of Class – which enters agreement with determiners and modifiers of N, and the inflections immediately following the root. The latter are instead sensitive to inflectional class. The treatment of inflectional class by Oltra-Massuet and Arregi (2005), Kramer (2015) has a

---

partition is subset formation, with each class/subset defined by a particular semantic feature ... And since the set of semantic features is not fixed, languages vary with respect to which features, and how many, they recruit for N-classes".

2 Note that the tree is left-branching. Indeed, we do not assume that trees are necessarily right-branching (Kayne 1994), nor that head movement is necessary to insure mirror orders. Rather we follow Chomsky (2013) in assuming that the only syntactic ordering relation is dominance. Precedence is introduced at externalization, and we assume that it can yield a left-branching or a right-branching structure.

Th(ematic vowel) node adjoined to Class/*n* postsyntactically. The content of Th are diacritics such as [I] for I inflectional class, etc. and the latter are in turn spelled out as *-a, -o*, etc. (e.g. in Latin, in Spanish, etc.). The countercyclic adjunction of Th after the syntactic derivation (contra Chomsky's (1995) Extension Condition) takes place in the Morphological Structure component, in the sense of Halle and Marantz (1993: 114–115 ff.), and is not compatible with the present framework.

The structures that we will be using throughout are introduced in (2) for Italian *gatt-o* 'he-cat' and *gatt-a* 'she-cat'. We assign the inflectional vowel of Italian to an Infl position (our own label) which embeds both the root and the Class node. The property 'cat' is compatible with both a feminine and a masculine Class, depending on the sex denoted.

(2)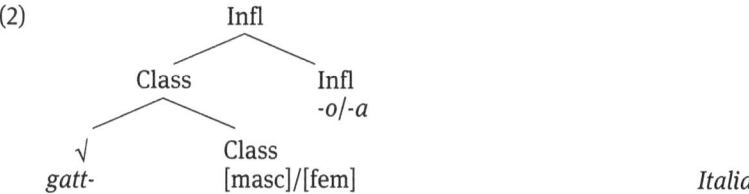
                                Italian

While languages like Spanish have an independent lexicalization for the plural, namely *-s*, in Italian pluralization is obtained by a change of the inflectional morpheme. Following Manzini and Savoia (2017a, 2017b and references quoted there), we formalize plurality in terms of the ⊆ property, saying that the denotatum of the predicate can be partitioned into subsets. In these terms the plural of *gatto/gatta* in (2), namely *gatti* 'cats' *gatt-e* 'she-cats' has the structure in (3a), where the plural ⊆ property is construed as part of the Class node, exactly like gender specifications.

(3)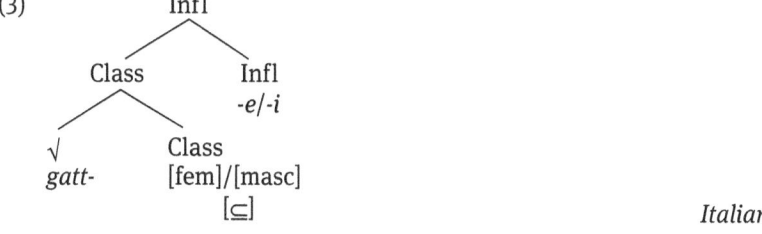
                                Italian

On the other hand, if we keep identifying the vocalic inflection of Spanish with the Infl position, it is evident that the specialized *-s* segment for plurality in Spanish must occur on top of Infl itself, as schematized for *libros/libras* 'books/pounds' in (4).

(4)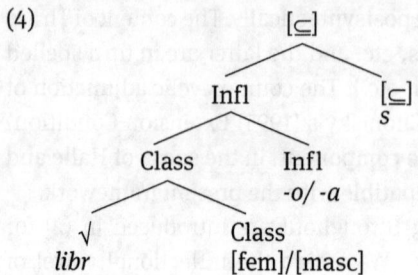
Spanish

The (⊆) property contributes plurality as schematized in (5) for structure (3) – namely by isolating a subset of the set (or set of sets) of all things that are 'cat'; in other words, (⊆) says that subsets can be partitioned off the set (the property) denoted by the lexical base.

(5) ∃x   [x (⊆) {cat}]
i.e. 'there is an x such that x is a subset of the set of individuals with the property 'cat'

A prediction generated from (3)–(4) is that since number may be expressed either by Class/Infl or by the specialized [⊆] node, it may be realized by both nodes at once. The prediction is not difficult to verify. For instance, Savoia et al. (2017) report data from Sardinian varities where the plural of nouns follows the Spanish system. Thus masculine singular *att-u* 'cat' pluralizes by the addition of the plural *-s/z* inflection in (a-a') and so does feminine singular *vemmin-a* 'woman'. Yet in the determiner system plurality is expressed by the *i* inflectional vowel, which can be seen to combine with the sigmatic plural in the pre-vocalic context in (5'c') yielding the duplication of the two plural morphemes *i-s/z* 'the(pl)'.

(5') a. s-u   att-u   a'. i   ɣatt-u-zu
       Det-M.SG   cat-M.SG   Det-PL   cat-M-PL
       'the cat'   'the cats'
    b. s-a   vemmin-a   b'. i   ʃemmin-a-za
       Det-FSG   woman-F.SG   Det-PL   woman-F-PL
       'the woman'   'the women'
    c. s   oriɣ-a   c'. iz   oriɣ-a-za
       Det   ear-F.SG   Det-PL   ear-F-PL
       'the ear'   'the ears'   *Orroli*

The layered structuring of gender is independently advocated in current literature. For Steriopolo and Wiltschko (2012), gender can be distributed over at least three nodes, namely the root, the *n* node and the D node (cf. also the Inner and Outer NAsp of Dèchaine et al 2014). Fassi Fehri (2015) discusses Arabic *-at*, which has both a singulative and a plurative use. In the singulative use, *-at* forms a Noun "denoting a discrete unit entity from a kind ... base, and it controls feminine agreement", as in *naḥl-at* 'bee-unit/a bee' from *naḥl* 'bee/bees'. In the plurative use *-at* "forms a group or a collection individual" from an individual, as in *saakin-at* 'inhabitants/population' from *saakin* 'inhabitant'. For Fassi Fehri, singulative *-at* is merged in Class under Num; plurative *-at* results from a reversal of the structure where gender takes scope over number.

Let us then assume that we have a working model of the categories and structures involved in nominal inflection. This still leaves several questions. One has to do with the correct pairing of roots with their gender. Indeed, the gender is not necessarily predictable from the root – even when sexed referents are involved. Thus Italian *la guida* 'the guide' is feminine even when referring to a male guide – and Italian *il contralto* is masculine even when referring to a female singer (as it normally does). The other problem has to do with pairing root, gender and number units with their appropriate inflection.

In order to proceed with the discussion, it is worth noting that the various matches required can be obtained, if necessary, by stipulation – without recourse to anything but the standard syntactic mechanism of selection. For Kramer (2015) the diacritics [I], [II], [III] in, say, Spanish, are inserted under Th and then interpreted as vocalic endings, namely *-a* for [II], etc. Technically the rule that inserts the class diacritics is sensitive to the context determined by certain sets of roots: insert *-e* in the context √*padr*, √*madr*, etc. But this means that we are in the presence of a selectional restriction. Indeed, this is the position taken by Kayne (2010: 73–74). Furthermore, Kramer (2015: 54) explicitly endorses the view that gender she terms 'arbitrary', is selected by the root. A similar approach is suggested by Acquaviva (2009: 5), namely that "morphological and semantic information can be dependent on the choice of a root without being encoded on the root itself". To say that "a noun has gender X", for instance, means in this perspective "a root Vocabulary item is licensed in the context of [n] with gender X". In other words, the standard syntactic notion of selectional restriction is powerful enough to encode the fact that a certain Class content is associated with a certain lexical base and not with others.

Theorists generally agree that Class/*n* is sometimes interpreted and sometimes not (i.e. it is arbitrary). We reject modelling in terms of the [interpretable] feature (Kramer 2015), since this cannot be understood as an extension of the [interpretable] feature of Chomsky (1995ff.). According to Chomsky, a given category is never associated with both interpretable and uninterpretable features; for instance, N is always associated with interpretable phi-features, while *v* or T are always associated with uninterpretable phi-features. In the same way, we would expect Class/*n* to be always interpretable or always uninterpretable – which is precisely not the case.

Interpreted gender arises in two configurations. First, in examples like Italian *donn-a* 'woman' (feminine) or *marit-o* 'husband' (masculine), the root contains female vs. male sex properties which are matched by feminine and masculine Class respectively. Furthermore, there are human and other animate terms, which are in principle compatible with either sex denotation and can co-occur with either gender. In this instance, choice of gender determines reference to sex as in *gatt-o, gatt-a* in (4) or, to take a human referent, *zi-o* 'uncle', masculine vs. *zi-a* 'aunt', feminine. In other words, we may simplify matters by assuming that all gender is alike; its composition with the root yields a sex interpretation only in case the root has the relevant content. Therefore, interpreted gender is a property of the configuration or ultimately of the root, not of the Class feature.

Summarizing so far, a Noun results from the merger of a root with a Class system including such partitions as masculine/feminine (or conventional gender) and count/mass (or conventional number), while inflectional classes are taken into account by a node Infl (our label). Selection restrictions account for the matching of certain roots with certain Classes and with certain Infls. As desired, the framework is entirely syntax internal and is sufficient to yield N structures like those in (3)–(5') covering the Romance languages, which are our object of study here.

2 Neuter -*o*

In this section we consider the so-called 'neuter gender' of Central Italian varieties (Rohlfs 1968 [1949]: §419), associated with the -*o* inflection, which has been observed to correlate with mass content. Thus on the one hand, a Class category like the traditional neuter, seems to have a content related to the interpretive count/mass distinction. On the other hand, some inflectional morphology, here -*o*, may specialize for a given Class (neuter/mass). This potentially calls into question the idea that inflectional class endings are pure morphological devices and suggests that they may have a stake in the syntactico-semantic economy of the Noun.

In the variety of Monte Giberto (Marche), three genders are traditionally distinguished both on Ds and on lexical categories (nouns, adjectives, participles).

We begin by illustrating the feminine gender in (6). This is shown to determine agreement with Ds and As in (6a), with unaccusative perfect participles in (6b) and with the clitic 'her' in (6c).

(6) a. l-a vokk-a rapɛrt-a
    the-F.SG mouth-F.SG open-F.SG
    'the open mouth'
  b. ɛ vvinut-a
    is come-F.SG
    'She has come'
  c. l-a ɣatt-a a l-a veðo
    the-F.SG cat-F.SG Cl her-F.SG I.see
    'I see the cat'   *Monte Giberto*

The masculine gender is exemplified in (7). It again determines agreement with determiners and adjectives in (7a-b), with unaccusative perfect participles in (7c) and with the clitic 'him' in (7d).

(7) a. l-u nas-u ruʃʃ-u
    the-M.SG nose-M.SG red-M.SG
    'the red nose'
  b. kwill-u ka ɛ bbell-u
    that-M.SG dog.M.SG is beautiful-M.SG
    'That dog is beautiful'
  c. ɛ vvinut-u un ɔm-u
    has come-M.SG a man-M.SG
    'A man has come'
  d. l-u ka a l-u veðo
    the-M.SG dog.M.SG Cl him-M.SG I.see
    'I see the dog'   *Monte Giberto*

The traditional neuter gender is exemplified in (8). Neuter agreement can be seen on determiners in (8a), on adjectives in (8b) and on unaccusative perfect participles in (8d). (8c) shows that a mass noun belonging to the *-e* class like *latt-* 'milk' triggers the dedicated *-o* neuter inflection on determiners and adjectives – from which it can be inferred that the noun has the neuter property.

(8) a. l-o kaʃ-o
    the-N.SG cheese-N.SG
    'the cheese'

b. kwell-o/l-o   vi(n-o)   vɛcc-o/roʃʃ-o
    that-N.SG/the-N.SG wine-N.SG   old-n.sg/red-N.SG
    'that/the old/red wine'
c. ɛ   kkaʃkat-o   l-o   pa
    has   fallen-N.SG the-N.SG   bread.N.SG
    'The bread dropped'
d. l-o   latt-e   jattʃ-o
    the-N.SG   milk-N.SG   cold-N.SG
    'The cold milk'   Monte Giberto

In addition, neuter agreement -o is found as the invariable inflection on participles of meteorological verbs, as in (8'd), of unergative verbs, as in (8'b), and of transitive verbs with lexical objects, as in (8'd). Furthermore, in (8'a) it is found as the inflection of the clitic *l-o* 'it' with eventive/propositional denotation. Indeed, the verb *sapere* 'know' in Italian takes only propositional complements; 'know' with individual complements is *conoscere*. Importantly, the data in (8)–(8') show that all neuters are mass terms in Center-South Italian varieties (the same holds in Ibero-Romance). However, the reverse is not true – in other words masculine and feminine nouns may be mass or count.

(8') a. l-o   sapete
        it-N.SG   you.know
        'You know it'
    b. sɔ   ddurmit-o
        I.am   slept-N.SG
        'I have slept'
    c. sɔ   rrapɛrt-o   l-a   pɔrt-a
        I.am   opened-N.SG   the-F.SG   door-F.SG
        'I have opened the door'
    d. a   pjɔt-o
        it.has   rained-N.SG
        'It has rained'   Monte Giberto

The data in (9) illustrate a different type of language, in which the -o inflection is limited to the determiners. In the Mascioni (Abruzzo) variety, the mass noun *vin-u* 'wine' is associated with -u inflection, as is the adjective modifying it in (9b). However, all of the determiners of the noun have a different -o inflection, which in the Mascioni language is uniquely associated with determiners of mass nouns. Similarly, in (9c) the pronoun can only refer to a mass referent (not to an individual).

(9) a. l-o/   kweʃt-o/   kwell-o   vin-u
        the-N.SG/this-N.SG/that-N.SG   wine-M.SG
        'the/this/that wine'
    b. kwell-o   vin-u   vecc-u
        that-N.SG   wine-M.SG   old-M.SG
        'that old wine'
    c. l-o   viju
        it-N.SG I.see
        'I see it'   *Mascioni*

In traditional terms, in a language like that of *Monte Giberto* there are three genders, namely masculine, feminine and neuter – for instance, *-o* corresponds to neuter gender in the traditional sense of the terms, deprived of any interpretive significance, for Loporcaro and Paciaroni (2011). The neuter corresponds to the Elsewhere gender, so that it will show up in environments where invariable inflections are selected in Romance varieties, such as in (8'). Apart from this, however, it characterizes only mass nouns and eventive/propositional contents. This association of neuter with mass denotation appears to be a characteristic of Italo- and Ibero-Romance languages and is what makes them interesting to us here. This is not a characteristic of neuter even in closely related languages; thus Latin neuters include count inanimates such as *donum* 'gift' or even animates such as *animal* 'animal'.

Pomino and Stark (2009) discuss standard Spanish, where only Ds have the special, neuter inflection; Spanish therefore is essentially like Mascioni.[3] In their terms, the traditional neuter corresponds to a non-individuated property; feminine and masculine are subclasses of [+individuated]. However, as pointed out by Loporcaro and Paciaroni (2011), in Center-South dialects of the Monte Giberto type not all masculine or feminine Ns are count nouns; rather masculine and feminine nouns equally include mass terms. Kučerova and Moro (2011) address Center-South Italian data of the type of Mascioni in (9). According to them, "a mass noun is structurally an NP, and as such has no number projection", i.e. no DivP in the sense of Borer (2005). Furthermore, "since gender is dependent on number, mass nouns are necessarily genderless". In their words, "if a mass noun can be interpreted as <e,t> ... the overt agreement is realized as the morphological default. In our case we obtain M.SG. on predicative adjectives. In contrast, if the structure requires type <e>, ... an additional structure must be introduced. The

---

[3] Similarly, in Portuguese the neuter appears only in the paradigm of demonstratives, i.e. mass *isto/isso/aquilo* vs. count *êste/êsse/aquêle*.

marked morphological realization we see in these cases – our "third" gender – is a direct reflex of the last-resort semantic process implemented as a structural adjustment". The authors acknowledge that there is an implementation problem concerning 'structural adjustment'. Apart from this, Kučerova and Moro do not make clear what the relation between language with -*o* only on determiners, that they consider, and other types of Romance varieties may be, including for instance Monte Giberto.

Let us then apply the structural analysis in section 1 to Monte Giberto's examples in (8), for instance *lo kaʃo* 'the cheese'. Following Chierchia (2010), we construe mass status in terms of a notion of aggregate of parts. Specifically, the elementary [aggr] content applies to the root 'cheese' in (15a) saying that 'cheese' admits to be factored into smaller parts, i.e. under existential closure, there is some x such that x is a part of the whole 'cheese', as in (15b).

(10) a. [√*kaʃ*-] [Class aggr]
     b. there is an x such that x is a part of the whole 'cheese'

Thus we obtain a representation like (10), which does away with the traditional Class neuter in favour of the Class [aggr]. Therefore Classes triggering agreement in the Monte Giberto language include [masc], [fem] and [aggr]; agreement with respect to [aggr] can be seen to take place in (10') between the determiner and the noun. The -*o* inflection in turn corresponds to the presence of the Class node [aggr]. In fact, in the Monte Giberto language, the -*o* nominal inflection is strictly constrained to [aggr] contexts; therefore, it is actually possible to associate -*o* with Class content, as we have suggested in the lexical entry in (10'b).

(10') a.

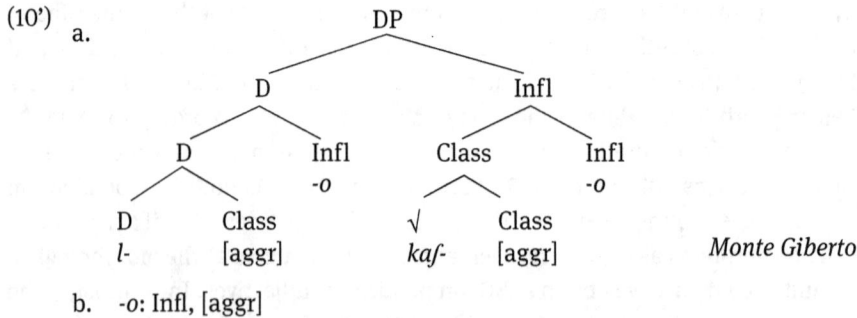

   Monte Giberto

b. -*o*: Infl, [aggr]

We mentioned at the outset the conception of number as a nominal class element Div proposed by Borer (2005). The analysis in (16) is incompatible with Borer's (2005) idea that mass status depends on the mere absence of the Div category (hence with Kucerova and Moro's analysis based on this idea). Rather mass has its own positively specified Class content – which is the same conclusion reached by Déchaine et al. (2014) for Bantu.[4]

We have seen in (8) that the neuter -*o* inflection on the determiner may combine with the -*e* inflection on the noun, as in *l-o latt-e* 'the milk'. We analyze the data as in (11). The mass base *latt-* is merged with the Class [aggr]; since agreement is governed by Class, the specialized -*o* [aggr] inflection can be seen to surface on the D. The reason why -*e* surfaces on *latt-* is that, as we have assumed in section 1, inflections partition lexical bases amongst themselves without any necessary correspondence with Class content. Thus -*e* selects *latt-* independently its Class content. However the D base, *l-*, is compatible with the -*a*, -*u*, -*o* set of inflections (or selected by them, if one prefers), leading to the surfacing of [aggr] Class agreement in (11).

(11)

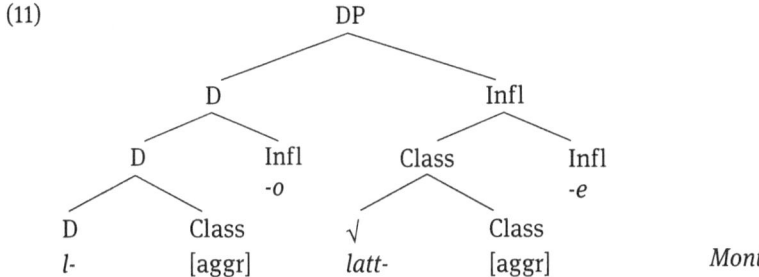

Monte Giberto

In the structures in (10)–(11) the property denoted by Class, i.e. mass/aggregate, restrict the argument open at the root; in other words the properties denoted by the root and by Class conjunctively apply to the argument. Therefore [aggr] is like the natural or interpreted gender associated with roots like 'cat' in section 1. What is interesting about the [aggr] Class is that it is always interpreted – unlike what is generally held of the feminine or masculine class. This raises the issue of -*o* occurring on pronouns referring to an event or a situation, as in *lo sapete* 'you know it', as in (8'). A tentative characterization of such examples can refer

---

4 An anonymous reviewer suggests that a negatively specified [-count] feature could be employed rather than the positively specified [aggr] property. There are two aspects to this proposal. One is formal; it may be noticed that we are using only positively specified (privative) features – in keeping with the privative characterization of syntactic categories. Another aspect of the issue is empirical. The anonymous reviewer suggests that eventive/propositional contents provide potential argument in favour of a negative characterization of the neuter (i.e. whatever it is, it is not count). We return to events in the text below.

to the closeness between mass terms, as aggregates of smaller unindividuated elements (Chierchia 2010), and the representation of the temporal continuum underlying an event, as 'aggregate[s] of components/ atoms of imaginable continuums (substances/ events)'. In other words, event/situation contents may be associated with the [aggr] Class – which in turn surfaces as the -o inflection with lexical bases, such as the l- D base, that are compatible with it.

The examples in (8') displaying -o on a perfect participle are more complex, since they involve a model of perfect participle agreement. Suppose we make the standard assumption (Chomsky 2000, 2001) that where the clitic agrees with the participle (e.g. ɛ vvinutu un ɔmu 'there has come a man') the participle in v has an agreement probe, whose closest goal is the internal argument clitic. In the examples in (8'), where the perfect participle takes the invariable -o inflection, we are forced to conclude that there is no suitable internal argument goal. This is obviously so with unergative verbs (e.g. durmito 'slept'), where there is no internal argument. The fact that Agree does not take place in transitive V-DP enviroments (e.g. sɔ rrapɛrto la pɔrta 'I have opend the door') corresponds to the generalization of Kayne (1989) whereby participial agreement in languages like Italian takes place only when the internal argument overtly raises to vP (or AgrO in Kayne's terms) for independent reasons (passivization, cliticization).

What is directly relevant for present purposes is what happens in the absence of an internal argument goal. The traditional approach to the invariable inflection showing up on the verb is to say that it is a morphological default. Recall however that we have concluded that events are treated like mass. This suggests an alternative to the view that invariable verb inflections are defaults. Thus in the absence of a suitable internal argument, the verb inflection may probe for the event argument that is also part of the argument structure of the verb according to event semantics (Higginbotham 2009). What we are offering is essentially an explanation of why neuter always ends up as the default agreement in languages that have it. In present terms, Agree with the Event shows up in the descriptive neuter, because mass terms and events share the common property of being aggregates and are therefore expected to correspond to the [aggr] Class. In other words, we explain why in (8') the participle take the same form as the pronoun referring to propositional content.

Summarizing so far, the descriptive neuter Class of the Monte Giberto language has an [aggr] content and the -o inflection has the same content, selecting only for mass/aggregate arguments. Let us then consider the Mascioni language, where mass nouns otherwise agreeing in the masculine are picked up by -o inflected Ds and -o inflected pronouns. In connection with *Mascioni*, it is useful to cast a glance back to Italian (3), where we assumed that gender properties and plural properties could both be hosted in Class. The characterization that we have proposed here for the Romance neuter has the further advantage that being a count/mass Class predicate, i.e. in traditional terminology a number property, it is not necessarily in complementary distribution with traditional gender properties.

Therefore, we propose the structure in (12) for Mascioni's *l-o vin-u* 'the wine'. The idea is that Mascioni's nouns may be associated with two different Class features, namely [aggr] and [masc] (see Ledgeway (2009) for a compatible approach to Neapolitan) – essentially like Italian 'cats' in (3) is associated with both [fem]/[masc] and [⊆] features. Crucially *-o*, which we assume specializes for [masc] [aggr], is available only for a few D bases (*l-, kweʃt-, kwill-*). With those bases, [masc] [aggr] agreement takes place. On the other hand, for the majority of bases [masc][aggr] agreement is not possible; these have [masc] agreement. What Mascioni crucially shares with Monte Giberto is that *-o* has a specialized entry for [aggr] (and [masc]) which means that it will surface in [aggr] agreement contexts like (12).[5]

(12)

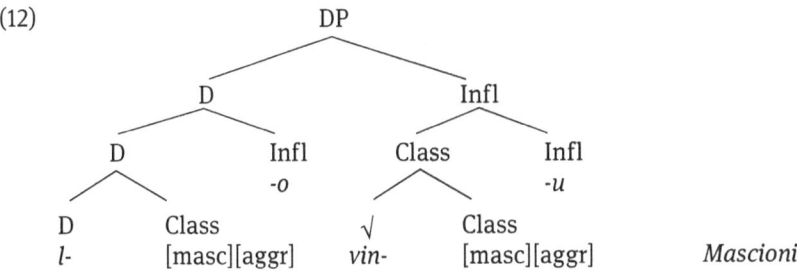

Mascioni

From a theoretical point of view, the main conclusion that emerges from the descriptive neuter of Central Italian varieties is that it is best characterized in terms of a number-like [aggr] property. This property is connected to the mass nature of the lexical base with which it merges; hence it is similar to non-arbitrary gender, which depends on the intrinsic sex properties of the bases to which it attaches. The reason why this result is appealing is that it strengthens the idea that (root, Class) structures have an interpreted core. The latter remains accessible to the computation even in languages with a highly impoverished Class system and therefore a largely arbitrary partition of lexical bases among nominal Classes. An accessory conclusion is that the *-o* inflectional vowel, and the inflectional class it defines, are associated only with [aggr] content. This means that Class content

---

5 The structure in (12) raises the obvious question why there wouldn't be a Class [fem] [aggr]. We will return to this matter in discussing the interaction between the I class *-a* inflection and the [aggr] Class in section 3.2.

may be transparently related to inflectional exponents even in Romance, even though in these languages (and in Indo-European languages generally) inflectional exponents are normally opaque with respect to Class, and directly reflect only a partition of lexical bases among declension classes.

3 Plural -*a*

Consider the nominal inflection vowel -*a* in Indo-European languages (see Clackson 2007 for a review of the question in historical terms). In Latin and Classical Greek, -*a* is associated with feminine singular and with neuter plural. A comparison can usefully be made with other language families that have genders, for instance the Semitic languages (Fassi Fehri 2015; Kramer 2015), which display the same syncretism between feminine singular and plural (non-gender specific), despite the fact that unrelated morphology is involved. In Italian, -*a* appears in the feminine singular, as in (13a); however (apart from occurrences as masculine singular, e.g. *poet-a* 'poet'), it also introduces the plural of a small set of nouns, as illustrated in (13d). The singular of these nouns is masculine, as in (13b) and it sometimes displays a regular masculine plural with a pure count interpretation such as (13c), while in this instance the -*a* plural is interpreted as collective. Romance languages have only two target genders (in the sense of Corbett 1991), namely masculine and feminine – and the -*a* plural agrees in the feminine with determiners and adjectives in (13d).

(13) a. l-a   cas-a   bianc-a
        the-F.SG   house-F.SG   white-F.SG
        'the white house'
    b. il   mur-o   solid-o
        the.M.SG   wall-M.SG   solid-M.SG
        'the wall'
    c. i   mur-i   solid-i
        the.M.PL   wall-M.PL   solid-M.PL
        'the solid walls (e.g. of the house)'
    d. l-e   mur-a   solid-e
        the-F.PL   wall-'A'PL   solid-F.PL
        'the solid walls (e.g. of Rome)'

As we saw in the previous sections, recent formal syntax and semantics studies revise the traditional oppositions of singular and plural, and of gender and number – yielding potential insights into their syncretism. First, underlying the standard number opposition singular/plural, there is an interpretive tripartition between mass nouns, count singulars and count plurals. More to the point mass singulars overlap in many respects with count plurals (Chierchia 2010). Another stream of generative literature (which occasionally overlaps with the previous one) calls into questions the tradition gender/number distinction. The similarity between the genders of, say, Romance languages and the nominal class system of Bantu has been remarked more than once by the literature (Kihm 2005; Carstens 2008; Déchaine et al. 2014). Genders and nominal classes are understood by the relevant literature to be essentially classification systems of nominal roots – and as such equivalent to (and perhaps formally unifiable with) classifiers proper. Recall now that for Borer (2005) number (*qua* countability), as formally represented by her category Div, is also a classifier. In this perspective, gender and number (countability) are simply different facets of nominal classification. We may therefore expect that there are syncretisms between them; indeed, a well-known fact about Bantu nominal classes is that there are no specialized number morphemes; the same morphology forms the singular of one class, and the plural of another.

So, on the one hand it is rather to be expected that the same exponent may lexicalize the apparently disjoint traditional categories of gender and number – conceived as manifestations of nominal class. On the other hand, it may also be expected that singular (qua mass singular) and plural may share a lexicalization.

For Italian we rely on the detailed studies of the two dozen or so -*a* plurals by Acquaviva (2008), Thornton (2010–11). Acquaviva (2008: 149–150) points out correctly that just one of them has collective meaning, namely *mura* in (13b). Some of the others are mass plurals (e.g. *budella* 'guts', *cervella* 'brains') and others yet denote body parts that naturally occur in pairs or sets (*labbra* 'lips', *membra* 'limbs'). Finally -*a* plurals characterize measure units (e.g. *paia* 'pairs', *migliaia* 'thousands'), leaving essentially only *uova* 'eggs' as a collection of individuals, (but "weakly differentiated ones" for Acquaviva). The empirical focus here will be on Central/Southern Italian varieties, where -*a* plurals are rather more productive.

3.1 Empirical evidence and previous approaches

Consider the variety of S. Gregorio Matese (Campania), which is relatively easy to process in that it preserves final vowels. This variety has a masculine agreement Class, corresponding to the -*u* and -*e* inflectional classes, as in (14) – and a feminine agreement Class, corresponding to the -*a* and -*e* inflections as in (15). In addition, there is a singular neuter, i.e. what we have called an [aggr] Class, morphologically distinguished only on Determiners of the noun, as illustrated in (16).

(14) a. r-u   jatt-u   a' r-i   jatt-i
        Det-M.SG cat-M.SG   Det-M.PL cat-M.PL
        'the cat'   'the cats'
    b. l-u   furn-u   b' r-i   furn-i
        Det-M.SG oven-M.SG   Det-M.PL oven-M.PL
        'the oven'   'the ovens'
    c. r-u   mes-e   c' r-i   mis-i
        Det-M.SG month-M.SG   Det-M.PL month-M.PL
        'the month'   'the months'
    d. r-u pɛr-e   d' r-i   per-i
        Det-M.SG foot-M.SG   Det-M.PL foot-M.PL
        'the foot'   'the feet'
    e. n-u rɛnt-e   e' r-i   rent-i
        Det-M.SG tooth-M.SG   Det-M.PL tooth-M.PL
        'a tooth'   'the teeth'

(15) a. l-a   kɔʃʃ-a   a' l-e   kɔʃʃ-e
        Det-F.SG thigh-F.SG   Det-F.PL thigh-F.PL
        'the thigh'   'the thighs'
    b. l   oɲɲ-a   b' l   oɲɲ-e
        Det-F.SG nail-F.SG   Det-F.PL nail-F.PL
        'the nail'   'the nails'
    c. l-a   noʃ-e   c' l-e   nuʃ-i
        Det-F.SG walnut-F.SG   Det-F.PL walnut-F.PL
        'the walnut'   'the walnuts'
    d. l-a   volep-e   d' l-e   vulip-i
        Det-F.SG fox-F.SG   Det-F.PL fox-F.PL
        'the fox'   'the foxes'

(16) a. l-o   kas-u   friʃk-u
        the-N.SG   cheese-M.SG   fresh-M.SG
        'the fresh cheese'
    b. l-o   sal-e   ɛ   kkarut-u
        the-N.SG   salt-M.SG   is   fallen-M.SG
        'The salt has tumbled down'   S. Gregorio Matese

What interests us here directly is the existence of -*a* plurals as in (17), whose singular counterparts belong to the masculine Class. The -*a* plurals trigger target feminine agreement on their determiners (and modifiers).

(17) a. r-u   riut-u   a' r-e   reut-a
        Det-M.SG   finger-M.SG   Det-M.PL   finger-'A'PL
        'the finger'   'the fingers'
     b. r-u   vratts-u   b' l-e   vratts-a
        Det-M.SG   arm-M.SG   Det-M.PL   arm-'A'PL
        'the arm'   'the arms'
     c. ov-o   c' ɔv-a
        egg-M.SG   egg-'A'PL
        'egg'   'eggs'   S. Gregorio Matese

Before proceeding to the analysis of the data, we illustrate the variety of Guardiaregia (Molise), where the data are quite robust,[6] though more difficult to process because of the neutralization of final vowels other than -a. The data in (18) exemplify the masculine class, those in (19) the feminine class, those in (20) the neuter singular, i.e. the [aggr] Class in the terms of section 2. The gender and number inflections of Guardiaregia are externalized on the determiners (pre-tonic, rather than final in the phonological word) and through metaphony of the stressed nucleus of the noun (Calabrese 1998a; Savoia 2015). Metaphony opposes etymological -u masculine and -i plural nouns, which present higher or tensed stressed nuclei, to other nouns, which present lower or laxed stressed nuclei.

(18) a. r-u   pɛt-ə   a' r-i   pet-ə
        Det-M.SG   foot-M.SG   Det-M.PL   foot-M.PL
        'the foot'   'the feet'
     b. r-u   marteʎʎ-ə   b' r-i   marteʎʎ-ə
        Det-M.SG   hammer-M.SG   Det-M.PL   hammer-M.PL
        'the hammer'   'the hammers'
     c. r-u   ferr-ə
        Det-M.SG   iron-M.SG
        'the iron'

---

6 Other Romance varieties with productive -a plurals include those of Corsica, where according to the data in Manzini and Savoia (2005), the -a inflection extends to a wider ensemble of roots, including the animate 'brother', and the III class (-i inflection) 'foot'.
(i) u frateɖu/i frateɖa
    'the brother/the brothers'
(ii) u peði/i peða
    'the foot/the feet'   Zonza (Corsica)

d. r-u fok-ə
Det-M.SG fire-M.SG
'the fire'

(19) a. l-a recc-a   a' l-ə recc-ə
Det-F.SG ear-F.SG   Det-F.PL ear-F.PL
'the ear'   'the ears'
b. l-a rɔt-a   b' l-ə rɔt-ə
Det-F.SG wheel-F.SG   Det-F.PL wheel-F.PL
'the wheel'   'the wheels'
c. l-a furmik-a   c' l-ə furmik-ə
Det-F.SG ant-F.SG   Det-F.PL ant-F.PL
'the ant'   'the ants'
d. l-a notʃ-ə   d' l-ə nutʃ-ə
Det-F.SG nut-F.SG   Det-F.PL nut-F.PL
'the nut'   'the nuts'
e. l akkw-a
Det-F.SG water-F.SG
'the water'

(20) a. l-ə latt-ə
the-N.SG milk-M.SG
'the milk'
b. l-ə kaʃ-ə
the-N.SG cheese-M.SG
'the cheese'
c. l-ə vin-ə
the-N.SG wine-M.SG
'the wine'
d. l-ə mɛl-ə
the-N.SG honey-M.SG
'the honey'
e. l-ə sal-ə
the-N.SG salt-M.SG
'the salt'

Guardiaregia

We provide further examples of definite determiners and clitics inserted in a sentential context in (21). As already indicated, adjectives display or not metaphony according to the noun's agreement Class, even in the presence of identical final schwa inflections. We further note that Guardiaregia follows the pattern of Mascioni in section 2, in that the neuter singular/[aggr] Class is visible only on determiners. Definite determiners are differentiated three-ways (masculine, feminine and neuter/aggregate).

(21) a. r-u / l-ə   siŋgə kott-ə
        it-m.sg/it-N-SG I.am   cooked-M.SG
        'I cooked it'
   b. l-a   siŋgə kɔtt-a
        it-F.SG   I.am   cooked-F.SG
        'I cooked it'
   c. dammə   l-ə pan-ə/   n-u məlon-ə   frisk-ə
        give.me the-N.SG bread-M.SG/ a-M.SG melon-M.SG fresh-M.SG
        'Give me the fresh bread/a fresh melon'
   d. dammə   l-ə vin-ə/   n-u ʎibbr-ə   nov-ə
        give-me the-N.SG wine-M.SG/ a-M.SG book-M.SG new-M.SG
        'Give me the new wine/a new book'
   c. lə   sattʃə
        it-n.sg   I.know
        'I know it'   Guardiaregia

Demonstratives, 'this' in (22) and 'that' in (23), have a metaphonic form for the masculine different from that of the feminine and the neuter. On the other hand, with nouns and adjectives the neuter patterns with the masculine in all respects.

(22) a. kuʃt-ə   jɛ   n-u   kanə   bbonə
        this-M.SG is   a-M.SG dog-M.SG   good-M.SG
        'This is a good dog'
   b. keʃt-ə   kaʃ-ə   ɛ   bbon-ə/   jɛ ffrisk-ə
        this-N.SG cheese-M.SG   is   good-M.SG /   is fresh-M.SG
        'This cheese is good/fresh'
   c. keʃt   akkw-a   jɛ   ffresk-a
        this.F.SG water-F.SG   is   fresh-F.SG
        'This water is fresh'

(23) a. kuʎʎ-ə   kanə   veccə
        that-M.SG   dog-M.SG   old-M.SG
        'that old dog'
   b. kell-ə   vin-ə   vecc-ə
        that-N.SG   wine-M.SG   old-M.SG
        'that old wine'

c. kell-a   sɛddʒ-a   vɛcc-a
that-F.SG   chair-F.SG   old-F.SG
'that old chair'   *Guardiaregia*

Finally, in (24) we exemplify -*a* plurals, which are predominantly masculine in the singular (but see 'nail' for an example belonging to the feminine Class). In the plural, the -*a* inflectional class agrees with its modifiers in the feminine as can be seen by the lack of metaphony, e.g. the low/lax properties of the stressed nucleus, for instance on 'long' in (25). An interesting variant on this general schema is illustrated in (26). Rather than pluralizing by means of the simple –*a* inflection, the -*ər*- extension is used, yielding -*ər-a* plurals.

(24) a. r-u   vrattʃ-ə   a' l-ə   vrattʃ-a
         Det-M.SG arm-M.SG   Det-F.PL arm-'A'PL
         'the arm'   'the arms'
     b. ʎ   ossə   b' l   ɔss-a
         Det-M.SG bone-M.SG   Det-F.PL bone-'A'PL
         'the bone'   'the bones'
     c. ʎ   ovə   c' l ɔv-a
         Det-M.SG egg-M.SG   Det-F.PL egg-'A'PL
         'the egg'   'the eggs'
     d. r-u   dit-ə   d' l-ə   det-a
         Det-M.SG arm-M.SG   Det-F.PL arm-'A'PL
         'the finger'   'the fingers'
     e. r-u   dit-iʎʎ-ə   e' l-ə   dət-ell-a
         Det-M.SG arm-dim-M.SG   Det-F.PL arm-dim-'A'PL
         'the finger (diminutive)'   'the fingers (diminutive)'
     f. l   oɲɲ-a   f' l   oɲɲ-a
         Det-F.SG nail-F.SG   Det-F.PL nail-'A'PL
         'the nail'   'the nails'

(25) a. l-ə   det-a   lɔŋg-ə
         the-F.PL   finger-'A'PL   long-F.PL
         'the long fingers'
     b. l   oɲɲ-a   lɔŋg-ə
         the.F.SG/PL nail-F.SG/'A'PL long-F.SG/PL
         'the long nail(s)'

(26) a. r-u   puts-ə   a' lə   pots-ər-a
         Det-M.SG wrist-M.SG   Det-F.PL wrist-Suff-'A'PL
         'the wrist'   'the wrists'

b.	ʎ	ortə	b'	l	ɔrt-ər-a
	Det-M.SG	garden-M.SG		Det-F.PL	garden-Suff-'A'PL
	'the vegetable garden'			'the vegetable garden'	
c.	ʎ	aneʎʎ-ə	c'	l	anɛll-ər-a
	Det-M.SG	ring-M.SG		Det-F.PL	ring-Suff-'A'PL
	'the ring'			'the rings'	*Guardiaregia*

Recall from section 2 that Loporcaro and Paciaroni (2011) treat mass singulars in Italian dialects as a third, neuter gender adding to masculine and feminine. As for the class of *-a* feminine plurals, they construe it as a fourth gender. Using Corbett's (1991) terminology, this fourth controller gender determines target masculine agreement in the singular and feminine target agreement in the plural; it is therefore a *genus alternans* (an alternating gender). Loporcaro and Paciaroni conclude that Center-South Italian varieties exemplify four gender systems that are formally similar to the four gender system (masculine, feminine, count neuter, mass neuter) of, say, the isolate language Burushaski. Loporcaro and Paciaroni point out that plural *-a* cannot simply be seen as defining an inflectional class (D'Achille and Thornton 2003 for Italian); in our own examples from S. Gregorio at least two inflectional classes are defined, namely *-e/-a* and *-u/-a*.

Acquaviva (2008) differs from most other approaches in assuming that *-a* is not a bona fide plural inflection, but an exponent for a "lexeme deriving process". However, in the Central Calabria variety of Iacurso, discussed by Manzini and Savoia (2017b), there is a single inflection *-i* for all determiners and modifiers of the noun, independently of the masculine or feminine Class of the noun – and hence of the *-a* or *-i* pluralization, as in (27). More importantly, under the tests suggested by Acquaviva (2008), *-a* plurals in Central Calabrian must be construed as masculine, as their singular counterparts, as illustrated in (28). Therefore *-a* introduces plural without gender change, or any other indications that anything but an inflectional process is at play, weakening Acquaviva's case.[7]

---

[7] One of the reasons why Acquaviva proposes a derivational treatment for Italian *-a* plurals is the fact that they are associated with the special semantics of "weakly differentiated" parts. Our data involve elicited productions and do not include grammaticality judgements. However, as detailed by Manzini and Savoia (2017b), the range of nouns covered by *-a* plurals in Calabrian is the same as in Center-South Italian varieties (body parts, eggs, etc.). In the specific instance of (27), recall that even in English the relevant objects can be denoted by a plural 'knives' or included in the collective singular 'cutlery'.

(27) piɟɟa   kir-i   du-i   kurtɛɾ-a/ kurtiɐɾ-i
     take   those-PL   two-PL   knives-'A'PL/knives-PL
     'Take those two knives'

(28) a. mi   kattɛru l   ɔv-a   e   mi   s   inda   ruppiu   un-u
        to.me   fell   the   egg-'A'PL and to.me REFL of.them   broke   one-M.SG
        'I let the eggs fall and one of them broke'
     b. un-u   dɛ   kir(-i)   ɔv-a
        one-M.SG   of   that-pl   egg-'A'PL
        'one of those eggs'
     c. un-u   dɛ   kiri   lɛtt-a   ɛ   bbiɐcc-u
        one-M.SG   of   that-pl   bed-'A'PL   is   old-M.SG
        'One of those beds is old'   *Iacurso*

The same examples of Central Calabrian are also a counterexample to Loporcaro and Paciaroni's idea that -*a* plurals configure a so-called *genus alternans*, as defined above; this characterization cannot be extended to the -*a* plurals in (27)–(28), which do not alternate between masculine and feminine but are consistently masculine. What is more, note that in the corpus of Guardiaregia, there are examples of -*a* plurals of feminine nouns, in particular 'nail' – which again would seem to indicate that the *genus alternans* characterization does not capture the essence of the phenomenon. Summarizing so far, we reject Loporcaro and Paciaroni's characterization of -*a* plurals as a *genus alternans* as not general enough to apply for instance to the Iacurso variety.

3.2 Aggregate -*a*

The nouns associated with -*a* plurals in the S. Gregorio and Guardiaregia varieties prominently include body parts, e.g. 'knees', 'lips', 'fingers' and 'bones' as well as 'eggs'. Other foodstuff with the same weak differentiation properties as 'eggs' such as 'pears' and 'apples' also appear with -*a* plurals in the variety of Guardiaregia. In addition, -*a* plurals attach to artifacts; in this respect, note that English also uses the singular 'cutlery' (or speaks of a 'knife set'). In general, it is tempting to conclude that where both an -*i* and an -*a* inflection are available, -*i* corresponds to a set whose members are individuated atoms, while -*a* may correspond to a set whose members are rather more like parts of a whole.

The question is how best to formalize this intuition. The analyses of standard Italian count plurals ('cats') in section 1 and of Central Italian mass singular ('cheese') in section 2 imply an elementary ontology of number properties represented under the Class node, including [⊆] for count plurals and [aggr] for mass singulars. It is natural to entertain the hypothesis that the two properties could be combined, allowing the combination [⊆], [aggr] to express pluralities, as implied by [⊆], but of parts rather than of individuals, as implied by [aggr], as schematized in (29) for *reut-a* in (17). The question as to the interpretive import of *-a* plurals is therefore answered by (29) if we assume that the [⊆], [aggr] Class node selects lexical bases that have a collective or mass plural interpretation or a plural interpretation covering sets of what Acquaviva (2008) calls "weakly differentiated" individuals.

(29)

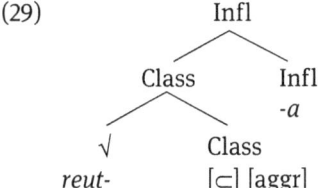

S. Gregorio Matese

The classical question that started the present investigation – namely the syncretism of plural and singular (I class, normally feminine) *-a* may also be answered by the hypothesis in (29). In principle the complex Class [⊆], [aggr] could be externalized by plural [⊆] morphology[8] or by aggregate [aggr] morphology. We surmise that the latter scenario is realized by *-a* forms – in other words that the Infl element *-a* is associated with the interpretive content [aggr]. Importantly, the [aggr] property of *-a* may be deployed in singular mass nouns, as exemplified by *akkw-a* 'water' in Guardiaregia in (19) (or *acqu-a* 'water' in standard Italian).[9] At the same time, when *-a* selects roots with individual content (e.g. *donn-a* 'woman' etc.), the [aggr] property cannot be associated with it. Therefore in (30) we associated *-a* with the interpretive [aggr] content optionally.

(30)   *-a*: Infl, ([aggr])

---

8 Manzini and Savoia (2017a) propose that the mass neuters of Albanian belong to the Class [⊆ aggregate], and that [⊆] plural morphology externalizes this Class content – proving a nice mirror solution to the one adopted by Italian.
9 In addition, the *-a* inflection is associated with aggregate content with property-denoting and eventive Ns, which have a mass behaviour, for reasons connected to the conception of property/event continua commented on in relation to the Central Italian neuter in section 2. For instance, deadjectival nominalizations in Italian largely belong to the *-a* inflectional class (Grossmann and Rainer 2004); so do several deverbal eventive Ns (*nomina actionis*). The same holds in Latin, where the I class includes *farina* 'flour', *aqua* 'water' as well as abstract nouns such *vita* 'life' and most deadjectival nouns. Other feminine eventive nouns belong to the III class (notably the *-io/ionis* nouns, as well as and *mors* 'death' etc.).

In turn, -*i*, specialized for (count) plurals, is associated with the [⊆] content, as in (30'). The readiness with which -*i* plurals freely alternate with -*a* plurals in standard Italian and in Italian varieties (for instance *kurtɛr-a/kurtier-i* 'knives' in (27)) could be taken as an indication that the [⊆] [aggr] complex Class characterization is indeed correct and can indeed in principle be externalized as [aggr] or as [⊆].

(30') -*i*: Infl, [⊆]

-*a* plurals where the root is enlarged by the -*ər* suffix receive a similar analysis. Manzini and Savoia (2017a) discuss the same suffix loaned into Albanian and associate it with the Class node. Following their lead, we may assign the structure in (31) to *pots-ər-a* 'wrists'. In essence the suffix -*ər* is an externalization of [⊆] [aggr] Class selected by -*a* aggregate inflections.

(31)

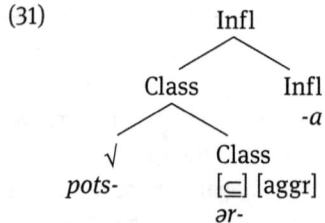

Guardiaregia

Recall that at the end of section 2 we proposed a complex Class content [masc], [aggr] for the language of Mascioni, leaving open the question as to why there wouldn't be a [fem], [aggr] class (see fn. 5). What we have now proposed is that the -*a* Infl, externalizing [fem] I class, is also associated with an [aggr] property. Therefore, [fem], [aggr] may in fact be taken to be present in the language of Mascioni, and to be externalized by -*a*. Vice versa, the -*o* inflection specializes for the externalization of the [aggr], [masc] Class on the D system.[10]

Summing up so far, -*a* is associated with [aggr] content and may surface either in singular or in plural contexts including the [aggr] specification. In other words, we can point to a property of -*a*, namely [aggr], that bridges between singular

---

[10] Similarly, in the language of Monte Giberto the [aggr] -*o* class includes what are historically II class [masc] nouns in Latin.

and plural. In virtue of this property [aggr], -*a* turns up both as a singular and a plural Infl.[11]

We are now ready to consider the question why -*a* plurals trigger [fem] agreement, given that their singular counterparts are normally II class masculine nouns. Let us review the facts first. Acquaviva (2008) argues that in Italian, distributive singular predicates taking an -*a* plural as antecedent, obligatorily surface in the feminine – yielding the feminine alternative in examples like (32) and excluding the masculine one. Loporcaro and Paciaroni (2011) by contrast report that only one speaker (from Rome) replicates Acquaviva's judgements. Southern Italian speakers all show some degree of acceptability of the masculine. The authors of this work (from Northern Italy and Tuscany) accept both feminine and masculine, as indicated in (32)–(33). Loporcaro and Paciaroni (2011) also reproduce data comparable to (32)–(33) for the dialect of Treia. The judgements should be compared to those relating to ordinary feminine plurals in (34), where masculine agreement is thoroughly inaccessible. It is tempting to suggest that to the extent that Acquaviva's (2008) stricter judgements hold for Italian speakers, they reflect normative pressures.

(32) a. L-e   uov-a   costano trenta centesimi l'un-a/l'un-o
       the-F.PL egg-'A'.PL cost   thirty cents   each-F.SG/each-M.SG
       'Eggs cost 30 cents each'
    b. L-e   bracci-a   di Ugo sono un-a   più   lung-a   dell'   altr-a
       the-F.PL arm-'A'.PL of Ugo are   one-F.SG more long-F.SG than.the other-F.SG
       'Ugo's arms are one longer than the other'
    b' L-e   bracci-a   di Ugo sono un-o   più   lung-o   dell'   altr-o
       the-F.PL arm-'A'.PL of Ugo are   one-M.SG more long-M.SG than.the other-M.SG

(33) a. Io mi sono rotto   un dit-o   e lui se   ne
       I REFL am   broken-M.SG   a finger-M.SG   and he REFL of.them
       è rott-e   divers-e
       is broken-F.PL several-F.PL
       'I broke a finger and he broke several'
     a' Io mi sono rott-o   un dit-o   e lui se   ne
        I REFL am   broken-M.SG   a finger-M.SG   and he REFL of.them
        è rott-i   divers-i
        is broken-M.PL several-M.PL

---

11 According to historical accounts (Clackson 2007:107 and references quoted there), the original Indo-European neuter (collective etc.) plural -*a* was extended to an inflectional class for collective/abstract singulars – which only secondarily came to coincide with the default class for feminine animates. This reconstruction is compatible with what we are proposing, namely that -*a* has a core [aggr] feature for mass/collective plurals and for mass/eventive singulars – though this feature is optional and does not prevent count singulars from also belonging to the -*a* class.

b. Io ho fatto cadere un uov-o   e   lui ne   ha fatt-e   cadere
   I have made drop   an egg-M.SG and he.of them has made-F.PL drop
   molt-e
   many-F.PL

b'. Io ho fatto cadere un uov-o   e   lui ne   ha fatt-i   cadere
    I have made drop   an egg-M.SG and he of.them has made-F.PL drop
    molt-i
    many-F.PL

(34) a. L-e   tazz-e   sono un-a/*o   più   bell-a/*o   dell'
        the-F.PL cup-F.PL are one-F/M.SG more nice-F/M.SG than.the
        altr-a/*o
        other-F/M.SG
        'The cups are one nicer than the other'

  b. Ho fatto cadere un-a   tazz-a   ma lui ne   ha fatt-e/*i   cadere
     I made drop   a-F.SG cup-F.SG but he of.them has made-F/M.SG drop
     molte/*i
     many-F/M.SG
     'I dropped a cup but he dropped many'

The coordination of two masculine singular nouns which admit or favour -*a* plurals triggers masculine plural agreement on the predicate, as in (35a) – while feminine is inaccessible. This is comparable to the coordination of two ordinary masculine nouns, as in (35b).[12]

(35) a. Il   bracci-o e il   ginocchi-o sono ancora
        the.M.SG arm-M.SG and the.M.SG knee-M.SG are still
        buon-i/*buon-e
        good-M.PL/good-F.PL
        'The arm and the knee are still good'

  b. Il   lett-o   e l'   armadi-o   sono ancora
     the.M.SG bed-M.SG and the.M.SG wardrobe-M.SG are still
     buon-i/*buon-e
     good-M.PL/good-F.PL
     'The bed and the wardrobe are still good'

The possibility of masculine agreement in (32)–(33) means that the [masc] Class, selected by the lexical base in the singular, remains accessible in the plural. This is

---

[12] Loporcaro and Paciaroni (2011) report the availability of both options for a speaker from Avigliano, which we leave as an open issue here.

difficult to express formally, if the plural is associated with the [fem] Class – since the Classes [masc] and [fem] are otherwise in complementary distribution.[13] At the same time, DP-internal contexts tend to confirm Acquaviva's judgements. In the partitive DP in (32'a), only [fem] agreement with the -*a* plural is truly acceptable even for laxer speakers (like the authors of this article). Interestingly, both [fem] and [masc] agreement are again acceptable in DP contexts like (32'b). Therefore, stricter judgements do not appear to depend on DP-internal agreement per se.

(32') a. Un-a/*un-o   dell-e   mi-e   dit-a   è rott-a/ *rott-o
        one-F.SG/one-M.SG of.the-F.PL my-F.PL finger-'A'PL is broken-F.SG/broken-M.SG
        'One of my fingers is broken'
   b. Un-a/un-o   su mille   uova è rott-a/   rott-o
      one-F.SG/one-M.SG in thousand eggs is broken-F.SG/broken-M.SG
      'One in a thousand eggs is broken'

Given the evidence in (32), (33), (32'b), two paths are in principle open, one more conservative, but frankly stipulative – and one potentially more rewarding, but at odds with grammatical tradition. The more conservative assumption is that [aggr] plurals must co-occur with the [fem] class, and that the latter determines agreement. Nothing in what we have said prevents us from following this option. Besides being stipulative, this analysis leaves us with no explanation as to the accessibility of masculine agreement in the plural/singular mismatches in (32)–(33). In the next section, we will therefore begin by exploring an alternative analysis, based on denying that there is any switch from masculine in the singular to feminine in the plural.

3.3 Aggregate -*e*

For Monte Giberto in section 2 we proposed the tripartite agreement system, [masc], [fem] and [aggr] in the singular. Languages like standard Italian, or like S. Gregorio and Guardiaregia in section 3.2 could be taken to have three Classes

---

[13] The ambigenerics/neuters of Romanian display a consistently different behaviour from Italian -*a* plurals. In contexts of the type in (35), all the literature reports that the conjunction of two neuters/ambigenerics triggers feminine plural agreement on the predicate – though an added complication is that feminine is the default gender in the plural, while masculine is the default gender in Italian. In examples of the type in (33), the plural quantifier preceding the ellipsis site is reported to be feminine. The formal literature mostly subscribes to underspecification analyses. Kramer (2015) proposes that the third gender of Romanian comes to coincide with the masculine singular and the feminine plural via rules of morphological Impoverishment (in the sense of DM). One of the possibilities entertained by Giurgea (2014) is that the third gender

freely combining with the plural, namely [masc], [fem] and [aggr]. The [aggr] Class is neither [masc] nor [fem]; therefore we get the effects of equal availability of the two genders in the anaphoric contexts in (32)–(33).

But how come the *-e* inflection, otherwise associated exclusively with [fem] plurals is obligatorily present on determiners and modifiers of *-a* plurals? For instance, in S. Gregorio we find *l-e reut-a* 'the fingers' while **l-i reut-a* is impossible (same in Italian, *l-e dit-a* 'the fingers' vs. **i dit-a*). Formally speaking, we see a single option open, if we do not want to abandon the basic idea that *-a* plurals are neither [masc] nor [fem] but just [aggr]. This is to say that the *-e* inflections is also endowed with [aggr] content. In other words, the lexical entry for *-e* parallels the entry for *-a*, as indicated in (36). There is an important property that *-e* shares with *-a* namely that both appear both as singular inflections and as plural ones. Specifically, *-e* is the III class inflection in the singular (for both genders). As expected, the *-e* inflectional class contains several mass singulars, for instance *latte* 'milk', as in structure (11) for Monte Giberto in section 2, or the feminine eventive nouns in *-zione* in standard Italian (see fn. 9).

(36) *-e*: Infl, ([aggr])

The structure of *le reuta* 'the fingers' is then as in (37). Agreement takes place with respect to the [⊆][aggr] cluster and not with respect to the [⊆][fem] cluster as in traditional descriptions. Since *-e* also is the I class ending for [fem] plural, *-a* plurals are described as feminine; in reality they are neither feminine not masculine, they are [aggr]. It is the [aggr] property of *-e* which determines its occurrence on determiners, quantifiers and adjectival modifiers belonging to the I class, excluding the pure plural *-i* on these lexical bases.

(37)

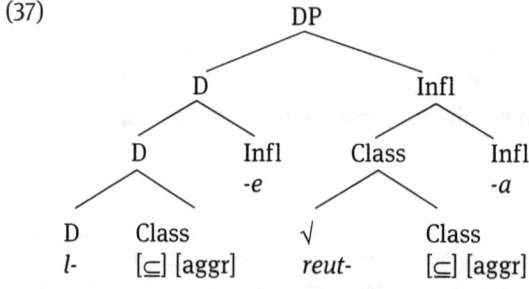

S. Gregorio Matese

IS absence of gender; masculine in the singular and feminine in the plural are just defaults. We do not take position on Romanian; a default/Elsewhere analysis does not seem appropriate for Italian, precisely because the [masc] gender of the singular remains accessible in the plural.

Let us go back to contexts with number mismatch in (32), (33). Recall that -*a* plurals can agree both with a [fem] or a [masc] singular, as in (32) – or vice versa a masculine singular with -*a* plural can again agree with a [fem] or a [masc] plural, as in (33). We account for these data in terms of the -*a* plurals belonging to the [aggr] Class and therefore being indeterminate as to the choice between [masc] and [fem].

Nevertheless, we also need an account as to why -*a* plurals must be matched with a [fem] singular at least in the partitive in (32'a). This piece of data suggests a partial retreat into the conventional idea that the relevant DPs are [fem]. We maintain that the -*a* plural does not trigger [fem] agreement. Rather -*e* Determiners and modifiers trigger it, on the grounds that -*e* is always [fem] in the non-[aggr] plural. Contexts like (32'b) involve a DP structure and an -*a* plural like those in (32b'), but they embed morphologically invariable elements (the numeral); since by itself, the -*a* plural does not trigger [fem] agreement, both [fem] and [masc] agreement are possible.

In short, -*a* plurals agree with respect to the [aggr] feature. This means that I class adjectives and determiners select the -*e* plural, because -*e* has the [aggr] feature. Agreement with the -*a* DP under number mismatch gives rise to great uncertainty in most speakers. In essence, it appears that both the [fem] feature normally associated with plural -*e* and the [masc] feature associated with the singular of the noun may prevail. In the standard variety, speakers take the first option in partitive constructions (32'a) (possibly defined by a single DP-phase and no ellipsis); some speakers may be prefer it in general, but not all speakers.

The question that now needs to be asked is whether there is independent support for the various assumptions made in this section. We conclude by arguing that at least the characterization of the -*e* inflection in (30) is independently supported again by the data of Monte Giberto. Apart from the singular neuter in section 2, this variety has a [masc] Class as in (38), a [fem] Class as in (39) and a Class traditionally described as alternating between a masculine singular and a feminine plural, as in (40). This latter Class implies no specialized -*a* inflection in the plural, but just the ordinary feminine plural -*e* inflection. At the same time, it is associated with many of the same Nouns that display -*a* plurals in standard Italian and in the varieties of section 3.2, notably body parts. The data in Loporcaro and Paciaroni (2011) show that the pattern in (40) is not mutually exclusive with the -*a* pattern considered so far; the two coexist for instance in the variety of Treia.

(38) a. l-u   jorn-u   a' l-i   jorn-i
        Det-M.SG   day-M.SG   Det-M.PL   day-M.PL
        'the day'   'the days'
     b. l-u   kortell-u   b' l-i   kurtell-i
        Det-M.SG   knife-M.SG   Det-M.PL   knife-M.PL
        'the knife'   'the knives'

    c. l-u   mes-e   c' l-i   mes-i
       Det-M.SG   month-M.SG   Det-M.PL   month-M.PL
       'the month'   'the months'

(39) a. l-a   recc-a   a' l-e   recc-e
       Det-F.SG   ear-F.SG   Det-F.PL   ear-F.PL
       'the ear'   'the ears'
    b. l-a   man-o   b' l-e   man-e
       Det-F.SG   hand-F.SG   Det-F.PL   ear-F.PL
       'the hand'   'the hands'
    c. l-a   vɔrb-e   c' l-e   vɔrb-e
       Det-F.SG   fox-F.SG   Det-F.PL   fox-F.PL
       'the fox'   'the foxes'

(40) a. l-u   ðit-u   a' l-e   ðet-e
       Det-M.SG   finger-M.SG   Det-F.PL   ear-F.PL
       'the finger'   'the fingers'
    b. l-u   vrattʃ-u   b' l-e   vrattʃ-e
       Det-M.SG   arm-M.SG   Det-F.PL   arm-F.PL
       'the arm'   'the arms'   *Monte Giberto*

If we apply the schema of explanation proposed in (37) to the Monte Giberto data in (40), we obtain structures of the type in (41), where we impute the [⊆] [aggr] Class to the ðet- 'finger' root.

Recall that we have maintained that the syncretism between -*a* plurals and -*a* singulars is due the fact that the [aggr] property bridges singular and plural. Evidently, the same can be said of the -*e* inflection. This provides evidence for the lexical entry in (36), quite independently of the need for -*e* to agree with -*a* in (37). The optionality of the [aggr] property in (36) on the other hand allows -*e* to be compatible with non-[aggr] singulars, belonging both to the [masc] or [fem] Classes, as in (38c) and (39c) respectively.

(41)

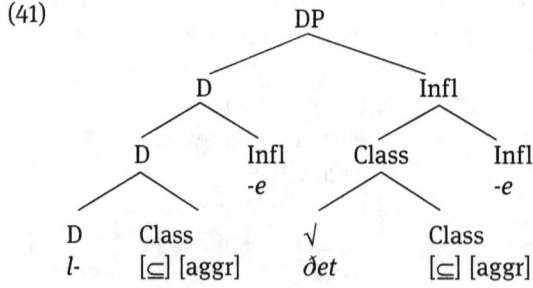

Monte Giberto

4 Conclusions

In present terms, varieties like Monte Giberto (sections 2, 3.3), Mascioni (section 2), S. Gregorio and Guardiaregia (section 3.1–3.2) have four Classes determining agreement, namely the conventional genders [masc] and [fem] – and what would be traditionally called two numbers, namely [aggr] for mass singulars and plurals, and a [⊆] Class corresponding to the count plural, as illustrated in (42). In fact, standard Italian also displays these four Classes. Other Romance languages do not display evidence of the [aggr] class, for instance French or many Northern Italian dialects. While [masc] and [fem] are mutually exclusive, they can combine with the number classes, which can equally combine with one another. It is possible that the mutual exclusion of [masc] and [fem] depends on their incompatibility as natural genders.

(42) Classes in Central Italian varieties/standard Italian
    a. [masc]
    b. [fem]
    c. [⊆]
    d. [aggr]

Besides proposing the introduction of the [aggr] Class, we also reached the conclusion that inflectional morphemes in Italian varieties, while not intrinsically endowed with gender properties, nevertheless may bear mass/plural properties. Specifically, the Infl system of a Central Italian variety may be as complex as (43). The *-i* Infl specializes for count plural (and for dative case on clitics, see Manzini and Savoia 2007, 2011). The *-a* and *-e* Infls both occur as mass plurals or plurals of weakly differentiated individuals; we take this characteristics to depend on an optional [aggr] feature. The [aggr] feature may be realized in the singular, with mass nouns; it is not realized in count singulars. This leaves the *-o* and *-u* Infls which never occur as plurals. The *-o* Infl specializes for the [aggr] feature and can only be associated with mass; the *-u* Infl apparently lacks any number property.

(43) Infls in Central Italian varieties
    -o: Infl, [aggr]
    -a: Infl, ([aggr])
    -e: Infl, ([aggr])
    -i: Infl, [⊆]
    -u: Infl

References

Acquaviva, Paolo. 2008. *Lexical plurals*. Oxford: Oxford University Press.
Acquaviva, Paolo. 2009. Roots and lexicality in Distributed Morphology. In Alexandra Galani, Daniel Redinger & Norman Yeo (eds.), *York Working Papers – Special Issue York-Essex Morphology Meeting May 2009*, 1–21.
Arregi, Karlos & Andrew Nevins. 2017. Beware Occam's syntactic razor: Morphotactic analysis and Spanish mesoclisis. lingbuzz/003365
Borer, Hagit 2005. *Structuring sense, vol. 1: In name only*. Oxford: Oxford University Press.
Calabrese, Andrea. 1998a. Metaphony revisited. *Rivista di linguistica* 10. 7–68.
Calabrese, Andrea. 1998b. Some remarks on the Latin case system and its development in Romance. In José Lema & Esthela Trevino (eds.), *Theoretical advances on Romance lLanguages*, 71–126. Amsterdam: John Benjamins.
Calabrese, Andrea. 2008. On absolute and contextual syncretism. In Andrew Nevins & Asaf Bachrach (eds.), *The bases of inflectional identity*, 156–205. Oxford: Oxford University Press.
Carstens, Vicki. 2008. DP in Bantu and Romance. In Cécile De Cat & Katherine Demuth (eds.), *The Bantu-Romance connection*, 131–166. Amsterdam: John Benjamins.
Chierchia, Gennaro. 2010. Mass nouns, vagueness and semantic variation. *Synthese* 174. 99–149.
Chomsky, Noam. 1995. *The minimalist program*. Cambridge, MA: The MIT Press.
Chomsky, Noam. 2000. Minimalist inquiries: The framework. In Roger Martin, David Michaels & Juan Uriagereka (eds.), *Step by step, essays on minimalist syntax in honor of Howard Lasnik*, 89–155. Cambridge, MA: MIT Press.
Chomsky, Noam. 2001. Derivation by Phase. In Michael Kenstowicz (ed.), *Ken Hale: A life in language*, 1–54. Cambridge, MA: The MIT Press.
Chomsky, Noam. 2013. Problems of projection. *Lingua* 130. 33–49.
Clackson, James. 2007. *Indo-European linguistics*. Cambridge: Cambridge University Press.
Corbett, Greville. 1991. *Gender*. Cambridge: Cambridge University Press.
Crisma, Paola, Lutz Marten & Rint Sybesma. 2011. The Point of Bantu, Chinese and Romance nominal classification. *Italian Journal of Linguistics* 23. 251–299.
D'Achille, Paolo & Anna M. Thornton. 2003. La flessione del nome dall'italiano antico all'italiano contemporaneo. In Nicoletta Maraschio & Teresa Poggi Salani (eds.), *Italia linguistica anno Mille – Italia linguistica anno Duemila, Atti del XXXIV congresso internazionale di studi della SLI*, 211–230. Roma: Bulzoni.
Déchaine, Rose-Marie, Raphaël Girard, Calisto Mudzingwa & Martina Wiltschko. 2014. The internal syntax of Shona class prefixes. *Language Sciences* 43. 18–46.
Fassi Fehri, Abdelkader. 2016. Semantic gender diversity and its architecture in the grammar of Arabic. *Brill's Journal of Afroasiatic Languages and Linguistics* 8. 154–199.
Ferrari Bridgers, Franca. 2008. A unified syntactic analysis of Italian and Luganda nouns. In Cécile De Cat & Katherine Demuth (eds.), *The Bantu-Romance connection*, 239–260. Amsterdam: John Benjamins.
Giurgea, Ion. 2014. Possible syntactic implementations of the controller vs. target gender distinction: the view from ambigenerics. *Language Sciences* 43. 47–61.
Grossmann, Maria & Franz Rainer (eds.). 2004. *La formazione delle parole in italiano*. Tübingen: Max Niemeyer Verlag.
Halle, Morris & Alec Marantz. 1993. Distributed morphology and the pieces of inflection. In Kenneth Hale & Samuel J. Keyser (eds.), *The view from Building 20*, 111–176. Cambridge, MA.: The MIT Press.

Halle, Morris & Bert Vaux. 1998. Theoretical aspects of Indo-European nominal morphology: The nominal declensions of Latin and Armenian. In Jay Jasanoff, H. Craig Melchert & Lisi Oliver (eds.), *Mír Curad: Studies in honor of Calvert Watkins,* 223–240. Innsbruck: Innsbrucker Beitraege zur Sprachwissenschaft.
Higginbotham, James. 1985. On semantics. *Linguistic Inquiry* 16. 547–621.
Higginbotham, James. 2009. *Tense, aspect, and indexicality.* Oxford: Oxford University Press.
Kayne, Richard. 1989. Facets of Romance past participle agreement. In Paola Benincà (ed.), *Dialect variation and the theory of grammar*, 85–103. Dordrecht: Foris.
Kayne, Richard. 1994. *The antisymmetry of syntax.* Cambridge, MA: The MIT Press
Kayne, Richard. 2010. *Comparisons and contrasts.* New York: Oxford University Press
Kihm, Alain. 2005. Noun class, gender, and the lexicon/syntax/morphology interfaces: a comparative study of Niger-Congo and Romance languages. In Guglielmo Cinque & Richard Kayne (eds.), *The Oxford handbook of comparative syntax*, 459–512. Oxford: Oxford University Press.
Kramer, Ruth. 2014. Gender in Amharic: A morphosyntactic approach to natural and grammatical gender. *Language Sciences* 43. 102–115.
Kramer, Ruth. 2015. *The morphosyntax of gender.* Oxford: Oxford University Press.
Kučerová, Ivona & Anna Moro. 2011. On mass nouns in Romance: semantic markedness and structural underspecification. In *Proceedings of the 2011 annual conference of the Canadian Linguistic Association.*
Ledgeway, Adam. 2009. *Grammatica diacronica del dialetto napoletano.* Tübingen: Niemeyer.
Loporcaro, Michele & Tania Paciaroni. 2011. Four gender-systems in Indo-European. *Folia Linguistica* XLV. 389–433.
Manzini, M. Rita & Leonardo M. Savoia. 2005. *I dialetti italiani e romanci.* Alessandria: Edizioni dell'Orso
Manzini, M. Rita & Leonardo M. Savoia. 2007. *A unification of morphology and syntax. investigations into Romance and Albanian dialects.* London: Routledge.
Manzini, M. Rita & Leonardo M. Savoia. 2011. *Grammatical categories.* Cambridge: Cambridge University Press.
Manzini, M. Rita & Leonardo M. Savoia. 2017a. N morphology and its interpretation: The neuter in Italian and Albanian varieties. In Anna Bloch-Rozmej & Anna Bondaruk (eds.), *Constraints on language structure (Proceedings of the LingBaw Conference, Lublin 2015),* 213–236. Frankfurt: Peter Lang.
Manzini, M. Rita & Savoia, Leonardo M. 2017b. Gender, number and inflectional class in Romance. In *Proceedings of the Olomouc Linguistics Colloquium, 'Categorial features of Nouns and their projections'* June 9–11.
Marantz, Alec. 1997. No escape from syntax: Don't try morphological analysis in the privacy of your own lexicon. *University of Pennsylvania Working Papers in Linguistics* 4. 201–25.
Oltra-Massuet, Isabel & Karlos Arregi, 2005. Stress-by-structure in Spanish. *Linguistic Inquiry* 36(1). 43–84.
Percus, Orin. 2011. Gender features and interpretation: a case study. *Morphology* 21. 167–196.
Picallo, Carme. 2008. Gender and number in Romance. *Lingue e Linguaggio* VII. 47–66.
Pomino, Natascha & Elizabeth Stark. 2011. How the Latin neuter pronominal forms became markers of non-individuation in Spanish. In Katerina Stathi, Elke Gehweiler & Ekkehard König (eds.), *Grammaticalization: Current views and issues,* 273–293. Amsterdam: John Benjamins.
Rohlfs, Gerhard. 1968 [1949]. *Grammatica storica della lingua italiana e dei suoi dialetti. Morfologia.* Torino: Einaudi.

Savoia, Leonardo M. 2015. *I dialetti italiani. Sistemi e processi fonologici nelle varietà di area italiana e romancia*. Pisa: Pacini.

Savoia, Leonardo M., Benedetta Baldi & M. Rita Manzini. 2017. Sigmatic plural systems in Romance varieties spoken in Italy. Paper presented at TEAM 2017, Università di Padova, 22–24 June.

Steriopolo, Olga & Martina Wiltschko. 2010. Distributed Gender hypothesis. In Gerhild *Zybatow*, Philip Dudchuk, Serge Minor & Ekaterina Pshehotskaya (eds.), *Formal studies in Slavic linguistics*, 155–172. New York: Peter Lang.

Thornton, Anna. 2010–11. La non canonicità del tipo it. braccio // braccia / bracci: sovrabbondanza, difettività o iperdifferenziazione? *Studi di grammatica Italiana* 29–30. 419–477.

Williams, Edwin. 1994. *Thematic structure in syntax*. Cambridge, MA: MIT Press.

Andrew Nevins
Copying and resolution in South Slavic and South Bantu Conjunct Agreement

1 Introduction: Four strategies for conjunct agreement

When two noun phrases of different genders are conjoined, agreement targets often show a range of options. For example, partial agreement (i.e. First Conjunct Agreement or Closest Conjunct Agreement) can pick one of the two conjuncts as the controller. Often, however, languages choose another option, namely an agreement value which may not be coming from either of the individual conjuncts in the coordination, but from the coordination head *i* 'and', syntactically represented by the category &P, itself. This leads to what is typically called 'resolution' in conjunct agreement, and sometimes 'default' agreement, and the choice among all of these options is often revealing of grammar-internal mechanisms such as the computation of locality (how can an individual conjunct be chosen? What is the internal structure of a coordination), the markedness relations among genders (why in certain combinations are the options limited?), and the influence of number on gender (why is closest conjunct agreement more prevalent for gender than number, and why is it often limited to the plural?). This has led to a broad array of theoretical and experimental studies, particularly on languages with three or more genders, such as the South Slavic family. By exploring questions of markedness relations among genders, the relation between number and gender, and the very modelling of tradeoffs between hierarchical, linear, and feature-relativized locality, conjunct agreement provides an exciting testbed for these topics through the manipulation of a fairly small structure purely in terms of combinatorics – and indeed, one can additionally focus on, say, DP-internal concord vs verbal agreement with such coordinations as an additional variable.

The present paper focuses on the implementation of the resolution strategy for gender values in conjunct agreement, ultimately couched in a theory of copying and nondistinctness. As the resolution mechanism is implemented in terms of an agreement mechanism initiated within the &P, it draws on tools of feature-based computation found elsewhere in the grammar. However, &P-internal agreement is unique within the grammar in that the two participating goals (namely, each conjunct) are equidistant from the &P head in question (assuming it is specified as needing to probe twice). As a result, existing mechanisms such as Multiple Agree (Hiraiwa, 2001, Anagnostopoulou, 2005), which are based on one goal being hierarchically higher than the other, and employed in accounts such as the Person-Case Constraint, are inapplicable. Instead, the closest grammatical parallels to an agreement mechanism with equidistant goals are found in phonology, and it will be proposed that precisely such a mechanism is shared in these two domains, even though they instantiate distinct modules of the grammar. As such, the analysis offered in this paper instantiates a case of Crossmodular Structural Parallelism, a hypothesis about the reuse of operations such as featural agreement, featural deletion, and feature co-occurrence constraints across domains of morphosyntactic and phonological features, and one that has been a fruitful part of linguistic theory throughout the work of Andrea Calabrese (e.g. Calabrese 1998) and many works inspired by it.

Resolution is the terminology employed in works such as Corbett (1991) to refer to how verbal or other agreement is computed for a subject noun phrase that has a mixed gender, such as in French below:

(1) *Resolution of mixed genders to masculine in French*:
    a. [Le garçon et la fille] sont compétents / *compétentes
       [The boy and the girl] aux.PL competent.M.PL / *competent.F.PL
       'The boy and girl are competent'

In languages such as French, with two genders, a conjunction of masculine and feminine, when employing resolution for agreement, chooses masculine. In fact, in such cases, there is no way to tell apart what might be called 'resolution agreement' (a function that chooses a particular gender value given a set of two nonidentical ones) from 'default agreement' – which simply chooses a single gender value as the default when ordinary agreement 'fails'.

This is what seems to happen in Icelandic, which has three genders. Mixed-gender combinations of masculine (M) + feminine (F) result in a resolution value with *neither* of these, but instead neuter (Corbett 1991, Wechsler 2009):

(2) *Resolution of mixed genders to neuter in Icelandic*:
    a. Drengurinn og telpan eru dhreytt
       boy.def.M. and girl.def.F are tired.N.PL
       'The boy and the girl are tired'

The neuter value here presumably reflects the *default* value that any conjunction has. Formally speaking, we could localize the [neuter] feature on the &P that heads the entire conjunction, assuming a structure like as representing the language-specific nature of &P in Icelandic as lexically neuter.

(3) *Representation of the gender value on &P in Icelandic:*

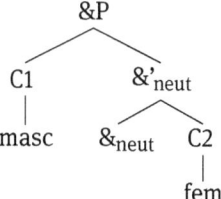

As such, the default gender – that which is lexically specified on the conjunction head – in French is masculine, and in Icelandic, it is neuter, and these are the result of agreement when the conjunction head itself is chosen as the controller. Icelandic does allow resolution: when both conjuncts are masculine, masculine is possible, and when both conjuncts are feminine, feminine is possible. But mixed conjunction requires the neuter.

Matters are even more complex, however, in South Slavic (Bosnian/Croatian/Serbian, Slovenian), where there are three genders, and there is the possibility of closest-conjunct agreement – namely agreement with one of the individual conjuncts, instead of resolution or default agreement. For South Slavic, conjunct agreement has been argued to show three distinct strategies: Highest Conjunct Agreement (HCA), Closest Conjunct Agreement (CCA) and Default Agreement. In the present paper, we put aside the first two completely (see Marušič et al. (2015), Murphy & Puškar (2018) inter alia for accounts of HCA and CCA), and focus on Default Agreement, arguing that in fact it should be cleft into *two distinct* agreement strategies, namely Default vs Resolution (see Willer-Gold et al. (2016) for a prior development of this claim).

There is a long tradition of study of conjunct agreement in South Slavic. Only recently, however, have new experimental results come to light that may cause re-evaluation of the empirical picture previously established in the literature. For example, Corbett & Mtenje (1987, 25) comparing Chichewa and Serbo-Croat (which was what they called then what is now B/C/S) contend that "a difference between the two languages is that in the cases of plural conjuncts requiring the same agreement form, resolution is excluded in Serbo-Croat", by which they mean Neuter & Neuter (N&N) in particular. What Corbett & Mtenje were referring to was the claim, repeated in Wechsler (2009, 569) that while N&M or F&M can yield M, and even F&N can yield M, N&N should yield only M – with no possibility of resolved neuter agreement, as claimed below:

(4) *Claimed lack of neuter resolution in B/C/S:*
   a. Ogledalo   i   nalivpero   su   bili   / *bila
      Mirror.N.SG and fountain.pen.N.SG aux.PL were. M.PL / *were.N.PL
      na stolu
      on table
      'The mirror and fountain pen were on the table'

However, as it turns out, when one turns to judgements of the cases in which both neuter conjuncts are *plural*, and once large-scale elicitation patterns are carried out across a range of South Slavic sites with native speakers who are not linguists and whose task is free production, rather than prescriptively-influenced judgements, NPl &NPl conjunctions can yield *either* N or M as agreement patterns. In Willer-Gold et al. (2016), we experimentally elicited these patterns across 6 sites where South Slavic languages are spoken, and Figure 1 shows the overall averages for conjunctions of inanimate plurals. In the discussion that follows, we restrict our attention to cases in which both conjuncts are plural, until Section 5.

Of even greater interest, visible in the graph, is the fact that N agreement is consistently stronger than F. Thus, t-tests show a statistically significant difference between closest conjunct agreement when preverbal conditions with Conj2

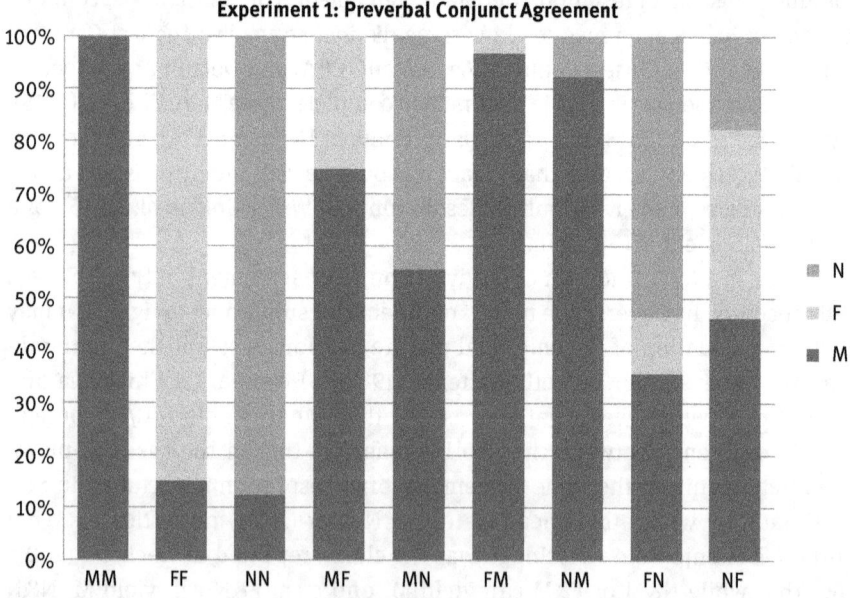

Figure 1: Preverbal Conjunct Agreement (pl&pl) production (n=180), results from Willer-Gold et al (2016). Compare N and F in columns 2 vs 3, 4 vs 5, 6 vs 7, and 8 vs 9.

as F vs N are compared (i.e. the grey bar in column 8 versus the light grey bar in column 9; p < .001), and a statistically significant difference between Preverbal HCA when Conj1 as F vs N are compared (i.e., the grey bar in column 9 versus the light grey bar in column 8; p < .001), In Willer-Gold et al. (2016), it was proposed that the source of this neuter agreement is an additional *fourth* agreement strategy, specifically Resolution.

(5) *Default vs Resolution in South Slavic conjunct agreement:*
    a. Default &P agreement: a fixed value of masculine plural, independent of the values of either conjunct
    b. Resolution &P agreement: a computation that depends on the feature values of each conjunct and their relation to each other

The extra 'edge', therefore, found for Neuter agreement (over Feminine) across all 8 conditions of interest comes from this fourth mechanism. How? In Willer-Gold et al. (2016), we proposed the following input-output functions for South Slavic. As shown in Figure 1, anytime there is an N present, the function outputs an N. Otherwise anytime there is an M present, the function outputs an M. Otherwise, it outputs an F (only, specifically, in the case where two Fs are present).

(6) *Gender Resolution outcomes for 9 possible gender combinations (only when both are plural):*

Uniform-gender conjuncts:	F&F	→ F
Uniform-gender conjuncts:	M&M	→ M
Uniform-gender conjuncts:	N&N	→ N
Presence of Masculine:	M&F, F&M	→ M
Presence of Neuter:	M&N, N&M	→ N
Presence of Neuter:	F&N, N&F	→ N

Moreover, Willer-Gold et al. (2016) claimed that default agreement, as found in (5), reflects what is called *index* agreement of the &P (a prespecified masculine value), whereas resolution in (5) is *concord* agreement of the &P, and results from the computation specified in (6). Importantly, our focus is on inanimate nouns, so semantic agreement is not at stake (though cf. Wechsler 2009 for highly pertinent discussion of what can go on with animates, where semantic agreement affects the purely grammatical computation based on the gender features of each conjunct). For agreement, either index or concord agreement values are in principle available.

In the remainder of this paper, we will focus on the mechanisms responsible for index agreement (default, prespecified masculine) and concord agreement (a resolution-based computation specified in (6)). These mechanisms are distinct, but only visible as such under the right conditions and with the right combinations. Thus, when conjoined Nsg&Nsg yield Ndual in languages such as Slovenian, this is resolution – as only resolution has the potential to inspect the two conjuncts for their number and gender values and compute that the result should be neuter when there are two neuters, and dual when there are two singulars. On the other hand, when a combination of Nsg&Nsg yields MPl in Slovenian, this must be prespecified default agreement, which has a fixed value of masculine and a fixed value of plural, regardless of the values of the individual conjuncts. Such a distinction is implicitly acknowledged in Corbett (1991, 302), where the masculine plural default is found even when conjuncts "consist entirely of feminine nouns" (alongside expected FPl). The need for a distinction between resolution, therefore, which looks at the individual values of the conjuncts and chooses a number and gender output on that basis, versus a fixed, prespecified default, is empirically necessary even outside the context of neuters, as can be seen in column 2 of Figure 1.

Further evidence for the proposed distinction comes from the fact, presented in Willer-Gold et al. (2016), that &P default agreement dwindles postverbally, while resolution remains as a possibility. In other words, conjunct agreement can take place when the coordination itself is postverbal, but the results are not symmetric with what happens when the coordination is preverbal. In particular, in postverbal position, masculine agreement (reflecting prespecification with the features of &P) is greatly reduced in availability for all coordinations besides M&F, M&N, and M&M. These results parallel what is found with the absence of index agreement elsewhere, as argued by Smith (2017b), on the basis of British English patterns like *There are a committee in the room*, concluding that index agreement requires that the controller surface c-command the target.

In what follows, we assume that default agreement is index agreement, reflecting agreement with the prespecified features on the &P head, following work by Arsenijević & Mitić (2016). The &P head bears both index and concord features, where the former are inherently specified as masculine plural, and the latter are the result of a computation. Following Marušič et al (2015), agreement with an &P can choose among Highest Conjunct Agreement, Closest Conjunct Agreement, or &P agreement. When &P agreement is chosen, however, either index or concord agreement can be chosen (assuming that Smith's condition on c-command is met for index agreement, otherwise it is unavailable). In the remainder of this paper, therefore, our focus is on the computation of concord agreement, and a formal means for providing the function specified in (6).

2 Failure of set-theoretic tools

An intriguing paper by Dalrymple & Kaplan (2000) proposes a set-theoretic union operation to derive resolution rules, whereby for two-gender languages, Fem is represented as an empty set ={ }. This therefore leads to the following resolution rule for languages like French, as was illustrated in (1) above:

(7) *Gender Resolution through Set-Theoretic Union:*
Set-union for M&F = M: {M} ∪ { } = {M}
Set-union for M&M = M: {M} ∪ {M} = {M}
Set-union for F&F = F: { } ∪ { } = { }

According to this formalism, masculine is the resolution value because it is formally present, whereas feminine is formally absent. Set-union thus provides tools for *deriving* why the function is what it is, based on existing operations that we already presume might exist in computing the logical basis for combinations like conjunction. This representation, however, does not square with the markedness relations in South Slavic. For three-gender languages with the resolution pattern of Icelandic, they propose that Neuter is composed of a set {M,F}, which predicts that Masc+Fem (i.e. {M} ∪ {F} = {M,F}), will yield Neuter. Thus, any mixed gender combinations (or N+N combinations) will yield Neuter, as a resolution rule.

However, as we have seen, unlike in Icelandic, in South Slavic, M&F yields M as a resolution value. On a more general level, this problem arises because there is no way to achieve a multi-level theory of resolution (like the one in (6), where M&F = M but M & N = N) with privative features and set-theoretic union. While this mechanism could perhaps be made to work if, say, feminine were maximally unmarked/underspecified in South Slavic, this would seem at odds with the general properties of markedness found in the language.

A way out for South Slavic could arise if it were the case that the resolution value were always M. In fact, for Slovenian, Dalrymple & Kaplan (2000) argue, based on Corbett (1983, 186), that N&N = M. However, as Figure 1 shows, our results show little support for this, as N&N also yields N (and much more so than M); see also Marušič et al. (2015) for Slovenian. Given these same features, set-intersection (instead of union) would also founder, as N&N would yield *only* N, and not allow M. Recall that under our model, the latter pattern is actually *not* resolution, but default. What is needed, therefore, is a model in which the resolution function, as specified in (6), delivers N for these cases, alongside a distinct grammatical option of index agreement (always yielding prespecified M).

Dalrymple & Kaplan (2000) in fact suggest that default values in addition to resolution may be necessary. They note, on the basis of parallel patterns with noun class resolution in Lama (Yu, 1988), that the coordination head itself can provide an additional gender value. Lama is a Gur language with default noun classes used in cases of coordination, and as Yu (1988) points out, highly similar to Bantu languauges in this respect. In Section 4, where we discuss Bantu conjunct agreement strategies, we will return to the kind of data that motivated this conclusion.

Returning to the issue of set-theoretic tools to derive resolution, Ingria (1990) recognized the generalized problem of resolution patterns of this sort for unification-based approaches. He proposed, instead of union or intersection as a means for determining the output function based on the feature-values of the conjuncts, a mechanism of *nondistinctness*, which we take up here.

3 Nondistinctness

We now provide a resolution function that will yield (6). Recall that masculine plural is a fixed &P default value. However, in South Slavic overall, neuter is the least specified. Evidence for this claim comes from a wide range of sources, especially the fact that clauses with no nominative subject, or with 5&Up quantified noun phrases (which cause failure of agreement), consistently yield *neuter* on the verb. Outside of &P, there is no debate that neuter is the least marked gender: it is what is chosen alongside singular for numerally-quantified noun phrases, which otherwise lack agreement features. We thus take neuter as the absence of gender specification in South Slavic; see Kramer (2015) and Willer-Gold et al. (2016) for additional discussion.[1] Let us suppose a Germanic-type system in which Feminine and Masculine are grouped by a feature [+common] (crucially, for inanimates as well), as Dutch has a system with 'common gender' vs 'neuter gender'. Extending this grouping of M and F to the exclusion of N via the feature [± common], we may propose the following system, where only positive feature-values are shown.

(8) *Proposed Feature-System for South Slavic Gender*:
F = [+common, +fem]
M = [+common]
N = [ ]

---

[1] Despić (2017) provides relevant discussion of markedness relations among gender in South Slavic, although focuses strictly on animate nouns. It may be that neuter is the default in inanimates, but as it is largely absent from animates (and in fact neuter plural is syncretic with feminine singular), masculine steps in as the default for animates.

Let us turn to nondistinctness as the implementation of resolution. In order to provide a computation underlying the the function in (6), the resolution procedure on &P (eventually yielding the concord value) inspects the features of the two conjuncts, and only keeps the least-specified feature(s) in the pair (again, only when both are plural).

(9)   M&M: [+common] & [+common]:   &-head: [+common] (M)
     F&F: [+comm, +fem] & [+common, +fem]:   &-head: [+common, +fem] (F)
     M&F: [+comm, +fem] & [+common]:   &-head: [+common] (M)
     M&N: [+common] & [ ]:   &-head: [ ] (N)
     F&N:[+common, +fem] & [ ]:   &-head: [ ] (N)

The notion of nondistinctness therefore correctly yields the empirically-attested pattern. But how is nondistinctness achieved within a grammatical model? There are no other phenomena that look quite like this within agreement systems, and ideally the grammar would employ (or reuse) some existing machinery. Despić (2017, 293), focusing on conjunct agreement, also proposes that in cases of resolution 'CoordP will be marked for a gender value only if every conjunct is marked with a [+] gender value of the same kind (i.e. there is no mismatch)', but provides no specific mechanism. It is to the formal implementation that we turn.

Murphy & Puškar (2018), in their work on &P-agreement, speculate that resolution is achieved by impoverishment on &P feeding agreement with an external conjunct, a view we are sympathetic towards in spirit. However, the implementation of impoverishment rules that would underly nondistinctness-based concord of the precise type specified above would require overly powerful statements:

(10) *An Attempt at Implementing Nondistinctness via Impoverishment:*
    a. Impoverish [+common] on an NP-daughter of &P if it is the only NP in &P with this feature
    b. Impoverish [+fem] on an NP-daughter of &P if it is the only NP in &P with this feature

Impoverishment rules generally do not require this kind of quantification in their statements of context, and we therefore contend that it is not the right mechanism to provide nondistinctness. Instead, we localize the nondistinctness mechanism in an agreement mechanism driven by &P itself, to which we turn.

Although *Multiple Agree* with various feature-compatibility conditions has been proposed (e.g. for PCC effects; Nevins 2007), it was for cases where one goal was necessarily more local (and hence imposed conditions of priority, which has thus far proven to be irrelevant in resolution). Thus within the &P this is not applicable, and a bidirectional version of Multiple Agree is required, although bidirectional (e.g. equally local) goals have no precursors in syntax. There *is*, however, an extant such copying mechanism from a case of bidirectional vowel harmony in Woleaian, as analyzed in Nevins (2010). In this language, a thematic vowel occurring between the stem and an inflectional suffix shows bidirectional height harmony. Specifically, the underlying vowel /a/ will raise to [e] only if the closest vowels *on both sides* are [− low]:

(11) Bidirectional *[−low] VH of theme vowel in Woleaian*:
    a. /ülü m-a-mu/ → {ülü m-e-m^w} 'cup-2sg'
    b. /ülü m-a-la/ → {ülü m-a-l} 'cup-3sg'
    c. /mat-a-mu/ → {mat-a-m^w} 'eye-2sg'

As (11) shows, only in the (a) case, where both flanking vowels are [− low], can harmony occur. This phonological configuration instantiates a case where goals are equally local, and copying of [− low] only succeeds if found on both goals. The same condition, imported to copying the features [+comm] and [+fem] with South Slavic &P, yields (6).

Specifically, assume that within the syntax, the &-head probes upwards and downwards simultaneously. Given a two-step Agree (with Agree-Link in the syntax, and Agree-Copy in PF; cf. Arregi & Nevins 2012, Bhatt & Walkow 2013), in PF, the &P upon beginning copying will inspect the features of both conjuncts, copying from them only after it has found a certain feature on both of them. This yields the resolution value on &P (available alongside its prespecified M.PL index feature). Thus, only when the feature [+comm] is found on both conjuncts can it be copied to &P's concord feature, and thus only combinations of M&F or M&M can yield [+comm] on &P. The same holds for [+fem], and thus only combinations of F&F can yield [+fem] on &P. Otherwise, no values are copied, as cases of F&N or F&M do not find the relevant features on both goals. As a result, the resolution value in such cases will be empty, yielding neuter, and providing the function in (6).[2]

---

[2] It may be that the Nondistinctness effect in ConjP gender resolution is related to more general properties of &P in requiring a category label from one of its conjuncts. For example, an &P that conjoins two DPs shows the overall distribution of a DP, and an &P that conjoins two VPs shows the overall distribution of a VP. If the mechanism responsible for this category-labeling involves projection, the gender resolution property may be related to the need for nondistinctness in projection, requiring featural decomposition in cases of coordination of unlikes (e.g. *Pat is wealthy and a Republican*: Sag 2002). For a proposal of how Labelling as a primitive operation in Minimalist syntax can provide the means for number resolution, see Larson (2013).

The application of Crossmodular Structural Parallelism in this case goes in a less usual direction: much previous work, for example, has examined the extent to which principles of syntax apply to phonological representations, while the application of phonological principles to syntactic phenomena is less commonly explored. However, given that equidistant goals in a search arguably arise much less often in syntax (given hierarchical structure), this is a domain in which the flat structures of phonological search domains prove helpful in understanding a syntactic configuration. The ConjP assumed here is not flat, but is lexically specified as needing to probe twice, and thereby must agree with both the element in its complement and in its specifier, given the structure of &P assumed in Section 1.

4 Default agreement, humanness, and ineffability in Southern Bantu

As mentioned above, three-gender languages such as Icelandic and South Slavic provide evidence for a default value of &P, distinct from the result that occurs as the output of resolution, a conclusion already anticipated in Dalrymple & Kaplan's (2000) reference to the Lama data in Yu (1988). The evidence for a default value on &P arises particularly clearly in Bantu noun class systems, which we can essentially consider as gender systems here, where the even numbers refer to plural number cases. Consider Southern Bantu, on the basis of data reported in Mitchley (2015). Xitsonga conjunct agreement shows clear evidence for default &P, with class 2 as the default for [+human], and class 8 for [−human]. Thus, when two class 6 humans are conjoined, verbal agreement (notated below as SM for 'subject marker') is class 2, which by hypothesis reflects the prespecified gender on a [+human] &P.[3]

(12) *Default [+human] agreement in Xitsonga:*
 a. A   ma-hahla ni   ma-jaha   vo   tira
     the 6-twin   and 6-young.man   SM2   work

In parallel, when two class 10 non-humans are conjoined, verbal agreement is class 8, which by hypothesis reflects the prespecified gender on a [− human] &P.

---

3 See also Smith (2017a) for the proposal that default gender, as found in Chichewa, is semantic/index agreement.

(13) *Default [–human] agreement in Xitsonga:*
 a. A tim-fenhe ni tim-byana swa lwa
   the 10-baboon and 10-dog SM8 fight

This pattern of default prespecification in Xitsonga is distinct from that found in Sesotho, as discussed by Mitchley, which by contrast has resolution for cases parallel to (12) and hence does allow agreement to resolve to the value shared by each conjunct. Compare Sesotho's resolution for the equivalent of (12):

(14) *Resolved [+human] agreement in Sesotho:*
 a. ma-shodu le ma-polesa a lwana
   6-thief and 6-policeman SM6 fight

Thus, it seems that Xitsonga differs from Sesotho in only allowing the default, prespecified version of &P, and indeed, that there are two versions of &P, depending on their value for [±human]. Confirmation of the fact that the class 2 and class 8 values, respectively, are defaults for (12) and (13), comes from the fact that it is ineffable to combine a [+human] and [–human] NP within a &P. Strikingly, this ineffability, as found in (15), with two idiosyncratically class 10 nouns, one [+human] and [–human], disallows the default [+human] gender value, the default [–human] gender value, *and* the gender value for which both nouns are accidentally syncretic!

(15) *Ineffable mixed [±human] agreement in Xitsonga:*
 a. A tin-anga na tim-byana *va/*swa/*ta famba
   the 10-doctor and 10-dog SM2/8/10 walk

This ineffability occurs, by hypothesis, because no &P can fit two such conflicting conjuncts: in Xitsonga, an &P must be either [+human] or [–human], and its individual conjuncts must both match this choice.[4] The cases of ineffable mixed [+human] and [–human] cases suggest that in languages such as Xitsonga, unlike with gender specification in South Slavic, *both* values of [± human] are visible. No 'default default' is available; only a [+human] default and a [–human] default. Interestingly enough, a similar phenomenon is actually found to a certain extent even in English, as pointed out by Ad Neeleman (pers. comm.):

---

4 It may also be possible to assume a more refined, hierarchical or multi-feature system, whereby class 6 nouns bear features for class 6 as well as a subset that match class 2, and that class 10 nouns bear features for class 10 as well as a subset that match class 8.

(16) *Ungrammatical mixed [±animate] agreement in English:*
   a. Where is the boy scout and his pet dog? They're in the waiting room.
      (i) Where is boy scout manual and the compass? They're in the waiting room.
      (ii) Where is the boy scout and his merit badge sash? %They're in the waiting room.

These facts are all the more striking because they suggest that English plural *they* does correspond to two underlying syntactic versions, a [+animate] one (the plural of *he/she*), and a [–animate] one, the plural of *it*. Surprisingly, the impossibility of mixing these two for downstream agreement is visible even in pronominal anaphora in (16). Similar, mixed animacy coordinations are disallowed in Mi'gmaq (Gordon, 2016):

(17) *Ungrammatical mixed [±animate] agreement in Mi'gmaq:*
   a. *nemi'-gig   epit   aq pata'uti
      see-1>3.PL.AN   woman.AN and table.IN
      (Intended) 'I see the women and the table'

Although the discussion of Southern Bantu here is largely included in order to demonstrate the distinction of default agreement versus resolution in the Xitsonga vs Sesotho contrast discussed in Mitchley's (2015) data, it is worth mentioning that CCA and HCA strategies parallel to those found within South Slavic occur in the third language she studied, namely isiXhosa, which allows CCA:[5]

(18) *Closest conjunct agreement in isiXhosa:*
   a. Ama-doda nemi-nqathe i-se   gadi-ni
      6-man   and.4-carrot SM4.loc garden.loc
      'The men and the carrots are in the garden'

This closest conjunct agreement, by hypothesis, results from the proposal in Marušič et al. (2015) that languages differ in whether they allow agreement with &P itself (and subsequently, a distinction between index and concord features of &P, yielding default vs resolution, respectively) or allow partial agreement, namely with a single individual conjunct. Now ordinarily when a language allows partial agreement, it will allow either CCA or HCA preverbally

---

[5] Though see Voeltz (1971, footnote 3) for discussion of a Xhosa pattern akin to the one described for Xitsonga in the text.

(these two strategies converging of course in postverbal contexts, where the highest conjunct *is* the closest), although naturally with preferences based on whether the locality principle at stake is hierarchical or linear. Perhaps, therefore, we would expect that HCA should be possible in some cases in isiXhosa, even if ordinarily dispreferred. In fact, HCA can be found in a specific configuration: when the closest conjunct is singular (as in the odd-numbered second conjunct below):

(19) *Highest conjunct agreement in isiXhosa:*
    a. Ama-hashe nen-komo a-tya ingca
        6-horse   and.9-cow 6-eat grass
        'The horses and the cow are eating grass'

This pattern instantiates the Consistency Principle that Marušič et al. (2015) found for Slovenian: in order for gender agreement to occur with potential &P controller C, C must bear the value of *number* agreement already chosen (thus, fem.pl & neut.sg will not yield neut.sg agreement). In Slovenian and in isiXhosa, therefore, it seems that number resolution happens first, before any kind of gender agreement – be it resolution or otherwise. Once number resolution has taken place, however, the choice of a gender controller, if based on CCA/HCA, must respect the number decision already recorded on the agreement target (see also Boskovic 2009, Sec 3.4). Thus, in (19), assuming number resolution occurs first, the second conjunct becomes ineligible as a controller for partial agreement. Put differently, number resolution seems to happen first, and restricts the space of possible gender controllers. In the last section of this paper, we suggest an answer for why number resolution may come earlier in the derivation.

5 Conclusion and future directions

Everything discussed above for B/C/S looked at plural conjuncts. But in fact, when both conjuncts are singular, gender resolution doesn't happen at all. In particular, when there is N.SG & N.SG, only M.PL (default) is possible, and resolution is not an option.[6] This instantiates the Consistency Principle, as mentioned above, in the sense that in order for resolution to even be possible (as opposed to

---

[6] See Arsenijević (2016) for discussion of this fact, and for a different view from the present one, developing the interesting proposal that neuter plurals are collectives, not formed from neuter singulars.

simply default), the conjuncts must bear the appropriate number. An individual conjunct can only be looked at for gender agreement (whether for CCA, HCA, or the computation of resolution) if it already bears the 'right' value for number. This depends, of course, on number agreement being computed first.[7]

In this section we suggest a tentative explanation for why number resolution comes first – that is, why gender agreement depends on prior number agreement. While one can clearly always simply state that gender is dependent on number in a feature-geometric sense, our goal here is to see whether this potentially can be related to a difference in the nature of number resolution versus gender resolution themselves. Thinking about the resolution function for number, recall from the generalization for gender resolution is that in cases of nonidentical specifications, the least marked gender is the one that survives. This is clearly not the operative principle for number in Slovenian:

(20) *Number Resolution outcomes for 6 possible number combinations:*
  sg & sg   → dual
  sg & dual   → plural
  sg & pl   → plural
  dual & dual   → dual or plural
  dual & plural   → plural
  plural & plural → plural

Neither bidirectional agreement nor impoverishment nor set union suffice to derive number resolution. Number resolution in &P takes place in apparently a wholly different manner, not necessarily one that works based on the feature values of [±singular], [±augmented], as there is no way to take the two [−augmented] features in dual & dual and end up with [+augmented] plural resolution.[8] Number resolution simply does not involve preservation, nondistinctness, union, or intersection of the participating features, but rather the construction of a potentially new value based on the inputs.

This construction of a new value in cases of coordination may be akin to cases of the Multiple Agree mechanisms proposed by Trommer (2006) and Gluck-

---

[7] Convergent evidence for number agreement being first and restricting the choices for gender agreement can be found in Despić (2017), where it is argued that for honorific 2nd person *Vi*, the option of plural agreement subsequently restricts the options for gender agreement.
[8] See, however, Šuligoj (2017) for a discussion of how dual & dual may yield dual, as potentially a kind of CCA for number.

man (2016), who analyze 'constructed plural': in languages like Nocte and Tupi-Guaraní where the subject and object can jointly contribute in a transitive verb.

(21) *Constructed Plural in Nocte:*
    a. Ni   roantang rang-ka-e
        1pl   always   asp-go-1pl
        'We always go'
    b. nga-ma   nang   hetho-e
        1sg-nom   2sg   teach-1pl
        'I shall teach you'

Thus, the 1pl ending *-e* is found both for true 1pl subjects and for 'summative' cases of a 1sg subject and a 2sg object. A similar phenomenon, although interacting with the inclusive/exclusive distinction, is found in Tupi-Guaraní with the prefix *oro-*. In these cases, the number features of the object make their way to the subject – though not necessarily as a portmanteau a la Georgi (2012), but in a conceptually similar manner. The function specified in (21) involves construction of a new value rather than nondistinctness-based selection. We suggest that this is why it necessarily comes earlier in the derivation.

While one can appeal to the nature of features where gender is dependent on number in a general sense to understand the consistency principle effect (and indeed, a variety of psycholinguistic studies have found evidence for number as more prominent than gender, e.g. Carminati 2005, Nevins et al. 2008), we suggest this results from a more general property, whereby constructive resolution necessarily precedes selective resolution (this seems clearly operative for person resolution as well), and await its verification with other features (e.g. humanness/animacy). Selective resolution and nondistinctness based on morphosyntactic features, as developed here, have a 'later' character, potentially related to the more morphophonological factors explored in Pullum & Zwicky (1986). In other words, number resolution, being constructive resolution is part of an earlier submodule than gender resolution, and the latter is not even broached if the individual conjuncts do not bear the requisite number features established earlier. This architectural move of distinct timing of operation types with different natures (constructive vs selective resolution) in their sequencing at PF, in the spirit of Arregi & Nevins (2012), potentially obviates the need to extrinsically order these two resolution types.

Acknowledgments: Thanks to Boban Arsenijević, Lanko Marušič, Zorica Puškar, Peter W. Smith, Jana Willer-Gold, the editors of this volume, and two anonymous reviewers.

References

Anagnostopoulou, Elena. 2005. Strong and weak person restrictions: A feature checking analysis. In L. Heggie and F. Ordóñez (ed.), *Clitics and affixation*, 199–235. Amsterdam: John Benjamins.

Arregi, Karlos & A. Nevins. 2012. *Morphotactics: Basque auxiliaries and the structure of Spellout*. Dordrecht: Springer.

Arsenijević, Boban. 2016. Gender, like classifiers, specifies the type of partition: evidence from Serbo Croatian. Paper presented at Chicago Linguistic Society 52.

Arsenijević, Boban & I. Mitić. 2016. On the number-gender (in)dependence in agreement with coordinated subjects. *Journal of Slavic Linguistics* 24. 41–69.

Bhatt, Rajesh & M. Walkow. 2013. Locating agreement in grammar: An argument from agreement in conjunctions. *Natural Language and Linguistic Theory* 31. 951–1013.

Bošković, Željko. 2009. Unifying first and last conjunct agreement. *Natural Language and Linguistic Theory* 27(3). 455–496.

Calabrese, Andrea. 1998. Some remarks on the Latin case system and its development in Romance. In J. Lema & E. Treviño (eds.), *Theoretical advances on Romance languages*, 71–126. Amsterdam: John Benjamins.

Carminati, M. N. 2005. Processing reflexes of the feature hierarchy (person > number > gender) and implications for linguistic theory. *Lingua* 115. 259–285.

Corbett, G.G. & A. D. Mtenje. 1987. Gender agreement in Chichewa. *Studies in African Linguistics* 18. 1–38.

Corbett, Greville G. 1983. *Hierarchies, Targets and Controllers: Agreement patterns in Slavic*. London: Croom Helm.

Corbett, Greville G. 1991. *Gender*. Cambridge: Cambridge University Press.

Dalrymple, Mary & R. M. Kaplan. 2000. Feature Indeterminacy and Feature Resolution. *Language* 76. 759–798.

Despić, Miloje. 2017. Investigations on mixed agreement: polite plurals, hybrid nouns and coordinate structures. *Morphology* 27. 253–310.

Georgi, Doreen. 2012. A relativized probing approach to person encoding in local scenarios. *Linguistic Variation* 12. 153–210.

Gluckman, John. 2016. Decomposing Morphological Number in Local Contexts. In Kyeong min Kim, Pocholo Umbal, Trevor Block, Queenie Chan, Tanie Cheng, Kelli Finney, Mara Katz, Sophie Nickel Thompson & Lisa Shorten (eds.), *Proceedings of the 33rd West Coast Conference of Formal Linguistics*, Somerville, MA: Cascadilla Proceedings Project.

Gordon, Douglas. 2016. Animate-inanimate Coordination in Migmaq: Consequences for Conjunction Reduction. McGill Canadian Conference for Linguistics Undergraduates.

Hiraiwa, Ken. 2001. Multiple Agree and the defective intervention constraint in Japanese. In Ora Matushansky (ed.), *Proceedings of the 1st HUMIT student conference in language research (HUMIT 2000)*, vol. 40 MIT Working Papers in Linguistics, 67–80. MITWPL, MIT, Cambridge, Mass.

Ingria, Robert. 1990. The limits of unification. *Proceedings of the 28th Annual meeting of the ACL, Pittsburgh* 194–204.

Kramer, Ruth. 2015. *The morphosyntax of gender*. Oxford University Press.

Larson, Bradley. 2013. Arabic conjunct-sensitive agreement and Primitive Operations. *Linguistic Inquiry* 44(4). 611–631.

Marušič, Franc, A. Nevins & B. Badecker. 2015. The grammars of conjunction agreement in Slovenian. *Syntax* 18(1). 39–77.

Mitchley, Hazel. 2015. *Agreement and coordination in Xitsonga, Sesotho and isiXhosa: an Optimality Theoretic perspective*. Rhodes University MA thesis.
Murphy, Andrew & Z. Puškar. 2018. Closest conjunct agreement is an illusion. *Natural Language and Linguistic Theory* 1–55.
Nevins, Andrew. 2007. The representation of third person and its consequences for person-case effects. *Natural Language and Linguistic Theory* 25(2). 273–313.
Nevins, Andrew. 2010. *Locality in vowel harmony*. Cambridge, Mass.: MIT Press.
Nevins, Andrew, B. Dillon, S. Malhotra & C. Phillips. 2008. The role of feature-number and feature-type in processing Hindi verb agreement violations. *Brain Research* 1164. 81–94.
Pullum, Geoffrey K. & A. M. Zwicky. 1986. Phonological resolution of syntactic feature conflict. *Language* 62. 751–773.
Sag, Ivan. 2002. Coordination and Underspecification. In *Proceedings of the 9th International Conference on Head-Driven Phrase Structure Grammar*, 267–291. Stanford, CSLI Publications. http://cslipublications.stanford.edu/HPSG/3/.
Smith, Peter W. 2017a. Possible and Impossible Agreement Mismatches. Ms., Univ. Frankfurt.
Smith, Peter W. 2017b. The syntax of semantic agreement in English. *Journal of Linguistics* 53(4). 823–863.
Trommer, Jochen. 2006. Plural insertion is constructed plural. *Linguistische Arbeits Berichte* 84. 197–228.
Voeltz, Erhard. 1971. Surface constraints and agreement resolution: some evidence from Xhosa. *Studies in African Linguistics* 2. 37–60.
Šuligoj, Tina. 2017. Categorizing Number: Agreement in the Case of Coordination. Paper presented at Resolving Conflicts Across Borders, Dubrovnik.
Wechsler, Stephen. 2009. Elsewhere in Gender Resolution. In Kristin Hanson & Sharon Inkelas (eds.), *The Nature of the Word: Essays in Honor of Paul Kiparsky*, 567–586. MIT Press.
Willer-Gold, Jana, B. Arsenijević, M. Batinić, N. Čordalija, M. Kresić, N. Leko, F. L. Marušič, T. Milićev, N. Milićević, I. Mitić, A. Nevins, A. Peti-Stantić, B. Stanković, T. Šuligoj & J. Tušek. 2016. Conjunct agreement and gender in South Slavic: From theory to experiments to theory. *Journal of Slavic Linguistics* 24. 187–224.
Yu, Ella Ozier. 1988. Agreement in left dislocation of coordinate structures. *Chicago Linguistic Society* 24.2. 322–336.

Diego Pescarini
Subject and impersonal clitics in northern Italian dialects

1 Introduction

This paper examines the interaction between subject clitics and the clitic *si/se* triggering an arbitrary interpretation (henceforth s_{arb}; Manzini 1986; Cinque 1988 a.o.). S_{arb} constructions feature an implicit argument denoting a set of human individuals that may contain the speaker. The null argument usually corresponds to the external argument of transitive and unergative verbs and, to a lesser extent, the internal argument of unaccusatives (Dobrovie Sorin 1998, 2006; Parry 1998). In what follows, I focus on the alternation between two s_{arb} constructions featuring transitive verbs (on terminological issues, see also D'Alessandro 2007: 39):

i. the passive-like construction (PASS), in which the subject is the (third-person) internal argument, see (1);[1]
ii. the impersonal construction *stricto sensu* (IMP),[2] in which the verb takes an accusative argument, which is usually realised as a clitic pronoun or, to a lesser extent, as a DP.[3]

(1) Questa   sera   si   leggono   due   libri   (PASS)
     This   evening   s=[4]   read.3PL   two   books
     'This evening we will read two books'

---

1 Besides the two constructions illustrated above, it is worth mentioning a third one, usually dubbed 'the middle *si* construction', which is a kind of passive-like construction without specific time reference (Cinque 1988). Middles differ from passive-like constructions in that the former have a property reading and occur more readily with a preverbal subject (more on this in section 3).

(i) Quel   libro   si   legge   facilmente.   (middle)
     That   book   s=   reads   easily
     'That book is easy to read'

2 Some scholars – Cennamo (1993, 1995, 1997); Parry (1998) among others – use the term *passive* to refer to *s-* constructions having the subject in preverbal position. However, I will argue that preverbal subjects of passive-like constructions are in A' position (see §3 and Raposo & Uriagereka 1996; Pescarini 2018).
3 According to D'Alessandro (2007: 55), the agreeing variant in (1) denotes accomplishment predicates, while the nonagreeing variant in (2a) denotes activity predicates. In what follows I will concentrate on the former, disregarding the latter, which is accepted by a subset of speakers.
4 Following the Leipzig Glossing Rules, cliticization is signalled with the symbol "=".

(2) a. %*Questa sera si legge due libri* (IMP)
    This evening s= read.3SG two books
    'This evening we will read two books'
 b. *Questa sera li si legge*
    This evening them= s= read
    'This evening we will read them (two books)'

I show that, although s_{arb} does not behave as a fully-fledged subject clitic, it nonetheless exhibits a puzzling interaction with subject clitics. I argue that the peculiar behaviour of northern Italian dialects (henceforth NIDs) results from the Multiple-Agree relation holding between T, s_{arb}, and the argument of passive-like constructions (D'Alessandro 2007), coupled with language-specific constraints on the realisation of T's features (Calabrese & Pescarini 2014).

The structure of the paper is as follows: sections 2, 3, and 4 overview the main features of s_{arb} constructions in western NIDs, Venetan, and Friulian dialects, respectively; section 5 deals with further irregularities in the placement of s_{arb} with respect to other clitic elements.

2 Western NIDs

In Romance languages, the IMP construction is attested in a subset of the languages allowing the PASS construction. In languages lacking the IMP construction, such as Romanian, s_{arb} cannot occur with object clitics, as shown in (3). Furthermore, since double passives are generally not allowed, s_{arb} cannot occur with passives in IMP-less dialects, as shown in (4) (Dobrovie Sorin 1998, 2006)

(3) a. *(Le materie umanistiche) le si studia in questa università*
       (Italian)
 b. **(Stiinţele umane) le se predă în această universitate*
       (Romanian)
    (the humanities)   them= s= studies in this   university
    'You can study the humanities in this university'

(4) a. *Spesso si è traditi dai falsi amici* (Italian)
 b. **Adesea se este trădat de prieteni falşi* (Romanian)
    Frequently s= is betrayed by friends false
    'One is frequently betrayed by false friends'

Similar restrictions are found in Italo-Romance dialects (Parry 1998; 2005: 216–219). Eastern NIDs such as Venetan, Lombard, and Friulian dialects allow both PASS and IMP constructions, while western NIDs such as Ligurian and Piedmontese exhibit a pattern akin to the one in Romanian, in which s_{arb} cannot occur in passives or co-occur with accusative clitics; see (5) and (6):

(5) a. Quando che se vien veci, se ze desmentegà dai zovini
When that s= come old, s= is forgotten by.the young
(Vicentino, east. NID)
b. *Quand ch' as ven vej, as ven dësmentià dai giovo
When that s= come old, s= come forgotten by.the young
(Pied., Parry 1998: 91)
'When one becomes old, one is forgotten by the young'

(6) a. Lo se magna doman (Vicentino)
it= s= eats tomorrow
b. U s (*lu) mångia adman (Pied.; Monregalese)
SCL= s= it= eats tomorrow
'We will eat it tomorrow'

Notice that, like Romanian, western NIDs do not allow s_{arb} to combine with accusative clitics, but dative, locative and partitive clitics are free to co-occur with s_{arb}, as shown in (7). This means that the above restriction does not result from a generalised ban on clitic combinations, but instead hinges on the Case-licensing mechanism.

(7) a. a s jë disìa (Pied., Parry 1998: 87)
SCL= s= to.him/her/them= say.impf
'One used to say to them'
b. a s në contratavo minca ann quatr mila chilo
SCL= s= of.them exchanged.hands each year four thousand kilos
'Each year four thousand kilos of them exchanges hands'

Some western NIDs such as Genovese (Ligurian) are more liberal than the others as they allow first or second person accusative clitics to co-occur with s_{arb} (Mendikoetxea & Battye 1990). I will not discuss here the variation across western NIDs; for a principled account, see Pescarini (2018).

(8) a. Finalmente me/te se vedde (Genovese)
At last me/you= s= sees
'At last, one sees me'

b. *I   se leza
   them= s= reads
   'one reads them'

3 Venetan

Eastern NIDs have been reported to allow both IMP and PASS constructions, but in this section I will show that the alternation is less clear than previously thought.

The distinction between PASS and IMP constructions is often blurred when the subject of PASS is postverbal. In many Venetan dialects, postverbal subjects of PASS cannot be distinguished from objects of IMP because postverbal subjects are not doubled by subject clitics and the verb shows no plural agreement in the third person.

To observe a contrast between IMP and PASS constructions, we must turn to preverbal subjects. Crucially, with preverbal subjects, PASS sentences are degraded. For Trentino, Zubizarreta (1982: 150ff) reports the ungrammaticality of the PASS construction in (9a) (contrasted with the IMP counterpart in (9b), while for Paduan and Venetian, Cinque (1988: 573–574) concludes that they "appear not to allow for passive *si* with specific time reference (Paola Benincà (personal communication) and Lepschy (1984, 71)), but only to allow for it with generic time reference." (more on this below):

(9) a. *Le   castagne   se magna col   vin   caldo
                                              (Trentino, Cinque 1988: 573)
       The   chestnuts s= eats   with.the wine hot
       'Chestnuts are eaten with hot wine.'
    b. Le   castagne, se le   magna   col   vin   caldo
       The   chestnuts s= them=   eats   with.the wine hot
       'Chestnuts se (one) eats them with hot wine.'

(10) a. *Maria   se ga   invità   na   volta   (Paduan, Cinque 1988: 574)
        Maria   s= has   invited   one   time
        'Maria was invited once.'
     b. *Ana   dovaria   verse   ciamà   do   volte
        Ana   should   have=s   called two   times
        'Ana should have been called twice.'
     c. *Mario   se ga   visto   in   strada   poco   fa
        Mario   s= has   seen   in   street   a.while ago
        'Mario was seen in the street a while ago.'

In what follows, I claim that the marginality of (9) and (10) is related to the position of preverbal subjects in PASS constructions and, in turn, to the syntax of subject clitics. First, I will show that the preverbal subjects of PASS occupy an A' position (for a similar conclusion, see Raposo & Uriagereka 1996; Pescarini 2018); second, since topicalised subjects are expected to co-occur with subject clitics (Benincà & Poletto 2004), I will argue that the ungrammaticality of (9) and (10) results from an incompatibility between s_{arb} and subject clitics.

As for preverbal subjects, notice that a sentence with the order *subject* > s_{arb} > *verb* cannot be uttered in wide focus environments as (11), meaning that preverbal subjects of PASS constructions yield a topic/comment partition. Furthermore, unlike canonical subjects in A position, the preverbal subject of s_{arb} constructions cannot be a controller, as shown in (12) (Belletti 1982a, 1982b), and cannot be pronominalized by the It. weak subject pronoun *egli* 'he', as in (13).

(11)   – *Cos'è successo?*
      'What happened?'
  – #*Una torta si è mangiata*   (vs *si è mangiata una torta*)
    A   cake s= is eaten
    'we ate a cake'

(12) *I miei genitori$_i$ si sono salutati prima di PRO$_{*i}$ partire*
    The my   parents   s= are   greeted   before of   leaving
    'We greeted my parents before we/*they left'

(13) **egli/lui si è scelto*
    He   s= is chosen
    'He has been chosen'

The tests in (11)–(13) confirm that the preverbal subject of PASS constructions is in fact topicalised and, as such, it is expected to be resumed by a subject clitic. Benincà and Poletto (2004) show that, with preverbal subjects, the clitic seems to be optional, see (14). However, if a dislocated object intervenes between the subject and the verb as in (14), then the clitic cannot be omitted. This means that the clitic is obligatory whenever the subject is left dislocated and that the optionality of (14a) is only apparent, as the presence of the clitic ultimately depends on the A/A' position of the subject.

(14) a. *Mario (l)   compra na casa*
       Mario (he=) buys   a   house
       'Mario is going to buy a house'

b. *Mario, na casa, no *(l) la compra*
   Mario, a house, not (he=) it= will.buy
   'Mario is not going to buy a house'

To summarize, subject clitics are expected to double topicalised subjects, including the preverbal subjects of PASS. If this analysis is on the right track, we expect Venetan to allow PASS sentences in which a topicalised/null subject is resumed/doubled by a subject clitic. In fact, Lepschy (1983/1989, 1984/1989) claims that PASS constructions featuring a subject clitic (which precedes s_{arb}) are fine and alternate freely with the IMP construction, in which the internal argument is pronominalized by an accusative clitic, which follows s_{arb}:

(15) a. *La se vede ~~Maria~~*   (PASS; Venetian, Lepschy 1986)
       She= s= sees
       'One sees her'
   b. *Se la vede ~~Maria~~*   (IMP)
       s= her= sees
       'One sees her'

However, for many Venetan speakers, the PASS structure in (15a) is less acceptable than the IMP one in (15b). I illustrate the contrast with data from the Venetan dialect of Palmanova (Laura Vanelli, p.c.): the PASS structure in (16a) is far less acceptable than that in (16b), in which the internal argument is left dislocated and resumed by an accusative clitic.

(16) a. **?(Le patate) le se magna doman*   (Palmanova, Ven.)
       The potatoes they= s= eats tomorrow
       'Potatoes will be eaten tomorrow'
   b. *(Le patate), se le magna doman*
       The potatoes s= them= eats tomorrow
       'Potatoes will be eaten tomorrow'

Notice that the contrast becomes stronger if we turn to a masculine singular clitic (Pescarini 2015). In fact, the contrast between the PASS and IMP constructions in sentences like (15) and (16) is partly blurred as object and subject clitics are identical. One might therefore accept (15a) and (16a) as instances of the IMP construction with a deviant clitic order; we will see in section 5 that in several NIDs the order of s_{arb} with respect to other object clitics is not fixed and it is worth noting that the order accusative > s_{arb} is the one in Italian. However, if we turn to cases in which the subject form (e.g. *el*) differs from the accusative one (e.g. *lo* 'him/it'), the contrast between PASS and IMP construction is clearer:

(17) a. *(El formajo)   el   se magna doman   (Palmanova, Ven.)
        (The cheese)   it.NOM=   s= eats   tomorrow
        'Tomorrow we will eat cheese'
    b. (El formajo)   se lo   magna   doman
        (The cheese)   s= it.ACC=   eats   tomorrow
        'Tomorrow we will eat cheese'

The data in (16) and (17) show that the asymmetry between PASS and IMP constructions holds even if the subject clitic is present. Hence, given the above data, one may argue that the marginality/ungrammaticality of PASS constructions *results* from the incompatibility between s_{arb} and subject clitics; subject clitics are mandatory with dislocated subjects, but they cannot co-occur with s_{arb} in PASS.

Before exploring this hypothesis, it is worth addressing the aforementioned asymmetry between PASS constructions with and without specific time reference, namely the PASS *stricto sensu* and the so-called middle construction (fn. 2; Cinque 1988: 558–566). From a semantic point of view, PASS constructions denote an event, while middle constructions trigger a property reading. As shown in the following examples, the subject of the middle construction, unlike that of PASS, behaves as a canonical preverbal subject that can occur under wide focus and can control into an adjunct clause, cf. (19):

(18) a. la pasta si mangia facilmente
         property reading: 'pasta is easy to eat, anybody can eat pasta'   → middle
         *event reading: 'we are likely to eat pasta'   → PASS
    b. facilmente si mangia la pasta
         *property reading: 'pasta is easy to eat, anybody can   → middle
         eat pasta'
         event reading: 'we are likely to eat pasta'   → PASS

(19) a. la $pasta_i$ si mangia facilmente   (a patto   d' PRO_i essere
         The   pasta   s= eats   easily   (provided   to   be
         senza   sugo)
         without   sauce)
         'Pasta is easy to eat (if it does not have sauce)'
    b. domani   la $pasta_i$ si mangia di sicuro   (a patto   d' PRO_{*i}
         Tomorrow   the   pasta   s= eats   for sure   (provided   to
         essere   senza   sugo)
         be   without   sauce)
         'Tomorrow we will certainly eat pasta (if it does not have sauce)'

This may explain why in languages like Paduan and Venetian the PASS construction is ungrammatical with specific time reference (see Cinque's quote above): sentences like (9) and (10) are degraded because the subject is dislocated and, as such, must be resumed by a subject clitic (Benincà and Poletto 2004). Conversely, sentences without specific time reference are fine because the subject can occupy an A position, where it can occur without being doubled by a subject clitic.

Let us summarise the overall scenario:
1) the PASS construction is forbidden in the context in which subject clitics are mandatory, i.e. when the subject of the PASS construction is left-dislocated.
2) the PASS construction is grammatical when the preverbal subject is in an A position as in the middle construction with generic time reference. Recall that, with preverbal subjects in A position, subject clitics are not mandatory (Benincà & Poletto 2004).
3) The PASS construction is fine when the subject occurs postverbally. In this case, subject clitics do not occur, but the PASS construction (often) becomes identical to the IMP one as the verb does not show number agreement.

Given the above data, I ultimately advance the hypothesis that the marginality of the PASS construction in Venetan follows from a restriction on the co-occurrence of subject clitics and s_{arb}.

This hypothesis allows us to account for the Venetan pattern without discarding the sound parametric analysis of arbitrary constructions put forth in works such as Cinque 1988, Roberts 2010. These works build on the generalisation that the IMP construction is allowed iff the PASS construction is allowed, which is at odds with the Venetan data. As Cinque 1988: 577 observes, "I see no simple way to reconcile the Venetian/Paduan case with that of the remaining Romance languages." However, if we account for the Venetan pattern as an orthogonal agreement restriction ruling out subject clitics in the context of s_{arb}, then we may keep the overall parametric analysis unchanged.

The remainder of this section shows that the hypothesized restriction results from the specific agreement pattern holding in s_{arb} constructions. To do so, some remarks on the representation of clitics are in order. Unlike (non-colloquial) French subject clitics, NIDs subject clitics are usually analysed as agr-like elements licensing a *pro* or doubling an overt DP subject. For the sake of clarity, in what follows I adopt a split representation in which T's features are scattered across several positions. I remain agnostic as to whether the template below results from fission (à la Roberts 2010, 2012, 2014) or exists *a priori* (à la Poletto 2000; Manzini & Savoia 2005). Following Roberts (2010), clitics are represented as bundles of agreement features resulting from the Agree relation holding between a T probe and a (defective) argument:

(20) $[_{T1}\, i\varphi_T \,...\, [_{T2}\, v\, ...$
       ↓
       SCL

Given the above analysis of subject clitics, let us introduce object clitics in the representation. Object clitics, like subject clitics, will be represented as bundles of φ features. Object clitics, including s_{arb}, are always lower than subject clitics and, unlike subject clitics, move along with the inflected verb under T-to-C movement. I therefore assume that object clitics (and s_{arb}, cf. Manzini & Savoia 2001: 251) are merged with the verb in a previous stage of the derivation (Roberts 2010; Calabrese & Pescarini 2011) and then moved to T. Whether the [... v] constituent is a complex head (Roberts 2010) or a remnant phrase (Poletto & Pollock 2009) is orthogonal to the present analysis.

(21) $[_{T1}\, i\varphi_T \,...\, [_{T2}\, [i\varphi\, v]\, ...$
       ↓   ↓
       SCL   OCL

Under this representation, no interaction is supposed to hold between subject and object clitics and, *mutatis mutandis*, between subject clitics/agreement and s_{arb}.

However, this is not the case (more on this below). What is of interest here is that s_{arb}, even if placed in [... v], triggers a clear agreement restriction on T, banning first or second person subjects, cf. (22a) vs (22b):

(22)   a.   Lui   si   vede   spesso   in   televisione
       b.   *Tu   si   vedi   spesso   in   televisione
            he/*you s=   see   often   on   TV
            'One can often see him/*you on TV'

D'Alessandro (2007) argues that the ungrammaticality of (22) is due to a condition on Multiple-Agree (Anagnostopoulou 2003) in which T probes s_{arb} and the subject at the same time. This disallows the occurrence of subjects whose Person features are incompatible with the {arb} specification of s_{arb}. Rephrasing D'Alessandro's claim, let us assume that when s_{arb} occurs, the {arb} specification spreads across T projections, thus restricting the range of T's possible goals to third person, i.e. non-person, arguments (for an alternative account, see Stegovec 2017):

(23)   ◄--------
       $[_{T1}\, \{arb\} \,...\, [_{T2}\, [\{arb\}\, v]$
                         ↓
                         si

Under (23), the restriction on Venetan subject clitics begins to receive a principled, though tentative explanation: besides preventing T from agreeing with a first or second person subject, as in (22), the configuration in (23) prevents the occurrence of further agreement markers such as eastern NIDs subject clitics. I will resume this point later, dealing with Friulian data.

Before turning to another group of dialects, however, one may wonder why the restriction in PASS constructions is not attested in western NIDs, which exhibit subject clitics as well. As a tentative answer, I would point to the fact that in Piedmontese and Ligurian the subject of PASS constructions – but the same holds for any type of impersonal construction *lato sensu* – is doubled by a non-agreeing nominative clitic, e.g. *a*:

(24) A se sciairs nen bin (ël cel / la montagna) (Parry 1998: 86)
 SCL= s= sees not well (the sky / the mountain)
 'the sky/the mountain cannot be seen well'

Hence, while Venetan subject clitics are agreement markers, which undergo agreement restrictions when combined with s_{arb}, in Piedmontese and Liguarian the subject clitic is an invariable particle, acting as an expletive element (for a sound typology of subject clitic pronouns, see Poletto 2000).

4 Friulian

Friulian dialects allow the IMP construction, as s_{arb} occurs in passives and sentences with accusative clitics, see (25) and (26). Vanelli (1998: 126) notices that, in certain varieties the object clitic is exceptionally placed in enclisis to the finite verb (on related phenomena, see section 5):

(25) a. Si è pajas masa pouc (Campone)
 b. Si è pajas masa puc (S. Michele al Tagliamento)
 s= is paid too little
 'people are paid too little'

(26) a. si lu vjo:t
 s= it/him= sees
 'One sees it/him'
 b. %si vjodi-lu
 s= sees=it/him
 'One sees it/him'

The PASS construction is allowed as well, but subject clitics must be omitted:[5]

(27) a. *Patatas*   *a(*l) si mangjan spess*   (Campone)[6]
 b. *Li patatis*   *(*al) si mangin spess*   (S. Michele al Tagliamento)
 c. *Lis patatis*   *(*al) si mangjn simpri*   (Palmanova, Friulian)
    The potatoes SCL= s= eat often/always

The pattern above may follow from an orthogonal phenomenon as Friulian dialects are subject to a generalized restriction on the co-occurrence of subject and object clitics (what Roberts 1993 dubs 'object clitic for subject clitic'). As shown in (28), subject clitics tend to be dropped in the presence of object clitics. Analogous phenomena are reported for Valdôtain (Roberts 1993) and Romagnol dialects (Manzini & Savoia 2004; Pescarini 2012).

(28) a. *O   vin   cantá:t*   (Friul., Benincà & Vanelli 2005: 67)
     we= have sung
     'We sang'
 b. *(*O) lu vin cantá:t*
     we= it= have sung
     'We sang it'

Hence, Friulian differs from western NIDs in allowing the IMP construction and differs from Venetan in allowing the PASS construction. In the latter, however, subject clitics are dropped because of an orthogonal process that deletes subject clitics when co-occurring with object clitics or s_{arb}.

To clarify the mechanism, I focus on the analysis of a single dialect, the one spoken in Campone (Masutti & Casalicchio 2015). I chose the dialect of Campone because it has a richer array of subject clitics than other Friulian dialects and, by virtue of its complexity, the Camponese system can clarify the behaviour of other eastern NIDs.

---

[5] The subject clitic is allowed when occurring in enclisis as a consequence of V-to-C movement in interrogative clauses:
(i) a. *Si   vjo:t   la   lune*
      s=   see   the moon
      'One sees the moon'
 b. *Si vjodi-al?*
      s= sees = SCL
      'Can you see it (the moon)?'

[6] According to orthographic conventions, in Friulian <gj> stands for /ɟ/.

First, Camponese has a double subject clitic system, i.e. subject clitics are expressed by two formatives: one – usually a vowel – occurring above negation and the other occurring after negation.[7] The latter realises gender and number agreement features (Poletto 2000; Manzini & Savoia 2009; Calabrese & Pescarini 2014 a.o.).

(29) a. A   no l'   ha   studia:t (Campone, Masutti & Casalicchio 2015)
        SCL= not M.SG= has studied
        'He did not study'
    b. A   no i   vi:f   uchì
        SCL= not M.PL= live   here
        'They do not live here'

We can therefore assume for Camponese the following template, in which two kinds of T's features (D and φ features, respectively) are checked by two probes separated by the position of the negative (clitic?) marker:

(30)   iD$_T$ ... iΣ ... iφ$_T$ ...

Camponese third-person subject clitics can be therefore decomposed as follows (see also Calabrese & Pescarini 2011 on the nearby dialect of Forni di Sotto):

(31) a. *al* 'he'
         a   'she'
         ai 'they.M'
         as 'they.F'
     b. *a-* ↔ [D]
         -l ↔ [Person: __; Gender: m; Number: sg]
         -i ↔ [Person: __; Gender: m; Number: pl]
         -s ↔ [Person: __; Gender: f; Number: pl]

Although the verb always agrees with postverbal subjects, the clitic formatives *l/i/s* do not occur with indefinite postverbal subjects (Masutti & Casalicchio 2015).

(32) a. A _   son   rivaz   trei   canais
        SCL= are   arrived three boys
        'There arrived three boys'
     b. A _   son   rivaz   duciu   tarc
        SCL= are   arrived all   late
        'They all arrived late/ Everybody arrived late'

---

[7] The latter is often dropped whenever an object clitic is present, while the vowel *a* is never affected by the presence of other clitic material.

However, in the PASS construction the clitic formatives *l/i/s* are dropped not only with indefinite subjects, but also with definite ones, see (33).

(33) a. A   (*-s) si   manghian patatas
        SCL= F.PL= S=   eats   potatoes
        'people eat potatoes'
    b. A   (*-s) si   manghian las patatas …
        SCL= F.PL= S=   eats   the potatoes that I bought yesterday
        'people eat the potatoes that bought yesterday'

With intransitive verbs, the clitic *a* does not occur. This confirms the hypothesis that *a* expresses a D feature, thus occurring if T probes a DP.

(34) a. (*a) si è   pajas   masa pouc
            S= is paid   too   little
            'people are paid too little'
    b. (*a) si durmis benon uchì
            S= sleep   well   here
            'people sleep well here'
    c. (*a) si partis   doma:n
            S= leaves tomorrow
            'we will leave tomorrow'

Let us focus on the incompatibility in (33) between s_{arb} and the subject clitics expressing T's φ-features. The deletion of the subject clitic formative is not exceptional since Camponese is one of the many Friulian dialects that exhibit the 'object clitic for subject clitic' pattern (Roberts 1993, 2015). In Camponese, the subject clitics *l/i/s* are omitted whenever a third-person object clitic is present, while the D clitic *a* is never dropped (Masutti & Casalicchio 2015: fn. 30):

(35) A   no   (*l)   l'   ha   chiatat
     SCL= not   =M.SG =it   has   found
     'He has not found it'

Roberts (2015) argues that object clitic for subject clitic effects are due to operations of fission and fusion. Similar operations have been assumed in the analysis of the nearby dialect of Forni di Sotto by Calabrese & Pescarini (2011). In Roberts's terms, T's and v's φ-features, i.e. subject and object agreement markers, are fused under adjacency into a single feature bundle:

(36) $[_{T1} i\varphi_T ... [_{T2} [i\varphi \text{ } v] ... \rightarrow [_{T1/2} [i\varphi_T i\varphi \text{ } v] ...$

Then, feature specifications are deleted/simplified, giving rise to the object clitic for subject clitic effect (recall that the clitic *a* can be spelled out because it realizes a D feature, which is located in a higher position):

(37) $[i\varphi_T i\varphi \, v] \rightarrow [i\varphi \, v]$

The same holds for clitic combinations featuring s_{arb}: after T's and v's features are fused, s_{arb}'s features obliterate T's features, thus impeding the insertion of the subject clitic. In these dialects, however, the agreement restriction banning subjects clitics does not yield ungrammaticality as subject clitics are ruled out by the 'object clitic for subject clitic' effect in (37), which acts as a *repair strategy* (Calabrese 2005; 1994, 2011 on clitics) avoiding the presence of subject clitics in the PASS construction.

In conclusion, I argued that the marginality of PASS in Venetan results from an agreement restriction banning the co-occurrence of subject clitics and s_{arb}. Western NIDs do not exhibit any restriction as the subject clitic occurring in PASS construction is a non-agreeing, expletive clitic, while in Friulian, PASS constructions are grammatical because the restriction is overridden by an orthogonal process, namely the 'object clitic for subject clitic' repair.

5 An aside on placement phenomena

Given the above interactions between s_{arb} and T's features, one might wonder whether in NIDs s_{arb} can be eventually treated as a subject clitic itself. Since s_{arb} pronominalizes the grammatical subject of IMP constructions and the logical subject of PASS constructions, the hypothesis has already been advanced in the literature. However, the only convincing clue in favour of this hypothesis comes from the dialect of Borgomanero (Tortora 2015), where complement clitics, including the reflexive *si*, stand enclitic to the inflected verb, while subject clitics and – crucially – the arbitrary *as* occur in preverbal position:

(38) a. *Al vônga   =si*   (Borgomanerese, Tortora 2015)
          He= sees   =himself
          'He sees himself'
      b. *As môngia   bej   chilonsé*
          s= eat   well   here
          'You eat well here'

This led Tortora to conclude that "[b]ecause there are no OCLs in Borgomanerese which otherwise appear proclitically, the pre-verbal position of impersonal *s* in (115) [=(38)b] suggests that this is in fact a subject clitic." (Tortora 2015: 115). The conclusion, however, cannot be extended straightforwardly to all the northern dialects as, under many respects, s_{arb} does not exhibit the peculiar behaviour of fully-fledged subject clitics (see also Manzini & Savoia 2001: 251). For instance, s_{arb} never undergoes inversion in the dialects exhibiting subject-clitic inversion in interrogative clauses, cf. (39a) vs (39b):

(39) a. magne-li mia ancò?   (Vicentino, Venetan)
        eat=they not today
        'Don't they eat today?'
    b. se magna / *magne=semia ancò?
       s= eat   not today
       'Don't we/they eat today?'

(40) a. I   mevol   ben
        they=   me=   wish.3PL   well
        'They love me'
    b. me   vol-i   ben?
        me.F= wish.3PL=they   well
        'Do they love me'

If we analyse inversion as movement of the [iφ v] constituent above the position hosting subject clitics, the data above show that s_{arb} moves along with the finite verb, as illustrated below:

(41) [C   [T1 iφT ... [T2 [iφ v]] ...
            ↓   ↓
           SCL s_{arb}

However, even if s_{arb} does not behave as a fully-fledged subject clitic, it is fair to conclude that it does not behave as a proper object clitic, either. Outside of Borgomanerese, the exceptionality of the impersonal s_{arb} is confirmed by further data from other dialects of Piedmont, where enclisis of object pronouns is allowed only in compound tenses and restructuring environments. Until the 18th century, these contexts allowed a pattern of clitic copying (Parry 1998: 107–110) in which two instances of the object clitic occur, one in enclisis and the other in proclisis (see also Tortora 2014a, 2014b). In present-day dialects, by contrast, the proclitic copy cannot occur anymore, as shown in (42b). However, as shown in (43), the impersonal s- differs from *plain* complement clitics like *lo* as it is still allowed to occur twice and, in contexts where it occurs once, as in (43b), it is allowed to stand proclitic to the modal verb:

(42) a. *a   l   peul   di-lo*   (18th century Piedm., Parry 1998: 108)
          (S)he=   it=can   say=it
      b. *a   *(l) peul   di-lo*   (present day Piedm.)
          (S)he=   it=can   say=it
          '(S)he can say'

(43) a. *a   s   peul   di-sse*
          EXPL=   s=   can   say=s
      b. *a   s   peul   di*
          EXPL=   s=   can   say
      c. *a   peul   di-sse*
          EXPL=   can   say=s
          'One can say'

Another clue of the peculiar status of s_{arb} comes from Venetan dialects like Venetian (Lepschy 1984/1989). In Venetian, the partitive clitic is *ghene*, which can be analysed as a compound formed by two clitic items (*ghe+ne*). The former element (*ghe*) is dropped if another complement clitic precedes the partitive, see (44a) (Benincà & Vanelli 1982, 14). However, after a subject clitic or s_{arb}, *ghe* cannot be dropped, see (44b) and (44c) respectively:

(44) a. *el   me   (*ghe)ne   parla*
          he=   to.me=   of.it=   speaks
          'He speaks to me about it'
      b. *el   *(ghe)ne   parla*
          he=   of.it=   speaks
          'He speaks about it'
      c. *se   *(ghe)ne   parla*
          s=   of.it=   speaks
          'One speaks about it'

Given (44a) and (44b-c), one might argue that *ghe* is dropped when another clitic occurs in the same local domain, i.e. in [... v], while *ghe* is not dropped if a clitic occurs in T, cf. (45a) vs (45b). Under this analysis, the pattern in (44b-c) means that, when s_{arb} is placed in [... v], something happens, preventing *ghe* from being dropped (more on this below).

(45) a. [$_{T1}$ el ... [$_{T2}$ *[me (*ghe)ne v]* ...
      b. [$_{T1}$ el ... [$_{T2}$ *[*(ghe)ne v]* ...

Further evidence of the exceptionality of s_{arb} comes from the placement of s_{arb} with respect to other complement clitics (Manzini & Savoia 2001) as it turns out that the order in many NIDs is not rigid. Lepschy 1983/1989; 1984/1989) notices that in modern Venetian, the impersonal *se* precedes the accusative clitic, as shown in (46). However, besides the order in (46), several authors of the 19th century also allow the opposite order (viz, accusative > impersonal), which is in fact attested in other Venetan vernaculars. According to Lepschy, similar alternations are found in combinations with first and second person dative clitics as well.

(46) a. *se lo tol* (Venetian, 20th and 19th c.)
s= it=take
'one takes it'
b. *no la se ga da mandar via* (Venetian, 19th c.)
not it/her= s= has of send away
'one should not turn her away'

Vicentino, another Venetan dialect, exhibits a similar alternation, but in combination with the third person dative clitic *ghe*:

(47) a. *Ghe se porta un libro* (Vicentino)
to.him= s= bring a book
'One brings him a book'
b. *Se ghe porta un libro*
s= to.him= bring a book
'One brings him a book'

Mendrisiotto, a dialect spoken in Ticino (Lurà 1987: 162), exhibits the same pattern of alternation with either dative or accusative clitics. The latter alternation is attested in other dialects of Ticino such as Bellinzonese (Cattaneo 2009):

(48) a. *a la mam granda, sa ga / ga sa dava dal vö*
to the mum great s= to.her= / to.her= s= give the vö
(Mendrisiotto, Tic.)
'We were used to addressing the grandmother with the vö form'
b. *a sa l / al sa tö migna*
PART s= it= / it= s= takes NEG
'One does not take it'

(49) a. *Sa la ved tüt i matin in piaza* (Bellinzonese, Tic.)
s= it/her= sees all the morning in square
'One sees her/it in the square every morning'
b. *La sa ved tüt i matin in piaza*
it/her= s= sees all the morning in square
'One sees her/it in the square every morning'

An account of these alternations is provided by Cattaneo (2009), who argues that third-person object clitics like *la* can 'rebel' and exceptionally climb to the positions dedicated to the homophonous third person subject clitics. The analysis builds on Lepschy's intuition that these alternations result from the identity of third person subject and object clitics. If we assume the hypothesis that subject and object clitics are merged in different positions of the functional spine of the clause, then Cattaneo's analysis can be reformulated as follows:

(50) a. [T1 *la* ... [T2 **[*sa la* v]** ...
              ↑_____|

Cattaneo's analysis is supported by the behaviour of the particle *a* (Lurà 1987: 157; Cattaneo 2009: 27–49), which can combine with the object *la*, but is ungrammatical in combination with the homophonous subject clitic:

(51) a. *(A) la   legi, la riviscta*
             SCl her= read the magazine
             'I read it, the magazine'
      b. *(*A) la   va   a Padova*
             SCl she= goes   to Padova
             'She goes to Padova'

Crucially, when the rebelling object clitic *la* precedes the impersonal *sa*, *a* is ruled out, see (52). This led Cattaneo to conclude that the rebelled *la* is not in its canonical position in [... v], but occupies a higher T position, as illustrated in (53).

(52) a. *(A) sa   la   ved   tüt i   matin   in piaza*
             SCL s= her= see.3sg all the morning in square
             'One sees her/it in the square every morning'
      b. *(*A) la   sa ved   tüt i   matin   in piaza*
             SCL her= s= see.3sg all the morning in square
             'One sees her/it in the square every morning'

(53) a. [T1 (*a) *la* ... [T2 **[*sa la* v]** ...
              ↑_____|

This analysis, however, cannot hold for the cases in which s_{arb} can either precede or follow another complement clitic such as the dative *ga/ghe*, cf. (47) and (48). In fact, no probing head is expected to trigger the rebellion of dative clitics. However, I think that Cattaneo's analysis can be maintained once it is assumed that the rebelling clitic is s_{arb}, which in certain dialects and under certain conditions can realise a higher bundle of T features, thus giving rise to the above alternations.

It is worth recalling the D'Alessandro-style analysis of agreement provided in the previous sections (repeated below for the sake of clarity): I argued that *s*'s {arb} feature spreads across T projections, thus giving rise to agreement restrictions and ruling out agreeing subject clitics in eastern NIDs.

(54)   spreading
       [T1 {*arb*} ... [T2 [{*arb*} v]
                        ↓
                        si

Given (54) and assuming a late insertion model (Halle & Marantz 1993; Calabrese 2003), one might therefore expect that, in languages with subject clitics, the formative *s* may eventually realise the higher feature bundle in T rather than the lower one in v:

(55)   spreading
       [T1 {*arb*} ... [T2 [{*arb*} v]
        ↓   ↓
        si   (si)

Arguably, the environment triggering/allowing (55) is subject to further subconditions, which give rise to the kaleidoscopic variation introduced so far. Due to space limitations, I cannot go into details, but it seems to me that the mechanism in (55) provides a promising explanation of all the puzzles introduced in the present section.

Lastly, this hypothesis may shed light on the behaviour of sequences formed by an impersonal and a reflexive clitic, which are a major source of variation across Italian vernaculars. Three main patterns are attested: Italian-type languages, in which the combination is morphologically opaque as one of the two clitics is replaced by another clitic item (e.g. *ci* in (56)a); Venetan/Lombard-type languages, in which the combination is grammatical and transparent as two *s*-'s elements can co-occur; Piedmontese-type languages, in which the combination is impossible and speakers must retreat to an indefinite pronoun meaning 'one'/'man'.

(56) a. ci/*si si lava   (Italian)
      b. se se lava   (Venetian)
      c. un/*s as lava   (Piedmontese, Parry 1998:91)
          'One washes him/herself'

As suggested by Grimshaw (1997, 2000), Maiden (2000), Pescarini (2010) among others, the opacity of clusters displayed by Italian-type languages is probably triggered by an identity-avoidance principle preventing two occurrences of the same exponent within the same cluster. In the light of the previous analysis, one might argue that Venetan-type dialects allow *se se* sequences as s_{arb} can 'rebel', i.e. realise T's highest head. If so, a sequence of two *se*'s becomes grammatical since the two *se*'s realise feature bundles that are not in the same local domain.

6 Conclusion

In this paper, I have summarised data concerning the distribution of PASS and IMP constructions in NIDs. Western NIDs seem to lack the IMP construction, thus banning (clitic) objects in arbitrary constructions. Conversely, in Venetan dialects, the most marginal construction is the PASS one, even if the distinction between the two is often blurred because subject clitics do not occur with postverbal subjects, third person subject and object clitics are often identical, and verbs do not exhibit plural agreement in the third person. Lastly, Friulian allow both PASS and IMP constructions, but in the former subject clitics are always dropped, arguably because of an 'object clitic for subject clitic' effect.

The type of restriction exhibited by western NIDs has already been accounted for in works such as Cinque (1988), Dobrovie Sorin (1998, 2006), Roberts (2010) on the basis of data from Romanian. On the contrary, the restrictions exhibited by Venetan and Friulian dialects, which challenge previous parametric analyses, have remained almost unnoticed.

I argued that the above restrictions follow from the agreement relation holding between T, the argument of the PASS clause, and s_{arb}. Besides giving rise to the ban against first or second person subjects in PASS (D'Alessandro 2007), I have entertained the hypothesis that the same mechanism may account for the syntax of subject clitics in PASS constructions and for other puzzling phenomena regarding the placement of s_{arb} exponents.

Acknowledgments: To Andrea, my mentor.
For comments and suggestions, I thank audiences in Padua, Zurich, Leiden, and two anonymous reviewers.

References

Anagnostopoulou, Elena. 2003. *The syntax of ditransitives: Evidence from clitics*. Berlin: Mouton De Gruyter.
Belletti, Adriana. 1982a. 'Morphological' passive and Pro-Drop: the impersonal construction in Italian. *Journal of linguistic research* 2. 1–34.

Belletti, Adriana. 1982b. On the anaphoric status of the reciprocal construction in Italian. *The Linguistic Review* 2. 101–37.
Benincà, Paola & Cecilia Poletto. 2004. Topic, Focus and V2: Defining the CP sublayers. In Luigi Rizzi (ed.), *The structure of CP and IP*, 52–75. Oxford and New York: Oxford University Press.
Benincà, Paola & Laura Vanelli. 1982. Appunti di sintassi veneta. In Manlio Cortelazzo, *Guida ai dialetti veneti IV*, 7–38. Padova: CLEUP.
Benincà Paola & Laura Vanelli. 2005. *Linguistica Friulana*. Padova: Unipress.
Calabrese, Andrea. 1994. Syncretism phenomena in the clitic systems of Italian and Sardinian dialects and the notion or morphological change. In J.N. Beckman (ed.), *Proceedings of NELS* 25.2, 151–174. Amherst (Mass.): GLSA.
Calabrese, Andrea. 2003. On impoverishment and fission in the verbal morphology of the dialect of Livinallongo. In Christina Tortora, *The syntax of Italian*, 3–33. New York and Oxford: Oxford University Press.
Calabrese, Andrea. 2005. *Markedness and economy in a derivational model of phonology*. Berlin: Mouton de Gruyter.
Calabrese, Andrea. 2011. Investigations on markedness, syncretism and zero exponence in morphology. *Morphology* 21. 283–325.
Calabrese, Andrea & Diego Pescarini. 2014. Clitic metathesis in the Friulian dialect of Forni di Sotto. *Probus* 26(2). 275–308.
Cattaneo, Andrea. 2009. *It is all about clitics: The case of a northern Italian Dialect like Bellinzonese*. New York University, doctoral dissertation.
Cennamo, Michela. 1993. *The reanalysis of reflexives: a diachronic perspective*. Napoli: Liguori.
Cennamo, Michela. 1995. Transitivity and VS order in Italian reflexives. *STUF* 48. 84–105.
Cennamo Michela. 1997. Passive and impersonal constructions. In Mair Parry & Martin Maiden, *The dialects of Italy*, 145–161. London: Routledge.
Cinque Guglielmo. 1988. On si constructions and the theory of *arb*. *Linguistic Inquiry* 19. 521–582.
D'Alessandro, Roberta. 2007. *Impersonal* si *constructions*. Berlin: Mouton De Gruyter.
Dobrovie-Sorin Carmen. 1998. Impersonal se constructions in Romance and the passivization of unergatives. *Linguistic Inquiry* 29(3). 399–437.
Dobrovie-Sorin Carmen. 2006. The SE-anaphor and its role in argument realization. In Martin Everaert & Henk van Riemsdijk (eds.), *The Blackwell companion to syntax*, vol. 4, 118–179. Oxford: Blackwell.
Grimshaw, Jane. 1997. The best clitic: constraint interaction in morphosyntax. In Liliane Haegeman (ed.), *Elements of grammar: Handbook of generative syntax,* 169–196. Dordrecht: Kluwer.
Grimshaw, Jane. 2000. Optimal clitic positions and the lexicon in Romance clitic systems. In G. Legendre, J. Grimshaw, S. Vikner (eds.), *Optimality theoretic syntax*, 205–240. Cambridge, MA: MIT Press.
Halle, Morris & Alec Marantz. 1993. Distributed Morphology and the pieces of inflection. In Kenneth Hale & S. Jay Keyser, *The view from building 20*, 111–176. Cambridge, MA: MIT Press.
Lepschy, Giulio C. 1983/1989. Clitici veneziani. In G. Holtus & M. Metzeltin (eds), *Linguistica e dialettologia veneta. Studi offerti a Manlio Cortelazzo dai colleghi stranieri*, 71–77. Tubingen: Narr, 71-7. (republished in Giulio C. Lepschy, *Nuovi saggi di linguistica italiana*, 119–127. Bologna, Il Mulino.)
Lepschy Giulio C. 1984/1989. Costruzioni impersonali con se in veneziano. In Manlio Cortelazzo (ed.), *Guida ai dialetti veneti VI*, 69–79. Padova, CLEUP. (republished in Giulio C. Lepschy, *Nuovi saggi di linguistica italiana,* 129–142. Bologna: Il Mulino).

Lurà, Franco. 1987. *Il dialetto del Mendrisiotto: descrizione sincronica e diacroniaca e confronto con l'italiano.* Mendrisio-Chiasso: Edizioni Unione di Branche Svizzere.

Maiden, Maiden. 2000. Phonological dissimilation and clitic morphology in Italo-Romance. In Lori Repetti (ed.), *phonological theory and the dialects of Italy*, 137–168. Amsterdam, Benjamins.

Manzini, M. Rita. 1986. The syntax of pronominal clitics. *Syntax and Semantics* 19. 241–262.

Manzini, M. Rita & Leonardo Savoia. 1997. Null subjects without *pro*. *UCL Working Papers in Linguistics* 9. 1–12.

Manzini, M. Rita & Leonardo Savoia. 2000. The syntax of object clitics: *si* in Italian dialects. In Guglielmo Cinque & Giampaolo Salvi (eds), *Current studies in Italian syntax. Essays offered to Lorenzo Renzi*, 225–255. Amsterdam: North-Holland.

Manzini, M. Rita & Leonardo Savoia. 2004. Clitics: Co-occurrence and mutual exclusion patterns. In Luigi Rizzi (ed.), *The structure of CP and IP*, 211–250. New York: Oxford University Press.

Manzini, M. Rita & Leonardo Savoia. 2009. Morphology dissolves into syntax: Infixation and doubling in Romance languages. *Annali online dell'università di Ferrara. Sezione lettere* 4(1). 1–28.

Masutti, Vania & Jan Casalicchio. 2015. A syntactic analysis of the subject clitic *a* in the friulian variety of Campone. *Isogloss* (Special Issue on the morphosyntax of Italo-Romance, ed. by Diego Pescarini & Silvia Rossi). 103–132.

Mendikoetxea, Amaya & Adrian Battye. 1990. Arb *se/si* in transitive contexts: a comparative study. *Rivista di grammatica generativa* 15. 161–195.

Parry, Mair. 1997. Preverbal negation and clitic ordering, with particular reference to a group of North-West Italian dialects. *Zeitschrift für Romanische Philologie* 113(2). 243–270.

Parry, Mair. 1998. The reinterpretation of the reflexive in Piedmontese: 'Impersonal' SE constructions. *Transactions of the Philological Society* 96. 63–116.

Parry, Mair. 2005. *Parluma 'd Còiri. Sociolinguistica e grammatica storica del dialetto di Cairo Montenotte.* Savona: Società savonese di storia patria.

Pescarini, Diego. 2010. Elsewhere in Romance: evidence from clitic clusters. *Linguistic Inquiry* 41(3). 427–444.

Pescarini, Diego. 2012. Osservazioni sui clitici soggetto nei dialetti Romagnoli e Marchigiani. *Quaderni di lavoro ASIt* 15. 45–60.

Pescarini, Diego. 2015. *Le costruzioni con si. Italiano, dialetti, lingue romanze.* Roma: Carocci.

Pescarini Diego. 2018. Parametrising arbitrary constructions. *Probus* 30(1). 67–92.

Poletto, Cecilia. 2000. *The higher functional field. Evidence from Northern Italian dialects.* New York and Oxford, Oxford University Press.

Poletto Cecilia & Jean-Yves Pollock. 2009. Another look at wh-questions in Romance: the case of medrisiotto and its consequences for the analysis of French wh-in-situ and embedded interrogatives. In Leo Wentzel, *Romance languages and linguistic theory 2006: Selected papers from 'going Romance'*, 199–258. Amsterdam, John Benjamins.

Raposo, Eduardo & Juan Uriagereka. 1996. Indefinite SE. *Natural Language and Linguistic Theory* 14. 749–810.

Roberts, Ian. 1993. The nature of subject clitics in Franco-Provençal Valdôtain. In Adriana Belletti (ed.), *Dialects of Italy*, 319–353. Turin: Rosenberg & Sellier.

Roberts, Ian. 2010. *Agreement and head movement. Clitics, incorporation, and defective goals.* Cambridge, MA: MIT Press.

Roberts, Ian. 2012. On the nature of syntactic parameters: a programme for research. In J. Avelar et al., *Diachronic Syntax,* 318–334. Oxford: Oxford University Press.
Roberts, Ian. 2014. Subject clitics and macroparameters. In Paola Benincà, Adam Ledgeway & Nigel Vincent (eds), *Diachrony and dialects. Grammatical change in the dialects of Italy*, 177–201. Oxford: Oxford University Press.
Roberts, Ian. 2015. Subject- and object-licensing interactions: OCL-for-SCL in Piedmontese and Valdôtain revisited. Talk given at the *International Dialect Meeting*, Leiden, 22–24 June 2015.
Salvi, Giampaolo. 2008a. La formazione della costruzione impersonale in italiano. *Revista de Estudos Linguísticos da Universidade do Porto* 3. 13–37.
Salvi, Giampaolo. 2008b. Imperfect systems and diachronic change. In Ulrich Detges & Richard Waltereit, *The paradox of grammatical change: Perspectives from Romance*, 127–146. Amsterdam: Benjamins.
Stegovec, Adrian. 2017. Two's company, three's a crowd: Strength implications in syntactic person restrictions. Talk given at *GLOW* 20, 15th March 2017.
Tortora, Christina. 2014a. Patterns of variation and diachronic change in Piedmontese object clitic syntax. In Paola Benincà, Adam Ledgeway & Nigel Vincent (eds.), *Diachrony and dialects. Grammatical change in the dialects of Italy*, 218–240. Oxford: Oxford University Press.
Tortora, Christina. 2014b. On the relation between functional architecture and patterns of change in Romance clitic syntax. In M.-H. Côté & E. Mathieu (eds.), *Variation within and across Romance Languages*, 331–348. Amsterdam: Benjamins.
Tortora, Christina. 2015. *A comparative grammar of Borgomanerese.* Oxford and New York: Oxford University Press.
Vanelli, Laura. 1998. *I dialetti italiani settentrionali nel panorama romanzo.* Roma: Bulzoni.
Zubizzareta, Maria-Luisa. 1982. *On the relationship of the lexicon to syntax.* Cambridge, MA: MIT dissertation.

Susi Wurmbrand
Markedness as a condition on feature sharing

1 Introduction

Germanic languages, like many other languages, show a distributional gap in the inventory of pronouns: only third person pronouns distinguish gender. This is illustrated for English, Dutch, German, and Icelandic in *Table 1*: English, Dutch and German only show gender distinctions in the third person singular; in Icelandic, gender is distinguished in the third person singular and plural.

Table 1: Pronouns in English, Dutch, German, and Icelandic

	English	Dutch	German	Icelandic	
1.SG	I	ik	ich	ég	
2.SG	you	jij	du	þú	
3.MASC.SG	he	hij	er	hann	
3.FEM.SG	she	zij	sie	hún	
3.NEU.SG	it	het	es	það	
1.PL	we	wij	wir	við	
2.PL	you	jullie	ihr	þið	
3.PL	they	zij	sie	MASC:	þeir
				FEM:	þær
				NEUT:	þau

Calabrese 2011 proposes a markedness approach to distributional gaps in paradigms (see also Noyer 1998, Nevins 2011, Bobaljik 2017, among others). If a markedness constraint such as (1) is active in a language, illicit feature combinations (in this case, 1/2.FEM) need to get repaired. One specific mechanism suggested is *obliteration*, whereby a marked morphological category is removed as in (2). In our specific case, first and second person (i.e., [+PARTICIPANT]) pronouns always end up without a gender branch, hence no pronominal form can distinguish gender in these persons. A similar markedness constraint, *[GENDER, PLURAL] (Bobaljik 2017: 9, (17b)),[1] can be assumed to be active in English, Dutch, and

---

[1] This constraint and the one given in (1) use different feature notations. Below, we will see that for our purposes, (1) has to be modified as *[GENDER, PARTICIPANT] (see (14)), which makes the two constraints parallel.

https://doi.org/10.1515/9781501506734-015

German, however, not in Icelandic, to derive the lack of gender distinctions in the third person plural in the former three languages.

(1) *[+PARTICIPANT, +FEMININE] [Calabrese 2011: 295, (14)]

(2) 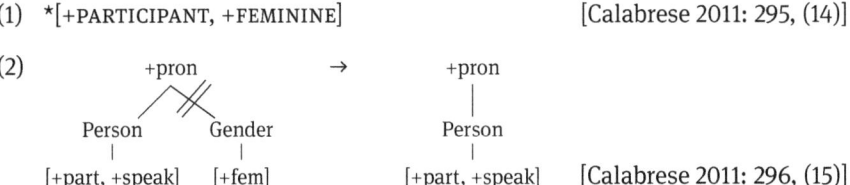   [Calabrese 2011: 296, (15)]

In this squib, I discuss a distributional restriction of a specific type of pronoun – first and second person pronouns that are interpreted as bound variables rather than indexical pronouns. I show that the availability of bound readings of first and second person pronouns in certain relative clause contexts correlates with the richness of agreement displayed by the head DPs and relative pronouns in the four Germanic languages above, and I suggest that markedness constraints of the type developed in Calabrese 2011 may also play a role in syntax in the process of feature valuation.

2 Fake indexicals

In contexts such as (3), first and second person pronouns are interpreted as bound variables rather than indexical pronouns: the interpretation is that only the addressee did his/her best, and no other people in the comparison set did their best (since one cannot do someone else's best, such sentences can in fact only involve a bound variable interpretation and a referential/indexical interpretation is not available). Indexicals that are interpreted as bound variables are referred to as *fake indexicals* [FIs].

(3) a. *Only I did my best.*
    b. *Only you did your best.*

As shown in (4), Dutch, German, and Icelandic also allow bound variable interpretations of indexicals.

(4) a. Alleen   ik   heb   m'n/*haar   best   gedaan.   Dutch
       only   I   have   my/*her   best   done   (P. Fenger, p.c.)
    b. Nur   ich   habe   mein/*ihr   Bestes gegeben.   German
       only   I   have   my/*her   best   given
    c. Aðeins ég   geri   mitt/* hennar besta.   Icelandic
       only   I   do   my/*her   best   (G. Harðarson, p.c.)

An interesting difference arises in these languages when indexical pronouns are embedded in a relative clause headed by *the only one*. As shown in (5) through (7), English and Dutch allow fake indexicals in this context, whereas German and Icelandic prohibit them. In the latter, a first person pronoun can only be interpreted as referring to the speaker, in other words, the meaning can only be that nobody in the comparison set can take care of the speaker's child/children. If an indexical interpretation is not possible, as in the *do your best* contexts in (6c) and (7c), morphologically first (and second) person pronouns are excluded altogether.

(5) English, Dutch: FIs possible
   a. *I am the only one who takes care of her/my son.*
      Possible: Nobody else is taking care of their son.
   b. *Ik ben de enige die m'n best gedaan heeft.*
      I am the.only.one who my best done has.3.SG
      'I am the only one who has done my best.'
      [Maier and de Schepper 2010: 4, (11)]

(6) German: FIs impossible
   a. *Ich bin die einzige, die ihren Sohn versorgen kann.*
      I am the.FEM.SG only who.FEM.SG her son take.care.of can.1/3.SG
      'I am the only one who can take care of her son.'
      Possible: Nobody else can take care of their son. [based on Kratzer 2009]
   b. *Ich bin die einzige, die meinen Sohn versorgen kann.*
      I am the.FEM.SG only who.FEM.SG my son take.care.of can.1/3.SG
      'I am the only one who can take care of my (= the speaker's) son.'
      Impossible: Nobody else can take care of their son. [based on Kratzer 2009]
   c. *Ich bin die einzige, die *mein / √ihr Bestes geben will.*
      I am the.FEM.SG only who.FEM.SG *my / √her best give want.1/3.SG
      'I am the only one who wants to do *my/her best.'

(7) Icelandic: FIs impossible (G. Harðarson, p.c.)[2]
   a. *Ég er sá eini hérna sem getur séð um börnin sín.*
      I am DEM.MASC.SG only here that can.3.SG see about children SELF
      'I am the only one here who can take care of his/her children.'
      Possible: Nobody else here can take care of their children.

---

[2] The situation is more complex in Icelandic, once verb agreement and the distribution of empty subjects is considered (see Wurmbrand 2017b). In this paper, I concentrate on the configuration in (7).

b. Ég   er   sá eini   hérna sem getur   séð um börnin   mín.
   I   am   DEM.MASC.SG only   here that can.3.SG see about children my
   'I am the only one here who can take care of my (= the speaker's) children.'
   Impossible: Nobody else here can take care of their children.

c. Ég   er   sá eini   sem   gerir   *mitt / ✓sitt   besta.
   I   am   DEM.MASC.SG only that   do.3.SG   *my   / ✓SELF's best
   'I am the only one who does his/her best.'

In Kratzer 2009 it is proposed that the difference in the availability of FIs between English and German lies in the morphology. While the specific morphological approach proposed there does not extend to Dutch and Icelandic (see Wurmbrand 2015, 2017a for various issues), I will show that morphological properties, specifically the feature make-up of relative DPs, are indeed a major factor in the distribution of FIs in these configurations.

3 Dependencies in 'the only one' contexts

In contrast to simple sentences with FIs such as (3)/(4), which involve a direct dependency between the (true) indexical pronoun and the FI, the connection between the fake and the true indexical in cases such as (5)/(7) is only indirect in that it is mediated by various other dependencies. It is this difference that lies at the heart of the (un)availability of FIs. While the direct dependency in (3)/(4) can be treated as regular binding and feature transfer, thus allowing FIs in all four languages, I suggest that the additional dependencies in (5)/(7) interfere with feature transfer in a way to be spelled out below. Specifically, the morpho-syntactic and semantic dependencies in these cases are predication, relativization (it is not relevant for the current purpose whether relative clauses involve a matching or head-internal derivation), subject – T agreement, and binding (see (8)). Predication is a predominantly semantic dependency which does not involve morphological feature sharing in the languages under consideration (cf. *I* [1.SG] – *the only one* [3.SG]). Subject – T agreement is a morphological or syntactic dependency which typically does not feed into semantics. Binding is a syntactic dependency which is interpreted semantically and shows morphological effects. Lastly, relativization is also a syntactic and semantic dependency, however, it shows morphological effects only in some of the languages examined here. As shown in *Table 2*, English and Dutch determiners, adjectives, and relative pronouns do not distinguish (animate) gender whereas German and Icelandic DPs do (in German, relative pronouns also distinguish gender; Icelandic has no relative pronouns).

(8)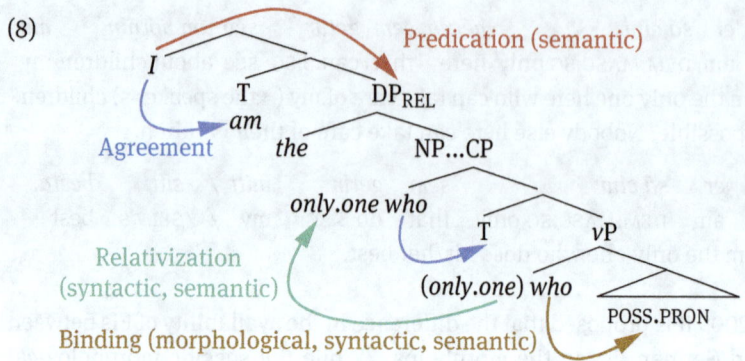

Table 2: 'the only one who' in English, Dutch, German, and Icelandic

	English	Dutch	German	Icelandic
FEM.SG	the only one who	de enige die	die einzige die	sú eina
MASC.SG	the only one who	de enige die	der einzige der	sá eini
FEM.PL	the only ones who	de enigen die	die einzigen die	þær einu
MASC.PL	the only ones who	de enigen die	die einzigen die	þeir einu

In what follows, I propose that the difference in the availability of FIs in contexts such as (5) and (7) is rooted in the morphological properties of relative DPs: In English and Dutch, the relative DP only shows number distinctions (*the only one* vs. *the only ones*), whereas it also shows gender distinctions in German and Icelandic (in German only in the singular).

4 Establishing the dependencies

Let us see how the dependencies and features relations are established in a bottom-up derivation in English. The first relation, ①, is the binding relation, established between the relative pronoun (or the relative NP in a head-internal derivation) and the possessive pronoun. I follow the common view that syntactic binding is accompanied by feature transfer from the antecedent to the bindee. Assuming that third person is the lack of person (participant) features, the relative DP/pronoun *the only one who* is only specified for number in English, and the number value is transferred to the possessive pronoun during binding. The next step is agreement between the subject and T (whether before or after the subject moves to Spec,TP does not concern us here). The last operation in the embedded clause is relativization, ②, which moves the relative pronoun (or the relative NP) to the CP domain. In the matrix clause the subject and predicate are in a predication configuration, ③, and the subject agrees with matrix T. If no further operation takes place, the sentence is pronounced as in (9a). Lastly, as for the gender feature on the possessive pronoun, I assume that it is freely inserted in syntax or morphology, perhaps as a last resort, and it is evaluated contextually whether the morphosyntactic value chosen is appropriate given the contextual referent of "I" (similarly to cross-sentential gender 'agreement').

(9) a. *I am the only one who takes care of her son.*

b.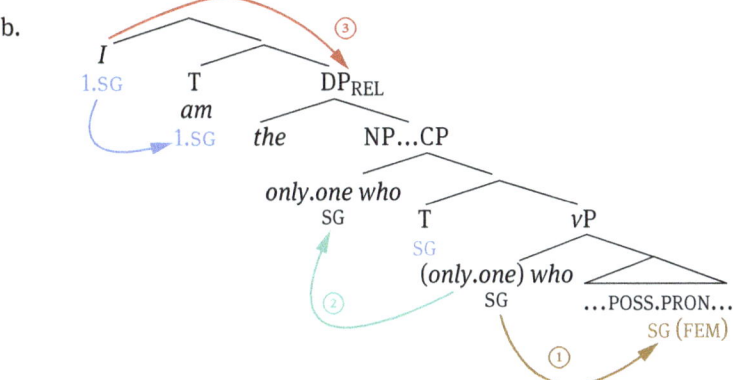

The configuration with a FI possessive pronoun proceeds the same way. Since the matrix subject is indirectly connected to the possessive pronoun via the three dependencies (①, ②, ③), I propose that a further feature sharing process is possible as in (10) (④), as long as it does not over-write or conflict with any of the features present already (which, as we will see, will be the case in German and Icelandic).

(10) a. *I am the only one who takes care of my son.*

b.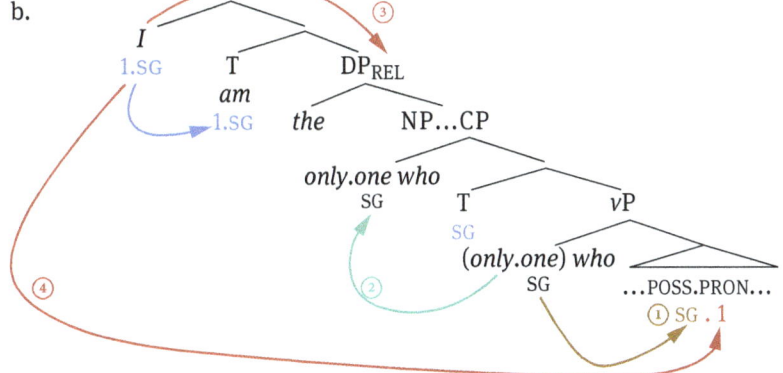

I suggest that the operation in ④ is a syntactic feature dependency analogous to feature transfer in binding (e.g., whether this is termed Agree or differently is not essential for the current purpose). In contrast to the (free and contextually evaluated) appearance of the gender feature in (9), a syntactic dependency is sensitive to the syntactic configuration, in particular c-command. The following facts motivate this distinction. As shown in (11), the option of FIs disappears in inverted (specificational) contexts in both English and Dutch. Since the matrix subject does not c-command into the relative clause in these cases, an additional syntactic agreement dependency between *I* and the possessive pronoun cannot be established. Note that in both languages, bound variable interpretations are not in principle excluded in these contexts. They are only possible, however, through the relative DP – i.e., only with third person pronouns. As shown in (11), like in (9), (contextual) feminine is again available, but a FI is not. The availability of feminine marking in both (9) and (11) together with the difference in FIs in (10) vs. (11) support the claim that the two features arise via different mechanisms – the first person feature in (10) can only be transmitted via a syntactic binding-like relation, whereas the gender feature in (9) and (11) is contextual.

(11) a. *The only one who has done *my/✓her best is me.*
 b. *De enige   die   *m'n / ✓haar best gedaan heeft   ben   ik.*
    the only.one who   *my / ✓her best done   has.3.SG am.1.SG I
    'The only one who has done her best is me.'   (P. Fenger, p.c.)

Finally, an additional feature transfer relation triggered by the matrix subject in (10) is only possible for dependencies that can apply long-distance (such as variable binding) and not for operations like subject – T agreement which are strictly local in the languages under consideration. Thus, although the embedded possessive pronoun can receive features from the matrix subject in (10), the embedded T can only be valued by its local subject, the relative pronoun, and hence remains third person, independently of what form the possessive pronoun takes (see also Wurmbrand 2017a, b for further discussion of the relation between FIs and verb agreement).

In the next section, I return to the difference in the availability of FIs between English/Dutch and German/Icelandic.

5 A markedness account

As mentioned above, in German and Icelandic, relative DPs display a richer feature inventory since in addition to number, gender is also distinguished on attributive elements (in German also on the relative pronoun). Thus, the features of the relative clause in (12a) are as in (12b).³

(12) a. Ich bin die einzige,   die   ihren / meinen*FI   Sohn
         I   am   the.FEM.SG only who.FEM.SG her   / my*FI   son
         versorgen   kann.
         take.care.of can.1/3.SG
         'I am the only one who can take care of his/my son.'

[based on Kratzer 2009]

b.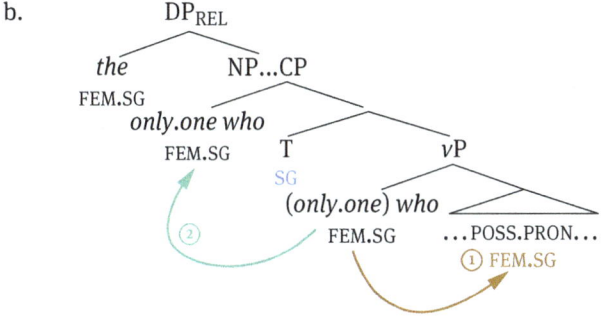

The major difference between German (12b) and English (9)/(10) is that in the German case, the possessive pronoun is valued FEM.SG via the binding dependency (I assume that feature sharing must apply exhaustively to all features present in the target and the source whenever possible). If, in this scenario, a further Agree relation is established between the matrix subject and the possessive pronoun, as in (13), an illicit feature combination would be created: +PARTICIPANT, +FEMININE. I propose that this markedness violation is what excludes FIs in German and Icelandic.

---

3 Since non-pronominal DPs distinguish gender in German and Icelandic, whereas they don't in English and Dutch (or only in a very limited way in the latter), I assume that a gender feature is always present in the former but (can be) absent in the latter. As in the case of 3rd person possessive pronouns in (9), the gender value on 'the only' may be inserted freely in syntax/morphology and evaluated contextually.

(13)

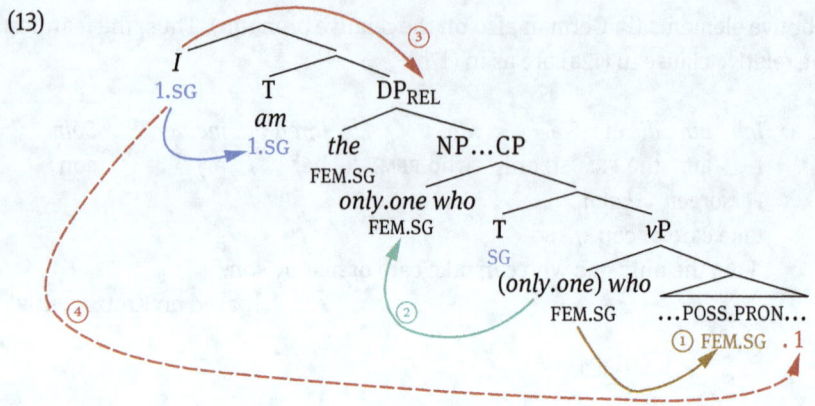

At this point the question arises of how markedness applies in these cases.⁴ If markedness constraints apply (solely) in morphology, we would expect that in (13) the gender feature/branch gets deleted, exactly as in (2) (which we have seen is operative in German and Icelandic). However, this would create the wrong result for the distribution of FIs. It would be predicted that the possessive pronoun ends up as 1.SG – i.e., a FI, which is exactly the form it cannot take. One could assume that in this case, the person feature is deleted, but it is not clear how such an assumption could be motivated. The alternative I would like to suggest is that in addition to triggering rules like obliteration that repair illicit configurations, markedness constraints may also constrain the application of rules that would otherwise create an illicit configuration. Specifically, I suggest that markedness also plays a role for syntactically established feature dependencies that manipulate features, such as feature transfer in binding yielding (morphological) agreement. Since FIs are also excluded in the context of masculine relative DPs in German and Icelandic, the restriction to feminine in Calabrese 2011's original constraint would not be sufficient. Instead I propose the general markedness constraint in (14). In essence, operation ④ in (13) is excluded since adding the feature first person to the already existing feature bundle FEM.SG would create an illicit configuration violating (14).

(14)   *[GENDER, PARTICIPANT]   (Ge/Ice)   [based on Calabrese 2011]

Further motivation for this approach may come from FIs in plural contexts in German. Recall from *Table 2* that German does not show gender distinctions in

---

4 Thanks to Jonathan Bobaljik, Heidi Harley, Beata Moskal, and Pete Smith for discussion of this point.

the plural. If this corresponds to the lack of gender features, the markedness approach proposed here predicts that FIs should be possible in the plural since no markedness violation would arise if a participant feature is added via the operation in ④ in (13). Although the judgments are subject to speaker variation (in particular in second person plural configurations), the data in (15) from Kratzer 2009 support this prediction.

(15) a. Wir sind die einzigen,   die   unseren   Sohn   versorgen
         we   are   the only.ones   who.PL   our.ACC   son   take.care.of.1/3.PL
         'We are the only ones who are taking care of   [Kratzer 2009: 191, (7)]
         our son.'

    b. Ihr   seid die einzigen   die   euren   Sohn   versorgt.
        you   are   the only.ones who.PL   your.ACC son   take.care.of.2.PL
        'You are the only ones who are taking care   [Kratzer 2009: 192, (9)]
        of your son.'

Finally, I'd like to speculate about the question of where/when the markedness constraint in (14) applies. Although markedness is restricted to morphology in Calabrese 2011, the current proposal is not necessarily against the spirit of Calabrese's account. While operation ④ in (13) has to involve a core syntactic component (due to its sensitivity to c-command), the actual application of the markedness constraint in (14) could nevertheless be seen as a morphological phenomenon. To achieve this technically, let us assume that operation ④ is an Agree dependency, which accompanies operations such as syntactic binding. Agree is often split into two subparts (Chomsky 2000, 2001, Bhatt and Walkow 2013) – a part that establishes a syntactically conditioned link between two matching elements, and a part that copies and transfers feature values (cf. Bhatt and Walkow 2013's notions of *Match* and *Value*). It is then possible to situate the two parts of Agree in different components – Match in syntax, and Value in morphology. Thus, while the Match part of ④ in (13) is only subject to syntactic conditions, the morphological Value part would be constrained by markedness.

6 Conclusion

In this squib, I have shown that the distribution of fake indexicals in four Germanic languages shows a connection between the richness of agreement and the availability of bound readings. I have suggested that markedness constraints of the type developed in Calabrese 2011 are involved in restricting certain feature combinations in the morphological feature valuation part of Agree dependencies. Following Calabrese 2011, purely syntactic operations such as Merge or Move are not (or rather unlikely) to be subject to markedness constraints. The only syntactic(ally established) dependencies for which markedness constraints are relevant are dependencies that feed into morphological agreement. Given the ambivalent status of agreement as a syntactic and/or morphological operation, having morphological constraints participate in regulating (partly) syntactic operations pertaining to agreement may not be a big adjustment to the general workings of markedness, or so I hope.

Acknowledgments: Mille grazie, Andrea – having you as a colleague has been very inspiring (linguistically and personally), comforting, and fun!

References

Bhatt, Rajesh, and Martin Walkow. 2013. Locating agreement in Grammar: An argument from agreement in conjunctions. *Natural Language and Linguistic Theory* 31(4). 951-1013.

Bobaljik, Jonathan D. 2017. Distributed morphology. In *Oxford research encyclopedia of linguistics*. Oxford/New York: Oxford University Press.

Calabrese, Andrea. 2011. Investigations on markedness, syncretism and zero exponence in morphology. *Morphology* 21(2). 283–325.

Chomsky, Noam. 2000. Minimalist inquiries: The framework. In Roger Martin, David Michaels and Juan Uriagereka (eds.), *Step by step: Essays on minimalist syntax in honor of Howard Lasnik*, 89-155. Cambridge, MA: MIT Press.

Chomsky, Noam. 2001. Derivation by phase. In Michael Kenstowicz (ed.), *Ken Hale: A life in language*, 1–52. Cambridge, MA: MIT Press.

Kratzer, Angelika. 2009. Making a pronoun: Fake indexicals as windows into the properties of pronouns. *Linguistic Inquiry* 40(2). 187–237.

Maier, Emar, and Kees de Schepper. 2010. Fake indexicals in Dutch: A challenge for Kratzer (2009). Ms.

Nevins, Andrew. 2011. Marked targets vs. marked targets and impoverishment of the dual. *Linguistic Inquiry* 42. 413–444.

Noyer, Rolf. 1998. Impoverishment theory and morphosyntactic markedness. In Steven G. Lapointe, Diane K. Brentari and Patrick M. Farrell (eds.), *Morphology and its relation to phonology and syntax*, 264–285. Stanford, CA: CSLI Publications.

Wurmbrand, Susi. 2015. Fake indexicals, feature sharing, and the importance of gendered relatives. Colloquium talk, MIT, Cambridge, MA.

Wurmbrand, Susi. 2017a. Feature sharing or how I value my son. In Claire Halpert, Hadas Kotek and Coppe van Urk (eds.), *The Pesky set: Papers for David Pesetsky*, 173–182. Cambridge, MA: MIT Working Papers in Linguistics.

Wurmbrand, Susi. 2017b. Icelandic as a partial null subject language – Evidence from fake indexicals. In Laura Bailey and Michelle Sheehan (eds.), *Order and structure in syntax*. Language Science Press.

Part IV: *Issues* in Syntax

Adriana Belletti
On *a*-marking of object topics in the Italian left periphery

1 Introduction

Standard Italian is known not to mark lexical direct objects through use of a preposition.[1] This is in contrast with southern varieties, in which lexical direct objects are typically introduced by preposition *a*, as an instance of the Differential Object Marking/DOM phenomenon, found in several languages (Manzini and Franco 2016 for recent assessment of the phenomenon). In the closely related standard Spanish, to mention a well-known case, lexical direct objects are introduced by the same preposition *a*, with constraints depending on the nature of the direct object (such as e.g., its specificity and animacy). Thus, speakers of standard Italian judge sentences like (1) as ungrammatical, or else they typically attribute to these sentences a clear "southern" flavor:

(1) a. *Ho salutato a Maria*
 (I) have greeted to Maria
 'I have greeted Maria'
 b. *Hanno arrestato al colpevole*
 (they) have arrested to the guilty
 'They have arrested the guilty'

However, when *a* (typically, animate) lexical direct object is realized as a left peripheral topic, also standard Italian allows it to be introduced by preposition *a*, at different levels of marginality for different speakers. This is especially possible when the object is an Experiencer object. Belletti & Rizzi (1988) report examples like those in (2)a, b originally pointed out by Paola Benincà (Benincà 1986, also reviewed in Berretta 1989):

(2) a. *? A Gianni, questi argomenti non l'hanno convinto*
 to Gianni, these arguments him-CL have not convinced
 'Gianni, these arguments have not convinced him'

---

[1] I will use the term Standard Italian throughout having in mind the variety of Italian that is most widespread. This is utilized and taught in school and to L2 learners, used on television and in written or formal communication and which is historically based on (literary) Tuscan.

https://doi.org/10.1515/9781501506734-016

b. *A Gianni, la gente non lo conosce
   to Gianni, people him-CL do not know
                          (Belletti & Rizzi 1988, footnote 27)

Whereas (2)a is considered relatively acceptable by speakers of standard Italian, although at different levels of marginality depending on the speaker as mentioned, (2)b is judged as deviant by all speakers, thus indicating that the possibility of *a*-marking of the direct object preferably goes with Experiencer objects. Interestingly, in the Clitic Left Dislocation/ClLD structures of the type in (2), presence of the *a*-marked topic does not have any effect on the type of resumptive clitic in the following clause, which remains an accusative clitic (*lo* in 2a). Hence, *a*-marking of the topic does not transform the pre-posed object into a dative Experiencer, a possibility found in Italian with, e.g., the *piacere/like* class of psych-verbs. With the *piacere/like* class the resumptive pronoun in ClLD structures is a dative clitic:

(3) *A Gianni, questi argomenti non gli sono mai piaciuti*
     to Gianni, these arguments to-him-CL have never liked
     'Gianni never liked these arguments'

The impossibility of both (4)a and (4)b following indicates an interesting property of the Italian *a*-marking of direct objects: not only is it preferably limited to Experiencer objects, it also is only available when the object is a left peripheral topic. Thus, *a*-marking of the clause internal Experiencer object in (4)a is as impossible as the *a*-marking of the object in (4)b, which is not an Experiencer. Both (4)a and (4)b are ungrammatical for speakers of standard Italian at the same level as the examples in (1), with no difference due to the thematic interpretation of the object:

(4) a. **Questi argomenti non hanno convinto a Gianni*
        these arguments have not convince to Gianni
     b. **La gente non conosce a Gianni*
        people do not know to Gianni

The *a*-marking available in standard Italian for Experiencers of the *piacere/like* class, can sometimes extend to verbs of the *preoccupare/worry* class, which normally mark the Experiencer with accusative. For instance, this is the case for a verb like *interessare/interest*, as is indicated in (5) a,b where both the *a*-marked option and the accusative option for the Experiencer are possible for the majority of standard Italian speakers.[2] However, this is not the case for the verb *preoccupare/worry* in (6)b below, much as for the verb *convincere/convince* in (4)a above, for which the *a*-marked Experiencer is not an option for any speaker:

(5) a. *Questa idea interessa gli studiosi*
       this idea interests the researchers
    b. (?)*Questa idea interessa agli studiosi*
       this idea interests to the researchers

(6) a. *Questo comportamento preoccupa i responsabili*
       this behavior   worries the responsibles
    b. **Questo comportamento preoccupa ai responsabili*
       this behavior   worries the responsibles

The contrast between (5) a, b on the one side and (6) a, b and (4)a on the other thus indicates clearly that *a*-marking is not a property associated exclusively with the Experiencer role and it is not directly associated with the argument structure of the verb nor with the Th-role of the object.

Hence, something different than just a property of the object Experiencer must be at play with Left-peripheral *a*-Topics of the type in (2)a. The following pages highlight some (of the) interpretive property (-ies) that *a*-Topics may express as well as some aspects of their syntax. Recent results from acquisition will also inspire and guide the investigation.

---

[2] Note that the dative *a*-Experiencer of the *piacere* type can be pre-posed as a Topic with no resumptive dative clitic in the following clause, an option always available when the pre-posed topic is a PP (PP-pre-posing):

(i) a. *A Gianni, questa idea interessa*
       to Gianni this   idea interests
    b. *A Gianni, questa idea piace*
       to Gianni, this idea likes

No such option is available for the *a*-Topic possible with verbs of the *preoccupare* class, as illustrated by the impossiblity of ii., in contrast with the (marginal) possibility of (2)a in the text:

(ii) **A Gianni, questi argomenti non hanno convinto*
      to Gianni, these arguments have not convinced

This further indicates that the *a*-Topic remains a direct object DP and is not a PP: direct object topics obligatorily require an accusative clitic in the clause following the pre-posed topic, in ClLD structures.

2 *a*-Marking of Object Topics as a property of the Left periphery: Aspects of their distribution

I would like to explore the hypothesis according to which *a*-marking is primarily a property of the (Italian) Left Periphery that may be associated with pre-posed (animate) direct objects when they fill the peripheral topic position in ClLD structures.

Consider first the observation due to Leonetti (2004), according to which a tight relation between *a*-marking and topicality emerges in the Spanish DOM phenomenon, to the effect that left dislocated direct objects in ClLDs are always obligatorily *a*-marked. A particularly interesting illustration of this relation is provided by verbs allowing for optional DOM of the direct object when it is clause internal; if the object is left dislocated, however, *a*-marking becomes obligatory with the same verbs with the same type of object (see also Laca 1987). Relevant contrasts are illustrated in (7)–(8). The indefinite direct object is interpreted as a specific topic in (8):

(7) a. *Ya conocía (a) muchos estudiantes*
already (I) knew many students
b. *Habían incluido (a) dos catedráticos en la lista*
(they) had included two professors in the list

(8) CLLD:
a. **(A) muchos estudiantes, ya los conocía*
many students, (I) alreadu knew them(cl)
b. **(A) dos catedráticos, los habían incluido en la lista*
two professors, (they) had included them(cl) in the list
(Leonetti 2004: (12)a, b)

It is tempting to propose that the Italian *a*-marking of topics illustrated in (2)a, manifests the same option available in Spanish.[3] In the latter language *a*-marking is obligatory in the left-peripheral position, whereas in Italian it is only an option, often a marginal one. Examples like those in (9)a, b, d below, also discussed in

---

3 Indeed, as pointed out by a reviewer to whom the following example i. is due, *a*-marking of a non-specific indefinite object topic is excluded in Italian as well also with object experiencers in cases similar to (2):

(i) *(*A) un mulo, non lo convincerai di certo con questi metodi*
(*to) a mule, (you) will not convince it-CL with these methods
'You will certainly not convince a mule with these methods'
Only possible if the intended referent is a specific mule.

Berretta (1989) (see also Renzi 1988), in which the topic is a first or second person pronoun constitute an exception, as the *a*-marking is in fact quasi-obligatory in these cases in (non southern varieties of) standard Italian; a bit more marginally, also a third person pronoun can tolerate *a*-marking (9c). In (9)a the left dislocated object is an Experiencer object. In the other examples in (9) it is not, yet *a*-marking is possible in fact much favored thus confirming that relation with the Experiencer role is not a necessary condition for *a*-marking:

(9) a. *A me/*?Me non mi si inganna*
    to me/me   one does not me-CL cheat
    'Nobody cheats me'
  b. *A te/*?te ti licenziano di sicuro*
    to you/you they you-CL fire for sure
    'They will certainly fore you'
  c. *?A lui/✓lui lo rispettano tutti*
    to him/him they him-CL respect all
    'Everybody respects him'
  d. *A noi sul lavoro non ci assume più nessuno*
    to us on work nobody us-hire anymore
    'Nobody will hire us anymore'

As pointed out in Berretta (1989) the above sentences without the *a*-marking of the pronoun have the flavor of a northern regional variety of Italian, in which *a*-marking is excluded from the left peripheral topic position in the core possible case of personal-pronoun-Topics (and not just with lexical noun phrases, or in the clause internal direct object position as an instance of DOM); northern varieties are, in this respect, a kind of mirror image of southern varieties. Be as it may, the proper description of the phenomenon for standard Italian (corresponding to central-northern varieties) is then that *a*-marking of left peripheral topics with a lexical noun phrase is marginal, *a*-marking of left peripheral topics that are personal pronouns, especially first and second person ones, is perfectly acceptable in fact required. It would then seem that *a*-marking of lexical left peripheral topics is an extension of the standard option at work for first and second personal pronouns.

2.1 Only topic, never focus

In concluding this descriptive section, it should also be noted that *a*-marking is indeed an option that solely concerns topics. Consider in this respect the very clear contrasts in (10):

(10) a. *TE assumeranno __ (non Maria)*
   YOU they will hire (not Maria)
   b. **A TE assumeranno __ (non Maria)*
   TO YOU the will hire
   c. *TE questi argomenti convincono (non certo me)*
   YOU these arguments convince (not me for sure)
   d. **A TE questi argomenti convincono (non certo me)*
   TO YOU these arguments convince (not me for sure)
   e. *A te, questi argomenti non ti hanno mai convinto*
   to you, these arguments you-CL have never convinced

(10)b (with a non-psych verb) in which the contrastive/corrective fronted focus is introduced by prepostion *a* contrasts with (10)a in which there is no such preposition, similarly (10)d (with a psych-verb) contrasts with (10)c; (10)b and (10)d are just ungrammatical for all speakers of standard (non southern) Italian, also those who tend to accept *a*-Topics with object Experiencers, as in (2)a; (10)d contrasts in turn with the perfect status of (10)e, with a second person pronominal *a*-Topic.

2.2 Same distribution and interpretive possibilities as simple left peripheral non-*a*-marked topics

As for the distribution of *a*-Topics, the examples in (11) indicate that the *a*-marker can be associated with the different Topic positions of the Italian Left Periphery, above and below Focus (hence possibly different types of topics, along the lines of Bianchi and Frascarelli 2010, Frascarelli and Hinterhölzl 2007, appear to be compatible with *a*-marking).

(11) a. *Al bambino, LA MAMMA, (con la giacca) lo vestirà*
   to-the kid, THE MUM (with the jacket) him-CL will dress
   b. *(con la giacca), LA MAMMA, al bambino lo vestirà*
   (with the jacket) THE MUM, to-the kid, him-CL will dress

Long distance *a*-Topics are also possible:

(12) *Al bambino la ragazza pensa che la mamma lo vestirà con la giacca*
   to the kid the girl thinks that the mother him-CL will dress with the jacket

Since a crucial property of an *a*-Topic is that of being associated with a direct object, it follows that there can be just one *a*-Topic per clause/per verb. Hence, there cannot be iteration of *a*-Topics even in a multiple topic language like Italian (Rizzi 1997).

Also from the point of view of their possible coreference possibilities, *a*-Topics behave like simple non *a*-marked topics. As observed by Calabrese (1986) a left dislocated Topic cannot easily co-refer with a null *pro* subject of the clause following it. This is illustrated by the following Calabres's example:

(13)   *Poiché a Mario$_j$, Carla$_i$ gli ha dato un bacio, pro$_{i/*j}$ è felice*
       since to Mario Carla gave a kiss, (she) pro is happy
                              (Calabrese 1986: 32, example 28)

An *a*-Topic, has the same interpretive possibilities as a left dislocated topic not introduced by preposition *a*. Consider (14) in this respect, with the same structure as (13) above:

(14)   a. *Poiché Mario$_j$/lui$_j$, Carla$_i$ l'ha convinto, pro$_{i/*?j}$ è felice*
           since Mario, Carla him-cl has convinced, (she) *pro* is happy
       b. *Poiché a Mario$_j$/a lui$_j$, Carla$_i$ l'ha convinto, pro$_{i/*?j}$ è felice*
           since to Mario, Carla him-cl has convinced, (she) *pro* is happy

Dative experiencers of the *piacere* class behave as subjects, in fact as so-called Quirky subjects (Belletti & Rizzi 1988). They have a number of subject-like properties. Among these properties, we find that, as noted again by Calabrese (1986), they can co-refer with a silent null subject *pro* in the following clause. The examples in (15) illustrate this possibility:

(15)   a. *Poiché a Gianni$_i$ piace Maria$_j$, pro$_{i/*j}$ va sempre nel bar dove si sono conosciuti*
           Since (to) Gianni likes Maria, (he) *pro* always goes to the bar where they first met
       b. *Poiché ad Andrea$_i$ interessa l'iconografia, pro$_i$ abbandonerà con piacere la linguistica*
           since Andrea is interested in iconography, (he) *pro* will abandon linguistics with pleasure   (Calabrese 1986: 28, ex. 10)
       c. *Quando a Lori$_i$ è venuta voglia di gelato, pro$_i$ si è messa a tremare*
           when Lori got the urge to eat an ice cream, (she) *pro* began to tremble
                              (Calabrese 1986: 28, ex. 11)

Therefore, an *a*-Topic does not behave as a dative experiencer. This interpretive fact is consistent with the Case property already noted: an *a*-Topic is not a dative.

Having established some basic distributional properties of *a*-Topics and (some of) their interpretive possibilities, in the following section some salient features of their discourse value will be highlighted. In the analysis that will be sketched out the somewhat privileged status of Experiencers as the most felicitous *a*-Topics (even when lexical) as well as the privileged status of first and second person pronouns as the best instances of *a*-marked Topics will find a natural *raison d'être*.

3 On the nature of left peripheral *a*-Topics

I would like to entertain the hypothesis that *a*-Topics express some psychological affectedness/involvement of the object in the action/feeling/overall event expressed by the verb. This involvement may also result in the expression of a certain amount of "empathy", in the sense of Kuno and Kaburaki (1977) and subsequent work. More specifically, according to this idea, *a*-Topics are psychologically affected/involved objects that express an empathic point of view; this is done by means of use of the overt marker *a*.[4] If a psychologically affected empathic point of view is expressed, it is not surprising that *a*-marking of topics be a property of the left periphery, as is generally the case for properties characteristically connected with the discourse context: the closest area at the interface with the contextual discourse is precisely the left periphery of the clause (Rizzi 1997 and much subsequent work on the syntactic cartography of this area of the clause). Quoting Kuno and Kaburaki (1977):

(16) "Empathy is the speaker's identification (which may vary in degree) with a person/thing that participates in the event or state that he describes in a sentence."

(Kuno and Kaburaki 1977:3)

The difference between a simple topic and an *a*-Topic, would then be that the latter involves an empathic point of view.[5] Hence not just a topic, with the specificity and giveness that the topic interpretation carries along, but a topic with respect to which the speaker feels a certain empathy.

---

4 In Italian *a* is the same preposition utilized to express a dative experiencer, a goal and also a benefactive, the additional argument of a transitive action (as in e.g. ho letto una storia ai bambini/ *I have read a story to the children*). The benefactive interpretation expresses a similar type of affectedness/involvement as the one outlined in the text for *a*-Topics.
5 Thanks to V. Bianchi for suggesting a possible relation with "empathy" in these cases.

To the extent that this is a good enough approximation to an appropriate characterization of some crucial aspect of the interpretation of *a*-Topics, two of the distributional properties singled out in the previous descriptive sections may find a natural account: i. Object Experiencers are the most preferred *a*-Topics in standard Italian probably because an Experiencer is, by definition, psychologically affected/involved by the event described by the verb; ii. first and second person pronouns are the most likely *a*-Topics as first and second person pronouns directly participate in the speech event and express the point of view of the speaker/hearer (Speas & Tenny 2003). In this case, it is an empathic point of view, according to the characterization above (Sigürdhsson 2004, Bianchi 2006 for the role of the feature person in the left periphery of the clause).[6]

Some recent results from acquisition, presented in the following section, lend support to a characterization along these lines.

3.1 Some reflections from acquisition

Recent experimental results presented in Belletti & Manetti (2017) on the elicited production of overt direct object topics by Italian speaking young children (4;1 to 5;11) have revealed a significant use of *a*-marking of topics in their ClLD structures. Indeed, children's vast majority of the produced ClLDs (88% of the cases) had the left dislocated object realized as an *a*-Topic rather than as a simple non-*a*-marked topic (12% of the cases). Since the tested children were all speakers of Tuscan varieties of Italian, such marking cannot be assimilated to a manifestation of DOM of the southern variety type.

A further crucial feature of children's productions in the elicitation experiment is that *a*-marking is limited to object topics when they are pre-posed into the Left Periphery; indeed, never is the direct object *a*-marked in the children's productions when it is a clause internal direct object. The following example of a sentences produced by one child in the elicitation experiment presented in the reference quoted, offers a kind of natural minimal pair: the pre-posed object topic in the answer in (17)A is marked with *a* in the second sentence of the child's answer in which it is left dislocated, but it is not marked by *a* in the first sentence of the same answer in which it is realized in the object position. The first sentence of the child's answer is expressed in the form of a simple SVO declarative clause with no ClLD:

---

6 In the case of first person *a*-Topics the empathy reaches in a sense its highest degree, given the coincidence between the speaker and the *a*-Topic.

(17) Q: *Che cosa succede ai miei amici, il pinguino e la mucca?*
 what happens to my friends, the pinguin and the cow
 A: *La giraffa sta leccando* **la mucca**, *e il coniglio* **al pinguino**
 the giraffe is licking the cow and the rabbit to the penguin it-CL
 lo sta grattando
 is scratching

(Omar, 5 y.o.)

Hence, children's *a*-marking of topics is a property of the left periphery much as is the case in adult standard Italian and it is not the manifestation of DOM (as seen in e.g. Spanish).

We have seen in section 2 that *a*-marking of topics is characteristically realized with Experiencer objects in adult standard Italian (when the topic is a lexical noun phrase). However, preliminary results have indicated that adult speakers of Italian who have been asked to judge the CILD sentences produced by children containing the pre-posed *a*-Topics tended to find them relatively acceptable, irrespective of the thematic interpretation of the object, which was never a psychological Experiencer in the experimental stimuli. Further results from a larger adult population are currently being collected. It is natural to speculate that in their productions young children have somewhat overextended the possibility of a-marking of pre-posed object topics, also available in standard Italian to a certain degree, as described in the previous section. And such an extension is relatively accepted by adult speakers in spite of the fact that non-Experiencer *a*-Topics are only acceptable with first and second person pronouns in the adult language.

As indicated in (17), in the experimental setting of Belletti and Manetti (2017), children answered patient oriented questions of the type "what happens to X?". These patient-oriented questions aimed at favoring the production by children of an overt left dislocated object topic (and they indeed succeeded in this aim). The questions always referred to a situation that was described to the children by the experimenter with the help of pictures illustrating some animal (e.g. a giraffe and a rabbit, the subjects/agents) performing an action (wash, dry …) over another animal (e.g. a cow and a penguin, the objects/patients) and ending with the question, e.g. "What happens to my friends the penguin and the cow?". It is reasonable to think that children, who actively participated in this type of game setting, tended to identify themselves with the pre-posed left dislocated topic (the patient of the described event), or that they felt involved in the event that affected it. Thus, children may have found themselves in a situation in which the expression of an empathic point of view was particularly natural for them. In other words, the experimental setting appears to have created a situation in which the expression of the topic in the form of an *a*-Topic was particularly appropriate. As discussed in detail in Belletti and Manetti (2017) use of the *a*-Topic also allowed children to cope with a ClLD in which the object A'-dependency between the left dislocated topic and the clitic in the following sentence had to be established across an intervening lexical subject, an intervention situation that is known to be hard for children to properly master at that age (along the lines of Friedmann, Belletti, Rizzi 2009; Manetti et al. 2016). This aspect of the children's use of *a*-Topics in the described experiments, although crucial in other respects, is not relevant to the present discussion. For all details concerning both the experimental design and the articulated results the reader is referred to the reference quoted.

Here the following considerations should be highlighted: the frequent use of *a*-Topics in children's productions was somewhat unexpected since the phenomenon is rather limited in adult standard Italian, as seen in the previous sections. At the same time, children's productions do not sound so deviant to the adult Italian speakers' ear, as was also confirmed by the (preliminary results on) judgments provided by adults on the children's productions mentioned above. Hence, once again, also viewed from this angle, children appear to have adopted a possibility available in standard Italian, and to have overextended it (Belletti 2017). They have done so in two respects: they have *a*-marked direct objects that were not Experiencers and they have *a*-marked direct objects that were always lexical noun phrases (as opposed to being first or second person pronouns). Children's productions are reminiscent of the Spanish examples quoted in (7) and (8) from Leonetti (2004); in those Spanish examples (obligatory) *a*-marking of left dislocated objects was dissociated by their (optional) *a*-marking in the direct object position, as an instance of DOM. Also in those cases, as underscored by Leonetti (2004), *a*-marking can be primarily seen as a property of the left periphery associated with the topicality of the direct object. We have hypothesized that psychological affectedness and empathy can be added as features linked to *a*-marking. Furthermore, Spanish seems to have gone one step further compared to child-Italian: whereas *a*-marking of the left peripheral topic is favored in Italian speaking children's productions (also for the locality reasons hinted at above), it is not obligatory (12% of children's CLLDs contain a simple non-*a*-marked Topic) contrary to Spanish; and *a*-marking of the direct object is never an option when it remains in sentence internal position, as is instead the case in the Spanish examples in (7).

As seen in (17), in the experimental setting of Belletti and Manetti (2017), children answered patient oriented questions of the type "what happened to my friends, X and Y?". The question always contained a dative Experiencer. It cannot be excluded that this also contributed to somehow prime the use of *a*-marking of the topic in the children's answers. However, it is a fact that the left dislocated object topic was treated as a direct object by children and not as a dative as shown by the fact the resumptive clitic in the following clause was systematically an accusative clitic.[7] In contrast to the children, in the first informal pilot grammaticality judgment task mentioned above, the Italian speaking adults interviewed had been given no context for the expression of their judgment; in particular there was no question-answer setting; hence there was no "primed" a-dative Experiencer. Nevertheless, they did not generally rule out the children's ClLDs containing the *a*-Topics. Again this confirms that the *a*-marker has an autonomous status in the Left periphery of standard Italian and that an a-Experiencer argument does not need to be present in the immediate context to (more or less directly) license it. Overall, the acquisition data reviewed in this section, combined with the adults' reactions to them support the view that *a*-marking is a Left Peripheral phenomenon in standard Italian, characteristically affecting pre-posed object topics.

3.2 Why only objects

But why is it that only objects can be *a*-Topics? In this section we offer some speculative considerations relevant to this question.

One issue is: Why couldn't a PP argument also be an *a*-Topic? Since PPs can be clitic left dislocated as illustrated in (18), one should wonder why (18)a is possible but (18)b is not; this would be parallel to the (marginal according to the description above) possibility of the left dislocated object as an *a*-Topic in (18)c as compared to the simple topic in (18)d:

(18) a. *Con Gianni, ci parlo domani*
  with Gianni, (I) with him-CL will speak tomorrow
  'With Gianni I will speak tomorrow'
 b. **A con Gianni, ci parlo domani*
  to with Gianni, (I) with him-CL will speak tomorrow
 c. *A Maria, non la convince nessuno*
  to Maria, nobody her-CL convince
 d. *Maria, non la convince nessuno*
  Maria, nobody her-CL convince
  'Maria, nobody convinces her'

---

7 The clitic was (correctly) a dative clitic only if the verb of the sentence was realized by children with a periphrastic expression requiring a dative goal, as in "dare un bacio a ./give a kiss to..." instead of "baciare/kiss". In many cases the verb of the sentence was realized as a simple transitive verb requiring an accusative object, which the children correctly realized through use of an accusative resumptive clitic in the sentence following the *a*-Topic.

The contrast between (18)a and (18)b in a sense already contains the answer to the question: a PP cannot be or be introduced as the complement of a further preposition. Whatever the precise characterization of this constraint turns out to be in terms of its expression in the clause structure (e.g. along the lines of an approach à la Kayne 2004), the described major violation is clearly responsible for the complete impossibility of (18)b.[8]

Direct objects are not introduced by a preposition, hence no analogous problem arises for them in this respect: a DP can be introduced by preposition *a* with no problem, as indicated by the possibility of (18)c, and, more generally, the existence of datives introduced by *a*. The following discourse related property of direct objects can also be observed. Characteristically, direct objects constitute the focus of new information in a clause containing a transitive verb: they either express the narrow focus, or, alternatively, they are part of the focus of new information expressed by an all-new clause. The two possibilities are illustrated by examples like (19)a and b respectively, uttered in the contexts indicated:

(19) (Context: *Chi hanno convinto?*/Whom have they convinced?)
   a. *Hanno convinto Maria*
      they have convinced Maria
   b. (Context: *Che cosa è successo?*/ What happened?)
      Hanno convinto Maria
      they have convinced Maria

It is tempting to suggest that *a*-marking on an overtly realized object is a way to mark it when it is not the focus or part of the focus. In other words, objects are(/can be) marked through *a*- when they are topics (cf. Leonetti 2004 quoted above on the relation between *a*-marking and topicality).

When an object is mentioned in the previous context and hence qualifies as a topic, it is normally expressed by a pronoun. Consider the simple discourse exchange in (20):

(20) (Context: *Che cosa è successo a Maria?*/What happened to Maria?)
   L'hanno convinta
   they her-CL have convinced

---

[8] So called "complex prepositions" are a different case. They are typically formed by an adverbial element + a (light) preposition (*a/to, di/of, da/from* in Italian), e.g. *vicino a/next to, sopra di/above of, lontano da/far from*, etc. (see Rizzi 1988 for systematic description).

Normally in a question-answer situation like (20), the topic (*Maria*) is not repeated in the answer, where it remains silent. However, if more than one object is present in the relevant context, the left dislocated topic is expressed; this is in fact the only way to solve the contrast, as in e.g. the contrastive topic situation in (21).[9]

(21) (Context: *Che cosa succede a Gianni e Maria?*/What happens to Gianni and Maria?)
(a) *Gianni lo assumono e (a) Maria la promuovono*
(to) Gianni him-CL they hire and (to) Maria her-CL they promote
'They will hire Gianni and they will promote Maria'

In these cases the topic can be expressed in the form of an *a*-Topic, with the described constraints holding in standard Italian, i.e preference for Experiencers when the object is a lexical noun phrase and in a more general fashion if it is a first or second person pronoun.

What about a subject DP? Subjects cannot be *a*-marked, even if they are Experiencers, as in (22):

(22) *A Maria teme me*
to Maria fears me

(22) is totally ungrammatical in standard Italian under any condition. A way to characterize the clear impossibility of (22) may be the following: although the subject of the psych-verb *fear* can be considered psychologically affected by her/his fear, *a*-marking reduces this noun phrase to a Quirky subject, making the *a*-Topic analysis unavailable. If the *a*-marked DP is a Quirky subject introduced by preposition *a*, this means that it is analyzed as a dative, hence the verb is analyzed in turn as a verb of the *piacere/like* class in Italian, whose object is nominative. This amounts to claiming that *a*-marking of the DP subject in a preverbal position leads to a Quirky subject analysis of this DP, hence it must be clause internal and fill (the relevant) subject position.[10]

This excludes the alternative possible analysis of the subject as a left peripheral *a*-Topic, with a resumptive null *pro* in the following clause. In the latter analysis *pro* would be the equivalent of the resumptive object clitic present when the

---

[9] Note that the contrastive topic situation is precisely the discourse condition of the acquisition experiment described in section 3.1 and indeed the object topics were overtly expressed in the answers provided by the children, as discussed.
[10] See Cardinaletti (2004), Rizzi and Shlonsky (2007), Bianchi and Chesi (2014) for considerations and proposals on different properties of subject positions in the clause structure (within TP).

a-Topic is the object.¹¹ Essentially, the analysis in (23)a is excluded. This contrasts with the possibility of (23)b, the analysis of a ClLD with an object *a*-Topic:

(23) a. *A Maria$_i$, pro$_i$ teme me
 to Maria fears me
 b. A Maria$_i$, la$_i$ convinceranno presto
 to Maria, (they) her-CL will convince soon

Subjects are distinct from topics (Calabrese 1986). Subjects are the argument about which the sentence predicates a property (Rizzi 2005, this volume, Reinhart 1981). From the discourse point of view, there is an *aboutness* relation between the subject and the following clause, which is close to the one between a topic and the following clause. Subjects are not necessarily also topics, though: They need not be given in the previous context in the same way as topics. This, however, does not exclude the possibility for a subject to also be a topic, given appropriate discourse conditions (cf. Belletti & Manetti 2017 for relevant discussion). For instance, in the discourse fragment in (24), the subject is also a topic. (24)a answers the question and could in principle be analyzed as in (24)b:

(24) Q: *Che cosa temono Gianni e Maria?*
 What do Gianni and Maria fear?
 A:
 a. *Gianni teme il terremoto e Maria teme il caldo*
 Gianni fears the earthquake and Maria fears the heath
 b. *Gianni$_i$, pro$_i$ teme il terremoto e Maria$_j$, pro$_j$ teme il caldo*
 Gianni pro fears the earthquake and Maria pro fears the heath

If our reasoning concerning the impossibility of (23)a is on the right track, it suggests that the analysis in (24)b is in fact not selected for an *a*-DP subject; an *a*-DP subject is rather analyzed as the argument about which the sentence predicates a property even when it is also a discourse topic. Hence, from the point of view of *a*-marking, a subject tolerates the marker only if it can be interpreted as a dative Experiencer, i.e. as a Quirky subject.¹²

---

11 There are no overt resumptive subject clitics in null subject Italian.
12 Thus, *a*-marking is just excluded in cases in which marking the subject with *a* is incompatible with its thematic interpretation, i.e. when it is not an Experiencer (e.g.: *A Gianni legge il libro*/To Gianni reads the book). In this situation a possible different analysis of the structure (in which the *a*-DP is a dative in subject position, with the verb reanalyzed as belonging to the *piacere/like* class and *a* as the marker of dative) is not available.

A subject does not tolerate *a*-marking if it can only be analyzed as a left peripheral topic. This is confirmed by the fact that in a multiple topics situation in which both subject and object are topics, to the extent that *a*-marking is available it necessarily goes on the object:

(25) a. *Gianni a Francesco l'ha convinto, Piero a Filippo l'ha deluso*
Gianni to Francesco him-CL has convinced, Piero to Filippo him-CL has deceived
b. *a Francesco Gianni l'ha convinto, a Filippo Piero l'ha deluso*
to Francesco Gianni him-CL has convinced, to Filippo Piero him-CL has deceived

Gianni and *Piero* are interpreted as the subject in both (25)a and b . With the order in (25)b, *Gianni* and *Piero* could be analyzed as filling a clause internal subject position. However, this is not the case in (25)a, where both the DPs and the a-DPs are necessarily pre-posed into the left periphery. Thus, (25)a is particularly relevant for our discussion as in this sentence both *Gianni* and *Piero* unambiguously occupy a high topic position in the left periphery, which is above the one of the left dislocated *a*-Topic in an iterated multiple topic construction. As noted, the only interpretation of the sentence (25)a is one in which *Gianni* and *Piero* are the subject of the respective following clause; they cannot be interpreted as the object, with *a Francesco* and *a Filippo* consequently interpreted as the subject. This confirms that that *a*-marking is indeed generally excluded for subjects in the left periphery. As discussed, *a*-marking of subjects is only limited to subject Experiencers in a clause internal subject position, in which *a*-marking is in fact dative marking (of a Quirky subject). Taken together (25)a, b indicate the impossibility of *a*-marking a subject in a left peripheral topic position, clearly external to TP. So, when there is *a*-marking with a subject, it is a clause internal Quirky subject.

The conclusion is that, indeed, *a*-marking of topics only concerns objects, when they are topics.[13] As topics are primarily expressed in the left periphery,

---

[13] The only instances of *a*-marking of a subject we are aware of are presented in Manzini and Savoia (2005, examples 256), quoting Rohlfs (1969). The relevant cases are all cases of long distance wh-extraction of an embedded subject, in languages with systematic DOM. See Chomky (1981), Kiss (1987), quoted by Manzini and Savoia in this respect for comparable data in English and Hungarian (in which accusative appears on a long-distant moved subject). The crucial property common to these cases is the long distance extraction process, and, related to that, the wh- nature of the subject. *a*-Marking thus appears to be a feature of long wh-extraction. Although extremely interesting and worth further investigation, this type of *a*-marking has (at least in part) a different nature from the one we have been investigating: in the case of *a*-Topics, the *a*-marker typically appears on a

a-marking is a left peripheral phenomenon in its core manifestation, as discussed in section 2. This is the case in standard Italian, as we have described it here. The following representation schematically illustrates the derivation of an *a*-Topic object moved to the Topic position in the articulated left periphery (Rizzi 1997, Rizzi and Bocci 2016 for recent developments) from its merge position as the Internal Argument/IA of the verb. In (26) the further movement of the preposition into a higher (Case?) head is also illustrated as a way to express the pre- positional order of the *a*-marker, which precedes the topic (Kayne 2004); movement of the DP External Argument/EA is also indicated in (26):

(26)

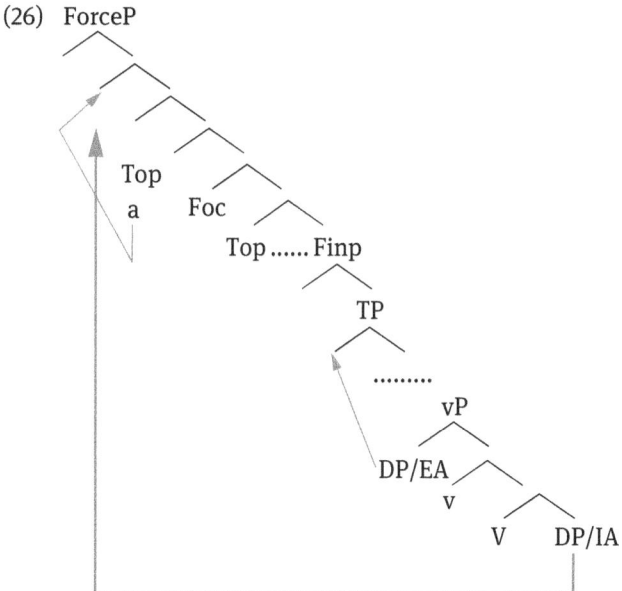

We conclude this section with a further speculative consideration, which deals with the phenomenon of *a*-marking in perspective. In section 3.1 we interpreted children's use of *a*-Topics as an extension of the *a*-marking that is possible to a much more limited extent in present day adult standard Italian. It is tempting to suggest that this behavior by children may indicate a step toward a possible syntactic change, which may eventually lead to a wider use of *a*-marking and

---

locally pre-posed topic. We have seen that the *a*-marker can also appear on a long distance extracted topic (example 12), but the point is that an *a*-marked topic need not have undergone long-distance movement, in contrast with the *a*-marked wh-extracted subjects quoted by Manzini & Savoia (2005). The issue is left open for future research. See Manzini and Savoia (2005) for a first proposal.

then possibly to the introduction of DOM in standard Italian.¹⁴ A possible way to express this idea could be the following. If, as is proposed in various analyses (Belletti 2004, Jayaseelan 2001, Tsai 2015), the low part of the clause contains a vP-periphery with discourse related positions similar to those found in the clause external left periphery, it is tempting to suggest that also the low topic position could be endowed with the *a*-marker. If this is the case, a clause internal direct object could be *a*-marked in the low vP-periphery. This might express the core property of the DOM phenomenon: *a*-marking of direct objects in their topic interpretation (hence, affected, typically human/animate and specific). The syntax of this (clause internal) *a*-marking would be the same as that of the clause external one, but the process would occur lower down in the structure, as sketched out in (27):¹⁵

---

14 Thanks to Ian Roberts for pointing out this possibility, in line with Lightfoot's (1999) approach to syntactic change as a process induced by innovative children's behaviors. The described experimental findings may have spotted a change on its way. See also Berretta (1989) for comparable considerations on a possible under way development of DOM in standard Italian. It is a fact that the phenomenon of *a*-marking described here already shares a number of features with classical DOM, often expressed through scales in the relevant literature, e.g. animacy, person, specificity (Bossong (1991), Leonetti (2008), Aissen (2003), a.o.).
15 I assume that movement of the DP/IA over the DP/EA (either in Spec-vP or in Spec-TP) in both (26) and (27) does not yield a violation of (featural) Relativized Minimality/fRM as the target position of the direct object is precisely endowed with the Topic feature. On the featural interpretation of the locality principle RM, Starke (2001), Rizzi (2004); for its relevance in acquisition, also mentioned in section 3.1, Friedmann, Belletti, Rizzi (2009) and much subsequent literature. See also Snyder & Hyams (2015) for related considerations on the development of passive in children.
Note that cases like the following in i. and ii. can be analyzed as instances of right peripheral *a*-Topics exploiting the low vP-periphery. Interestingly, also in these cases, much like in the left-peripheral ones, (first and second) personal pronouns require *a*-marking semi-obligatorily, whereas lexical *a*-marked low topics remain rather marginal, possibly more so than the left peripheral ones, even when they correspond to object experiencers:

(i) *Non mi si inganna, a me/?*me*
    one does not me-CL cheat, to me/me
(ii) *L'abbiamo convinto, Gianni/??a Gianni*
    we have convinced him-CL, Gianni/to Gianni

Possibly, overall *a*-marking of personal pronouns may be at a more advanced stage of grammaticalization. This is an interesting question, in need of further elaboration. Thanks to a reviewer for pointing out the comparison with right topics.

(27)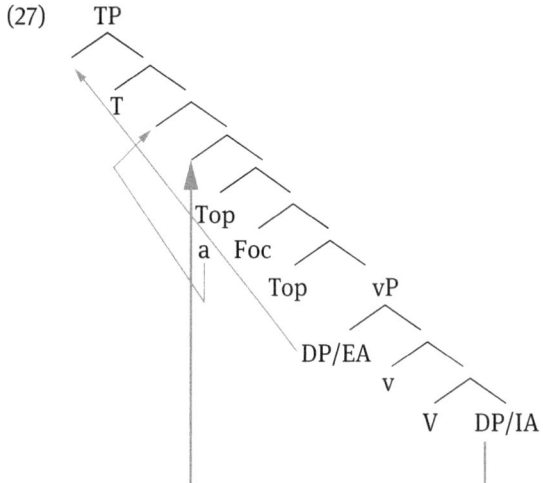

We leave the hypothesis, currently under investigation, at this speculative level, as a worth exploring route of a possible (ongoing) language change.[16]

4 Concluding remarks

In this article a characterization of the possibility of *a*-marking object topics in standard (non-southern) Italian has been proposed. The possibility is somewhat marginal for adult speakers of Italian, as it depends on the thematic interpretation of the object and on its lexical or pronominal nature; in contrast, it appears to be widely adopted by young Italian speaking children, as has emerged under eliciting experimental conditions. Despite this difference, *a*-marking for both children and adults is a process only involving direct objects when they are topics (and not focus or part it) and fill a topic position in the Italian left periphery. We have speculated that children may be overextending the recourse to *a*-Topics compared to adults and that this may be the symptom of a possible linguistic

---

[16] The change could then go even further, making the relation with the topic interpretation (correlating with animacy, specificity....) less strict. This would give rise to a more widespread use of *a*-marking of direct objects. This is a possible way toward a characterization of the current situation of *a*-marking in Spanish, and of *o*-marking of objects in Japanese (as described by Leonetti 2004 and related literature quoted therein). It is also possible that, in the described situation of grammaticalization, the *a*-marker may end up being located lower down in the structure, ultimately realizing (one of) the functional small *v* head(s). See Belletti (2004) for a proposal relating the latter option to an account of the possible VSO order of Spanish - an order that is not equally allowed in standard Italian. See Belletti (forthcoming) for further elaboration of this point.

change under way eventually leading to a more extended use of differentially marking direct objects in standard Italian.

Acknowledgments: The research presented here was funded in part by the European Research Council/ERC Advanced Grant 340297 SynCart – "Syntactic cartography and locality in adult grammars and language acquisition" which is here acknowledged.

References

Aissen, Judith. 2003. Differential object marking: Iconicity vs economy. *Natural Language and Linguistic Theory* 21. 435–483.
Belletti Adriana. 2004. Aspects of the low IP area. In Luigi Rizzi (ed.), *The structure of CP and IP*, 16–51. New York: Oxford University Press.
Belletti, Adriana & Luigi Rizzi. 1988. Psych verbs and Th-Theory. *Natural Language and Linguistic Theory* 6(3). 291–352.
Belletti, Adriana. 2017. Internal grammar and children's grammatical creativity against poor inputs. *Frontiers in Psychology*, 01 December 2017. https://doi.org/10.3389/fpsyg.2017.02074.
Belletti Adriana. Forthcoming. Objects and Subjects in the Left Periphery: The case of a-Topics. In Mirko Grimaldi, Rosangela Lai, Ludovico Franco and Benedetta Baldi (eds.), *Structuring variation in Romance Linguistics and Beyond*. (Linguistik Aktuell/Linguistics Today [LA]), Amsterdam: John Benjamins.
Belletti, Adriana & Claudia Manetti. 2017. Topics and passives in Italian-speaking children and adults. Paper presented at IGG42, University of Salento, Lecce, February 18–20. University of Geneva-University of Siena manuscript, submitted.
Belletti, Adriana & Claudia Manetti 2017. Topics and Passives in Italian-speaking children and adults. Accepted for publication in Language Acquisition.
Benincà, Paola. 1986. Il lato sinistro della frase italiana. *ATI Journal* 47. 57–85.
Berretta, Monica. 1989. Sulla presenza dell'accusativo preposizionale nell'italiano settentrionale: note tipologiche. *Vox Romanica* 48. 13–37.
Bianchi, Valentina.2006. On the syntax of personal arguments. *Lingua* 116. 2023–2067.
Bianchi, Valentina & Mara Frascarelli. 2010. Is Topic a Root Phenomenon? *Iberia* 2. 43–48.
Bianchi, Valentina & Cristiano Chesi 2014. Subject islands, reconstruction, and the flow of the computation. *Linguistic Inquiry* 45(4). 525–569.
Bossong, Georg. 1991. Differential object marking in Romance and beyond. In Dieter Wanner and Dougla A. Kibbe (eds.), *New Analyses in Romance Linguistics. Selected Papers from the XVIII Linguistic Symposium on Romance Languages 1988*, 143–170. Amsterdam: John Benjamins.
Calabrese, Andrea. 1986. Some properties of the Italian pronominal system. An analysis based on the notion of *Thema* as subject of predication. In Harro Stammerjohann (ed.), *Tema-Rema in Italiano/Theme-Rheme in Italian/Thema-Rhema im Italienischen*, 25–36. Tübingen: Gunter Narr Verlag.

Cardinaletti, Anna. 2004. Toward a cartography of subject positions. In Luigi Rizzi (ed.), *The structure of CP and IP. The cartography of syntactic structures*, Volume 2. 115–165. New York: Oxford University Press.
Chomsky, Noam. 1981. *Lectures on government and binding*. Dordrecht: Foris.
Frascarelli, Mara & Roland Hinterhölzl. 2007. Types of topics in German and Italian. In Susanne Winkler and Kerstin Schwabe (eds.), *On information structure, meaning and form*, 87–116. Amsterdam: John Benjamins.
Friedmann, Naama, Adriana Belletti & Luigi Rizzi 2009. Relativized relatives: Types of intervention in the acquisition of A-bar dependencies. *Lingua* 119: 67–88.
Jayaseelan, K.A. 2001. IP-internal topic and focus phrases. *Studia Linguistica* 55(1). 39–75.
Kayne, Richard. 2004. Prepositions as probes. In Adriana Belletti (ed.), *Structures and yeyond – The cartography of syntactic structures*, Vol 3, 192–212. New York: Oxford University Press.
Kiss, Katalin. 1987. *Configurationality in Hungarian*. Springer.
Kuno, Susumu. and Etsuko Kaburaki 1977. Empathy and syntax. *Linguistic Inquiry* 8(4). 627–672.
Laca, Brenda 1987. Sobre el uso del acusativo preposicional en espanol. In Carmen Pensado (ed.), *El complement directo preposicional*, 61–91. Madrid: Viso.
Leonetti, Manuel. 2004. Specificity and Differential Object Marking in Spanish. *Catalan Journal of Linguistics* 3. 75–114.
Leonetti, Manuel. 2008. Specificity in Clitic Doubling and in Differential Object Marking. *Probus* 20. 35–69.
Lightfoot, David. 1999. *The development of language: Acquisition, change, and evolution*. Oxford: Blackwell.
Manetti, Claudia, Vincenzo Moscati, Luigi Rizzi & Adriana Belletti. 2016. The role of number and gender features in the comprehension of Italian clitic left dislocations. In Jennifer Scott and Deb Waughtal (eds.), *Proceedings of the 40th annual Boston University Conference on Language Development [BUCLD40]*, 229–240. Somerville MA: Cascadilla Press.
Manzini, Maria Rita & Leonardo Savoia 2005. *I dialetti italiani e romanci. Morfosintassi generativa. Vol 2 (3 vols.)*. Alessandria: Edizioni dell'Orso.
Manzini, Maria Rita & Ludovico Franco. 2016. Goal and DOM datives. *Natural Language and Linguistic Theory* 34. 197–240.
Reinhart, Tanya. 1981. Pragmatics and linguistics: An analysis of sentence topics in pragmatics and philosophy. *Philosphica* 27(1). 53–94.
Renzi, Lorenzo. 1988. *Grande grammatica Italiana di consultazione*, vol. 1, *La frase*. Bologna: Il Mulino.
Rizzi, Luigi. 1988. Il sintagma reposizionale. In L. Renzi (ed.), *Grande grammatica italiana di consultazione*, 507–531. Bologna: Il Mulino.
Rizzi, Luigi. 1997. The fine structure of the Left Periphery. In Liliane Haegeman (ed.), *Elements of grammar*, 281–337. Dordrecht: Kluwer.
Rizzi, Luigi. 2004. Locality and Left Periphery. In Adriana Belletti (ed.) *Structures and beyond: The cartography of syntactic structures*, Vol 3, 223–251. New York: Oxford University Press.
Rizzi, Luigi. 2005. On some properties of subjects and topics. In Laura Brugé, Giuliana Giusti, Nicola Munaro, Walter Schweikert and Giuseppina Turano (eds.), *Proceedings of the XXX Incontro di Grammatica Generativa*, 203–224. Venezia: Cafoscarina.
Rizzi, Luigi & Giuliano Bocci 2016. The left periphery of the clause – Primarily illustrated for Italian. Forthcoming in *the Blackwell companion to syntax*, II edition.

Rizzi, Luigi & Ur Shlonsky 2007. Strategies of subject extraction. In Hans-Marti Gärtner and Uli Sauerland (eds). *Interfaces + Recursion = Language? Chomsky's minimalism and the view from syntax-semantics*, 115–160. Berlin: Mouton de Gruyter.

Rohlfs, Gerhard. 1969. *Grammatica storica della lingua italiana e dei suoi dialetti*. 3 vols. Torino: Einaudi.

Sigurdhsson, Halldór A. 2004. The syntax of person, tense, and speech features. *Italian Journal of Linguistics* 16. 219–251.

Snyder, William & Nina Hyams. 2015. Minimality effects in children's passives. In Elisa Di Domenico, Cornelia Hamann and Simona Matteini (eds.), *Structures, strategies and beyond,* Linguistik Aktuell/Linguistics Today 223, 343–368. Amsterdam/Philadelphia: John Benjamin.

Speas, Margaret & Carol Tenny. 2003. Configurational properties of point of view roles. In Anna Maria Di Sciullo (ed.), *Asymmetry in grammar*, Volume 1: *Syntax and Semantics*, 315–343. Amsterdam: John Benjamins.

Starke, Michal. 2001. *Move dissolves into merge*. University of Geneva, doctoral dissertation.

Tsai, Wei-Tien Dylan. 2015. A tale of two peripheries: Evidence from Chinese adverbials, light verbs, applicatives and object fronting. In Wei-Tien Dylan Tsai (ed.), T*he cartography of Chinese syntax. The cartography of syntactic structures,* vol. 11, 1–32. New York: Oxford University Press.

Giuliano Bocci and Silvio Cruschina
Postverbal subjects and nuclear pitch accent in Italian wh-questions

Ad Andrea, per tutto quello che ci ha insegnato,
trasmesso e cucinato

1 Introduction

In his seminal paper on the relationship between word order alternations, information structure, and phonology in Italian, Calabrese (1982) discusses two generalizations that, despite their relevance to the understanding of the derivation and prosody of wh-questions, have largely escaped the attention of the subsequent linguistic literature:[1]

(a) *Subject inversion in embedded clauses under long-distance movement*: In direct wh-questions, subjects tend to appear postverbally not only in matrix clauses in the case of short wh-movement (cf. 1b vs. 1a), but also in the embedded clauses from which the wh-element is extracted via successive cyclic movement to the matrix clause, i.e. via long wh-movement (cf. 2b vs. 2a);

(b) *Nuclear pitch accent (NPA) assignment*: In wh-questions, NPA is generally assigned to the verb (cf. 3).[2]

(1) a. * *Che cosa   Gianni   ha   portato?*
       what   Gianni   has   brought
   b. *Che cosa   ha   portato   Gianni?*
       what   has   brought   Gianni
       'What did Gianni bring?'

(2) a. ?? *Che cosa   hai   detto   che   Gianni   ha   portato?*
          what   have.2SG   said   that   Gianni   has   brought

---
[1] Note that the two generalizations do not hold for Italian yes/no-questions. Although it used to be a feature of Old Italian (cf. Munaro 2010), modern Italian yes/no-questions do not require subject inversion, either in the matrix or in an embedded clause (cf. Bocci & Pozzan 2014); nor do they display any special prosodic pattern with respect to the placement of NPA when compared to declarative sentences.
[2] When relevant to the discussion, in the examples the element associated with the NPA is marked in bold.

b. *Che cosa   hai   detto   che   ha   portato   Gianni?*
    what   have.2SG   said   that has   brought   Gianni
    'What did you say that Gianni brought?'

(3) *Chi   ha   **chiesto**   un   aumento?*
    who   has   asked   a   rise
    'Who asked for a pay rise?'

While several other syntactic and phonological aspects of focus constituents in declarative sentences have later been developed by other scholars, these two generalizations have somehow been relegated to a pool of mysteries that still revolve around the grammatical properties of wh-questions. The main aim of the present paper is to provide experimental evidence in support of the first empirical generalization and to redefine this property in the light of more recent theoretical developments. The second generalization will also be discussed, especially with regard to its relevance to the understanding of real nature of embedded subject inversion. However, for this latter generalization, we will mostly rely on the findings reported and examined in Bocci, Bianchi & Cruschina (2018).

Following Calabrese (1982), we show that subject inversion and NPA assignment in Italian wh-questions are the reflexes of the derivational history of wh-movement, and, accordingly, the result of a direct interaction between the syntactic and the phonological component. Unlike Calabrese, however, we argue that subject inversion is by nature a syntactic phenomenon, triggered by the successive cycling movement of the wh-phrase and not prosodically motivated. In particular, we claim that the very same syntactic mechanism that yields subject inversion (successive cycling movement) is also responsible for the prosodic properties characterizing Italian direct wh-questions. In other words, we defend a view on the division of labour between syntax and prosody in wh-questions whereby syntax tailors and delivers its instructions to prosody.

The structure of this chapter is as follows. We first illustrate the phenomenon of subject inversion in Italian wh-questions (§ 2). In Section 3, we present the results of a syntactic experiment on the distribution of subjects in the embedded clause of wh-questions. Our analysis is presented in Section 4, where we directly relate the syntactic and prosodic peculiarities of Italian wh-questions to the successive cyclic nature and to the intermediate positions of wh-movement. We show that while subject inversion is a phenomenon that involves the edge of the C-phrase, the assignment of NPA additionally involves the vP-edge. We then attempt to capture the observed patterns and to provide further support to our analysis by comparing direct and indirect wh-questions with respect to both subject inversion and their prosodic properties (§ 5). A summary and some final remarks close the chapter.

2 Subject inversion in wh-questions

Subject inversion in interrogative environments is a syntactic property common to many languages. In Italian, however, we do not observe the same rigid subject inversion pattern as in English or in German: used in reference to the Italian facts, then, the term itself might be misleading. The essential property of Italian wh-questions is the adjacency requirement between the wh-phrase and the verb. This has direct repercussions on the other constituents in the sentence, including the subject, which cannot appear in a preverbal position.[3] It is important to note, however, that the subject in Italian does not necessarily undergo inversion: in fact, it can be omitted or dislocated to the left. In neutral contexts where the subject does not have a valid antecedent in the context and resists dislocation or omission, the subject will tend to appear in a postverbal position: this is what we mean by subject inversion in this paper.

In what follows, we will first describe the phenomenon of subject inversion in the matrix clause of wh-questions, with short-distance movement. Subject inversion in embedded clauses in combination with long-distance movement will be discussed in the next subsection.

2.1 Matrix subject inversion and short-distance movement

It is well known that, in Italian wh-questions with bare wh-elements (with the exception of *perché* 'why' and *come mai* 'how come'), neither subjects nor other constituents can intervene between the wh-phrase and the verb – the subject, for instance, must occur postverbally, as shown in (4) (see Calabrese 1982; Rizzi 1996, 2001; Bocci 2013, a.o.; see also Bianchi, Bocci & Cruschina 2017 for an account of asymmetries between *perché* 'why' and the other bare wh-elements):[4]

(4) a. *Chi   ha   visto   Mario?*
       who   has   seen   Mario
    b. * *Chi   Mario   ha   visto?*
       who   Mario   has   seen
       'Who did Mario see?'

---

[3] Even if this is not essential to our analysis, we agree with Cardinaletti (2001, 2002) on the idea that postverbal subjects can stay in their base position and are not necessarily right-dislocated.
[4] Cardinaletti (2007) shows that certain elements, in particular specific types of adverb, can intervene between the wh-phrase and the verb. For simplicity, we here describe the adjacency requirement in its traditional terms and refer to her work for the relevant exceptions. Note also that in Italian, subjects cannot occur between the auxiliary and the verb in analytic verb forms (see, e.g., Rizzi 1996).

Calabrese (1982) treats this restriction as a consequence of a phonological requirement for the wh-phrase and the verb to form a single intonational phrase. Focal elements, including wh-phrases, receive a [F] feature ([N] for 'new' in Calabrese's original formulation) from the verb and must be string-adjacent to it: the phonological group consisting of the verb and the [F]-marked elements forms a single and independent intonational phrase that constitutes the main intonational phrase of the sentence whose rightmost constituent is thus assigned NPA. In wh-questions, the wh-phrase in the CP inherits [F] from its trace in the base-generation position and must be adjacent to the verb. Any potential intervener must be syntactically displaced. For Calabrese, therefore, the same phonological requirement is responsible for both subject inversion and NPA assignment.

A variety of accounts – largely syntactic – have been proposed to explain the adjacency requirement in more recent years. According to Rizzi (1996 et seq.), wh-movement is driven by the Wh-Criterion,[5] which requires a wh-phrase carrying the feature [wh] to be in a Spec-Head agree-relation with a head endowed with the same feature. This criterial configuration must be satisfied in a dedicated CP-projection of the left periphery, namely, FocP. The head that carries the feature [wh] in wh-questions is T: thus, the wh-phrase ends up in Spec/FocP, while T moves to Foc° and brings the [wh] feature along with it. In the criterial approach, therefore, T-to-C movement takes place in order to yield the Spec-Head configuration which, in turn, ensures adjacency between the two elements and prevents any other constituent from intervening between them (for a different technical implementation of this analysis, see Rizzi 2006). More recently, adopting the view that there are several preverbal subject positions specialized for different types of subject (see Cardinaletti 1997, 2004), the intervention restriction has been selectively limited to SubjP – that is, the projection that hosts strong and overt preverbal subjects functioning as subjects of the predication, as opposed to weak or null pronouns which occur in Spec/TP or in lower positions. More specifically, it has been proposed that T-to-C movement prevents the subject from moving to SubjP (cf. Rizzi & Shlonsky 2007): the subject must therefore either remain in a lower position or be dislocated.

Cardinaletti (2007) adopts a different position. She still assumes that Spec/SubjP is unavailable in wh-questions, but also argues against the hypothesis that the wh-phrase and the verb occur in one and the same projection. She claims that "only subjects in specSubjP are excluded from occurring between the wh-phrase

---

[5] The Wh-Criterion is one of the Criteria that require a phrase with feature [α] to be in a Spec-Head configuration with a functional head carrying [α]. See Rizzi (2006) for more details.

and the verb in wh-questions, whereas subjects in specTP (or lower subject positions [...]) are permitted" (Cardinaletti 2007: 66).

Irrespective of the motivation behind the ban on intervening subjects in wh-questions (see also Bianchi, Bocci & Cruschina forthcoming), these syntactic approaches only address the issue with respect to matrix wh-questions,[6] neglecting what happens within the left periphery of a possible embedded clause from which wh-movement takes place. As observed by Calabrese (1982), in fact, subject inversion occurs both with short- and long-distance movement.[7] Moreover, the syntactic approaches do not address the issue of NPA assignment and, in fact, their explanation does not offer any means of accounting for the special prosodic contour of wh-questions.

2.2 Embedded subject inversion and long-distance movement

As already mentioned, Calabrese (1982: 39–40) makes an important empirical observation: when the wh-phrase is moved from an embedded clause, the embedded subject must appear postverbally:

(5) a. ?? *Che cosa gli hai detto che Carlo ha fatto?*
         what thing him.DAT have.2SG said that Carlo has done

     b. *Che cosa gli hai detto che ha fatto Carlo?*
         what thing him.DAT have.2SG said that has done Carlo
         'What did you say Carlo has done?'

The wh-phrase *che cosa* ('what') in (5) is extracted from the embedded clause of the direct wh-question. In combination with this long-distance movement,[8] a preverbal embedded subject proves rather marginal (cf. 5a), while subject inversion would make the sentence fully grammatical. Calabrese relates this constraint to the phonological requirement for the phonological phrase containing the verb and the phonological phrase of the constituent bearing the [F] feature to form the

---

[6] Several observations about the special properties of indirect wh-questions are discussed in Rizzi (2001).

[7] This observation is also discussed in Torrego (1983, 1984), where subject inversion in Spanish wh-questions with long-distance movement is investigated. Her analysis will be considered in the next section.

[8] By long-distance movement, or more simply long movement, we mean extraction via successive cyclic movement from an embedded clause. As will be explained in detail below, subject inversion is more specifically triggered by the intermediate movement of the wh-phrase through the CP– or CPs– that are crossed between the extraction and the landing site.

main intonational phrase of the sentence. In the case of long-distance movement (5b), the embedded verb containing the trace of the wh-chain will be grouped within the same intonational phrase (i.e. IP) as the F-marked constituent:[9]

(5′) b.   [[Che cosa]$_\Phi$ [gli hai detto]$_\Phi$ [che ha **fatto**]$_\Phi$ *t*]$_{IP}$ [Carlo]$_\Phi$?

In other words, when the wh-phrase is extracted from an embedded clause, the main intonational phrase of the sentence must include the head and the foot (i.e. the lowest trace) of the wh-chain, as well as both the embedded and the matrix verb: adjacency throughout all these elements is required, and NPA is assigned to the rightmost (phonologically non-null) element within this intonational phrase, i.e. to the embedded lexical verb. As a consequence of this phonological constraint, the embedded subject *Carlo* must be right dislocated or marginalized (cf. 5a) (see also Antinucci & Cinque 1977, Cardinaletti 2002, 2007). No content elements other than verbs can be included within this sequence.

Around the same time, the same phenomenon was observed by Torrego (1983, 1984) for Spanish. Unlike Calabrese, however, Torrego analyses embedded subject inversion in wh-questions as a syntactic phenomenon: a direct reflex of successive cyclic movement. In particular, she argues that when an operator such as the wh-phrase moves to Spec/CP, the verb must reach the head of CP in order to establish the required configuration with the wh-element. In her account, therefore, T-to-C movement also takes place in the case of long extraction:

(6) a.   *¿Qué   querían   esos   dos?*
         what   wanted   these   two
         'What did those two want?'
    b.   **¿Qué   esos   dos   querían?*
         what   these   two   wanted
         (Torrego 1984: 103)

(7) a.   *¿Qué   pensaba   Juan   que   le   había   dicho   Pedro   que*
         what   thought   John   that   him   had   told   Peter   that
         había   publicado   la   revista [t]?
         had   published   the   journal
         'What did John think that Peter had told him that the journal had published?'

---

[9] The relevant tone is assigned to lexical heads only (Calabrese 1982: 19), therefore excluding auxiliaries and complementizers (see also Nespor & Vogel 1986).

b. * ¿Qué pensaba Juan que Pedro le había dicho que
   what thought John that Peter him had told that
   la revista había publicado?
   the journal had published
   (Torrego 1984: 109)

Under Torrego's analysis, T-to-C-movement applies not only in the matrix clause (6), but also in all embedded left peripheries hosting the wh-phrases in intermediate positions on its way to the final (matrix) landing site (7): subject inversion takes place along the whole movement path (see also Kayne & Pollock 1978 on stylistic inversion in French and Henry 1995 on Belfast English). In our analysis, we combine elements of both analyses, i.e. Calabrese's phonological account and Torrego's syntactic account. Before outlining our proposal in detail (cf. § 4), let us now go back to Italian and consider some empirical evidence in support of embedded subject inversion.

3 The distribution of embedded subjects: A syntactic experiment

In order to experimentally support Calabrese's observation on embedded subject inversion, we carried out a forced-choice experiment where participants had to express their preference for the pre- or postverbal placement of the subject in the complement clause of direct wh-questions. The design, methodology, and results of this experiment are discussed in this section.

3.1 Design and methodology

We carried out a web-based forced choice experiment (hosted by Ibex Farm). 59 Italian native speakers, recruited via Facebook, participated in the experiment. Two independent binary factors in a 2*2 factorial design were tested:
a) type of wh-dependency: long extraction (from an embedded clause) vs. short extraction (from the matrix clause);
b) type of verb in the embedded clause: transitive vs. intransitive.[10]

Factor (a) is directly related to the issue of subject inversion in wh-questions, while factor (b) was included in order to verify whether, especially in the case of

---

10 We deliberately avoided testing unaccusative verbs since they license subject inversion more freely and independently of the presence of a syntactic trigger such as wh-movement (see Belletti & Bianchi 2016 for an overview and relevant references).

long extraction from an embedded clause, the type of verb has any influence on the position of the embedded subject.

We tested 24 items. Type of wh-dependency was manipulated between items, while verb-type was manipulated within items. In other words, we tested 12 items with intransitive verbs and 12 items with transitive verbs. Each item included the variants with the long- and short-distance movement. For the resulting 48 experimental sentences (12 items * 2 verb types * 2 dependency types), we then created the two alternative versions that minimally differed with respect to the position of the subject in the embedded clause: either preverbal or postverbal. This amounts to a total of 96 stimuli.

The two independent factors were manipulated within participants and the experimental sentences were arranged in a Latin-square design. We divided the experimental sentences into 4 lists so that each list included one experimental sentence per item. Each list consisted of 24 experimental sentences (for each of them we presented the two alternatives) and 24 fillers.

Each trial started with a brief description of a hypothetical context. The subject of the target sentences was never mentioned in this introductory context in order to avoid the postverbal, sentence-final subject being interpreted as given and, hence, as syntactically right-dislocated. The matrix verb was always the verb of saying *dire*. The stimuli were presented in a pseudo-randomized order.

In each trial, two alternative sentences which varied only with respect to the position of the subject were presented and the participants were asked to express their preference for either version. The participants had to express their preference for either version by clicking on the preferred alternative. It is important to emphasize that the target sentences were also controlled with respect to the type of wh-dependency: they were nearly identical in the long- and short-movement condition, except for the position of a dative clitic pronoun which forced one interpretation against the other. For example, the clitic pronoun *ti* 'to you' in sentence (9) was necessary to avoid the wh-phrase being interpreted as the dative argument of the matrix verb *dire* 'say/tell'.

Moreover, for each item the short- and the long-distance sentences were introduced by the same context. Let us look at some examples. In (8) and in (9), we have an intransitive verb (*disobbedire* 'disobey') in combination with short (8) and long movement (9), respectively. The two sentences in (8) and (9) only differ with respect to the position of the embedded subject: the a-sentences contain a preverbal subject, while the b-sentences include a postverbal subject.

(8) SHORT MOVEMENT, INTRANSITIVE V

Ad un consiglio dei docenti, si tirano le somme e si decidono i voti in condotta. Ma ci sono alcuni disaccordi tra colleghi, e la direttrice, per assicurarsi di aver capito bene, chiede a Lucia, l'insegnante di ginnastica:

'At a meeting, teachers take stock and decide the grades for behaviour. There are some disagreements among colleagues, and the principal, to make sure that she understood correctly, asks Lucia, the physical education teacher:'

   a. A chi   hanno   detto   che   Giulio   ti   ha   disobbedito? (SV)
       to who   have.3PL   said   that   Giulio   you   has   disobeyed

   b. A chi   hanno   detto   che   ti   ha   disobbedito Giulio? (VS)
       to who   have.3PL   said   that   you   has   disobeyed   Giulio
       'Who did they tell that Giulio disobeyed you?'

(9)   LONG MOVEMENT, INTRANSITIVE V

Ad un consiglio dei docenti, si tirano le somme e si decidono i voti in condotta. Ma ci sono alcuni disaccordi tra colleghi, e la direttrice, per assicurarsi di aver capito bene, chiede a Lucia, l'insegnante di ginnastica:

'At a meeting, teachers take stock and decide the grades for behaviour. There are some disagreements among colleagues, and the principal, to make sure that she understood correctly, asks Lucia, the physical education teacher:'

   a. A chi   ti   hanno   detto   che   Giulio   ha   disobbedito? (SV)
       to who   you   have.3PL   said   that   Giulio   has   disobeyed

   b. A chi   ti   hanno   detto   che   ha   disobbedito Giulio? (VS)
       to who   you   have.3PL   said   that   has   disobeyed   Giulio
       'Who did they tell you that Giulio disobeyed?'

The same design and structure was maintained for the 12 items involving a transitive embedded verb, such as *insultare* 'insult' in (10) and in (11):

(10)   SHORT MOVEMENT, TRANSITIVE V

Francesco è il nuovo insegnante di filosofia di un liceo. Durante il primo giorno di lavoro, un collega gli racconta un episodio spiacevole sul quale non è ancora stato preso nessun provvedimento. Francesco, un po' perplesso, gli chiede:

'Francesco is the new philosophy teacher in a high school. During his first day at work, a colleague tells him about an unpleasant incident, for which no disciplinary action has yet been taken. Francesco, a bit puzzled, asks him:'

   a. A chi   hai   detto che   gli studenti   ti   hanno   insultato? (SV)
       to who   have.2SG   said that   the students   you   have.3PL   insulted

   b. A chi   hai   detto che   ti   hanno   insultato gli studenti? (VS)
       to who   have.2SG   said that   you   have.3PL   insulted   the students
       'Who did you tell that the students insulted you?'

(11) LONG MOVEMENT, TRANSITIVE V

Francesco è il nuovo insegnante di filosofia di un liceo. Durante il primo giorno di lavoro, un collega gli racconta un episodio spiacevole sul quale non è ancora stato preso nessun provvedimento. Francesco, un po' perplesso, gli chiede:
'Francesco is the new philosophy teacher in a high school. During his first day at work, a colleague tells him about an unpleasant incident, for which no disciplinary action has yet been taken. Francesco, a bit puzzled, asks him:'

a. Chi   hai   detto che   gli studenti hanno   insultato? (SV)
   who   have.2SG   said   that the students have.3PL insulted

b. Chi   hai   detto che   hanno   insultato gli studenti? (VS)
   who   have.2SG   said   that have.3PL insulted the students
   'Who did you say that the students insulted?'

In short-movement contexts, the wh-phrase is an argument of the matrix verb and thus undergoes short-distance movement, while in long-distance contexts the wh-phrase is an argument of the embedded verb and therefore gives rise to a long-distance dependency.

3.2 The results

As mentioned earlier, the results of this syntactic experiment confirm Calabrese's observation: the embedded subjects of wh-questions tend to appear postverbally when the wh-phrase is extracted from the embedded clause. The results are illustrated in Figure 1 with respect to the first factor, namely, type of wh-dependency. Crucially, this tendency only emerges with long-movement contexts, i.e. when the wh-phrase is extracted from within the embedded clause, where postverbal subjects are preferred in 79% of cases. In short-movement contexts, by contrast, subjects of the embedded clause are preferred in preverbal position (67%).

If we integrate the second factor into this picture, very little changes. See Figure 2.

We carried out statistical analyses based on multi-level mixed effects regressions with log odds of a postverbal subject response as the dependent variable, type of movement (short vs. long wh-movement), and type of VP (transitive vs. intransitive) as fixed effects. The best random structure justified by the data included random intercepts for subjects and items, as well as by-subject and

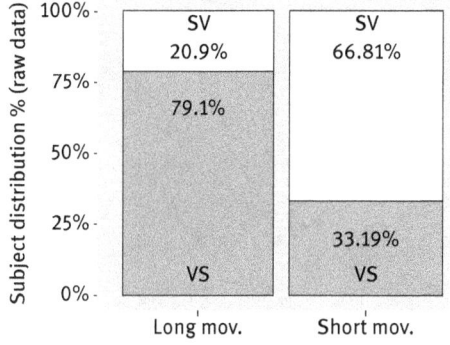

Figure 1: First syntactic experiment: preferences for SV vs. VS in direct wh-questions across dependency type

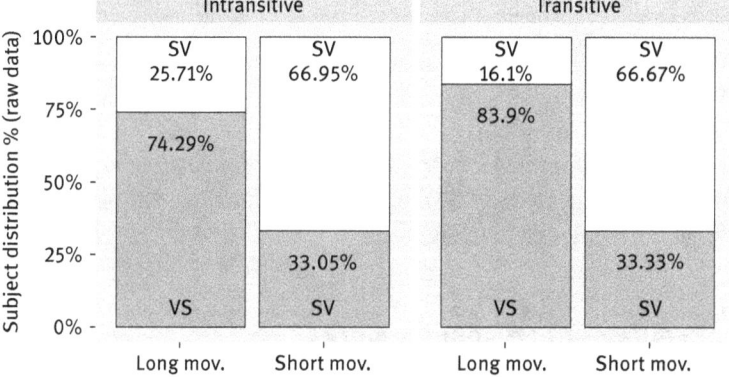

Figure 2: First syntactic experiment: preferences for SV vs. VS in direct wh-questions across dependency type and verb type

by-item random slopes for the effect of movement type and by-subject random slopes for the type of verb. For both fixed factors, we specified the contrasts with a deviation coding scheme.

The type of wh-movement (short vs. long) has a significant impact on the preference for the position of the embedded subject: under the long wh-movement condition the probability of postverbal subject is significantly higher than under the short wh-movement condition (*Estimate* = 2.63, SE = .228, p < .001). The main effect of VP type is not significant (*Estimate* = .40, SE = .270, p > .1). However, the interaction between type of movement and type of verb approaches the significance threshold (*Estimate* = 0.632, SE = .354, p = .074), indicating that the probability for postverbal subjects is higher for transitive verbs than intransitives

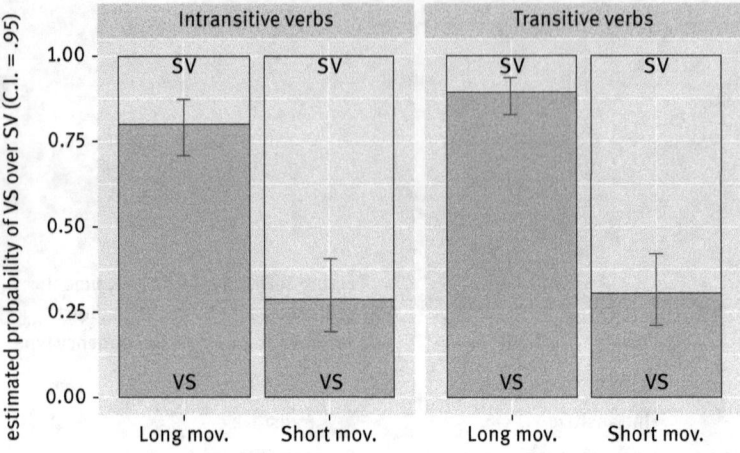

Figure 3: Estimated probabilities of VS over SV across dependency type and verb type

in the case of long-distance movement.[11] We extracted the coefficients and the confidence intervals (calculated at 0.95) from the model, and converted them to estimated probabilities, plotted in in Figure 3.

3.3 Lack of ceiling effect: some remarks

While the results of the syntactic experiment confirm subject inversion with long extraction, the lack of ceiling effect is evident and raises important questions: why is SV still chosen in 21% of long-movement cases? Two possible answers come to mind. It could be that the deviant pattern is simply the consequence of the structural complexity of wh-question with long extraction: this would imply that our participants fail to interpret correctly the relevant experimental stimuli in the corresponding number of cases (i.e. 21%). Alternatively, it could well be that the preference for SV is not to be attributed to a processing difficulty, but rather to a different interpretation of the preverbal subject that would still be compatible with the long-distance interpretation. Even if we specifically tried to control for (and prevent) such an interpretation (by avoiding any mention of the subject in the introductory context and, hence, that it could be interpreted as a given), it could be that, in this smaller percentage of the cases, the preverbal

---

11 Given that it does not reach the significance threshold, for the time being we leave this tendency aside and simply report it for completeness.

subject was perceived as left-dislocated, namely, in a TopP position. Given that order Topic>wh>verb is always possible, a topical subject in TopP would not intervene between the wh-trace in the embedded CP and the lower verb. As an alternative, we tentatively suggest that the adjacency requirement is somewhat weaker when the (intermediate) movement to CP is triggered by a formal rather than a criterial feature (see Rizzi 2006 for the distinction between formal and criterial features).

A similar lack of floor effect can be observed with short extraction: even when the wh-phrase is not extracted from the embedded clause, VS is preferred in the 33% of cases. Again, we unfortunately do not have a sound explanation for this issue. More experimental evidence is needed before a more solid analysis of both deviant patterns can be pursued. For the time being, we leave this task for future work.

4 Moving through the edges: A phase-based analysis

Building on Calabrese's original insights, we offer an analysis that simultaneously accounts for both embedded subject inversion and the placement of NPA. In fact, we propose that both phenomena are the reflexes of successive cycle movement and, more specifically, under current minimalist theory, of the Phase Impenetrability Condition (Chomsky 2008), according to which wh-movement must pass through the edge of every *v*P and CP phase between the base-generation position and the final landing site. We additionally assume that, in direct wh-questions, an interrogative wh-phrase bears a wh/focal feature and that, when it passes through the edge of a phase (v° or C°), the wh-phrase shares a wh/focal feature with the relevant phase head. At the syntax-prosody interface, the NPA is assigned to the rightmost element in the sentence that is endowed with the wh/focal feature and is not phonologically null. Crucially, the prosodic computation does not differentiate between interpretable and uninterpretable instances of the wh/focal feature. See Bocci, Bianchi & Cruschina (2018).

A question featuring long extraction such as (12a) is thus analysed as illustrated in (12b). The wh-element is cyclically extracted from the vP of the embedded clause and, on its way to the CP of the matrix clause, it shares its wh-focal feature (shortened as [wh] in the illustrations below) with the head of each phase it passes through. As a result, in the syntactic structure visible to the phonological component, the past participle *rubato* 'stolen' counts as the rightmost element endowed with the wh/focal feature that is not phonologically null. It is therefore associated with the NPA.

(12) a. *A chi ti ha detto che hanno rubato la macchina?*
to who you.CL has said that have.3PL stolen the car
'Who did he tell you that they stole the car from?'

b.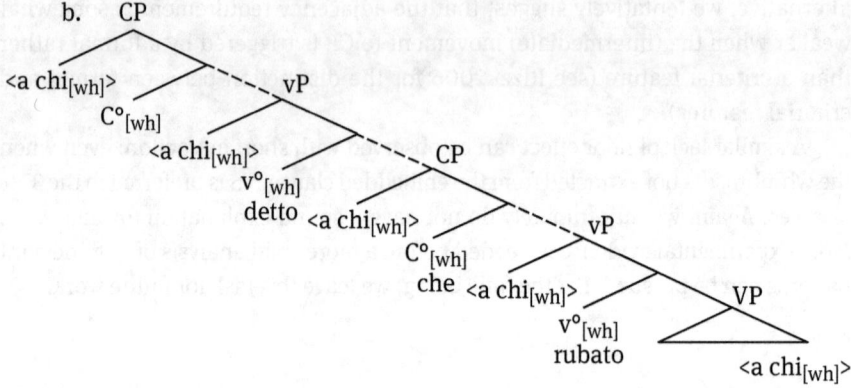

By contrast, in the case of short movement, as in (13a), the wh-phrase starts off from within the vP of the matrix clause and only shares its wh/focal feature with the phase heads in the matrix clause (cf. 13b). Consequently, the rightmost phonologically-realized element that is specified for the wh/focal feature is the matrix lexical verb *detto* 'said'. The NPA must be associated with this element and can never fall on the embedded verb which lacks the wh/focal feature.

(13) a. *A chi hai detto che ti hanno rubato la macchina?*
to who have.2SG said that you.cl have.3PL stolen the car
'Who did you tell that they stole your car?'

b.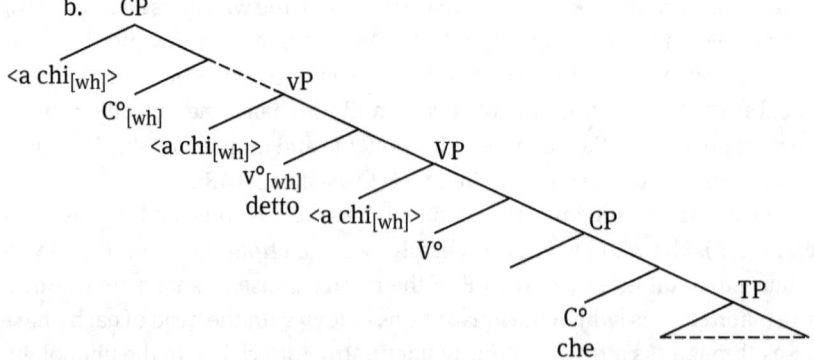

This analysis correctly predicts that an embedded verb is visible to phonology for the assignment of NPA only in the case of long-distance movement, given that the wh-phrase must move through the edge of the *v* phase head. By contrast, only the matrix verb is a possible candidate for NPA assignment because no feature sharing occurs in the embedded clause.

If the intermediate movement through the edge of each phase is responsible for the distribution of NPA, we argue that intermediate movement through the edge of the CP triggers subject inversion. Irrespective of whether or not this is to be related to the Wh-Criterion and to T-to-C movement (we leave this question open for future research), the intermediate passage of the wh-phrase through the edge of the C-phase prevents subjects from moving to their regular preverbal position in the TP domain (i.e. SubjP). Embedded subjects must therefore occur in a lower position, that is, in a subject-inversion configuration.

5 Further observations and experimental evidence

As mentioned in the previous section, along the lines of Calabrese (1982) and Torrego (1983, 1984) (cf. § 2.2), we claim that subject inversion (VS) in the main and in the embedded clauses from which wh-extraction takes place is determined by successive cyclic movement, i.e. the (transitory or final) movement of the wh-phrase to the left periphery (the edge of the C°). Our analysis, more specifically, puts together elements from both Calabrese's phonological account and Torrego's syntactic proposal. We do subscribe to the idea that the NPA is associated with the (lexical) verb in case of long wh-movement. Unlike Calabrese, however, and following Torrego's insight more closely, we argue that embedded subject inversion is a direct reflex of the syntactic derivation, i.e. successive cyclic movement, rather than prosodic well-formedness requirements as in Calabrese's analysis. In particular, we propose that the same mechanism that triggers subject inversion in matrix clauses and that makes SubjP unavailable to (preverbal) subjects (cf. § 2.1) also operates in embedded clauses. Our analysis relies on three empirical observations, each supported by the relevant experimental data:

(i) in direct wh-questions with bare wh-elements (other than *perché* 'why' and *come mai* 'how come'), NPA is by default assigned to the lexical verb; it is assigned to the embedded lexical verb only with long-distance movement;

(ii) in indirect wh-questions, as in declarative sentences, NPA is assigned by default to the rightmost constituent of the sentence, unless a constituent that qualifies as narrow focus attracts NPA;

(iii) subject inversion also occurs in indirect wh-questions.

A direct and close comparison between the syntax and the prosody of direct and indirect wh-questions shows that embedded subject inversion in direct wh-questions with long extraction cannot be triggered by a prosodic requirement on focussed elements because inversion also takes place in indirect questions where a different prosodic pattern is observed (see also Bocci & Pozzan 2014). We devote the rest of this section to the three observations mentioned above, the discussion of which will lead us to a more precise definition of the phenomena in support of our proposal based on successive cyclic movement and feature sharing in intermediate positions.

5.1 NPA assignment in direct wh-questions

The assignment of NPA in wh-questions is a phenomenon that has not yet been fully understood or accounted for. In line with a widespread view (e.g. Horvath 1981/1986, É. Kiss 1995; see Haida 2007: §7.2 for an overview), Calabrese (1982) argues that the wh-element in wh-questions is endowed with a focus feature on a par with the focus constituent of declaratives. However, while in assertions the focus constituent must be assigned NPA, in wh-questions with bare wh-phrases NPA falls on to the lexical verb. This implies that the verb carries NPA even when it is not interpreted as focus. To account for this syntax-prosody mismatch, Calabrese proposes an analysis based on two assumptions (cf. §2.2): (i) the focus feature is assigned to the wh-phrase in its base-generated position, connected to the surface position by means of an A'-chain and thus guaranteeing the correct interpretation; (ii) the main pitch accent of the sentence is then assigned to the last phonological phrase within the main intonational phrase, i.e. the prosodic unit made up by the wh-phrase and the adjacent verb.

Bocci, Bianchi & Cruschina (2018) substantiate this observation through the results of a dedicated production experiment aimed at investigating the placement of NPA in wh-questions. Ten native speakers of Tuscan Italian had to read 24 stimuli (12 items), alternating short-distance wh-movement (14a) and long-distance wh-movement (14b), together with 24 fillers, which were presented in a pseudo-randomized order:

(14) a. Chi **pensa** che ti dovrei presentare al direttore?
 who thinks that you should.1SG introduce to-the director
 'Who thinks that I should introduce you to the director?'
 b. Chi pensi che dovrei **presentare** al direttore?
 who think.2SG that should.1SG introduce to-the director
 'Who do you think that I should introduce to the director?'

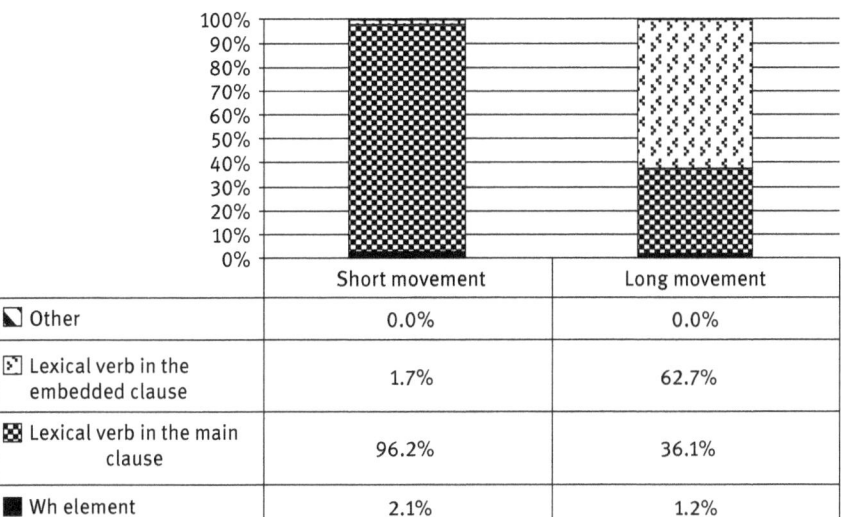

Figure 4: Distribution of NPA across type of wh-movement

The results, summarized in Figure 4, show that in complex wh-questions consisting of a matrix and an embedded clause NPA is assigned to the verb, either to the main lexical verb or to the embedded lexical verb. NPA on the wh-element is very marginal. In particular, the experimental findings demonstrate that when the wh-element is extracted from the matrix clause, via short-distance movement (14a), NPA is assigned to the lexical verb of the matrix clause. Figure 5 illustrates a pitch contour of a sentence produced with this pattern. Crucially, as shown in Figure 4, NPA is virtually never assigned to the embedded lexical verb (only 1.7%). By contrast, with long-distance movement (14b), NPA is much more likely to be associated with the lexical verb of the embedded clause, rather than the matrix lexical verb. Figure 6 illustrates an example of this prosodic pattern.

It is worth noting that in both conditions (short and long) NPA is never (0%) assigned to the rightmost element of the sentence, which is the default position for NPA assignment in Italian. We refer to Bocci, Bianchi & Cruschina (2018) for more details relating to the experiments and their results.[12]

---

[12] See Bocci, Bianchi & Cruschina (2018) also for arguments and evidence against Calabrese's proposal that the phonological computation directly refers to the wh-trace in its base-generation position.

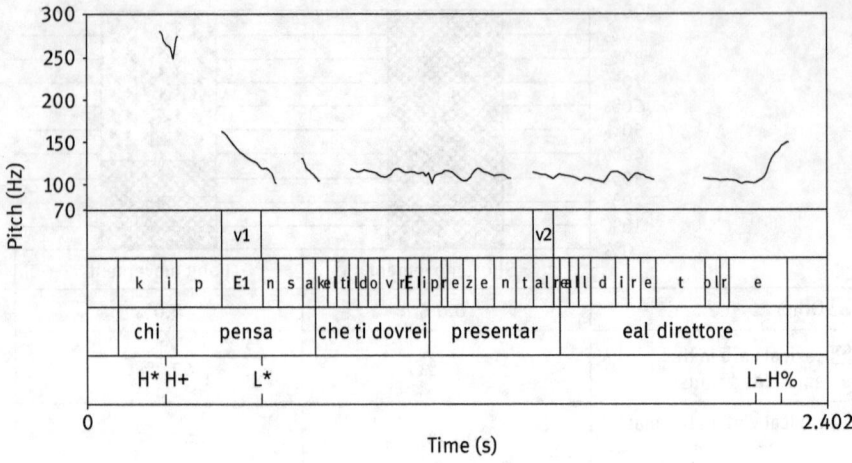

Figure 5: Pitch contour of an utterance produced after (14a): wh-question with short movement

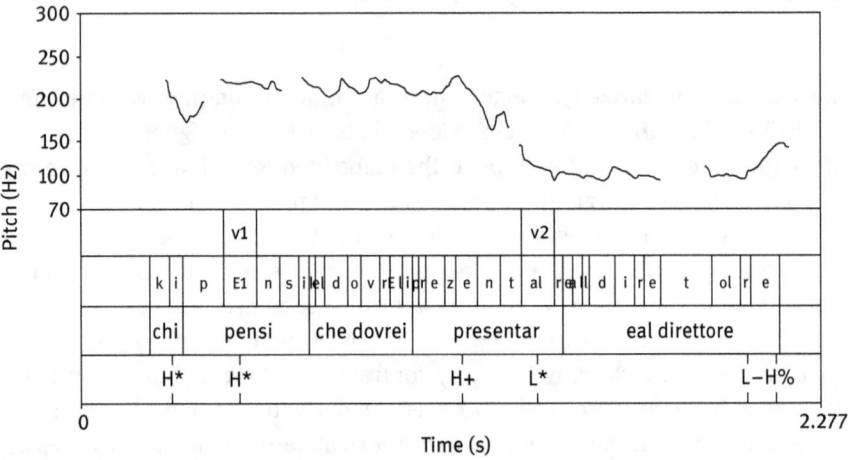

Figure 6: Pitch contour of an utterance produced after (14b): wh-question with long movement

5.2 NPA assignment in indirect wh-questions: the prosodic experiment

Since Calabrese's account connects subject inversion in wh-questions with the special prosodic properties of wh-questions, we tested the same two properties in indirect wh-questions. In this section, we discuss the prosodic properties of indirect wh-questions on the basis of the results of a production experiment, while in the next section we report the results of forced-choice experiment on the distribution of the subject in indirect wh-questions.

We carried out a production experiment to investigate the prosodic properties of indirect questions. The stimuli of this experiment were included in the experiment described in Bianchi, Bocci & Cruschina (2017) and discussed in Section 5.1. The 10 native speakers of Tuscan Italian (8 women, 2 men) who took part in the experiment had to read short scripts. Each script consisted of a description of a fictional context followed by a target indirect question. The contexts were set up in order to prevent the speaker from assigning a narrow focus interpretation to any constituent of the target sentences. Moreover, the referents present in the target sentences were not mentioned in the contexts. This was done in order to disfavour a right-dislocation interpretation of the postverbal constituents in the target sentences.

The experiment comprised of 24 stimuli divided into three groups on the basis of the wh-phrase being tested: 8 stimuli with direct object *chi* 'whom', 8 with indirect object *a chi* 'to whom', and 8 with locative *dove* 'where'. For each wh-type group, we manipulated the type of matrix clause selecting the indirect question: 2 stimuli with *mi domando* 'I ask myself', 2 stimuli with *mi chiedo* 'I ask myself', 2 stimuli with *non so* 'I don't know', and 2 stimuli with *vorrei sapere* 'I would like to know'). This design allowed us to evaluate and compare the extent to which the type of bare wh-element and the type of matrix clause have an impact on NPA placement in indirect questions produced in neutral contexts. The 24 experimental stimuli were pseudo-randomized along with an equal number of fillers, ensuring a rigid alternation between the two types of stimuli.

We collected 4 repetitions for each trial. From the sentences produced we randomly picked 2 disfluency free repetitions, whenever available, for the prosodic analysis, and discarded the sentences that included segmental disfluency (and false starts). The overall corpus analysed consisted thus of 470 indirect wh-questions: 10 speakers * 24 stimuli * 2 disfluency-free repetitions.[13]

We downsampled the sentences from 48kHz to 16kHz, and automatically segmented them into phonemes by means of the WebMAUS aligner (Schiel 1999, Kisler et al. 2016) – the segmentation was then carefully corrected manually. We transcribed the sentences intonationally. In particular, the NPA label was assigned to the rightmost PA after which the pitch contour is completely compressed and

---

[13] The two disfluency-free repetitions per speaker were always available except in 10 cases. This is why we had a total of 470 sentences to analyse rather than the expected 480.

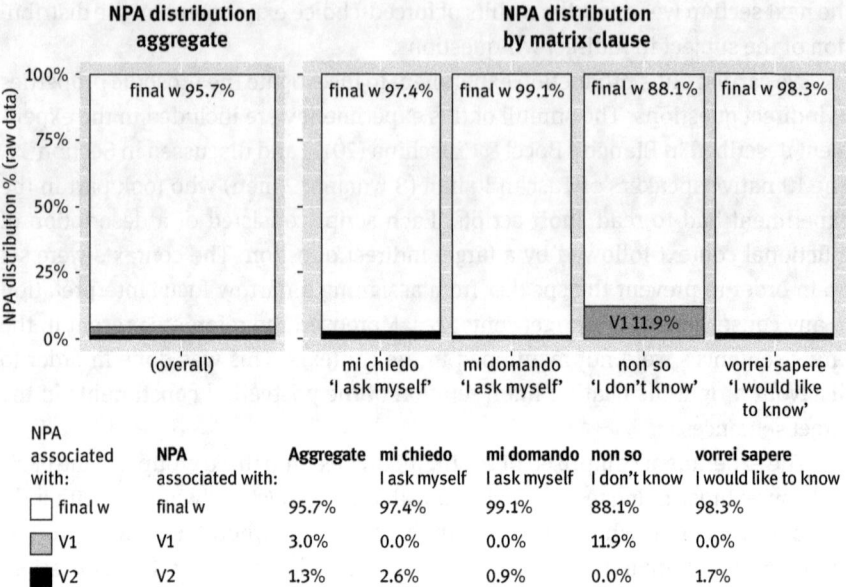

Figure 7: The prosodic experiment: NPA distribution in indirect wh-questions

no fully-fledged PA is observable (Gili Fivela et al. 2016). The NPA placement results are shown in Figure 7.[14]

In our data, the NPA was overwhelmingly assigned to the rightmost constituent of the sentence, indicated as 'final w(ord)' in Figure 7. Overall, this pattern is observed in 95.7% of the data.[15] In the remaining cases, the NPA falls either on the lexical verb of the matrix clause (V1) or on the lexical verb of the embedded wh-question (V2), in 3% and 1.3% of cases, respectively.

An example of the most common prosodic pattern observed in our data is illustrated in Figure 8, which shows the contour produced after the experimental sentence in (15) (an indirect wh-question with *a chi* 'to whom'). As the reader can

---

[14] It is worth mentioning that only 1 sentence out of 470 was realized with a final rise (i.e. L-H%). All the other sentences were characterized by a low final boundary tone (i.e. L-L%). Together with the use of the subjunctive mood for the embedded verb, this consistent prosodic pattern rules out any possibility that participants might have interpreted the embedded clause as a direct, rather than indirect, question.

[15] Given these results, we could not statistically test the distribution with a mixed model analysis: the distribution is too extreme and there is no variability in several conditions. However, this clearly does not undermine our findings.

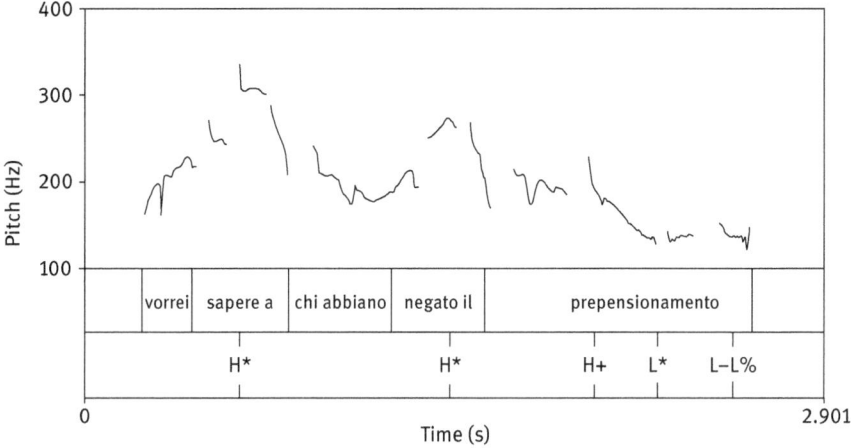

Figure 8: Pitch contour of an utterance produced after the indirect wh-question in (15)

observe, the H+L* NPA is associated with the stressed syllable of the rightmost constituent of the sentence.

(15) CONTEXT: *In ufficio è appena arrivato il piano delle mansioni per l'anno prossimo. Amalia e Rosa discutono il documento inviato dalle risorse umane e Rosa commenta così*:
'The work schedule for next year has just arrived in the office. Amalia and Rosa discuss the document sent by Human Resources and Rosa comments:'
Vorrei   sapere   a   chi   abbiano   negato
want.COND.1SG know.INF   to   whom   have.SBJV.3PL denied
il   prepensionamento.
the   early-retirement
'I'd like to know whom they deny an early retirement to.'

While the type of wh-element did not appear to have an impact on the distribution of NPA, the nature of the matrix verb showed a limited effect on the NPA placement. In fact, the NPA was assigned to the matrix verb only in sentences introduced by *non so* 'I don't know'. With this type of matrix clause, the NPA is assigned to the matrix verb in 11.9% of cases. We hypothesize that this prosodic pattern is due to the presence of negation in the matrix clause. We propose that when the NPA was assigned to the matrix verb *so* 'know', the speakers interpreted the matrix verb as a narrow focus associated with the negation, which frequently functions as a focus sensitive element (cf., e.g., Rooth 1996). This may explain why it is only with this matrix clause that the NPA is – albeit in a limited number of cases – on the matrix verb. In the majority of cases, however, the contexts provided disfavoured such an interpretation and, as a result, the NPA was assigned on the rightmost constituent.

Finally, it is worth emphasizing that, in contrast to direct wh-questions (see Bianchi, Bocci & Cruschina 2017), NPA in indirect wh-questions was assigned to the verb of the clause from which the wh-element is extracted only in a marginal number of cases (1.3%).

In conclusion, the results of the prosodic experiment show that under a neutral context, NPA is assigned to the rightmost constituent of the sentence. Crucially, this corresponds to the default prominence placement for Italian declaratives and contrasts with the prominence placement observed in direct wh-questions (cf. § 5.2). Our findings, therefore, lead us to the generalization that the prosody of indirect wh-questions patterns with that of declarative sentence rather than with the prosody of direct wh-questions.

5.3 Subject inversion in indirect wh-questions: second syntactic experiment

In the previous section, we saw that in indirect wh-questions, NPA is not necessarily assigned to the verb or to the wh-element: in other words, in this environment, Calabrese's phonological requirement is not at play. Subject inversion, nevertheless, systematically occurs in indirect wh-questions. Bocci & Pozzan (2014) investigated the distribution of subjects in direct and indirect questions. On the basis of three experimental studies, Bocci & Pozzan (2014) show that, when the discourse conditions disallow a topic or narrow focus interpretation of the subject, postverbal subjects are preferred and rated more highly than preverbal subjects in questions with *dove* 'where', while the reverse pattern is found in wh-questions with *perché* 'why' and yes-no questions. These patterns were observed both in direct and indirect questions.

The distinct behaviour of *perché* 'why' as opposed to the other wh-phrases is expected in light of the existing literature. *Perché* is base-generated in the left periphery and does not undergo wh-movement (Rizzi 2001), while *dove* 'where', which we chose as representative of the class of bare wh-phrases that also include 'who', 'what', 'how', undergoes wh-movement to the embedded left periphery and thus triggers subject inversion (for discussion and experimental evidence see Bianchi, Bocci & Cruschina 2017). Similarly, indirect yes/no-questions introduced by *se* 'if' do not involve wh-movement and do not induce subject inversion. In conclusion, since subject inversion is observed in indirect wh-questions and since the indirect questions are not characterized by the same special prosodic properties of direct wh-questions, subject inversion cannot be triggered by a prosodic requirement.

The indirect questions tested in Bocci & Pozzan's (2014) experiment included an embedded verb in the indicative mood. Even if the indicative is not the favourite option for most speakers in this context, it is generally accepted at the colloquial level. Prescriptively, however, the subjunctive is required in Italian indirect questions, and this option is often preferred by native speakers, although there is a strong variability across speakers. The mood of the embedded verb is not immaterial with respect to the issue under investigation here, namely, the distribution of subjects. It has been reported that it has a direct impact on the subject position, as observed by Calabrese (1982: 66–67) himself, and that it plays a relevant role in the licensing of preverbal subjects (see Rizzi 1996, 2001, Giorgi & Pianesi 1997, Poletto 2000). For this reason, we wanted to assess the different impact of the subjunctive mood and carried out a web-based forced choice experiment with two alternatives using similar materials as in Bocci and Pozzan's (2014) experiment and taking the mood of the embedded verb as a factor. Unlike in Bocci and Pozzan, we only considered indirect questions in this study.

The two experimental factors were: (i) 'embedded mood' with two levels, i.e. indicative vs. subjunctive, and (ii) 'question type' with three levels: wh-question with *dove* 'where', wh-questions with *perché* 'why', and yes/no-questions introduced by *se* 'if'.[16] The two factors were manipulated within items in a fully crossed design. We tested 30 items under 6 conditions (=3*2), leading to a total of 180 target sentences. For each target sentence, we had two versions: with the subject of the embedded clause either in preverbal or in postverbal position. All target sentences consisted of indirect questions in which the embedded clause contained only a subject (full DP) and an unergative verb in present (syncretic) tense. Below are examples for each condition:

(16) A: *Perché non metti un po' di musica?* [*dove*, **indicative**]
 'Why don't you put some music on?'
 B: *Meglio di no. Non so dove Claudia studia.* (SV)
 B': *Meglio di no. Non so dove studia Claudia.* (VS)
 better of not not know where Claudia studies Claudia
 'Better if I don't. I don't know where Claudia is studying.'

(17) A: *Perché non metti un po' di musica?* [*dove*, **subjunctive**]
 'Why don't you put some music on?'

---

16 We added this latter type of question, namely *if*-questions, to see which positions subjects occupy within indirect yes/no-questions. Since this article deals with wh-questions, we will not comment on the results and on their theoretical implications. See Bocci & Pozzan (2014) for discussion.

B: Meglio di no. Non so dove Claudia studi. (SV)
  B': Meglio di no. Non so dove studi Claudia. (VS)
  better of not not know where Claudia studies Claudia
  'Better if I don't. I don't know where Claudia is studying.'

(18) A: *Ma gli esami non sono stati rinviati?* [*perché*, **indicative**]
  'Haven't the exams been postponed?'
  B: Sì, di due mesi. Non so perché Claudia studia. (SV)
  B': Sì, di due mesi. Non so perché studia Claudia. (VS)
  yes of two months not know why Claudia studies Claudia
  'Yes, by two months. I don't know why Claudia is studying.'

(19) A: *Ma gli esami non sono stati rinviati?* [*perché*, **subjunctive**]
  'Haven't the exams been postponed?'
  B: Sì, di due mesi. Non so perché Claudia studi. (SV)
  B': Sì, di due mesi. Non so perché studi Claudia. (VS)
  yes of two months not know why Claudia studies Claudia
  'Yes, by two months. I don't know why Claudia is studying.'

(20) A: *Perché non metti un po' di musica?* [*se*, **indicative**]
  'Why don't you put some music on?'
  B: Meglio di no. Non so se Claudia studia. (SV)
  B': Meglio di no. Non so se studia Claudia. (VS)
  better of not not know if Claudia studies Claudia
  'Better if I don't. I don't know if Claudia is studying.'

(21) A: *Perché non metti un po' di musica?* [*se*, **subjunctive**]
  'Why don't you put some music on?'
  B: *Meglio di no. Non so se Claudia studi.* (SV)
  B': *Meglio di no. Non so se studi Claudia.* (VS)
  better of not not know if Claudia studies Claudia
  'Better if I don't. I don't know if Claudia is studying.'

The target sentences were divided into 6 lists following a Latin square design. The two factors 'embedded mood' and 'question type' were manipulated within participants, so that each list consisted of 30 experimental item. Each participant was thus presented with the experimental stimuli of a certain item only under one condition. 30 fillers were added to the trials, and the order of the trials was pseudo-randomized. The experimental trials and the fillers alternated.

The sentence pairs were presented as parts of brief written exchanges between two speakers (A and B) (cf. 16–21). The contexts were designed in order to disfavour as much as possible a focus or topic interpretation of the subject

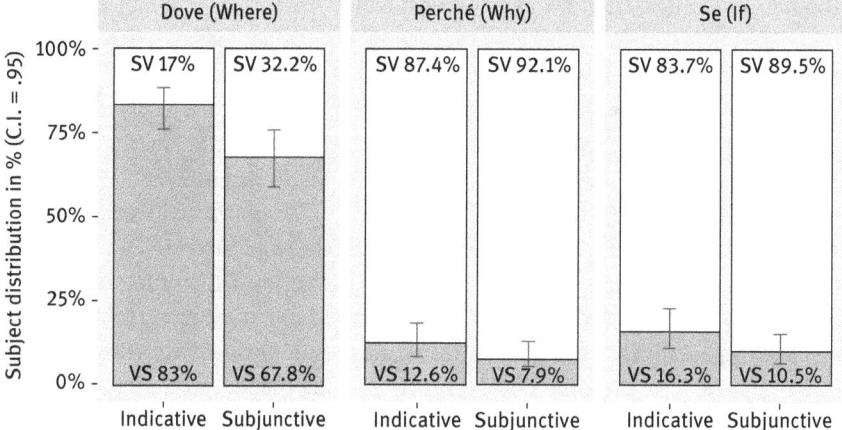

Figure 9: Second syntactic experiment: preferences for SV or VS in the three types of indirect question, with indicative or subjunctive mood

in the embedded clause. For each item, *se*-questions and *dove*-questions were presented within the same dialogue, while *perché*-questions were introduced by different dialogues. Participants were asked to choose between the two alternative orders (SV vs. VS); 60 native speakers of Italian residing in Italy participated in the experiment. Figure 9 shows the results.

Statistical analyses were based on multi-level mixed effects regressions with log odds of a postverbal subject response as the dependent variable, mood (subjunctive vs. indicative), question-type (*se*-, *perché*-, and *dove*-questions) as fixed effects. The random structure included by-subject and by-item random intercepts, and by-subject and by-item slopes for question-type.

A first statistical model, with question-type specified with backward difference schema, showed that subject distribution in *se*- and *perché*-questions is not significantly different (*Estimate* = –.560, *SE* = .36, p > .1), while *perché*-questions significantly differ from *dove*-questions (*Estimate* = 4.043, SE = .438, p < .001). The main effect of mood was extremely significant (*Estimate* = .009, SE = .2, p < .001). To understand the role of mood with respect to *perché*-questions and *dove*-questions, we fitted a second model that included only *perché*- and *dove*-questions. This model revealed that *dove*-questions with subjunctive mood (the baseline) significantly differ from *dove*-questions with indicative mood (*Estimate* = 1.112, SE = .271, p < .001) since in the latter condition the preference for postverbal subjects increases. Notably, *dove*-questions with subjunctive mood also significantly differ from *perché*-questions with subjunctive mood (*Estimate* = –3.724, SE = .488, p < .001) since the probability of VS in the latter condition is much lower. There is no marginal interaction for *perché*-questions with indicative mood (*Estimate*= −.595, SE = . 0.444, p > .1) indicating that the type of mood does not affect the distribution of subjects in *perché*-questions.

These results show that, in the absence of contextual conditions that could favour a focus or topic interpretation, postverbal subjects are clearly preferred in *dove*-questions, but dispreferred with *perché*- and *se*-questions. The pattern observed with the indicative is also present with the subjunctive: although the inverting effect of *dove* is slightly reduced with the subjunctive, VS is still the prevailing pattern in *dove*-questions with the subjunctive. This contrasts with the preference for SV observed for *perché*-questions with the same mood (cf. Figure 9) (see Bianchi, Bocci & Cruschina 2017 for an account for this asymmetry).

In sum, we have experimental evidence showing that the subjunctive slightly diminishes the preference for postverbal subjects in indirect questions. However, even if less compelling, exactly the same preference patterns observed with the indicative are reproduced with the subjunctive, showing that the factor that ultimately counts is the question type.

6 Conclusion

The derivational history of the wh-phrase, i.e. its successive cyclic movement, is essential to understand the constraints on the subject position and on the placement of NPA in wh-questions, both with short and long movement. Our first experiment shows that subject inversion in the embedded clause of a complex wh-question is strongly preferred only when the wh-phrase originates from within that clause and has moved to the main clause. Further experimental data (see in particular Bocci, Bianchi & Cruschina 2018) add prosodic evidence in favour of the essential role of the successive cyclic movement in the determination of the syntactic and prosodic properties of wh-questions. Our results confirm that in complex wh-questions the placement of NPA is sensitive to the extraction process of the wh-element. The differences and similarities between direct and indirect wh-questions are crucial in this respect. On the one hand, the adjacency requirement between the wh-element and the verb is active in direct wh-questions as well as in indirect wh-questions, both with the subjunctive and the indicative mood. On the other, with respect to their prosodic properties, indirect wh-questions pattern with declarative sentences rather than with direct wh-questions, insofar as NPA is placed by default on the rightmost element of the sentence.

We thus conclude that subject inversion in wh-questions does not result from a prosodic requirement, but is instead syntactic in nature. While there is no direct causal relation between NPA placement and subject inversion, both phenomena are independently rooted in the syntactic computation. Subject inversion in both direct and indirect questions is a syntactic phenomenon and is sensitive to successive cyclic movement. Similarly, the prosodic mechanism originally observed by Calabrese that leads to the NPA placement in direct wh-questions is syntactically determined and must also be viewed as a reflex of successive cyclic movement.

Acknowledgments: We would like to thank Valentina Bianchi and Lucia Pozzan for invaluable help and discussion. Giuliano Bocci's research was supported by the ERC Advanced Grant 340297 SynCart.

References

Antinucci, Francesco & Guglielmo Cinque. 1977. Sull'ordine delle parole in Italiano. L'emarginazione. *Studi di Grammatica Italiana* 6. 121–146.
Belletti, Adriana. 2004. Aspects of the low IP area. In Luigi Rizzi (ed.), *The structure of IP and CP. The cartography of syntactic structures, Vol. 2*, 16–51. Oxford & New York: Oxford University Press.
Belletti, Adriana & Valentina Bianchi. 2016. Definiteness effect and unaccusative subjects: An overview and some new thoughts. In Susann Fischer, Tanja Kupisch & Esther Rinke (eds.), *Definiteness effects: bilingual, typological and diachronic variation*, 14–65. Cambridge: Cambridge Scholars Publishing.
Bianchi, Valentina, Giuliano Bocci & Silvio Cruschina. 2017. Two types of subject inversion in Italian wh-questions. *Revue roumaine de linguistique* 62(3): 233–252.
Bianchi, Valentina, Giuliano Bocci & Silvio Cruschina. forthcoming. The syntactic and prosodic effects of long-distance wh-movement in Italian. *Italian Journal of Linguistics*.
Bocci, Giuliano & Lucia Pozzan. 2014. Questions (and experimental answers) about Italian subjects. Subject positions in main and indirect question in L1 and attrition. In Carla Contemori & Lena Dal Pozzo (eds.), *Inquiries into linguistic theory and language acquisition. Papers offered to Adriana Belletti*, 28–44. Siena: CISCL Press.
Bocci, Giuliano. 2013. *The Syntax–Prosody Interface: a cartographic perspective with evidence from Italian*. Amsterdam: John Benjamins.
Bocci, Giuliano, Valentina Bianchi & Silvio Cruschina. 2018. The syntactic role of focus: Evidence from Italian wh-questions. Manuscript.
Calabrese, Andrea. 1982. Alcune ipotesi sulla struttura informazionale della frase in Italiano e sul suo rapporto con la struttura fonologica. *Rivista di Grammatica Generativa* 13. 489–526.
Cardinaletti, Anna. 2001. A second thought on *emarginazione*: Destressing vs 'Right Dislocation'. In Guglielmo Cinque & Giampaolo Salvi (eds.), *Current studies in Italian syntax. Essays offered to Lorenzo Renzi*, 117–135. Amsterdam: Elsevier.
Cardinaletti, Anna. 2002. Against optional and null clitics. Right dislocation vs. marginalization. *Studia Linguistica* 56(1). 29–57.

Cardinaletti, Anna. 2007. Subjects and wh-questions. Some new generalizations. In Jose Camacho et al. (eds.), *Romance linguistics 2006: Selected papers from the 36th Linguistic Symposium on Romance Languages (LSRL)*, 57–79. Amsterdam & Philadelphia: John Benjamins.

Chomsky, Noam. 2008. On phases. In Robert Freidin, Carlos P. Otero, and Maria Luisa Zubizarreta (eds.), *Foundational issues in linguistic theory: Essays in honor of Jean-Roger Vergnaud*. Cambridge, MA: MIT Press.

É. Kiss, Katalin. 1995. Introduction. In Katalin É. Kiss (ed.), *Discourse configurational languages*, 3–27. Oxford & New York: Oxford University Press.

Giorgi, Alessandra & Fabio Pianesi. 1997. *Tense and aspect. From semantics to morphosyntax*. Oxford & New York: Oxford University Press.

Haida, Andreas. 2007. *The indefiniteness and focusing of wh-words*. Berlin: Humboldt-Universität PhD dissertation.

Henry, Alison. 1995. *Belfast English and Standard English: dialect variation and parameter setting*. Oxford & New York: Oxford University Press.

Horvath, Julia. 1981. *Aspects of Hungarian syntax and the theory of grammar*. Los Angeles: UCLA PhD dissertation.

Horvath, Julia. 1986. *FOCUS in the theory of grammar and the syntax of Hungarian*. Dordrecht: Foris.

Kayne, Richard S. & Jean-Yves Pollock. 1978. Stylistic inversion, successive cyclicity and move NP in French. *Linguistic Inquiry* 9. 595–621.

Kisler Thomas, Uwe D. Reichel, Florian Schiel, Christoph Draxler, Bernhard Jackl & Nina Pörner. 2016. BAS Speech Science Web Services – an update of current developments. In *Proceedings of the 10th International Conference on Language Resources and Evaluation (LREC 2016)*, Portorož, Slovenia, 3880–3885.

Munaro, Nicola. 2010. La frase interrogativa. In Lorenzo Renzi & Giampaolo Salvi (eds.), *Grammatica dell'italiano antico*, 1147–1185. Bologna: Il Mulino.

Nespor, Marina & Irene Vogel. 1986. *Prosodic phonology*. Dordrecht: Foris.

Poletto, Cecilia. 2000. *The higher functional field: evidence from Northern Italian dialects*. Oxford & New York: Oxford University Press.

Rizzi, Luigi & Ur Shlonsky. 2007. Strategies of subject extraction. In H.-M. Gärtner & U. Sauerland (eds.), *Interfaces + recursion = language? Chomsky's minimalism and the view from syntax-semantics*, 115–160. Berlin: Mouton de Gruyter.

Rizzi, Luigi. 1996. Residual verb-second and the wh-criterion. In Adriana Belletti & Luigi Rizzi (eds.), *Parameters and functional heads. Essays in comparative syntax*, 63–90 Oxford & New York: Oxford University Press.

Rizzi, Luigi. 2001. On the position Int(errogative) in the left periphery of the clause. In Guglielmo Cinque & Giampaolo Salvi (eds.), *Current studies in Italian syntax. Essays offered to Lorenzo Renzi*, 287–296. Amsterdam: Elsevier.

Rizzi, Luigi. 2006. On the form of chains: Criterial positions and ECP effects. In Lisa Lai-Shen Cheng & Norbert Corver (eds.), *Wh-movement. moving on*, 97–133. Cambridge, MA: MIT Press.

Rooth, Mats. 1996. Focus. In Shalom Lappin (ed.), *The handbook of contemporary semantic theory*, 271–297. Oxford: Blackwell.

Schiel, Florian. 1999. Automatic phonetic transcription of non-prompted speech. *Proceedings of the International Congress of Phonetic Sciences* 1999. 607–610.

Torrego, Esther. 1983. More effects of successive cyclic movement. *Linguistic Inquiry* 14. 561–565.

Torrego, Esther. 1984. On inversion in Spanish and some of its effects. *Linguistic Inquiry* 15. 103–129.

Guglielmo Cinque
On the Merge position of additive and associative plurals

1 Introduction

Differently from the additive plural, which refers to several instances of X, the associative plural refers to a group consisting of X and other individuals associated with X.[1] As noted in fn. 1, in some languages (e.g., Turkish, Ainu, Japanese) 'additive' plurals and 'associative' plurals are expressed by one and the same morpheme; in others (Bangla (Biswas 2013, 2014), Garo (Burling 2004: 179f), Hungarian (see below)), by distinct morphemes. This suggests that the two plural notions share some common component while differing with respect to other components. Some languages capitalize on the shared component thus using one and the same morpheme (lexically underspecified with respect to the two notions), while other languages capitalize on the differentiating components thus using different morphemes, according to a pervasive source of lexical variation among languages (Cinque 2015a).[2] In this article just one aspect of their syntax will be in focus: their Merge position within the extended projection of the NP, where they appear to occupy two distinct positions.

---

[1] I thank Paola Benincà, Richard Kayne and two anonymous reviewers for their helpful comments. For a general discussion of associative plurals see Corbett and Mithun (1966), Corbett (2000: 107-110), Moravcsik (1994, 2003), Kibort (2008), Daniel and Moravcsik (2005, 2013), and the other references given below. Languages differ as to how many categories in the so-called 'Animacy Hierarchy', (1st and 2nd person pronominals > 3rd person pronominal > proper names > kinship terms > human definite nouns > other animate (> inanimate)) accept an associative plural (interpretation). While English and Italian restrict their associative expressions to (plural) 1st and 2nd person pronominals, Central Alaskan Yup'ik draws the line between proper names and the rest (Corbett 2000: 107-8). Hungarian allows associative to be formed from pronominals, proper names, kin terms, title nouns and the noun 'neighbour', but not other definite nouns (Moravcsik 2003: 472; Dekany 2011: §9.4), while the split in Slovenian is between human definite and other animate nouns (Lanko Marušič, p.c.). Whether 'associative plurality' should be considered a number, as (additive) plurals, duals, etc., or not (Corbett 2000: §4.3.4 argues that it should be regarded as a category distinct from 'number') is not crucial here. Nonetheless the fact that in nearly half of Daniel and Moravcsik's (2013) sample of languages associative and additive plurals are morphologically identical seems to suggest that they belong to the same category.

[2] Alternatively, the single morpheme which expresses the shared component is accompanied by different silent elements, while the two distinct morphemes are specialized to express the differentiating components of meaning.

2 The evidence

That associative and additive plurals are merged in two different positions is particularly evident in certain languages, including Turkish, Ainu, Hungarian and Japanese.

As Görgülü (2011) notes, in Turkish, the additive plural morpheme is closer to the noun than possessives (see 1a.), while the same morpheme in its associative interpretation is further away from the noun than possessives (see 1b.):[3]

(1) a. *abi-**ler**-im*   (additive plural)
       brother-**PL**-1SG.Poss
       'my brothers'
       (Görgülü 2011,72 and Jaklin Kornfilt, p.c.)
    b. *abi-m-**ler***   (associative plural)
       brother-1SG.Poss-**PL**
       'My brother and his family/associates/friends'
       (Görgülü 2011,73 and Jaklin Kornfilt, p.c.)

With Görgülü (2011) and Nakanishi and Ritter (2009) I take this to mean that the two plurals occupy two distinct projections. Under the Mirror Principle, which yields the predominant, though not the exclusive, order of suffixes (cf. the Yupik case below) the associative plural projection turns out to be higher than the projection hosting possessives, which in turn must be higher than that hosting additive plurals. See (2):

---

[3] Görgülü (2011) also argues that in addition to their different morphosyntactic properties additive and associative plurals also differ semantically. The former, attaching to proper names, kinship terms and common nouns, induces both collective and distributive interpretations while the latter, attaching just to proper names and kinship terms induces only a collective/group interpretation (with a focal referent). Richard Kayne mentions the possibility that the associative *-ler* is actually the same additive *-ler* appended to a silent AND FRIEND (*abi-m*-AND-FRIEND-*ler*), thinking of *my brother and his friends, my brother and company* in English. As a matter of fact the associative plural in Basque is expressed by 'and' following a proper name ("John and" = John and FRIENDS/OTHERS) (Data Point – Basque/ The Associtive Plural, WALS online: http://wals.info/valuesets/36A-bsq; perhaps Spanish and Venetian 1st person plural pronouns *nosotros/n(o)ialtri* ‹'we' is a type of associative ('I and others›). Also see colloquial Italian (**noi*) *siamo andati con Maria al cinema* (we = I and Maria) went.1st.pl with Maria to the movies).

(2)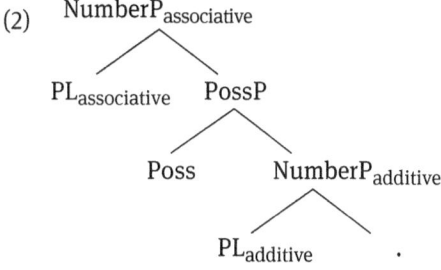

Exactly the same pattern is found in Ainu (language isolate). See (3):[4]

(3) a. *ku-yup-**utar**-i*   (additive plural)
    1sg-elder.brother-**PL**-poss
    'my elder brothers'
  b. *ku-yup-i-**utar***   (associative plural)
    1sg-elder.brother-poss-**PL**
    'my elder brother and others'

A similar case is provided by Hungarian, which differently from Turkish and Ainu, distinguishes morphologically the two plurals, but appears to merge them in the same two different positions, with additive plurals preceding (4a.), and associative plurals following, the possessive suffix (4b.)

(4) a. *barát-**ai**-m*   (additive plural)
    friend-**PL**$_{additive}$-my
    'my friends'
    (Hirose 2004,335)
  b. *a barát-om-**ék*** (associative plural)
    det friend-my-**PL**$_{associative}$
    'my friend and his associates'
    (Hirose 2004: 335)

In Hungarian the two plurals can even co-occur on the same noun, in the expected order N-PL$_{additive}$-Poss-PL$_{associative}$. See (5):

---

4 From WALS online Feature 36A: The Associative Plural of WALS. Also see Hirose (2004: §3.1), based on Shibatani (1990: 32).

(5) a. *barát-**ai**-m-ék*   (Julia Horvath, p.c.)[5]
    friend-PL$_{Additive}$ (of possessed)-1SG possessor-PL$_{Associative}$
    'my friends and their associates'
   b. *barát-a-**i**-d-ék-at*   (Dékány 2011: §9.4, ex.(29))[6]
    friend-Poss-PL$_{additive}$-Poss.2sg-PL$_{associative}$-Acc
    'your friends and their associates'

Japanese as well gives evidence that the two plurals occupy distinct positions. Even if morphologically identical, so that a single occurrence of the suffix (*-tachi-/-tati-*) is ambiguous between an additive or associative interpretation (see (6)), the two suffixes can co-occur, in the order N > PL$_{Additive}$ > PL$_{Associative}$, as in (7):

(6) a. *kyooju-tachi-ga*
    professor-PL-NOM
   b. 'More than one professor'
   c. 'The professor and some others'
    (Hirose 2004: 332)[7]

(7) *gakusei-tati-tati*
    student-TATI$_{Additive}$-TATI$_{Associative}$
    'the students and their associates'
    (Ueda and Haraguchi 2008: 237)[8]

---

5 Julia Horvath tells me (p.c.) that the associates must be interpreted as joint/shared among my friends. They cannot be distributive, i.e., cannot be different associates for each friend.
6 Hungarian has another possessive suffix, lower than additive plurals.
7 See also Nakanishi and Tomioka (2004). Hirose (2004) explicitly proposes that while additive plurals adjoin to NP associative plurals adjoin to DP, and discusses (§4.1) some consequences which follow from the higher merger of associative plurals in Japanese.
8 The associative plural (ia.) (though not the additive one (ib.)) can apparently be reiterated, modifying a complex DP, already modified by one instance of the associative plural:
(i) a. *Taroo-tati-tati*
    Taroo-TATI-TATI
    'Taroo and his associates and their associates'
    (Ueda and Haraguchi 2008: 237)
   b. *gakusei-tati-tati*
    student-TATI(PL)-TATI(PL)
    '*the students'
    'the students and their associates'
    (Ueda and Haraguchi 2008: 237)
Not all speakers accept (7) and (i) above. I thank a reviewer for pointing this out to me.

I thus take the order N-PL$_{Additive}$-PL$_{Associative}$(-Case) of Japanese to be derived from a structure in which the additive plural is lower than the associative plural by raising the NP with *pictures-of-whom* pied piping around the 'heads' PL$_{Additive}$, PL$_{Associative}$ (and Case) as is typical of well-behaved head-final languages (cf. Cinque 2017a).

The opposite order N-PL$_{Associative}$-PL$_{Additive}$, which is found in Yup'ik (Corbett and Mithun 1996:12) (cf. (8) and (9)) must instead derive from the same structure by raising the NP in one fell swoop (without reversing their order):[9]

(8) *cuna-nku-t*
Cuna-PL$_{associative}$-PL$_{additive}$
'Cuna and his associates'

(9) *cuna-nku-k*
Cuna-PLassociative-Dual
'Cuna and his associate (refers to two people)'

3 The respective position of additive and associative plurals

3.1 Additive plurals

Clearer evidence on the position of additive plurals within the nominal extended projection comes from those languages where additive plurals are expressed by a free morpheme.[10] Cross-linguistic evidence appears to point

---

[9] One reviewer wonders whether "the additive morpheme here modifies the number of associates of Cuna, rather than the noun itself (being the latter a proper name)". If so the behaviour of the additive morpheme would be different from its typical one of changing the number of the noun. However, the fact that in (9) the dual interpretation is not on the number of associates, but on the number made up by Cuna and his associate makes one think that in (8) too the plural refers to a plurality made up by Cuna and associates rather than by just the associates. This recalls the colloquial Italian case mentioned in fn. 3 above.

[10] Bound morphemes, which end up being affixed to the noun (and often, for concord, to other nominal modifiers as well) do not give as transparent an indication of their position of Merge.

I limit here reference to 'Plural', rather than the more general 'Number', as it is not at all clear whether other additive numbers (dual, trial, paucal) occupy the same position of Merge. As a matter of fact, Henderson (1995: 73) reports that in the Papuan language Yele dual and plural

to a location of Plural (Number) between cardinal numerals and adjectives (cf. also Dryer 1989).[11] Interestingly, this position appears to correspond to the unique semantic scope position of Number, which Vennemann (1973: 44f) and Heycock and Zamparelli (2005: §4) locate between Cardinal numerals and adjectives.[12]

Here we present a number of representative cases, first of the 'direct' order Numeral$_{Cardinal}$ PL <Adjective> N <Adjective>, and then of the mirror-image order N Adjective PL Numeral$_{Cardinal}$. The two orders are arguably derived from a unique order reflecting the relative scope of the elements (i.e. Dem Num$_{Card}$ CFL PL Adj N) via movement of NP involving pied piping of the *picture-of-whom* type and of the *whose-picture* type, respectively (see Cinque 2017a). Other orders, like that of Zaiwa (Dem N Adj Num$_{Card}$ CLF PL – Wannemacher 2010) are presumably derived with a mixture of movements (raising of NP above AP and then raising of NP AP without pied piping above Num$_{Card}$ CLF PL – see Cinque 2005, 2017a for the derivation of different orders).

The direct order of Numeral$_{Cardinal}$ > Plural > Adjective (modulo the Adjective in postnominal position for some of them) is found in Oto-Manguean (Hnonho, Copala Trique), Mayan (Sipakapense Maya), in Austronesian (Hawaiian), and non-Austronesian Papuan (Kuot). See for example (10) to (14):

(10) ár   'bede yoho **ya** ndo   Ø   mí=n-jödö
     SG.3POS story two   **PL** man   REL   3.IMP=MED-brothers

---

can co-occur (see (i)), thus betraying their distinct Merge position ("[t]wo number markers are used, *dê* for dual items and *yoo* for plural animate items"):

(i) U   kpâm   dê   y:oo
     His   wife   DU   PL
     'his two wives'

Also see the co-occurrence of dual and nonsingular (plural) in the Papua New Guinea language isolate Kuot (Lindström 2002:147), with raising of the noun around the two morphemes without pied piping:

(ii) alaŋ   alaŋ-ip   alaŋ-ip-ien
     road(sg)   road-nsg   road-nsg-dl
     'road'   'roads'   'two roads'

As well as the co-occurrence of dual and plural in the Austronesian language Biak (Dalrymple and Mofu 2013: 48).

11 More precisely, between numeral classifiers, themselves below cardinal numerals, and adjectives. See below.

12 Pace Sauerland (2003), who locates Number above DP. On the original proposal for a separate projection of (Additive) NumberP below DP see Ritter (1991), and also Picallo (2008).

'the story of two men who were brothers'
(Hnonho Otomi – Oto-Manguean – Palancar 2009:163)[13]

(11) wahnux1 **nix** nee zah1 yoh
 three **PL** knife good that
 'those three good knives'
 (Copala Trique – Oto-Manguean – Hollenbach 1992:280)[14]

(12) keb' **ke'q** nim-a tz'i'
 two **PL** big-aff dogs
 'two big dogs'
 (Sipakapense Maya – Mayan – Barrett 1999:200)

(13) élua a'u **mau** ia
 two my **PL** fish
 'my two fishes'
 (Hawaiian – Austronesian – Dryer 1989, 866; from Elbert and Pukui 1979: 159)[15]

(14) miro naien **ma** kamilip mila murum
 this three **PL** yam Rel good
 'these three good yams'
 (Kuot – East Papuan – Chung and Chung 1993: 19)

The mirror-image of Numeral$_{Cardinal}$, Plural and Adjective is found in several other languages including the following:

(15) nìsì wòngjúwe **ɐ́** cúk
 eyes red **PL** two
 'two red eyes'
 (Fali – Adamawa – Kramer 2014: 231)[16]

(16) Nέb sɔɔn **bəd** ʔiirā
 person good **PL** two

---

[13] The more detailed DP internal order of Hnonho Otomi is: Dem Num$_{Card}$ PL Adj-N (Palancar 2009: 92ff).
[14] The order of Copala Trique nominal modifiers is: Num$_{Card}$ PL N Adj Dem. Another Mixtecan language with the same order is Ocotepec Mixtec (Alexander 1988: 220).
[15] The order of Hawaiian nominal modifiers is: Dem Num$_{Card}$ PL N A.
[16] The order of nominal modifiers in Fali given by Kramer (2014: 233) is: N Adj PL Num$_{Card}$ Dem Q$_{all}$.

'two good people'
(Samba Leko – Adamawa – Fabre 2004: 194f)[17]

(17) naŋ ŋu ɔvu zam voŋ ɲiu **hai** sam
 this 1sg GEN house be big big **PL** three
 'These three big houses of mine'
 (Leinong Naga – Sino-Tibetan (Kuki-Chin) – Ohn 2010: 88)[18]

(18) sira kokan la telu nene nap~a sup~e **la** a-pisi pani-la
 female small PL three these Rel chief **PL** 3Pl-spoke to-3Pl
 'These three girls that the chiefs reprimanded'
 (Lewo – Oceanic – Early 1994:65)[19]

(19) baha waitnika araska karna **nani** wâl ba
 these man horses strong **PL** two def/top
 'these two strong horses of the man'
 (Miskito – Misumalpan – Salamanca 2008: 116)

As noted above, in languages that have numeral classifiers co-occurring with cardinal numerals and additive plurals, additive plurals appear between the numeral classifier, itself below cardinals, and adjectives, in the orders in (20), arguably derived from Dem Num$_{Card}$ CLF PL Adj N via different options of NP raising with *whose-pictures* or *pictures-of-whom* pied piping – cf. Cinque (2017a). See (21)-(25) for some examples:[20]

(20) a. **Num CLF PL** Adj N Dem (Mayan: Jakaltek; Jucatec,..)
 b. Dem **Num CLF PL** N Adj (Mon-Khmer: Khasi,..)
 c. **Num CLF PL** N Adj Dem (Malayo-Polynesian: Northern Roglai; Tai-Kadai: Nùng,..)

(21) **caw-aŋ** **heb** naj winaj
 two-numeralCLF **PL** nominalCLF (gender?) man

---

[17] The order of Samba Leko nominal modifiers is: N Adj PL Num$_{Card}$ Dem.
[18] Another Sino-Tibetan language displaying the same order is Dzongkha (Gelles 2010: 3).
[19] Other Oceanic languages displaying the order N Adj PL Num$_{Card}$ are Daakaka (von Prince 2012:91), Lenakel (Lynch 1978: 74), Sinaugoro (Kolia 1975: 124), Ske (Johnson 2014: §2.4), and Tawala (Ezard 1997: 147).
[20] Although in many languages numeral classifiers and number markers cannot co-occur, a fact that has been elevated to a universal (Borer 2005: Chapter 4, p. 8–10), these languages show that there is no absolute ban on their co-occurrence. See also Gebhardt (2009).

'two men'
(Jacaltec – Maya – Craig Grinevald 1977:143)

(22) ʔaar tllii kii miaw
 two CLF PL cat
 'two cats'
 (Khasi – Mon-Khmer – Rabel 1961: 52; from Dryer 1989: 874)[21]

(23) **Cáh mạhn** khỏhn ɖáhm-ɖihc
 CLF PL feather black
 'the feathers were pitch black'
 (Nùng – Tai-Kadai – Saul and Freiberger Wilson 1980: 24)[22]

(24) **dua ia:k labuʔ** ʔañā? sia:p ñũ ʔanĩ la sa:k
 two CLF PL child good 3p this in house
 'these two good children of his in the new house'
 (Northern Roglai – Malayo-Polynesian – Thurgood, Thurgood and Li 2014: 149)

(25) to **upat** no **buuk** no **mgo** kamuti
 DET **four** LK **unit** LK **PL** camote
 'four (units of) camote' (four camotes)
 (Agusan Manobo – Austronesian (Philippine) – Schumacher and Schumacher 2008: 22)

3.2 Associative plurals

The fact that nominal extended projections containing associative plurals are necessarily definite (pronominals, proper names, and definite NPs) suggests that associative plurals can only modify (definite) DPs, nothing smaller; that is to say, they must c-command a definite DP. This is natural if one considers the fact that associative number applies to individuals rather than to something which is still a predicate (as is arguably the case with additive plurals – Kiparsky 2014:118f – among others). Interesting confirmation for a Merge position of the associative

---

21 The order of nominal modifiers given in Rabel (1961:131) is <Qall> Dem Num CLF PL N Adj <Qall>.
22 The overall order of nominal modifiers given by Saul and Freiberger Wilson (1980) is: Num CLF PL N Adj Poss Dem. With numeral 'one' the order is: CLF N Adj Num (p.14).

plural higher than DP comes from the relative pre-nominal word order of the Associative Plural morpheme and the determiner in Muna. See (26):

(26) no-hamba **ndo** **Wa** Marangkululi
3sR-chase **PL**$_{Associative}$ **art** Marangkululi
'He chased Marangkululi and her friends'
(Muna -Malayo-Polynesian, (van den) Berg 1989: 108)

and the mirror-image order N-art-Associative Trial of Urama in (27):[23]

(27) Karika=i=obi asio p-a'ai bi=mo
Karika=DEF=TRIAL sneeze DPST-do TR=PL
'Karika and two others sneezed.'
(Urama – Papuan (Trans-New Guinea) – Brown, Muir, Craig, and Anea 2016: 25)

This proposal is reminiscent of Li's (1999) idea that the Chinese associative plural morpheme -*men* raises from Number to the proper name in D, and Hirose's (2004, 333) proposal that the Japanese associative -*tati*- adjoins to DP (also see Ueda and Haraguchi (2008: 237) -*tati*- as a D°). Biswas (2013, 2014), following Chacón (2011), also assume that the Bangla associative plural marker -*ra* is higher than DP, and so does Forbes (2013) for the associative plural morpheme *dip* in Gitksan (Tsimshianic). Nakanishi and Ritter (2008) have similarly suggested that associative plurals are merged in a group phrase, GrP, projected outside DP.

4 Conclusion

The partial map of the fragment of the nominal extended projection encompassing additive and associative plurals thus seems to be[24]:

---

[23] "Within the noun phrase, the trial clitic =*obi* appears outside of the definite article clitic. [(26)] represents an associative trial" (Brown, Muir, Craig, and Anea 2016: 25).
[24] The Hungarian example (4)b and the Japanese example (5)a above, and the Chuvash (Turkic) example in (i) from WALS online, seem to indicate, under the Mirror Principle (Baker 1985), holding pervasively but not exclusively (see the case of Yup'ik above, in (8) and (9)), that the associative Plural projection is below the Case projection (see Dékány 2011: §9.4.1 on Hungarian and Forbes 2013 on Gitxsan):

(i) ivăl - se - n - e kaj - sa kil - t - ĕm
son - **PL**$_{Associative}$ - **obl** – DA go - CONV come - pfv - 1
'I went to my son's (to my son and his family)'

(28)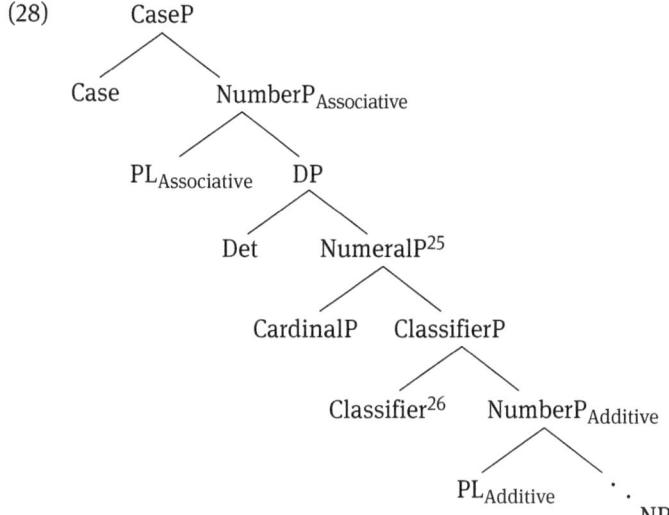

Actual orders like the (Case) PL$_{associative}$ Det N of Muna above, or the mirror-image N-PL$_{associative}$- Case one of Japanese are derived via the two options in which the core of the extended projection, the NP, raises to derive the canonical head-initial and head-final word orders (*whose-picture* pied piping and *picture-of whom* pied piping – Cinque 2017a), with the consequent segregation of heads on one side of the N and phrases on the other side.[25]

Acknowledgments: Ad Andrea, in ricordo dei suoi anni da studente a Padova e a Campi.

References

Alexander, Ruth Mary. 1988. A syntactic sketch in Ocotepec Mixtec. In C.H.Bradley & B.E. Hollenbach (eds.), *Studies in the syntax of Mixtecan languages* 1, 153–304. Dallas: Summer Institute of linguistics and The University of Texas at Arlington.

Aghul and Bagvalal (Northeast Caucasian), Khakas (Turkic), Meithei (Tibeto-Burman) also show the order N-PL$_{Associative}$-Case in the WALS online Feature 36A (The Associative Plural). In the same archive Dani (Lower Grand Valley) (Papuan) shows that the associative plural suffix can be followed by Case and Topic suffixes.

25 But see Cinque (2017b) for the possibility of reconciling such apparent segregation of heads and phrases with Kayne's (2016) idea that heads are invariably silent. For a different movement analysis altogether, see Vassilieva (2005, 2008).

Baker, Mark. 1985. The mirror principle and morphosyntactic explantion. *Linguistic Inquiry* 16. 373–415.
Barrett, Edward Rush, III. 1999. *A grammar of Sipakapense Maya*. University of Texas at Austin, Ph.D. dissertation.
Berg, René van den. 1989. *A grammar of the Muna Language*. Universiteit Leiden Ph.D. dissertation. http://www-01.sil.org/silepubs/pubs/928474552170/ebook_52_van_den_berg_muna_12-11-12.pdf.
Biswas, Priyanka. 2013. Plurality in a classifier language: Two types of plurals in Bangla. *The Proceedings of GLOW in Asia IX 2012*, Mie University, Japan. http://faculty.human.mie-u.ac.jp/~glow_mie/IX_Proceedings_Poster/03Biswas.pdf.
Biswas, Priyanka. 2014. Bangla associative plural *-ra*: A Cross-linguistic comparison with Chinese *men* and Japanese *-tachi*. In R.E.Santana-LaBarge (ed.), *Proceedings of the 31st West Coast Conference on Formal Linguistics*, 56–65. http://www.lingref.com/cpp/wccfl/31/paper3007.pdf.
Borer, Hagit. 2005. *Structuring sense, vol I: In name only*. Oxford: Oxford University Press.
Brown, Jason, Alex Muir, Kimberley Craig & Karika Anea. 2016. *A short grammar of Urama*. Canberra: Asia-Pacific Linguistics (The Australian National University). http://hdl.handle.net/1885/111328.
Burling, Robbins. 2004. *The language of the Modhupur Mandi, Garo. vol.1, grammar*. New Delhi: Bibliophile South Asia.
Chacón, D. A. 2011. Bangla and company: the distribution of associative plurals in Bangla, Japanese, and Mandarin Chinese. Handout in *Formal Approaches to South Asian Languages* (FASAL I), University of Massachusetts, Amherst.
Chung, Chul-Hwa & Kyung-Ja Chung. 1996. Kuot grammar essentials. In J.M.Clifton (ed.), *Two non-Austronesian grammars from the islands* (Data Papers on Papua New Guinea Languages 42). 1–75. Ukarumpa: Summer Institute of Linguistics. http://www.sil.org/pacific/png/abstract.asp?id=37101.
Cinque, Guglielmo. 2005. Deriving Greenberg's Universal 20 and its exceptions. *Linguistic Inquiry* 36. 315–332 http://lear.unive.it/jspui/bitstream/11707/82/1/Greenberg-LI.pdf.
Cinque, Guglielmo. 2015a. A source of parametric variation in the lexicon. In A. Gallego & C.Potts (eds.), *50 Years later: Reflections on Chomsky's aspects* (MIT Working Papers in Linguistics). http://filcat.uab.cat/clt/publicacions/Aspects-50-years-later/50YearsLaterMITWPL.pdf.
Cinque, Guglielmo. 2015b. A note on 'other'. In E. Brandner, A. Czypionka, C. Freitag & A. Trotzke (eds.), *Charting the landscape of linguistics. Webschrift for Josef Bayer*, 22–27. Konstanz: Universität Konstanz. http://ling.uni-konstanz.de/pages/WebschriftBayer/2015/title.html.
Cinque, Guglielmo. 2017a. A microparametric approach to word order typology. In S.Karimi & M.Piattelli Palmarini (eds.), *Parameters* (*Linguistic Analysis* 41.309–366). http://lear.unive.it/jspui/handle/11707/5762.
Cinque, Guglielmo. 2017b. On the status of functional categories (heads or phrases?). *Language and Linguistics* 18.521–576.
Corbett, Greville G. 2000. *Number*. Cambridge: Cambridge University Press.
Corbett, Greville G. & Marianne Mithun. 1996. Associative forms in a typology of number systems: evidence from Yup'ik. *Journal of Linguistics* 32. 1–17 http://www.linguistics.ucsb.edu/faculty/mithun/pdfs/1996%20Associative%20forms%20in%20a%20typology%20of%20number%20systems.pdf.

Craig Grinevald, Colette. 1977. *The structure of Jacaltec*. Austin: University of Texas Press.
Dalrymple, Mary & Suriel Mofu. 2013. Semantics of number in Biak. *Language and Linguistics in Melanesia* 31(1). 42–55. http://www.langlxmelanesia.com/LLM%20Vol.%2031(1)_Dalrymple%20&%20Mofu_with%20page%20breaks.pdf.
Daniel, Michael & Edith Moravcsik. 2005. Associative plurals. In M.S. Dryer, M. Haspelmath, D. Gil & B. Comrie (eds.), *World atlas of language structures*, 150–153. Oxford: Oxford University Press. http://amor.cms.hu-berlin.de/~h2816i3x/Lehre/2007_VL_Typologie/03_Daniel_AssociativePlural.pdf.
Daniel, Michael & Edith Moravcsik. 2013. The associative plural. In M.S. Dryer & M. Haspelmath (eds.), *The world atlas of language structures online*. Leipzig: Max Planck Institute for Evolutionary Anthropology. http://wals.info/chapter/36.
Dékány, Eva Katalin. 2011. *A profile of the Hungarian DP. The interaction of lexicalization, agreement and linearization with the functional sequence*. University of Tromsø Ph.D. dissertation. http://real-phd.mtak.hu/57/1/thesis_dekany.pdf.
Dryer, Matthew S. 1989. Plural words. *Linguistics* 27. 865–895 http://wings.buffalo.edu/linguistics/people/faculty/dryer/dryer/DryerPluralWords.PDF.
Early, Robert. 1994. *A grammar of Lewo, Vanuatu*. Australian National University Ph.D. dissertation. https://www.academia.edu/1059215/A_grammar_of_Lewo_Vanuatu.
Elbert, Samuel H. & Mary Kawena Pukui. 1979. *Hawaiian grammar*. Honolulu: University Press of Hawaiʻi.
Ezard, Bryan. 1997. *A grammar of Tawala: an Austronesian language of the Milne Bay area, Papua New Guinea*. Canberra: Pacific Linguistics.
Fabre, Gwenaëlle. 2004. *Le samba leko, langue Adamawa du Cameroun*. München: Lincom Europa.
Forbes, Clarissa. 2013. Associative plurality in the Gitksan nominal domain. In *Proceedings of the 2013 Annual Conference of the Canadian Linguistic Association*. http://homes.chass.utoronto.ca/~cla-acl/actes2013/Forbes-2013.pdf
Gebhardt, Lewis. 2009. *Numeral classifiers and the structure of DP*. Northwestern University, Ph.D. dissertation. http://www.linguistics.northwestern.edu/documents/dissertations/linguistics-research-graduate-dissertations-gebhardtdissertation2008.pdf.
Gelles, Bryan Donald. 2010. *On the structure of nominal phrases in Dzongkha*. San Diego State University M.A. thesis. http://sdsu-dspace.calstate.edu/xmlui/bitstream/handle/10211.10/297/Gelles_Bryan.pdf?sequence=1.
Görgülü, Emrah. 2011. Plural marking in Turkish: Additive or associative? *Working Papers of the Linguistics Circle of the University of Victoria* 21.70–80. http://journals.uvic.ca/index.php/WPLC/article/view/5814/2680.
Henderson, James. 1995. *Phonology and grammar of Yele, Papua New Guinea* (Pacific Linguistics B-112.) Canberra: The Australian National University.
Heycock, Caroline & Roberto Zamparelli. 2005. Friends and colleagues: plurality, coordination, and the structure of DP. *Natural language semantics* 13. 201–270. http://semanticsarchive.net/Archive/jdmMTdkN/friends-colleagues-04-revised.pdf.
Hirose, Tomio. 2004. N-Plural vs. D-Plural. *WCCFL Proceedings* 23. 332–345.
Hollenbach, Barbara E. 1992. A syntactic sketch of Copala Trique. In C.H.Bradley & B.E. Hollenbach (eds.), *Studies in the syntax of Mixtecan languages* 4, 173–431. Dallas: Summer Institute of Linguistics and University of Texas at Arlington.
Johnson, Kay. 2014. *Static spatial expression in Ske: an Oceanic language of Vanuatu*. SOAS, University of London Ph.D. dissertation. http://eprints.soas.ac.uk/18443/.

Kayne, Richard S. 2016. The silence of heads. *Studies in Chinese Linguistics* 37. 1–37. http://www.degruyter.com/downloadpdf/j/scl.2016.37.issue-1/scl-2016-0001/scl-2016-0001.xml.

Kibort, Anna. 2008. Grammatical features inventory: associativity. University of Surrey. http://www.smg.surrey.ac.uk/features/morphosemantic/associativity.

Kiparsky, Paul. 2014. The two plurals: A case for allosemy. *Olomouc Linguistics Colloquium. Book of Abstracts*. Palacký University, Olomouc, Czech Republic. http://olinco.upol.cz/wp-content/uploads/2015/11/olinco2014_book-of-abstracts_web.pdf.

Kolia, J. A. 1975. A Balawaia grammar sketch and vocabulary. In T.E.Dutton (ed.), *Studies in languages of Central and Southeast Papua*, 107–226. Canberra: Australian National University.

Kramer, Raija. 2014. *Die Sprache der Fali in Nordkamerun: eine funktionale Beschreibung*. Köln: Köppe.

Li, Y-H. Audrey. 1999. Plurality in classifier language. *Journal of East Asian Linguistics* 8. 75–99

Lindström, Eva 2002. *Topics in the grammar of Kuot, a non-Austronesian language of New Ireland, Papua New Guinea*. Stockholm University, Ph.D. dissertation. http://www2.ling.su.se/eastpapuan/html.

Lynch, John. 1978. *A grammar of Lenakel*. Canberra: Pacific Linguistics.

Moravcsik, Edith. 1994. Group plural – associative plural or cohort plural. E-mail document, LINGUIST List 5.681, 11 June 1994.

Moravcsik, Edith. 2003. A semantic analysis of associative plurals. *Studies in Language* 27. 469–503

Nakanishi, Kimiko & Elizabeth Ritter. 2009. Plurality in languages without a count-mass distinction. Paper presented at *the Mass/Count Workshop*. University of Toronto. file:///C:/Users/cinque/Downloads/PLURALITY_IN_LANGUAGES_WITHOUT_A_COUNT-MASS_DISTIN%20(1).pdf.

Nakanishi, Kimiko & Satoshi Tomioka. 2004. Japanese plurals are exceptional. *Journal of East Asian Linguistics* 13. 113–140.

Ohn, Mar Htun Gwa [Esther Wayesha]. 2010. *A comparison of imperfectivity in Leinong Naga, Burmese, and Lisu*. Payap University M.A. thesis. http://ic.payap.ac.th/graduate/linguistics/theses/Esther_Wayesha_Thesis.pdf.

Palancar, Enrique L. 2009. *Gramática y Textos del Hñöñhö Otomí de San Ildefonso Tultepec, Querétaro. Vol I. Gramática*. Madrid: Plaza y Valdéz Editores. http://www.academia.edu/860683/Gramatica_del_Otomi_de_San_Ildefonso_Tultepec.

Picallo, M. Carme. 2008. Gender and number in Romance. *Lingue e Linguaggio* VII. 47–66 http://filcat.uab.es/clt/membres/professors/picallo/GenderandNumber.pdf.

Rabel, Lili. 1961. *Khasi: a language of Assam*. Baton Rouge: Louisiana State University Press.

Ritter, Elizabeth. 1991. Two functional categories in noun phrases: evidence from Modern Hebrew. In *Syntax and semantics* 25 (*Perspectives on phrase structure: Heads and licensing*), 37–60. New York. Academic Press.

Salamanca, Danilo. 2008. El idioma miskito: estado de la lengua y características tipológicas. *Letras* 43. 91–122. http://www.revistas.una.ac.cr/index.php/letras/article/view/296.

Sauerland, Uli. 2003. A new semantics for number. *Proceedings of SALT* 13, 258–275. Ithaca, NY: CLC-Publications, Cornell University.

Saul, Janice E. & Nancy Freiberger Wilson. 1980. *Nung grammar*. Dallas: Summer Institute of Linguistics and the University of Texas at Arlington.

Schumacher, Donna & Ron Schumacher. 2008. *Agusan Manobo noun phrase*. Manila: Summer Institute of Linguistics. http://www.sil.org/asia/philippines/ling/msm_Noun_Phrase_paper_2010.pdf.

Shibatani, Masayoshi. 1990. *The languages of Japan*. Cambridge: Cambridge University Press.

Simpson, Andrew. 2005. Classifiers and DP structure in Southeast Asia. In G. Cinque & R.S. Kayne (eds.), *The Oxford handbook of comparative syntax*, 806–838. New York: Oxford University Press.

Testelec, Yakov G. 1998. Word order in Daghestanian languages. In A. Siewierska (ed.), *Constituent order in the languages of Europe*, 257–280. Berlin: Mouton de Gruyter.

Thurgood, Graham, Ela Thurgood & Fenxiang Li. 2014. *A grammatical sketch of Hainan Cham. History, contact, and phonology*. Berlin: De Gruyter Mouton.

Ueda, Yasuki. 2009. Number in Japanese and Chinese. *Nanzan Linguistics* 5. 105–130 http://www.ic.nanzan-u.ac.jp/LINGUISTICS/publication/pdf/NL5-6-ueda.pdf.

Ueda, Yasuki & Tomoko Haraguchi. 2008. Plurality in Japanese and Chinese. *Nanzan Linguistics* (Special Issue 3) 2. 229–242 http://www.ic.nanzan-u.ac.jp/LINGUISTICS/publication/pdf/NLSI3_2-12-ueda_haraguchi.pdf.

Vassilieva, Masha. 2005. *Associative and pronominal plurality*. SUNY Stony Brook, Ph.D. dissertation. https://linguistics.stonybrook.edu/sites/default/files/uploads/Vassilieva2005.pdf.

Vassilieva, Masha. 2008. A syntactic analysis of nominal and pronominal associative plurals. *University of Pennsylvania Working Papers in Linguistics* 14 (issue 1). http://repository.upenn.edu/cgi/viewcontent.cgi?article=1042&context=pwpl.

Venneman, Theo. 1973. Explanation in syntax. In J. Kimball (ed.), *Syntax and semantics* 2, 1–50. New York: Seminar Press.

Wannemacher, Mark. 2010. The basic structure of the Zaiwa noun phrase. *Linguistics of the Tibeto-Burman Area* 33. 85–135.

Luigi Rizzi
Subjects, topics and the interpretation of *pro*

1 Introduction

In this paper I would like to address the classical issue of the similarities and differences between subject and topic positions. In doing so, I will build on seminal work by Andrea Calabrese, particularly Calabrese (1986) on pronominal interpretation. This paper, as well as other contributions on prosody, syntax and information structure (Calabrese 1982, 1992) anticipated and inspired a view of the syntax-pragmatics interface which turned out to be of crucial importance for cartographic projects.

The theoretical context for the analysis of subject positions is offered by the recent discussion on freezing and labeling, and the "halting problem" for movement. Certain syntactic positions are "halting sites" for syntactic movement, and give rise to freezing effects. These are the criterial positions in the sense of Rizzi (1997), for instance the position hosting the wh-element in questions, but also focus and topic positions. A restrictive approach to labeling (Chomsky 2013, 2015: Rizzi 2015a, b, 2016; see also the papers in Bošković 2016) has been recently shown to offer a comprehensive account of the halting problem, capturing both cases in which movement must continue from an intermediate position, and cases in which movement must stop.

The criterial-labeling approach, originally motivated by properties of A'-syntax, naturally extends to A-syntax. The subject position is the typical "halting site" of A-movement. Under the approach just outlined, it is expected to be a criterial position, expressing a Subject Criterion analogous, *mutatis mutandis*, to the Q Criterion, the Focus Criterion and the Topic Criterion of A'-syntax. One would therefore expect the subject position to manifest the kind of scope-discourse interpretive properties which are typical of criterial positions, i.e., giving rise to an articulation akin to topic – comment, focus – presupposition, operator – scope domain, as in familiar A'-constructions. In Rizzi (2005, 2006, and much related work) I have argued that the subject position occurring in the high part of the IP structure expresses the argument "about which" the event expressed by the predicate is presented. This aboutness property is independent from information structure (see section 4), and has consequences for discourse organization and anaphora resolution. Calabrese (1986) observed that in a null subject language like Italian, *pro* in the following sentence (in certain structural configurations) picks out the aboutness subject: this is what I will refer to henceforth as "the Calabrese effect".

The "aboutness" approach makes the subject position akin to the topic position, which also involves "aboutness" (as well as other properties which distinguish topics from subjects: see section 5): the comment is a statement made about the topic; nevertheless subjects and topics should be distinguished, even in Null Subject Languages in which a full assimilation is at first sight very plausible. In this paper, I will address the different formal and interpretive properties of subjects and topics, taking as a point of departure Calabrese's insight on their role in anaphora resolution. The goal is to arrive at a comprehensive analysis of these positions in the context of the cartographic study of structures and interfaces.

2 The "halting problem" for phrasal movement

Phrasal movement proceeds in successive steps, in accordance with fundamental locality principles (Chomsky 1973). Some intermediate positions require movement to continue (transiting positions), whereas other positions require movement to stop (halting position). Familiar illustrations of these effects are provided by A-bar movement, e.g., wh-movement from the clausal complements of different verbs. A verb like *think* in English requires the complementizer system of its complement clause to function as a transiting position. From an initial representation like (1)a, the wh element must transit through the embedded complementizer system, yielding an intermediate representation like (1)b; but (1)b cannot be the final representation, the embedded C-system is a transiting position, from which the wh-element must move further, yielding the main question (1)c:

(1) a. John thinks [C [Bill read [which book]]]
    b. * John thinks [[which book] [C [Bill read __]]]
    c.   [[Which book] [does [John think [__ C [Bill read __]]]]]?

(that the wh-element transits through the embedded C-system, as predicted by locality, is straightforwardly shown, e.g., in languages with overtly "agreeing complementizers", which morphologically mark the transit of the element: see van Urk 2016 for recent discussion). The reciprocal pattern is offered by the complement of a verb like *wonder*:

(2) a.   John wonders [C [Bill read [which book]]]
    b.   John wonders [[which book] [C [Bill read __]]]
    c. * [[which book] [does [John wonder [__ C [Bill read __]]]

movement to the embedded complementizer, as in (2)b yields a well-formed structure here, an embedded question. But this is now a halting position: movement cannot continue as in (2)c, we have a freezing effect in the halting position.

The notions of halting and transiting positions are, of course, descriptive categories: ideally the status of a position wrt movement should be derived from fundamental ingredients of linguistic computations. An approach to the halting problem based on the labeling algorithm is presented in Chomsky (2013, 2015), Rizzi (2015a-b, 2016) (see also the other papers in Bošković 2016).

The crucial structural property here is the "criterial configuration", the fact that in the embedded C-system of (2)b the wh-element and the C agree in criterial feature +Q, the feature designating questions:

(2') b' John wonders [$_\alpha$ [which$_{+Q}$ book] [+Q [Bill read ___]]]

Here both phrases *[which$_{+Q}$ book]* and *[+Q [Bill read ___]]*, (internally) merged together yielding an XP-YP configuration, carry the criterial feature +Q on their most prominent element. So, both give consistent instructions for the labeling of the mother node α, which can be labeled as Q, an indirect question. The wh-phrase can therefore remain in the embedded C-system, as far as labeling is concerned. Moreover, it must remain there because of the maximality principle of Rizzi (2015a-b, 2016), stating that only maximal objects with a given label can be moved, so that we have the freezing effect illustrated by the ban on (2)c. In a nutshell, after labeling of α has taken place in (2')b, *which book* is not anymore the maximal object carrying the categorial feature Q, as it is immediately dominated by a node labeled as Q, hence it is unmovable in accordance with maximality. Reciprocally, labeling of the embedded clause would not be possible in (1)b (XP and YP do not provide a coherent labeling instruction here), so that further movement of the wh-phrase is required to permit labeling of the embedded clausal node, and its C-system necessarily is a transiting position. The halting or transiting status of a position can thus be derived in a principled way, ultimately from the labeling algorithm and the maximality principle.

If we now consider the A-system, we also find transiting positions, such as the subject position of an untensed raising verb (3)b, and halting positions, such as the subject position of a tensed complement (4)b:

(3) a.　(it) seems [to have been arrested John]
　　 b.　* (it) seems [John to have been arrested ___]
　　 c.　John seems [___ to have been arrested ___]

(4) a. (it) seems [could have been arrested John]
    b. (it) seems [John could have been arrested __]
    c. * John seems [__ could have been arrested __]

The crucial point here is that the subject position of a tensed clause is the fundamental halting position of A-movement, a position in which movement stops, and which arguably gives rise to freezing effects, as (4)c illustrates for A-movement (see Rizzi 2006, Rizzi & Shlonsky 2007 and much related work for freezing effects connected to the subject position with respect to both A- and A'-movement).[1]

If halting positions typically are criterial positions, the halting property of the high, clause initial subject position (the EPP position in GB syntax) leads us to the following hypothesis:

(5) There is a subject criterion

Criterial positions are normally associated to special scope-discourse effects such as, in the A'-system, the expression of articulations such as topic – comment, focus – presupposition, operator – scope domain. So, what could be the interpretive property, relevant for scope-discourse interpretation, associated to a subject criterial position?

Here it is important to distinguish between different positions which can be referred to as "subject positions": the thematic position of the subject (Spec-vP in non-unaccusative structures), the low subject position used for subject focalization in (some) Null Subject Languages (Belletti 2004), the high, clause initial, subject position corresponding to the EPP position of GB syntax (with the possibility of a further proliferation of non-thematic subject positions in the high IP field: Cardinaletti 2004). The position which is central to our discussion is the latter: the canonical subject position, the typical final landing site of A-movement. What is the contribution of this position to interpretation?

In Rizzi (2005, 2006, and much related work) I have argued that this subject position expresses the argument which is selected as the starting point in the

---

[1] A reviewer raises the question of whether and how the classical distinction between A and A' movement has an impact on freezing. The analysis developed in the references quoted in the text gives rise to the expectation that a criterial position (be it A', as the specifier of Q in an indirect question, or A, as a subject position) always gives rise to freezing effects, and for both A- and A'-movement. In fact, in the references quoted, that-trace effects are analyzed as cases of freezing, an analysis which implies that criterial subject positions disallow further A' movement. If subjects are indeed harder than objects to extract, languages often allow subject extraction in special configurations (special complementizer forms, etc.), which are analyzed in the references quoted as devices to allow a subject wh to avoid the freezing position and remain extractable. See, in particular, Rizzi & Shlonsky (2007).

description of the event: the subject is the argument "about which" the event expressed by the predicate is presented. The "aboutness" effect is clearly illustrated by active-passive pairs:

(6) a. Piero ha colpito Gianni
       'Piero has hit Gianni'
    b. Gianni è stato colpito da Piero
       'Gianni has been hit by Piero'

The same "hitting" event is presented as being about the agent in (6)a, and about the patient in (6)b. So, passivisation may be seen as a device to shift aboutness from one argument to another in the argument structure of the verb.

3 The Calabrese effect (Calabrese 1986)

The aboutness property seems to be very subtle and elusive, but years ago, Andrea Calabrese discovered a clear test sensitive to aboutness subjects. The null pronominal subject *pro* in Italian picks out the aboutness subject of the immediately preceding clause in certain structural contexts. The effect is particularly clear in the core configuration that Calabrese discusses, i.e., when an adverbial clause precedes the matrix clause (his ex. (1)):

(7) Quando Mario$_i$ ha picchiato Antonio$_k$, pro$_{i,*k}$ era ubriaco
    'When Mario hit Antonio, pro was drunk' (pro = Mario)

Calabrese observes that *pro* can also pick out another salient referent from the previous discourse. For instance, if in the discourse context preceding (7) we have been talking about Francesco, *pro* in (7) could refer to him; e.g., if Francesco is a hanging topic:

(7') (A proposito di) Francesco$_j$, Quando Mario$_i$ ha picchiato Antonio$_k$, pro$_j$ era ubriaco
     '(As for) Francesco, when Mario hit Antonio, pro was drunk' (pro = Francesco)

but if we want to search for the antecedent of *pro* in the immediately preceding adverbial clause, *pro* must pick out the subject of predication. In the configuration at issue, if we want to express the fact that Antonio was drunk, we must use the overt subject pronoun *lui*:

(7") Quando Mario$_i$ ha picchiato Antonio$_k$, lui$_{*i,k}$ era ubriaco
     'When Mario hit Antonio, pro was drunk' (pro = Antonio)

Calabrese also shows that the fact of picking out the aboutness subject is a specificity of *pro* and does not extend to other weak pronominal forms in Italian. A clitic pronoun can refer to both the subject and the object (his ex. (3)):

(8) Quando Mario$_i$ ha picchiato Antonio$_k$, io lo$_{i,k}$ ho visto sanguinare
'When Mario hit Antonio, I saw him bleed' (ambiguous)

Calabrese treats this effect through two principles (his (6) and (5)):

(9) Use a stressed pronoun only when the occurrence of its referent is not expected

(10) A subject pronoun is expected to have the referent of another subject (in the immediate context)

Principle (9) may be seen as a variant (or perhaps the natural complement) of the Avoid pronoun principle of Chomsky (1981): if there is an alternation between a stressed and a null form, use the null form for expected referents, and the stressed form for unexpected referents. Principle (10) says something specific to subjects, in our sense of aboutness subjects (Calabrese's subject of predication, what he calls "thema"): distinct predicates, in the same local domain, tend to be predicated about the same referent, perhaps a particular case of the functional linguistics' notion of "topic continuity" (Givon 1983), Calabrese argues.[2]

We can now go back to an active-passive pair: in the context identified by Calabrese, *pro* always picks out the aboutness subject, the agent in the active and the patient in the passive:

(11) a. Quando Mario$_i$ ha picchiato Antonio$_k$, *pro*$_{i,*k}$ era ubriaco
'When Mario hit Antonio, pro was drunk' (pro = Mario)
b. Quando Antonio$_k$ è stato picchiato da Mario$_i$, *pro*$_{*i,k}$ era ubriaco
'When Antonio was hit by Antonio, pro was drunk' (pro = Antonio)

So, Calabrese's effect offers a reliable way to detect an interpretive property that goes with the aboutness subject. As criterial positions typically involve special interpretive properties, this finding supports the view that the aboutness subject position is a criterial position.

---

[2] The basic pattern observed by Calabrese seems to require full native command of null subject properties: in an experimental study, Belletti, Bennati & Sorace (2007) found out that near-native L2 speakers of Italian were significantly more lenient than native speakers in admitting coreference between an overt pronominal and a previous subject.

4 An apparent exception to the Calabrese effect: the relevance of c-command

Calabrese also observes that the system does not seem to work when we have a configuration with a main and a complement clause:

(12) Francesca ha fatto notare a Maria che *pro* era molto stanca
 'Francesca made Maria realize that pro was very tired'

In fact, the interpretation of *pro* here is fully ambiguous, *pro* could equally well refer to Francesca or Maria.

I believe that what is going on in this case is that both DP's c-command *pro*, which suggests another principle like

(10') A subject pronoun is expected to have the referent of a c-commanding DP

That c-command may be relevant here is shown by the following:

(13) Francesca ha fatto notare alla sorella di Maria che *pro* era molto stanca
 'Francesca made Maria's sister realize that pro was very tired'

Here *pro* can naturally refer to Francesca or to Maria's sister, but not to Maria. To express that interpretation, the overt pronominal subject must be used (even though the exclusion of the null form in the intended interpretation may be less sharp than in the previous cases, the preference pattern seems to me to be clear):

(13') Francesca ha fatto notare alla sorella di Maria$_i$ che *lei*$_i$ era molto stanca
 'Francesca made Maria's sister realize that pro was very tired'

This pattern follows from the combined action of (9) and (10'): by (10'), both DP's *Francesca* and *La sorella di Maria* are expected to be antecedents of the subject pronoun, which, by (9), can be *pro* in that interpretation. In contrast, *Maria* does not c-command the pronoun, so that it is not an expected antecedent (it is not a subject either, so that (10) is not operative, either); therefore, under (9), the pronoun must be overt in that interpretation.

As c-command makes every DP an expected antecedent for a pronoun, the Calabrese effect is fully visible only in cases in which c-command (and principle (10')) does not hold, so that only principle (10) is operative in determining what an expected antecedent can be: this happens with preposed adverbials, and also in discourse sequences, as we will see in a moment.

The relevance of c-command and principle (10') also allows us to address another puzzle in the interpretive properties of *pro*. Consider the coreference possibilities in "scene setting" environments, such as those discussed by Reinhart (1983):

(14) In this picture of Mary, she looks sick

In the equivalent in Italian, if we want to express the interpretation in which Mary looks sick, the overt pronominal *lei* must be used:

(15) In questa foto di Maria$_j$, *pro$_i$ / lei$_i$ sembra malata
      'In this picture of Maria, pro / she looks sick'

Pro is of course possible, but it must refer to another salient referent, not to Maria.[3] Why is it so? Clearly, here neither (10) nor (10') apply, because Maria is not an aboutness subject, nor does it c-command the main subject. So, Maria is not the expected antecedent of the pronominal subject, therefore *pro* cannot be used, and the overt pronominal must be used to express coreference with Maria.

Back to the main line of argumentation, we can also notice that *pro* naturally picks out a preverbal subject, but not a postverbal subject in a language like Italian, which permits both positions:

(16) a.   Quando Gianni$_i$ ha telefonato, *pro$_i$* era ubriaco
           'When Gianni telephoned, pro was drunk'
      b. * Quando ha telefonato Gianni$_i$, *pro$_i$* era ubriaco
           'When telephoned Gianni, pro was drunk'

Coreference in (16)a is fine because Gianni is the subject of predication here, as in the cases considered previously. A postverbal subject is not in the aboutness subject position, hence it is expected that it may not be the antecedent of *pro*, as in (16)b. But there may be an additional reason excluding that dependency. The postverbal subject position is focal (Belletti 2004, 2009), therefore the relevant construal may be excluded by whatever property excludes the construal of a pronoun with a non c-commanding focal element. In fact, as Calabrese (1986) observes, (16)b remains deviant also when the main pronominal subject is overt:

(16) b'. *? Quando ha telefonato Gianni$_i$, lui$_i$ era ubriaco
           'When telephoned Gianni, he was drunk'

---

3 For instance, if Francesca is a (hanging) topic, a *pro* coreferential to Francesca is possible:
  (i) (A proposito di) Francesca$_k$, in questa foto di Maria$_j$, *pro$_k$* sembra malata
       '(As for) Francesca, in this picture of Maria, she looks sick'
Here, *di Maria* would naturally designate the possessor of the picture, rather than the person reproduced in it.

The persistence of the ill-formedness in (16)b' shows that a more demanding principle is violated here than the requirements of the system in (9)–(10).

Calabrese (1986, fn. 3) reports an observation due to Lidia Lonzi according to which construal with a postverbal subject considerably improves when *pro* is in an adverbial clause following the postverbal subject:

(17)   Ha parlato Carlo$_j$, dopo che *pro*$_i$ è arrivato
       'Spoke Carlo (subj), after pro arrived'

Apart from the necessity of a strong pause between the postverbal subject and the adverbial clause, which Calabrese notices, in this case *pro* may be c-commanded by the focal subject: this would come about if the focal subject is locally moved to an IP-internal focus position (as in Belletti 2004), and this position is high enough to c-command clause-final adjunct clauses. This configuration would make *pro* bindable by the focal element, and would make the case analogous to these in which the antecedent c-commands *pro*, such as (12), etc. The c-command option is clearly excluded in cases like (16)b, as the postverbal focal subject is in an embedded adverbial. C-command is also excluded in (16)a, but here *pro* has the other option of picking out a local aboutness subject, an option not available in (16)b.

5 Aboutness is independent from new-given information

In general, the "aboutness" argument tends to be associated with given information, whereas a predicate-internal argument is not. So, there could be a confound between aboutness and givenness: could it be that what *pro* really picks out is given information?

In fact, the link between the aboutness argument and givenness is not necessary. When the subject is not given, for instance in an all-new context, it still functions as the antecedent of *pro*. Here we cannot use the core context discussed by Calabrese, with a preposed adverbial and a main clause, which would often not sound natural in an all-new context: the selective effect on the choice of the antecedent of *pro* is also found, as Calabrese (1986) points out, in the immediately following clause in discourse. Consider for instance a context in which a speaker asks question (18)Q, thus setting up a natural context for a possible all-new sentence (for instance, a speaker may utter (18)Q when he perceives that some action is going on without knowing what kind of event is happening and who the participants are), and the interlocutor answers with sentence (18)A, and then continues with (18)A':

(18) Q: Che cosa è successo?
'What happened?'
A: Un ragazzo$_i$ ha buttato a terra un vecchio$_k$
'A boy threw an old man to the ground'
A': ... poi pro$_{i, *k}$ ha cominciato a urlare
'...then pro started to scream'

In (18)A, both a boy and an old man are new information, and still *pro* in the immediately following sentence is restricted to pick out the subject. So, the test is not sensitive to the informational property of givenness, but to the structural position of the antecedent.[4] Again, if the subject of (18)A' is the overt pronoun *lui*, the coreference option shifts, and the natural interpretation is that the old man started screaming.

We have parallel effects when the all-new sentence is passivized: the interlocutor can choose to answer question (19)Q with a passive sentence, as in (19) A; again, in the following sentence (19)A', *pro* picks out the surface subject of predication, in this case the patient of the passive sentence:[5]

(19) Q: Che cosa è successo?
'What happened?'
A: Un vecchio$_k$ è stato buttato a terra da un ragazzo$_i$
'An old man was thrown to the ground by a boy'

---

[4] Giuliano Bocci raises the question of whether in this context the effect is restricted to *pro*, or it also extends to other weak pronominal forms. In fact, it seems to me that, here as before, an object clitic can pick out both arguments. For instance two continuations like the following
  (i) ... poi, lo ho visto sanguinante
    '... then, I saw him bleeding'
  (ii) ... poi, lo ho visto ammanettato
    '...then, I saw him handcuffed'
seem to me to be both possible (pragmatically, (i) is natural with an old man as antecedent, (ii) with a boy as antecedent)

[5] Cardinaletti (2004) argued that (at least) two subject positions are to be specified in the high IP field. Building on that, Bianchi & Chesi (2013) argued that the higher and the lower positions correspond to two distinct interpretations, akin to Kuroda's (1973) "categorical" and "thetic" judgments. Given these ideas, the question arises of whether the Calabrese effect involves both subject positions, or is restricted to just one. I will not fully addressed this issue here. Let me just notice that such example as (18), (19) in all-new contexts should instantiate Kuroda's thetic judgments, and they do give rise to the Calabrese effect. If thetic judgments involve the lower subject position, the conclusion seems to be that the Calabrese effect is triggered by this position as well.

A'   ... poi *pro*_{k, *i} ha cominciato a urlare
     '...then pro started to scream'

That the aboutness property is independent from informational structure is also underscored by the reciprocal case wrt (18)–(19). In fact, we have an identifiable effect also in contexts in which both arguments are given, like the following:

(20) Q: Come mai Gianni e Piero sono così arrabbiati?
          'Why are Gianni and Piero so angry?
      A: Beh, è successo che Gianni$_i$ ha insultato Piero$_k$ davanti a tutti
          'Well, it happened that Gianni insulted Piero in front of everyone'
      A' ... e subito dopo *pro*$_{i, *k}$ ha lasciato la riunione
          '...and immediately after pro left the meeting'

One could also answer the questions in (20)Q (=(21)Q) with a passive sentence, as in (21)A; in that case the coreference possibilities are reversed, and *pro* in the following sentence (21)A' must refer to the surface subject of passive, the patient:

(21) Q: Come mai Gianni e Piero sono così arrabbiati?
          'Why are Gianni and Piero so angry?'
      A: Beh, è successo che Piero$_k$ è stato insultato da Gianni$_i$ davanti a tutti
          'Well, it happened that Piero was insulted by Gianni in front of everyone'
      A' ... e subito dopo *pro*$_{*i, k}$ ha lasciato la riunione
          '...and immediately after pro left the meeting'

In conclusion, the Calabrese effect is independent from the new or given character of the relevant referent: what the effect is sensitive to is the aboutness property, in accordance with (10), and it holds whether the aboutness subject qualifying as the expected antecedent is new or given information.

6 Subject vs Topic

Reference to "aboutness" stresses the similarity between subjects and topics. In this section and in section 7, I would like to discuss similarities and differences between the two notions, and try to address the question of whether the Calabrese effect singles out subjects, or concerns both.

A classical line of research (e.g., Li & Thompson 1976) addresses similarities and differences between subjects and topics. Let us focus on this issue on the basis of the analysis developed so far. Both subject and topic involve aboutness.

In a subject – predicate configuration, the predicate says something about the subject; in a topic – comment configuration, the comment says something about the topic (Reinhart 1981).

The appropriateness conditions for the use of topics are stricter, though: in "what happened?" contexts, a subject can be felicitously used, as in (18)A, (19)A, but a topic cannot:

(22) Q: Che cosa è successo?
 'What happened?'
 A: # Un vecchio, un ragazzo lo ha buttato a terra
 'An old man, a boy threw him to the ground'

In this context, the topic structure is not felicitous either when the subject is preverbal, as in (22)A, or when it is postverbal, as in the following A':

 A': # Un vecchio, lo ha buttato a terra un ragazzo
 'An old man, threw him to the ground a boy(subj)'

Could the difference between subject and topic be that topics cannot be indefinite? Indeed, various languages put a requirement of definiteness and/or of specificity on topics, and certain cases of topics seem to require definiteness. This is the case, for instance, for hanging topics introduced by prefixes such as *per quanto riguarda X, quanto a X*, etc. (as far as X is concerned, as for X):

(23) Quanto a Maria/questa ragazza/alla ragazza/*una ragazza, parlerò presto con lei
 'As for Maria/this girl/the girl/*a girl, I will talk soon with her'

Nevertheless, in Italian it is not impossible to have an indefinite topic in the clitic left dislocation construction, even a non-specific indefinite, as the following felicitous exchange shows:

(24) Q: Perchè la direttrice è così preoccupata per il dipartimento?
 'Why is the head of department so worries about the dept?
 A: Una segretaria che sappia tenere la contabilità, non riesce a trovarla
 'A secretary who can(subjunctive) keep the accounting, she cannot find'

The topic is indefinite and non-specific here, as is shown by the subjunctive mood of the verb in the relative clause. Still, the topic structure is felicitous, as the topic directly connects to the context (the accounting of the department).

Examples (22)A, A' can also be made felicitous, e.g., in the following conversational exchange:

(25) Q: Che cosa è successo? E' vero delle persone anziane sono state portate
'What happened? Is it true that some elderly people have been taken to
all'ospedale?
the hospital?'
A: Io ho visto solo che un vecchio, un ragazzo lo ha buttato a terra
'I have only seen that an old man, a boy threw him to the ground'
A': Io ho visto solo che un vecchio, lo ha buttato a terra un ragazzo
'I have only seen that an old man, threw him to the ground a boy(subj)'

Question (25)Q introduces a group of elderly people, and (25)A, A' take up a member of this group (albeit indefinite) as a topic.

In order to have a felicitous topic, some kind of connection with a contextually given set appears to be necessary. An indefinite topic is also possible in Italian, when an unknown individual is linked to a contextually given set (e.g., an old man is connected to the set of elderly people evoked in the immediately previous discourse in (25)). This distinguishes the case in which a topic is possible and impossible, as in (22)A, A'. This link to a contextually given set is clearly reminiscent of D-linking (Pesetsky 1987) (but of relevance may also be Enç's 1984 notion of "partitivity").

This component of connection to the discourse context in the licensing of topics is particularly clear in certain cases (here my presentation is based on Rizzi 2005). Consider a context in which a father is checking on his son's preparation of an exam. If the father says sentence (26), the son could reply with (27) or (27'):

(26) Father: Oggi non hai fatto niente per preparare l'esame...
'Today, you did nothing to prepare the exam...'

(27) Son: Beh, ho letto un libro...
'Well, I read a book...?

(27') Son: Beh, un libro l'ho letto...
'Well, a book, I read it...'

Both replies are felicitous, but they are not interpretively equivalent. Reply (27') involves a clitic left dislocation of the indefinite object *un libro* (a book): the sentence implies that this book is part of the program for the preparation of the exam: i.e., "a book among those required for preparing the exam, I read it". No such implication is associated with reply (27), in which *a book* remains in object position. The sentence can be very naturally interpreted as "ok, I didn't do anything for the preparation of the exam, but I spent time in another worthwhile activity, reading a book", with the book in question completely disconnected

from the program of the exam. The special interpretation associated with (27')
thus suggests that topics must be licensed by this (explicit or implicit) partitive
connection to a set established in discourse, here the set of documents necessary
for the preparation of the exam.

We may express the interpretive rules triggered by Top at the interface as
follows:

(28) **Top**: a. Interpret the Spec as a D-linked argument about which a comment is made
b. Interpret the complement as the comment about the Spec.

Beninca' & Poletto (2004), Frascarelli & Hinterhoeltz (2007), Bianchi & Frascarelli (2011) propose a finer typology of topics: aboutness shift, contrastive, and familiarity topics. I think aboutness is a common feature of all kinds of topics (including aboutness shift: "so far we have been talking about topic X, now I want to shift to a different topic Y"), and D-linking, or the relevant notion of partitivity, may also be. So, one can think of (28) as the common interpretive core that different kinds of topics share.

The aboutness Subject, Calabrese's notion of Thema, shares the aboutness property of topics, but does not require D-linking. So, a non-D-linked phrase as *un ragazzo, un vecchio* in contexts like (18), (19), (22) can be a subject, but cannot be a topic:

(29) **Subj**: a. Interpret the Spec as the argument which the predicate is about.
b: Interpret the complement as the predicate

Does the Calabrese effect distinguish subject and topic? Calabrese discusses examples like (30) in which *pro* is unable to pick out the dative topic *a Gianni* of a preceding sentence, whereas it can take the subject *Carla* as antecedent (his example (28)):

(30) Poiché a Gianni$_k$ Carla$_i$ gli ha dato un bacio, $pro_{i, *k}$ è felice
'Because to Gianni Carla to-him gave a kiss, pro is happy'

I find the judgment clear in the case in which the topic is a dative, as in (30). When the topic is a direct object, my judgment becomes less sharp. Consider the following:

(31) a. Poiché Mario, Carlo lo ha severamente criticato, *pro* era piuttosto imbarazzato
'Because Mario, Carlo severely him criticized, pro was rather embarrassed'

b. Quando Francesco, Gianni lo ha presentato a Piero, *pro* era molto contento
 'When Francesco, Gianni him introduced to Piero, pro vas very happy'

These judgments are difficult, perhaps I still have a preference for binding of *pro* by the previous aboutness subject, but binding by the topic does not seem to me to be excluded. If binding by a topic is disambiguated by gender agreement of the predicate, i.e., with subject and topic mismatching in gender, binding by the topic sounds ok to me:

(32) a. Poiché Mario$_i$, Carla lo ha severamente criticato, *pro*$_i$ era piuttosto
 'Because Mario, Carla severely him criticized, pro was rather
 imbarazzato
 embarrassed'
 b. Quando Francesco$_k$, Giovanna lo ha presentato a Piero, *pro*$_k$ era molto
 'When Francesco, Giovanna him introduced to Piero, pro vas very
 contento
 happy'

Notice that, when the object is not topicalized but *in situ* in object position, gender mismatch does not seem to help:

(33) a. Poiché Carla ha severamente criticato Mario$_i$, *pro*$_{*i}$ era piuttosto
 'Because Carla severely criticized Mario, pro was rather
 imbarazzato
 embarrassed'
 b. Quando Giovanna ha presentato Francesco$_k$ a Piero, *pro*$_{*k}$ era molto contento
 'When Giovanna introduced Francesco to Piero, pro vas very happy'

(*pro* in (33)a–b can obviously refer to another male referent, e.g. Antonio which was mentioned in previous discourse; coreference with the object becomes natural in (33) if the overt pronominal form *lui* is used, as before).

Given the contrast between (32) and (33), topicality of an object seems to at least improve the possibility of coreference with a successive *pro*. If this is so, it would seem that the Calabrese effect is sensitive to aboutness, a property that subjects and topics have in common: we could then restate (10) to the effect that a pronominal subject is expected to have the reference of a +aboutness position (in this view, the degraded character of (30) would be due to some other property, presumably connected to the dative case of that example). Given the less than straightforward nature of the relevant judgments, I will leave the question open of whether (10) is indeed to be revised along these lines, or it selectively picks out subjects, as in Calabrese's original formulation.

7 More evidence that preverbal subjects and topics are distinct positions in Null Subject Languages

In a non-null subject language like French, whether a subject is in subject or topic position is straightforwardly shown by the presence of a resumptive subject clitic in the latter case:

(34) a. Jean a rencontré Marie
'Jean met Marie'
b. Jean, il a rencontré Marie
'Jean, he met Marie'

In (34)a, *Jean* is in subject position, where it is not clitic-resumed, whereas in (34)b it is in topic position, and it is obligatorily clitic resumed in the French clitic left dislocation construction. The obligatoriness of clitic resumption is illustrated by a case like the following:

(35) a. Jean, ton livre, il le lira demain
'Jean, your book, he it will read tomorrow'
b. *Jean, ton livre, _ le lira demain
'Jean, your book, _ it will read tomorrow'

In (35), Jean necessarily is in a left-peripheral topic position, because it is followed by an object topic; and here clitic resumption is obligatory, as the ill-formedness of (35)b shows.

In a Null Subject Language like Italian, the evidence distinguishing preverbal subjects and subject topics is less straightforward because the resumptive pronoun corresponding the a subject topic is null, so a string like (36) is in principle structurally ambiguous between the two representations of (37):

(36) Gianni ha incontrato Maria
'Gianni met Maria'

(37) a. [$_{IP}$ Gianni ha incontrato Maria]
'Gianni has met Maria'
b. [$_{TopP}$ Gianni Top [$_{IP}$ *pro* ha incontrato Maria]
'Gianni has met Maria'

One could observe that the two representations of (37) would correspond to two distinct intonational contours, but intonation does not seem to offer completely reliable cues to distinguish between preverbal subjects and topics (Bocci 2013).

This state of affairs has sometimes led to the hypothesis that perhaps Null Subject Languages make a more drastic choice in these cases: perhaps, the preverbal subject position is always filled by *pro* in Null Subject Languages, and "preverbal subjects" are in fact always in the left peripheral topic position. I.e., according to this view, the representation of (36) always is (37)b.

We have already seen one clear piece of evidence against this view. In all new contexts, preverbal subjects are legitimate, but topics are not (see (22)), a pattern which I will now illustrate with another example. In a "what happened" context like (38)Q, SV answers are possible, both in active and passive, as in(38)A, A', but topics are not allowed (as in (38)B, B'). So, (38)A, A' (and previous examples like (18), (19)), illustrate a case of a preverbal subject which is not a topic.

(38) Q Cosa è successo?
 'What happened?'
 A Un camion ha tamponato un autobus
 'A truck bumped into a bus'
 A' Un autobus è stato tamponato da un camion
 'A bus was bumped into by a truck'
 B # Un autobus, un camion lo ha tamponato
 'A bus, a truck it bumped into'
 B' # Un autobus, lo ha tamponato un camion
 'A bus (obj), it bumped into a truck (subj)'

Another kind of evidence leading to the same conclusion, discussed in Rizzi (1985), is provided by the fact that certain quantified expressions, particularly when the quantifier is bare, cannot naturally function as topics:

(39) a. Non ho incontrato nessuno
 'I met noone'
 b. * Nessuno, lo ho incontrato
 'Noone, I met him'

(40) a. Ho capito tutto
 'I understood everything'
 b. * Tutto, lo ho capito
 'Everything, I understood it

And still these elements can be found in preverbal subject position:

(41) Nessuno ha aiutato Maria
 'Nobody helped Maria'

(42) Tutto è successo nella notte
'Everything happened during the night'

So, it appears that preverbal subjects are not necessarily topics in Null Subject Languages: they can be topics in the left periphery and bind *pro* in IP internal position if their interpretive properties and the discourse conditions are consistent with topicality, but they can also be expressed in the IP internal subject position, much as in non Null Subject Languages.

We can now trace back the deviance of (39)b, (40)b to the interpretive procedure associated to Top in (28). This makes a prediction. If indeed (39)b, (40)b are ruled out because the D-linking element necessarily involved in topicality is missing there, one would expect that by making such elements D-linked the possibility of topicalizing quantified expressions should improve. In fact the following are sharply improved, compared to (39)b, (40)b:

(43) Nessuno di loro, lo ho incontrato alla festa
'None of them I him met at the party'

(44) Tutto questo, lo ho capito
'All this, I it understood'

The partitive expression *di loro* (of them) and the demonstrative *questo* (this) link the quantified expressions to the discourse context, and make the use of such expressions as topics felicitous. No connection to the context of this sort is needed for quantified expressions in subject position in (41), (42), which follows from the assumed difference in interpretive properties between subject and topic positions.

Conclusions

The preverbal subject position is the typical final landing site of A-movement. Recent approaches to the "halting problem" identify halting positions of phrasal movement chains as criterial positions. If this is correct, we are led to assume a "subject criterion" to be satisfied in the higher part of the IP zone. The natural interpretive property associated to this criterial position is "aboutness": it identifies the argument "about which" the event is presented, with a detectable shift, for instance, from agent to patient aboutness in active-passive pairs. Andrea Calabrese discovered a property which is clearly sensitive to aboutness in this sense: a *pro* subject in Null Subject Languages picks out the aboutness subject of an immediately preceding sentence in a local environment (Calabrese 1986).

The Calabrese effect thus shows that subjecthood is crucial for the structuring of subsequent discourse and anaphora resolution, a scope-discourse property that we may expect to hold for a criterial position.

Topics share with subjects the aboutness property, in the obvious sense that a comment states something about the topic. Nevertheless topics are more demanding than subjects, in that they can be used felicitously only if some kind of connection to the previous discourse (D-linking, or partitivity) can be established. Preverbal subjects are thus possible in "what happened" contexts, but topics are not. Even in Null Subject Languages, in which an identification of preverbal subjects and topics has often been proposed, "what happened" contexts clearly differentiate the two cases. This kind of evidence converges with evidence based on the distributional properties of bare quantified expressions, possible in subject but not in topic positions, a distributional difference which also is ultimately deducible from the different interpretive procedures for subjects and topics.

Acknowledgment: This research was supported by the ERC AG n. 340297 "SynCart".

References

Belletti, Adriana. 2004. Aspects of the low IP area. In Luigi Rizzi (ed.), *The structure of CP and IP: the cartography of syntactic structures*, vol. 2. New York: Oxford University Press.
Belletti, Adriana. 2009. *Structures and strategies*. London and New York: Routledge.
Belletti Adriana, Elisa Bennati, & Antonella Sorace. 2007. Theoretical and developmental issues in the syntax of subjects: evidence from near native Italian. *Natural Language and Linguistic Theory* 25(4). 657–689.
Benincà, Paola and Cecilia Poletto. 2004. Topic, focus and V2: Defining the CP sublayers. In Luigi Rizzi (ed.), *The structure of CP and IP*, 52–75. New York: Oxford University Press.
Bianchi, Valentina & Cristiano Chesi. 2014. Subject islands, reconstruction, and the flow of the computation. *Linguistic Inquiry* 45(4). 525–569.
Bianchi, Valentina & Mara Frascarelli. 2010. Is topic a root phenomenon? *Iberia* 2. 43–48.
Bocci, Giuliano. 2013. *The Syntax–Prosody Interface: a cartographic perspective with evidence from Italian*. Amsterdam: John Benjamins.
Bošković, Željko (ed.). 2016. *The Linguistic Review* 33 (1). Special Issue on Labeling.
Calabrese, Andrea. 1982. Alcune ipotesi sulla struttura informazionale della frase in italiano e sul suo rapporto con la struttura fonologica. *Rivista di grammatica generativa* 7.
Calabrese, Andrea. 1986. Some properties of the Italian pronominal system: An analysis based on the notion of thema as subject of predication. In H. Stammerjohann (ed.), *Tema-Rema in Italiano*, 25–36. Tübingen: Gunter Narr Verlag.
Calabrese, Andrea. 1992. Some remarks on focus and logical structures in Italian. *Harvard Working Papers in Linguistics* I. 19–27.

Cardinaletti, Anna. 2004. Towards a cartography of subject positions. In Luigi Rizzi (ed.), *The structure of CP and IP*, 115–165. New York: Oxford University Press.
Chomsky, Noam. 1973. Conditions on transformations. In S. Anderson & P. Kiparsky (eds.), *A Festschrift for Morris Halle*. New York: Holt Rinehart and Winston.
Chomsky, Noam. 1981. *Lectures on government and binding*. Dordrecht: Foris.
Chomsky, Noam. 2013. Problems of projection. *Lingua* 130. Special Issue, Core ideas and results in syntax, 33–49.
Chomsky, Noam. 2015. Problems of projection: extensions. In E. Di Domenico, C. Hamann & S. Matteini (eds.), *Structures, strategies and beyond – Studies in honour of Adriana Belletti*, 3–16. Amsterdam: John Benjamins.
Frascarelli, Mara & Roland Hinterhölzl. 2007. Types of topics in German and Italian. In Susanne Winkler and Kerstin Schwabe (eds.), *On information structure, meaning and form*, 87–116. Amsterdam: John Benjamins.
Givón, Talmy. 1983. *Topic continuity in discourse: a quantitative cross language study*. (Typological Studies in Language 3). Amsterdam: John Benjamins.
Kuroda, Sige-Yuki. 1972. The categorical and thetic judgement: evidence from Japanese syntax. *Foundations of Language* 9. 153–185.
Li, Charles N. and Sandra A. Thompson. 1976. Subject and topic: a new typology of language. In Charles N. Li (ed.), *Subject and topic*, 457–461. New York: Academic Press.
Pesetsky, David. 1987. Wh in situ: movement and unselective binding. In E. Reuland & A ter Meulen (eds.), *The representation of (In)definiteness*, 98–129. Cambridge, MA: MIT Press.
Reinhart, Tanya. 1981. Pragmatics and linguistics: An analysis of sentence topics in pragmatics and philosophy I. *Philosophica anc Studia Philosophica Gandensia Gent* 27. 53–94.
Reinhart, Tanya. 1983. *Anaphora and semantic interpretation*. Chicago: The University of Chicago Press.
Rizzi, Luigi. 1986. On the status of subject clitics in Romance. In Jaeggli & Corvalan (eds.), *Studies in Romance linguistics*, 391–419. Dordrecht: Foris Publications.
Rizzi, Luigi. 1997. The fine structure of the left periphery. In L. Haegeman (ed.), *Elements of grammar*, 281–337. Dordrecht: Kluwer.
Rizzi, Luigi. 2005. On some properties of subjects and topics. In Laura Brugé, Giuliana Giusti, Nicola Munaro, Walter Schweikert & Giuseppina Turano (eds.), *Proceedings of the XXX Incontro di Grammatica Generativa*, 203–224. Venezia: Cafoscarina.
Rizzi, Luigi. 2006. On the form of chains: criterial positions and ECP effects. In L. Cheng, N. Corver (eds.), *On wh movement*, 97–133. Cambridge, MA: MIT Press.
Rizzi, Luigi. 2015a. Cartography, criteria, and labeling. In U. Shlonsky (ed.), *Beyond functional sequence – the cartography of syntactic structures, vol. 10*, 314–338. New York: Oxford University Press.
Rizzi, Luigi. 2015b. Notes on labeling and subject positions. In E. Di Domenico, C. Hamann & S. Matteini (eds.), *Structures, strategies and beyond – Studies in honour of Adriana Belletti*, 17–46. Amsterdam: John Benjamins.
Rizzi, Luigi. 2016. Labeling, maximality, and the head – phrase distinction. *The Linguistic Review* 33(1). 103–127.
Rizzi, Luigi & Shlonsky, Ur. 2007. Strategies of subject extraction. In Hans-Martin Gärtner & Uli Sauerland (eds.), *Interfaces + recursion = language? Chomsky's minimalism and the view from syntax-semantics*, 115–160. Berlin: Mouton de Gruyter.
Van Urk, Coppe. 2015. *A uniform syntax for phrasal movement: A Dinka Bor case study*. Cambridge, MA: MIT dissertation.

Index

∀-attraction 123
∀-element 120–124
1H-system 116
2H-system 116

Ablaut 161, 189, 204, 206, 222–226, 269–277, 279, 280–287, 289, 291
Aboutness 459, 510, 511, 514, 515, 517, 518–520, 523, 524, 525, 527, 528
Accentuation 59, 146, 174, 266, 269, 270–292, 467–493
Acoustic outputs 65, 76, 92
A-deletion 125
A-element 124, 125
Affection 123, 308
Affix attrition 257, 258, 264
After-perfect 349
Aggregate (aggr) 366–369, 372, 373, 375, 378–381, 383–387
Agree 136, 187, 212, 336, 358, 361, 368, 385, 386, 392, 399, 400, 401, 405, 410, 416, 417, 438, 439, 441, 442, 469, 470, 512
– copy 400
– link 400
– Multiple Agree 392, 399, 400, 405, 410, 417
Agreement 120, 170, 198, 199, 205, 222, 224, 234, 243, 337, 341, 342, 344, 348, 358, 361, 363–368, 371, 372, 374, 377, 381–385, 387, 391–406, 412, 416–418, 420–422, 427, 428, 433–438, 440–442, 524
Ainu 495–497
Allomorphy 3, 15, 16, 19, 20, 24, 27, 182, 193, 195, 200, 202, 205, 207, 211, 212, 224, 225, 239–244, 268, 278, 279, 285, 288–290, 292, 295–323
Alutor 163, 168, 176
Analysis by synthesis 65
Angus 149
a-Topic 447, 450–464
ATR 104, 109, 112–117, 120, 123, 149, 163, 167, 177, 214, 253

– dominance 117–119
– harmony 117, 163
Attraction 58, 121, 123–125
Austronesian 500, 501, 503

Balmagee 142
Balmaghie 140, 141, 144, 146
Balto-Finnic languages 112
Bangla 495, 504
Basic Accentual Principle(BAP) 273–277, 279–282, 285, 286, 292
Belfast English 473
Biak 500
Binary 31, 65, 76, 90, 94, 104, 105, 110, 111, 124, 473
– feet 124
– system 110, 111
Binding 435, 436, 438–441, 524
Blocking 9, 124, 164, 237, 306

Cardinal numerals 500, 502
Cartographic description 330
Categorical
– perception 68, 79, 85, 90, 107
– processing 68
c-command 396, 438, 441, 503, 516–518
Celtic 129–132
Chukchi 163–168, 176, 182, 183, 188, 189
Chukotko-Kamchatkan 161–169, 175, 180, 188, 189
Circumstantial complement 331, 333, 336, 337, 341
Classes 58, 76, 105–108, 138, 215, 268, 357, 358, 362, 365, 366, 369–371, 377, 383, 386, 387, 398
Classical Gaelic 130, 132, 134, 135, 137, 138, 149–153
Clitic Left Dislocation/ClLD 446, 447, 448, 453, 454, 455, 456, 459
Closest Conjunct Agreement (CCA) 391, 393, 394, 396, 403–405
Compounding 165

Contour
- pitch 483, 484, 485, 487
- prosodic 471
- unary 104, 105, 113
Copying 121, 122, 391–406, 423
CP 251, 436, 437, 439, 440, 470–472, 479–481
Crossmodular Structural Parallelism 392, 401
Cycle 195, 202, 209–212, 216, 228–232, 235, 244, 286, 289, 290, 301, 467, 468, 471, 472, 481, 482, 492, 493

D-domain 317
Deictic 329–334, 336, 337, 339, 340, 341, 342, 344, 345, 346, 348, 350–354
- adverbs 336, 337, 339, 341
Delinking repair 141, 143, 152
Dependency Phonology 104–106
Determiners 295–324
Diacritic 163, 166–168, 170, 182, 183, 189, 224, 244, 290, 359, 361
Dietro 'behind' 340, 349
Differential Object Marking/DOM 445, 448, 449, 453, 454, 455, 460, 462
Diminutives 218, 226, 227
Diphthong 3–13, 17, 18, 20, 21, 25, 27, 114, 115, 122, 150, 249
- falling diphthong 3–7, 11–13, 22, 25, 27, 144
- rising diphthong 4, 6, 11, 12, 18, 20–22, 25, 134
Dislocation 469, 485, 521, 522, 525
Distributed Morphology 241, 266, 267, 269, 287, 288, 291, 299, 357
D-linking 522, 523, 527, 528
Dominant-recessive systems 111, 163, 188
Dutch 30, 348, 398, 432, 433, 434, 435, 436, 438, 439

ECoG 71, 84, 94
EEG 70, 71, 74, 80–83, 85, 94
- oscillations 80, 81
Elements 17, 82, 104–125, 210, 279, 330, 332, 340, 344, 346, 348–354, 358, 368, 385, 410, 416, 427, 439, 441, 469, 470, 472, 473, 481, 482, 495, 500, 526, 527

English 17, 32, 43, 85, 121, 129, 131–135, 137–146, 148–153, 178, 180, 186, 199, 210–213, 226, 238, 243, 266, 267, 329–354, 377, 378, 396, 402, 403, 432, 434–436, 438, 439, 460, 469, 473, 495, 496, 511
Entro 335, 352
Event 71, 73–87, 108, 110, 138, 154, 161, 166, 183, 329–331, 334, 336, 345, 346, 350–352, 354, 358, 367, 368, 379, 415, 452–454, 510, 514, 518, 527
Event-related magnetic fields (ERMFs) 71, 73–80
Event-related potentials (ERPs) 71, 73–80, 82, 84
Exceptionality 182, 183, 193–196, 200–217, 219, 228, 234, 235, 240, 241, 264, 421, 423, 424
Extraction 87, 88, 95, 460, 471–474, 478, 479
- long extraction 472–474, 478, 479, 482
- short extraction 473, 479

Fake indexicals 433, 434, 441
Falling tone 249–251, 253, 255, 259, 260–264
Features
- distinctive 65–67, 70, 75, 76, 80, 88, 90, 92, 93, 94, 95
- floating 120, 194, 196, 287, 312
- focus 482
- geometry 106
- sharing 432–442, 481, 482
- transfer 435, 436, 438, 440
- valuation 433, 442
- wh/focal 479, 480
Focus 32, 59, 105, 161, 202, 213, 216, 244, 245, 249, 272, 279, 347, 371, 391, 393, 395, 396, 409, 413, 415, 419, 421, 449–450, 457, 463, 468, 481, 482, 485, 487, 488, 490, 492, 495, 510, 513, 518, 520
Forni di Sotto 420, 421
Freezing 510, 512, 513
French 139, 141, 143, 151, 301, 344, 387, 392, 393, 397, 416, 525

Friulian 410, 411, 418–422, 428
Future deixis 352

Gaelic 129–132, 134, 135–138, 145, 147–153
Garo 495
Gender 296, 299, 308–310, 357–359,
   361–363, 365–371, 375, 377, 383, 384,
   387, 391–393, 395–402, 404–406, 420,
   432, 433, 435–441, 524
– default gender 383, 393, 401
– feminine 120, 203, 214, 296, 297, 305,
   306, 318, 321, 324, 359–365, 367, 370,
   371–373, 375–379, 381–385, 392, 393,
   395–398, 438, 440
– neuter 132, 357–387, 392–398, 400
German 30, 44, 77, 180, 195, 202, 213,
   217–235, 238, 244, 432–440, 469
– Germanic 19, 30, 44, 120, 143, 204, 270,
   353, 398, 432, 433, 441
Già 335, 336, 337, 338, 339, 341, 343
Glide
– off-glide 3, 5, 6, 8, 10–13, 17, 18, 22, 25, 27
– on-glide 3, 5, 6, 8, 10, 11, 13–26, 27
Gorgia 15
Government Phonology (GP) 104, 107, 111, 125
Grammaticalization 329–355, 462, 463
Great Vowel Shift 121

Harmony
– bidirectional vowel harmony 400
– disharmonic roots 110, 187, 188, 189
– non-stress-induced harmony 123
– parasitic harmony 112
– stress-induced harmony 123
– vowel harmony 104, 106, 110–112, 124,
   161–189, 400
Hiatus 3–5, 7–10, 16, 17, 19, 26, 27, 133, 270,
   279, 289, 296, 300, 301, 304, 305, 310,
   311, 317, 323, 324
Hiberno 139, 349
Hungarian 460, 495–498, 504

Icelandic 151, 203–206, 209, 232, 392, 393,
   397, 401, 432–440
Indexical pronouns 433, 434, 435
Indicative 207, 208, 226, 337–339, 343, 345,
   347, 348, 350, 358, 493, 495, 496

Insertion 111, 125, 133, 200, 237, 238–242,
   255, 256, 261, 263–265, 267, 278, 279,
   281, 282, 284, 286, 288, 290, 299, 312,
   332, 351, 357, 422, 427
Intervention 112, 200– 209, 216, 221– 223,
   228, 236, 243, 279, 455, 470, 471
Intonational phrase 470, 472, 482
Irish 129–154
isiXhosa 403, 404
Italian 3–27, 113–124, 143, 198, 206, 207,
   268, 295–324, 329–354, 357–387,
   409–428, 445–464, 467–493, 495, 496,
   499, 510, 514, 515, 517, 521, 522, 525
Italian dialects 113–124, 330, 342, 343, 377,
   387, 409–428
– Arpinate 213, 214, 215, 216, 219, 234
– Bellinzonese 425
– Borgomanerese 422, 423
– Campone 418, 419, 420, 421
– Calvello 114, 118, 122
– Foggia 115, 118, 119
– Forni di Sotto 420, 421
– Friulian 410, 411, 418–422, 428
– Genovese 411
– Grado 115, 118, 120
– Servigliano 114, 117
– Ischia 198, 199, 200, 209, 213, 243
– Italo-Romance 198, 213, 295, 296, 301,
   315, 316–323, 411
– Ligurian 411, 418
– Lombard 411
– Mendrisiotto 425
– Neapolitan 316, 319, 321–324, 345, 369
– Paduan 412, 416
– Palmanova 414, 415, 419
– Piedmont 423
– Piedmontese 411, 418, 427
– Romagnol 419
– Romanesco 320, 321
– S. Michele al Tagliamento 418, 419
– Salentino 321
– Servigliano 117
– Teramo 115
– Trentino 412
– Valdôtain 419
– Venetan 410–419, 422, 423, 424, 425, 427,
   428

Italian dialects (*continued*)
– Venetian 412, 414, 416, 424, 425, 427, 496
– Vicentino 411, 423, 425
Itelmen 161–190

Japanese 463, 495, 496, 498, 499, 504, 505
Jumjum 256–258, 262

Kashaya 208–209, 210
Kerek 163, 177
Koryak 161, 163, 168, 170, 175–177, 182, 183, 189, 190
Kuot 500, 501

Language shift 183, 184, 188, 189
Learnability 162, 178, 180, 185–188
Left periphery 449–468, 474, 475, 477, 485, 492, 529, 530, 531
Lexicon 5, 7–9, 80, 110, 111, 186, 187, 233, 291, 314
– lexical stratification 185, 186
– lexical stratum 185
Licensing 30–33, 52, 53, 58, 59, 106, 111, 112, 117, 120, 122, 124, 411, 416, 489, 522
Loanword 6, 7, 19, 24, 25, 33, 40, 43, 50, 58, 176, 184, 185–188
Locality 111, 112, 123, 124, 195–197, 199, 201–204, 206, 207, 209, 216, 221, 222, 227, 232, 233, 235, 237, 239, 240, 242–244, 268, 317, 391, 404, 455, 462, 511
– bridge locality 111, 112

Mabaan 249–265
Markedness 34, 49, 58, 59, 105, 314, 391, 397, 398, 432–442
Mass 358, 362–369, 371, 377, 378, 379, 381, 384, 387
Match 46, 48, 441
Mayak 258, 259, 264
MEG 71, 74, 80
Metaphony 104–125, 198, 200, 201, 213–216, 234, 243, 268, 373, 376
Mi'gmaq 403
Micro-parameterization 315
Middle Irish 130, 134–137, 140, 141, 149–153

Mirror Principle 496, 504
Mixed animacy 403
MMN 73, 79–80, 88
Modularity 268, 289
Monophthongization 17, 115, 136–137, 150–153
Morphological boundary 4, 9, 12, 303
Morphologization 116, 165–167, 238
Morphophonology 193–201, 213, 228, 231, 232, 235, 237, 240, 241, 242, 244
Movement 78, 86, 121, 124, 125, 344, 417, 423, 461, 467, 468, 469–483, 492, 493, 500, 510–514, 527
– long-distance 461, 467, 469, 471–473, 478, 480, 481, 483
– long 476, 478
– long wh 467, 476, 477, 481
– short 474–476, 480, 484
– short wh- 467, 477
– short-distance 469–471, 474, 476, 483
– short-distance wh- 482
– successive cyclic 467, 471, 472, 481, 482, 492, 493
– wh- 467, 468, 470, 471, 473, 476, 477, 479, 481, 482, 488, 511
Mutation 123, 133

N1 71, 73, 75, 76, 87, 88
Neapolitan 316, 319, 321–324, 345, 369
Neurobiology of language 65–95
Neuronal excitability 90, 91, 94
Neurophysiological states 70, 91–95
New-given information 518–520
Nilotic 44, 249, 259, 265
Nuer-Dinka 265
Null Subject languages 510, 511, 513, 525–528
Number 180, 185, 207, 259, 273, 299, 300, 308, 310, 336, 357, 358, 361, 369, 371, 373, 387, 391, 396, 401, 404–406, 420, 438
Numeral classifiers 500, 502

Obligatory Contour Principle (OCP) 253–255, 264, 265
Oggi 314, 335–339, 341, 522
Old French 344

Index —— 535

Old Irish 129, 130, 132–134, 136–137, 138, 141, 144, 150, 152
Old Italian 20, 329, 330, 333, 334–344, 353, 354, 467
Opponent Principle 107–109
Ora 335–339, 341, 354
Oscillators 86, 90
Oscillatory rhythms 70, 93
– beta band 83–87, 92, 94
– delta bands 86
– gamma rhythms 84
– nested cortical oscillatory rhythms 70, 93
– theta band 83, 84, 86, 87, 89, 90, 92–94
Oto-Manguean 500, 501
Overapplication 212, 222, 228–231, 234

Partitivity 522, 523, 528
Pharyngeal 109
Phase 38, 44, 46, 48, 49, 58, 73, 81, 82, 83, 85–87, 89, 93, 95, 195, 196, 201, 202, 209–212, 216, 228, 229, 232, 233, 235, 241, 244, 290, 385, 479–481
– cyclicity 202, 210
– Phase Impenetrability Condition 479
Phonemochrony 73
Phonemotopy principle 72
Phonetic *implementation* 109, 118, 251
Phonetic Interpretation Functions 108
Phonetic merger 118
Plural 180, 208, 214, 215, 258, 261, 262, 273, 274, 277–284, 286–289, 291, 297, 302, 320, 321, 324, 341, 348, 357–387, 393–396, 401, 403, 405, 428, 440, 441, 495–505
– *a* plural(s) 348, 370–373, 376, 377–386, 499
– additive plural 495, 496, 497, 499
– associative plural 495–505
Postverbal subject 412, 420, 428, 467–493, 517, 518
Predication 342, 435, 437, 470, 514, 515, 517, 519
Prefixes 30, 111, 164, 208, 406, 521
Prepositions 303–305, 329, 331, 339, 340, 344, 344, 346, 348, 349, 350, 352, 445, 450, 451, 457, 458, 461
Prima 31, 329–332, 344, 345, 346, 350, 351

Primitive Irish 130
Pro 416, 451, 458, 510–528
Productivity 170, 179, 180, 185, 186, 215, 216
Prominence 488
Proper prepositions 333
Proto-Romance 15, 18

Raddoppiamento 11, 12
Radical CV Phonology 104–106
Raising 31, 113–124, 142, 143, 198, 213, 214, 499, 502, 512
Recursive Splitting 109
Resolution 71, 121, 123–125, 304, 323, 391–406, 510, 511, 528
Right-dislocation 485
Romance dialects 105, 125, 411
Romance languages 8, 17, 20, 329–354, 357, 362, 365, 371, 387, 410, 416
Romanian 383, 384, 410, 411, 428
Rules 67, 76, 78, 79, 92, 185, 186, 196–206, 209, 210, 216, 224, 225, 235–238, 240, 241, 249, 265, 266–292, 300, 316, 397, 399, 440, 523
– morpho-phonological rules 120, 297, 302, 305, 319
– readjustment rules 237, 266–292, 316
Russian 50, 79, 161, 162, 176, 183–186, 188, 189

Scottish Gaelic 129–132, 134–139, 141, 143, 144, 147, 148, 149, 151, 153
Sesotho 402, 403
Sopra 'above' 349
Sotto 'under' 349, 351
South Slavic 391–406
Spanish 8, 10, 17, 20, 123, 198, 329, 330, 333–336, 339, 353, 354, 357, 359–361, 365, 445, 448, 455, 472
Spectro-temporal states 70, 91–95
Spell-Out 92, 299, 315
Stamattina 345
Step-wise raising 121
Strengthening 123, 124
Stress 4, 8, 11, 21, 59, 113, 119, 120, 123, 124, 174, 186, 196, 213, 220, 273, 292, 320
– stressed vowel 6, 11, 13, 25, 113, 117, 120, 121, 123–125, 198, 220

Subject(s) 19, 26, 30, 52, 53, 55, 66, 68, 71,
   73, 79, 86, 111, 175, 190, 198, 202, 203,
   209, 213, 233, 264, 268, 275, 291, 292,
   308, 322, 333, 337, 342, 344, 347, 348,
   392, 398, 401, 406, 409–428, 434–439,
   441, 442, 451, 454, 455, 458–461,
   467–493, 510–528
– clitic(s) 347, 409, 410, 412–424, 426–428,
   459, 525
– inversion 467–473, 478, 479, 481, 482,
   484, 488, 489, 492, 493
– SubjP 470, 481
Subjunctive 204, 205, 222–226, 486,
   489–492, 521
Successive Division Algorithm (SDA) 109,
   110, 117
Suffixes 111, 175, 180, 188, 203, 205, 208,
   249, 251–253, 255, 256, 258–260, 262,
   264, 265, 277, 284, 286, 287, 291, 496,
   498, 505
Sundanese 17
Suppletion/Suppletive 193, 199, 236, 239,
   240, 242–244, 267–269, 278, 279, 280,
   287, 303, 315–317
Surkum 262, 264

Tolerance Principle 178, 183, 186
Tone 249–265, 287, 472, 486
– tonal inventory 249, 253, 262
– tonotopic principle 72, 92
Topic 201, 206, 213, 245, 272, 391, 413,
   445–464, 479, 488, 490, 492, 510–528

Tra/fra 303, 352
Troncamento 300–306, 310, 311, 315, 317,
   321
T-to-C 417, 470, 472, 473, 481
Turkish 75, 76, 88, 186–188, 289, 495–497

Ulster 133, 136–138, 140–142, 144, 145, 148,
   150, 151, 154
Umlaut 120, 123, 124, 195, 196, 202–206,
   209, 212, 213, 216–239, 241, 242, 244
Unarism 105
Uninterpretable features 362
Utterance Time (UT) 329, 353

Vedic Sanskrit 266–292
Verb *essere* 330, 337
Verb *fare* 329, 332, 333, 335, 336, 344, 348
Vocabulary Insertion 200, 238–242, 267,
   278, 299, 312, 357
Vowel systems 75, 76, 110, 112, 116–120, 249
vP 368, 400, 462, 476, 477, 479, 480, 513
– edge 468

Weakening 123, 124, 377
wh-questions 467, 468, 471, 473, 477, 479,
   482, 492

Xitsonga 401–403

Yup'ik 495, 499, 504

Zaiwa 500